APPLIED ETHICS

Arctic Ocean

Bering Sea

Russian Federated Republic

Sea of Okhotsk

Estonia
Latvia
Lithuania

elarus

Kazakhstan

Jkraine

ira

Black Sea

Caspian Sea

Aral Sea

Uzbekistan

Kyrgyzstan

Mongolia

Turkey

Azerbaijan

Turkmenistan

Tajikistan

Sea of Japan

Syria

Armenia

China

N. Korea

S. Korea

Japan

Israel

Jordan

Iran

Afghanistan

Egypt

Kuwait

Pakistan

Nepal

Bhutan

East China Sea

Saudi Arabia

U.A.E.

India

Myanmar

Vietnam

Taiwan

Pacific Ocean

Oman

Laos

Hong Kong

Philippine Sea

Sudan

Yemen

Bangladesh

Thailand

South China Sea

Philippines

can

Ethiopia

Somalia

Sri Lanka

Kampuchea

Uganda

Kenya

Brunei

Malaysia

Papua New Guinea

anda

Tanzania

Malaysia

nyika

Singapore

Indonesia

Solomon Islands

Indian Ocean

Arafura Sea

Malawi

bia

Mbzambique

Coral Sea

Zimbabwe

Madagascar

Australia

wana

aziland

Estonia
Latvia
Lithuania

Russian Federated Republic

Byelarus

New Zealand

Ukraine

Moldova

Kazakhstan

Romania

Caspian Sea

Aral Sea

Bulgaria

Black Sea

Georgia

Uzbekistan

Kyrgyzstan

Macedonia

Azerbaijan

Greece

Turkey

Turkmenistan

China

Armenia

Syria

Lebanon
Israel

Iran

Afghanistan

Iraq

Egypt

Jordan

Pakistan

Kuwait

APPLIED ETHICS
A Multicultural
Approach

edited by

Larry May
Washington University

Shari Collins-Chobanian
Arizona State University West

Kai Wong
Washington University

PRENTICE HALL, Upper Saddle River, New Jersey 07458

Library of Congress Cataloging-in-Publication Data

Applied ethics : a multicultural approach / edited by Larry May, Shari
    Collins-Chobanian, and Kai Wong. — 2nd ed.
        p.   cm.
    ISBN 0-13-575291-4
    1. Applied ethics.   2. Multiculturalism.   I. May, Larry.
II. Collins-Chobanian, Shari.   III. Wong, Kai.
BJ1031.A66   1998   97-29594
170—dc21   CIP

Editorial director: Charlyce Jones Owen
Acquisitions editor: Angie Stone
Production editor: Edie Riker
Cover design: Bruce Kenselaar
Cover art from Letraset Phototone
Buyer: Tricia Kenny

This book was set in 10/12 New Century Schoolbook by DM Cradle Associates
and was printed and bound by Courier Companies, Inc. The cover was
printed by Phoenix Color Corp.

 © 1998, 1994 by Prentice-Hall, Inc.
Simon & Schuster / A Viacom Company
Upper Saddle River, New Jersey 07458

Printed in the United States of America

10   9   8   7   6   5   4   3   2   1

ISBN   0-13-575291-4

Prentice-Hall International (UK) Limited, *London*
Prentice Hall of Australia Pty, Limited, *Sydney*
Prentice-Hall Canada Inc., *Toronto*
Prentice-Hall Hispanoamericana, S.A., *Mexico*
Prentice-Hall of India Private Limited, *New Delhi*
Prentice-Hall of Japan, Inc., *Tokyo*
Simon & Schuster Asia Pte. Ltd., *Singapore*
Editoria Prentice-Hall do Brasil, Ltda., *Rio de Janeiro*

Contents

Preface

This book has filled an existing gap in the literature used in applied ethics courses. The major anthologies in applied ethics contain essays written almost exclusively by American social and moral philosophers. These anthologies leave the student with the impression that there are no viewpoints other than those expressed by Americans, and that ethical and social philosophy has little to do with perspectives of other nations and cultures. More and more courses that include the perspectives of diverse cultures are being added to the curriculum. There is no applied ethics volume comparable to ours—indeed philosophy has been very slow to respond to the call for multiculturalism in our curricula.

Our volume addresses various topics in applied ethics from Western and non-western perspectives. As a result, the typical instructor will have an easier time approaching the material than if the material were segregated, or if the issues were not already well known in the West. Nonetheless, since our book devotes significant attention to the moral perspectives of many different cultures and ethnicities, students will come away from our text having a deeper appreciation for other cultures. We believe that the increasing emphasis on multiculturalism and internationalism across disciplines has set the stage for a very positive reception for a book like ours.

Let us briefly address some of the terminology in the book. We have chosen to use the term "American Indian" rather than "Native American" because of the increasing use of the former instead of the latter in such titles as "American Indian Studies" and because many American Indian people believe that the term "Native American" does not adequately capture their identity since many non-Indians may also claim to be Native Americans. We have used the term "African American" when referring to Blacks living in America and have retained the term "Blacks" when the designated group was not restricted to Americans.

Many people provided us with valuable suggestions and assistance throughout the years that we worked on this project. We would like to thank Margaret Battin, Karen Warren, Iris Young, Mary Mahowald, Marilyn Friedman, Denward Wilson, and Gloria Cuádraz for valuable suggestions about the book's format and selections. We are especially grateful to Dana Klar from Washington University's Center for American Indian Studies for help with some of the multicultural material. In addition, Kenneth Sharratt, Marilyn Broughton, and Debi Katz have helped in the more technical phases of the book's production. The following reviewers provided helpful suggestions and useful insights: Richard Farr, University of Hawaii at Manoa; James A. Gould, University of South Florida; Karen Hanson, Indiana University; Howard McGary, Rutgers University; Elane O'Rourke, Moorpark College; Donald Porter, College of San Mateo; Robert W. Smith, Mesa Community College; and Maurine Stein, Prairie State College. Joel Anderson, Kate Parsons, Jennifer Stiff, Dennis Cooley, William Tolhurst and many others who used the first edition gave valuable help on the second edition, as did our students. And finally we would like to thank Ted Bolen, Wayne Spohr, Rob DeGeorge, Nicole Gray, Angela Stone, and the rest of the Prentice Hall staff for their invaluable help and support.

INTRODUCTION

Our first resource is human compassion, gained through the clear use of our minds, which will allow us to make the best use of the human family. And another of our best resources emerges when we think clearly about the peoples who have alterative answers to the questions that are not being answered by our society. For the first time . . . it is possible . . . to make the world our library.

—John Mohawk[1]

This anthology presents a new approach to the study of applied ethics. Its premise is that the issues in applied ethics are addressed too often from narrow North American perspectives, with little attention paid to viewpoints from other cultures. The 58 essays collected here attempt to present a wide view of the standard issues in contemporary applied ethics such as abortion, euthanasia, world hunger, discrimination, war, and the environment. To these standard issues we have added discussions of gender roles, violence, human rights, and AIDS. We have attempted to find the very best recent literature—indeed, over half the essays in our book have been written in the last five years. In addition, more than half the essays either take a non-Western perspective or address themselves to the international context of an applied ethics issue, and many of the essays are written by people who are indigenous to the cultures about which they are writing.

Each section of our anthology begins with a well-known essay on a major issue such as hunger, war, or abortion. This is followed by a very recent essay, usually responding to the "classical" essay. In addition, each section includes several essays that approach the topic from Third World perspectives, and many sections have pieces that relate the topic of the section to relevant international issues. It is our intention to broaden the range of perspectives, in addition to making the issues come alive in ways they often do not when a more limited range of perspectives is considered.

THE CASE FOR A MULTICULTURAL APPROACH TO ETHICS

Lawrence Blum offers the following definition of multiculturalism:

> Multiculturalism involves an understanding, appreciation and valuing of one's own culture, and an informed respect and curiosity about the ethnic cultures of others. It involves a valuing of other cultures, not in the sense of approving of all aspects of those cultures, but of attempting to see how a given culture can express value to its own members.[2]

In this view—a view we largely share—a multicultural approach to ethics, or any subject, does not require that we be uncritical of the practices and beliefs of other cultures. Indeed, just as a consideration of the many distinctly North American perspectives on abortion does not require that we agree with all of these views, so a consideration of the many diverse cultural perspectives on applied ethics issues does not require that we agree with all of these views either.

Our approach to multiculturalism begins with a sincere belief in the words written 100 years ago by John Stuart Mill:

> Only through diversity of opinion is there, in the existing state of human intellect, a chance of fair play to all sides of the truth.[3]

The key component in the case for multiculturalism is diversity of opinion. To give just one example: In the contemporary American debate on abortion, virtually no one defends late-term abortions. But we have included an essay by several Chinese physicians who defend this practice in countries such as theirs which are struggling to curb a population explosion. We have included this essay not because we necessarily agree with it, but because we think that it is important that this opinion be heard and reflected upon to see whether there is any part of the truth that is revealed by such a consideration.

Another important part of the case for multicultural approaches to ethics, and to other subjects, is to combat the ethnocentrism and racism that often result from ignorance of other peoples and cultures. There is little doubt that our ignorance of people who are different from ourselves has, historically, contributed to much hatred and violence. By remaining uninformed about people of other cultures, we miss the opportunity to see how much alike they are to us and avoid having to try to understand the basis for our differences.

Yet another argument in favor of a multicultural approach to ethics, or to any other subject, has to do with the importance of understanding those who are our competitors, and those who we hope will eventually be our partners in the development of the global village. In the past, the restricted vision of traditional approaches in the West worked to a limited extent only because the world was cut into many self-contained units. In a fragmented world, one group could survive simply by closing its doors and regarding everyone else as the enemy. With increasing global interdependence this narrow approach is becoming counterproductive. John Mohawk makes the case well when he says:

> We are living in a world in which difference is just a simple fact of life, but our collective thinking has yet to truly come to grips with this reality. This *has* to change. A workable world mentality means that we are going to have to make peace with those who are different from us.[4]

The reach of many issues today—environmental degradation, racial and sexual oppression, the AIDS epidemic—is global. Intellectual disciplines such as applied ethics cannot afford to be myopic, since the survival of the West will surely depend in the near future on its ability to understand the much more populous areas of the Third World, as well as disparate cultures that exist side by side with, and sometimes within, Western cultures.

Finally, there is a strong moral case for discussions of cultures different from one's own. Such discussions foster respect for others. Respect is generally recognized as a moral value by most cultures. And the most important component of respect is an appreciation for another person as different from oneself. An appreciation for different cultures will make us better able to appreciate differences among individuals, especially between ourselves and those who in many minor, and some major, ways are different from us. If it is true that understanding breeds respect, then a consideration of a diverse set of cultural perspectives, such as those contained in this anthology, will advance the moral goal of increasing respect among peoples and individuals in the world.

WHAT DOES ETHICS CONCERN?

According to many Western and non-Western perspectives, ethics generally is understood to address the question: How ought we to lead our lives? Ethics, as a branch of philosophy, raises a number of questions that can be addressed conceptually or theoretically, namely:

- Is ethical knowledge possible?
- What are the sources of such knowledge?
- What are the theoretical strategies for resolving conflicts among these sources?
- Which are the most important values and how are they related to each other?

Applied ethics pursues these various conceptual or theoretical questions within the framework of particular contemporary issues.

In Western thought, it is common to distinguish between two large subgroups of questions in ethics. *Personal ethics* deals with the questions

- What determines the rightness or wrongness of particular actions?
- What determines how social responsibility will divide into the individual shares of responsibility for the members of a community?

Then there are large-scale, collective issues in ethics, which we will call *social ethics*, such as

- What determines the rightness or wrongness of various social policies?
- What are communities collectively responsible for?

There is a long-standing controversy in Western thought about the relationship between personal and social ethics. Some thinkers have believed that ethics mainly concerns what one's individual conscience tells one to do, and that one should not be concerned about what the society at large could do. Others, such as the utilitarians, have thought that ethics primarily concerns deciding what is best for the society at large, with each person's own happiness counting for no more than any other person's happiness. Some non-Western approaches deny that there is a significant difference between these two approaches.

Neither of these approaches, personal or social, excludes the other. Indeed, environmental ethics is a clear case of a blend between the two: It involves a set of issues that ultimately require collective action, yet it also involves issues that individuals in North America, for instance, face every day in the way they decide about such personal matters as whether to use a recycling bin. All issues in ethics have a personal dimension in that they have an effect on individual lives and call for some kind of judgment on the individual's part. In addition, most ethical issues have a social dimension in that, for their resolution, they require some sort of group action by the community at large. In this text, we will stress social ethics first, in order to push ourselves to think about the effects of our actions on distant parts of the world, thereby extending the horizon of our ethical gaze.

WHERE DO WE BEGIN?

In any study of ethics, the first and most difficult question we face concerns the subject matter itself: What do we study in an ethics course? What data, if any, are we concerned with? There are three types of "data" most commonly mentioned in ethics:

- Intuitions
- Rules and codes
- Social roles

Some philosophers would also include *reason* as a major source of ethical knowledge. But it seems to us that reason alone cannot tell us very much in ethics, unless it has something to operate on. Although rationality is terribly important in ethics, since it sets the ground rules for discussion and deliberation, an appeal to reason alone is unlikely to lead very far in ethics.

The most commonly cited "data," especially in Western approaches to ethics, are people's *intuitions*. Intuitions concern what people actually think, especially after they have engaged in reflection about what is right and wrong. Most discussions of ethics begin with what people think is wrong about such issues as starvation or murder. Of course, there is significant disagreement about such things, and so an appeal to intuitions alone will not resolve many ethical questions. What one can hope for, indeed what our book aims at, is an increasingly reflective approach toward one's intuitions, informed by an understanding of the intuitions and reasoning of a wide spectrum of the population. As we will see, there is an emerging consensus concerning issues raised in certain ethical questions. On some other issues, we are far away from anything remotely resembling a consensus.

Rules and *codes* are another important starting point in ethics. Most communities have explicit or implicit sets of moral rules and taboos, and many societies have codes of conduct that are enforced against their members in much the same way that civil laws are enforced. These rules and codes often reflect the considered judgments of many people over many generations. In this sense, rules and codes often represent an intergenerational consensus about what is right or wrong. But codes and rules can conflict with an individual person's intuitions when applied to a particular case. In such cases of conflict it is not clear that the rules or codes should be given priority over one's intuitions. One such example is Huck Finn's dilemma: He was drawn toward his friend, Jim, and was inclined not to turn him in as a runaway slave; but Huck was also strongly motivated by the rules of his society, which dictated that slaves were property, and when they escaped they were in effect stealing from their masters. It is extremely important that we not treat any code or set of rules (or intuition) as unchallengeable, for like the slavery rules, even the consensus of a community may be ethically flawed.

Social roles are another interesting starting point for ethics discussions. Taking on, or having been thrust into, a particular role, such as "father" or "mother," "teacher" or "friend," "employer" or "employee," is often thought to involve a change in one's moral status. Social roles create obligations or expand our responsibilities. Understanding what is the status of these roles may be an important first step toward understanding what is right or wrong to do in a given situation. But like rules and codes, social roles may conflict with intuitions, and worse yet, the different roles each person assumes may offer conflicting guidance about what is right or wrong in particular cases. So again, we should not, indeed we cannot, regard social roles as unimpeachable sources of ethics. Rather, we need to consider intuitions, rules, codes, and social roles as each providing input into a process of ethical deliberation. What is crucial in such a process is the ability to resolve conflicts that exist among these sources of ethical knowledge.

HOW ARE MORAL JUDGMENTS MADE?

In Western thought there are three standard ways of making moral judgments, especially in cases in which there are conflicts among our sources of ethical knowledge:

- Consequentialism—of which utilitarianism is the most prominent variation.
- Deontological theory—of which Kantianism and rights theory are the most prominent variations.
- Virtue theory—of which Aristotelianism and Thomistic theory are the most prominent variations.

Each of these theoretical perspectives has achieved prominence, and for each perspective there are significant groups of defenders among contemporary moral philosophers.

Consequentialism is the view that judgments about whether an action is morally right should be made based on an assessment of the probable effects, or consequences, of alternative acts that are open to the person in question. Consequentialists contend that an act is morally right insofar as it maximizes the best results for everyone. But there is considerable disagreement about how to assess what is the best consequence. Is pleasure or happiness the main basis for deciding what is best? Or is there some other criterion, such as goodness, that should be the basis for deciding what is best for everyone? Another question that arises is this: Should greater emphasis be placed on short-term or long-term effects? And also, should we take account of the effects that application of a particular rule would have on the society at large?

Some consequentialists, such as classical utilitarians, believe that a person can measure the quantity of happiness likely to be produced by an act, and the quantity of happiness likely to be produced by all alterative acts, and then by comparing these quantities decide which act is morally best. Duties and rights are reconceived as merely rules of thumb for guiding us toward what is best for everyone. Our second reading, an excerpt from John Stuart Mill's book *Utilitarianism*, ends by arguing that rights are merely highly likely to advance the greatest happiness for the greatest number. Rights, on this view, have no intrinsic value.

Other consequentialists, such as rule utilitarians, take a more subtle view of moral duties and rights. Rather than weighing the likely consequences of alternative acts, these consequentialists weigh the likely consequences of alternative rules. If a rule, such as "honesty is the best policy," has been proven to be productive of very good consequences, and no other more useful rule is applicable, then the right thing to do is to conform to the rule of honesty. Both duties and rights are understood as forms of rule. On this view it would be right to act according to a weighty rule, such as the honesty rule, even though it appears that better consequences could be had in this one case by acting dishonestly. Duties and rights have weight here, but the weight is still a function of their ability to produce the best consequences in the society as a whole.

Deontological theory is the view that we should perform those acts that conform to duties and rights, quite independently of the consequences. In general, deontological views characterize morally right acts as those that display the most intrinsic value. The value of an act is determined by examining the act in light of moral principles. Here are two common deontological principles:

- Always treat a person as an end, never as a means only.
- Treat people the way you would want to be treated.

Deontological theorists are generally concerned about what a person intends to do, rather than about the actual results of what that person does. Some deontological theorists believe that the principles used to assess acts must be universal in scope, and others believe that it is sufficient that the principles reflect a consensus in a particular society.

Our third reading is by Ronald Dworkin, one of the best-known contemporary defenders of a deontological approach to rights. Dworkin argues that rights should be treated as trump cards. Whenever they are applicable, they should not be overridden by considerations of social well-being. If a government is willing to disregard a person's fundamental rights for some useful social purpose, that government fails to respect the dignity of the person, and thereby undermines the idea of equality and justice within its domain. For example, when a government denies fundamental rights of free speech to one of its citizens, Dworkin argues, that government insults the citizen, and the government thereby undermines respect for law. Deontological theory is attractive because of its firm stand against the denial of rights to any citizen. Many of the essays in our book embrace such a perspective, especially the United Nations Declaration and the essay by O'Neill.

Virtue theory is the view that judgments about what is morally right should be made in terms of promoting good character or other natural ends. The key to making good judgments is to have developed good habits to which one can merely refer now that one is uncertain about what to do. Morality is very much a matter of context as well as habit; the virtuous person is supposed to have developed a fine sense of appropriateness that is sensitive to differences in context. In this respect, virtue theory shares much in common with various non-Western perspectives, such as Buddhism. Unlike consequentialism and deontological theory, virtue theory focuses on the person's character rather than the person's behavior.

One way of understanding the virtuous life is in terms of conforming to what is "natural." In deciding what to do, one should pursue the path that is most in keeping with what is most natural in a given context. In this sense, virtue theory and *natural law* theory share much in common. Natural law theory is the view that morality is grounded in something larger than our human circumstances, namely in a natural (in many cases God-given) order. Natural law theory is most prominently espoused by Catholic theorists and by other theorists who support a strong connection between religion and ethics. Natural law has been understood, at least since Thomas Aquinas, as God's eternal law applied to natural entities, most especially to humans. In its more recent manifestations, there has been much controversy in natural law theory as to what precisely is the relationship between God's law and human laws.

Each of these theories may give a different answer to the question of how to resolve a particular conflict between sources of ethical knowledge. There is no consensus about which of these theories is best. Our view is that each of these theories contains a grain of truth, and that some combination of these theoretical perspectives may turn out to be the best overall theory. Until such a combination is devised, it is worthwhile to consider each perspective seriously whenever one is faced with a conflict of sources of ethical knowledge. This may seem unsatisfactory to those who were hoping that ethics would always provide a single solution to any ethical question. On our view, ethics is not a science that provides such solutions; rather, the study of ethics enriches one's deliberations but leaves the conclusion of those deliberations often unresolved.

WHAT ARE SOME OF THE CHIEF VALUES?

In most Western discussions of ethics, from a philosophical perspective, various values are subjected to the most intense conceptual scrutiny. Each of these values can be understood from the standpoint of personal or social ethics. Among the chief values are

- autonomy
- justice
- responsibility
- care

Autonomy is often thought to be a paradigmatic value in personal ethics. Being autonomous means being true to our own principles and acting in a way which we have chosen or which we endorse. Autonomy is closely connected to self-respect, for the person who is true to his or her own principles generally esteems himself or herself. Autonomy also has a social ethics dimension. For autonomy to be maintained and maximized in a population it is crucial that social institutions be designed to minimize interference with the life choices of individuals. Highly intrusive institutions will make it much more difficult for individuals to attain autonomy. In the field of medicine, the more fully patients are informed about treatment options, the more likely they are to make autonomous decisions.

Justice is also sometimes characterized as a value of personal ethics. In this view, justice is best understood as giving to each person his or her due, based on what that individual has a legitimate right to. When rights are understood as a contract between two equal parties, they undergird a personal ethics conception of justice. But justice is also concerned with the fair distribution of goods and services within a society. The fairness of distributions is not solely determined by contractual rights. This is especially true, as we will see in several of our essays, when we approach distributive justice from a global perspective. It may be true that no one is owed our help to be saved from starvation, but it seems to many philosophers that it would be unjust to spend one's resources on luxuries while others die highly painful deaths from starvation because they have no resources with which to purchase food.

Responsibility, like justice, has a personal and social orientation. Responsibility can be understood as accountability for the consequences that one has explicitly and directly caused. According to this understanding, one can limit one's responsibility simply by not doing very much that has effects in the world. But if we think of the consequences of what people have failed to do, as well as what they have explicitly done, then responsibility can be seen as a social category that is related to our membership in various communities. This latter sense of responsibility implies that in order to avoid acting irresponsibly, people will have to worry about their contribution, or lack of contribution, to group action as well as about their own individual personal actions. For example, racist violence on one's campus may not seem to be a particular student's responsibility if that student did not engage in the violence. But if the student could have helped in preventing the violence, but chose not to, there is a sense in which the student may share responsibility for that violence.

Care has recently been discussed as a decidedly different value from justice. Justice, even in its social, distributive form, calls for us to be impartial in assigning to people what is considered their due. But care calls for partiality, especially toward those who cannot protect themselves and to whom we are in special relationships. Our own children may not be owed any more than children in distant parts of the world; indeed our own children are probably owed less, given their already privileged position. But there is a value in preferring one's own child and striving to aid him or her. In our section on gender roles, we will encounter a recent dispute on whether and to what extent justice and care are different.

This concludes a brief overview of some of the main currents in contemporary Western philosophical approaches to ethics. In the next section we will explain how an emphasis on multiculturalism will further enrich our deliberations about both personal and social ethics.

A BRIEF ACCOUNT OF SOME NON-WESTERN PERSPECTIVES

The main non-Western perspectives represented in this anthology are these:

- African
- Confucian
- Buddhist
- Indian Hindu
- Islamic
- American Indian

We have also included a significant number of both Western and non-Western feminist pieces. As will become clear, there is considerable overlap among many of these non-Western perspectives. It is for this reason that it is sometimes appropriate to talk of a Third World perspective, even though each of these non-Western perspectives is unique. In the remainder of this introduction we will give a very brief overview of these perspectives.

The question of whether there is a single, distinct African perspective is hotly debated. What most of our authors mean by an African perspective is one that is centered on several traditional key ideas. Ifeanyi Menkiti provides a good summary of some of these ideas. Africans deny that the concept of a person

> can be defined by focusing on this or that physical or psychological characteristic
> of the lone individual. Rather man is defined by reference to the environing com-

munity . . . the reality of the community takes precedence over the reality of individual life histories, whatever these may be . . . persons become persons only after a process of incorporation. Without incorporation into this or that community, individuals are considered to be mere danglers, to whom the description "person" does not fully apply.[5]

In addition, as we will see, the experiences of poverty and hunger, so prevalent in many parts of Africa, have meant that Africans put much more emphasis on economic considerations than on political rights such as the right to free speech. Furthermore, the well-being of the community is paramount, and the well-being of the individual is inextricably linked to that of the community. Claude Ake's essay on African conceptions of human rights is a good place to begin to understand the ethical perspective that is connected to the view of personhood central to traditional African thought.

The traditional Confucian ethical perspective, to some degree resembling the African perspective, also emphasizes the importance of the community to the individual. In order for one to realize one's identity and sense of value, one has to fulfill a set of obligations defined by one's roles in a nexus of relationships. And by living in harmony with others through the proper execution of these obligations, the individual nurtures and develops his or her human nature which is held to be fundamentally good. The failure to live up to these duties and to find one's roles would reduce a person to insignificance and render him or her unable to lead a virtuous life. Nonetheless, it is important to add that for the truly virtuous individual, occasions may arise when he or she has to stand up for what is right in spite of opposition from the community at large.

Like Confucian ethics, the Buddhist outlook places no less weight on the interrelatedness of the individual with other people and nature. However, the way in which the Buddhist regards self, others, and nature could not differ more from a Confucian. Whereas a Confucian locates his or her sense of value and significance in a virtuous life within a fabric of relationships, the Buddhist assumes an attitude of nonattachment toward persons and things in the world, however valuable they are. By "nonattachment," the Buddhist does *not* mean that one should totally drop out of commitments and relationships, but rather one should not be encumbered by or ensnared in anything in the world, whether it is something as vicious as greed or hatred or even as good as justice or friendship. For it is precisely this "clinging" and "grasping" attitude that accounts for suffering in this world. Once one realizes that one's own existence, one's relationships, and the world are products of contingency and transitoriness, one is willing to let go of the things one holds dear to when the time comes. Only with this orientation of nonattachment can one live with an openness that is free to show patience and compassion to humanity and all of creation which struggle and suffer in the same way. (For more on the Buddhist perspective, see Inada and the editors' notes that accompany it.)

Indian Hindu perspectives on ethics share many features in common with Buddhist perspectives, but there are also important differences. I. C. Sharma has provided a good summary of some of the key Indian ethical ideas. Indian philosophies all start with the idea of a person who is suffering, and "who is to be rescued from endless torture, misery, disease, destruction, old age, even death."[6] For most Indian philosophers, the path to take in ending suffering is as important as the ending of suffering itself. Mohandas Gandhi epitomizes one of the great differences between Hindu and Buddhist ethical perspectives. Gandhi stressed an active intervention into the world to make it better, whereas Buddhists often prefer a more patient and passive approach. Gandhi's nonviolence and pacifism, as we will see, are inspired by a drive toward mitigating as much suffering as one can in the present. This orientation can also be seen in the essay by Guha in the section on environmental ethics, in which he criticizes those who place wilderness preservation ahead of relieving human suffering.

Traditional Islamic perspectives on ethics are deeply intertwined with religious conceptions. Like some Hindu perspectives, Islamic ethics is highly activist and interventionist. Most interestingly for our purposes, Islamic ethics are highly partialist. The Koran specifies that there will be strict rules for the ethical conduct of males, and quite different, some would say even stricter, rules for women. In addition, non-Muslims are to be treated quite differently from Muslims. This ethical perspective shares some features in common with those Western philosophers in the virtue ethics tradition who have argued for different sets of norms for how one behaves toward one's family members and toward those who are outside of one's family. But the Islamic perspective is especially difficult to reconcile with any claims of universal human rights, or of women's equal rights, as we will see in the essays about Islam in the sections on human rights and on gender roles.

American Indian perspectives, although often quite different from tribe to tribe, are deeply infused with a respect for the group, as is true for African perspectives. Added to this is a respect for

> the integrity and inherent importance of the natural world. . . . This is a very central belief which seems consistent across many Native American cultures—that the Earth is a living, conscious being that must be treated with respect and loving care.[7]

American Indians are also deeply affected by the extreme forms of suffering and discrimination their people have been forced to withstand while living in a dominant white society. Their insights are particularly important, as we will see, both in discussions of environmental ethics and in those on racial and gender discrimination.

Finally, let us say just a few words about feminism, a perspective that falls in between Western and non-Western philosophies. Many recent feminist writings have stressed the importance of relationships and interdependence rather than autonomy and individual rights. In this respect some feminist perspectives share many views in common with African and American Indian perspectives.[8] Most feminists have offered often cogent critiques of Western ethical views, especially concerning the nature and importance of justice, the commitment to universal principles, the rigidity of gender roles, as well as the status of pregnant women and the distribution of health care. Essays addressing these subjects can be found in the following sections of our anthology.

Let us end this introduction with a comment about method. While we have tried to provide a representative sample of Western and non-Western perspectives on applied ethics, we have not provided a sample of differences in method that exist in non-Western philosophical writing about ethics. Rather we have tried to find pieces that all have an argument that can be analyzed in terms of Western philosophical methods. In this sense, the essays all speak to one another, in terms of arguments and counterarguments, even though this method may not be common in the cultures in question. Nonetheless, even though most of our essays are Western in form, we feel that they are not so "Westernized" as to misrepresent their cultural perspectives.

It is our hope that this anthology will spawn future works in applied ethics by those who take non-Western perspectives. In constructing our book we found a large literature—larger than most Western-trained philosophers would expect to find. Hopefully, our success will cause other Western philosophers to explore Third World perspectives on applied ethics in greater depth. We would be grateful to hear from anyone who is working in this area or who knows of good essays that we have not included here. We have provided a brief bibliography at the end of each chapter to point the reader toward some of the essays that we were not able to include in this book.

NOTES

1. John Mohawk, "Epilogue: Looking for Columbus." *The State of Native America,* edited by M. Annette Jaimes. (Boston: South End Press, 1992), p. 443.
2. Lawrence Blum, "Antiracism, Multiculturalism, and Interracial Community: Three Educational Values for a Multicultural Society," a monograph published by the University of Massachusetts, Boston, 1991.
3. John Stuart Mill, *On Liberty* [1859] (Indianapolis: Hackett Publishing, 1978), p. 46.
4. John Mohawk, "Epilogue," p. 442.
5. Ifeanyi Menkiti, "Person and Community in African Traditional Thought," in *African Philosophy*, 3rd ed. edited by Richard Wright (Lanham, MD: University Press of America, 1984), pp. 171-72.
6. I. C. Sharma, *Ethical Philosophies of India* (New York: Harper & Row, 1965), p. 55.
7. Annie Booth and Harvey Jacobs, "Ties that Bind: Native American Beliefs as a Foundation for Environmental Consciousness," *Environmental Ethics,* vol. 12 (Spring 1990), pp. 30, 32.
8. See Sandra Harding's fascinating essay, "The Curious Coincidence of Feminine and African Moralities," in Eva Kittay and Diana Meyers, eds., *Women and Moral Theory* (Totowa, NJ: Rowman and Littlefield, 1987).

Antiracism, Multiculturalism, and Interracial Community: Three Educational Values for a Multicultural Society

Lawrence A. Blum

Lawrence Blum is a professor of philosophy at University of Massachusetts at Amherst. He is the author of many articles in ethics and of Friendship, Altruism and Morality *(1980),* A Truer Liberty: Simone Weil and Marxism *(1989 and* Moral Perception and Particularity *(1994). He is also actively involved in programs promoting intercultural understanding, both at the higher and secondary levels of education.*

Blum maintains that central to education for a multicultural society are four distinct but interrelated values—antiracism, multiculturalism, interracial community and respect for persons as individuals, of which the first three are the focus of this article. The value of antiracism education is to counter those attitudes of superiority that seek to perpetuate unjustified advantages of one group over another's. The value of multiculturalism involves the appreciation of values different from those of one's culture, and the value of sense of a community is to foster solidarity amongst various groups in spite of their ethnic and cultural differences.

I want to argue that there are a plurality of values that one would want taught in schools and families. None of these can be reduced to the others, nor can any take the place of the others. Without claiming comprehensiveness for my list I want to suggest that there are at least four values, or families of values, essential to a program of value education for a multiracial society. . . .

The first value is *antiracism* or *opposition* to racism:

> Racism is the denial of the fundamental moral equality of all human beings. It involves the expression of attitudes of superior worth or merit justifying or underpinning the domination or unjust advantage of some groups over others. Antiracism as a value involves striving to be without racist attitudes oneself as well as being prepared to work against both racist attitudes in others and racial injustice in society more generally.

The second value is *multiculturalism*:

Multiculturalism involves an understanding, appreciation and valuing of one's own culture, and an informed respect and curiosity about the ethnic culture of others. It involves a valuing of other cultures, not in the sense of approving of all aspects of those cultures, but of attempting to see how a given culture can express value to its own members.

The third value is a sense of *community,* and in particular an *interracial community*:

This involves a sense, not necessarily explicit or articulated, that one possesses human bonds with persons of other races and ethnicities. The bonds may, and ideally should, be so broad as to encompass all of humanity; but they may also be limited to the bonds formed in friendships, schools, workplaces, and the like.

The fourth value is *treating persons as individuals:*

This involves recognizing the individuality of each person–specifically, that while an individual person is a member of an ethnic or racial group, and while that aspect may be an important part of who she is, she is more than that ethnic or racial identity. It is the lived appreciation of this individuality, not simply paying lip service to it, that constitutes the value I will call treating persons as individuals. . . .

Again, I claim that these four are distinct though related values, and that all of them are essential to multicultural value education. Failure to appreciate their distinctness poses the danger that one of them will be neglected in a value education program. At the same time there are natural convergences and complementarities among the four values taken in any combination; there are ways of teaching each value that support the promotion of each one of the other values. On the other hand, I will claim, there can also be tensions, both practical and theoretical, between various of the values; that is, some ways of teaching one of the values may work against the conveying of one of the others. Since the values can be either convergent or in tension, it will be crucial to search for ways of teaching them that minimize the tension and support the convergences.

I have designated *antiracism* as the first value for this value education. In contrast to the three others, this one is stated negatively—in opposition to something rather than as a positive goal to be striven for. Why do I not refer to this value positively as "racial equality" or "racial justice"? One reason is that the oppositional definition brings out that a central aspect of the value of antiracism involves countering an evil and not just promoting a good. An important component of what children need to be taught is how to notice, to confront, to oppose, and to work toward the elimination of manifestations of racism. Particular moral abilities and traits of character, involving certain forms of empowerment, are required for activities of *opposition* that are not required merely for the promotion of a good goal. Of course, antiracism does presuppose the positive value of racial justice; hence, the positive element is implicitly contained in the value of antiracism.

To understand the value of antiracism we must first understand *racism*. The term racism, while a highly charged and condemnatory one, has no generally agreed upon meaning. On the one hand all can agree that using a racial slur, telling a Chicano student that one does not like Chicanos and wishes they were not in one's school, or carving "KKK" on . . . [an] African-American student's door, are racist acts. At the same time the conservative writer Dinesh D'Souza has given voice to a suspicion, shared I am sure by others, that the term "racism" is in danger of losing its meaning and moral force through a too broad usage.

I agree that there has sometimes been a tendency to inflate the meaning of the word racism so it becomes virtually a catchall term for any behavior concerning race or race relations that its user strongly condemns. This development ill serves those like myself who wish racism to be taken more seriously than it presently is. Like the boy who cried "wolf," the inflation of the concept of racism to encompass phenomena with questionable connection to its core meaning desensitizes people to the danger, horror, and wrongfulness of true racism.

Here is my definition of racism, which I present without further defense: Racism refers both to an institutional or social structure of racial domination or injustice—as when we speak of a racist institution—and also to individual actions, beliefs, and attitudes, whether consciously held or not, which express, support or justify the superiority of one racial group to another. Thus, on both the individual and institutional levels, racism involves denying or violating the equal dignity and worth of all human beings independent of race; and, on both levels, racism is bound up with dominance and hierarchy.

There are three components of (the value of) *antiracism* as I see it.

One is the belief in the equal worth of all persons regardless of race, not just as an intellectual matter, but rooted more deeply in one's attitudes and emotions; this is to have what one might call a *nonracist* moral consciousness. But it is not enough to learn to be nonracist as an individual; students must also be taught to *understand* the particularity of racism as a psychological and historical phenomenon. This is partly because one aspect of antiracism is learning to perceive racism and to recognize when it is occurring. Just being nonracist cannot guarantee this. For one may sincerely subscribe to the right principles of racial justice and yet not see particular instances of racism right under one's nose, in either institutional or individual forms; for example, not recognizing unintended patterns of exclusion of people of color, or not recognizing a racial stereotype.

There are three components to this second feature of antiracism (understanding racism). The first is the *psychological* dynamic of racism, such as scapegoating and stereotyping, rigidity and fear of difference, rationalization of privilege and power, projecting of unwanted wishes onto others, and other psychological processes contributing to racist attitudes. The second is the *historical* dynamic of racism in its particular forms: slavery, colonialism, segregation, Nazism, the mistreatment of native Americans, and the like. Involved also must be learning about movements *against* racism, such as abolitionism, civil rights movements, and the black power movement; and learning about institutional racism as well. The third component is the role of *individuals* in sustaining or resisting racist institutions, patterns, and systems—how individuals can change racist structures; how they may contribute to or help to perpetuate racist patterns even if they themselves are not actually racist.

Studying the historical dynamics of racism necessarily involves teaching the victimization of some groups by others. While some conservative critics of multicultural education ridicule and derogate focusing on a group's history as victims as racism, it would nevertheless be intellectually irresponsible not to do so. One can hardly understand the historical experience of African-Americans without slavery, of Jews without the Holocaust, of Asian-Americans without the historic barriers to citizenship and to family life and without the World War II internment camps.

Nevertheless, from the point of view of historical accuracy as well as that of value education, it is vital not to *confine* the presentation of a group to its status as victim. One needs to see subordinate groups as agents in their own history— not just as suffering victimization but as responding to it, sometimes by active resistance both cultural and political, sometimes by passive resistance, sometimes by accommodation. The study of social history is invaluable here in providing the framework for seeing that victims made their own history in the face of their victimization, and for giving concrete embodiment to the philosophical truth that human beings retain the capacity for agency even when oppressed and dominated by others.

The third component of antiracist education (in addition to nonracism and understanding racism) is *opposition to racism*; for nonracism implies only that one does all one can to avoid racism in *one's own* actions and attitudes. This is insufficient, for students need also to develop a sense of responsibility concerning manifestations of racism in other persons and in the society more generally. For example, since students will almost inevitably witness racist acts, to confine their own responsibility simply to ensuring that they individually do not participate in such actions themselves is to give students a mixed message about how seriously they are being asked to take racism.

• • •

The second educational value, *multiculturalism,* encompasses the following three subvalues: (a) affirming one's own cultural identity; learning about and valuing one's own cultural heritage; (b) respecting and desiring to understand and learn about (and from) cultures other than one's own; (c) valuing and taking delight in cultural diversity itself; that is, regarding the existence of distinct cultural groups within one's own society as a positive good to be treasured and nurtured. The kind of respect involved in the second condition (respecting others) is meant to be an informed (and not uncritical) respect grounded in an understanding of another culture. It involves an attempt to see the culture from the point of view of its members and in particular to see how members of that culture value the expression of their own culture. It involves an active interest in and ability in some way to enter into and to enjoy the cultural expressions of other groups.

Such an understanding of another culture in no way requires an affirmation of every feature of that culture as positively good, as some critics of multiculturalism fear (or at least charge). It does not preclude criticism, on the basis either of norms of that culture itself which particular practices in that culture might violate, or of standards external to that culture. Of course when it is legitimate to use a standard external to a culture (e.g., a particular standard of equality between men and women drawn from the Western liberal tradition) is a complex issue. And multiculturalism always warns both against using a legitimate criticism of some feature of a culture as moral leverage to condemn the culture as a whole—declaring it not worthy of serious curricular attention, or disqualifying it as a source of moral insight to those outside that culture, for example—as well as alerting us to the difficult-to-avoid failure to scrutinize the basis of that criticism for its own cultural bias. Nevertheless, multiculturalism need not and should not identify itself with the view that members of one culture never have the moral standing to make an informed criticism of the practices of another culture.

The outward directedness of the second feature of multiculturalism (respecting other cultures) is an important complement to the inward focus of the first feature (learning about and valuing one's own culture). This dual orientation meets the criticism sometimes made of multiculturalism that it creates divisions between students. For the second feature prescribes a reaching out beyond one's own group and thus explicitly counters the balkanizing effect of the first dimension of multiculturalism alone. Nevertheless, that first feature—learning about and valuing one's own culture—is an integral part of multiculturalism, not merely something to be tolerated, treated as a response to political pressure, or justified simply on the grounds of boosting self-esteem. An individual's cultural identity is a deeply significant element of herself, and understanding of her own culture should be a vital part of the task of education. An understanding of one's own culture as contributing to the society of which one is a part is a significant part of that first element of multiculturalism.

The third component of multiculturalism is the valuing of diversity itself. Not only do we want our young people to respect specific other cultures but also to value a school, a city, a society in which diverse cultural groups exist. While this diversity may certainly present problems for young people, one wants them to see the diversity primarily as something to value, prefer, and cherish.

Three dimensions of culture seem to be deserving of curricular and other forms of educational attention in schools. The first is the *ancestor culture* of the ethnic group, nation, or civilization of origin. For Chinese-Americans this would involve understanding Chinese culture, including ancient Chinese cultures, philosophies, religions, and the like. For Irish-Americans it would be Irish history and culture. For Mexican-Americans it would include attention to some of the diverse cultures of Mexico—the Aztec, the Mayan, as well as the Spanish, and then the hybrid Spanish/indigenous culture which forms modern Mexican culture.

While all ethnic cultures have an ancestor culture, not all current groups bear the same relationship to that ancestor culture. For example, African-Americans' connection to their ancestor culture is importantly different from that of immigrant groups like Italians, Eastern European Jews, and Irish. Although scholars disagree about the actual extent of influence of various African "cultures on current African-American cultural forms, it was a general feature of American slavery systematically to attempt to deprive African slaves of their African culture. By contrast voluntary immigrant groups brought with them an intact culture, which they renegotiated in the new conditions of the United States. In fact the label "African-American" can be seen as an attempt to forge a stronger analogy between the experience of black Americans and that of other immigrant groups than do other expressions, such as "black" or even "Afro-American." The former conceptualization emphasizes that American blacks are not simply a product of America but do indeed possess an ancestor culture, no matter how brutally that culture was attacked. Note, however, that there is an important difference between this use of "African-American" and that applied, for example, to "second-generation Ethiopian-Americans. The latter is truer parallel to white ethnic "hyphenate Americans."

Other differences among groups, such as the current ethnic group's distance in time from its original emigration, variations and pressures to assimilate once in the United States, and the effects of racism affect the significance of the ancestor culture for a current ethnic group. Nevertheless ancestor culture plays some role for every group.

A second dimension of culture to be encompassed by multicultural education is the *historical experience* of the ethnic group within the United States. Generally it will attend to the historical experiences, ways of life, triumphs and setbacks, art and literature, contributions and achievements, of ethnic groups in the United States. The latter point is uncontroversial; all proponents of multicultural education agree in the need to correct the omission in traditional curricula and text books of many ethnic groups' experiences and contributions to our national life. But distinguishing this dimension from the ancestor culture and giving attention to both of them is crucial. For the culture of the Chinese-American is *not* the same as the culture of traditional or modern China; it is a culture with its own integrity: neither the purer form of ancestor culture nor that of middle-America. It can be called "intercultural," influenced by more than one

culture (as indeed the ancestor culture itself may have been), yet forming a culture in its own right.

A third dimension of culture is the *current ethnic culture* of the group in question. This is the dimension most directly embodied in the student member of that culture. This current ethnic culture—family ethnic rituals, foods, customs regarding family roles and interactions, values, musical and other cultural preferences, philosophies of life, and the like—bears complex relationships to the ancestor culture as well as to the group's historical ethnic experience in the United States. It changes over time and is affected in myriad ways by the outer society. As with ancestor culture and historical ethnic experience, the student's current ethnic culture must be given respect. What such respect consists in is a complex matter, as the following examples indicate.

In one case respect can involve allowing Arab girls to wear traditional headgear in school if they so desire. In another it can mean seeing a child's remark in class as containing insight stemming from her cultural perspective that might otherwise be missed or seem off the mark. Another form of respect for culture involves, for example, recognizing that a Vietnamese child's failure to look a teacher in the eye is not a sign of evasiveness or lack of interest but a way of expressing a deference to teachers and authority, culturally regarded as appropriate. Thus, respect for ethnic cultures sometimes involves a direct valorizing of a part of that culture; at other times neither valorizing nor disvaluing, but allowing for its expression because it is important to the student. In another context, it can involve reshaping one's own sense of what is educationally essential, to take into account another culture's difference. Finally, it can sometimes involve seeing a cultural manifestation as a genuine obstacle to learning but respecting the cultural setting in which it is embedded and the student's own attachment to that cultural feature, and finding ways to work with or around that obstacle to accomplish an educational goal.

In summary, ancestor culture, ethnic historical experience in the United States, and current ethnic culture are three dimensions of ethnic culture requiring attention in a multicultural education. They are all dimensions that children need to be taught and taught to respect—both in their own and other's cultures.

The context of multicultural education presupposes a larger society consisting of various cultures. Thus, teaching an attitude of appreciation toward a particular one of these cultures in the three dimensions just mentioned will have both a particular and general aspect. We will want students to appreciate cultures in their own right, but also in their relationship to the larger society. This simple point can help us to avoid two familiar, and contrasting, pitfalls of multicultural education, that can be illustrated with the example of Martin Luther King, Jr.

One pitfall would be exemplified by a teacher who portrayed King as an important leader of the black community, but who failed to emphasize that he should be seen as a great *American* leader more generally—as a true hero for all Americans, indeed for all humanity, and not *only* for or of African-Americans. The teacher fails to show the non-African-American students that they too have a connection with King simply as Americans.

Yet an exactly opposite pitfall is to teach appreciation of the contribution of members of particular cultures *only* insofar as those contributions can be seen in universal terms or in terms of benefiting the entire society. This pitfall would be exemplified by seeing Dr. King only in terms of his contribution to humanity or to American society more generally, but *not* acknowledging him as a product and leader specifically of the African-American community. Multicultural education needs to enable non-African-American students (whether white or not) to be able to appreciate a leader of the African-American community in that role itself, and not *only* by showing that the leader in question made a contribution to everyone in the society. Thus, multicultural education needs to emphasize both the general or full society dimension of each culture's contributions and heroes and also the particular or culture-specific dimension.

Many people associate multiculturalism with the idea of moral *relativism* or cultural relativism and specifically with the view that because no one from one culture is in a position to judge another culture, no one is in a position to say which culture should be given priority in the allocation of respect, curricular inclusion, and the like. Therefore, according to this way of thinking, every culture has a claim to equal inclusion and respect, because no one is in a position to say which ones are *more* worthy of respect. While the philosophic relativism on which this version of multiculturalism rests needs to be taken seriously—it has a long and distinguished philosophic history—there is an alternative, quite different and nonrelativistic, philosophic foundation for multiculturalism as well. This view—which might be called *pluralistic*—agrees that cultures manifest different values but affirms that the values of a given culture can be, or can come to be, appreciated (as well as assessed) by someone from a different culture. Thus, while cultures are different, they are at least partly accessible to one another.

According to this pluralist, nonrelativist line of thought, multicultural education should involve exposing students to, and helping them to appreciate the range of, values embodied in different cultures. Both whites and Cambodian immigrant students can come to appreciate Toni Morrison's novels of black life in America. African-American students can come to understand and appreciate Confucian philosophy. This pluralist view should not minimize the work often necessary to see beyond the parochial assumptions and perspectives of one's own culture in order to appreciate the values of another culture. Indeed, one of the undoubted contributions of the multicultural movement has been to reveal those obstacles as well as the dominant culture's resistance to acknowledging them. Nevertheless, the fact that such an effort can be even partially successful provides a goal of multicultural education that is barely conceivable within the pure relativist position.

• • •

The third value for an educational program that I want to discuss is the *sense of community*—specifically a sense of community that embraces racial and cultural differences. While the idea of a multiracial integrated community has historically been linked with the struggle against racism, I think there is reason for focusing on it as a value distinct from antiracism. The sense of community that I mean involves a sense of bond with other persons, a sense of shared identification with the community in question (be it a class, a

school or workplace), a sense of loyalty to and involvement with this community. I will make the further assumption that the experience of interracial community in such institutions is an important contributor to being able fully to experience members of other races and cultures as fellow citizens and fellow human beings throughout one's life.

It is true that the achievement of or the experience of interracial community is likely to contribute to a firm commitment to nonracist and antiracist values. Nevertheless, there is an important difference between the two families of values. A sense of community is defeated not only by racist attitudes, in which members of one group feel themselves superior to members of another group, but simply by experiencing members of other races and cultural groups as *other,* as distant from oneself, as people with whom one does not feel comfortable, and has little in common. . . . What defeats a sense of community is to see members of a group primarily as *they,* as a kind of undifferentiated group counterposed to a *we,* defined by the group one identifies with oneself. One becomes blind to the individuality of members of the *they* group. One experiences this group as deeply different from oneself, even if one cannot always account for or explain that sense of difference. This anticommunal consciousness can exist in the absence of actual racist attitudes towards the other group, although the former is a natural stepping stone toward the latter. I think many students in schools, of all races and cultures, never do achieve the experience of interracial community, never learn to feel comfortable with members of other racial and ethnic groups, even though these students do not really have racist attitudes in the strict sense. Rather, the sense of group difference simply overwhelms any experiencing of commonality and sharing that is necessary for developing a sense of community.

Fortunately, we need not choose between the values of interracial community and antiracism; rather, we should search for ways of teaching antiracist values that minimize the potential for harming or preventing interracial community. I will briefly mention two general guidelines in this regard. One is constantly to emphasize the internal variety within a group being studied; not to say "whites" and "blacks" all the time as if these were monolithic groups. For example, in discussing slavery, make clear that not all blacks were slaves during the period of slavery, that there were many free blacks. Similarly, most whites did *not* own slaves, and a few whites even actively aligned themselves with the cause of abolition, aiding free blacks who organized the underground railroads and the like. Exhibiting such internal variety within "white," "black," and other groups helps to prevent the formation of rigid or undifferentiated images of racial groups that lend themselves readily to a *we / they* consciousness that undermines community.

A second guideline is to try to give students the experience (in imagination at least) of being both discriminated against, excluded, or demeaned, and also being the discriminator, the excluder, the advantaged one. . . .

Encouraging students to attempt as much as possible to experience the vantage points of advantaged and disadvantaged, included and excluded, and the like, provides an important buffer to a "we/they" consciousness in the racial

domain. This buffering is accomplished not so much by encouraging, as the first guideline does, the appreciation of internal diversity in a given group, as by bridging the gulf between the experience of the dominant and that of the subordinate. This is achieved by showing children that there is at least *some* dimension of life on which they occupy the dominant, and on others the subordinate, position (even if these dimensions are not of equal significance).

Some broad guidelines are the following: (a) Invite children's participation in cultures studied, so as to make "other" cultures as accessible as possible to nonmembers. For example, have children in the class interview one another, posing questions about each others' cultures that the questioners feel will help them to comprehend the culture in question. Establish an "intercultural dialogue" among students. This approach will use a recognition of genuine cultural differences to bring children together rather than keep them apart. (b) Recognize cultures' internal variety (even contradictory strands within a given culture), their change over time, and (where appropriate) their interaction with other cultures—rather than presenting cultures as frozen in time, monolithic, and totally self-contained. (c) Recognize cultural universals and commonalities. It is not contrary to the spirit of multiculturalism—to the acknowledgment of authentic cultural differences—to see that distinct cultures may share certain broad features. For example, every culture responds to certain universal features of human life, such as birth, death, the rearing of children, a search for meaning in life. Both (b) and (c) prevent an inaccurate and community-impairing "theyness" in the presentation of other cultures.

Finally, our conception of interracial community must itself allow for the recognition of difference. A powerful, but misleading, tradition in our thinking about community is that people only feel a sense of community when they think of themselves as "the same" as the other members of the community. But, as Robert Bellah and his colleagues argue in *Habits of the Heart,* the kind of community needed in the United States is *pluralistic* community, one which involves a sense of bond and connection stemming from shared activity, condition, task, location, and the like—and grounded ultimately in an experience of shared humanity—yet recognizing and valuing cultural differences (and other kinds of differences as well).[1]

NOTES

1. Robert Bellah, et al., *Habits of the Heart: Individualism and Commitment in American Life* (Berkeley: University of California Press, 1985).

I

HUMAN RIGHTS
AND JUSTICE

In each of our chapters, rights play a prominent role, so it is important to begin by understanding what rights are. Human rights are rights that people have by virtue of simply being human. Such rights are thought to exist universally. This universality is attested to by the fact that the United Nations' Universal Declaration of Human Rights was ratified with no dissenting votes. But in spite of this fact, there is quite a lively debate about the nature, extent, justification, and enumeration of human rights. We begin our anthology with this topic because it is central to all of the subsequent discussions—environmental rights; the right to be fed; the rights of those fighting in, or the right not to have to fight in, wars; the rights of sexual and racial equality; the right to health care; the right to free choice; as well as the right to life and the right to die.

In general, rights are considered to be extremely important moral considerations. Rights form the basis upon which individuals can make claims against other individuals or against whole societies or governments. If Jones has a right of free speech, then she has a strong basis for complaint if someone tries to prevent her from speaking, regardless of whether anyone wants to hear what she says. Indeed, according to the deontological tradition, the existence of a right provides an individual with a nearly unchallengeable basis for exercising that right, even when the vast majority of fellow citizens would be better off if the individual were not allowed to exercise her right. From a deontological point of view, rights are anti-majoritarian, or as Ronald Dworkin puts it, trump cards, which outweigh considerations of collective happiness or well-being.

Hardly anyone, at least in Western societies, denies that there are human rights, but there is a long-standing debate about what is the basis of these rights and about which are the most fundamental human rights. The latter debate has centered around the distinction between civil and economic rights. Civil rights concern the basic political status of members of a society and include such things as the rights to vote, speak, assemble, and participate equally in political affairs. Economic rights concern the livelihood and survival of a person in terms of food, shelter, clothing, and medical supplies. Many socialists, feminists and members of certain non-Western societies have challenged the Western-oriented dominance of civil over economic rights.

In some non-Western societies, as we will see, there is also a serious question raised about whether there are human rights that are universal in scope, or whether rights vary according to gender or race. Another challenge often brought against conceptions of human rights is that they are too focused on the individual rather than on the group. Ancient and medieval discussions of ethics in the West, especially discussions of natural rights, did not have this emphasis. The universalistic and individualistic dimensions of a Western conception of rights are products of the modern age. In a sense, some of the non-Western approaches we will examine resemble ancient and medieval Western conceptions much more than they do modern ones, and there are interesting parallels between premodern and non-Western approaches that would be interesting to explore.

To set the stage for our discussion, we begin with what many believe to be the authoritative statement of human rights—the United Nations' Universal Declaration of Human Rights. Passed by the General Assembly in 1948, this document was created in the aftermath of World War II as a resolution on the part of the founders of the United Nations to prevent future massive violations of persons' rights. It enumerates the variety of civil, political, legal, economic, and welfare rights that each individual, independent of sex, race, religion, social status, and national origin, is entitled to enjoy. Notice that while these human rights may not be effective until a government implements them through legislation or a society integrates them into their practice, they are nonetheless normative standards which any government or legal system is expected to respect and on the basis of which their practices can be criticized. It is also important to bear in mind that these rights constitute only minimum standards for "decent social and governmental practice."[1] They are not meant to be directives for comprehensive solutions of moral problems.

Our second reading is one of the best-known discussions of consequentialist ethics in general. John Stuart Mill, a defender of utilitarianism, presents one of the most plausible interpretations of utilitarianism, that is, the theory of ethics that equates moral rightness with the maximization of pleasure and the minimization of pain. Mill explains the importance of distinguishing between pleasures qualitatively. He argues that the test for deciding which of two pleasures is the best is simply which is preferred by those who have experienced both. Mill's general defense of the principle of utility proceeds from the idea that only when people prefer or desire something do we have any basis for regarding that thing as good. He then proceeds to show that happiness is the only thing that is desired for its own sake. Virtue and rights are valued in terms of their promotion of happiness or utility. At the end, Mill recognizes that justice is a term for various moral requirements that protect rights, and that while justice is merely a form of social utility, it is an especially important and weighty kind of utility.

Our third reading presents a simplified account of a dominant deonotological approach rivalling Mill's consequentialism—the ethics of Kant. In this selection, Onora O'Neill explicates the Formula of the End in Itself, one of the key formulations of Kant's fundamental moral principle, the Categorical Imperative. According to this formulation, moral rightness consists in treating oneself and others always as an end and not merely as a means. To treat a person as an end, on O'Neill's analysis, is in essence to allow the person at least in principle a choice between consenting and rejecting one's proposed course of action, which Kant calls a *maxim*. Absent such a choice, whether due to coercion or deception, the other person is treated merely as a means, and one's intended act cannot be morally acceptable. O'Neill proceeds to point out that unlike Mill's utilitarianism, which sees an individual's value as capable of compromise or sacrifice for the happiness of all, Kant's deontology rules out this possibility.

The next reading is taken from one of the most prominent defenders of rights, Ronald Dworkin. Dworkin is a defender of a deontological approach to ethics. In his essay he explains why rights need to be conceived as things that are not just very weighty forms of utility and hence as not being subject to legislative negotiation. The members of any society need to know that their government will respect them, and not exploit them for the betterment of the society against their will. On his account, rights operate as protectors of individual dignity, and as guarantors of equal respect within societies. To this end, Dworkin, like most other Western theorists, focuses on civil or political rights as the most fundamental of human rights.

Charlotte Bunch challenges the priority assigned to civil and political rights over socioeconomic rights in the Western conception of human rights in light of women' s situation. She observes that since the oppression and the violence directed against women across the globe are carried out by men who hold positions of power over them, protecting women's civil or political rights will not necessarily end such practices as sexual slavery, nor will it diminish the extent to which men are able to exercise arbitrary power over their social and economic status. Notice that Bunch does not claim that human rights are unimportant. She only intends to bring out the fact that unless the actual problems faced by women are treated of equal concern as the problems faced by men, human rights discussions will not have much to offer women.

In contrast with Bunch, Abdullahi Ahmed An-Na'im discusses a society in which the very legitimacy of human rights is called into question by the practices of the religious leadership. An-Na'im points out that some societies, such as those in the Islamic world, do not clearly endorse the view that all people should be accorded the same fundamental protections. Islamic society is partialist, in the sense that non-Muslims are treated quite differently from Muslims. The equal respect which Dworkin holds to be the hallmark of human rights theory is lacking in practice, although arguably it is something that can be justified by reference to some main Islamic texts. In those societies that do not accept the principle of equal respect, talk of human rights will not have much meaning, he concludes.

Similar to Charlotte Bunch, Claude Ake argues that individual civil and political liberties are of little benefit to communities of people suffering from hunger, poverty, and disease. In his view the best society is the one that leads to the greatest amount of economic development and liberation for the members of society. Thus, economic considerations should outweigh civil or political considerations. Furthermore, to better account for the African context, which views a person's interests as inextricably bound up with those of the community as a whole, the idea of human rights should be expanded from the rights of the individuals to include communities as rights-bearers, that is, collective human rights.

In some ways akin to the African view of the person, the Confucian moral perspective emphasizes an individual's finding his or her value and significance in a community. Roger T. Ames explores how the Confucian practice of ceremonial civility constitutes and expresses an ethical dimension of the individual who strives to feel and realize his or her nature and personality through a set of role-defined duties and obligations in harmony with others. Ames adds that this stress on extralegal responsibilities encompasses a moral import above and beyond what the Western conception of human rights can offer with its narrower focus on the individual and the protection of minimum standards for all.

We end this section with a discussion of Buddhist conception of ethics and the application of Buddhism to the human rights debate. Despite its surface affinities to the Confucian perspective due to a similar emphasis on the interconnectedness of nature and people, Buddhism differs from Confucian in its fundamental conception of human nature and attitudes to self, others, and the world. Kenneth Inada spends most of his essay discussing this Buddhist conception. On Inada's analysis, the Buddhist approach is characterized by an openness to and interrelatedness in experience, a recognition of emptiness and a realization of the ultimate contingency and fortuity in the constitution of one's self and the world. It is on this understanding of the ephemerality and fragility of existence that one should open oneself to human beings with compassion. Rights theorists tend to ignore such things and to focus instead, in a legalistic way, on theories and strategies for confronting offending institutions and governments that have abused the human rights of their members. Such an aggressive adversarial approach is quite inconsistent with the patient, compassionate, cooperative approach that characterizes the Buddhist perspective.

The discussions of Confucian, Buddhist, and Islamic perspectives could lead to a broader discussion of approaches to the field of ethics. In the West, ethics is often seen as similar to law. The pursuit of human rights is thus seen as quite similar to the pursuit of legal rights through the adversarial court system. But perhaps ethics should not be conceived in such a legalistic fashion. Perhaps ethics is, and should be, more concerned with cooperation and compassion than with the positing of claims by one person against another person. This is a subtext of our anthology and will recur in several other contexts.

—Kai Wong

NOTES

1. James Nickel, *Making Sense of Human Rights* (Berkeley: University of California Press, 1987), p. 4.

United Nations Universal Declaration of Human Rights

The Universal Declaration of Human Rights was approved unanimously by the General Assembly of the United Nations on December 10, 1948, by forty-eight nations with eight abstentions (including six members in the Soviet bloc at the time, South Africa, and Saudi Arabia) to be the common universal standard of human rights for all nations and peoples. The Declaration enumerates all rights and freedoms that each individual is to enjoy irrespective of "race, color, sex, language, religion, political or other opinion, national or social origin, property, birth or other status."

THE GENERAL ASSEMBLY

proclaims

This universal declaration of human rights as a common standard of achievement for all peoples and all nations, to the end that every individual and every organ of society, keeping this Declaration constantly in mind, shall strive by teaching and education to promote respect for these rights and freedoms and by progressive measures, national and international, to secure their universal and effective recognition and observance, both among the peoples of Member States themselves and among the peoples of territories under their jurisdiction.

ARTICLE 1

All human beings are born free and equal in dignity and rights. They are endowed with reason and conscience and should act towards one another in a spirit of brotherhood.

ARTICLE 2

Everyone is entitled to all the rights and freedoms set forth in this Declaration, without distinction of any kind, such as race, colour, sex, language, religion, political or other opinion, national or social origin, property, birth or other status.

Furthermore, no distinction shall be made on the basis of the political, jurisdictional or international status of the country or territory to which a person belongs, whether it be independent, trust, non-self-governing or under any other limitation of sovereignty.

ARTICLE 3

Everyone has the right to life, liberty and security of person.

ARTICLE 4

No one shall be held in slavery or servitude; slavery and the slave trade shall be prohibited in all their forms.

Reprinted with the permission of United Nations Publications. [Edited]

ARTICLE 5

No one shall be subjected to torture or to cruel, inhuman or degrading treatment or punishment.

ARTICLE 6

Everyone has the right to recognition everywhere as a person before the law.

ARTICLE 7

All are equal before the law and are entitled without any discrimination to equal protection of the law. All are entitled to equal protection against any discrimination in violation of this Declaration and against any incitement to such discrimination.

ARTICLE 8

Everyone has the right to an effective remedy by the competent national tribunals for acts violating the fundamental rights granted him by the constitution or by law.

ARTICLE 9

No one shall be subjected to arbitrary arrest, detention or exile.

ARTICLE 10

Everyone is entitled in full equality to a fair and public hearing by an independent and impartial tribunal, in the determination of his rights and obligations and of any criminal charge against him.

ARTICLE 11

1. Everyone charged with a penal offence has the right to be presumed innocent until proved guilty according to law in a public trial at which he has had all the guarantees necessary for his defence.

2. No one shall be held guilty of any penal offence on account of any act or omission which did not constitute a penal offence, under national or international law, at the time when it was commited. Nor shall a heavier penalty be imposed than the one that was applicable at the time the penal offence was committed.

ARTICLE 12

No one shall be subjected to arbitrary interference with his privacy, family, home or correspondence, nor to attacks upon his honour and reputation. Everyone has the right to the protection of the law against such interference or attacks.

ARTICLE 13

I. Everyone has the right to freedom of movement and residence within the borders of each state.

2. Everyone has the right to leave any country, including his own, and to return to his country.

ARTICLE 14

1. Everyone has the right to seek and to enjoy in other countries asylum from persecution.

2. This right may not be invoked in the case of prosecutions genuinely arising from non-political crimes or from acts contrary to the purposes and principles of the United Nations.

ARTICLE 15

1. Everyone has the right to a nationality.

2. No one shall be arbitrarily deprived of his nationality nor denied the right to change his nationality.

ARTICLE 16

1. Men and women of full age, without any limitation due to race, nationality or religion, have the right to marry and to found a family. They are entitled to equal

rights as to marriage, during marriage and at its dissolution.

2. Marriage shall be entered into only with the free and full consent of the intending spouses.

3. The family is the natural and fundamental group unit of society and is entitled to protection by society and the State.

ARTICLE 17

1. Everyone has the right to own property alone as well as in association with others.

2. No one shall be arbitrarily deprived of his property.

ARTICLE 18

Everyone has the right to freedom of thought, conscience and religion; this right includes freedom to change his religion or belief, and freedom, either alone or in community with others and in public or private, to manifest his religion or belief in teaching, practice, worship and observance.

ARTICLE 19

Everyone has the right to freedom of opinion and expression; this right includes freedom to hold opinions without interference and to seek, receive and impart information and ideas through any media and regardless of frontiers.

ARTICLE 20

1. Everyone has the right to freedom of peaceful assembly and association.

2. No one may be compelled to belong to an association.

ARTICLE 21

1. Everyone has the right to take part in the govemment of his country, directly or through freely chosen representatives.

2. Everyone has the right of equal access to public service in his country.

3. The will of the people shall be the basis of the authority of government; this will shall be expressed in periodic and genuine elections which shall be by universal and equal suffrage and shall be held by secret vote or by equivalent free voting procedures.

ARTICLE 22

Everyone, as a member of society, has the right to social security and is entitled to realization, through national effort and international co-operation and in accordance with the organization and resources of each State, of the economic, social and cultural rights indispensable for his dignity and the free development of his personality.

ARTICLE 23

1. Everyone has the right to work, to free choice of employment, to just and favourable conditions of work and to protection against unemployment.

2. Everyone, without any discrimination, has the right to equal pay for equal work.

3. Everyone who works has the right to just and favourable remuneration ensuring for himself and his family an existence worthy of human dignity, and supplemented, if necessary, by other means of social protection.

4. Everyone has the right to form and to join trade unions for the protection of his interests.

ARTICLE 24

Everyone has the right to rest and leisure, including reasonable limitation of working hours and periodic holidays with pay.

ARTICLE 25

Everyone has the right to a standard of living adequate for the health and well-being of himself and of his family, including food, clothing, housing and medical care and necessary social services, and the right to security in the event of unemployment, sickness, disability, widowhood, old age or other lack of livelihood in circumstances beyond his control.

1. Motherhood and childhood are entitled to special care and assistance. All children, whether born in or out of wedlock, shall enjoy the same social protection.

ARTICLE 26

1. Everyone has the right to education. Education shall be free, at least in the elementary and fundamental stages. Elementary education shall be compulsory. Technical and professional education shall be made generally available and higher education shall be equally accessible to all on the basis of merit.

2. Education shall be directed to the full development of the human personality and to the strengthening of respect for human rights and fundamental freedoms. It shall promote understanding, tolerance and friendship among all nations, racial or religious groups, and shall further the activities of the United Nations for the maintenance of peace.

2. Parents have a prior right to choose the kind of education that shall be given to their children.

ARTICLE 27

1. Everyone has the right freely to participate in the cultural life of the community, to enjoy the arts and to share in scientific advancement and its benefits.

2. Everyone has the right to the protection of the moral and material interests resulting from any scientific, literary or artistic production of which he is the author.

ARTICLE 28

Everyone is entitled to a social and international order in which the rights and freedoms set forth in this Declaration can be fully realized.

ARTICLE 29

1. Everyone has duties to the community in which alone the free and full development of his personality is possible.

2. In the exercise of his rights and freedoms, everyone shall be subject only to such limitations as are determined by law solely for the purpose of securing due recognition and respect for the rights and freedoms of others and of meeting the just requirements of morality, public order and the general welfare in a democratic society.

3. These rights and freedoms may in no case be exercised contrary to the purposes and principles of the United Nations.

ARTICLE 30

Nothing in this Declaration may be interpreted as implying for any State, group or person any right to engage in any activity or to perform any act aimed at the destruction of any of the rights and freedoms set forth herein.

Utilitarianism

John Stuart Mill

John Stuart Mill was one of the leading intellectuals of the nineteenth century. He was a member of Parliament as well as a popular philosopher. He is the author of A System of Logic *(1843),* On Liberty *(1859),* Utilitarianism *(1861),* Considerations on Representative Government *(1861),* The Subjection of Women *(1869), and* Principles of Political Economy *(1871).*

Mill's defense of the principle of utility is the most influential modern account of a consequentialist moral theory. In this excerpt from his book Utilitarianism, *Mill clearly sets out the principle of the greatest happiness for the greatest number and defends it against several of the most obvious objections. He then offers a limited defense of the principle. He ends by explaining the intimate relationship between utility and rights.*

WHAT UTILITARIANISM IS

The creed which accepts as the foundation of morals "utility" or the "greatest happiness principle" holds that actions are right in proportion as they tend to promote happiness; wrong as they tend to produce the reverse of happiness. By happiness is intended pleasure and the absence of pain; by unhappiness, pain and the privation of pleasure. To give a clear view of the moral standard set up by the theory, much more requires to be said; in particular, what things it includes in the ideas of pain and pleasure, and to what extent this is left an open question. But these supplementary explanations do not affect the theory of life on which this theory of morality is grounded—namely, that pleasure and freedom from pain are the only things desirable as ends; and that all desirable things (which are as numerous in the utilitarian as in any other scheme) are desirable either for pleasure inherent in themselves or as means to the promotion of pleasure and the prevention of pain.

Now such a theory of life excites in many minds, and among them in some of the most estimable in feeling and purpose, inveterate dislike. To suppose that life has (as they express it) no higher end than pleasure—no better and nobler object of desire and pursuit—they designate as utterly mean and groveling, as a doctrine worthy only of swine, to whom the followers of Epicurus were, at a very early period, contemptuously likened; and modern holders of the doctrine are occasionally made the subject of equally polite comparisons by its German, French, and English assailants.

When thus attacked, the Epicureans have always answered that it is not they, but their accusers, who represent human nature in a degrading light, since the

Reprinted with permission of Hackett Publishing Co., from *Utilitarianism,* by John Stuart Mill, edited by George Sher, 1979. [Edited]

accusation supposes human beings to be capable of no pleasures except those of which swine are capable. If this supposition were true, the charge could not be gainsaid, but would then be no longer an imputation; for if the sources of pleasure were precisely the same to human beings and to swine, the rule of life which is good enough for the one would be good enough for the other. The comparison of the Epicurean life to that of beasts is felt as degrading, precisely because a beast's pleasures do not satisfy a human being's conceptions of happiness. Human beings have faculties more elevated than the animal appetites and, when once made conscious of them, do not regard anything as happiness which does not include their gratification. I do not indeed, consider the Epicureans to have been by any means faultless in drawing out their scheme of consequences from the utilitarian principle. To do this in any sufficient manner, many Stoic, as well as Christian, elements require to be included. But there is no known Epicurean theory of life which does not assign to the pleasures of the intellect, of the feelings and imagination, and of the moral sentiments a much higher value as pleasures than to those of mere sensation. It must be admitted, however, that utilitarian writers in general have placed the superiority of mental over bodily pleasures chiefly in the greater permanency, safety, uncostliness, etc., of the former— that is, in their circumstantial advantages rather than in their intrinsic nature. And on all these points utilitarians have fully proved their case; but they might have taken the other and, as it may be called, higher ground with entire consistency. It is quite compatible with the principle of utility to recognize the fact that some kinds of pleasure are more desirable and more valuable than others. It would be absurd that, while in estimating all other things quality is considered as well as quantity, the estimation of pleasure should be supposed to depend on quantity alone.

If I am asked what I mean by difference of quality in pleasures, or what makes one pleasure more valuable than another, merely as a pleasure, except its being greater in amount, there is but one possible answer. Of two pleasures, if there be one to which all or almost all who have experience of both give a decided preference, irrespective of any feeling of moral obligation to prefer it, that is the more desirable pleasure. If one of the two is, by those who are competently acquainted with both, placed so far above the other that they prefer it, even though knowing it to be attended with a greater amount of discontent, and would not resign it for any quantity of the other pleasure which their nature is capable of, we are justified in ascribing to the preferred enjoyment a superiority in quality so far outweighing quantity as to render it, in comparison, of small account.

Now it is an unquestionable fact that those who are equally acquainted with and equally capable of appreciating and enjoying both do give a most marked preference to the manner of existence which employs their higher faculties. Few human creatures would consent to be changed into any of the lower animals for a promise of the fullest allowance of a beast's pleasures; no intelligent human being would consent to be a fool, no instructed person would be an ignoramus, no person of feeling and conscience would be selfish and base, even though they should be persuaded that the fool, the dunce, or the rascal is better satisfied with his lot than they are with theirs. They would not resign what they possess more than he for the most complete satisfaction of all the desires which they have in common with him. If they ever fancy they would, it is only in cases of unhappiness so extreme that to escape from it they would exchange their lot for almost any other, however undesirable in their own eyes. A being of higher faculties requires more to make him happy, is capable probably of more acute suffering, and certainly accessible to it at more points, than one of an inferior type; but in spite of these liabilities, he can never really wish to sink into what he feels to be a lower grade of existence. We may give what explanation we please of this unwillingness; we may attribute it to pride, a name which is given indiscriminately to some of the most and to some of the least estimable feelings of which mankind are capable; we may refer it to the love of liberty and personal independence, an appeal to which was with the Stoics one of the most effective means for the inculcation of it; to the love of power or to the love of excitement, both of which do really enter into and contribute to it; but its most appropriate appellation is a sense of dignity, which all human beings possess in one form or other, and in some, though by no means in exact, proportion to their higher faculties, and which is so essential a part of the happiness of those in whom it is strong that nothing which conflicts with it could be otherwise than momentarily an object of desire to them. Whoever supposes that this preference takes place at a sacrifice of happiness— that the superior being, in anything like equal circumstances, is not happier than the inferior—confounds the two very different ideas of happiness and content. It

is indisputable that the being whose capacities of enjoyment are low has the greatest chance of having them fully satisfied; and a highly endowed being will always feel that any happiness which he can look for, as the world is constituted, is imperfect. But he can learn to bear its imperfections, if they are at all bearable; and they will not make him envy the being who is indeed unconscious of the imperfections, but only because he feels not at all the good which those imperfections qualify. It is better to be a human being dissatisfied than a pig satisfied; better to be Socrates dissatisfied than a fool satisfied. And if the fool, or the pig, are of a different opinion, it is because they only know their own side of the question. The other party to the comparison knows both sides.

It may be objected that many who are capable of the higher pleasures occasionally, under the influence of temptation, postpone them to the lower. But this is quite compatible with a full appreciation of the intrinsic superiority of the higher. Men often, from infirmity of character, make their election for the nearer good, though they know it to be the less valuable; and this no less when the choice is between two bodily pleasures than when it is between bodily and mental. They pursue sensual indulgences to the injury of health, though perfectly aware that health is the greater good. It may be further objected that many who begin with youthful enthusiasm for everything noble, as they advance in years, sink into indolence and selfishness. But I do not believe that those who undergo this very common change voluntarily choose the lower description of pleasures in preference to the higher. I believe that, before they devote themselves exclusively to the one, they have already become incapable of the other. Capacity for the nobler feelings is in most natures a very tender plant, easily killed, not only by hostile influences, but by mere want of sustenance; and in the majority of young persons it speedily dies away if the occupations to which their position in life has devoted them, and the society into which it has thrown them, are not favorable to keeping that higher capacity in exercise. Men lose their high aspirations as they lose their intellectual tastes, because they have not time or opportunity for indulging them; and they addict themselves to inferior pleasures, not because they deliberately prefer them, but because they are either the only ones to which they have access or the only ones which they are any longer capable of enjoying. It may be questioned whether anyone who has remained equally susceptible to both classes of pleasures ever knowingly and calmly preferred the lower, though many, in all ages, have broken down in an ineffectual attempt to combine both.

From this verdict of the only competent judges, I apprehend there can be no appeal. On a question which is the best worth having of two pleasures, or which of two modes of existence is the most grateful to the feelings, apart from its moral attributes and from its consequences, the judgment of these who are qualified by knowledge of both, or, if they differ, that of the majority among them, must be admitted as final. And there needs be the less hesitation to accept this judgment respecting the quality of pleasures, since there is no other tribunal to be referred to even on the question of quantity. What means are there of determining which is the acutest of two pains, or the intensest of two pleasurable sensations, except the general suffrage of those who are familiar with both? Neither pains nor pleasures are homogeneous, and pain is always heterogeneous with pleasure. What is there to decide whether a particular pleasure is worth purchasing at the cost of a particular pain, except the feelings and judgment of the experienced? When, therefore, those feelings and judgment declare the pleasures derived from the higher faculties to be preferable *in kind*, apart from the question of intensity, to those of which the animal nature, disjoined from the higher faculties, is susceptible, they are entitled on this subject to the same regard.

I have dwelt on this point as being part of a perfectly just conception of utility or happiness considered as the directive rule of human conduct. But it is by no means an indispensable condition to the acceptance of the utilitarian standard; for that standard is not the agent's own greatest happiness, but the greatest amount of happiness altogether; and if it may possibly be doubted whether a noble character is always the happier for its nobleness, there can be no doubt that it makes other people happier, and that the world in general is immensely a gainer by it. Utilitarianism, therefore, could only attain its end by the general cultivation of nobleness of character, even if each individual were only benefited by the nobleness of others, and his own, so far as happiness is concerned, were a sheer deduction from the benefit. But the bare enunciation of such an absurdity as this last renders refutation superfluous.

According to the greatest happiness principle, as above explained, the ultimate end, with reference to and for the sake of which all other things are desirable—whether we are considering our own good or that of other people—is an existence exempt as far as possible from pain, and as rich as possible in enjoyments, both in point of quantity and quality; the test of quality and the rule for measuring it against quantity being the preference felt by those who, in their opportunities of experience, to which must be added their habits of self-consciousness and self-observation, are best furnished with the means of comparison. This, being according to the utlitarian opinion the end of human action, is necessarily also the standard of morality, which may accordingly be defined "the rules and precepts for human conduct," by the observance of which an existence such as has been described might be, to the greatest extent possible, secured to all mankind; and not to them only, but, so far as the nature of things admits, to the whole sentient creation. . . .

OF WHAT SORT OF PROOF THE PRINCIPLE OF UTILITY IS SUSCEPTIBLE

It has already been remarked that questions of ultimate ends do not admit of proof, in the ordinary acceptation of the term. To be incapable of proof by reasoning is common to all first principles, to the first premises of our knowledge, as well as to those of our conduct. But the former, being matters of fact, may be the subject of a direct appeal to the faculties which judge of fact—namely, our senses and our internal consciousness. Can an appeal be made to the same faculties on questions of practical ends? Or by what other faculty is cognizance taken of them?

Questions about ends are, in other words, questions of what things are desirable. The utilitarian doctrine is that happiness is desirable, and the only thing desirable, as an end; all other things being only desirable as means to that end. What ought to be required of this doctrine, what conditions is it requisite that the doctrine should fulfill—to make good its claim to be believed?

The only proof capable of being given that an object is visible is that people actually see it. The only proof that a sound is audible is that people hear it; and so of the other sources of our experience. In like manner, I apprehend, the sole evidence it is possible to produce that anything is desirable is that people do actually desire it. If the end which the utilitarian doctrine proposes to itself were not, in theory and in practice, acknowledged to be an end, nothing could ever convince any person that it was so. No reason can be given why the general happiness is desirable, except that each person, so far as he believes it to be attainable, desires his own happiness. This, however, being a fact, we have not only all the proof which the case admits of, but all which it is possible to require, that happiness is a good, that each person's happiness is a good to that person, and the general happiness, therefore, a good to the aggregate of all persons. Happiness has made out its title as *one* of the ends of conduct and, consequently, one of the criteria of morality.

But it has not, by this alone, proved itself to be the sole criterion. To do that, it would seem, by the same rule, necessary to show, not only that people desire happiness, but that they never desire anything else. Now it is palpable that they do desire things which, in common language, are decidedly distinguished from happiness. They desire, for example, virtue and the absence of vice no less really than pleasure and the absence of pain. The desire of virtue is not as universal, but it is as authentic a fact as the desire of happiness. And hence the opponents of the utilitarian standard deem that they have a right to infer that there are other ends of human action besides happiness, and that happiness is not the standard of approbation and disapprobation.

But does the utilitarian doctrine deny that people desire virtue, or maintain that virtue is not a thing to be desired? The very reverse. It maintains not only that virtue is to be desired, but that it is to be desired disinterestedly, for itself. Whatever may be the opinion of utilitarian moralists as to the original conditions by which virtue is made virtue, however they may believe (as they do) that actions and dispositions are only virtuous because they promote another end than virtue, yet this being granted, and it having been decided, from considerations of this description, what *is* virtuous, they not only place virtue at the very head of the things which are good as means to the ultimate end, but they also recognize as a psychological fact the possibility of its being, to the individual, a good in itself, without looking to any end beyond it; and hold that the mind is not in a right state, not in a state conformable to utility, not in the state most conducive to the general happiness, unless it does love virtue in this manner—as a thing desirable in itself, even although, in the individual instance, it should not produce those other desirable consequences which it tends to produce, and on account of which it is held to be virtue. This opinion is not, in the smallest degree, a departure from the happiness principle. The ingredients of happiness are very various, and each of them is desirable in itself, and not merely when considered as swelling an aggregate. The principle of utility does not

mean that any given pleasure, as music, for instance, or any given exemption from pain, as for example health, is to be looked upon as means to a collective something termed happiness, and to be desired on that account. They are desired and desirable in and for themselves; besides being means, they are a part of the end. Virtue, according to the utilitarian doctrine, is not naturally and originally a part of the end, but it is capable of becoming so; and in those who live it disinterestedly it has become so, and is desired and cherished, not as a means to happiness, but as a part of their happiness.

To illustrate this further, we may remember that virtue is not the only thing originally a means, and which if it were not a means to anything else would be and remain indifferent, but which by association with what it is a means to comes to be desired for itself, and that too with the utmost intensity. What, for example, shall we say of the love of money? There is nothing originally more desirable about money than about any heap of glittering pebbles. Its worth is solely that of the things which it will buy; the desires for other things than itself, which it is a means of gratifying. Yet the love of money is not only one of the strongest moving forces of human life, but money is, in many cases, desired in and for itself; the desire to possess it is often stronger than the desire to use it, and goes on increasing when all the desires which point to ends beyond it, to be compassed by it, are falling off. It may, then, be said truly that money is desired not for the sake of an end, but as part of the end. From being a means to happiness, it has come to be itself a principal ingredient of the individual's conception of happiness. The same may be said of the majority of the great objects of human life: power, for example, or fame, except that to each of these there is a certain amount of immediate pleasure annexed, which has at least the semblance of being naturally inherent in them—a thing which cannot be said of money. Still, however, the strongest natural attraction, both of power and of fame, is the immense aid they give to the attainment of our other wishes; and it is the strong association thus generated between them and all our objects of desire which gives to the direct desire of them the intensity it often assumes, so as in some characters to surpass in strength all other desires. In these cases the means have become a part of the end, and a more important part of it than any of the things which they are means to. What was once desired as an instrument for the attainment of happiness has come to be desired for its own sake. In being desired for its own sake it is, however, desired as *part* of happiness. The person is made, or thinks he would be made, happy by its mere possession; and is made unhappy by failure to obtain it. The desire of it is not a different thing from the desire of happiness any more than the love of music or the desire of health. They are included in happiness. They are some of the elements of which the desire of happiness is made up. Happiness is not an abstract idea but a concrete whole; and these are some of its parts. And the utilitarian standard sanctions and approves their being so. Life would be a poor thing, very ill provided with sources of happiness, if there were not this provision of nature by which things originally indifferent, but conducive to, or otherwise associated with, the satisfaction of our primitive desires, become in themselves sources of pleasure more valuable than the primitive pleasures, both in permanency, in the space of human existence that they are capable of covering, and even in intensity.

Virtue, according to the utilitarian conception, is a good of this description. There was no original desire of it, or motive to it, save its conduciveness to pleasure, and especially to protection from pain. But through the association thus formed it may be felt a good in itself, and desired as such with as great intensity as any other good; and with this difference between it and the love of money, of power, or of fame—that all of these may, and often do, render the individual noxious to the other members of the society to which he belongs, whereas there is nothing which makes him so much a blessing to them as the cultivation of the disinterested love of virtue. And consequently, the utilitarian standard, while it tolerates and approves those other acquired desires, up to the point beyond which they would be more injurious to the general happiness than promotive of it, enjoins and requires the cultivation of the love of virtue up to the greatest strength possible, as being above all things important to the general happiness.

It results from the preceding considerations that there is in reality nothing desired except happiness. Whatever is desired otherwise than as a means to some end beyond itself, and ultimately to happiness, is desired as itself a part of happiness, and is not desired for itself until it has become so. . . .

ON THE CONNECTION BETWEEN JUSTICE AND UTILITY

In all ages of speculation one of the strongest obstacles to the reception of the doctrine that utility or happiness is the criterion of right and wrong has been drawn from the idea of justice. The powerful sentiment and apparently clear perception which that word recalls with a rapidity and certainty resembling an instinct have seemed to the majority of thinkers to point to an inherent quality in things; to show that the just must have an existence in nature as something absolute, generically distinct from every variety of the expedient and, in idea, opposed to it, though (as is commonly acknowledged) never, in the long run, disjoined from it in fact. . . .

The idea of justice supposes two things—a rule of conduct and a sentiment which sanctions the rule. The first must be supposed common to all mankind and intended for their good. The other (the sentiment) is a desire that punishment may be suffered by those who infringe the rule. There is involved, in addition, the conception of some definite person who suffers by the infringement, whose rights (to use the expression appropriated to the case) are violated by it. And the sentiment of justice appears to me to be the animal desire to repel or retaliate a hurt or damage to oneself or to those with whom one sympathizes, widened so as to include all persons, by the human capacity of enlarged sympathy and the human conception of intelligent self-interest. From the latter elements the feeling derives its morality; from the former, its peculiar impressiveness and energy of self-assertion.

I have, throughout, treated the idea of a *right* residing in the injured person and violated by the injury, not as a separate element in the composition of the idea and sentiment, but as one of the forms in which the other two elements clothe themselves. These elements are a hurt to some assignable person or persons, on the one hand, and a demand for punishment, on the other. An examination of our own minds, I think, will show that these two things include all that we mean when we speak of violation of a right. When we call anything a person's right, we mean that he has a valid claim on society to protect him in the possession of it, either by the force of law or by that of education and opinion. If he has what we consider a sufficient claim, on whatever account, to have something guaranteed to him by society, we say that he has a right to it. If we desire to prove that anything does not belong to him by right, we think this done as soon as it is admitted that society ought not to take measure for securing it to him, but should leave him to chance or to his own exertions. Thus a person is said to have a right to what he can earn in fair professional competition, because society ought not to allow any other person to hinder him from endeavoring to earn in that manner as much as he can. But he has not a right to three hundred a year, though he may happen to be earning it; because society is not called on to provide that he shall earn that sum. On the contrary, if he owns ten thousand pounds three-per-cent stock, he *has* a right to three hundred a year because society has come under an obligation to provide him with an income of that amount.

To have a right, then, is, I conceive, to have something which society ought to defend me in the possession of. If the objector goes on to ask why it ought, I can give him no other reason than general utility. If that expression does not seem to convey a sufficient feeling of the strength of the obligation, nor to account for the peculiar energy of the feeling, it is because there goes to the composition of the sentiment, not a rational only but also an animal element—the thirst for retaliation; and this thirst derives its intensity, as well as its moral justification, from the extraordinarily important and impressive kind of utility which is concerned. The interest involved is that of security, to everyone's feelings the most vital of all interests. All other earthly benefits are needed by one person, not needed by another; and many of them can, if necessary, be cheerfully forgone or replaced by something else; but security no human being can possibly do without; on it we depend for all our immunity from evil and for the whole value of all and every good, beyond the passing moment, since nothing but the gratification of the instant could be of any worth to us if we could be deprived of everything the next instant by whoever was momentarily stronger than ourselves. Now this most indispensable of all necessaries, after physical nutriment, cannot be had unless the machinery for providing it is kept unintermittedly in active play. Our notion, therefore, of the claim we have on our fellow creatures to join in making safe for us the very groundwork of our existence gathers feelings around it so much more intense than those concerned in any of the more common cases of utility that the difference in degree (as is often the case in psychology) becomes a real difference in kind. The claim assumes that character of absoluteness, that apparent infinity and incommensurability with all other considerations which constitute the distinction between the feeling of right and wrong and that of ordinary expediency and inexpediency. The feelings concerned are so powerful, and we count so positively on finding a responsive feeling in others (all being alike interested) that *ought* and *should* grow into *must,* and recognized indispensability becomes a moral necessity,

analogous to physical, and often not inferior to it in binding force.

If the preceding analysis, or something resembling it, be not the correct account of the notion of justice—if justice be totally independent of utility, and be a standard *per se*, which the mind can recognize by simple introspection of itself—it is hard to understand why that internal oracle is so ambiguous, and why so many things appear either just or unjust, according to the light in which they are regarded. . . .

It appears from what has been said that justice is a name for certain moral requirements which, regarded collectively, stand higher in the scale of social utility, and are therefore of more paramount obligation, than any others, though particular cases may occur in which some other social duty is so important as to overrule any one of the general maxims of justice. Thus, to save a life, it may not only be allowable, but a duty, to steal or take by force the necessary food or medicine, or to kidnap and compel to officiate the only qualified medical practitioner. In such cases, as we do not call anything justice which is not a virtue, we usually say, not that justice must give way to some other moral principle, but that what is just in ordinary cases is, by reason of that other principle, not just in the particular case. By this useful accommodation of language, the character of indefeasibility attributed to justice is kept up, and we are saved from the necessity of maintaining that there can be laudable injustice.

The considerations which have not been adduced resolve, I conceive, the only real difficulty in the utilitarian theory of morals. It has always been evident that all cases of justice are also cases of expediency; the difference is in the peculiar sentiment which attaches to the former, as contradistinguished from the latter. If this characteristic sentiment has been sufficiently accounted for; if there is no necessity to assume for it any peculiarity of origin; if it is simply the natural feeling of resentment, moralized by being made coextensive with the demands of social good; and if this feeling not only does but ought to exist in all the classes of cases to which the idea of justice corresponds—that idea no longer presents itself as a stumbling block to the utilitarian ethics. Justice remains the appropriate name for certain social utilities which are vastly more important, and therefore more absolute and imperative, than any others are as a class (though not more so than others may be in particular cases); and which, therefore, ought to be, as well as naturally are, guarded by a sentiment, not only different in degree, but also in kind; distinguished from the milder feeling which attaches to the mere idea of promoting human pleasure or convenience at once by the more definite nature of its commands and by the sterner character of its sanctions.

A Simplified Account
of Kant's Ethics

Onora O'Neill

Onora O'Neill is now principal of Newnham College, Cambridge University. She has taught philosophy at the University of Essex and Bernard College. She has published articles on ethics and is also the author of Acting on Principle *(1975),* Faces of Hunger *(1986), and* Constructions of Reason *(1989).*

Kant's ethics represents the prevailing approach to deontological moral theory. In this selection, O'Neill elucidates and provides an interpretation of one of the formulations of the Categorical Imperative, The Formula of the End in Itself, in terms of the notion of consent. She also highlights the differences between utilitarianism and Kantian ethics on the value of human life.

Kant's moral theory has acquired the reputation of being forbiddingly difficult to understand and, once understood, excessively demanding in its requirements. I don't believe that this reputation has been wholly earned, and I am going to try to undermine it. . . . I shall try to reduce some of the difficulties. . . . Finally, I shall compare Kantian and utilitarian approaches and assess their strengths and weaknesses.

The main method by which I propose to avoid some of the difficulties of Kant's moral theory is by explaining only one part of the theory. This does not seem to me to be an irresponsible approach in this case. One of the things that makes Kant's moral theory hard to understand is that

"A Simplified Account of Kant's Ethics," by Onora O'Neill from *Matters of Life and Death*, ed. Tom Regan, 1986, McGraw-Hill Publishing Company. Reprinted by permission of McGraw-Hill. [Edited]

he gives a number of different versions of the principle that he calls the Supreme Principle of Morality, and these different versions don't look at all like one another. They also don't look at all like the utilitarians' Greatest Happiness Principle. But the Kantian principle is supposed to play a similar role in arguments about what to do.

Kant calls his Supreme Principle the *Categorical Imperative*; its various versions also have sonorous names. One is called the Formula of Universal Law; another is the Formula of the Kingdom of Ends. The one on which I shall concentrate is known as the *Formula of the End in Itself*. To understand why Kant thinks that these picturesquely named principles are equivalent to one another takes quite a lot of close and detailed analysis of Kant's philosophy. I shall avoid this and concentrate on showing the implications of this version of the Categorical Imperative.

THE FORMULA OF THE END IN ITSELF

Kant states the Formula of the End in Itself as follows:

> Act in such a way that you always treat humanity, whether in your own person or in the person of any other, never simply as a means but always at the same time as an end.

To understand this we need to know what it is to treat a person as a means or as an end. According to Kant, each of our acts reflects one or more *maxims*. The maxim of the act is the principle on which one sees oneself as acting. A maxim expresses a person's policy, or if he or she has no settled policy, the principle underlying the particular intention or decision on which he or she acts. Thus, a person who decides "This year I'll give 10 percent of my income to famine relief" has as a maxim the principle of tithing his or her income for famine relief. In practice, the difference between intentions and maxims is of little importance, for given any intention, we can formulate the corresponding maxim by deleting references to particular times, places, and persons. In what follows I shall take the terms 'maxim' and 'intention' as equivalent.

Whenever we act intentionally, we have at least one maxim and can, if we reflect, state what it is. (There is of course room for self-deception here—"I'm only keeping the wolf from the door" we may claim as we wolf down enough to keep ourselves overweight, or, more to the point, enough to feed someone else who hasn't enough food.)

When we want to work out whether an act we propose to do is right or wrong, according to Kant, we should look at our maxims and not at how much misery or happiness the act is likely to produce, and whether it does better at increasing happiness than other available acts. We just have to check that the act we have in mind will not use anyone as a mere means, and, if possible, that it will treat other persons as ends in themselves.

USING PERSONS AS MERE MEANS

To use someone as a *mere means* is to involve them in a scheme of action *to which they could not in principle consent.* Kant does not say that there is anything wrong about using someone as a means. Evidently we have to do so in any cooperative scheme of action. If I cash a check I use the teller as a means, without whom I could not lay my hands on the cash; the teller in turn uses me as a means to earn his or her living. But in this case, each party consents to her or his part in the transaction. Kant would say that though they use one another as means, they do not use one another as *mere* means. Each person assumes that the other has maxims of his or her own and is not just a thing or a prop to be manipulated.

But there are other situations where one person uses another in a way to which the other could not in principle consent. For example, one person may make a promise to another with every intention of breaking it. If the promise is accepted, then the person to whom it was given must be ignorant of what the promisor's intention (maxim) really is. If one knew that the promisor did not intend to do what he or she was promising, one would, after all, not accept or rely on the promise. It would be as though there had been no promise made. Successful false promising depends on deceiving the person to whom the promise is made about what one's real maxim is. And since the person who is deceived doesn't know that real maxim, he or she can't in principle consent to his or her part in the proposed scheme of action. The person who is deceived is as it were, a prop or a tool—a mere means—in the false promisor's scheme. A person who promises falsely treats the acceptor of the promise as a prop or a thing and not as a person. In Kant's view, it is this that makes false promising wrong.

One standard way of using others as mere means is by deceiving them. By getting someone involved in a business scheme or a criminal activity on false pretenses, or by giving a misleading account of what one is about, or by making a false promise or a fraudulent contract, one involves another in something to which he or she in principle cannot consent, since the scheme requires that he or she doesn't know what is going on. Another standard way of using others as mere means is by coercing them. If a rich or powerful person threatens a debtor with bankruptcy unless he or she joins in some scheme, then the creditor's intention is to coerce; and the debtor, if coerced, cannot consent to his or her part in the creditor's scheme. To make the example more specific: If a moneylender in an Indian village threatens not to renew a vital loan unless he is given the debtor's land, then he uses the debtor as a mere means. He coerces the debtor, who cannot truly consent to this "offer he can't refuse." (Of course the outward form of such transactions may look like ordinary commercial dealings, but we know very well that some offers and demands couched in that form are coercive.)

In Kant's view, acts that are done on maxims that require deception or coercion of others and so cannot have the consent of those others (for consent precludes both deception and coercion), are wrong. When we act on such maxims, we treat others as mere means, as things rather than as ends in themselves. If we act on such maxims, our acts are not only wrong but unjust: such acts wrong the particular others who are deceived or coerced.

TREATING PERSONS AS ENDS IN THEMSELVES

Duties of justice are, in Kant's view (as in many others'), the most important of our duties. When we fail in these duties, we have used some other or others as mere means. But there are also cases where, though we do not use others as mere means, still we fail to use them as ends in themselves in the fullest possible way. To treat someone as an end in him or herself requires in the first place that one not use him or her as mere means, that one respect each as a rational person with his or her own maxims. But beyond that, one may also seek to foster others' plans and maxims by sharing some of their ends. To act beneficently is to seek others' happiness, therefore to intend to achieve some of the things that those others aim at with their maxims. If I want to make others happy, I will adopt maxims that not merely do not manipulate them but that foster some of their plans and activities. Beneficent acts try to achieve what others want. However, we cannot seek everything that others want; their wants are too numerous and diverse, and, of course, sometimes incompatible. It follows that beneficence has to be selective.

There is then quite a sharp distinction between the requirements of justice and of beneficence in Kantian ethics. Justice requires that we act on *no* maxims that use others as mere means. Beneficence requires that we act on *some* maxims that foster others' ends, though it is a matter for judgment and discretion which of their ends we foster. Some maxims no doubt ought not to be fostered because it would be unjust to do so. Kantians are not committed to working interminably through a list of happiness-producing and misery-reducing acts; but there are some acts whose obligatoriness utilitarians may need to debate as they try to compare total outcomes of different choices, to which Kantians are stringently bound. Kantians will claim that they have done nothing wrong if none of their acts is unjust, and that their duty is complete if in addition their life plans have in the circumstances been reasonably beneficent.

In making sure that they meet all the demands of justice, Kantians do not try to compare all available acts and see which has the best effects. They consider only the proposals for action that occur to them and check that these proposals use no other as mere means. If they do not, the act is permissible; if omitting the act would use another as mere means, the act is obligatory. Kant's theory has less scope than utilitarianism. Kantians do not claim to discover whether acts whose maxims they don't know fully are just. They may be reluctant to judge others' acts or policies that cannot be regarded as the maxim of any person or institution. They cannot rank acts in order of merit. Yet, the theory offers more precision than utilitarianism when data are scarce. One can usually tell whether one's act would use others as mere means, even when its impact on human happiness is thoroughly obscure.

THE LIMITS OF KANTIAN ETHICS: INTENTIONS AND RESULTS

Kantian ethics differs from utilitarian ethics both in its scope and in the precision with which it guides action. Every action, whether of a person or of an agency, can be assessed by utilitarian methods, provided only that information is available about all the consequences of the act. The theory has unlimited scope, but owing to lack of data, often lacks precision. Kantian ethics has a more restricted scope. Since it assesses actions by looking at the maxims of agents, it can only assess intentional acts. This means that it is most at home in assessing individuals' acts; but it can be extended to assess acts of agencies that (like corporations and governments and student unions) have decision-making procedures. It can do nothing to assess patterns of action that reflect no intention or policy, hence it cannot assess the acts of groups lacking decision-making procedures, such as the student movement, the women's movement, or the consumer movement.

It may seem a great limitation of Kantian ethics that it concentrates on intentions to the neglect of results. It might seem that all conscientious Kantians have to do is to make sure that they never intend to use others as mere means, and that they sometimes intend to foster other's ends. And, as we all know, good intentions sometimes lead to bad results and correspondingly, bad intentions sometimes do no harm, or even produce good. If Hardin is right, the good intentions of those who feed the starving lead to dreadful results in the long run. If some traditional arguments in favor of capitalism are right, the greed and selfishness of the profit motive have produced unparalleled prosperity for many.

But such discrepancies between intentions and results are the exception and not the rule. For we cannot just *claim* that our intentions are good and do what we will. Our intentions reflect what we expect the immediate results of our action to be. Nobody credits the "intentions" of a couple who practice neither celibacy nor contraception but still insist "we never meant to have (more) children." Conception is likely (and known to be likely) in such cases. Where people's expressed intentions ignore the normal and predictable results of what they do, we infer that (if they are not amazingly ignorant) their words do not express their true intentions. The Formula of the End in Itself applies to the intentions on which one acts—not to some prettified version that one may avow. Provided this intention—the agent's real intention—uses no other as mere means, he or she does nothing unjust. If some of his or her intentions foster others' ends, then he or she is sometimes beneficent. It is therefore possible for people to test their proposals by Kantian arguments even when they lack the comprehensive causal knowledge that utilitarianism requires. Conscientious Kantians can work out whether they will be doing wrong by some act even though it blurs the implications of the theory. If we peer through the blur, we see that the utilitarian view is that lives may indeed be sacrificed for the sake of a greater good even when the persons are not willing. There is nothing wrong with using another as a mere means provided that the end for which the person is so used is a happier result than could have been achieved any other way, taking into account the misery the means have caused. In utilitarian thought persons are not ends in themselves. Their special moral status derives from their being

means to the production of happiness. Human life has therefore a high though derivative value, and one life may be taken for the sake of greater happiness in other lives, or for ending of misery in that life. Nor is there any deep difference between ending a life for the sake of others' happiness by not helping (e.g., by triaging) and doing so by harming. Because the distinction between justice and beneficence is not sharply made within utilitarianism, it is not possible to say that triaging is a matter of not benefiting, while other interventions are a matter of injustice.

Utilitarian moral theory has then a rather paradoxical view of the value of human life. Living, conscious humans are (along with other sentient beings) necessary for the existence of everything utilitarians value. But it is not their being alive but the state of their consciousness that is of value. Hence, the best results may require certain lives to be lost—by whatever means—for the sake of the total happiness and absence of misery that can be produced.

KANT AND RESPECT FOR PERSONS

Kantians reach different conclusions about human life. Human life is valuable because humans (and conceivable other beings, e.g., angels or apes) are the bearers of rational life. Humans are able to choose and to plan. This capacity and its exercise are of such value that they ought not to be sacrificed for anything of lesser value. Therefore, no one rational or autonomous creature should be treated as mere means for the enjoyment or even the happiness of another. We may in Kant's view justifiably—even nobly—risk or sacrifice our lives for others. For in doing so we follow our own maxim and nobody uses us as mere means. But no others may use either our lives or our bodies for a scheme that they have either coerced or deceived us into joining. For in doing so they would fail to treat us as rational beings; they would use us as mere means and not as ends in ourselves.

It is conceivable that a society of Kantians, all of whom took pains to use no other as mere means, would end up with less happiness or with fewer persons alive than would some societies of complying utilitarians. For since the Kantians would be strictly bound only to justice, they might without wrongdoing be quite selective in their beneficence and fail to maximize either survival rates or happiness, or even to achieve as much of either as a strenuous group of utilitarians, who they know that their foresight is limited and that they may cause some harm or fail to cause some benefit. But they will not cause harms that they can foresee without this being reflected in their intentions.

UTILITARIANISM AND RESPECT FOR LIFE

From the differing implications that Kantian and utilitarian moral theories have for our actions towards those who do or may suffer famine, we can discover two sharply contrasting views of the value of human life. Utilitarians value happiness and the absence or reduction of misery. As a utilitarian one ought (if conscientious) to devote one's life to achieving the best possible balance of happiness over misery. If one's life plan remains in doubt, this will be because the means to this end are often

unclear. But whenever the causal tendency of acts is clear, utilitarians will be able to discern the acts they should successively do in order to improve the world's balance of happiness over unhappiness.

This task is not one for the fainthearted. First, it is dauntingly long, indeed interminable. Second, it may at times require the sacrifice of happiness, and even of lives, for the sake of a greater happiness. Such sacrifice may be morally required not only when the person whose happiness or even whose life is at stake volunteers to make the sacrifice. It may be necessary to sacrifice some lives for the sake of others. As our control over the means of ending and presenting human life has increased, analogous dilemmas have arisen in many areas for utilitarians. Should life be preserved at the cost of pain when modern medicine makes this possible? Should life be preserved without hope of consciousness? Should triage policies, because they may maximize the number of survivors, be used to determine who should be left to starve? Should population growth be fostered wherever it will increase the total of human happiness—or on some views so long as average happiness is not reduced? All these questions can be fitted into utilitarian frameworks and answered *if* we have the relevant information. And sometimes the answer will be that human happiness demands the sacrifice of lives, including the sacrifice of unwilling lives. Further, for most utilitarians, it makes no difference if the unwilling sacrifices involve acts of injustice to those whose lives are to be lost. It might, for example, prove necessary for maximal happiness that some persons have their allotted rations, or their hardearned income, diverted for others' benefit. Or it might turn out that some generations must sacrifice comforts or liberties and even lives to rear "the fabric of felicity" for their successors. Utilitarians do not deny these possibilities, though the imprecision of our knowledge of consequences often somehow make the right calculations. On the other hand, nobody will have been made an instrument of others' survival or happiness in the society of complying Kantians.

Taking Rights Seriously

Ronald Dworkin

Ronald Dworkin is professor of jurisprudence at Oxford and professor of law at New York University. His books include Taking Rights Seriously *(1977),* A Matter of Principle *(1985),* Law's Empire *(1986) and* A Bill of Rights for Britain *(1990).*

This is one of the best-known recent statements of the deontological approach to rights. Dworkin argues that rights must be understood as extremely important moral concerns, and cannot be outweighed merely because a majority would be better off by violating the rights of an individual. Rights need extremely strong protection because they are necessary for the dignity and equal respect of individuals, especially when those individuals form a minority within a society. Dworkin believes that the right to free speech is a paradigm example of a right that should be given extremely strong weight—what he elsewhere has called treating rights as trump cards. Dworkin concludes that only when governments respect rights will respect for the law be generally reestablished.

THE RIGHTS OF CITIZENS

The language of rights now dominates political debate in the United States. Does the Government respect the moral and political rights of its citizens? Or does the Government's foreign policy, or its race policy, fly in the face of these rights? Do the minorities whose rights have been violated have the right to violate the law in return? Or does the silent majority itself have rights, including the right that those who break the law be punished? It is not surprising that these questions are now prominent. The concept of rights, and particularly the concept of rights against the

Reprinted with permission of Ronald Dworkin, from *Taking Rights Seriously*, by Ronald Dworkin, Harvard University Press, 1977. [Edited]

Government, has its most natural use when a political society is divided, and appeals to cooperation or a common goal are pointless.

The debate does not include the issue of whether citizens have *some* moral rights against their Government. It seems accepted on all sides that they do. Conventional lawyers and politicians take it as a point of pride that our legal system recognizes, for example, individual rights of free speech, equality, and due process. They base their claim that our law deserves respect, at least in part, on that fact, for they would not claim that totalitarian systems deserve the same loyalty.

Some philosophers, of course, reject the idea that citizens have rights apart from what the law happens to give them. Bentham thought that the idea of moral rights was "nonsense on stilts." But that view has never been part of our orthodox political theory, and politicians of both parties appeal to the rights of the people to justify a great part of what they want to do. I shall not be concerned, in this essay, to defend the thesis that citizens have moral rights against their governments; I want instead to explore the implications of that thesis for those, including the present United States Government, who profess to accept it.

It is much in dispute, of course, what *particular* rights citizens have. Does the acknowledged right to free speech, for example, include the right to participate in nuisance demonstrations? In practice the Government will have the last word on what an individual's rights are, because its police will do what its officials and courts say. But that does not mean that the Government's view is necessarily the correct view; anyone who thinks it does must believe that men and women have only such moral rights as Government chooses to grant, which means that they have no moral rights at all.

All this is sometimes obscured in the United States by the constitutional system. The American Constitution provides a set of individual *legal* rights in the First Amendment, and in the due process, equal protection, and similar clauses. Under present legal practice the Supreme Court has the power to declare an act of Congress or of a state legislature void if the Court finds that the act offends these provisions. This practice has led some commentators to suppose that individual moral rights are fully protected by this system, but that is hardly so, nor could it be so.

The Constitution fuses legal and moral issues, by making the validity of a law depend on the answer to complex moral problems, like the problem of whether a particular statute respects the inherent equality of all men. This fusion has important consequences for the debates about civil disobedience; I have described these elsewhere[1] and I shall refer to them later. But it leaves open two prominent questions. It does not tell us whether the Constitution, even properly interpreted, recognizes all the moral rights that citizens have, and it does not tell us whether, as many suppose, citizens would have a duty to obey the law even if it did invade their moral rights.

Both questions become crucial when some minority claims moral rights which the law denies, like the right to run its local school system, and which lawyers agree are not protected by the Constitution. The second question becomes crucial when, as now, the majority is sufficiently aroused so that Constitutional amendments to eliminate rights, like the right against self-incrimination, are seriously proposed. It is also crucial in nations, like the United Kingdom, that have no constitution of a comparable nature.

Even if the Constitution were perfect, of course, and the majority left it alone, it would not follow that the Supreme Court could guarantee the individual rights of citizens. A Supreme Court decision is still a legal decision, and it must take into account precedent and institutional considerations like relations between the Court and Congress, as well as morality. And no judicial decision is necessarily the right decision. Judges stand for different positions on controversial issues of law and morals and, as the fights over Nixon's Supreme Court nominations showed, a President is entitled to appoint judges of his own persuasion, provided that they are honest and capable.

So, though the constitutional system adds something to the protection of moral rights against the Government, it falls far short of guaranteeing these rights, or even establishing what they are. It means that, on some occasions, a department other than the legislature has the last word on these issues, which can hardly satisfy someone who thinks such a department profoundly wrong.

It is of course inevitable that some department of government will have the final say on what law will be enforced. When men disagree about moral rights, there will be no way for either side to prove its case, and some decision must stand if there is not to be anarchy. But that piece of orthodox wisdom must be the beginning and not the end of a philosophy of legislation and enforcement. If we cannot insist that the Government reach the right answers about the rights of its citizens, we can insist at least that it try. We can insist that it take rights seriously, follow a coherent theory of what these rights are, and act consistently with its own professions. I shall try to show what that means, and how it bears on the present political debates. . . .

CONTROVERSIAL RIGHTS

The argument so far has been hypothetical: if a man has a particular moral right against the Government, that right survives contrary legislation or adjudication. But this does not tell us what rights he has, and it is notorious that reasonable men disagree about that. There is wide agreement on certain clearcut cases; almost everyone who believes in rights at all would admit, for example, that a man has a moral right to speak his mind in a nonprovocative way on matters of political concern, and that this is an important right that the State must go to great pains to protect. But there is great controversy as to the limits of such paradigm rights, and the so-called "anti-riot" law involved in the famous Chicago Seven trial of the last decade is a case in point.

The defendants were accused of conspiring to cross state lines with the intention of causing a riot. This charge is vague—perhaps unconstitutionally vague—but the law apparently defines as criminal emotional speeches which argue that violence is justified in order to secure political equality. Does the right of free speech protect this sort of speech? That, of course, is a legal issue, because it invokes the free-speech clause of the First Amendment of the Constitution. But it is also a moral issue, because, as I said, we must treat the First Amendment as an attempt to protect a moral right. It is part of the job of governing to "define" moral rights through statutes and judical decisions, that is, to declare officially the extent that moral rights will be taken to have in law. Congress faced this task in voting on the anti-riot bill, and the Supreme Court has faced it in countless cases. How should the different departments of government go about defining moral rights?

They should begin with a sense that whatever they decide might be wrong. History and their descendants may judge that they acted unjustly when they thought they were right. If they take their duty seriously, they must try to limit their mistakes, and they must therefore try to discover where the dangers of mistake lie.

They might choose one of two different models for this purpose. The first model recommends striking a balance between the rights of the individual and the demands of society at large. If the Government *infringes* on a moral right (for example, by defining the right of free speech more narrowly than justice requires), then it has done the individual a wrong. On the other hand, if the Government *inflates* a right (by defining it more broadly than justice requires) then it cheats society of some general benefit, like safe streets, that there is no reason it should not have. So a mistake on one side is as serious as a mistake on the other. The course of government is to steer to the middle, to balance the general good and personal rights, giving to each its due.

When the Government, or any of its branches, defines a right, it must bear in mind, according to the first model, the social cost of different proposals and make the necessary adjustments. It must not grant the same freedom to noisy demonstrations as it grants to calm political discussion, for example, because the former causes much more trouble than the latter. Once it decides how much of a right to recognize, it must enforce its decision to the full. That means permitting an individual to act within his rights, as the Government has defined them, but not beyond, so that if anyone breaks the law, even on grounds of conscience, he must be punished. No doubt any government will make mistakes, and will regret decisions once taken. That is inevitable. But this middle policy will ensure that errors on one side will balance out errors on the other over the long run.

The first model, described in this way, has great plausibility, and most laymen and lawyers, I think, would respond to it warmly. The metaphor of balancing the public interest against personal claims is established in our political and judicial rhetoric, and this metaphor gives the model both familiarity and appeal. Nevertheless, the first model is a false one, certainly in the case of rights generally regarded as important, and the metaphor is the heart of its error.

The institution of rights against the Government is not a gift of God, or an ancient ritual, or a national sport. It is a complex and troublesome practice that makes the Government's job of securing the general benefit more difficult and more expensive, and it would be a frivolous and wrongful practice unless it served some point. Anyone who professes to take rights seriously, and who praises our Government for respecting them, must have some sense of what that point is. He must accept, at the minimum, one or both of two important ideas. The first is the vague but powerful idea of human dignity. This idea, associated with Kant, but defended by philosophers of different schools, supposes that there are ways of treating a man that are inconsistent with recognizing him as a full member of the human community, and holds that such treatment is profoundly unjust.

The second is the more familiar idea of political equality. This supposes that the weaker members of a political community are entitled to the same concern and respect of their government as the more powerful members have secured for themselves, so that if some men have freedom of decision whatever the effect on the general good, then all men must have the same freedom. I do not want to defend or elaborate these ideas here, but only to insist that anyone who claims that citizens have rights must accept ideas very close to these.[2]

It makes sense to say that a man has a fundamental right against the Government, in the strong sense, like free speech, if that right is necessary to protect his dignity, or his standing as equally entitled to concern and respect, or some other personal value of like consequence. It does not make sense otherwise.

So if rights make sense at all, then the invasion of a relatively important right must be a very serious matter. It means treating a man as less than a man, or as less worthy of concern than other men. The institution of rights rests on the conviction that this is a grave injustice, and that it is worth paying the incremental cost in social policy or efficiency that is necessary to prevent it. But then it must be wrong to say that inflating rights is as serious as invading them. If the Government errs on the side of the individual, then it simply pays a little more in social efficiency than it has to pay; it pays a little more, that is, of the same coin that it has already decided must be spent. But if it errs against the individual it inflicts an insult upon him that, on its own reckoning, it is worth a great deal of that coin to avoid.

So the first model is indefensible. It rests, in fact, on a mistake I discussed earlier, namely the confusion of society's rights with the rights of members of society. "Balancing" is appropriate when the Government must choose between competing claims of right—between the Southerner's claim to freedom of association, for example, and the black man's claim to an equal education. Then the Government can do nothing but estimate the merits of the competing claims, and act on its estimate. The first model assumes that the "right" of the majority is a competing right that must be balanced in this way; but that, as I argued before, is a confusion that threatens to destroy the concept of individual rights. It is worth noticing that the community rejects the first model in that area where the stakes for the individual are highest, the criminal process. We say that it is better that a great many guilty men go free than that one innocent man be punished, and that homily rests on the choice of the second model for government.

The second model treats abridging a right as much more serious than inflating one, and its recommendations follow from that judgment. It stipulates that once a right is recognized in clear-cut cases, then the Government should act to cut off that right only when some compelling reason is presented, some reason that is consistent with the suppositions on which the original right must be based. It cannot be an argument for curtailing a right, once granted, simply that society would pay a further price for extending it. There must be something special about that further cost, or there must be some other feature of the case, that makes it sensible to say that although great social cost is warranted to protect the original right, this particular cost is not necessary. Otherwise, the Government's failure to extend the right will show that its recognition of the right in the original case is a sham, a promise that it intends to keep only until that becomes inconvenient.

How can we show that a particular cost is not worth paying without taking back the initial recognition of a right? I can think of only three sorts of grounds that can consistently be used to limit the definition of a particular right. First, the Government might show that the values protected by the original right are not really at stake in the marginal case, or are at stake only in some attenuated form. Second, it might show that if the right is defined to include the marginal case, then some competing right, in the strong sense

I described earlier, would be abridged. Third, it might show that if the right were so defined, then the cost to society would not be simply incremental, but would be of a degree far beyond the cost paid to grant the original right, a degree great enough to justify whatever assault on dignity or equality might be involved.

It is fairly easy to apply these grounds to one group of problems the Supreme Court faced, imbedded in constitutional issues. The draft law provided an exemption for conscientious objectors, but this exemption, as interpreted by the draft boards, has been limited to those who object to *all* wars on *religious* grounds. If we suppose that the exemption is justified on the ground that an individual has a moral right not to kill in violation of his own principles, then the question is raised whether it is proper to exclude those whose morality is not based on religion, or whose morality is sufficiently complex to distinguish among wars. The Supreme Court held, as a matter of Constitutional law, that the draft boards were wrong to exclude the former, but competent to exclude the latter.

None of the three grounds I listed can justify either of these exclusions as a matter of political morality. The invasion of personality in forcing men to kill when they believe killing immoral is just as great when these beliefs are based on secular grounds, or take account of the fact that wars differ in morally relevant ways, and there is no pertinent difference in competing rights or in national emergency. There are differences among the cases, of course, but they are insufficient to justify the distinction. A government that is secular on principle cannot prefer a religious to a nonreligious morality as such. There are utilitarian arguments in favor of limiting the exception to religious or universal grounds—an exemption so limited may be less expensive to administer, and may allow easier discrimination between sincere and insincere applicants. But these utilitarian reasons are irrelevant, because they cannot count as grounds for limiting a right.

What about the anti-riot law, as applied in the Chicago trial? Does the law represent an improper limitation of the right to free speech, supposedly protected by the First Amendment? If we were to apply the first model for government to this issue, the argument for the anti-riot law would look strong. But if we set aside talk of balancing as inappropriate, and turn to the proper grounds for limiting a right, then the argument becomes a great deal weaker. The original right of free speech must suppose that it is an assault on human personality to stop a man from expressing what he honestly believes, particularly on issues affecting how he is governed. Surely the assault is greater, and not less, when he is stopped from expressing those principles of political morality that he holds most passionately, in the face of what he takes to be outrageous violations of these principles.

It may be said that the anti-riot law leaves him free to express these principles in a non-provocative way. But that misses the point of the connection between expression and dignity. A man cannot express himself freely when he cannot match his rhetoric to his outrage, or when he must trim his sails to protect values he counts as nothing next to those he is trying to vindicate. It is true that some political dissenters speak in ways that shock the majority, but it is arrogant for the majority to suppose that the orthodox methods of expression are the proper ways to speak, for this is a denial of equal concern and respect. If the point of the right is to protect the dignity of dissenters, then we must make judgments about appropriate speech with the personalities of the dissenters in mind, not the personality of the "silent" majority for whom the anti-riot law is no restraint at all.

So the argument fails, that the personal values protected by the original right are less at stake in this marginal case. We must consider whether competing rights, or some grave threat to society, nevertheless justify the anti-riot law. We can consider these two grounds together, because the only plausible competing rights are rights to be free from violence, and violence is the only plausible threat to society that the context provides.

I have no right to burn your house, or stone you or your car, or swing a bicycle chain against your skull, even if I find these to be natural means of expression. But the defendants in the Chicago trial were not accused of direct violence; the argument runs that the acts of speech they planned made it likely that others would do acts of violence, either in support of or out of hostility to what they said. Does this provide a justification?

The question would be different if we could say with any confidence how much and what sort of violence the anti-riot law might be expected to prevent. Will it save two lives a year, or two hundred, or two thousand? Two thousand dollars of property, or two hundred thousand, or two million? No one can say, not simply because prediction is next to impossible, but because we have no firm understanding of the process by which demonstration disintegrates into riot, and in particular of the part played by inflammatory speech, as distinct from poverty, police brutality,

blood lust, and all the rest of human and economic failure. The Government must try, of course, to reduce the violent waste of lives and property, but it must recognize that any attempt to locate and remove a cause of riot, short of a reorganization of society, must be an exercise in speculation, trial, and error. It must make its decisions under conditions of high uncertainty, and the institution of rights, taken seriously, limits its freedom to experiment under such conditions.

It forces the Government to bear in mind that preventing a man from speaking or demonstrating offers him a certain and profound insult, in return for a speculative benefit that may in any event be achieved in other if more expensive ways. When lawyers say that rights may be limited to protect other rights, or to prevent catastrophe, they have in mind cases in which cause and effect are relatively clear, like the familiar example of a man falsely crying "Fire!" in a crowded theater.

But the Chicago story shows how obscure the causal connections can become. Were the speeches of Hoffman or Rubin necessary conditions of the riot? Or had thousands of people come to Chicago for the purposes of rioting anyway, as the Government also argues? Were they in any case sufficient conditions? Or could the police have contained the violence if they had not been so busy contributing to it, as the staff of the President's Commission on Violence said they were?

These are not easy questions, but if rights mean anything, then the Government cannot simply assume answers that justify its conduct. If a man has a right to speak, if the reasons that support that right extend to provocative political speech, and if the effects of such speech on violence are unclear, then the Government is not entitled to make its first attack on that problem by denying that right. It may be that abridging the right to speak is the least expensive course, or the least damaging to police morale, or the most popular politically. But these are utilitarian arguments in favor of starting one place rather than another, and such arguments are ruled out by the concept of rights.

This point may be obscured by the popular belief that political activists look forward to violence and "ask for trouble" in what they say. They can hardly complain, in the general view, if they are taken to be the authors of the violence they expect, and treated accordingly. But this repeats the confusion I tried to explain earlier between having a right and doing the right thing. The speaker's motives may be relevant in deciding whether he does the right thing in speaking passionately about issues that may inflame or enrage the audience. But if he has a right to speak, because the danger in allowing him to speak is speculative, his motives cannot count as independent evidence in the argument that justifies stopping him.

But what of the individual rights of those who will be destroyed by a riot, of the passer-by who will be killed by a sniper's bullet or the shopkeeper who will be ruined by looting? To put the issue in this way, as a question of competing rights, suggests a principle that would undercut the effect of uncertainty. Shall we say that some rights to protection are so important that the Government is justified in doing all it can to maintain them? Shall we therefore say that the Government may abridge the rights of others to act when their acts might simply increase the risk, by however slight or speculative a margin,

that some person's right to life or property will be violated?

Some such principle is relied on by those who oppose the Supreme Court's recent liberal rulings on police procedure. These rulings increase the chance that a guilty man will go free, and therefore marginally increase the risk that any particular member of the community will be murdered, raped, or robbed. Some critics believe that the Court's decisions must therefore be wrong.

But no society that purports to recognize a variety of rights, on the ground that a man's dignity or equality may be invaded in a variety of ways, can accept such a principle. If forcing a man to testify against himself, or forbidding him to speak, does the damage that the rights against self-incrimination and the right of free speech assume, then it would be contemptuous for the State to tell a man that he must suffer this damage against the possibility that other men's risk of loss may be marginally reduced. If rights make sense, then the degrees of their importance cannot be so different that some count not at all when others are mentioned.

Of course the Government may discriminate and may stop a man from exercising his right to speak when there is a clear and substantial risk that his speech will do great damage to the person or property of others, and no other means of preventing this are at hand, as in the case of the man shouting "Fire!" in a theater. But we must reject the suggested principle that the Government can simply ignore rights to speak when life and property are in question. So long as the impact of speech on these other rights remains speculative and marginal, it must look elsewhere for levers to pull.

WHY TAKE RIGHTS SERIOUSLY?

I said at the beginning of this essay that I wanted to show what a government must do that professes to recognize individual rights. It must dispense with the claim that citizens never have a right to break its law, and it must not define citizens' rights so that these are cut off for supposed reasons of the general good. Any Government's harsh treatment of civil disobedience, or campaign against vocal protest, may therefore be thought to count against its sincerity.

One might well ask, however, whether it is wise to take rights all that seriously after all. America's genius, at least in her own legend, lies in not taking any abstract doctrine to its logical extreme. It may be time to ignore abstractions, and concentrate instead on giving the majority of our citizens a new sense of their Government's concern for their welfare, and of their title to rule.

That, in any event, is what former Vice President Agnew seemed to believe. In a policy statement on the issue of "weirdos" and social misfits, he said that the liberals' concern for individual rights was a headwind blowing in the face of the ship of state. That is a poor metaphor, but the philosophical point it expresses is very well taken. He recognized, as many liberals do not, that the majority cannot travel as fast or as far as it would like if it recognizes the rights of individuals to do what, in the majority's terms, is the wrong thing to do.

Spiro Agnew supposed that rights are divisive, and that national unity and a new respect for law may be developed by taking them more skeptically. But he is wrong. America will continue to be divided by its social and foreign policy, and if the economy grows weaker again the divisions will become more bitter. If we want our laws and our legal institutions to provide the ground rules within which these issues will be contested then these ground rules must not be the conqueror's law that the dominant class imposes on the weaker, as Marx supposed the law of a capitalist society must be. The bulk of the law—that part which defines and implements social, economic, and foreign policy—cannot be neutral. It must state, in its greatest part, the majority's view of the common good. The institution of rights is therefore crucial, because it represents the majority's promise to the minorities that their dignity and equality will be respected. When the divisions among the groups are most violent, then this gesture, if law is to work, must be most sincere.

The institution requires an act of faith on the part of the minorities, because the scope of their rights will be controversial whenever they are important, and because the officers of the majority will act on their own notions of what these rights really are. Of course these officials will disagree with many of the claims that a minority makes. That makes it all the more important that they take their decisions gravely. They must show that they understand what rights are, and they must not cheat on the full implications of the doctrine. The Government will not re-establish respect for law without giving the law some claim to respect. It cannot do that if it neglects the one feature that distinguishes law from ordered brutality. If the Government does not take rights seriously, then it does not take law seriously either.

NOTES

1. See Chapter 8.
2. He need not consider these ideas to be axiomatic. He may, that is, have reasons for insisting

that dignity or equality are important values, and these reasons may be utilitarian. He may believe, for example, that the general good will be advanced, *in the long run,* only if we treat indignity or inequality as very great injustices, and never allow our *opinions* about the general good to justify them. I do not know of any good arguments for or against this sort of "institutional" utilitarianism, but it is consistent with my point, because it argues that we must treat violations of dignity and equality as special moral crimes, beyond the reach of ordinary utilitarian justification.

Women's Rights as Human Rights: Toward a Re-Vision of Human Rights

Charlotte Bunch

Charlotte Bunch is the director of the Center for Global Issues and Women's Leadership at Rutgers University. She is the author of Passionate Politics: Feminist Theory in Action *(1987). She is the editor of seven books, including* Class and Feminism *(1974) and* Learning Our Way: Essays in Feminist Education *(1983).*

Bunch criticizes the Western conception of human rights as leaving women's rights largely out of the picture. Many women's rights are socioeconomic—that is, centered on food, shelter, and work. In addition, political oppression and systematic forms of violence against women are not taken as seriously as rights to free speech and press—rights that are only marginally important to many women, especially those in the Third World. Bunch concludes with some practical guidelines for transforming Western conceptions of human rights to ensure that women's rights are also counted as human rights.

Significant numbers of the world's population are routinely subject to torture, starvation, terrorism, humiliation, mutilation and even murder simply because they are female. Crimes such as these against any group other than women would be recognized as a civil and political emergency as well as a gross violation of the victims' humanity. Yet, despite a clear record of deaths and demonstrable abuse, women's rights are not commonly classified as human rights. This is problematic both theoretically and practically, because it

Reprinted by permission of *Human Rights Quarterly*, Volume 12, Number 4, November 1990.

has grave consequences for the way society views and treats the fundamental issues of women's lives. This paper questions why women's rights and human rights are viewed as distinct, looks at the policy implications of this schism, and discusses different approaches to changing it.

Women's human rights are violated in a variety of ways. Of course, women sometimes suffer abuses such as political repression that are similar to abuses suffered by men. In these situations, female victims are often invisible, because the dominant image of the political actor in our world is male. However, many violations of women's human rights are distinctly connected to being female—that is, women are discriminated against and abused on the basis of gender. Women also experience sexual abuse in situations where their other human rights are being vlolated, as political prisoners or members of persecuted ethnic groups, for example. In this paper I address those abuses in which gender is a primary or related factor because gender-related abuse has been most neglected and offers the greatest challenge to the field of human rights today.

The concept of human rights is one of the few moral visions ascribed to internationally. Although its scope is not universally agreed upon, it strikes deep chords of response among many. Promotion of human rights is a widely accepted goal and thus provides a useful framework for seeking redress of gender abuse. Further it is one of the few concepts that speaks to the need for transnational activism and concern about the lives of people globally. The Universal Declaration of Human Rights,[1] adopted in 1948, symbolizes this world vision and defines human rights broadly. While not much is said about women, Article 2 entitles all to "the rights and freedoms set forth in this Declaration, without distinction of any kind, such as race, colour, sex, language, religion, political or other opinion, national or social origin, property, birth or other status." Eleanor Roosevelt and the Latin American women who fought for the inclusion of sex in the Declaration and for its passage clearly intended that it would address the problem of women's subordination.[2]

Since 1948 the world community has continuously debated varying interpretations of human rights in response to global developments. Little of this discussion, however, has addressed questions of gender, and only recently have significant

challenges been made to a vision of human rights which excludes much of women's experiences. The concept of human rights, like all vibrant visions, is not static or the property of any one group; rather, its meaning expands as people reconceive of their needs and hopes in relation to it. In this spirit, feminists redefine human rights abuses to include the degradation and violation of women. The specific experiences of women must be added to traditional approaches to human rights in order to make women more visible and to transform the concept and practice of human rights in our culture so that it takes better account of women's lives.

In the next part of this article, I will explore both the importance and the difficulty of connecting women's rights to human rights, and then I will outline four basic approaches that have been used in the effort to make this connection.

BEYOND RHETORIC: POLITICAL IMPLICATIONS

Few governments exhibit more than token commitment to women's equality as a basic human right in domestic or foreign policy. No government determines its policies toward other countries on the basis of their treatment of women, even when some aid and trade decisions are said to be based on a country's human rights record. Among nongovernmental organizations, women are rarely a priority, and Human Rights Day programs on 10 December seldom include discussion of issues like violence against women or reproductive rights. When it is suggested that governments and human rights organizations should respond to women's rights as concerns that deserve such attention, a number of excuses are offered for why this cannot be done. The responses tend to follow one or more of these lines: (1) sex discrimination is too trivial, or not as important, or will come after larger issues of survival that require more serious attention; (2) abuse of women, while regrettable, is a cultural, private, or individual issue and not a political matter requiring state action; (3) while appropriate for other action, women's rights are not human rights per se; or (4) when the abuse of women is recognized, it is considered inevitable or so pervasive that any consideration of it is futile or will overwhelm other human rights questions. It is important to challenge these responses.

The narrow definition of human rights, recognized by many in the West as solely a matter of state violation of civil and political liberties, impedes consideration of women's rights. In the United States the concept has been further limited by some who have used it as a weapon in the cold war almost exclusively to challenge human rights abuses perpetrated in communist countries. Even then, many abuses that affected women, such as forced pregnancy in Romania, were ignored.

Some important aspects of women's rights do fit into a civil liberties framework, but much of the abuse against women is part of a larger socioeconomic web that entraps women, making them vulnerable to abuses which cannot be delineated as exclusively political or solely caused by states. The inclusion of "second generation" or socioeconomic human rights to food, shelter, and work—which are clearly delineated as part of the Universal Declaration of Human Rights—is vital to addressing women's concerns fully. Further, the assumption that states are not respon-

sible for most violations of women's rights ignores the fact that such abuses, although committed perhaps by private citizens, are often condoned or even sanctioned by states. I will return to the question of state responsibility after responding to other instances of resistance to women's rights as human rights.

The most insidious myth about women's rights is that they are trivial or secondary to the concerns of life and death. Nothing could be farther from the truth: sexism kills. There is increasing documentation of the many ways in which being female is life-threatening. The following are a few examples:

- Before birth: Amniocentesis is used for sex selection leading to the abortion of more female fetuses at rates as high as 99 percent in Bombay, India; in China and India, the two most populous nations, more males than females are born even though natural birth ratios would produce more females.[3]
- During childhood: The World Health Organization reports that in many countries, girls are fed less, breast fed for shorter periods of time, taken to doctors less frequently, and die or are physically and mentally maimed by malnutrition at higher rates than boys.[4]
- In adulthood: the denial of women's rights to control their bodies in reproduction threatens women's lives, especially where this is combined with poverty and poor health services. In Latin America, complications from illegal abortions are the leading cause of death for women between the ages of fifteen and thirty-nine.[5]

Sex discrimination kills women daily. When combined with race, class, and other forms of oppression, it constitutes a deadly denial of women's right to life and liberty on a large scale throughout the world. The most pervasive violation of females is violence against women in all its manifestations, from wife battery, incest, and rape, to dowry deaths,[6] genital mutilation,[7] and female sexual slavery. These abuses occur in every country and are found in the home and in the workplace, on streets, on campuses, and in prisons and refugee camps. They cross class, race, age, and national lines; and at the same time, the forms this violence takes often reinforce other oppressions such as racism, "able-bodyism," and imperialism. Case in point: in order to feed their families, poor women in brothels around U.S. military bases in places like the Philippines bear the burden of sexual, racial, and national imperialism in repeated and often brutal violation of their bodies.

Even a short review of random statistics reveals that the extent of violence against women globally is staggering:

- In the United States, battery is the leading cause of injury to adult women, and a rape is committed every six minutes.[8]
- In Peru, 70 percent of all crimes reported to police involve women who are beaten by their partners; and in Lima (a city of seven million people), 168,970 rapes were reported in 1987 alone.[9]
- In India, eight out of ten wives are victims of violence, either domestic battery, dowry-related abuse, or among the least fortunate, murder.[10]
- In France, 95 percent of the victims of violence are women; 51 percent at the hands of a spouse or lover. Similar statistics from places as diverse as Bangladesh, Canada, Kenya, and Thailand demonstrate that more than 50 percent of female homicides were committed by family members.[11]

Where recorded, domestic battery figures range from 40 percent to 80 percent of women beaten, usually repeatedly, indicating that the home is the most dangerous place for women and frequently the site of cruelty and torture. As the Carol Stuart murder in Boston demonstrated,

sexist and racist attitudes in the United States often cover up the real threat to women; a woman is murdered in Massachusetts by a husband or lover every 22 days.[12]

Such numbers do not reflect the full extent of the problem of violence against women, much of which remains hidden. Yet rather than receiving recognition as a major world conflict, this violence is accepted as normal or even dismissed as an individual or cultural matter. Georgina Ashworth notes that:

> The greatest restriction of liberty, dignity and movement and at the same time, direct violation of the person is the threat and realization of violence. . . . However violence against the female sex, on a scale which far exceeds the list of Amnesty International victims, is tolerated publicly; indeed some acts of violation are not crimes in law, others are legitimized in custom or court opinion, and most are blamed on the victims themselves.[13]

Violence against women is a touchstone that illustrates the limited concept of human rights and highlights the political nature of the abuse of women. As Lori Heise states: "This is not random violence. . . . [T]he risk factor is being female."[14] Victims are chosen because of their gender. The message is domination: stay in your place or be afraid. Contrary to the argument that such violence is only personal or cultural, it is profoundly political. It results from the structural relationships of power, domination, and privilege between men and women in society. Violence against women is central to maintaining those political relations at home, at work, and in all public spheres.

Failure to see the oppression of women as political also results in the exclusion of sex discrimination and violence against women from the human rights agenda.

Female subordination runs so deep that it is still viewed as inevitable or natural, rather than seen as a politically constructed reality maintained by patriarchal interests, ideology, and institutions. But I do not believe that male violation of women is inevitable or natural. Such a belief requires a narrow and pessimistic view of men. If violence and domination are understood as a politically constructed reality, it is possible to imagine deconstructing that system and building more just interactions between the sexes.

The physical territory of this political struggle over what constitutes women's human rights is women's bodies. The importance of control over women can be seen in the intensity of resistance to laws and social changes that put control of women's bodies in women's hands: reproductive rights, freedom of sexuality whether heterosexual or lesbian, laws that criminalize rape in marriage, etc. Denial of reproductive rights and homophobia are also political means of maintaining control over women and perpetuating sex roles and thus have human rights implications. The physical abuse of women is a reminder of this territorial domination and is sometimes accompanied by other forms of human rights abuse such as slavery (forced prostitution), sexual terrorism (rape), imprisonment (confinement to the home), and torture (systematic battery). Some cases are extreme, such as the women in Thailand who died in a brothel fire because they were chained to their beds. Most situations are more ordinary like denying women decent educations or jobs which leaves them prey to abusive marriages, exploitative work, and prostitution.

This raises once again the question of the state's responsibility for protecting women's human rights. Feminists have shown how the distinction between private and public abuse is a dichotomy often used to justify female subordination in the home. Governments regulate many matters in the family and individual spheres. For example, human rights activists pressure states to prevent slavery or racial discrimination and segregation even when these are conducted by nongovernmental forces in private or proclaimed as cultural traditions as they have been in both the southern United States and in South Africa. The real questions are: (1) who decides what are legitimate human rights; and (2) when should the state become involved and for what purposes. Riane Eisler argues that:

> the issue is what types of private acts are and are not protected by the right to privacy and/or the principle of family autonomy. Even more specifically, the issue is whether violations of human rights within the family such as genital mutilation, wife beating, and other forms of violence designed to maintain patriarchal control should be within the purview of human rights theory and action. . . . [T]he underlying problem for human rights theory, as for most other fields of theory, is that the yardstick that has been developed for defining and measuring human rights has been based on the male as the norm.[15]

The human rights community must move beyond its male defined norms in order to respond to the brutal and systematic violation of women globally. This does not mean that every human rights group must alter the focus of its work. However it does require examining patriarchal biases and acknowledging the rights of women as human rights. Governments must seek to end the politically and culturally constructed war on women rather than continue to perpetuate it. Every state has the responsibility to intervene in the abuse of women's rights within its borders and to end its collusion with the forces that perpetrate such violations in other countries.

TOWARD ACTION: PRACTICAL APPROACHES

The classification of human rights is more than just a semantics problem because it has practical policy consequences. Human rights are still considered to be more important than women's rights. The distinction perpetuates the idea that the rights of women are of a lesser order than the "rights of man," and, as Eisler describes it, "serves to justify practices that do not accord women full and equal status."[16] In the United Nations, the Human Rights Commission has more power to hear and investigate cases than the Commission on the Status of Women, more staff and budget, and better mechanisms for implementing its findings. Thus it makes a difference in what can be done if a case is deemed a violation of women's rights and not of human rights.[17]

The determination of refugee status illustrates how the definition of human rights affects people's lives. The Dutch Refugee Association, in its pioneering efforts to convince other nations to recognize sexual persecution and violence against women as justifications for granting refugee status, found that some European governments would take sexual persecution into account as an aspect of other forms of political repression, but none would make it the grounds for refugee status per se.[18] The implications of such a distinction are clear when examining a situation like that of the Bangladeshi women, who having been raped during the Pakistan–Bangladesh war, subsequently faced death at the hands of male relatives to preserve "family honor." Western powers professed outrage but did not offer asylum to these victims of human rights abuse.

I have observed four basic approaches to linking women's rights to human rights. These approaches are presented separately here in order to identify each more clearly. In practice, these approaches often overlap, and while each raises questions about the others, I see them as complementary. These approaches can be applied to many issues, but I will illustrate them primarily in terms of how they address violence against women in order to show the implications of their differences on a concrete issue.

1. Women's Rights as Political and Civil Rights. Taking women's specific needs into consideration as part of the already recognized "first generation" political and civil liberties is the first approach. This involves both raising the visibility of women who suffer general human rights violations as well as calling attention to particular abuses women encounter because they are female. Thus, issues of violence against women are raised when they connect to other forms of violation such as the sexual torture of women political prisoners in South America.[19] Groups like the Women's Task Force of Amnesty International have taken this approach in pushing for Amnesty to launch a campaign on behalf of women political prisoners which would address the sexual abuse and rape of women in custody, their lack of maternal care in detention, and the resulting human rights abuse of their children.

Documenting the problems of women refugees and developing responsive policies are other illustrations of this approach. Women and children make up more than 80 percent of those in refugee camps, yet few refugee policies are specifically shaped to meet the needs of these vulnerable populations who face considerable sexual abuse. For example, in one camp where men were allocated the community's rations, some gave food to women and their children in exchange for sex. Revealing this abuse led to new policies that allocated food directly to the women.[20]

The political and civil rights approach is a useful starting point for many human rights groups; by considering women's experiences, these groups can expand their efforts in areas where they are already working. This approach also raises contradictions that reveal the limits of a narrow civil liberties view. One contradiction is to define rape as a human rights abuse only when it occurs in state custody but not on the streets or in the home. Another is to say that a violation of the right to free speech occurs when someone is jailed for defending gay rights, but not when someone is jailed or even tortured and killed for homosexuality. Thus while this approach of adding women and stirring them into existing first generation human rights categories is useful, it is not enough by itself.

2. Women's Rights as Socioeconomic Rights.
The second approach includes the particular plight of women with regard to "second generation" human rights such as the rights to food, shelter, health care, and employment. This is an approach favored by those who see the dominant Western human rights tradition and international law as too individualistic and identify women's oppression as primarily economic.

This tendency has its origins among socialists and labor activists who have long argued that political human rights are meaningless to many without economic rights as well. It focuses on the primacy of the need to end women's economic subordination as the key to other issues including women's vulnerability to violence. This particular focus has led to work on issues like women's right to organize as workers and opposition to violence in the workplace, especially in situations like the free trade zones which have targeted women as cheap, nonorganized labor. Another focus of this approach has been highlighting the feminization of poverty or what might better be called the increasing impoverishment of females. Poverty has not become strictly female, but females now comprise a higher percentage of the poor.

Looking at women's rights in the context of socioeconomic development is another example of this approach. Third world peoples have called for an understanding of socioeconomic development as a human rights issue. Within this demand, some have sought to integrate women's rights into development and have examined women's specific needs in relation to areas like land ownership or access to credit. Among those working on women in development, there is growing interest in violence against women as both a health and development issue. If violence is seen as having negative consequences for social productivity, it may get more attention. This type of narrow economic measure, however, should not determine whether such violence is seen as a human rights concern. Violence as a development issue is linked to the need to understand development not just as an economic issue but also as a question of empowerment and human growth.

One of the limitations of this second approach has been its tendency to reduce women's needs to the economic sphere which implies that women's rights will follow automatically with third world development, which may involve socialism. This has not proven to be the case. Many working from this approach are no longer trying to add women into either the Western capitalist or socialist development models, but rather seek a transformative development process that links women's political, economic, and cultural empowerment.

3. Women's Rights and the Law.
The creation of new legal mechanisms to counter sex discrimination characterizes the third approach to women's rights as human rights. These efforts seek to make existing legal and political institutions work for women and to expand the state's responsibility for the violation of women's human rights. National and local laws which address sex discrimination and violence against women are examples of this approach. These measures allow women to fight for their rights within the legal system. The primary international illustration is the Convention on the Elimination of All Forms of Discrimination Against Women.[21]

The Convention has been described as "essentially an international bill of rights for women and a framework for women's participation in the development process . . . [which] spells out internationally accepted principles and standards for achieving equality between women and men."[22] Adopted by the UN General Assembly in 1979, the Convention has been ratified or acceded to by 104 countries as of January 1990. In theory these countries are obligated to pursue policies in accordance with it and to report on their compliance to the Committee on the Elimination of Discrimination Against Women (CEDAW).

While the Convention addresses many issues of sex discrimination, one of its shortcomings is failure to directly address the question of violence against women. CEDAW passed a resolution at its eighth session in Vienna in 1989 expressing concern that this issue be on its agenda and instructing states to include in their periodic reports information about statistics, legislation, and support services in this area.[23] The Commonwealth Secretariat in its manual on the reporting process for the Convention also interprets the issue of violence against women as "clearly fundamental to the spirit of the Convention," especially in Article 5 which calls for the modification of social and cultural patterns, sex roles, and stereotyping that are based on the idea of the inferiority or the superiority of either sex.[24]

The Convention outlines a clear human rights agenda for women which, if accepted by governments, would mark an enormous step forward. It also carries the limitations of all such international documents in that there is little power to demand its implementation. Within the United Nations, it is not generally regarded as a convention with teeth, as illustrated by the difficulty that CEDAW has had in getting countries to report on compliance with its provisions. Further, it is still treated by governments and most nongovernmental organizations as a document dealing with women's (read "secondary") rights, not human rights. Nevertheless, it is a useful statement of principles endorsed by the United Nations around which women can organize to achieve legal and political change in their regions.

4. Feminist Transformation of Human Rights. Transforming the human rights concept from a feminist perspective, so that it will take greater account of women's lives, is the fourth approach. This approach relates women's rights and human rights, looking first at the violations of women's lives and then asking how the human rights concept can change to be more responsive to women. For example, the GABRIELA women's coalition in the Philippines simply stated that "Women's Rights are Human Rights" in launching a campaign last year. As Ninotchka Rosca explained, coalition members saw that "human rights are not reducible to a question of legal and due process. . . . In the case of women, human rights are affected by the entire society's traditional perception of what is proper or not proper for women."[25] Similarly, a panel at the 1990 International Women's Rights Action Watch conference asserted that "Violence Against Women is a Human Rights Issue." While work in the three previous approaches is often done from a feminist perspective, this last view is the most distinctly feminist with its woman-centered stance and its refusal to wait for permission from some authority to determine what is or is not a human rights issue.

This transformative approach can be taken toward any issue, but those working from this approach have tended to focus most on abuses that arise specifically out of gender, such as reproductive rights, female sexual slavery, violence against women, and "family crimes" like forced marriage, compulsory heterosexuality, and female mutilation. These are also the issues most often dismissed as not really human rights questions. This is therefore the most hotly contested area and

requires that barriers be broken down between public and private, state and nongovernmental responsibilities.

Those working to transform the human rights vision from this perspective can draw on the work of others who have expanded the understanding of human rights previously. For example, two decades ago there was no concept of "disappearances" as a human rights abuse. However, the women of the Plaza de Mayo in Argentina did not wait for an official declaration but stood up to demand state accountability for these crimes. In so doing, they helped to create a context for expanding the concept of responsibility for deaths at the hands of paramilitary or right-wing death squads which, even if not carried out by the state, were allowed by it to happen. Another example is the developing concept that civil rights violations include "hate crimes," violence that is racially motivated or directed against homosexuals, Jews or other minority groups. Many accept that states have an obligation to work to prevent such rights abuses, and getting violence against women seen as a hate crime is being pursued by some.

The practical applications of transforming the human rights concept from feminist perspectives need to be explored further. The danger in pursuing only this approach is the tendency to become isolated from and competitive with other human rights groups because they have been so reluctant to address gender violence and discrimination. Yet most women experience abuse on the grounds of sex, race, class, nation, age, sexual preference, and politics as interrelated, and little benefit comes from separating them as competing claims. The human rights community need not abandon other issues but should incorporate gender perspectives into them and see how these expand the terms of their work. By recognizing issues like violence against women as human rights concerns, human rights scholars and activists do not have to take these up as their primary tasks. However, they do have to stop gatekeeping and guarding their prerogative to determine what is considered a "legitimate" human rights issue.

As mentioned before, these four approaches are overlapping and many strategies for change involve elements of more than one. All of these approaches contain aspects of what is necessary to achieve women's rights. At a time when dualist ways of thinking and views of competing economic systems are in question, the creative task is to look for ways to connect these approaches and to see how we can go beyond exclusive views of what people need in their lives. In the words of an early feminist group, we need bread and roses, too. Women want food and liberty and the possibility of living lives of dignity free from domination and violence. In this struggle, the recognition of women's rights as human rights can play an important role.

NOTES

1. Universal Declaration of Human Rights, *adopted* 10 December 1948, G.A. Res. 217A(III), U.N. Doc. A/810 (1948).
2. Blanche Wiesen Cook, "Eleanor Roosevelt and Human Rights: The Battle for Peace and Planetary Decency," Edward P. Crapol, ed. *Women and American Foreign Policy: Lobbyists, Critics, and Insiders* (New York: Greenwood Press, 1987), 98–118; Georgina Ashworth. "Of Violence and Violation: Women and Human Rights," *Change Thinkbook II* (London, 1986).
3. Vibhuti Patel. *In Search of Our Bodies: A Feminist Look at Women, Health, and Reproduction in India* (Shakti, Bombay, 1987); Lori Heise, "Inrernational Dimensions of Violence Against Women," *Response*, vol. 12, no. 1 (1989): 3.
4. Sundari Ravindran, *Health Implications of Sex Discrimination in Childhood* (Geneva: World Health Organization, 1986). These problems and proposed social programs to counter them in India are discussed in detail in "Gender Violence: Gender Discrimination Between Boy and Girl in Parental Family," paper published by CHETNA (Child Health Education Training and Nutrition Awareness), Ahmedabad, 1989.
5. Debbie Taylor, ed., *Women: A World Report, A New Internationalist Book* (Oxford: Oxford University Press, 1985), 10. See Joni Seager and Ann Olson, eds., *Women In The World: An International Atlas* (London: Pluto Press, 1986) for more statistics on the effects of sex discrimination.
6. Frequently a husband will disguise the death of a bride as suicide or an accident in order to collect the marriage settlement paid him by the bride's parents. Although dowry is now illegal in many countries, official records for 1987 showed 1,786 dowry deaths in India alone. See Heise, note 3 above, 5.
7. For an in-depth examination of the practice of female circumcision see Alison T. Slack, "Female Circumcision: A Critical Appraisal," *Human Rights Quarterly* 10 (1988): 439.
8. C. Everen Koop, M.D. "Violence Against Women: A Global Problem," presentation by the Surgeon General of the U.S., Public Health Service, Washington D.C., 1989.
9. Ana Maria Portugal, "Cronica de Una Violacion Provocada?", *Fempress* especial "Contraviolencia," Santiago, 1988; Seager and Olson, note 5 above, 37.
10. Ashworth, note 2 above, 9.
11. "Violence Against Women in the Family," Centre for Social Development and Humanitarian Affairs, United Nations Office at Vienna, 1989.
12. Bella English, "Stereotypes Led Us Astray," *The Boston Globe*, 5 Jan. 1990, 17, col. 3. See also the statistics in *Women's International Network News*, 1989; United Nations Office, note 11 above; Ashworth, note 2 above; Heise, note 3 above; and *Fempress*, note 9 above.
13. Ashworth, note 2 above, 8.
14. Heise, note 3 above, 3.
15. Riane Eisler, "Human Rights: Toward an Integrated Theory for Action," *Human Rights Quarterly* 9 (1987):297. See also Alida Brill, *Nobody's Business: The Paradoxes of Privacy* (New York: Addison-Wesley, 1990).
16. Eisler, note 15 above, 291.
17. Sandra Coliver, "United Nations Machineries on Women's Rights: How Might They Better Help Women Whose Rights Are Being Violated?" in Ellen L. Lutz, Hurst Hannum, and Kathryn J.

Burke, eds., *New Directions in Human Rights* (Philadelphia: Univ. of Penn. Press, 1989).

18. Marijke Meyer, "Oppression of Women and Refugee Status," unpublished report to NGO Forum, Nairobi, Kenya, 1985 and "Sexual Violence Against Women Refugees" Ministry of Social Affairs and Labour, The Netherlands, June 1984.

19. Ximena Bunster describes this in Chile and Argentina in "The Torture of Women Political Prisoners: A Case Study in Female Sexual Slavery," in Kathleen Barry, Charlotte Bunch, and Shirley Castley, eds., *International Feminism: Networking Against Female Sexual Slavery* (New York: IWTC, 1984).

20. Report given by Margaret Groarke at Women's Panel, Amnesty International New York Regional Meeting, 24 Feb. 1990.

21. Convention on the Elimination of All Forms of Discrimination Against Women, G.A. Res. 34/180, (1980).

22. International Women's Rights Action Watch. "The Convention on the Elimination of All Forms of Discrimination Against Women" (Minneapolis: Humphrey Institute of Public Affairs, 1988), 1.

23. CEDAW Newsletter, 3rd Issue (13 Apr. 1989), 2 (summary of U.N. Report on the Eighth Session, U.N.Doc. A/44/38, 14 April 1989).

24. Commonwealth Secretariat, "The Convention on the Elimination of All Forms of Discrimination Against Women: The Reporting Process—A Manual for Commonwealth Jurisdictions," London, 1989.

25. Speech given by Ninotchka Rosca at Amnesty International New York Regional Conference, 24 Feb. 1990, 2.

Islam, Islamic Law and the Dilemma of Cultural Legitimacy for Universal Human Rights[1]

Abdullahi Ahmed An-Na'im

Abdullahi Ahmed An-Na'im is currently professor of law at the University of Khartoum. He is the author of Toward an Islamic Reformation: Civil Liberties, Human Rights and International Law *(1990). He has edited* Human Rights in Africa: Cross Cultural Perspectives *(1990), and* Human Rights in Cross Cultural Perspectives *(1992).*

Islamic societies, like African ones, generally do not place a high value on the protection of human rights. An-Na'im argues that human rights need to be perceived as culturally legitimate in order for them to be given more than lip service. Since countries are largely left unsupervised in terms of the protection of the human rights of their own citizens, the leaders must be persuaded that the human rights of all their citizens are deserving of equal respect. But in Islamic cultures a deep division exists between those who are Muslim and those who are not, as well as between men and women. As long as these divisions exist, appeals to universal human rights will continue to clash with deeply held cultural and religious views.

Although Islam is often discussed in the contexts of North Africa and the Middle East, in fact the majority of Muslims live outside this region. The clear majority of the Muslims of the world live in the Indian sub-continent.[2] The Muslim population of Indonesia alone is equal to the combined Muslim population of Egypt and Iran, the largest countries of the so-called Muslim heartland of North Africa and the Middle East. In terms of percentage to the total

Reprinted from *Asian Perspectives on Human Rights,* Claude E. Welch and Virginia Leary (editors), 1990, by permission of Westview Press, Boulder, Colorado. [Edited]

population, Muslims constitute 97% of the total population of Pakistan, 82.9% of that of Bangladesh and 80% of that of Indonesia. While Muslims constitute slightly less than half the population of Malaysia, Islam is perceived as an important element of Malay ethnicity which receives special protection under the constitution.[3] As we shall see, Pakistan has been struggling with the meaning and implications of its purported Islamic identity since independence. Bangladesh also appears to be heading in the same direction. It is therefore important to consider the Islamic dimension of human rights policy and practice in South and Southeast Asia.

It is important to note that Islamic norms may be more influential at an informal, almost subconscious psychological level than they are at the official legal or policy level. One should not therefore underestimate the Islamic factor simply because the particular state is not constituted as an Islamic state, or because its legal system does not purport to comply with historical Islamic law, commonly known as Shari'a.[4] Conversely, one should not overestimate the Islamic factor simply because the state and the legal system are publicly identified as such. This is particularly important from a human rights point of view where underlying social and political attitudes and values may defeat or frustrate the declared policy and formal legal principles.

This chapter is concerned with both the sociological as well as the legal and official impact of Islam on human rights. The chapter begins by explaining the paradox of declared commitment to human rights, on the one hand, and the low level of compliance with these standards in daily practice, on the other. It is my submission that this paradox can be understood in light of the competing claims of the universalism and relativism of human rights standards. It is my thesis that certain standards of human rights are frequently violated because they are not perceived to be culturally legitimate in the context of the particular country. To the extent that political regimes and other dominant social forces can explicitly or implicitly challenge the validity of certain human rights norms as alien or at least not specifically sanctioned by the primary values of the dominant indigenous culture, they can avoid the negative consequences of their violation.

Such analysis would seem to suggest the need for establishing cultural legitimacy for human rights standards in the context of the particular society. However, this enterprise raises another problem. If indigenous cultural values are to be asserted as a basis of human rights standards, we are likely to encounter "undesirable" aspects of the indigenous culture. In other words, while it may be useful to establish cultural legitimacy for human rights standards, certain elements of the indigenous culture may be antithetical to the human rights of some segments of the population. This chapter will illustrate the dilemma of cultural legitimacy for human rights in the Islamic tradition.

THE HUMAN RIGHTS PARADOX

1988 marked the fortieth anniversary of the Universal Declaration of Human Rights, which was adopted by the General Assembly of the United Nations on the 10th of December 1948.[5] Several U.N. and regional human rights conventions have since been ratified as binding international treaties by scores of countries from all parts of the world.[6] At the domestic level, many human rights receive strong endorsement in the constitutional and legal system of most countries of the world. Moreover, human rights issues are continuously covered by the news media as a supposedly important consideration in national and international politics.

Despite these formal commitments to human rights, and apparently strong concern with their violation, there is a mounting crisis in practical compliance with human rights standards throughout the world. Gross and consistent violations of human rights in many countries are recorded daily. Activist groups and non-governmental organizations continue to charge almost every government in the world of involvement or complicity in violating one or more human rights in its national and/or international policies.[7]

This glaring disparity between apparent commitment in theory and poor compliance in practice is what may be called the paradox of human rights. On the one hand, the idea of human rights is so powerful that no government in the world today can afford to reject it openly.[8] On the other hand, the most basic and fundamental human rights are being consistently violated in all parts of the world. It is therefore necessary to understand and resolve this paradox if human rights are to be respected and implemented in practice. As correctly stated by Jenks: "The potentially tragic implication of this paradox is the ever-present danger that the denial of human rights may, as in the past, express, permit and promote a worship of the State no less fatal to peace than to freedom; by failure to make a reality of the Universal Declaration of Human Rights and United Nations Covenants of Human Rights we may leave mankind at the mercy of new absolutism which will engulf the world."[9]

One obvious explanation of the dichotomy between the theory and practice of human rights is the cynical manipulation of a noble and enlightened concept by many governments and politicians in all countries of the world. It may therefore be said that this is merely the current manifestation of an ancient phenomenon in human affairs. However, without disputing the historical validity of this analysis, one can point to the other side of the coin as the concrete manifestation of another ancient phenomenon in human affairs, namely the capacity of people to assert and realize their rights and claims in the face of adversity and cynicism. From this perspective, what is therefore significant is not the cynical abuse of the human rights idea, but the fact that oppressive governments and ambitious politicians find expressing their support of human rights useful, if not necessary, for gaining popular support at home and legitimacy abroad. This tribute paid by vice to virtue is very significant and relevant to future efforts at bridging the gap between the theory and practice of human rights.

In order to hold governments to their declared commitment to human rights, it is essential to establish the principle that human rights violations are not matters within the exclusive domestic jurisdiction of any state in the world.[10] Under traditional international law, national sovereignty was taken to include the right of each state to treat its own subjects in whatever manner it deemed fit. Consequently, it was perceived to be unwarranted interference in the internal affairs of a sovereign state for other states to object to or protest any action or policy of that state towards its own subjects. The Charter of the United Nations (UN) apparently endorsed these notions. Article 2.7 expressly stated that the Charter does not "authorize the United Nations to intervene in matters which are essentially within the domestic jurisdiction of any state or shall require the Members to submit such matters to settlement under the present Charter." Other authoritative statements of international law continue to emphasize the traditional definition of national sovereignty. For example, these notions feature prominently in the 1970 UN Declaration on Principles of International Law Concerning Friendly Relations and Cooperation among States in Accordance with the Charter of the United Nations.[11]

However, Article 2.7 of the UN Charter stipulates that the principle of non-interference in matters essentially within the domestic jurisdiction of any state shall not apply to UN action with respect to threats to the peace, breaches of the peace and acts of aggression. It could be argued that serious and consistent violations of at least some fundamental human rights constitute a threat to international peace and security, and are therefore within this exception to the "essentially domestic jurisdiction" clause of the UN Charter. In other words, since serious and consistent violations of certain human rights constitute a threat to international peace and security, the UN can act against the offending state because the matter is beyond the "essentially domestic jurisdiction" of the state. It may also be possible to construe some of the language of the above cited 1970 UN Declaration on Friendly Relations as permitting international action in promoting and protecting at least some fundamental human rights.

Despite its problems, national sovereignty appears to be necessary for the exercise of the right of peoples to self-determination. In any case, it is too strongly entrenched to hope for its total repudiation in the foreseeable future. Nevertheless, it is imperative to overcome national sovereignty objections to international action for the protection and promotion of human rights without violating the legitimate scope of such sovereignty. "The renunciation of intervention [in the internal affairs of states] does not constitute a policy of nonintervention; it involves the development of some form of *collective intervention*."[12]

In order to support this position, it is necessary to repudiate any plausible argument which claims that action in support of human rights violates the national sovereignty of the country. It has been argued, for example, that the established international standards are not consistent with the cultural traditions or philosophical and ideological perspectives of the given country.[13] It is not enough to say that this argument may be used as a pretext for violating human rights because such manipulation would not be viable if there is no validity to the argument itself. In other words, this argument is useful as a pretext precisely because it has some validity which makes the excuse plausible. It is therefore incumbent upon human rights advocates to address the element of truth in this argument in order to prevent its cynical abuse in the future.

THE LEGITIMACY DILEMMA

If we take the UN Charter and the Universal Declaration of Human Rights as the starting point of the modern movement for the promotion and protection of human rights, we will find it true that the majority of the peoples of Africa and Asia had little opportunity for direct contribution to the formulation of these basic documents. Since the majority of the peoples of these two continents were still suffering from the denial of their collective human right to self-determination because of colonial rule and foreign domination at the time, they were unable to participate in the drafting and adoption processes.[14] It is true that some of the representatives of the older, mainly Western, nations were sensitive to the cultural traditions of the unrepresented peoples,[15] but that could have hardly been a sufficient substitute for direct representation.

Many more African and Asian countries subsequently achieved formal independence and were able to participate in the formulation of international human rights instruments. By ratifying the UN Charter and subscribing to the specialized international instruments which incorporated and elaborated upon the Universal Declaration of Human Rights, the emerging countries of Africa and Asia were deemed bound by those earlier documents in addition to the subsequent instruments in which they participated from the start. Thus, the vast majority of the countries of Africa and Asia can be seen as parties to the process by which international human rights standards are determined and formulated. Nevertheless, this official and formal participation does not seem to have achieved the desired result of legitimizing international human rights standards in the cultural traditions of these peoples. This failure is clearly illustrated, in my view, by the lack of sufficient popular awareness of and support for these standards among the majority of the population of the countries of Africa and Asia. Given this lack of awareness and support for the international standards, it is not surprising that governments and other actors are able to evade the negative consequences of their massive and gross violations of human rights throughout Africa and Asia.

It is my submission that formal participation in the formulation and implementation processes by the elites of African and Asian countries will never achieve practical respect and protection for human rights in those regions unless that participation reflects the genuine consensus of the population of those countries. I would further suggest that the peoples of these regions have not had the chance to develop such consensus by reexamining their own cultural traditions in terms of universal and international human rights. It seems that the elites of these countries have come to the international fora where human rights standards were determined and formulated without a clear mandate from their own peoples.

As an advocate of international human rights, I am not suggesting that the international community should scrap the present documents and start afresh. This would be an impracticable and dangerous course of action because we may never recover what would be lost through the repudiation of the present instruments and structures. What I am suggesting is that we should supplement the existing standards and continue to develop them through the genuine participation of the widest possible range of cultural traditions. In furtherance of this approach, it is incumbent on the advocates of human rights to work for legitimizing universal standards of human rights within their own traditions.

However, this approach presents us with the other horn of the dilemma. Almost every existing cultural tradition (including philosophical or ideological positions) in the world has some problems with respect to the full range of fundamental human rights. Generally speaking, for example, whereas the liberal tradition(s) of the West have difficulties in accepting economic, social and cultural rights and in conceiving of collective rights such as a right to development, the Marxist tradition has similar difficulties with respect to civil and political rights.[16]

More specifically, prevailing notions of freedom of speech under the Constitution of the United States, for instance, may protect forms of speech and expression which advocate racial hatred in violation of the international standards set by the Covenant for the Elimination of All Forms of Racial Discrimination of 1965.

The main difficulty in working to establish universal standards across cultural boundaries is the fact that each tradition has its own internal frame of reference and derives the validity of its precepts and norms from its own sources. When a cultural tradition relates to other traditions and perspectives, it is likely to do so in a negative and perhaps even hostile and antagonistic way. In order to claim the loyalty and conformity of its own members, a tradition would normally assert its own superiority over, and tend to dehumanize the adherents of, other traditions. This tendency would clearly undermine efforts to accord members of other traditions equality in status and rights, even if they happen to live within the political boundaries of the same country.[17]

Nevertheless, I believe that all the major cultural traditions adhere to the common normative principle that one should treat other people as he or she wishes to be treated by them. This golden rule, which may be called the principle of reciprocity, is shared by all the major traditions of the world. Moreover, the moral and logical force of this simple proposition can easily be appreciated by all human beings of whatever cultural tradition or philosophical persuasion. If construed in an enlightened manner so that the "other" includes all other human beings, this principle is capable of sustaining universal standards of human rights.

In accordance with this fundamental principle of reciprocity, I would take universal human rights to be those rights which I claim for myself, and must therefore concede to others. The practical implications of this fundamental principle would have to be negotiated through the political process to develop consensus around specific policies and concrete action on what the majority or other dominant segment of the population would accept for itself and would therefore have to concede to minorities and individuals. Although theoretical safeguards and structures may be devised to ensure the constitutional and human rights of all individuals and groups, the ultimate safeguard is the goodwill and sense of enlightened political expediency of the majority or other dominant segment of the population. Unless the majority or dominant segment of the population is persuaded to respect and promote the human rights of minorities and individuals, the whole society will drift into the politics of confrontation and subjugation rather than that of reconciliation and justice.

THE LEGITIMACY DILEMMA IN THE MUSLIM CONTEXT

When I consider Shari'a as the historical formulation of my own Islamic tradition I am immediately confronted with certain inadequacies in its conception of human rights as judged by the above stated principle of reciprocity and its supporting arguments. In particular, I am confronted by Shari'a's discrimination against Muslim women and non-Muslims and its restrictions on freedom of religion and belief. Unfortunately, most contemporary Muslim writings on the subject tend to provide a misleadingly glowing view of Shari'a on human rights without any reference to the above cited problematic aspects of Shari'a.[18] Moreover, some of those Muslim authors who are willing to candidly state the various features of conflict and tension between Shari'a and current standards of human rights tend to take an intransigent position in favor of Shari'a without considering the prospects of its reconciliation with current standards of human rights.[19]

It is true that Shari'a had introduced significant improvements in the status and rights of women as compared to its historical contemporaries between the seventh and nineteenth centuries A.D.[20] Under Shari'a, Muslim women enjoy full and independent legal personality to own and dispose of property and conclude other contracts in their own right. They are also guaranteed specific shares in inheritance, and other rights in family law. However, Shari'a did not achieve complete legal equality between Muslim men and women. Whereas a man is entitled to marry up to four wives and divorce any of them at will, a woman is restricted to one husband and can only seek judicial divorce on very limited and strict grounds. Women receive only half a share of a man in inheritance, and less monetary compensation for criminal bodily harm (*diya*). Women are generally incompetent to testify in serious criminal cases. Where their testimony is accepted in civil cases, it takes two women to make a single witness.[21] Other examples of inequality can be cited. In fact, the general rule of Shari'a is that men are the guardians of women, and as such have the license to discipline them to extent of beating them "lightly" if they fear them to become unruly.[22] Consequently, Shari'a holds that Muslim women may not hold any office

involving exercising authority over Muslim men.

Similarly, Shari'a granted non-Muslim believers, mainly Christians and Jews who submit to Muslim sovereignty, the status of *dhimma*, whereby they are secured in person and property and permitted to practice their religion and regulate their private affairs in accordance with their own law and custom in exchange for payment of a special tax, known as *jiziya*.[23] Those classified by Shari'a as unbelievers are not allowed to live within an Islamic state except with a special permit of safe conduct, known as *aman*, which defines their status and rights.[24] If the residence of a *musta'min*, an unbeliever allowed to stay within an Islamic state under *aman*, extends beyond one year, some Shari'a jurists would allow him to assume the status of *dhimma*. However, neither *dhimma* nor *aman* would qualify a non-Muslim to full citizenship of an Islamic state or guarantee such a person complete equality with Muslim citizens.[25] For example, Shari'a specifically requires that non-Muslims may never exercise authority over Muslims.[26] Consequently, non-Muslims are denied any public office which would involve exercising such authority.

The third example of serious human rights problems with Shari'a indicated above is freedom of religion and belief. It is true that *dhimma* and possibly *aman*, would guarantee a non-Muslim a measure of freedom of religion in that he would be free to practice his officially sanctioned religion. However, such freedom of religious practice is inhibited by the limitations imposed on non-Muslims in public life, including payment of *jiziya*, which is intended by Shari'a to be a humiliating tax.[27]

Another serious limitation of freedom of religion and belief is the Shari'a law of apostasy, *ridda*, whereby a Muslim would be subject to the death penalty if he should repudiate his faith in Islam, whether or not in favor of another religion.[28] Some modern Muslim writers have argued that apostasy should not be punishable by death.[29] However, this progressive view has not yet been accepted by the majority of Muslims. Moreover, even if the death penalty is abolished, other serious consequences will remain, such as the possibility of other punishment, confiscation of the property of the apostate and the nullification of his or her marriage to a Muslim spouse.[30] In contrast, non-Muslims, including Christians and Jews, are encouraged to embrace Islam. Whereas Muslims are supported by the State and community in their efforts to proselytize in order to convert non-Muslims to Islam, non-Muslims are positively prohibited from undertaking such activities.

All of the above features of discrimination against Muslim women and non-Muslims and restrictions on freedom of religion and belief are part of Shari'a to the present day. Those aspects of discrimination against Muslim women which fall within the scope of family law and inheritance are currently enforced throughout the Muslim world because Shari'a constitutes the personal law of Muslims even in those countries where it is not the formal legal system of the land.[31] Discrimination against non-Muslims and the Shari'a law of apostasy are enforced in those countries where Shari'a is the formal legal system. For example, Article 13 of the Constitution of the Islamic Republic of Iran expressly classifies Iranians in terms of their religious or sectarian belief.

By the terms of this Article, Baha'is are not a recognized religious minority, and as such are not entitled even to the status of second class citizens under the principle of *dhimma* explained above. Moreover, as recently as January 1985, a 76-year-old man was executed for apostasy in the Sudan.[32]

What is more significant for our present purposes, however, is the fact that all of these and other aspects of Shari'a are extremely influential in shaping Muslim attitudes and policies even where Shari'a is not the formal legal system. In other words, so long as these aspects of Shari'a are held by Muslim legislators, policy makers and executive officials to be part of their cultural tradition, we can only expect serious negative consequences for human rights in predominantly Muslim countries, regardless of whether or not Shari'a is the basis of the formal constitutional and legal system of the land. . . .

Conclusion: Revised Agenda for the Human Rights Movement

Thus, if we are to bridge the gap between the theory and practice of human rights in the contemporary world, we must all be ready to shed or modify those preconceptions which seem to obstruct or frustrate the efficacy of international cooperation in the field of human rights. This would require a modification of the concept of national sovereignty in order to enhance the principle of international accountability for violating human rights. The international community must firmly establish, as a matter of international law and, as well, of practice, that violations of universal human rights are not matters of "essentially domestic jurisdiction." The legal framework for such action can easily be established under the UN Charter and existing international and regional human rights instruments. What may be lacking is the political will among states to relinquish their traditional national pride in favor of the international rule of law.

Another concept that needs to be modified is the cultural conception of the term "right." In the Western liberal tradition, rights are primarily entitlements or claims which the individual person has against the state. This conception has led many Western governments and human rights advocates to deny human rights status to claims which they deem to be too vague or not amenable to enforcement against the state, such as economic rights and collective rights to development. Non-Western cultural traditions, in contrast, not only conceive of such claims as human rights, they insist that they must be granted that status. Some of the human rights treaties and literature already reflect a broader conception of rights than originally envisaged by liberal theory. However, there is little evidence to show that this is more than a token concession by liberal governments. The developed countries of the world should not expect other peoples of the world, including the Muslim peoples, to examine and reevaluate their cultural and philosophical traditions in the interest of more genuine respect for and greater compliance with international standards of human rights *unless* they (the developed countries) are willing to examine and re-evaluate their own cultural traditions.

It is my submission that these and other related considerations must now be injected into human rights discourse at official, scholarly and popular levels of debate and action. It is not difficult, for example, to develop the appropriate for-

mulations and implementation mechanisms and procedures for collective claims or entitlement as human rights which do not necessarily correspond to the established Western notion of "right." For this course of action to be useful, however, the existing human rights standards and mechanisms for their enforcement must be opened up for new ideas and influences. The process of definition, formulation and implementation of universal human rights must be genuinely universal and not merely Western in orientation and techniques.

In conclusion, the dilemma of cultural legitimacy must be resolved if the glaring disparity between the theory and practice of human rights is to be narrowed. To achieve this end, human rights advocates need to undertake a massive educational effort, drawing on all the religious and other normative resources of each community in support of universal human rights. They must build from the immediately local, through the national and regional levels, towards greater international cooperation in the promotion and protection of human rights. Greater emphasis must be placed on the role of grass-roots non-governmental organizations and the role of indigenous mechanisms for enhancing the cultural legitimacy of human rights.

NOTES

1. A first draft of this chapter was prepared under a grant from the Woodrow Wilson International Center for Scholars, Washington, D.C. The statements and views expressed herein are those of the author and are not necessarily those of the Wilson Center. I have prepared the final draft of this chapter while holding the position of Ariel F. Sallows Professor of Human Rights at the College of Law, University of Saskatchewan, Canada in 1989–90.
2. For statistics on Muslim peoples and their percentages of the total population of all the coun-

tries of the world see, Richard V. Weeks, ed., *Muslim Peoples, A World Ethnographic Survey,* second ed. (Westport CT.: Greenwood Press, 1984), pp. 882–911.

3. F. A. Trindade and H. P. Lee, editors, *The Constitution of Malaysia: Further Perspectives and Developments* (Singapore: Oxford University Press, 1986), pp. 5–12. See further the review of this book by Abdullahi A. An-Na'im in *Columbia Journal of Transnational Law* 26 (1988), pp. 1101–1107.

4. It is misleading to think of Shari'a as merely law in the strict modern sense of the term. Shari'a is the Islamic view of the whole duty of humankind, and includes moral and pastoral theology and ethics, high spiritual aspirations and detailed ritualistic and formal observance as well as legal rules in the formal sense. See S. G. Vesey-Fitzgerald, "The Nature and Sources of the Shari'a," in M. Khadduri and H. J. Liebesny, eds., *Law in the Middle East* (Washington: The Middle East Institute, 1955), pp. 85ff.; and Majid Khadduri, "Nature and Sources of Islamic Law," *George Washington Law Review* 22 (1953), pp. 6–10.

5. For the full text of the Universal Declaration of Human Rights see Ian Brownlie, ed., *Basic Documents on Human Rights,* second ed. (Oxford: Clarendon Press, 1981), pp. 21–27.

6. These include the International Convention on the Elimination of All Forms of Racial Discrimination of 1963; the International Covenant on Economic, Social and Cultural Rights and the International Covenant on Civil and Political Rights, both of 1966; and the Convention on the Elimination of All Forms of Discrimination Against Women of 1979. For the texts of these instruments, see *ibid.* pp. 150–63, pp. 118–27 and pp. 94–107, respectively. There are three regional conventions currently in force for Europe, the Americas and Africa. See *ibid.* pp. 242–57 and pp. 391–416 for the European and American Conventions respectively. The African Charter is included as Appendix I in Claude E. Welch, Jr. and Ronald I. Meltzer, eds., *Human Rights and Development in Africa* (Albany: State University of New York Press, 1984). pp. 317–29.

7. See, for example, the Annual Reports of Amnesty International, and the periodic reports of Human Rights Internet and the Minority Rights Group. Of special interest to the subject of this paper, see Lawyers Committee for Human Rights, *Zia's Law: Human Rights under Military Rule in Pakistan* (New York/Washington: The Lawyers Committee for Human Rights (1985). The Lawyers Committee has also published two other reports on human rights in Pakistan: *Violations of Human Rights in Pakistan* June 1981; and *Justice in Pakistan* July 1983.

8. Louis Henkin, Introduction, in Louis Henkin, ed., *The International Bill of Rights: The Covenant on Civil and Political Rights* (New York: Columbia University Press, 1981), p. 1.

9. C. Wilfred Jenks, *The World Beyond the Charter in Historical Perspective* (London: George Allen and Unwin, Ltd., 1969), pp. 130–31.

10. Henkin, *The International Bill of Rights,* pp. 3–8. See generally, Richard Falk, *Human Rights and State Sovereignty* (New York: Holmes & Meier, 1982).

11 G.A. Res. 2625 (XXXV 1970). For the full text of this Declaration see Louis Henkin, Richard C. Pugh, Oscar Schachter and Hans Smit, eds., *Basic Documents Supplement to International Law: Cases and Materials,* second ed. (St. Paul, MN.: West Publishing Co., 1987), pp. 75–83.

12. Richard Falk, *Legal Order in a Violent World* (Princeton: Princeton University Press, 1968), p. 339. Emphasis added.

13. This argument was recently advanced by official spokesmen of the Islamic Republic of Iran. See Edward Mortimer, "Islam and Human Rights," *Index on Censorship* (1983), p. 5.

14. Only eleven African and Asian countries were founding Members of the U.N., with seven more joining over the next ten years. Jenks, *The World Beyond the Chattel in Historical Perspective,* p. 92.

15. See, for example, "Human Rights, Comments and Interpretations," a symposium edited by UNESCO, London, 1949, reprinted in *Human Rights Teaching,* IV (1985), pp. 4–31.

16. These conceptual difficulties and cultural differences were the underlying cause of the development of two separate covenants, one for civil and political rights and the other for economic, social and cultural rights, rather than a single bill of human rights as originally envisaged. Henkin, *The International Bill of Rights.* pp. 5–6.

17. See, generally, Patrick Thornberry, "Is there a Phoenix in the Ashes? International Law and Minority Rights." *Texas International Law Journal* 15 (1980), p. 421.

18. See, for example, Ali Abedl Wahid Wafi, "Human Rights in Islam," *Islamic Quarterly* 11 (1967), p. 64; and Isma'il al-Faruqi, "Islam and Human Rights," *Islamic Quarterly* 27 (1983), p. 12. One of the better and more constructive works by contemporary Muslim authors is Riffat Hassan's "On Human Rights and the Qur'anic Perspectives," *Journal of Ecumenical Studies* 19 (1982), p. 51.

19. See, for example, Tabandeh, *A Muslim Commentary on the Universal Declaration of Human Rights* (London: F. T. Goulding and Co., 1970).

20. On the relative improvements in the status of women introduced by Shari'a, see Ameer Ali, *The Spirit of Islam* (London: Christophers,

1922), pp. 222–57; and Fazlur Rahman, "Status of Women in The Qur'an," in G. Nashat, ed., *Women and Revolution in Iran* (Boulder, CO.: Westview Press, 1983), p. 37.

21. For sources and discussion of these aspects of Shari'a, see Abdullahi Ahmed An-Na'im, "The Rights of Women and International Law in the Muslim Context," *Whittier Law Review* (1987), pp. 493–97.

22. Verse 4:34 of the Qur'an. The Qur'an is cited here by number of chapter followed by number of verse in that chapter.

23. Verse 9:29 of the Qur'an. See *The Encyclopedia of Islam, New Edition,* vol. II, p. 227; and Majid Khadduri, *War and Peace in the Law of Islam* (Baltimore: The Johns Hopkins Press, 1955), p. 177 and pp. 195–99.

24. Khadduri, *War and Peace in the Law of Islam,* pp. 163–69; Muhammad Hamidullah, *The Muslim Conduct of State,* 5th edition (Lahore: Sh. M. Ashraf, 1966), pp. 201–02.

25. Majid Khadduri, "Human Rights in Islam," *The Annals of the American Academy of Political and Social Science* 243 (1946), p. 79. Cf. Majid Khadduri, *The Islamic Concept of Justice* (Baltimore and London: The Johns Hopkins University Press, 1984), p. 233.

26. This is held to be so because verses of the Qur'an, such as 3:28, 4:144, 8:72 and 73, etc. prohibit Muslims from taking non-Muslims as *awliya,* guardians and supporters.

27. This connotation is reflected in the language of verse 9:29 of the Qur'an which requires that *dhimmis* pay *jiziya* in humiliation and submission.

28. Khadduri, *War and Peace in the Law of Islam,* p. 150; Rudoph Peters and Gert J. De Vries, "Apostasy in Islam," *Die Welt des Islams* XVII (1976–77), p. 1.

29. See, for example, A. Rahman, *Punishment of Apostasy in Islam* (Lahore: Institute of Islamic Culture, 1972).

30. On these other consequences of apostasy see Abdullahi Ahmed An-Naim, "The Islamic Law of Apostasy and its Modern Applicability: A Case from the Sudan," *Religion* 16 (1986), p. 212.

31. Coulson, *A History of Islamic Law.* p. 161; Herbert Liebesny. *The Law: of the Near and Middle East* (Albany: State of New York Press, 1975), p. 56.

32. For a full explanation and discussion of this case see An-Na'im, "The Islamic Law of Apostasy and its Modern Applicability: A Case from the Sudan."

The African Context
of Human Rights

Claude Ake

Claude Ake was professor of political science at the University of Port Harcourt in Nigeria. He was the author of A Theory of Political Integration *(1967),* Revolutionary Pressures in Africa *(1978) and* A Political Economy of Africa *(1981).*

Ake points out that Western conceptions of human rights are not very interesting or useful for African societies. He contends that if a person is starving to death, the right to free speech does not do him or her much good. Ake also argues that a strong emphasis on rights will block various development policies. He believes that socialism rather than what he calls procedural liberalism provides the best grounding for a conception of human rights that will effectively address the current problems of hunger and fascism in African countries. In this context, collective rights, especially those of disadvantaged groups, will be of greater concern than individual rights.

Nobody can accuse Africa of taking human rights seriously. In a world which sees concern for human rights as a mark of civilized sensitivity, this indifference has given Africa a bad name. It is not unlikely that many consider it symptomatic of the rawness of life which has always been associated with Africa. I am in no position to say with any confidence why Africa has not taken much interest in human rights but I see good reasons why she should not have done so.

Before going into these reasons let us be clear what we are talking about. The idea of human rights is quite simple. It is that human beings have certain rights simply by virtue of being human. These rights are a necessary condition for the good life. Because of their singular importance, individuals are entitled to, indeed, required to claim them and society is enjoined to allow them. Otherwise, the quality of life is seriously compromised.

The idea of human rights, or legal rights in general, presupposes a society which is atomized and individualistic, a society of endemic conflict. It presupposes a society of people conscious of their separateness and their particular interests and anxious to realize them. The legal right is a claim which the individual may make against other members of society, and simultaneously an obligation on the part of society to uphold this claim.

The values implicit in all this are clearly alien to those of our traditional societies. We put less emphasis on the individual and more on the collectivity, we do not allow that the individual has any claims which may override that of the

Reprinted by permission of *Africa Today,* Vol. 34, No. 142, pp. 5–13, © 1987.

society. We assume harmony, not divergence of interests, competition and conflict; we are more inclined to think of our obligations to other members of our society rather than our claims against them.

The Western notion of human rights stresses rights which are not very interesting in the context of African realities. There is much concern with the right to peaceful assembly, free speech and thought, fair trial, etc. The appeal of these rights is sociologically specific. They appeal to people with a full stomach who can now afford to pursue the more esoteric aspects of self-fulfillment. The vast majority of our people are not in this position. They are facing the struggle for existence in its brutal immediacy. Theirs is a totally consuming struggle. They have little or no time for reflection and hardly any use for free speech. They have little interest in choice for there is no choice in ignorance. There is no freedom for hungry people, or those eternally oppressed by disease. It is no wonder that the idea of human rights has tended to sound hollow in the African context.

The Western notion of human rights lacks concreteness. It ascribes abstract rights to abstract beings. There is not enough concern for the historical conditions in which human rights can actually be realized. As it turns out, only a few people are in a position to exercise the rights which society allows. The few who have the resources to exercise these rights do not need a bill of rights. Their power secures them. The many who do not have the resources to exercise their rights are not helped any by the existence of these rights. Their powerlessness dooms them.

The idea of human rights really came into its own as a tool for opposing democracy. The French Revolution had brought home forcefully to everyone the paradox of democracy, namely that its two central values, liberty and equality, come into conflict at critical points. There is no democracy where there is no liberty for self-expression or choice. At the same time there is no democracy where there is no equality, for inequality reduces human relations to subordination and domination. The French Revolution and Jean Jacques Rousseau revealed rather dramatically the paradoxical relation between these two central values of democracy by leaning heavily towards equality. They gave Europe a taste of what it would be like to take the idea of equality and the correlative idea of popular sovereignty seriously.

Bourgeois Europe was horrified. The idea of a popular sovereign insisting on equality and having unlimited power over every aspect of social life was unacceptable. For such power was a threat to the institution of private property as well as the conditions of accumulation. So they began to emphasize liberty rather than the collectivity. This emphasis was also a way of rejecting democracy in its pure form as popular sovereignty. That was the point of stressing the individual and his rights and holding that certain rights are inalienable. That was the point of holding that the individual could successfully sustain certain claims and certain immunities against the wishes of the sovereign or even the rest of society. It is ironical that all this is conveniently forgotten today and liberal democrats can pass as the veritable defenders of democracy.

CHANGING STATUS OF HUMAN RIGHTS IN AFRICA

Africa is at last beginning to take interest in human rights. For one thing, the Western conception of human rights has evolved in ways which have made it more relevant to the African experience, although its relevance still remains ambiguous. Because human rights is such an important part of the political ideology of the West, it was bound to register in Africa eventually. Human rights record is beginning to feature in Western decisions of how to relate to the countries and leaders of Africa. Western decisions on this score have been made with such cynical inconsistency that one wonders whether human rights record really matters to them at all. However, our leaders ever so eager to please are obliged to assume that it matters and to adjust their behavior accordingly. Also the authoritarian capitalism of Africa is under some pressure to be more liberal and thereby create political conditions more conducive to capitalist efficiency.

If these are the reasons why Africa is beginning to take more interest in human rights, they are by no means the reason why she ought to do so. The way I see it is that we ought to be interested in human rights because it will help us to combat social forces which threaten to send us back to barbarism. Because it will aid our struggle for the social transformation which we need to survive and to flourish. To appreciate this let us look at the historical conditions of contemporary Africa.

I hope we can all agree that for now, the most salient aspect of these conditions is the crisis. It has been with us for so long we might well talk of the permanent crisis. No one seems to know for sure what its character is but we know its devastating effects only too well. We Africans have never had it so bad. The tragic consequences of our development strategies have finally come home to us. Always oppressed by poverty and deprivation, our lives become harsher still with each passing day as real incomes continue to decline. We watch helplessly while millions of our people are threatened by famine and look pitifully to the rest of the world to feed us. Our social and political institutions are disintegrating under pressure from our flagging morale, our dwindling resources and the intense struggle to control them. What is the problem? I am not sure. But I am convinced that we are not dealing simply or even primarily with an economic phenomenon. There is a political dimension to it which is so critical, it may well be the most decisive factor.

This is the problem of democracy or the problem of political repression. A long time ago our leaders opted for political repression. Having abandoned democracy for repression, our leaders are delinked from our people. Operating in a vacuum, they proclaim their incarnation of the popular will, hear echoes of their own voices, and reassured, pursue with zeal, policies which have nothing to do with the aspirations of our people and which cannot, therefore, mobilize them. As their alienation from the people increases, they rely more and more on force and become even more alienated.

CONSEQUENCES OF THE PROBLEM OF DEMOCRACY

The consequences of this are disastrous. In the first place it means that there is no development. Political repression ensures that the ordinary people of Africa who are the object of development remain silent, so that in the end nobody really speaks for development and it never comes alive in practice. Development cannot be achieved by proxy. A people develops itself or not at all. And it can develop itself only through its commitment and its energy. That is where democracy comes in. Self-reliance is not possible unless the society is thoroughly democratic, unless the people are the end and not just the means of development. Development occurs, in so far as it amounts to the pursuit of objectives set by the people themselves in their own interest and pursued by means of their own resources.

Another consequence of repression is the brutalization of our people. Look around you. The willful brutalization of people occurring among us is appalling. Human life is taken lightly, especially if it is that of the underprivileged. All manner of inhuman treatment is meted out for minor offenses and sometimes for no offenses at all. Ordinary people are terrorized daily by wanton display of state power and its instruments of violence. Our prison conditions are guaranteed to traumatize. The only consensus we can mobilize is passive conformity arising from fear and resignation. As we continue to stagnate this gets worse.

Yet another disaster threatens us. I am referring to fascism. In all probability this is something which nobody wants. But we might get it anyway because circumstances are moving steadily in that direction. All the ingredients of fascism are present now in most parts of Africa: a political class which has failed even by its own standards, and which is now acutely conscious of its humiliation and baffled by a world it cannot control; a people who have little if any hope or sense of self-worth yearning for redeemers; a milieu of anomie; a conservative leadership pitted against a rising popular radicalism and poised to take cover in defensive radicalism. That is what it takes and it is there in plenty. If Africa succumbs it will be terrible—fascism has always been in all its historical manifestations.

It seems to me that for many African countries the specter of fascism is the most urgent and the most serious danger today. Unless we contain it effectively and within a very short time, then we are in a great deal of trouble.

If this analysis is correct, then our present agenda must be the task of preventing the rise of fascism. To have a chance of succeeding this task requires a broad coalition of radicals, populists, liberals and even humane conservatives. That is, a coalition of all those who value democracy not in the procedural liberal sense but in the concrete socialist sense. This is where the idea of human rights comes in. It is easily the best ideological framework for such a coalition.

AN AFRICAN CONCEPTION OF HUMAN RIGHTS

We have now seen the relevance of human rights in the African context. But on a level of generality which does not tell us very much and so does not really settle the question of the applicability of the Western concept of human rights. I do not see how we can mobilize the African masses or the intelligentsia against fascism or whatever by accepting uncritically the Western notion of human rights. We have to domesticate it, recreate it in the light of African conditions. Let me indicate very briefly how these conditions redefine the idea of human rights.

First, we have to understand that the idea of legal rights presupposes social atomization and individualism, and a conflict model of society for which legal rights are the necessary mediation. However, in most of Africa, the extent of social atomization is very limited mainly because of the limited penetration of capitalism and commodity relations. Many people are still locked into natural economies and have a sense of belonging to an organic whole, be it a family, a clan, a lineage or an ethnic group. The phenomenon of the legal subject, the largely autonomous individual conceived as a bundle of rights which are asserted against all comers has not really developed much especially outside the urban areas.

These are the conditions which explain the forms of consciousness which we insist on misunderstanding. For instance, ethnic consciousness and ethnic identity. It is the necessary consciousness associated with non-atomized social structures and mechanical solidarity. Ethnic consciousness will be with us as long as these structural features remain, no matter how we condemn it or try to engineer it out of existence.

All this means that abstract legal rights attributed to individuals will not make much sense for most of our people; neither will they be relevant to their consciousness and living conditions. It is necessary to extend the idea of human rights to include collective human rights for corporate social groups such as the family, the lineage, the ethnic group. Our people still think largely in terms of collective rights and express their commitment to it constantly in their behavior. This disposition underlies the zeal for community development and the enormous sacrifices which poor people readily make for it. It underlies the so-called tribalist voting pattern of our people, the willingness of the poor villager to believe that the minister from his village somehow represents his share of the national cake, our tradi-

tional land tenure systems, the high incidence of cooperative labor and relations of production in the rural areas. These forms of consciousness remain very important features of our lives. If the idea of human rights is to make any sense at all in the African context, it has to incorporate them in a concept of communal human rights.

For reasons which need not detain us here some of the rights important in the West are of no interest and no value to most Africans. For instance, freedom of speech and freedom of the press do not mean much for a largely illiterate rural community completely absorbed in the daily rigors of the struggle for survival.

African conditions shift the emphasis to a different kind of rights. Rights which can mean something for poor people fighting to survive and burdened by ignorance, poverty and disease, rights which can mean something for women who are cruelly used. Rights which can mean something for the youth whose future we render more improbable every day. If a bill of rights is to make any sense, it must include among others, a right to work and to a living wage, a right to shelter, to health, to education. That is the least we can strive for if we are ever going to have a society which realizes basic human needs.

Finally, in the African context, human rights have to be much more than the political correlate of commodity fetishism which is what they are in the Western tradition. In that tradition the rights are not only abstract, they are also ascribed to abstract persons. The rights are ascribed to the human being from whom all specific determinations have been abstracted: the rights have no content just as individuals who enjoy them have no determination and so do not really exist.

All these problems which usually lurk beneath the surface appear in clear relief when we confront them with empirical reality. Granted, I have the freedom of speech. But where is this freedom, this right? I cannot read, I cannot write. I am too busy trying to survive I have no time to reflect. I am so poor I am constantly at the mercy of others. So where is this right and what is it really? Granted, I have the right to seek public office. That is all very well. But how do I realize this right? I am a full-time public servant who cannot find the time or the necessary resources to put up the organization required to win office. If I take leave from my work, I cannot hold out for more than one month without a salary. I have no money to travel about and meet the voters, even to pay the registration fees for my candidature. If I am not in a position to realize this right, then what is the point of saying that I have it? Do I really have it?

In Africa liberal rights make less sense even as ideological representations. If rights are to be meaningful in the context of a people struggling to stay afloat under very adverse economic and political conditions, they have to be concrete. Concrete in the sense that their practical import is visible and relevant to the conditions of existence of the people to whom they apply. And most importantly, concrete in the sense that they can be realized by their beneficiaries.

To be sure, there are rights which are realizable and there are people in Africa who effectively realize their rights. However, the people who are in a position to realize their rights are very few. They are able to realize their rights by virtue of their wealth and power. The litmus test for rights is those who need protection. Unfortunately these are precisely the people who are in no position to enjoy rights. Clearly, that will not do in African conditions. People are not going to struggle for formalities and esoteric ideas which will not change their lives.

Therefore, a real need arises, namely, to put more emphasis on the realization of human rights. How is this to be? Not in the way we usually approach such matters: by giving more unrealizable rights to the powerless and by begging the powerful to make concessions to them in the name of enlightened self-interest, justice and humanity. That approach will fail us always. Rights, especially those that have any real significance for our lives are usually taken, not given—with the cooperation of those in power if possible, but without it if necessary. That is the way it was for other peoples and that is the way it is going to be in Africa.

The realization of rights is best guaranteed by the power of those who enjoy the rights. Following this, what is needed is the empowerment by whatever means, of the common people. This is not a matter of legislation, although legislation could help a little. It is rather a matter of redistributing economic and political power across the board. That means that it is in the final analysis a matter of political mobilization and struggle. And it will be a protracted and bitter struggle because those who are favored by the existing distribution of power will resist heartily.

CONCLUSION: HUMAN RIGHTS AND SOCIAL TRANSFORMATION

It is at this point that the ideal of human rights is fully articulated for it is now that we see its critical dialectical moment. Initially part of the ideological prop of liberal capitalism, the idea of human rights was a conservative force. It was meant to safeguard the interests of the men of property especially against the threatening egalitarianism of popular sovereignty. It was not of course presented as a tool of special interests but a universal value good for humanity. That went down well and it has been able to serve those who propagated it behind this mystification.

But ideas have their own dynamics which cannot easily be controlled by the people who brought them into being. In case of human rights, its dynamics soon trapped it in a contradiction somewhat to the dismay of its protagonists. Fashioned as a tool against democracy, the idea became an important source of legitima-tion for those seeking the expansion of democracy. But in Europe, this contradiction never fully matured. An agile and accommodating political class and unprecedented affluence saw to that.

In Africa, prevailing objective conditions will press matters much further, particularly the question of empowerment. In all probability, the empowerment of people will become the primary issue. Once this happens, the social contradictions will be immensely sharpened and the idea of human rights will become an asset of great value to radical social transformation. I cannot help thinking that Africa is where the critical issues in human rights will be fought out and where the idea will finally be consummated or betrayed.

Rites as Rights:
The Confucian Alternative

Roger T. Ames

Roger T. Ames is professor of philosophy at the University of Hawaii at Manoa. He is the translator, editor, and author of many books. His books include Thinking Through Confucius *(1987) and* Anticipating China *(1995).*

Ames discusses the concept of rites in Confucianism in connection with the contemporary Western understanding of human rights. Ames points out how this practice of ritual propriety constitutes a necessary component of the ethical life of the individual in search of personal and moral fulfillment in a community of relationships. Ames concludes that the nonlegal emphasis of the Confucian perspective opens up an ethical dimension above and beyond the sort of minimum standards sought by the Western conception of human rights.

I. INSIDE *LI*

The concept of *li* ("rites/ritual practice") is extremely broad, embracing everything from manners to mediums of communication to social and political institutions. It is the determinate fabric of Chinese culture and, further, defines sociopolitical order. Ritual practice is not, of course, a purely Chinese innovation, but its prominence as an apparatus for ordering society, and its dominance over formal legal institutions, give the Chinese *li* a somewhat unique definition.[1]

Contemporary Chinese attitudes toward human rights, influenced by the Western model, tend to be state-centered and political. As an alternative I want to examine *li*, the traditional, primarily social mechanism for constituting community and generating its sociopolitical order. I then will show ways in which *li* has done some of the work expected from human rights notions, and how it has influenced the way in which contemporary Chinese society has entertained our doctrine of universal human rights.

The character *li*, generally translated "rites," "ritual practice," and "propriety," has strong religious implications in the sense of "bonding." *Li* is cognate with the character *t'i*, which means "to embody, "to constitute a shape," and, by extension, "organic form." Ritual practices, then, are "per-formances": social practices that effect relationships through prescribed forms. The etymology of the English "rites" and "ritual" is suggestive. In Latin *rītus* derives from the base **ri* ("to count," "to enumerate"), which in turn is an enlargement of the base **ar* ("to join" as in "arithmetic" or "rhyme"). Ritual practice is the rhyme and rhythm of society.

The translation of *li* as "propriety" also has its justification. It indicates the proprietorial implications of ritual practice: making community one's own. To perform ritual is, on the one hand, to be incorporated as integral to the society it defines, and hence to be shaped and socialized by it. On the other hand, it is to contribute oneself to the pattern of relationships which ritual entails, and thereby to have determinative effect on society. Because of this contributory and participatory emphasis, *li* does not carry the pejorative connotations such as superficiality, formalism, and irrationality often associated with the Western understanding of *ritual*. *Li* is not passive deference to external patterns. It is a *making* of society that requires the investment of oneself and one's own sense of importance.

Ritual practices initially lure the performer into authorized and established social relationships, but these are not simply standards of appropriateness rigidly embedded in cultural tradition. Ritual practices have a creative dimension. They exhort more than they prohibit. Rituals inform the participant of what may be properly performed by him or her. Beyond the formal social patterning is an open texture of ritual that is personalized and accommodates the uniqueness of each participant. Ritual is a pliant body of practices for registering one's importance. It is a vehicle for establishing the insights of the cultivating person, enabling one ultimately to leave one's own mark on the tradition.

There are variable degrees of personalization in ritual practices, and the roles they establish are hierarchical. These roles form a kind of social syntax that generates meaning through coordinating patterns of deference. The process of extending and deepening these roles brings with it a greater felt significance. It follows, then, that individual autonomy is anathema to a ritually constituted society, suggesting idiocy or immorality. To be socially unresponsive is to be irresponsible. A community's cultural memory is therefore an inherited repertoire of formalized actions showing the meaning and importance (*yi*) of the tradition of one's cultural predecessors. Ritual preserves and transmits culture. Ritual socializes a person and makes one a member of a community. It informs one of shared values. It provides an opportunity to integrate oneself into the community in a way which maintains and enriches community life.

Confucius declares that the project of ritual practice is to effect social harmony: "The exemplary person (*chün tzu*) seeks harmony (*ho*) rather than agreement (*t'ung*); the small person does the opposite."[2] Ritual action is a necessary condition for Confucius' vision of social harmony because, by definition, it not only permits but actually requires personalization. This harmony assumes that people are unique and must be orchestrated into relationships which permit expression of this uniqueness.[3] A formal ceremony without this kind of personal commitment is hollow, meaningless, and antisocial; on the other hand, a ceremony that coordinates and expresses the genuineness of its participants is a source of social cohesion and enjoyment. Ritual actions are unique because they display the specific quality of the performers.[4]

Throughout the *Analects* the truly harmonious community, relying as it does upon quality people to refine themselves in ritual action and to assume the internal perspective entailed by a sense of shame, is defined as fundamentally self-ordering.[5] Where the definition of the community, constituted by an internal network of interpersonal patterns of deference, is immanent and emergent rather than imposed, the "ruler" does not rule.[6] The community is a project of disclosure. This inseparability of personal integrity and social integration collapses the means/end distinction, rendering each person both an end in himself or herself and a condition or means for everyone else in the community to be what they are. The model is one of mutuality.

In ritual-ordered community, particular persons stand in relationships defined by creativity rather than power. This distinction between power and creativity is essential for an understanding of community constituted by ritual action.[7] Community is programmatic—a future goal that is constantly pursued rather than an immediate reality or fixed ideal. It is an open-ended aesthetic achievement, contingent upon particular ingredients and inspiration like a work of art, not the product of formula or blueprint.

I stress the role of self-cultivation and personalization in the capacity of ritual practice to constitute community. Implicit in self-cultivation and communal deference to its achievements is cultural elitism. The greater one's excellence, the more outstanding and determinate one becomes. The converse is also true. In the absence of self-cultivation and participation, one does not emerge as either culturally determinate or determinative.

In the Chinese tradition humanity itself is not essentialistically defined. It is understood as a progressive cultural achievement. There is a qualitative ascendancy from brute (*ch'in shou*) to indeterminate masses (*min*) to determinate person (*jen*) and ultimately to authoritative person (*jen**) which reveals the degree of one's refinement through ritual actions. Those who violate social relations and the values they embody are truly brutes. Humanity is open-ended and can be ever increasingly refined.[8]

Because ritual action can only take account of a person to the extent that he or she is differentiated and distinguished, the indeterminate masses (*min*) necessarily have a more passive and deferential role.[9] This means also that the achieved community will in some important respect always be local. It thus falls to those who are the fullest participants in ritual practice to formulate and shape a future for their particular community.

The relationship between exhortative ritual action (*li*) and prohibitive penal law (*hsing*) in the tradition defined by Confucius is correlative. The conceptual content and function of penal law can only be understood against an appreciation for the way in which ritual practice works to constitute a person in society.[10] Penal law establishes a minimum standard for what it means to be human and draws the external perimeter on what is acceptable at any time within the jurisdiction of ritual practice.[11] Ritual provides a direction for refinement and aspiration. Law instructs with deterrent force in what is minimally acceptable. Where ritual action prompts creative cultural adventure and reifies what is most significant in cultural achievement, law secures the society, sets constraints on the existing social order, and surgically eliminates what is incorrigible.[12]

Although Confucius aspires to a state that is free of litigation,[13] he is keenly aware of the distance between present reality and the need for law.[14] On the other hand, several reasons can be given for Confucius' reluctance to entertain "disorder" (*luan*) as a topic for discussion, perhaps the most important being his preoccupation with the ritual structure of society.

II. OUTSIDE RIGHTS

The concepts of *human rights* and *ritual action* are both social practices which establish and define the limits of relationships among persons and between a person and the state. The English term *ritual* is often negative and formal while the Chinese counterpart, *li,* is generally not. *Ch'üan,* or "rights," has generally denoted "power," not in the positive sense of legitimated authority but as a provisional advantage that derives from exceptional circumstances.

When in the nineteenth century this expression, *ch'üan-li**, was employed in translation of the notion of *human rights*, the initial Chinese response to it must have been one of considerable bemusement.[15] Nonetheless, this oblique approximation of *rights* made its formal entry into the Chinese world and has even achieved a technical prominence in the many constitutions promulgated in this century. Even so, the rhetoric of rights which dominates Western political discussion is still very foreign in popular Chinese culture. This Chinese resistance to the notion of human rights is due to factors far more fundamental than bad translation. Rights as defined in the classical Western tradition entail assumptions that are in many ways incompatible with Chinese social considerations.

Historically, our conception of human rights has been influenced by the rupture between the small familial community, in which custom and tradition guaranteed fundamental dignities, and the modern nation-state, in which mobile and atomized populations must claim their humanity from an impersonal and often oppressive governmental machine. A persuasive argument can be made that the industrial revolution has altered our concept of community so that human rights is a reasonable response for protecting personal worth. This same argument can be reversed to explain why the Chinese have not been under the same compulsion to develop a scheme of individual rights.

The classical Chinese formulation of human nature, *jen hsing**, elaborated throughout the tradition, belongs to Mencius. For Mencius, strictly speaking, a human is not a sort of being, but a kind of doing—an achievement. The concept *hsing**, generally translated as "nature," is derived from and a refinement on *sheng*, meaning the whole process of birth, growth, and the ultimate demise of a living creature. In the human context it perhaps comes closer to "character," "personality," or "constitution" than what we generally understand by "nature"—either as *physis* or as *natura*.[16]

This human nature is not innate—in Chinese, "prior to nature" (*hsien t'ien te*). Donald Munro, having translated a classical passage in precisely these terms, concludes: "This means that a person's nature being so decreed, cannot be altered through human action; it is a 'given' that exists from birth."[17] T'ang Chün-i, however, has more appropriately understood *t'ien ming* to be the relationship that obtains between heaven (*t'ien*) and humankind, emphasizing the mutuality of the relationship and shying away from importing the very Western notion of irrevocable fate or destiny to the Chinese tradition.[18]

Mencius suggests that the human being emerges in the world as a spontaneously arising and ever-changing matrix of relationships through which, over a lifetime, one defines one's nature. This initial disposition is "good" in the sense that these bonds are elicited responses to the already formed dispositions of family and community. These bonds are then nurturable with varying degrees of deftness and style (*shan*). Nurturing these primordial ties sustains one as a human being and elevates one above the animal world.

Given this conception of human nature, Mencius is not moved to establish a distinction between nature as the actual process of being a human being and nature as some capacity that underlies the process of becoming human. One device for understanding this relational conception of human nature (*hsing**) is to reflect on the shared implications between it and its cognate, *hsing***, which denotes "family or clan name." Like the concept of human nature, one's family name is a generalization shared by a group of people that both defines them and is defined by them. It signifies a set of conditions suggesting both shared tendency and the opportunity for cultivation in particular ways by each member—an opportunity to attach one's personal name (*ming**) to it, as it were. Neither one's family name nor one's nature is an essential or innate faculty; both are a focus of relationships in which one participates.

The fact that the Chinese tradition has been largely persuaded by the Mencian-based definition of human nature described above rather than by any notion of discrete individuality has profound implications for the way in which the soil of China has responded to the human rights transplant.

First, there is no philosophical basis that will justify self as a locus of interests independent of and prior to society. Under the sway of a relational understanding of human nature, the mutuality of personal, societal, and political realization has been generally assumed.[19]

Much if not most of the commentary available on Chinese attitudes toward human rights has reinterpreted this fundamental presupposition as a kind of self-abnegation or "selflessness," a modern echo of Hegel's "hollow men" interpretation of Chinese culture.[20] Attributing selflessness to the Chinese tradition, however, sneaks both the public/private and individual/society distinctions in by the back door, and vitiates our claim that *person* in the Chinese tradition is irreducibly social. To be "selfless" in the sense that Munro presupposes requires first that an individual self exist, and then that it be sacrificed for some higher interest. The suggestion that there are "higher interests" on the part of either person or society covertly establishes a boundary between them that justifies an adversarial relationship.

This attribution of selflessness to the Chinese tradition, both ancient and modern, arises out of an equivocation between *selfish* and *selfless*. The Confucian position is that because self-realization is fundamentally a social undertaking, individualistic "selfish" concerns are an impediment to self-realization.[21] A central issue in Chinese philosophy that has spanned the centuries has been the possible opposition between selfish advantage (*li**) and that which is appropriate and meaningful to all concerned (*yi*), including oneself. The former is associated with retarded personal development (*hsiao jen*) while the latter is the mainstay of the self-realized and exemplary person (*chün tzu*).

Western commentators, in imposing a "selfless" ideal on the Chinese tradition, are appealing to a contest between state and individual that has separated liberal democratic and collectivist thinkers in our own experience but has only limited applicability to the Chinese model. Self-realization for the Chinese requires neither a high degree of individual autonomy nor capitulation to the general will. Rather, it involves benefiting and being benefitted by membership in a world of reciprocal loyalties and obligations which surround and stimulate a person and which define his or her own worth.

Having questioned this notion that selflessness is and has been a Chinese ideal, it is further necessary to examine the corollary assertion that the project of self-realization is in fact to be pursued through "obedience . . . to the chief relevant authority," where each higher level of authority takes precedence over the one below it, until reaching the emperor in imperial China and the Party leadership today.[22] Such a combination of "selflessness" and obedience if true would bring this model perilously close to Hegel's characterization of a Chinese totalitarianism.

This "top-down" interpretation is encouraged by the relative absence of the adversarial tensions introduced by separating private from public interests, and by the basic trust that colors the relationship between person and state in what Tu Wei-ming describes as the "fiduciary" community.[23] The coterminous relationship between strong person and strong state presumed in the Chinese model contrasts with the liberal Western concern to limit state powers.

In China, the traditional assumption has been that public order and personal order entail each other, with the broader configuration always emerging out of the more immediate and concrete.[24] When the

country succumbs to a disintegration of order, the exemplary person returns to his or her home or community to begin again to shape an appropriate order.[25] Confucius himself, on being asked why he did not have a formal position in government, replied that the achievement of order in the home is itself the basis on which any broader attainment of order depends.[26] The central doctrine of graduated love in which family plays such a vital role is predicated on the priority of the immediate and concrete over universal principles and ideals.

This traditional Chinese prejudice for the immediate and substantive tends to preclude any concept of universal human rights. At the same time, it does not permit the sanctioning of absolute state power. In the classical political rhetoric, a symbiosis between government and people is presumed in which the people have been construed as the more dominant value: "the people as root" (min pen). The participation and tolerance characteristic of a bottom-up emergent order provides an internal check on totalitarianism.

In China, from ancient times to the present, conflicts have almost invariably been settled through informal mechanisms for mediation and conciliation as close to the dispute as possible.[27] Society has largely been self-regulating and has thus required only minimal government. It is this same communal harmony that defines and dispenses order at the most immediate level which is also relied upon to define and express authoritative consensus without more obvious formal provisions for effecting popular sovereignty.

In China, political directives appear to take the form of broad and abstract slogans promulgated in the public institutions and the press. What is not apparent is the degree to which such directives require interpretation and application as they ramify back down through society. Communication and consensus are, in fact, arrived at by a much less abstract mechanism than would be characteristic of a society constituted of strictly autonomous individuals. This is true in large measure because the Chinese conception of humanness does not presuppose any notion of a moral order transcending the consensual order which could justify either demagogic appeals or appeals to individual conscience, and which might disrupt the consensus.

In the Chinese tradition morality is a cultural product that derives from the ethos or character of the society and is embodied in its ritual patterns of conduct. In place of a metaphysics of morals guaranteeing a concept of natural rights, there is a marketplace of morals where what is natural is open to negotiation. Given that order is defined from the bottom up, and concrete conditions temper generalizations to yield varying degrees of appropriateness, the notion of universalizability is certainly problematic. In fact, the Chinese have approached doctrines of *universals* with the caution of a culture fundamentally reluctant to leave the security of immediate experience for the more tentative reaches of transcendent principles. Evidence for this prejudice is everywhere in the culture: a mythology that evolves out of concrete historical events, a concept of divinity as a direct extension of the spirituality of particular human beings,[28] a concept of *reason* emerging out of and defended by appeal to concrete historical instances of reasonableness, a concept of morality articulated through analogy with particular historical exemplars,[29] a conception of

knowledge inseparably bound to practical efficacy, a self-originating cultural identity that is inward-looking to the point of being xenophobic, and so on.

A final and most important illustration of this Chinese reluctance to universalize is a difficulty in accommodating the notion of equality as we understand it. It is our concept of *individual* as unit measure that permits the quantitative sense of equality on which we rely—the possession of an equivalent degree of some essential quality or attribute that entitles one to be regarded and treated as an equal. Equality thus understood tends to make qualitative ("better than") assessments suspect if not even abhorrent, leading as they will to egoism, sexism, nationalism, racism, and so on. It is against an essential equality that we allow that people have differences in rank, dignity, power, ability, and excellence.

The Chinese conception of person as a specific matrix of roles will not tolerate our assertion of natural equality. There is another sense of equality, however, that is relevant. Although persons stand in hierarchical relationships that reflect fundamental differences among them, ritual practice serves the notion of qualitative parity in several ways. First, the dynamic nature of roles means that privileges and duties within one's community tend to even up across a lifetime. One's duties as a child are balanced by one's privileges as a parent. One's field of relationships over time produce a degree of parity in what is perceived as the most vital source of humanity—one's human relations.

Second, the notion of equality, like identity, is equivocal: it can be used to mean sameness between two or more things or, when applied to one thing, it can mean forbearance on the part of other things to allow it to be itself and not something else. Accommodation is thus a kind of equality. The first sense of equality proceeds from empathy with perceptible sameness; the second from tolerance and enjoyment of perceptible difference. There is an important sense of equality in the assertion that all things are different, and yet all ought to be allowed to realize their own premise. This sense of equality, or perhaps parity, is not entirely altruistic; in fact, it is decidedly self-serving in that diverse elements in one's environment contribute to one's own creative possibilities. Where rights-based order strives to guarantee a minimum and yet vital sameness, ritual-based order seeks to guarantee tolerance. For it is the basic nature of harmony, the aspiration of ritual practice, that it is enhanced by a coordinated diversity among its elements.[30] Given this long-standing preference for the substantive over the abstract and the immediate over the generalized, there is an inbuilt resistance to what must be perceived as the vagaries of the universal human rights rhetoric.

III. CONSTITUTION OR RITUAL CODE?

Andrew J. Nathan, whose work on the Chinese constitution figures prominently in my analysis, observes that a comparison of the American and Chinese constitutions reveals the "challenging combination of broad rhetorical similarities with deep differences in values and practices."[31] These deep differences suggest that the Chinese are still in some important measure looking to ritual practice (li) to do the work reserved in our

society for principles guaranteeing human rights.

Since the turn of the century China has promulgated nothing short of twelve official constitutions and numerous constitutional drafts of one kind or another.[32] Since in the Chinese tradition neither human nature nor the social order it defines is static, the constitution must remain open and be adaptable to its particular constituents in their particular circumstances.

A related feature of the adaptable Chinese constitutions is that they not only define an existing sociopolitical order but, further, are "programmatic" in looking ahead to some goals yet to be realized.[33] Like ritual practice, they do not seek to settle universally valid ideals but pursue changing configurations of harmony and refinement in more concrete terms. Any constitution is only the most recent manifesto of Party policies and aspirations. Changes are substantive and are not simply amendments that seek to clarify unalterable principles. Given the resistance to any universalization of order in the ritual community, the constitutionally guaranteed rights do not, as in our case, fix a boundary on the enactment of laws ("no law shall be enacted that . . ."). Rather, the changing social order in China requires that law and Party policy have a free hand in articulating the changing rights and duties of the community.

The Chinese constitution is more a social than a political document in that its primary function is to promote social harmony rather than to mediate disputes and resolve conflicts. Jerome Cohen in his discussion of the 1978 People's Republic of China Constitution, for example, asserts that it is not even what we mean by the term *constitution,* "for it is a formalization of existing power configurations rather than an authentic institutional framework for adjusting political forces that compete for power."[34] Where the American constitution is a basis for establishing laws, the Chinese constitution primarily establishes rituals. That is to say, the Chinese constitution formalizes status and defines privilege and obligation on the assumption of coterminous interests between person and community. There is no assumption that strengthening the authority of the community weakens the options of the particular persons that constitute it. Because the constitution is primarily a compact of cooperation formulated on a premise of trust between person and community, rather than a contract between potential adversaries, there are no independent provisions for the formal enforcement of rights claims against the state. The assumption is that order will be effected and guaranteed by informal community pressures that are more immediate to the circumstances and allow greater popular participation. As a last resort the constitution does provide for appeal to state organs, but, like appeal to law in traditional China, this is a no-win course of action. That is, one's very appearance in such circumstances almost in itself constitutes a tacit assumption of guilt.

Finally, another peculiar characteristic of the Chinese constitution is that rights derive solely from one's ongoing membership in society. While in our tradition the concept of the individual and his or her attendant rights serves to ground the notion of the individual's social and political relations, in the Chinese context humanity exists solely within the bounds of community. Rights are socially derived *proprieties* rather than individual *proper-*

ties. These proprieties, not unexpectedly, are primarily articulated as social welfare entitlements rather than individual political rights. Given that only social beings are human beings, it is thus conceivable in the Chinese case to disqualify oneself from rights considerations by withdrawing from community participation. This radically social definition of person is reflected in the inseparability of rights and duties in the Chinese document, where even a positive right such as the right to education is both a personal right and a social duty.

Constitutions, as isolated documents, are formal and abstract. But even at the level of abstraction required by our comparison of the Chinese and American constitutions, it is clear that these documents serve different worlds.

IV. A CULTURE-CENTERED PROGRAM OF PERSONAL RIGHTS

The campaign in China to forestall "bourgeois liberal" influences seems a clear condemnation of our human rights values. Yet their rejection of "bourgeois liberalism" is aimed at sustaining the direction and the momentum of *their own* social and economic development.

The Chinese are also taking Western ideas seriously. It is not clear that the reverse is true. I want now to leave the Chinese to their own devices and return to our conception of human rights to see if it cannot be strengthened in some way by appeal to the Chinese model.

It is not necessary to rehearse the many benefits that we derive from our commitment to human rights. In our world today these benefits are as obvious as they are important. I want rather to focus on certain of the weaknesses of rights theory.

A primary issue is the definition of the individual that grounds much rights theory. Henry Rosemont, Jr., has discussed this definition in his essay for this volume. There is much in the Confucian tradition that might be a resource for rethinking our notion of *autonomous individuality*, especially that aspect of the individual which, given its priority over society and environment, effectively renders context a means to individual ends. An obvious weakness here is the priority of individual freedoms over communal and environmental duties.

Corollary to a more contextual definition of person would be to reflect on the temptation to use individual rights to insist on always having all that is one's due. Individual autonomy does not necessarily enhance human dignity. In fact, if dignity is felt worth, the exaggeration of individuality might be anathema to the ultimate project of human rights, which is precisely to protect and foster human dignity. The Chinese concept of person is useful in making a distinction between individual autonomy and self-fulfillment.

In this same vein, the inordinate emotive importance that we are inclined to focus on human rights requires a better sense of proportion. The celebration of human rights as a means of realizing human dignity is of course overstated, unless by human dignity we mean the barest possible existence. To use human rights as a measure for the quality of life possible within community is like using minimum health standards as a universal index on the quality of restaurants. Human rights as law is ultimately a minimum standard, a last resort, the invocation of which signals a gross failure in the community.

The Confucian alternative suggests that almost all the actual rights and duties which define the sociopolitical order are sustained by extralegal institutions and practices and are enforced by social pressures rather than punishments. In fact, reliance upon the application of law and human rights as a subset of law, far from being a means of realizing human dignity, is fundamentally dehumanizing, impoverishing as it does the possibilities of mutual accommodation and compromising our *particular* responsibility to define what would be appropriate conduct. The introduction of obligation mediates and constricts the creative possibilities of a relationship. The emphasis on ritual, by contrast, is an effort toward the optimization of these same possibilities. The Chinese model suggests alternative nonlegal mechanisms for resolving conflicts. It tempers the readiness of the individual to pursue legal measures by providing reasonable alternatives. Movement away from formal procedures is also a movement toward a greater practicability.

The basically Marxian criticism that rights select out only particular aspects of human existence could be blunted by recognizing the immediate and inseparable relationship between cultural conditions and the variable content of abstractly defined human rights. A given right is constantly being redefined by factors that intrude upon it, including every manner of social and political pressure. A variable definition of human rights is only realistic and serves not only our own cultural development but our understanding of cultural differences.

China's resort to the Western model is enabling it to establish more formal and clearly defined guidelines for its changing sociopolitical order. Our recourse to the Chinese model can stimulate a clearer recognition of the ritual basis of human rights and provide us with a greater tolerance for cultural diversity: the capacity to recognize our own parochialisms and to cherish them as the actual substance of our human rights.

NOTES

1. Herbert Fingarette in his *Confucius: The Secular as Sacred* (New York: Harper & Row, 1972) has done a lot to bring out both the centrality and the uniqueness of ritual as it has functioned in the Confucian tradition.
2. *Analects* 13.23. See also 1.12, 2.14, and 15.22.
3. Ibid., 3.12.
4. Ibid., 3.3.
5. Ibid., 2.3.
6. Ibid., 15.5. See also 2.1.
7. David L. Hall, *The Uncertain Phoenix: Adventures toward a Post-Cultural Sensitivity* (New York: Fordham University Press, 1982), p. 249.
8. See D. C. Lau's Introduction to *Mencius* (Harmondsworth: Penguin, 1970); and for an analysis of its implications see Mark E. Lewis, "The Imperial Transformation of Violence," (Ph.D. diss., University of Chicago, 1985).
9. For this distinction between *jen* and *min* see David L. Hall and Roger T. Ames, *Thinking through Confucius* (Albany, N.Y.: SUNY Press, 1987), chap. 3.
10. *Li* is frequently used as shorthand for conceptual clusters. See Kenneth DeWoskin, *A Song for One or Two: Music and the Concept of Art in Early China* (Ann Arbor, Mich.: University of Michigan Press, 1982), esp. pp. 174ff.; and Hall, *Thinking through Confucius*, chap. 2.
11. See Bernhard Karlgren, *Grammata Serica Recensa*, Museum of Far Eastern Antiquities Bulletin no. 29 (Stockholm, 1987), p. 213.
12. See Brian E. McKnight, *The Quality of Mercy* (Honolulu: University of Hawaii Press, 1981). McKnight demonstrates that, amnesties being so frequent, China was in fact relying upon pressures within the community to restore all but the most egregious violations of social order.
13. *Analects* 12.13.
14. Ibid., 13.11–13.12.
15. *Hsün Tzu* brings these two terms together for the first time in the extant corpus with decidedly negative import: "For this reason, neither

16. promise of power (*ch'üan*) nor personal advantage (*li**) can subvert the exemplary person." See *Hsün Tzu*, Harvard-Yenching Sinological Index Series, supp. 22 (Taipei: Chinese Materials Center, 1966 reprint): 3.1.49.
16. See A. C. Graham, *Studies in Chinese Philosophy and Philosophical Literature* (Singapore: Institute of East Asian Philosophers, 1986), p. 8. He is keen to correct his earlier understanding of *hsing** as "that which one starts with" to make it more representative of the whole process of one's existence.
17. Donald J. Munro, *Concept of Man in Contemporary China* (Ann Arbor, Mich.: University of Michigan Press, 1979), pp. 19–20, 57. Munro develops the notion of an innate and unchanging nature.
18. See T'ang Chün-i, "The T'ien Ming ("Heavenly Ordinance") in Pre-Ch'in China," *Philosophy East and West* 11, no. 4 (1961): 195–218; and 12, no. 1 (1962): 29–50.
19. See *Analects* 6.30; and the *Ta-hsüeh* ("Great Learning"), which is the classic statement for this coextensive relationship.
20. Donald J. Munro, "The Shape of Chinese Values in the Eye of an American Philosopher," in *The China Difference*, ed. Ross Terrill (New York: Harper & Row, 1979), p. 40.
21. See *Analects* 12.1: "Authoritative humanity proceeds from oneself—how could it come from others?"
22. Munro, "Shape of Chinese Values," p. 41.
23. Tu Wei-ming, "Confucianism: Symbol and Substance in Recent Times," in *Value Change in Chinese Society*, ed. R. W. Wilson, A. A. Wilson, and S. L. Greenblatt (New York: Praeger, 1979), p. 46.
24. See *Analects* 12.17. See also 13.6 and 13.13.
25. Ibid., 8.13 and 15.17.
26. Ibid., 1.2 and 2.21.
27. See Victor H. Li, *Law without Lawyers* (Boulder, Colo.: Westview Press, 1978), esp. chap. 4.
28. See Emily M. Ahern, *Chinese Ritual and Politics* (Cambridge: At the University Press, 1981), p. 1; and Sarah Allan, "Shang Foundations of Modern Chinese Folk Religion," in *Legend, Lore and Religion in China*, ed. Alvin P. Cohen and Sarah Allan (San Francisco: Chinese Materials Center, 1979), p. 3. They argue, basically, that gods are dead people.
29. Henry Rosemont, Jr., "Kierkegaard and Confucius: On Following the Way," *Philosophy East and West* 36, no. 3 (1986), and *Confucianism and Contemporary Ethics* (forthcoming); and Fingarette, *Confucius: The Secular as Sacred*. The insights of these two scholars with respect to the nature of morality also apply to rationality; witness the relatively minor role of rational skepticism as a motive force in the tradition.

30. See Roger T. Ames, "Taoism and the Nature of Nature," *Environmental Ethics* 8, no. 4 (1986) for this argument.

31. Andrew J. Nathan, "Political Rights in the Chinese Constitutions," in *Human Rights in Contemporary China,* ed. R. Randle Edwards, Louis Henkin, and Andrew J. Nathan (New York: Columbia University Press, 1986), p. 79.

32. Ibid., pp. 82–83.

33. See, for example, Articles 14 and 19 of the 1982 People's Republic of China Constitution.

34. Cited in R. Randle Edwards, "Civil and Social Rights: Theory and Practice in Chinese Law Today," in *Human Rights in Contemporary China,* ed. Edwards.

A Buddhist Response
to the Nature
of Human Rights

Kenneth K. Inada

Kenneth K. Inada is a professor of philosophy at the State University of New York at Buffalo. He is the author of Nagarjuna (1970) and Guide to Buddhist Philosophy (1985). He edits the Journal of Buddhist Philosophy.

Inada contends that a Buddhist perspective places much more importance on the fluidity of human relationships than does a Western perspective. This means that a Buddhist conception of human rights will be softer, more accommodating, and more flexible than a Western conception of human rights; it will be more compassionate, more forgiving, and less inclined to set up strong oppositions between parties. In contrast to the Western perspective, a Buddhist conception of human rights is less interested in legal formalities and more interested in the nurturance of feelings that will promote humanistic existence.

It is incorrect to assume that the concept of human rights is readily identifiable in all societies of the world. The concept may perhaps be clear and distinct in legal quarters, but in actual practice suffers greatly from lack of clarity and gray areas due to impositions by different cultures. This is especially true in Asia, where the two great civilizations of India and China have spawned such outstanding systems as Hinduism, Buddhism, Jainism, Yoga, Confucianism, Taoism and Chinese Buddhism. These systems, together with other indigenous folk beliefs, attest to the cultural diversity at play that character-

Reprinted by permission of Westview Press, from *Asian Perspectives on Human Rights*, edited by Claude E. Walsh and Virginia Leary, 1990.

izes Asia proper. In focusing on the concept of human rights, however, we shall concentrate on Buddhism to bring out the common grounds of discourse.

Alone among the great systems of Asia, Buddhism has successfully crossed geographical and ideological borders and spread in time throughout the whole length and breadth of known Asia. Its doctrines are so universal and profound that they captured the imagination of all the peoples they touched and thereby established a subtle bond with all. What then is this bond? It must be something common to all systems of thought which opens up and allows spiritual discourse among them.

In examining the metaphysical ground of all systems, one finds that there is a basic feeling for a larger reality in one's own experience, a kind of reaching out for a greater cosmic dimension of being, as it were. It is a deep sense for the total nature of things. All this may seem so simple and hardly merits elaborating, but it is a genuine feeling common among Asians in their quest for ultimate knowledge based on the proper relationship of one's self in the world. It is an affirmation of a reality that includes but at once goes beyond the confines of sense faculties.

A good illustration of this metaphysical grounding is seen in the Brahmanic world of Hinduism. In it, the occluded nature of the self (*atman*) constantly works to cleanse itself of defilements by yogic discipline in the hope of ultimately identifying with the larger reality which is Brahman. In the process, the grounding in the larger reality is always kept intact, regardless of whether the self is impure or not. In other words, in the quest for the purity of things a larger framework of experience is involved from the beginning such that the ordinary self (*atman*) transforms into the larger Self (*Atman*) and finally merges into the ultimate ontological Brahman.

A similar metaphysical grounding is found in Chinese thought. Confucianism, for example, with its great doctrine of humanity (*jen*), involves the ever-widening and ever-deepening human relationship that issues forth in the famous statement, "All men are brothers." In this sense, humanity is not a mere abstract concept but one that extends concretely throughout the whole of sentient existence. Confucius once said that when he searched for *jen*, it is always close at hand.[1] It means that humanity is not something external to a person but that it is constitutive of the person's experience, regardless of whether there is conscious-

ness of it or not. It means moreover that in the relational nature of society, individual existence is always more than that which one assumes it to be. In this vein, all experiences must fit into the larger cosmological scheme normally spoken of in terms of heaven, earth and mankind. This triadic relationship is ever-present and ever-in-force, despite one's ignorance, negligence or outright intention to deny it. The concept that permeates and enlivens the triadic relationship is the *Tao*. The *Tao* is a seemingly catchall term, perhaps best translated as the natural way of life and the world. In its naturalness, it manifests all of existence; indeed, it is here, there and everywhere since it remains aloof from human contrivance and manipulation. In a paradoxical sense, it depicts action based on non-action (*wu-wei*), the deepest state of being achievable. The following story illustrates this point.

A cook named Ting is alleged to have used the same carving knife for some 19 years without sharpening it at all. When asked how that is possible, he simply replied:

> What I care about is the way (*Tao*), which goes beyond skill. When I first began cutting up oxen, all I could see was the ox itself. After three years I no longer saw the whole ox. And now—now I go at it by spirit and don't look with my eyes. Perception and understanding have come to a stop and spirit moves where it wants. I go along with the natural makeup, strike in the big hollows, guide the knife through the big openings, and follow things as they are. So I never touch the smallest ligament or tendon, much less a main joint. . . . I've had this knife of mine for nineteen years and I've cut up thousands of oxen with it, and yet the blade is as good as though it had just come from the grindstone.[2]*

Such then is the master craftsman at work, a master in harmonious triadic relationship based on the capture of the spirit of *Tao* where the function is not limited to a person and his or her use of a tool. And it is clear that such a spirit of *Tao* in craftsmanship is germane to all disciplined experiences we are capable of achieving in our daily activities.

Buddhism, too, has always directed our attention to the larger reality of existence. The original enlightenment of the historical Buddha told of a pure unencumbered experience which opened up all experiential doors in such a way that they touched everything sentient as well as insentient. A Zen story graphically illustrates this point.

Once a master and a disciple were walking through a dense forest. Suddenly, they heard the clean chopping strokes of the woodcutter's axe. The disciple was elated and remarked, "What beautiful sounds in the quiet of the forest!" To which the master immediately responded, "you have got it all upside down. The sounds only make obvious the deep silence of the forest!" The response by the Zen master sets in bold relief the Buddhist perception of reality. Although existential reality refers to the perception of the world as a singular unified whole, we ordinarily perceive it in fragmented ways because of our heavy reliance on the perceptual apparatus and its consequent understanding. That is to say, we perceive by a divisive and selective method which however glosses over much of reality and indeed misses its holistic nature. Certainly, the hewing sounds of the woodcutter's axe are clearly audible and delightful to the ears, but they are so at the expense of the basic silence of the forest (i.e., total reality). Or, the forest in its silence constitutes the

necessary background, indeed the basic source, from which all sounds (and all activities for that matter) originate. Put another way, sounds arising from the silence of the forest should in no way deprive nor intrude upon the very source of their own being. Only human beings make such intrusions by their crude discriminate habits of perception and, consequently, suffer a truncated form of existence, unknowingly for the most part.

Now that we have seen Asian lives in general grounded in a holistic cosmological framework, we would have to raise the following question: How does this framework appear in the presence of human rights? Or, contrarily, how does human rights function within this framework?

Admittedly, the concept of human rights is relatively new to Asians. From the very beginning, it did not sit well with their basic cosmological outlook. Indeed, the existence of such an outlook has prevented in profound ways a ready acceptance of foreign elements and has created tension and struggle between tradition and modernity. Yet, the key concept in the tension is that of human relationship. This is especially true in Buddhism, where the emphasis is not so much on the performative acts and individual rights as it is on the matter of manifestation of human nature itself. The Buddhist always takes human nature as the basic context in which all ancillary concepts, such as human rights, are understood and take on any value. Moreover, the context itself is in harmony with the extended experiential nature of things. And thus, where the Westerner is much more at home in treating legal matters detached from human nature as such and quite confident in forging ahead to establish human rights with a distinct emphasis on certain "rights," the Buddhist is much more reserved but open and seeks to understand the implications of human behavior, based on the fundamental nature of human beings, before turning his or her attention to the so-called "rights" of individuals.

An apparent sharp rift seems to exist between the Western and Buddhist views, but this is not really so. Actually, it is a matter of perspectives and calls for a more comprehensive understanding of what takes place in ordinary human relationships. For the basic premise is still one that is focused on human beings intimately living together in the selfsame world. A difference in perspectives does not mean noncommunication or a simple rejection of another's view, as there is still much more substance in the nature of conciliation, accommodation and absorption than what is initially thought of. Here we propose two contrasting but interlocking and complementary terms, namely, "hard relationship" and "soft relationship."

The Western view on human rights is generally based on a hard relationship. Persons are treated as separate and independent entities or even bodies, each having its own assumed identity or self-identity. It is a sheer "elemental" way of perceiving things due mainly to the strong influence by science and its methodology. As scientific methodology thrives on the dissective and analytic incursion into reality as such, this in turn has resulted in our perceiving and understanding things in terms of disparate realities. Although it makes way for easy understanding, the question still remains: Do we really understand what these realities are in their own respective fullness of existence? Apparently not. And to make matters worse, the methodology unfortunately has been uncritically extended over to the

human realm, into human nature and human relations. Witness its ready acceptance by the various descriptive and behavioral sciences, such as sociology, psychology and anthropology. On this matter, Cartesian dualism of mind and body has undoubtedly influenced our ordinary ways of thinking in such a manner that in our casual perception of things we habitually subscribe to the clearcut subject–object dichotomy. This dualistic perspective has naturally filtered down into human relationships and has eventually crystallized into what we refer to as the nature of a hard relationship. Thus, a hard relationship is a mechanistic treatment of human beings where the emphasis is on beings as such regardless of their inner nature and function in the fullest sense; it is an atomistic analysis of beings where the premium is placed on what is relatable and manipulable without regard for their true potentials for becoming. In a way it is externalization in the extreme, since the emphasis is heavily weighted on seizing the external character of beings themselves. Very little attention, if any, is given to the total ambience, inclusive of inner contents and values, in which the beings are at full play. In this regard, it can be said that postmodern thought is now attempting to correct this seemingly lopsided dichotomous view created by our inattention to the total experiential nature of things. We believe this is a great step in the right direction. Meanwhile, we trudge along with a heavy burden on our backs, though unaware of it for the most part, by associating with people on the basis of hard relationships.

To amplify on the nature of hard relationships, let us turn to a few modern examples. First, Thomas Hobbes, in his great work, *Leviathan*,[3] showed remarkable grasp of human psychology when he asserted that people are constantly at war with each other. Left in this "state of nature," people will never be able to live in peace and security. The only way out of this conundrum is for all to establish a reciprocal relationship of mutual trust that would work, i.e., to strike up a covenant by selfish beings that guarantees mutual benefits and gains, one in which each relinquishes certain rights in order to gain or realize a personal as well as an overall state of peace and security. This was undoubtedly a brilliant scheme. But the scheme is weak in that it treats human beings by and large mechanically, albeit psychologically too, as entities in a give-and-take affair, and thus perpetuates the condition of hard relationships.

Another example can be offered by way of the British utilitarian movement which later was consummated in American pragmatism. Jeremy Bentham's hedonic calculus[4] (e.g., intensity of pleasure or pain, duration of pleasure or pain, certainty or uncertainty of pleasure or pain, purity or impurity of pleasure or pain, etc.) is a classic example of quantification of human experience. Although this is a most expedient or utilitarian way to treat and legislate behavior, we must remind ourselves that we are by no means mere quantifiable entities. John Stuart Mill introduced the element of quality in order to curb and tone down the excesses of the quantification process,[5] but, in the final analysis, human nature and relationships are still set in hard relations. American pragmatism fares no better since actions by and large take place in a pluralistic world of realities and are framed within the scientific mode and therefore it is unable to relinquish the nature of hard relationships.

In contemporary times, the great work of John Rawls, *A Theory of Justice*,[6] has given us yet another twist in pragmatic and social contract theories. His basic concept of justice as fairness is an example of the reciprocal principle in action, i.e., in terms of realizing mutual advantage and benefit for the strongest to the weakest or the most favored to the least favored in a society. Each person exercises basic liberty with offices for its implementation always open and access available. It is moreover a highly intellectual or rational theory. It thus works extremely well on the theoretical level but, in actual situations, it is not as practical and applicable as it seems since it still retains hard relationships on mutual bases. Such being the case, feelings and consciousness relative to injustice and inequality are not so readily sported and corrected. That is to say, lacunae exist as a result of hard relationships and they keep on appearing until they are detected and finally remedied, but then the corrective process is painfully slow. Thus the theory's strongest point is its perpetually self-corrective nature which is so vital to the democratic process. Despite its shortcomings, however, Rawls' theory of justice is a singular contribution to contemporary legal and ethical thought.

By contrast, the Buddhist view of human rights is based on the assumption that human beings are primarily oriented in soft relationships; this relationship governs the understanding of the nature of human rights. Problems arise, on the other hand, when a hard relationship becomes the basis for treating human nature because it cannot delve deeply into that nature itself and functions purely on the peripheral aspects of things. It is another way of saying that a hard relationship causes rigid and stifling empirical conditions to arise and to which we become invariably attached.

A soft relationship has many facets. It is the Buddhist way to disclose a new dimension to human nature and behavior. It actually amounts to a novel perception or vision of reality. Though contrasted with a hard relationship, it is not in contention with it. If anything, it has an inclusive nature that "softens," if you will, all contacts and allows for the blending of any element that comes along, even incorporating the entities of hard relationships. This is not to say, however, that soft and hard relationships are equal or ultimately identical. For although the former could easily accommodate and absorb the latter, the reverse is not the case. Still, it must be noted that both belong to the same realm of experiential reality and in consequence ought to be conversive with each other. The non-conversive aspect arises on the part of the "hard" side and is attributable to the locked-in character of empirical elements which are considered to be hard stubborn facts worth perpetuating. But at some point, there must be a break in the lock, as it were, and this is made possible by knowledge of and intimacy with the "soft" side of human endeavors. For the "soft" side has a passive nature characterized by openness, extensiveness, depth, flexibility, absorptiveness, freshness and creativity simply because it remains unencumbered by "hardened" empirical conditions.

What has been discussed so far can be seen in modern Thailand where tradition and change are in dynamic tension. Due to the onslaught of elements of modernity, Buddhism is being questioned and challenged. Buddhist Thailand, however, has taken up the challenge in the person of a leading monk named Buddhadasa who has led the country to keep a steady course on traditional values.[7]

> The heart of Buddhadasa's teaching is that the Dhamma (Sanskrit, Dharma) or the truth of Buddhism is a universal truth. Dhamma is equated by Buddhadasa to the true nature of things. It is everything and everywhere. The most appropriate term to denote the nature of Dhamma is *sunnata* (Sanskrit, *sunyata*) or the void. The ordinary man considers the void to mean nothing when, in reality, it means everything—everything, that is, without reference to the self.

We will return to the discussion of the nature of the void or *sunnnta* later, but suffice it to say here that what constitutes the heart of Buddhist truth of existence is based on soft relationships where all forms and symbols are accommodated and allows for their universal usage.

Robert N. Bellah has defined religion as a set of normative symbols institutionalized in a society or internalized in a personality.[8] It is a rather good definition but does not go far enough when it comes to describing Buddhism, or Asian religions in general for that matter. To speak of symbols being institutionalized or internalized without the proper existential or ontological context seems to be a bit artificial and has strains of meanings oriented toward hard relationships. Bellah, being a social scientist, probably could not go beyond the strains of a hard relationship, for, otherwise, he would have ended in a nondescriptive realm. The only way out is to give more substance to the nature of religious doctrines themselves, as is the case in Buddhism. The Buddhist Dharma is one such doctrine which, if symbolized, must take on a wider and deeper meaning that strikes at the very heart of existence of the individual. In this respect, Donald

Swearer is on the right track when he says:

> the adaptation of symbols of Theravada Buddhism presupposes an underlying ontological structure. The symbol system of Buddhism, then, is not to be seen only in relationship to its wider empirical context, but also in relationship to its ontological structure. This structure is denoted by such terms as Dhamma or absolute Truth, emptiness and non-attachment. These terms are denotative of what Dhiravamsa calls "dynamic being." They are symbolic, but in a universalistic rather than a particularistic sense.[9]

Swearer's reference to an underlying ontological structure is in complete harmony with our use of the term soft relationship. And only when this ontological structure or soft relationship is brought into the dynamic tension between tradition and modernity can we give full accounting to the nature of human experience and the attendant creativity and change within a society.

Let us return to a fuller treatment of soft relationships. In human experience, they manifest themselves in terms of the intangible human traits that we live by, such as patience, humility, tolerance, deference, nonaction, humaneness, concern, pity, sympathy, altruism, sincerity, honesty, faith, responsibility, trust, respectfulness, reverence, love and compassion. Though potentially and pervasively present in any human relationship, they remain for the most part as silent but vibrant components in all experiences. Without them, human intercourse would be sapped of the human element and reduced to perfunctory activities. Indeed, this fact seems to constitute much of the order of the day where our passions are mainly directed to physical and materialistic matters.

The actualization and sustenance of these intangible human traits are basic to the Buddhist quest for an understanding of human nature and, by extension, the so-called rights of human beings. In order to derive a closer look at the nature of soft relationships, we shall focus on three characteristics, namely, mutuality, holism, and emptiness or void.

MUTUALITY

Our understanding of mutuality is generally limited to its abstract or theoretical nature. For example, it is defined in terms of a two-way action between two parties and where the action is invariably described with reference to elements of hard relationships. Except secondarily or deviously, nothing positive is mentioned about the substance of mutuality, such as the feelings of humility, trust and tolerance that transpire between the parties concerned. Although these feelings are present, unfortunately, they hardly ever surface in the relationship and almost always are overwhelmed by the physical aspect of things.

What is to be done? One must simply break away from the merely conceptual or theoretical understanding and fully engage oneself in the discipline that will bring the feelings of both parties to become vital components in the relationship. That is, both parties must equally sense the presence and value of these feelings and thus give substance and teeth to their actions.

Pursuing the notion of mutuality further, the Buddhist understands human experience as a totally open phenomenon, that persons should always be wide open in the living process. The phrase, "an open ontology," is used to describe the unclouded state of existence. An illustration of this is the newborn child. The child is completely an open organism at birth. The senses are wide open and will absorb practically anything without prejudice. At this stage, also, the child will begin to imitate because its absorptive power is at the highest level. This open textured nature should continue on and on. In other words, if we are free and open, there should be no persistence in attaching ourselves to hard elements within the underlying context of a dynamic world of experience. The unfortunate thing, however, is that the open texture of our existence begins to blemish and fade away in time, being obstructed and overwhelmed by self-imposed fragmentation, narrowness and restriction, which gradually develop into a closed nature of existence. In this way, the hard relationship rules. But the nature of an open ontology leads us onto the next characteristic.

HOLISM

Holism of course refers to the whole, the total nature of individual existence and thus describes the unrestrictive nature of one's experience. Yet, the dualistic relationship we maintain by our crude habits of perception remains a stumbling block. This stunted form of perception is not conducive to holistic understanding and instead fosters nothing but fractured types of ontological knowledge taking. Unconscious for the most part, an individual narrows his or her vision by indulging in dualism of all kinds, both mental and physical, and in so doing isolates the objects of perception from the total process to which they belong. In consequence, the

singular unified reality of each perceptual moment is fragmented and, what is more, fragmentation once settled breeds further fragmentation.

The Buddhist will appeal to the fact that one's experience must always be open to the total ambience of any momentary situation. But here we must be exposed to a unique, if not paradoxical, insight of the Buddhist. It is that the nature of totality is not a clearly defined phenomenon. In a cryptic sense, however, it means that the totality of experience has no borders to speak of. It is an open border totality, which is the very nature of the earlier mentioned "open ontology." It is a noncircumscribable totality, like a circle sensed which does not have a rounded line, a seamless circle, if you will. A strange phenomenon, indeed, but that is how the Buddhist sees the nature of individual existence as such. For the mystery of existence that haunts us is really the nature of one's own fullest momentary existence. Nothing else compares in profundity to this nature, so the Buddhist believes.

Now, the open framework in which experience takes place reveals that there is depth and substance in experience. But so long as one is caught up with the peripheral elements, so-called, of hard relationships one will be ensnared by them and will generate limitations on one's understanding accordingly. On the other hand, if openness is acknowledged as a fact of existence, then the way out of one's limitations will present itself. All sufferings (*duhkha*), from the Buddhist standpoint, are cases of limited ontological vision (*avidya*, ignorance) hindered by the attachment to all sorts of elements that obsess a person.

Holism is conversant with openness since an open experience means that all elements are fully and extensively involved. In many respects, holistic existence exhibits the fact that mutuality thrives only in unhindered openness. But there is still another vital characteristic to round out or complete momentary experience. For this we turn to the last characteristic.

EMPTINESS**

Emptiness in Sanskrit is *sunyata*.[10] Strictly speaking, the Sanskrit term, depicting zero or nothing, had been around prior to Buddhism, but it took the historical Buddha's supreme enlightenment (nirvana) to reveal an incomparable qualitative nature inherent to experience. Thus emptiness is not sheer voidness or nothingness in the nihilistic sense.

We ordinarily find it difficult to comprehend emptiness, much less to live a life grounded in it. Why? Again, we return to the nature of our crude habits of perception, which is laden with unwarranted forms. That is, our whole perpetual process is caught up in attachment to certain forms or elements which foster and turn into so-called empirical and cognitive biases. All of this is taking place in such minute and unknowing ways that we hardly, if ever, take notice of it until a crisis situation arises, such as the presence of certain obviously damaging prejudice or discrimination. Then and only then do we seriously wonder and search for the forms or elements that initially gave rise to those prejudicial or discriminatory forces.

Emptiness has two aspects. The first aspect alerts our perceptions to be always open and fluid, and to desist from attaching to any form or element. In this respect, emptiness technically functions as a force

of "epistemic nullity,"[11] in the sense that it nullifies any reference to a form or element as preexisting perception or even post-existing for that matter. Second and more importantly, emptiness points at a positive content of our experience. It underscores the possibility of total experience in any given moment because there is now nothing attached to or persisted in. This latter point brings us right back to the other characteristics of holism and mutuality. Now, we must note that emptiness is that dimension of experience which makes it possible for the function of mutuality and holism in each experience, since there is absolutely nothing that binds, hinders or wants in our experience. Everything is as it is (*tathata*), under the aegis of emptiness; emptiness enables one to spread out one's experience at will in all directions, so to speak, in terms of "vertical" and "horizontal" dimensions of being. As it is the key principle of enlightened existence, it makes everything both possible and impossible. Possible in the sense that all experiences function within the total empty nature, just as all writings are possible on a clean slate or, back to the zen story, where the sounds are possible in the silence (emptiness) of the forest. At the same time, impossible in the sense that all attachments to forms and elements are categorically denied in the ultimate fullness of experience. In this way, emptiness completes our experience of reality and at the same time, provides the grounds for the function of all human traits to become manifest in soft relationships.

It can now be seen that all three characteristics involve each other in the self-same momentary existence. Granted this, it should not be too difficult to accept the fact that the leading moral concept in Buddhism is compassion (*karuna*). Compassion literally means "passion for all" in an ontologically extensive sense. It covers the realm of all sentient beings, inclusive of non-sentients, for the doors of perception to total reality are always open. From the Buddhist viewpoint, then, all human beings are open entities with open feelings expressive of the highest form of humanity. This is well expressed in the famous concept of *bodhisattva* (enlightened being) in Mahayana Buddhism who has deepest concern for all beings and sympathetically delays his entrance to nirvana as long as there is suffering (ignorant existence) among sentient creatures. It depicts the coterminous nature of all creatures and may be taken as a philosophic myth in that it underscores the ideality of existence which promotes the greatest unified form of humankind based on compassion. This ideal form of existence, needless to say, is the aim and goal of all Buddhists.

As human beings we need to keep the channels of existential dialogue open at all times. When an act of violence is in progress, for example, we need to constantly nourish the silent and passive nature of nonviolence inherent in all human relations. Though nonviolence cannot counter violence on the latter's terms, still, its nourished presence serves as a reminder of the brighter side of existence and may even open the violator's mind to common or normal human traits such as tolerance, kindness and noninjury (*ahimsa*). Paradoxically and most unfortunately, acts of violence only emphasize the fact that peace and tranquillity are the normal course of human existence.

It can now be seen that the Buddhist view on human rights is dedicated to the understanding of persons in a parameter-free ambience, so to speak, where feelings that are extremely soft and tender, but nevertheless present and translated into human traits or virtues that we uphold, make up the very fiber of human relations. These relations, though their contents are largely intangible, precede any legal rights or justification accorded to human beings. In brief, human rights for the Buddhist are not only matters for legal deliberation and understanding, but they must be complemented by and based on something deeper and written in the very feelings of all sentients. The unique coexistent nature of rights and feelings constitutes the saving truth of humanistic existence.

NOTES

1. *Lu Yu* (The Analects of Confucius): VII, 29.
2. *The Complete Works of Chuang Tzu*, translated by Burton Watson (New York: Columbia University Press, 1960), pp. 50–51.
3. Thomas Hobbes, *Leviathan* (New York: Hafner, 1926).
4. Jeremy Bentham, *An Introduction to the Principles of Morals and Legislation* (New York: Hafner, 1948).
5. John Stuart Mill observed, "It is better to be a human being dissatisfied than a pig satisfied; better to be a Socrates dissatisfied than a fool satisfied." *Utilitarianism*, cited in Louis P. Pojman, *Philosophy: The Quest for Truth* (Belmont, CA: Wadsworth, 1989), p. 357.
6. John Rawls, *A Theory of Justice* (Cambridge: Harvard University Press, 1971). Rawls also has a chapter on civil disobedience but it too is treated under the same concept of justice as fairness and suffers accordingly from the elements of hard relationships.
7. Donald K. Swearer, "Thai Buddhism: Two Responses to Modernity," in Bardwell L. Smith, ed., *Contributions to Asian Studies*, Volume 4: *Tradition and Change in Theravada Buddhism* (Leiden: EJ. Brill, 1973), p. 80."Without reference to the self" means to uphold the Buddhist doctrine of non-self (Sanskrit, *anatman*) which underlies all momentary existence and avoids any dependence on a dichotomous self-oriented subject–object relationship. For an updated and comprehensive view of Buddhadasa's reformist's philosophy, see Donald K. Swearer, ed., *Me and*

Mine: Selected Essays on Bhikkhu Buddhadasa (Albany: State University of New York Press, 1989).

8. Robert N. Bellah, "Epilogue" in Bellah, ed., *Religion and Progress in Modern Asia* (New York: Free Press, 1965), p. 173.
9. Swearer, "Thai Buddhism," p. 92.
10. Etymologically *sunyata* (in Pali, *sunnata*) means the state of being swollen. as in pregnancy, or the state of fullness of being. Thus, from the outset the term depicted the pure, open and full textured nature of experiential reality.
11. Kenneth Inada, "Nagarjuna and Beyond," *Journal of Buddhist Philosophy* 2 (1984), pp. 65–76, for development of this concept.

EDITORS' NOTES

*On the Ting Story (p. 103)

As exaggerated as the story may sound, Ting's manual dexterity provides a vivid illustration of the centrality of the idea of embodiment in Taoism and in Eastern philosophy in general. Perhaps a different example may help toward understanding what Ting means by "the ox ceasing to be an ox" and "the spirit moves where it wants." Take for instance a person gone blind as a result of an injury to her eyes. She has to learn to go about her daily affairs with a walking stick. At the beginning of this new phase of her life, she is constantly aware of *the* stick—the pressure and the various sensations impinging on her hand as her stick comes into contact with the ground and different objects. But after habituating herself to the use of the stick, her attention is now transferred to the farther end of the stick, and she no longer needs to make self-conscious determinations of the distance between the two ends of the stick. In other words, the stick now *becomes* a part of her bodily extension—an extended hand: what was once only a tool, a thing, is now incorporated into her self.

The moral of Ting's story is that what stands out as alien object can be made "natural"

through this embodied integration into one's own self by a process of skillful habituation. Once the makeup of the ox, the tendons, the ligaments, the difficult joints become as familiar to the cook as his own body, the animal will cease to appear to be a thing that stands opposed to the cook and to have to be consciously mastered. With this embodied knowledge, the cook knows which parts of the animal's body most easily yield to his knife, and thus he can guide his knife as effortlessly as "the spirit moves where it wants." As dramatic as it sounds, after he submits thousands of oxen to the blade, it still remains as though "it had just come from the grindstone."

**On Emptiness (p. 110)

The idea of "emptiness" deserves a more detailed clarification here because of a very common but mistaken association that the term generates. There is a tendency among Western philosophers to construe this Buddhist idea of emptiness as nihilism, thanks to one of the most influential Western philosophers of the last century, Friedrich Nietzsche. (See, for example, his *Will to Power.*) But this characterization cannot be further from the truth. For one thing, Buddhism has always been a secular philosophy. There is no concept of a transcendent God, who is the ultimate source of all values. One's existence and place in the universe are contingent and in constant flux all along. The absence of God does not plunge one into a kind of despair that totally negates the ground of one's existence, because one's self-identification and sense of significance begin and end with the universe. More importantly, for the Buddhist, even when faced with extreme disappointment and misfortune, one should not "wallow" in meaninglessness and despair, because even meaninglessness and despair *are,* as paradoxical as it may sound, ultimately "empty." One should not hang onto good things such as friendship and justice any more than one should unpleasant feelings of meaninglessness and despair, because all of these will vanish in the ephemeral order of things after all, ignorance of which fact causes a person unnecessary suffering.

QUESTIONS: HUMAN RIGHTS AND JUSTICE

1. The United Nations Declaration of Human Rights claims to protect the rights of individuals. What problems do you see with this individual conception of human rights when the interests of ethnic or cultural minorities are taken into account, for example, when the rights of members of the majority to freedom of movement or to vote are restricted as a result of protecting the rights of minorities?

2. Outline Mill's discussion of the concept of justice. How is justice related to the principle of utility? What are some of the objections which might be brought against Mill's position?

3. What is a maxim, according to Onora O'Neill's understanding of Kant? In what sense does treating someone merely as a means reveal a failure to respect his or her maxim? In what sense does treating persons as ends involve consideration of his or her maxim?

4. Why is it that individual human rights are so important? What moral ideals are they supposed to uphold? What is Ronald Dworkin's answer? Do you think that the appeal to individual human rights can avoid completely considerations of utility? Explain.

5. How does Bunch relate violence against women to issues of human rights? What objections might be made against the identification of women's rights with human rights? Are these good objections? Why or why not?

6. Abdullahi Ahmed An-Na'im presents one cultural example of the rejection of universal human rights that is mandated and sanctified by religion. Given the goals and values of multiculturalism, how might we reject certain aspects of Shari'a while remaining respectful of others? Is such a piecemeal approach justified?

7. It is sometimes argued that the use of child labor (children as young as 14 years of age) in underdeveloped countries is morally justified on grounds that these children would be worse off because of the absence of independent means of support and the opportunity for education. In what ways does Claude Ake's perspective shed light on how we in the West consider the human rights situations in Third World countries?

8. How does Confucian ritual practice (ceremonial propriety) exhibit the notion of self and personhood in traditional Chinese society? How does this conception affect the way the idea of rights is understood in Chinese constitutions? In what ways does the Confucian alternative contribute to the current understanding of human rights? In what ways do you think that it is problematic?

9. Outline Inada's distinction between "hard relationships" and "soft relationships." How might taking this distinction seriously affect the way we talk about human rights—and would such a change be a good thing? Justify your response.

SUPPLEMENTARY READINGS: HUMAN RIGHTS AND JUSTICE

ABE, MASEO. "A Buddhist View of Human Rights." In *Human Rights and Religious Values: An Uneasy Relationship?* An-Na'im, Jansen, and Vroom, editors. Grand Rapids, MI: William B. Eerdmans Publishing Company, 1995.

ANAYA, S. JAMES, and CRIDER, S. TODD. "Indigenous Peoples, The Environment, and Commercial Forestry in Developing Countries: The Case of Awas Tingni, Nicaragua." *Human Rights Quarterly* vol. 18 (1996).

ANIKPO, MARK. "Human Rights and Self-Reliance in Africa." In *Emerging Human Rights,* Shepherd and Anikpo, editors. New York: Greenwood Press, 1990.

BADRAN, MARGOT. *Feminists, Islam, and Nation: Gender and the Making of Modern Egypt.* Princeton, NJ: Princeton University Press, 1995.

BELL, DANIEL A. "The East Asian Challenge to Human Rights: Reflections on an East West Dialogue." *Human Rights Quarterly* vol. 18 (1996).

BELL, DIANE. "Considering Gender: Are Human Rights for Women Too? An Australian Case." In *Human Rights in Cross Cultural Perspective*, An-Na'im, editor. Philadelphia: University of Pennsylvania Press, 1991.

COBBAH, JOSIAH. "African Values and the Human Rights Debate." *Human Rights Quarterly*, vol. 9(3), August 1987.

DONNELLEY, JACK. "Human Rights and Development: Complementary or Competing Concerns." In *Human Rights and Third World Development*, Shepherd and Nanda, editors. New York: Greenwood Press, 1985.

DROOGERS, ANDRE F. "Cultural Relativism and Universal Human Rights?" In *Human Rights and Religious Values: An Uneasy Relationship?* An-Na'im, Jansen, and Vroom, editors. Grand Rapids, MI: William B. Eerdmans Publishing Company, 1995.

HARE, R.M. "Rights and Justice." In *Moral Thinking*. Oxford: Oxford University Press, 1981.

LANE, SANDRA D., and RUBINSTEIN, ROBERT A. "Judging the Other: Responding to Traditional Female Genital Surgeries." *Hastings Center Report,* vol. 26(3) (1996).

LIXIAN, CHENG. "A Tentative Discussion of Human Rights." *Chinese Studies in Philosophy*, vol. 17(1), Fall 1985.

NIARCHOS, N. CATHERINE. "Women, War, and Rape: Challenges Facing the International Tribunal for the Former Yugoslavia." *Human Rights Quarterly,* vol. 17 (1995).

PENNOCK, J. ROLAND. "Rights, Natural Rights, and Human Rights—A General View." *NOMOS 23: Human Rights.* New York: New York University Press, 1981.

SCANLON, THOMAS. "Rights, Goals and Fairness." In *Public and Private Morality*, Hampshire, editor. Cambridge, England: Cambridge University Press, 1978.

TIBI, BASSAM. "The European Tradition of Human Rights and the Culture of Islam." In *Human Rights in Africa*, An-Na'im and Deng, editors. Washington, DC: The Brookings Institution, 1990.

VAN DER BERG, CHRISTIAAN J. G. "Fundamentalist Hindu Values and Human Rights: Two Worlds Apart?" In *Human Rights and Religious Values: An Uneasy Relationship?* An-Na'im, Jansen, and Vroom, editors. Grand Rapids, MI: William B. Eerdmans Publishing Company, 1995.

WIREDU, KWASI. "An Akan Perspective on Human Rights." In *Human Rights in Africa*, An-Na'im and Deng, editors. Washington. DC: The Brookings Institution, 1990.

ZEIDAN, SHAWKY. "A Human Rights Settlement: The West Bank and Gaza." In *Human Rights and Third World Development,* Shepherd and Nanda, editors. New York: Greenwood Press, 1985.

ZION, JAMES. "North American Indian Perspectives on Human Rights." in *Human Rights in Cross Cultural Perspectives*, An-Na'im, editor. Philadelphia: University of Pennsylvania Press, 1991.

II

ENVIRONMENTAL ETHICS

There is yet no ethic dealing with man's relation to land and to the animals and plants which grow upon it. Land . . . is still property. The land-relation is still strictly economic, entailing privileges but not obligations.

The extension of ethics to this third element in the human environment is, if I read the evidence correctly, an evolutionary possibility and an ecological necessity.

—Aldo Leopold[1]

Legally, the environment has no rights. Property rights are still the premier means of addressing the environment. Presently in the United States, the only way for natural objects or ecosystems to be protected is through the assertion of a human being's legal rights. In order to have a legal claim concerning an environmental harm, one must have "standing," which is the capacity to challenge an action in a court. The harm must be an "injury in fact"; can be in the past, present, or future; and must be capable of being redressed by the court. The environment may also be legally protected through legislation. However, in order to make any progress, one needs factual and conceptual arguments to persuade those in power that consideration for the environment goes beyond traditional property value concerns.

Many people link the environmental crisis to a general shortage of ethics. The historically unparalleled levels of consumption and the consequent environmental degradation have brought into question the earth's carrying capacity. Many assert that without reevaluations of and drastic changes in our ways of life, we will not come out of this crisis.

Environmental ethics considers limitations on the freedom of exercising property rights and concerns the further extension of our ethical duties to the environment. This reconceptualization of the environment as an object of moral concern carries with it a radical reconceptualization of key elements within the Western tradition.

Human rights, which were discussed in the previous section, and the environment are inextricably linked. Many have argued that the right to a clean, livable environment is an absolute prerequisite for all other human rights. Human rights approaches, or anthropocentric approaches, only consider the environment as it relates to human interests. Anthropocentrism asserts that we only have ethical duties to humans, thus precluding direct duties to the environment.

Others argue for a type of environmental rights, often to guarantee that differing property rights and competing interests will not further despoil the environment. It is asserted that we have ethical obligations to all of nature. To grant our obligations to all of nature is to recognize the interrelated nature of ecosystems, which are composed of living and nonliving entities. In direct contrast to the aforementioned views, it is claimed that both living and nonliving matter have inherent value and "standing" for ethical consideration. This view is often called "deep ecology" and is also known as the "biocentric" or "ecocentric" approach. Deep ecology broadens our ethical duties even further than a sentientist approach does. From the viewpoint of deep ecology, the entire ecosystem has intrinsic value and may not be used (as an instrument) to merely further specific interests. We are obliged to take the entire ecosystem into account as an object of moral concern while pursuing our human interests.

In our first selection, Aldo Leopold argues for the extension of moral concern to the land. Leopold begins by reminding us that some humans, Odysseus' slave girls in the example he provides, were thought to be property and thus treatment of these humans was not a moral issue, but one of property rights. Leopold points out that ethical principles were not lacking in Odysseus' Greece; however, the extension of those principles was not afforded to all human beings. While arguments that land despoliation is morally wrong have been advanced for thousands of years, society has not yet extended moral concern to the environment. Ethical principles were not extended to the environment when Leopold's work was published in 1949, and almost 50 years later the environment still lacks ethical standing.

Leopold argues for a "land ethic" which carries duties to the environment, including duties to love and respect the land and its (inherent) value. Leopold's land ethic states: "A thing is right when it tends to preserve the integrity, stability, and beauty of the biotic community. It is wrong when it tends otherwise."[2] He sees our adoption of this ethic as both possible and necessary.

In contrast, William Baxter embodies anthropocentrism. He begins with a case regarding penguins. In the 1970s scientists informed us that DDT use caused damage to penguin populations. Of what importance, he asks, is that to humans? Unless this damage (not harm) to penguins harms humans, he argues, this damage to penguins and other parts of the natural environment is "simply irrelevant." Baxter offers six reasons for this, including his fourth, that penguins and trees do not, and cannot, participate in decision-making processes about the public good. Ethical questions, Baxter argues, are unique to humans and are meaningless elsewhere. Although pollution can "damage" the environment and nonhuman creatures, it is not of moral concern unless it harms humans. Moreover, pollution is justified when it, overall, benefits human beings. Baxter's view is in stark contrast to traditional American Indian views as represented in the next essay.

J. Baird Callicott's essay brings the traditional American Indian views to the environmental ethics debate, and through his presentation we see yet another extension of the moral domain. Callicott asserts that traditional American Indian views did not draw a sharp line between living and nonliving matter and considered rocks, rivers, and other natural entities "very much alive." He asserts that for American Indians being "alive" means that the concept of consciousness and awareness that humans experience is considered to be shared with other entities, such as rivers and rocks. One's place in the world was dependent on maintaining good relations with all natural entities in the environment.

In some ways similar to the American Indian approach is that of Taoism. Chung-ying Cheng argues for the inclusion of the Tao and its teachings in environmental ethics. Cheng points out that Western attitudes toward nature center on the external relation of humans to their surroundings, premised upon a dichotomy between the human and nonhuman worlds. In contrast, the Chinese center on the internal relation of humans to their surroundings, premised upon an integrated and interdependent harmony of humans and the world. Westerners, while viewing themselves apart from nature, have studied and then manipulated, dominated, and exploited the world for their pursuits. The conception of humans as separate lends itself to the desire for and exercise of conquest and domination. In contrast, the Chinese tradition represented in both Confucianism and Taoism maintains an internalist, integrated view of nature. Cheng states that traditional Chinese views do not place humans opposite nature, in a hostile manner. Rather, in the Chinese view, it is necessary to cultivate the internal connection to nature, for one's own well-being. Cheng presents the "ecological principle of nature," which is derived from the Tao, and can teach us not to impose ourselves on things. This imposition has often been in the form of domination and exploitation. Shari Collins-Chobanian and Vandana Shiva address this type of imposition in the last two selections.

Environmental racism is a somewhat controversial topic that has become an important issue in the environmental justice movement. Environmental racism is the intentional targeting of communities where people of color live, for both the generation and storage of toxic waste. Collins-Chobanian discusses a case of environmental racism affecting American Indians. She first addresses those who contend that environmental racism is merely classism and argues that while poverty does overlap with racism, the phenomena cannot be reduced to classism. The issue of economic status is of particular relevance for American Indians who have been targeted for "temporary" storage of radioactive waste, a practice that is especially problematic in light of the legacy of radioactive contamination on American Indian lands. She argues that even if there appears to be consent to this siting, the targeting of American Indians is ethically unjustified.

Shiva challenges the assumption that women's economic status in the Third World is automatically improved by the postcolonial project of development. Shiva argues that although development programs were to improve everyone's well-being, rather than accomplishing this goal, development has impoverished numerous people, especially women. Development, she contends, is an extension of Western patriarchy, and is really "maldevelopment" that either introduces (where patriarchy has not previously held sway), or worsens man's domination over women and nature. The connection that she makes between patriarchal domination of women and nature is an example of an "ecofeminist" perspective.

Ecofeminism claims that there are similarities between the patriarchal domination of women and nature. Shiva points out that both women and nature are viewed as passive and are considered "unproductive" without "development." However, as she argues, the economic development programs are associated with enormous ecological costs, often to the point of destroying the regenerative ability of ecosystems. Shiva illuminates how these costs most affect women because this destruction threatens women's ability to provide subsistence for their families and themselves.

Shiva's essay is a good companion essay to Deane Curtin's in Chapter III. Both call into question many assumptions that people in the "developed" world hold concerning the universal benefits of our development programs. Both essays also illustrate some of the harm that occurs when Western cultural practices are imposed on other cultures, as well as providing insight into how these practices harm our enviornment and ourselves.

—Shari Collins-Chobanian

NOTES

1. Aldo Leopold, *A Sand County Almanac* (New York: Oxford University Press, 1966), p. 217.
2. Ibid., p. 262.

The Land Ethic

Aldo Leopold

Aldo Leopold was a United States Forest Service employee and the University of Wisconsin's first professor of Wildlife Management. Leopold is a very important and influential person in environmental ethics, with his book A Sand County Almanac *(1947) often considered the genesis of contemporary Western environmental ethics.*

Leopold urges us to consider our place in, as opposed to our control over, and our duties to, rather than merely our use of, the natural world. For determining the moral justifiability of our actions, he provides the "land ethic" as guidance. The land ethic places the preservation of the biotic community's integrity, stability, and beauty at the center of moral concern. However, he makes clear that this is a tentative ethic and will continue to evolve, as ethics overall is a product of social, intellectual, and emotional evolution and cannot therefore produce fixed, written rules.

When godlike Odysseus returned from the wars in Troy, he hanged all on one rope a dozen slave-girls of his household whom he suspected of misbehavior during his absence.

This hanging involved no question of propriety. The girls were property. The disposal of property was then, as now, a matter of expediency, not of right or wrong.

Concepts of right and wrong were not lacking from Odysseus' Greece: witness the fidelity of his wife through the long years before at last his black-prowed galleys clove the wine-dark seas for home. The ethical structure of that day covered wives, but had not yet been extended to human chattels. During the three thousand years which have since elapsed, ethical criteria have been extended to many fields of con-

duct, with corresponding shrinkages in those judged by expediency only.

THE ETHICAL SEQUENCE

This extension of ethics, so far studied only by philosophers, is actually a process in ecological evolution. Its sequences may be described in ecological as well as in philosophical terms. An ethic, ecologically, is a limitation on freedom of action in the struggle for existence. An ethic, philosophically, is a differentiation of social from antisocial conduct. These are two definitions of one thing. The thing has its origin in the tendency of interdependent individuals or groups to evolve modes of cooperation. The ecologist calls these symbioses. Politics and economics are advanced symbioses in which the original free-for-all competition has been replaced, in part, by cooperative mechanisms with an ethical content.

The complexity of cooperative mechanisms has increased with population density, and with the efficiency of tools. It was simpler, for example, to define the anti-social uses of sticks and stones in the days of the mastodons than of bullets and billboards in the age of motors.

The first ethics dealt with the relation between individuals; the Mosaic Decalogue is an example. Later accretions dealt with the relation between the individual and society. The Golden Rule tries to integrate the individual to society; democracy to integrate social organization to the individual.

There is as yet no ethic dealing with man's relation to land and to the animals and plants which grow upon it. Land, like Odysseus' slave-girls, is still property. The land-relation is still strictly economic, entailing privileges but not obligations.

The extension of ethics to this third element in human environment is, if I read the evidence correctly, an evolutionary possibility and an ecological necessity. It is the third step in a sequence. The first two have already been taken. Individual thinkers since the days of Ezekiel and Isaiah have asserted that the despoliation of land is not only inexpedient but wrong. Society, however, has not yet affirmed their belief. I regard the present conservation movement as the embryo of such an affirmation.

An ethic may be regarded as a mode of guidance for meeting ecological situations so new or intricate, or involving such deferred reactions, that the path of social expediency is not discernible to the average individual. Animal instincts are modes of guidance for the individual in meeting such situations. Ethics are possibly a kind of community instinct in-the-making.

THE COMMUNITY CONCEPT

All ethics so far evolved rest upon a single premise: that the individual is a member of a community of interdependent parts. His instincts prompt him to compete for his place in the community, but his ethics prompt him also to cooperate (perhaps in order that there may be a place to compete for).

The land ethic simply enlarges the boundaries of the community to include soils, waters, plants, and animals, or collectively: the land.

This sounds simple: do we not already sing our love for and obligation to the land of the free and the home of the brave? Yes, but just what and whom do we love? Certainly not the soil, which we are sending helter-skelter downriver. Certainly not the waters, which we assume have no function except to turn turbines, float barges, and carry off sewage. Certainly not the plants, of which we exterminate whole communities without batting an eye. Certainly not the animals, of which we have already extirpated many of the largest and most beautiful species. A land ethic of course cannot prevent the alteration, management, and use of these "resources," but it does affirm their right to continued existence, and, at least in spots, their continued existence in a natural state.

In short, a land ethic changes the role of *Homo sapiens* from conqueror of the land-community to plain member and citizen of it. It implies respect for his fellow-members, and also respect for the community as such.

In human history, we have learned (I hope) that the conqueror role is eventually self-defeating. Why? Because it is implicit in such a role that the conqueror knows, *ex cathedra,* just what makes the community clock tick, and just what and who is valuable, and what and who is worthless, in community life. It always turns out that he knows neither, and this is why his conquests eventually defeat themselves.

In the biotic community, a parallel situation exists. Abraham knew exactly what the land was for: it was to drip milk and honey into Abraham's mouth. At the present moment, the assurance with which we regard this assumption is inverse to the degree of our education.

The ordinary citizen today assumes that science knows what makes the community clock tick; the scientist is equally sure that he does not. He knows that the biotic mechanism is so complex that its workings may never be fully understood.

That man is, in fact, only a member of a biotic team is shown by an ecological interpretation of history. Many historical events, hitherto explained solely in terms of human enterprise, were actually biotic interactions between people and land. The characteristics of the land determined the facts quite as potently as the characteristics of the men who lived on it.

Consider, for example, the settlement of the Mississippi valley. In the years following the Revolution, three groups were contending for its control: the native Indian, the French and English traders, and the American settlers. Historians wonder what would have happened if the English at Detroit had thrown a little more weight into the Indian side of those tipsy scales which decided the outcome of the colonial migration into the cane-lands of Kentucky. It is time now to ponder the fact that the cane-lands, when subjected to the particular mixture of forces represented by the cow, plow, fire, and axe of the pioneer, became bluegrass. What if the plant succession inherent in this dark and bloody ground had, under the impact of these forces, given us some worthless sedge shrub, or weed? Would Boone and Kenton have held out? Would there have been any overflow into Ohio, Indiana, Illinois, and Missouri? Any Louisiana Purchase? Any transcontinental union of new states? Any Civil War?

Kentucky was one sentence in the drama of history. We are commonly told what the human actors in this drama tried to do, but we are seldom told that their success, or the lack of it, hung in large degree on the reaction of particular soils to the impact of the particular forces exerted by their occupancy. In the case of Kentucky, we do not even know where the bluegrass came from—whether it is a native species, or a stowaway from Europe.

Contrast the cane-lands with what hindsight tells us about the Southwest, where the pioneers were equally brave, resourceful, and persevering. The impact of the occupancy here brought no bluegrass, or other plant fitted to withstand the bumps and buffetings of hard use. This region, when grazed by livestock, reverted through a series of more and more worthless grasses, shrubs, and weeds to a condition of unstable equilibrium. Each recession of plant types bred erosion; each increment to erosion bred a further recession of plants. The result today is a progressive and mutual deterioration, not only of plants and soils, but of the animal community subsisting thereon. The early settlers did not expect this: on the ciénegas of New Mexico some even cut ditches to hasten it. So subtle has been its progress that few residents of the region are aware of it. It is quite invisible to the tourist who finds this wrecked landscape colorful and charming (as indeed it is, but it bears scant resemblance to what it was in 1848).

This same landscape was 'developed' once before, but with quite different results. The Pueblo Indians settled the Southwest in pre-Columbian times, but they happened *not* to be equipped with range livestock. Their civilization expired, but not because their land expired.

In India, regions devoid of any sod-forming grass have been settled, apparently without wrecking the land, by the simple expedient of carrying the grass to the cow, rather than vice versa. (Was this the result of some deep wisdom, or was it just good luck? I do not know.)

In short, the plant succession steered the course of history; the pioneer simply demonstrated, for good or ill, what successions inhered in the land. Is history taught in this spirit? It will be, once the concept of land as a community really penetrates our intellectual life.

THE ECOLOGICAL CONSCIENCE

Conservation is a state of harmony between men and land. Despite nearly a century of propaganda, conservation still proceeds at a snail's pace; progress still consists largely of letterhead pieties and convention oratory. On the back forty we still slip two steps backward for each forward stride.

The usual answer to this dilemma is "more conservation education." No one will debate this, but is it certain that only the *volume* of education needs stepping up? Is something lacking in the *content* as well?

It is difficult to give a fair summary of its content in brief form, but as I understand it, the content is substantially this: obey the law, vote right, join some organizations, and practice what conservation is profitable on your own land; the government will do the rest.

Is not this formula too easy to accomplish anything worthwhile? It defines no right or wrong, assigns no obligation, calls for no sacrifice, implies no change in the current philosophy of values. In respect of land-use, it urges only enlightened self-interest. Just how far will such education take us? An example will perhaps yield a partial answer.

By 1930 it had become clear to all except the ecologically blind that southwestern Wisconsin's topsoil was slipping seaward. In 1933 the farmers were told that if they would adopt certain remedial practices for five years, the public would donate CCC labor to install them, plus the necessary machinery and materials. The offer was widely accepted, but the practices were widely forgotten when the five-year contract period was up. The farmers continued only those practices that yielded an immediate and visible economic gain for themselves.

This led to the idea that maybe farmers would learn more quickly if they themselves wrote the rules. Accordingly the Wisconsin Legislature in 1937 passed the Soil Conservation District Law. This said to farmers, in effect: *We, the public, will furnish you free technical service and loan you specialized machinery, if you will write your own rules for land-use. Each county may write its own rules, and these will have the force of law.* Nearly all the counties promptly organized to accept the proffered help, but after a decade of operation, *no county has yet written a single rule.* There has been visible progress in such practices as strip-cropping, pasture renovation, and soil liming, but none in fencing woodlots against grazing, and none in excluding plow and cow from steep slopes. The farmers, in short, have selected those remedial practices which were profitable anyhow, and ignored those which were profitable to the community, but not clearly profitable to themselves.

When one asks why no rules have been written, one is told that the community is not yet ready to support them; education must precede rules. But the education actually in progress makes no mention of obligations to land over and above those dictated by self-interest. The net result is that we have more education but less soil, fewer healthy woods, and as many floods as in 1937.

The puzzling aspect of such situations is that the existence of obligations over and above self-interest is taken for granted in such rural community enterprise as the betterment of roads, schools, churches, and baseball teams. Their existence is not taken for granted, nor as yet seriously discussed, in bettering the behavior of the water that falls on the land, or in the preserving of the beauty or diversity of the farm landscape. Land-use ethics are still governed wholly by economic self-interest, just as social ethics were a century ago.

To sum up: we asked the farmer to do what he conveniently could to save his soil, and he has done just that, and only that. The farmer who clears the woods off a 75 per cent slope, turns his cows into the clearing, and dumps its rainfall, rocks, and soil into the community creek, is still (if otherwise decent) a respected member of society. If he puts lime on his fields and plants his crops on contour, he is still entitled to all the privileges and emoluments of his Soil Conservation District. The District is a beautiful piece of social machinery, but it is coughing along on two cylinders because we have been too timid, and too anxious for quick success, to tell the farmer the true magnitude of his obligations. Obligations have no meaning without conscience, and

the problem we face is the extension of the social conscience from people to land.

No important change in ethics was ever accomplished without an internal change in our intellectual emphasis, loyalties, affections, and convictions. The proof that conservation has not yet touched these foundations of conduct lies in the fact that philosophy and religion have not yet heard of it. In our attempt to make conservation easy, we have made it trivial.

SUBSTITUTES FOR A LAND ETHIC

When the logic of history hunger for bread and we hand out a stone, we are at pains to explain how much the stone resembles bread. I now describe some of the stones which serve in lieu of a land ethic.

One basic weakness in a conservation system based wholly on economic motives is that most members of the land community have no economic value. Wildflowers and songbirds are examples. Of the 22,000 higher plants and animals native to Wisconsin, it is doubtful whether more than 5 percent can be sold, fed, eaten, or otherwise put to economic use. Yet these creatures are members of the biotic community, and if (as I believe) its stability depends on its integrity, they are entitled to continuance.

When one of these non-economic categories is threatened, and if we happen to love it, we invent subterfuges to give it economic importance. At the beginning of the century songbirds were supposed to be disappearing. Ornithologists jumped to the rescue with some distinctly shaky evidence to the effect that insects would eat us up if birds failed to control them. The evidence had to be economic in order to be valid.

It is painful to read these circumlocutions today. We have no land ethic yet, but we have at least drawn nearer the point of admitting that birds should continue as a matter of biotic right, regardless of the presence or absence of economic advantage to us.

A parallel situation exists in respect of predatory mammals, raptorial birds, and fish-eating birds. Time was when biologists somewhat overworked the evidence that these creatures preserve the health of game by killing weaklings, or that they control rodents for the farmer, or that they prey only on "worthless" species. Here again, the evidence had to be economic in order to be valid. It is only in recent years that we hear the more honest argument that predators are members of the community, and that no special interest has the right to exterminate them for the sake of a benefit, real or fancied, to itself. Unfortunately this enlightened view is still in the talk stage. In the field the extermination of predators goes merrily on: witness the impending erasure of the timber wolf by fiat of Congress, the Conservation Bureaus, and many state legislatures.

Some species of trees have been "read out of the party" by economics-minded foresters because they grow too slowly, or have too low a sale value to pay as timber crops: white cedar, tamarack, cypress, beech, and hemlock are examples. In Europe, where forestry is ecologically more advanced, the non-commercial tree species are recognized as members of the native forest community, to be preserved as such, within reason. Moreover some (like beech) have been found to have a valuable function in building up soil fertility. The interdependence of the forest and its constituent tree species, ground flora, and fauna is taken for granted.

Lack of economic value is sometimes a character not only of species or groups, but of entire biotic communities: marshes, bogs, dunes, and "deserts" are examples. Our formula in such cases is to relegate their conservation to government as refuges, monuments, or parks. The difficulty is that these communities are usually interspersed with more valuable private lands; the government cannot possibly own or control such scattered parcels. The net effect is that we have relegated some of them to ultimate extinction over large areas. If the private owner were ecologically minded, he would be proud to be the custodian of a reasonable proportion of such areas, which add diversity and beauty to his farm and to his community.

In some instances, the assumed lack of profit in these "waste" areas has proved to be wrong, but only after most of them had been done away with. The present scramble to reflood muskrat marshes is a case in point.

There is a clear tendency in American conservation to relegate to government all necessary jobs that private landowners fail to perform. Government ownership, operation, subsidy, or regulation is now widely prevalent in forestry, range management, soil and watershed management, park and wilderness conservation, fisheries management, and migratory bird management, with more to come. Most of this growth in governmental conservation is proper and logical, some of it is inevitable. That I imply no disapproval of it is implicit in the fact that I have spent most of my life working for it. Nevertheless the question arises: What is the ultimate magnitude of the enterprise? Will the tax base carry its eventual ramifications? At what point will governmental conservation, like the mastodon, become handicapped by its own dimensions? The answer, if there is any, seems to be in a land ethic, or some other force which assigns more obligation to the private landowner.

Industrial landowners and users, especially lumbermen and stockmen, are inclined to wail long and loudly about the extension of government ownership and regulation to land, but (with notable exceptions) they show little disposition to develop the only visible alternative: the voluntary practice of conservation on their own lands.

When the private landowner is asked to perform some nonprofitable act for the good of the community, he today assents only with outstretched palm. If the act costs him cash this is fair and proper, but when it costs only forethought, open-mindedness, or time, the issue is at least debatable. The overwhelming growth of land-use subsidies in recent years must be ascribed, in large part, to the government's own agencies for conservation education: the land bureaus, the agricultural colleges, and the extension services. As far as I can detect, no ethical obligation toward land is taught in these institutions.

To sum up: a system of conservation based solely on economic self-interest is hopelessly lopsided. It tends to ignore, and thus eventually to eliminate, many elements in the land community that lack commercial value, but that are (as far as know) essential to its healthy functioning. It assumes, falsely, I think, that the economic parts of the biotic clock will function without the uneconomic parts. It tends to relegate to government many functions eventually too large, too complex, or too widely dispersed to be performed by government.

An ethical obligation on the part of the private owner is the only visible remedy for these situations.

THE LAND PYRAMID

An ethic to supplement and guide the economic relation to land presupposes the existence of some mental image of land as a biotic mechanism. We can be ethical only in relation to something we can see, feel, understand, love, or otherwise have faith in.

The image commonly employed in conservation education is "the balance of nature." For reasons too lengthy to detail here, this figure of speech fails to describe accurately what little we know about the land mechanism. A much truer image is the one employed in ecology: the biotic pyramid. I shall first sketch the pyramid as a symbol of land, and later develop some of its implications in terms of land-use.

Plants absorb energy from the sun. This energy flows through a circuit called the biota, which may be represented by a pyramid consisting of layers. The bottom layer is the soil. A plant layer rests on the soil, an insect layer on the plants, a bird and rodent layer on the insects, and so on up through various animal groups to the apex layer, which consists of the larger carnivores.

The species of a layer are alike not in where they came from, or in what they look like, but rather in what they eat. Each successive layer depends on those below it for food and often for other services, and each in turn furnishes food and services to those above. Proceeding upward, each successive layer decreases in numerical abundance. Thus, for every carnivore there are hundreds of his prey, thousands of their prey, millions of insects, uncountable plants. The pyramidal form of the system reflects this numerical progression from apex to base. Man shares an intermediate layer with the bears, raccoons, and squirrels which eat both meat and vegetables.

The lines of dependency for food and other services are called food chains. Thus soil-oak-deer-Indian is a chain that has now been largely converted to soil-corn-cow-farmer. Each species, including ourselves, is a link in many chains. The deer eats a hundred plants other than oak, and the cow a hundred plants other than corn. Both, then, are links in a hundred chains. The pyramid is a tangle of chains so complex as to seem disorderly, yet the stability of the system proves it to be a highly organized structure. Its functioning depends on the cooperation and competition of its diverse parts.

In the beginning, the pyramid of life was low and squat; the food chains short and simple. Evolution has added layer after layer, link after link. Man is one of thousands of accretions to the height and complexity of the pyramid. Science has given us many doubts, but it has given us at least one certainty: the trend of evolution is to elaborate and diversify the biota.

Land, then, is not merely soil; it is a fountain of energy flowing through a circuit of soils, plants, and animals. Food chains are the living channels which conduct energy upward; death and decay return it to the soil. The circuit is not closed; some energy is dissipated in decay, some is added by absorption from the air, some is stored in soils, peats, and long-lived forests; but it is a sustained circuit, like a slowly augmented revolving fund of life. There is always a net loss by downhill wash, but this is normally small and offset by the decay of rocks. It is deposited in the ocean and, in the course of geological time, raised to form new lands and new pyramids.

The velocity and character of the upward flow of energy depend on the complex structure of the plant and animal community, much as the upward flow of sap in a tree depends on its complex cellular organization. Without this complexity, normal circulation would presumably not occur. Structure means the characteristic numbers, as well as the characteristic kinds and functions, of the component species. This interdependence between the complex structure of the land and its smooth functioning as an energy unit is one of its basic attributes.

When a change occurs in one part of the circuit, many other parts must adjust themselves to it. Change does not necessarily obstruct or divert the flow of energy; evolution is a long series of self-induced changes, the net result of which has been to elaborate the flow mechanism and to lengthen the circuit. Evolutionary changes, however, are usually slow and local. Man's invention of tools has enabled him to make changes of unprecedented violence, rapidity, and scope.

One change is in the composition of floras and faunas. The larger predators are lopped off the apex of the pyramid; food chains, for the first time in history, become shorter rather than longer. Domesticated species from other lands are substituted for wild ones, and wild ones are moved to new habitats. In this worldwide pooling of faunas and floras, some species get out of bounds as pests and diseases, others are extinguished. Such effects are seldom intended or foreseen; they represent unpredicted and often untraceable readjustments in the structure. Agricultural science is largely a race between the emergence of new pests and the emergence of new techniques for their control.

Another change touches the flow of energy through plants and animals and its return to the soil. Fertility is the ability of soil to receive, store, and release energy. Agriculture, by overdrafts on the soil, or by too radical a substitution of domestic for native species in the superstructure, may derange the channels of flow or deplete storage. Soils depleted of their storage, or of the organic matter which anchors it, wash away faster than they form. This is erosion.

Waters, like soil, are part of the energy circuit. Industry, by polluting waters or obstructing them with dams, may exclude the plants and animals necessary to keep energy in circulation.

Transportation brings about another basic change: the plants or animals grown in one region are now consumed and returned to the soil in another. Transportation taps the energy stored in rocks, and in the air, and uses it elsewhere; thus we fertilize the garden with nitrogen gleaned by the guano birds from the fishes of seas on the other side of the Equator. Thus the formerly localized and self-contained circuits are pooled on a worldwide scale.

The process of altering the pyramid for human occupation releases stored energy, and this often gives rise, during the pioneering period, to a deceptive exuberance of plant and animal life, both wild and tame. These releases of biotic capital tend to becloud or postpone the penalties of violence.

This thumbnail sketch of land as an energy circuit conveys three basic ideas:

1. That land is not merely soil.
2. That the native plants and animals kept the energy circuit open; others may or may not.
3. That man-made changes are of a different order than evolutionary changes, and have effects more comprehensive than is intended or foreseen.

These ideas, collectively, raise two basic issues: Can the land adjust itself to the new order? Can the desired alterations be accomplished with less violence?

Biotas seem to differ in their capacity to sustain violent conversion. Western Europe, for example, carries a far different pyramid than Caesar found there. Some large animals are lost; swampy forests have become meadows or plowland; many new plants and animals are introduced, some of which escape as pests; the remaining natives are greatly changed in distribution and abundance. Yet the soil is still there and, with the help of imported nutrients, still fertile; the waters flow normally; the new structure seems to function and to persist. There is no visible stoppage or derangement of the circuit.

Western Europe, then, has a resistant biota. Its inner processes are tough, elastic, resistant to strain. No matter how violent the alterations, the pyramid, so far, has developed some new *modus vivendi* which preserves its habitability for man, and for most of the other natives.

Japan seems to present another instance of radical conversion without disorganization.

Most other civilized regions, and some as yet barely touched by civilization, display various stages of disorganization, varying from initial symptoms to advanced wastage. In Asia Minor and North Africa diagnosis is confused by climatic changes, which may have been either the cause or the effect of advanced wastage. In the United States the degree of disorganization varies locally; it is worst in the Southwest, the Ozarks, and parts of the South, and least in New England and the Northwest. Better land-uses may still arrest it in the less advanced regions. In parts of Mexico, South America, South Africa, and Australia a violent and accelerating wastage is in progress, but I cannot assess the prospects.

This almost world-wide display of disorganization in the land seems to be similar to disease in an animal, except that it never culminates in complete disorganization or death. The land recovers, but at some reduced level of complexity, and with a reduced carrying capacity for people, plants, and animals. Many biotas currently regarded as 'lands of opportunity' are in fact already subsisting on exploitative agriculture, i.e., they have already exceeded their sustained carrying capacity. Most of South America is overpopulated in this sense.

In arid regions we attempt to offset the process of wastage by reclamation, but it is only too evident that the prospective longevity of reclamation projects is often short. In our own West, the best of them may nor last a century.

The combined evidence of history and ecology seems to support one general deduction: the less violent the man-made changes, the greater the probability of successful readjustment in the pyramid. Violence, in turn, varies with human population density; a dense population requires a more violent conversion. In this respect, North America has a better chance for permanence than Europe, if she can contrive to limit her density.

This deduction runs counter to our current philosophy, which assumes that because a small increase in density enriched human life, that an indefinite increase will enrich it indefinitely. Ecology knows of no density relationship that holds for indefinitely wide limits. All gains from density are subject to a law of diminishing returns.

Whatever may be the equation for men and land, it is improbable that we as yet know all its terms. Recent discoveries in mineral and vitamin nutrition reveal unsuspected dependencies in the up-circuit: incredibly minute quantities of certain substances determine the value of soils to plants, of plants to animals. What of the down-circuit? What of the vanishing species, the preservation of which we now regard as an esthetic luxury? They helped build the soil; in what unsuspected ways may they be essential to its maintenance? Professor Weaver proposes that we use prairie flowers to reflocculate the wasting soils of the dust bowl; who knows for what purpose cranes and condors, otters and grizzlies may some day be used?

LAND HEALTH
AND THE A-B CLEAVAGE

A land ethic, then, reflects the existence of an ecological conscience, and this in turn reflects a conviction of individual responsibility for the health of the land. Health is the capacity of the land for self-renewal. Conservation is our effort to understand and preserve this capacity.

Conservationists are notorious for their dissensions. Superficially these seem to add up to mere confusion, but a more careful scrutiny reveals a single plane of cleavage common to many specialized fields. In each field one group (A) regards the land as soil and its function as commodity-production; another group (B) regards the land as a biota, and its function as something broader. How much broader is admittedly in a state of doubt and confusion.

In my own field, forestry, group A is quite content to grow trees like cabbages, with cellulose as the basic forest commodity. It feels no inhibition against violence; its ideology is agronomic. Group B, on the other hand, sees forestry as fundamentally different from agronomy because it employs natural species, and manages a natural environment rather than creating an artificial one. Group B prefers natural reproduction on principle. It worries on biotic as well as economic grounds about the loss of species like chestnut and the threatened loss of the white pines. It worries about a whole series of secondary forest functions: wildlife, recreation, watersheds, wilderness areas. To my mind, Group B feels the stirrings of an ecological conscience.

In the wildlife field, a parallel cleavage exists. For Group A the basic commodities are sport and meat; the yardsticks of production are ciphers of take in pheasants and trout. Artificial propagation is acceptable as a permanent as well as a temporary recourse—if its unit costs permit. Group B, on the other hand, worries about a whole series of biotic side-issues. What is the cost in predators of producing a game crop? Should we have further recourse to exotics? How can management restore the shrinking species, like prairie grouse, already hopeless as shootable game? How can management restore the threatened rarities, like trumpeter swan and whooping crane? Can management principles be extended to wildflowers? Here again it is clear to me that we have the same A-B cleavage as in forestry.

In the larger field of agriculture I am less competent to speak, but there seem to be somewhat parallel cleavages. Scientific agriculture was actively developing before ecology was born, hence a slower penetration of ecological concepts might be expected. Moreover the farmer, by the very nature of his techniques, must modify the biota more radically than the forester or the wildlife manager. Nevertheless, there are many discontents in agriculture which seem to add up to a new vision of 'biotic farming.'

Perhaps the most important of these is the new evidence that poundage or tonnage is no measure of the food-value of farm crops; the products of fertile soil may be qualitatively as well as quantitatively superior. We can bolster poundage from depleted soils by pouring on imported fertility, but we are not necessarily bolstering food-value. The possible ultimate ramifications of this idea are so immense that I must leave their exposition to abler pens.

The discontent that labels itself 'organic farming,' while bearing some of the earmarks of a cult, is nevertheless biotic in its direction, particularly in its insistence on the importance of soil flora and fauna.

The ecological fundamentals of agriculture are just as poorly known to the public as in other fields of land-use. For example, few educated people realize that the marvelous advances in technique made during recent decades are improvements in the pump, rather than the well. Acre for acre, they have barely sufficed to offset the sinking level of fertility.

In all of these cleavages, we see repeated the same basic paradoxes: man the conqueror *versus* man the biotic citizen; science the sharpener of his sword *versus* science the searchlight on his universe; land the slave and servant *versus* land the collective organism. Robinson's injunction to Tristram may well be applied, at this juncture, to *Homo sapiens* as a species in geological time:

> Whether you will or not
> You are a King, Tristram, for you are one
> Of the time-tested few that leave the world,
> When they are gone, not the same place it was.
> Mark what you leave.

THE OUTLOOK

It is inconceivable to me that an ethical relation to land can exist without love, respect, and admiration for land, and a high regard for its value. By value, I of course mean something far broader than mere economic value; I mean value in the philosophical sense.

Perhaps the most serious obstacle impeding the evolution of a land ethic is the fact that our educational and economic system is headed away from, rather than toward, an intense consciousness of land. Your true modern is separated from the land by many middlemen, and by innumerable physical gadgets. He has no vital relation to it; to him it is the space between cities on which crops grow. Turn him loose for a day on the land, and if the spot does not happen to be a golf links or a "scenic" area, he is bored stiff. If crops could be raised by hydroponics instead of farming, it would suit him very well. Synthetic substitutes for wood, leather, wool, and other natural land products suit him better than the originals. In short, land is something he has "outgrown."

Almost equally serious as an obstacle to a land ethic is the attitude of the farmer for whom the land is still an adversary, or a taskmaster that keeps him in slavery. Theoretically, the mechanization of farming ought to cut the farmer's chains, but whether it really does is debatable.

One of the requisites for an ecological comprehension of land is an understanding of ecology, and this is by no means coextensive with "education"; in fact, much higher education seems deliberately to avoid ecological concepts. An understanding of ecology does not necessarily originate in courses bearing ecological labels; it is quite as likely to be labeled geography, botany, agronomy, history, or economics. This is as it should be, but whatever the label, ecological training is scarce.

The case for a land ethic would appear hopeless but for the minority which is in obvious revolt against these "modern" trends.

The "key-log" which must be moved to release the evolutionary process for an ethic is simply this: quit thinking about decent land-use as solely an economic problem. Examine each question in terms of what is ethically and esthetically right, as well as what is economically expedient. A thing is right when it tends to preserve the integrity, stability, and beauty of the biotic community. It is wrong when it tends otherwise.

It of course goes without saying that economic feasibility limits the tether of what can or cannot be done for land. It always has and it always will. The fallacy the economic determinists have tied around our collective neck, and which we now need to cast off, is the belief that economics determines *all* land-use. This is simply not true. An innumerable host of actions and attitudes, comprising perhaps the bulk of all land relations, is determined by the land-users' tastes and predilections, rather than by his purse. The bulk of all land relations hinges on investments of time, forethought, skill, and faith rather than on investments of cash. As a land-user thinketh, so is he.

I have purposely presented the land ethic as a product of social evolution because nothing so important as an ethic is ever "written." Only the most superficial student of history supposes that Moses "wrote" the Decalogue; it evolved in the minds of a thinking community, and Moses wrote a tentative summary of it for a "seminar." I say tentative because evolution never stops.

The evolution of a land ethic is an intellectual as well as emotional process. Conservation is paved with good intentions which prove to be futile, or even dangerous, because they are devoid of critical understanding either of the land, or of economic land-use. I think it is a truism that as the ethical frontier advances from the individual to the community, its intellectual content increases.

The mechanism of operation is the same for any ethic: social approbation for right actions: social disapproval for wrong actions.

By and large, our present problem is one of attitudes and implements. We are remodeling the Alhambra with a steam-shovel, and we are proud of our yardage. We shall hardly relinquish the shovel, which after all has many good points, but we are in need of gentler and more objective criteria for its successful use.

A "Good" Environment: Just One of the Set of Human Objectives

William Baxter

William Baxter is professor of law at Stanford University. He is the author of People or Penguins: The Case for Optimal Pollution *(1974).*

Baxter addresses the issue of environmental pollution and argues from a thoroughly anthropocentric point of view. Pollution is the price we pay for the use of resources while in pursuit of benefits to human beings. Baxter does not advocate a "clean environment" but rather an "optimal level of pollution" to be determined by trade-offs between goods produced and methods of controlling pollution. These determinations are not made with any moral concern given to the environment and animals. Rather, these determinations are made in order to promote human good.

I start with the modest proposition that, in dealing with pollution, or indeed with any problem, it is helpful to know what one is attempting to accomplish. Agreement on how and whether to pursue a particular objective, such as pollution control, is not possible unless some more general objective has been identified and stated with reasonable precision. We talk loosely of having clean air and clean water, of preserving our wilderness areas, and so forth. But none of these is a sufficiently general objective: each is more accurately viewed as a means rather than as an end.

With regard to clean air, for example, one may ask, "how clean?" and "what does clean mean?" It is even reasonable to ask, "why have clean air?" Each of these questions is an implicit demand that a more general community goal be stated—a goal

sufficiently general in its scope and enjoying sufficiently general assent among the community of actors that such "why" questions no longer seem admissible with respect to that goal.

If, for example, one states as a goal the proposition that "every person should be free to do whatever he wishes in contexts where his actions do not interfere with the interests of other human beings," the speaker is unlikely to be met with a response of "why." The goal may be criticized as uncertain in its implications or difficult to implement, but it is so basic a tenet of our civilization—it reflects a cultural value so broadly shared, at least in the abstract—that the question "why" is seen as impertinent or imponderable or both.

I do not mean to suggest that everyone would agree with the "spheres of freedom" objective just stated. Still less do I mean to suggest that a society could subscribe to four or five such general objectives that would be adequate in their coverage to serve as testing criteria by which all other disagreements might be measured. One difficulty in the attempt to construct such a list is that each new goal added will conflict, in certain applications, with each prior goal listed; and thus each goal serves as a limited qualification on prior goals.

Without any expectation of obtaining unanimous consent to them, let me set forth four goals that I generally use as ultimate testing criteria in attempting to frame solutions to problems of human organization. My position regarding pollution stems from these four criteria. If the criteria appeal to you and any part of what appears hereafter does not, our disagreement will have a helpful focus: which of us is correct, analytically, in supposing that his position on pollution would better serve these general goals. If the criteria do not seem acceptable to you, then it is to be expected that our more particular judgments will differ, and the task will then be yours to identify the basic set of criteria upon which your particular judgments rest.

My criteria are as follows:

1. The spheres of freedom criterion stated above.
2. Waste is a bad thing. The dominant feature of human existence is scarcity—our available resources, our aggregate labors, and our skill in employing both have always been, and will continue for some time to be, inadequate to yield to every man all the tangible and intangible satisfactions he would like to have. Hence, none of those resources, or labors, or skills, should be wasted—that is, employed so as to yield less than they might yield in human satisfactions.
3. Every human being should be regarded as an end rather than as a means to be used for the betterment of another. Each should

be afforded dignity and regarded as having an absolute claim to an evenhanded application of such rules as the community may adopt for its governance.
4. Both the incentive and the opportunity to improve his share of satisfactions should be preserved to every individual. Preservation of incentive is dictated by the "no-waste" criterion and enjoins against the continuous, totally egalitarian redistribution of satisfactions, or wealth; but subject to that constraint, everyone should receive, by continuous redistribution if necessary, some minimal share of aggregate wealth so as to avoid a level of privation from which the opportunity to improve his situation becomes illusory.

The relationship of these highly general goals to the more specific environmental issues at hand may not be readily apparent, and I am not yet ready to demonstrate their pervasive implications. But let me give one indication of their implications. Recently scientists have informed us that use of DDT in food production is causing damage to the penguin population. For the present purposes let us accept that assertion as an indisputable scientific fact. The scientific fact is often asserted as if the correct implication—that we must stop agricultural use of DDT—followed from the mere statement of the fact of penguin damage. But plainly it does not follow if my criteria are employed.

My criteria are oriented to people, not penguins. Damage to penguins, or sugar pines, or geological marvels is, without more, simply irrelevant. One must go further, by my criteria, and say: Penguins are important because people enjoy seeing them walk about rocks; and furthermore, the well-being of people would be less impaired by halting use of DDT than by giving up penguins. In short, my observations about environmental problems will be people-oriented, as are my criteria. I have no interest in preserving penguins for their own sake.

It may be said by way of objection to this position, that it is very selfish of people to act as if each person represented one unit of importance and nothing else was of any importance. It is undeniably selfish. Nevertheless I think it is the only tenable starting place for analysis for several reasons. First, no other position corresponds to the way most people really think and act—i.e., corresponds to reality.

Second, this attitude does not portend any massive destruction of nonhuman flora and fauna, and they will be preserved because and to the degree that humans do depend on them.

Third, what is good for humans is, in many respects, good for penguins and pine trees—clean air for example. So that humans are, in these respects, surrogates for plant and animal life.

Fourth, I do not know how we could administer any other system. Our decisions are either private or collective. Insofar as Mr. Jones is free to act privately, he may give such preferences as he wishes to other forms of life: he may feed birds in winter and do with less himself, and he may even decline to resist an advancing polar bear on the ground that the bear's appetite is more important than those portions of himself that the bear may choose to eat. In short my basic premise does not rule out private altruism to competing life-forms. It does rule out, however, Mr. Jones' inclination to feed Mr. Smith to the bear, however hungry the bear, however despicable Mr. Smith.

Insofar as we act collectively on the other hand, only humans can be afforded an opportunity to participate in the collective decisions. Penguins cannot vote now and are unlikely subjects for the franchise—pine trees more unlikely still. Again

each individual is free to cast his vote so as to benefit sugar pines if that is his inclination. But many of the more extreme assertions that one hears from some conservationists amount to tacit assertions that they are specially appointed representatives of sugar pines, and hence that their preferences should be weighted more heavily than the preferences of other humans who do not enjoy equal rapport with "nature." The simplistic assertion that agricultural use of DDT must stop at once because it is harmful to penguins is of that type.

Fifth, if polar bears or pine trees or penguins, like men, are to be regarded as ends rather than means, if they are to count in our calculus of social organization, someone must tell me how much each one counts, and someone must tell me how these life-forms are to be permitted to express their preferences, for I do not know either answer. If the answer is that certain people are to hold their proxies, then I want to know how those proxy-holders are to be selected: self-appointment does not seem workable to me.

Sixth, and by way of summary of all the foregoing, let me point out that the set of environmental issues under discussion—although they raise very complex technical questions of how to achieve any objective—ultimately raise a normative question: what *ought* we to do. Questions of *ought* are unique to the human mind and world—they are meaningless as applied to a nonhuman situation.

I reject the proposition that we *ought* to respect the "balance of nature" or to "preserve the environment" unless the reason for doing so, express or implied, is the benefit of man.

I reject the idea that there is a "right" or "morally correct" state of nature to which we should return. The word "nature" has no normative connotation. Was it "right" or "wrong" for the earth's crust to heave in contortion and create mountains and seas? Was it "right" for the first amphibian to crawl up out of the primordial ooze? Was it "wrong" for plants to reproduce themselves and alter the atmospheric composition in favor of oxygen? For animals to alter the atmosphere in favor of carbon dioxide both by breathing oxygen and eating plants? No answers can be given to these questions because they are meaningless questions.

All this may seem obvious to the point of being tedious, but much of the present controversy over environment and pollution rests on tacit normative assumptions about just such nonnormative phenomena: that it is "wrong" to impair penguins with DDT, but not to slaughter cattle for prime rib roasts. That it is wrong to kill stands of sugar pines with industrial fumes, but not to cut sugar pines and build housing for the poor. Every man is entitled to his own preferred definition of Walden Pond, but there is no definition that has any moral superiority over another, except by reference to the selfish needs of the human race.

From the fact that there is no normative definition of the natural state, it follows that there is no normative definition of clean air or pure water—hence no definition of polluted air—or of pollution—except by reference to the needs of man. The "right" composition of the atmosphere is one which has some dust in it and some lead in it and some hydrogen sulfide in it—just those amounts that attend a sensibly organized society thoughtfully and knowledgeably pursuing the greatest possible satisfaction for its human members.

The first and most fundamental step toward solution of our environmental problems is a clear recognition that our objective is not pure air or water but rather some optimal state of pollution. That step immediately suggests the question: How do we define and attain the level of pollution that will yield the maximum possible amount of human satisfaction?

Low levels of pollution contribute to human satisfaction but so do food and shelter and education and music. To attain ever lower levels of pollution, we must pay the cost of having less of these other things. I contrast that view of the cost of pollution control with the more popular statement that pollution control will "cost" very large numbers of dollars. The popular statement is true in some senses, false in others; sorting out the true and false senses is of some importance. The first step in that sorting process is to achieve a clear understanding of the difference between dollars and resources. Resources are the wealth of our nation; dollars are merely claim checks upon those resources. Resources are of vital importance; dollars are comparatively trivial.

Four categories of resources are sufficient for our purposes: At any given time a nation, or a planet if you prefer, has a stock of labor, of technological skill, of capital goods, and of natural resources (such as mineral deposits, timber, water, land, etc.). These resources can be used in various combinations to yield goods and services of all kinds—in some limited quantity. The quantity will be larger if they are combined efficiently, smaller if combined inefficiently. But in either event the resource stock is limited, the goods and services that they can be made to yield are limited; even the most efficient use of them will yield less than our population, in the aggregate, would like to have.

If one considers building a new dam, it is appropriate to say that it will be costly in the sense that it will require x hours of labor, y tons of steel and concrete, and z amount of capital goods. If these resources are devoted to the dam, then they cannot be used to build hospitals, fishing rods, schools, or electric can openers. That is the meaningful sense in which the dam is costly.

Quite apart from the very important question of how wisely we can combine our resources to produce goods and services, is the very different question of how they get distributed—who gets how many goods? Dollars constitute the claim checks which are distributed among people and which control their share of national output. Dollars are nearly valueless pieces of paper except to the extent that they do represent claim checks to some fraction of the output of goods and services. Viewed as claim checks, all the dollars outstanding during any period of time are worth, in the aggregate, the goods and services that are available to be claimed with them during that period—neither more nor less.

It is far easier to increase the supply of dollars than to increase the production of goods and services—printing dollars is easy. But printing more dollars doesn't help because each dollar then simply becomes a claim to fewer goods, i.e., becomes worth less.

The point is this: many people fall into error upon hearing the statement that the decision to build a dam, or to clean up a river, will cost $X million. It is regrettably easy to say: "It's only money. This is a wealthy country, and we have lots of money." But you cannot build a dam or clean a river with $X million—unless you also have a match, you can't even make a fire. One builds a dam or cleans a river by diverting labor and steel and trucks and factories from making one kind of goods to making another. The cost in dollars is merely s shorthand way of describing the extent of the diversion necessary. If we build a dam for $X million, then we must recognize that we will have $X million less housing and food and medical care and electric can openers as a result.

Similarly, the costs of controlling pollution are best expressed in terms of the other goods we will have to give up to do the job. This is not to say the job should not be done. Badly as we need more housing, more medical care, and more can openers, and more symphony orchestras, we could do with somewhat less of them, in my judgment at least, in exchange for somewhat cleaner air and rivers. But that is the nature of the trade-off, and analysis of the problem is advanced if that unpleasant reality is kept in mind. Once the trade-off relationship is clearly perceived, it is possible to state in a very general way what the optimal level of pollution is. I would state it as follows:

People enjoy watching penguins. They enjoy relatively clean air and smog-free vistas. Their health is improved by relatively clean water and air. Each of these benefits is a type of good or service. As a society we would be well advised to give up one washing machine if the resources that would have gone into that washing machine can yield greater human satisfaction when diverted into pollution control. We should give up one hospital if the resources thereby freed would yield more human satisfaction when devoted to elimination of noise in our cities. And so on, trade-off by trade-off, we should divert our productive capacities from the production of existing goods and services to the production of a cleaner, quieter, more pastoral nation up to—and no further than—the point at which we value more highly the next washing machine or hospital that we would have to do without than we value the next unit of environmental improvement that the diverted resources would create.

Now this proposition seems to me unassailable but so general and abstract as to be unhelpful—at least unadministerable in the form stated. It assumes we can measure in some way the incremental units of human satisfaction yielded by very different types of goods. The proposition must remain a pious abstraction until I can explain how this measurement process can occur. In subsequent chapters I will attempt to show that we can do this—in some contexts with great precision and in other contexts only by rough approximation. But I insist that the proposition stated describes the result for which we should be striving—and again, that it is always useful to know what your target is even if your weapons are too crude to score a bull's eye.

Traditional American Indian and Western European Attitudes Toward Nature: An Overview

J. Baird Callicott

J. Baird Callicott is a professor of philosophy and natural resources at the University of Wisconsin, Stevens Point. He is the author of Companion to a Sand County Almanac: Interpretive and Critical Essays *(1987), and* In Defense of the Land Ethic: Essays in Environmental Philosophy *(1989), and coauthor of* Clothed in Fur and Other Tales: An Introduction to an Ojibwa World View *(1982).*

Callicott attempts to bring out the parallel between Aldo Leopold's land ethic and the land ethic of the traditional American Indians. Callicott acknowledges that there is no one world view of all North American Indians, and that the different tribes have richly varied cultures. However, Callicott emphasizes that there is a unity among the tribes concerning the attitudes and beliefs of the people in relation to the environment. Reverence and respect for nature is the unifying thread Callicott traces through various tribal accounts, settler accounts, and ethnographic reports. Callicott argues that this provides a fairly reliable record of American Indian attitudes towards nature. Callicott further argues that those who deny the relevant wisdom of American Indian world views for contemporary environmental ethics are mistaken.

I

In this paper I sketch (in broadest outline) the picture of nature endemic to two very different intellectual traditions: the familiar, globally dominant Western European civilization, on the one hand. and the presently beleaguered tribal cultures of the American Indians, on the other. I argue that the world view typical of American Indian peoples has included and supported an environmental ethic, while that of Europeans has encouraged human alien-

Reprinted by permission of J. Baird Callicott and *Environmental Ethics* from *Environmental Ethics*, Vol. 4, No. 4, 1982. [Edited]

ation from the natural environment and an exploitative practical relationship with it. I thus represent a romantic point of view; I argue that the North American "savages" were indeed more noble than "civilized" Europeans, at least in their outlook toward nature.

I do not enter into this discussion unaware of the difficulties and limitations which present themselves at the very outset. In the first place, there is no *one* thing that can be called *the* American Indian belief system. The aboriginal peoples of the North American continent lived in environments quite different from one another and had culturally adapted to these environments in quite different ways. For each tribe there were a cycle of myths and a set of ceremonies, and from these materials one might abstract *for each* a particular view of nature. However, recognition of the diversity and variety of American Indian cultures would not obscure a complementary unity to be found among them. Despite great internal differences there were common characteristics which culturally united American Indian peoples. Joseph Epes Brown claims that

> this common binding thread is found in beliefs and attitudes held by the people in the quality of their relationships to the natural environment. All American Indian peoples possessed what has been called a metaphysic of nature; all manifest a reverence for the myriad forms and forces of the natural world specific to their immediate environment; and for all their rich complexes of rites and ceremonies are expressed in terms which have reference to or utilize the forms of the natural world.[1]

Writing from a self-declared antiromantic perspective, Calvin Martin has more recently confirmed Brown's conjecture:

> What we are dealing with are two issues: the ideology of Indian land-use and the practical results of that ideology. Actually, there was a great diversity of ideologies, reflecting distinct cultural and ecological contexts. It is thus more than a little artificial to identify a single, monolithic ideology, as though all Native Americans were traditionally inspired by a universal ethos. Still, there were certain elements which many if not all these ideologies seemed to share, the most outstanding being a genuine respect for the welfare of other life forms.[2]

A second obvious difficulty bedeviling any discussion of American Indian views of nature is our limited ability accurately to reconstruct the abstract culture of New World peoples prior to their contact with (and influence from) Europeans. Documentary records of pre-contact Indian thought simply do not exist. American Indian metaphysics existed embedded in oral traditions. Left alone an oral culture may be very tenacious and persistent. If radically stressed, it may prove to be very fragile and liable to total extinction. Hence, *contemporary* accounts by contemporary American Indians of *traditional* American Indian philosophy are vulnerable to the charge of inauthenticity, since for several generations American Indian cultures, cultures preserved in the living memory of their members, have been both ubiquitously and violently disturbed by transplanted European civilization.

We ought, therefore, perhaps to rely where possible upon the earliest written observations of Europeans concerning American Indian belief. The accounts of the North American "savages" by sixteenth, seventeenth, and eighteenth-century Europeans, however, are invariably distorted by ethnocentrism, which to the cosmopolitan twentieth-century student appears so hopelessly abject as to be more entertaining than illuminating. The written observations of Europeans who first encountered American Indian cultures provide rather an instructive record of the implicit European metaphysic. Since Indians were not loyal to the Christian religion, it was assumed that they had to be mindfully servants of Satan, and that the spirits about which they talked and the powers which their shamans attempted to direct had to be so many demons from Hell. Concerning the Feast of the Dead among the Huron, Brebeuf wrote in 1636 that "nothing has ever better pictured for me the confusion among the damned."[3] His account, incidentally, is very informative and detailed concerning the physical requirements and artifacts of this ceremony, but the rigidity of his own system of belief makes it impossible for him to enter sympathetically that of the Huron.

Reconstructing the traditional Indian attitude toward nature is, therefore, to some extent a speculative matter. On the other hand, we must not abandon the inquiry as utterly hopeless. Post-contact American Indians do tell of their traditions and their conceptual heritage. Among the best of these nostalgic memoirs is Neihardt's classic, *Black Elk Speaks*, one of the most important and authentic resources available for the reconstruction of an American Indian attitude toward nature. The explorers', missionaries', and fur traders' accounts of woodland Indian attitudes are also useful, despite their ethnocentrism, since we may correct for the distortion of their biases and prejudices. Using these two sorts of sources, first contact European records and transcribed personal recollections of tribal beliefs by spiritually favored Indians, plus disciplined and methodical modern ethnographic reports, we may achieve a fairly reliable reconstruction of traditional Indian attitudes toward nature. . . .

II

The late John Fire Lame Deer, a reflective Sioux Indian, comments, straight to the point, in his biographical and philosophical narrative, *Lame Deer: Seeker of Visions*, that although the whites (i.e., members of the European cultural tradition) imagine earth, rocks, water and wind to be dead, they nevertheless "are very much alive."[4] In the previous section I tried to explain in what sense nature, as the *res extensa*, is conceived as "dead" in the mainstream of European natural thought. To say that

rocks and rivers are dead is perhaps misleading since what is now dead once was alive. Rather in the usual European view of things such objects are considered inert. But what does Lame Deer mean when he says that they are "very much alive"?

He doesn't explain this provocative assertion as discursively as one might wish, but he provides examples, dozens of examples, of what he calls the "power" in various natural entities. According to Lame Deer, "Every man needs a stone. . . . You ask stones for aid to find things which are lost or missing. Stones can give warning of an enemy, of approaching misfortune."[5] Butterflies, coyotes, grasshoppers, eagles, owls, deer, especially elk and bear all talk and possess and convey power. "You have to listen to all these creatures, listen with your mind. They have secrets to tell."[6]

It would seem that for Lame Deer the "aliveness" of natural entities (including stones which to most Europeans are merely "material objects" and epitomize lifelessness) means that they have a share in the same consciousness that we human beings enjoy. Granted, animals and plants (if not stones and rivers) are recognized to be "alive" by conventional European conceptualization, but they lack awareness in a mode and degree comparable to human awareness. Among the Cartesians, even animal behavior was regarded as altogether automatic, resembling in every way the behavior of a machine. A somewhat more liberal and enlightened view allows that animals have a dim sort of consciousness, but get around largely by "instinct," a concept altogether lacking a clear definition and one very nearly as obscure as the notorious occult qualities (the "soporific virtues," and so on) of the Schoolmen. Of course, plants are regarded as, although alive, totally lacking in sentience. In any case, we hear that only human beings possess *self*-consciousness, that is, are aware that they are aware and can thus distinguish between themselves and everything else!

Every sophomore student of philosophy has learned, or should have, that solipsism is a redoubtable philosophical position, and corollary to that, that every characterization of other minds—human as well as nonhuman—is a matter of conjecture. The Indian attitude, as represented by Lame Deer, apparently was based upon the consideration that since human beings have a physical body *and* an associated consciousness (conceptually hypostatized or reified as "spirit"), all other bodily things, animals, plants, and, yes, even stones, were also similar in this respect. Indeed, this strikes me as an eminently reasonable assumption. I can no more directly perceive another human being's consciousness than I can that of an animal or plant. I *assume* that another human being is conscious since he or she is perceptibly very like me (in other respects) and I am conscious. To anyone not hopelessly prejudiced by the metaphysical *apartheid* policy of Christianity and Western thought generally, human beings closely resemble in anatomy, physiology, and behavior other forms of life. The variety of organic forms themselves are clearly closely related and the organic world, in turn, is continuous with the whole of nature. Virtually all things might be supposed, without the least strain upon credence, like ourselves, to be "alive," i.e., conscious, aware, or possessed of spirit.

Lame Deer offers a brief, but most revealing and suggestive metaphysical explanation:

Nothing is so small and unimportant but it has a spirit given it by Wakan Tanka. Tunkan is what you might call a stone god, but he is also a part of the Great Spirit. The gods are separate beings, but they are all united in Wakan Tanka. It is hard to understand—something like the Holy Trinity. You can't explain it except by going back to the "circles within circles" idea, the spirit splitting itself up into stones, trees, tiny insects even, making them all *wakan* by his ever-presence. And in turn all these myriad of things which makes up the universe flowing back to their source, united in one Grandfather Spirit.[7]

This Lakota pantheism presents a conception of the world which is, to be sure, dualistic, but it is important to emphasize that, unlike the Pythagorean-Platonic-Cartesian tradition, it is not an *antagonistic* dualism in which body and spirit are conceived in contrary terms and pitted against one another in a moral struggle. Further, and most importantly for my subsequent remarks, the pervasiveness of spirit in nature, a spirit *in everything* which is a splinter of the Great Spirit, facilitates a perception of the human and natural realms as unified and akin.

Consider, complementary to this panpsychism, the basics of Siouan cosmogony. Black Elk rhetorically asks, "Is not the sky a father and the earth a mother, and are not all living things with feet or wings or roots their children?"[8] Accordingly, Black Elk prays, "Give me the strength to walk the soft earth, a relative to all that is!"[9] He speaks of the great natural kingdom as, simply, "green things," "the wings of the air," "the four-leggeds," and "the two-legged."[10] Not only does everything have a spirit, in the last analysis all things are related together as members of one universal family, born of one father, the sky, the Great Spirit, and one mother, the Earth herself.

More is popularly known about the Sioux metaphysical vision than about those of most other American Indian peoples. The concept of the Great Spirit and of the Earth Mother and the family-like relatedness of all creatures seems, however, to have been very nearly a universal American Indian idea, and likewise the concept of a spiritual dimension or aspect to all natural things. N. Scott Momaday remarked, " 'The earth is our mother. The sky is our father.' This concept of nature, which is at the center of the Native American world view, is familiar to us all. But it may well be that we do not understand entirely what the concept is in its ethical and philosophical implications."[11] And Ruth Underhill has written that "for the old time Indian, the world did not consist of inanimate materials. . . . It was alive, and everything in it could help or harm him."[12]

Concerning the Ojibwa Indians, who speak an Algonkian language and at the time of first contact maintained only hostile relations with the Sioux, Diamond Jenness reports:

> Thus, then, the Parry Island Ojibwa interprets his own being; and exactly the same interpretation he applies to everything around him. Not only men, but animals, trees, even rocks and water are tripartite, possessing bodies, souls, and shadows. They all have a life like the life in human beings, even if they have all been gifted with different powers and attributes. Consider the animals which most closely resemble human beings; they see and hear as we do, and clearly they reason about what they observe. The tree must have a life somewhat like our own, although it lacks the power of locomotion. . . . Water runs; it too must possess life, it too must have a soul and a shadow. Then observe how certain minerals cause the neighboring rocks to decompose and become loose and friable; evidently rocks too have power, and power means life, and life involves a soul and shadow. All things then have souls and shadows. And all things die. But their souls are reincarnated again, and what were dead return to life.[13]

Irving Hallowell has noted an especially significant consequence of the pan-spiritualism among the Ojibwa: "Not only animate properties," he writes, "but even 'person' attributes may be projected upon objects which to us clearly belong to a physical inanimate category."[14] Central to the concept of a person is the possibility of entering into social relations. Nonhuman persons may be spoken with, may be honored or insulted, may become allies or adversaries, no less than human persons.

The French fur traders and missionaries of the seventeenth century in the Great Lakes region were singularly impressed by the devotion of the savages with whom they lived to dreams. In 1648, Ragueneau speaking of the Huron, according to Kinietz, first suggested that dreams were "the language of the souls."[15] This expression lacks precision, but I think it goes very much to the core of the phenomenon. Through dreams and most dramatically through visions, one came into direct contact with the spirits of both human and nonhuman persons, as it were, naked of bodily vestments. In words somewhat reminiscent of Ragueneau's, Hallowell comments, "it is in dreams that the individual comes into direct communication with the *atiso'kanak*, the powerful 'persons' of the other-than-human class."[16] Given the animistic or pan-spiritualistic world view of the Indians, acute sensitivity and pragmatic response to dreaming makes perfectly good sense.

Dreams and waking experiences are sharply discriminated, but the theater of action disclosed in dreams and visions is continuous with and often the same as the ordinary world. In contrast to the psychologized contemporary Western view in which dreams are images of sorts (like afterimages) existing only "in the mind," the American Indian while dreaming experiences reality, often the same reality as in waking experience, in another form of consciousness, as it were, by means of another sensory modality.

As one lies asleep and experiences people and other animals, places and so on, it is natural to suppose that one's spirit becomes temporarily dissociated from the body and moves about encountering other spirits. Or, as Hallowell says, "when a human being is asleep and dreaming his *otcatcakwin* (vital part, soul), which is the core of the self, may become detached from the body (*miyo*). Viewed by another human being, a person's body may be easily located and observed in space. But his vital part may be somewhere else."[17] Dreaming indeed may be one element in the art of American Indian sorcery ("bear walking" among the Ojibwa). If the state of consciousness in dreams may be seized and controlled, and the phenomenal content of dreams volitionally directed, then the sorcerer may go where he wishes to spy upon his enemies or perhaps affect them in some malevolent way. It follows that dreams should have a higher degree of "truth" than ordinary waking experiences, since in the dream experience the person and everyone he meets is present in spirit, in essential self. This, notice, is precisely contrary to the European assumption that dreams are "false" or illusory and altogether private or subjective. E.g., in the second meditation Descartes, casting around for an example of the highest absurdity, says that it is, "as though I were to say 'I am awake now, and discern some truth; but I do not see it clearly enough; so I will set

about going to sleep, so that my dreams may give me a truer and clearer picture of the fact.'" Yet this, in all seriousness, is precisely what the Indian does. The following episode from Hallowell's discussion may serve as illustration. A boy claimed that during a thunderstorm he saw a thunderbird. His elders were skeptical, since to see a thunderbird in such fashion, i.e. with the waking eye, was almost unheard of. He was believed, however, when a man who had dreamed of the thunderbird was consulted and the boy's description was *"verified!"*[18]

The Ojibwa, the Sioux, and if we may safely generalize, most American Indians, lived in a world which was peopled not only by human persons, but by persons and personalities associated with all natural phenomena. In one's practical dealings in such a world it is necessary to one's well-being and that of one's family and tribe to maintain good social relations not only with proximate human persons, one's immediate tribal neighbors, but also with the nonhuman persons abounding in the immediate environment. For example, Hallowell reports that among the Ojibwa "when bears were sought out in their dens in the spring they were addressed, asked to come out so that they could be killed, and an apology was offered to them."[19]

In characterizing the American Indian attitude toward nature with an eye to its eventual comparison to ecological attitudes and conservation values and precepts I have tried to limit the discussion to concepts so fundamental and pervasive as to be capable of generalization. In sum, I have claimed that the typical traditional American Indian attitude was to regard all features of the environment as enspirited. These entities possessed a consciousness, reason, and volition, no less intense and complete than a human being's. The Earth itself, the sky, the winds, rocks, streams, trees, insects, birds, and all other animals therefore had personalities and were thus as fully persons as other human beings. In dreams and visions the spirits of things were directly encountered and could become powerful allies to the dreamer or visionary. We may therefore say that the Indian's social circle, his community, included all the nonhuman natural entities in his locale as well as his fellow clansmen and tribesmen.

Now a most significant conceptual connection obtains in all cultures between the concept of a person, on the one hand, and certain behavioral restraints, on the other. Toward persons it is necessary, whether for genuinely ethical or purely prudential reasons, to act in a careful and circumspect manner. Among the Ojibwa, for example, according to Hallowell, "a moral distinction is drawn between the kind of conduct demanded by the primary necessities of securing a livelihood, or defending oneself against aggression, and unnecessary acts of cruelty. The moral values implied document the consistency of the principle of *mutual obligations* which is inherent in all interactions with 'persons' throughout the Ojibwa world."[20]

The implicit overall metaphysic of American Indian cultures locates human beings in a larger *social,* as well as physical, environment. People belong not only to a human community, but to a community of all nature as well. Existence in this larger society, just as existence in a family and tribal context, place people in an environment in which reciprocal responsibilities and mutual obligations are taken for granted and assumed without question or reflection. Moreover, a person's basic cosmological representations in moments of

meditation or cosmic reflection place him or her in a world all parts of which are united through ties of kinship. All creatures, be they elemental, green, finned, winged, or legged, are children of one father and one mother. One blood flows through all; one spirit has divided itself and enlivened all things with a consciousness that is essentially the same. The world around, though immense and overwhelmingly diversified and complex, is bound together through bonds of kinship, mutuality, and reciprocity. It is a world in which a person might feel at home, a relative to all that is, comfortable and secure, as one feels as a child in the midst of a large family. As Brown reports:

> But very early in life the child began to realize that wisdom was all about and everywhere and that there were many things to know. There was no such thing as emptiness in the world. Even in the sky there were no vacant places. Everywhere there was life, visible and invisible, and every object gave us great interest to life. Even without human companionship one was never alone. The world teemed with life and wisdom, there was no complete solitude for the Lakota (Luther Standing Bear).[21]

III

I turn now to the claim made at the beginning of this discussion, viz., that in its practical consequences the American Indian view of nature is on the whole more productive of a cooperative symbiosis of people with their environment than is the view of nature predominant in the Western European tradition.

Respecting the latter, Ian McHarg writes that "it requires little effort to mobilize a sweeping indictment of the physical environment which is [Western] man's creation [and] it takes little more to identify the source of the value system which is the culprit."[22] According to McHarg, the culprit is "the Judeo-Christian-Humanist view which is so unknowing of nature and of man, which has bred and sustained his simple-minded anthropocentricism."[23]

Popular ecologists and environmentalists (perhaps most notably, Rachel Carson and Barry Commoner, along with McHarg and Lynn White, Jr.) have with almost loving attention recited a litany of environmental ills, spoken of "chlorinated hydrocarbons," "phosphate detergents," "nuclear tinkering," and "the gratified bulldozer" in language once reserved for detailing the precincts of Hell and abominating its seductive Prince. Given the frequency with which we are reminded of the symptoms of strain in the global biosphere and the apocalyptic rhetoric in which they are usually cast I may be excused if I omit this particular step from the present argument. Let us stipulate that modern technological civilization (European in its origins) has been neither restrained nor especially delicate in manipulating the natural world.

With somewhat more humor than other advocates of environmental reform Aldo Leopold characterized the modern Western approach to nature thus: "By and large our present problem is one of attitudes and implements. We are remodeling the Alhambra with a steam shovel, and we are proud of our yardage. We shall hardly relinquish the shovel, which after all has many good points, but we are in need of gentler and more objective criteria for its successful use."[24] So far as the historical roots of the environmental crisis are concerned, I have here suggested that the much maligned attitudes arising out of the Judeo-Christian tradition have not been so

potent a force in the work of remodeling as the tradition of Western natural philosophy originating among the ancient Greeks and consolidated in modern scientific thought. At least the latter has been as formative of the cultural milieu, one artifact of which is the steam shovel itself, as the former; and together, mixed and blended, so to speak, they create a mentality in which unrestrained environmental exploitation and degradation could almost be predicted in advance.

It seems obvious (especially to philosophers and historians of ideas) that attitudes and values *do* directly "determine" behavior by setting goals (e.g., to subdue the Earth, to have dominion) and, through a conceptual representation of the world, providing means (e.g., mechanics and other applied sciences). Skepticism regarding this assumption, however, has been forthcoming. Yi-Fu Tuan says in "Discrepancies between Environmental Attitude and Behavior: Examples from Europe and China":

> We may *believe* that a world-view which puts nature in subservience to man will lead to the exploitation of nature by man; and one that regards man as simply a component in nature will entail a modest view of his rights and capabilities, and so lead to the establishment of a harmonious relationship between man and his natural environment. But is this correct?[25]

Yi-Fu Tuan thinks not. The evidence from Chinese experience which he cites, however, is ambiguous. Concerning European experience, he marshalls examples and cases in point of large scale transformations imposed, with serious ecological consequences, upon the Mediterranean environment by the Greeks and Romans. They were, of course, nominally pagans. He concludes this part of his discussion with the remark that "against this background of the vast transformations of nature in the pagan world, the inroads made in the early centuries of the Christian era were relatively modest."[26] I believe, nevertheless, that my discussion in part two of this paper has explained the environmental impact of Greek and Roman civilization consistently with the general thesis that world view substantially affects behavior! Among the Chinese before Westernization, the facts which Yi-Fu Tuan presents, indicate as many congruencies as discrepancies between the traditional Taoist and Buddhist attitude toward nature and Chinese environmental behavior.

A simple deterministic model will not suffice with respect to the question, do cultural attitudes and values really affect the collective behavior of a culture? On the one hand, it seems incredible to think that all our conceptualizations, our representations of the nature of nature, are, as it were, mere entertainment, sort of epiphenomena of the mind, while our actions proceed in some blind way from instinctive or genetically programmed sources. After all, our picture of nature defines our theater of action. It defines both the possibilities and limitations which circumscribe human endeavor. On the other hand, the facts of history and everyday experience do not support any simple cause and effect relationship between a given conceptual and valuational set and what people do. My own view is that it is basic to human nature to both consume and modify the natural environment. Representations of the order of nature and the proper relationship of people to that order may have either a tempering, restraining effect on manipulative and exploitative tendencies or they may have an accelerating, exacerbating effect. They also give form and

direction to these inherently human drives and thus provide different cultures with their distinctive styles of doing things. It appears to me, further, that in the case of the predominant European mentality, shaped both by the Judeo-Christian and Greco-Roman images of nature and man, the effect was to accelerate the inherent human disposition to consume and modify surroundings. A kind of "takeoff" or (to mix metaphors) "quantum leap" occurred, and Western European civilization was propelled for better or worse into its industrial, technological stage with a proportional increase in ecological and environmental distress. The decisive ingredient, the *sine qua non*, may have been the particulars of the European world view.

If the predominant traditional Chinese view of nature and man is, as it has been characterized by Yi-Fu Tuan, "quiescent" and "adaptive," the American Indian view of the world has been characterized as in essence "ecological," for example, by Stewart Udall, in the *Quiet Crisis*. In "First Americans, First Ecologists" Udall nostalgically invokes the memory of Thoreau and attributes to his ghost the opinion that "the Indians were, in truth, the pioneer ecologists of this country."[27] To assert without qualification that the American Indians were ecologists is, to say the least, overly bold. Ecology is a part of biology, just as organic chemistry is a part of chemistry. It is a methodic and *quantitative* study of organisms in a contextual, functional relationship to conditions of their several ranges and habitats. Udall, of course, disclaims that he means to suggest that Indians were scientists. One might prefer to say that American Indians intuitively acquired an essentially ecological "outlook," "perspective," or "habit of mind." That would be roughly to say that Indians viewed nature as a matrix of mutually dependent functional components integrated systematically into an organic whole. It would suggest a kind of global or holistic viewpoint; it would also imply an acute sensitivity to the complex factors influencing the life cycles of living things.

To attribute to American Indians, on the one hand, a highly abstract conceptual schematism and, on the other, disinterested, systematic, disciplined, and meticulous observation of minutiae is to press the romantic interpretation of American Indian thought much too far. Much of the material which I have already cited *does* indicate that both woodland and plains Indians were careful students of their natural surroundings. Knowledge of animals and their ways, particularly those of utilitarian value, and knowledge of plants, especially edible and medicinal ones, is a well-known and much respected dimension of traditional Indian cultures. The American Indian pharmacopoeia alone certainly testifies to Indian botanical acumen. My impression, nonetheless, is that the typically Indian representation of nature is more animistic and symbolic than mechanical and functional. The "rules" governing hunting and fishing seem more cast in the direction of achieving the correct etiquette toward game species than *consciously* achieving maximum sustained yield of protein "resources." Medicinal plants were sought as much for their magical, symbolic, and representational virtues as for their chemical effects. Of course, in the case of hunting and fishing, proper manners *are* behavioral restraints and, more often than not, the outcome of their being followed—of correct social forms in respect to bear, beaver, and so on, being observed—was to limit exploitation and, therefore, incidentally, to achieve sustained yield.

To suggest that the Indians were (intuitive or natural or pioneer or even primitive) ecologists, in other words, strikes me as being very much like saying that Indian healers, like Black Elk, were intuitive (etc.) physicians. Indian medicine was not at an earlier stage of development than European medicine, as if moving along the same path some distance behind. It followed a different path altogether. As Black Elk explains, "It is from understanding that power comes; and the power in the [curing] ceremony was in understanding what it meant; for nothing can live well except in a manner that is suited to the way the sacred Power of the World lives and moves."[28] The power that Black Elk employed was, *in his view*, ceremonial and symbolic—what it meant, not what it *did* to the patient. The cure, thus, was effected through symbolism, not biological mechanism.

The general American Indian world view (at least the one central part of it to which I have called attention) deflected the inertia of day-to-day, year-to-year, subsistence in a way that resulted, on the average, in conservation. Conservation of resources may have been, but probably was not, a *consciously* posited goal, neither a personal ideal nor a tribal policy. *Deliberate* conservation would indeed, ironically, appear to be inconsistent with the spiritual and personal attributes which the Indians regarded as belonging to nature and natural things, since these are represented by most conservationists in the predominant Pinchot tradition as only commodities, subject to scarcity, and therefore in need of prudent "development" and "management." The American Indian posture toward nature was, I suggest, neither ecological nor conservative in the modern scientific sense so much as it was moral or ethical. Animals, plants, and minerals were treated as persons, and conceived to be coequal members of a natural social order.

My cautious claim that American Indians were neither deliberate conservationists nor ecologists in the conventional sense of these terms, but manifested rather a distinctly ethical attitude toward nature and the myriad variety of natural entities is based upon the following basic points. The American Indians, on the whole, viewed the natural world as enspirited. Natural beings therefore felt, perceived, deliberated, and responded voluntarily as persons. Persons are members of a social order (i.e., part of the operational concept of a person is the capacity for social interaction). Social interaction is limited by (culturally variable) behavioral restraints, rules of conduct, which we call, in sum, good manners, morals, and ethics. The American Indians, therefore, in Aldo Leopold's turn of phrase lived in accordance with a "land ethic." This view is also maintained by Scott Momaday: "Very old in the Native American world view is the conviction that the earth is vital, that there is a spiritual dimension to it, a dimension in which man rightly exists. It follows logically that there are ethical imperatives in this matter."[29]

To point to examples of wastage—buffaloes rotting on the plains under high cliffs or beaver all but trapped-out during the fur trade—which are supposed to deliver the *coup de grace* to all romantic illusions of the American Indian's reverence for nature[30] is very much like pointing to examples of murder and war in European history and concluding therefrom that Europeans were altogether without a humanistic ethic of any sort. What is lacking is a useful understanding of the function of ethics in human affairs. Ethics bear, as philosophers point out, a normative relation to behavior; they do not describe how people actually behave, but rather point out how people ought to behave. Therefore, people are free either to act in accordance with a given ethic or not. The fact that on some occasions some do not scarcely proves that ethics are not on the whole influential and effective behavioral restraints. The familiar Christian ethic has exerted a decisive influence within European civilization; it has inspired noble and even heroic deeds both of individuals and whole societies. The documented influence of the Christian ethic is not in the least diminished by monstrous crimes on the part of individuals. Nor do shameful episodes of national depravity, like the Spanish Inquisition, and genocide, as in Nazi Germany, refute the assertion that a humanistic ethic has palpably affected behavior among members of the European civilization and substantially shaped the character of that civilization itself. By parity of reasoning, examples of occasional destruction of nature on the pre-Columbian American continent and even the extirpation of species, especially during periods of enormous cultural stress, as in the fur trade era, do not, by themselves, refute the assertion that the American Indian lived not only by a tribal ethic but by a land ethic as well, the *overall* and *usual* effect of which was to establish a greater harmony between Indians and their environment than enjoyed by their European successors. . . .

NOTES

1. Joseph E. Brown, "Modes of Contemplation through Action: North American Indians," *Main Currents in Modern Thought* 30 (1973–74): 60.

2. Calvin Martin, *Keepers of the Game: Indian–Animal Relationships and the Fur Trade* (Berkeley and Los Angeles: University of California Press, 1978), p. 186.
3. W. Vernon Kinietz, *Indians of the Western Great Lakes, 1615–1760* (Ann Arbor: University of Michigan Press, 1965), p. 115.
4. Richard Erdoes, *Lame Deer: Seeker of Visions* (New York: Simon & Schuster, 1976), pp. 108–09.
5. Ibid., p. 101.
6. Ibid., p. 124.
7. Ibid., pp. 102–03.
8. John G. Neihardt, *Black Elk Speaks* (Lincoln: University of Nebraska Press, 1932), p. 3.
9. Ibid., p. 6.
10. Ibid., p. 7.
11. N. Scott Momaday, "A First American Views His Land," *National Geographic* 149 (1976): 14.
12. Ruth M. Underhill, *Red Man's Religion: Beliefs and Practices of the Indians North of Mexico* (Chicago: University of Chicago Press, 1965), p. 40.
13. Diamond Jenness, *The Ojibwa Indians of Parry Island, Their Social and Religious Life*, Canadian Department of Mines Bulletin no. 78, Museum of Canada Anthropological Series, no. 17 (Ottawa, 1935), pp. 20–21. The (Parry Island) Ojibwa, Jenness earlier details, divided spirit into two parts—soul and shadow—though, as Jenness admits, the distinction between the soul and shadow was far from clear and frequently confused by the people themselves.
14. A. Irving Hallowell, "Ojibwa Ontology, Behavior, and World View," *Culture in History: Essays in Honor of Paul Radin*, ed. S. Diamond (New York: Columbia University Press, 1960), p. 26.
15. Kinietz, *Indians of the Western Great Lakes*, p. 126.
16. Hallowell, "Ojibwa Ontology," p. 19.
17. Ibid., p. 41.
18. Ibid., p. 32.
19. Ibid., p. 35.
20. Ibid., p. 47 (emphasis added).
21. Brown, "Modes of Contemplation," p. 64.
22. Ian McHarg, "Values, Process, Form," from *The Fitness of Man's Environment* (Washington, D.C.: Smithsonian Institution Press, 1968) reprinted in Robert Disch, ed., *The Ecological Conscience* (Englewood Cliffs: Prentice-Hall, 1970), p. 25.
23. Ibid., p. 98.
24. Leopold, *Sand County Almanac*, pp. 225–26.
25. Yi-Fu Tuan, "Discrepancies between Environmental Attitude and Behavior," in *Ecology and Religion in History*, eds. Spring and Spring (New York: Harper and Row, 1974), p. 92.
26. Ibid., p. 98.
27. Stewart Udall, "First Americans, First Ecologists," *Look to the Mountain Top* (San Jose: Gousha Publications, 1972), p. 2.
28. Neihardt, *Black Elk Speaks*, p. 212.
29. Momaday, "First American Views," p. 18.
30. The most scurrilous example of this sort of argument with which I am acquainted is Daniel A. Guthre's "Primitive Man's Relationship to Nature," *BioScience* 21 (July 1971): 721–23. In addition to rotting buffalo, Guthrie cites alleged extirpation of pleistocene megafauna by Paleo-Indians, c. 10,000 B. P. (as if that were relevant), and his cheapest shot of all, "the litter of bottles and junked cars to be found on Indian reservations today."

On the Environmental Ethics
of the *Tao* and the *Ch'i*

Chung-ying Cheng

Chung-ying Cheng is a professor of philosophy at the University of Hawaii at Manoa, Hawaii. Cheng is the author of numerous articles and books on Chinese philosophy. He founded and edits Philosophical Review *and* The Journal of Chinese Philosophy, *and is editor of* Chinese Studies in Philosophy.

Cheng writes about how the Tao is applicable to our ecological understanding of the environment. Cheng states that the Tao is important to human well-being and complete ecological harmony with nature. The application of the Tao in this manner, he asserts, is important to both philosophers of the Tao and environmentalists. Cheng presents the ecological principle of nature, from which comes the most important point about nature in the Tao: That the Tao does not impose itself on things and stresses universal harmony, yet remains aware that there is constant flux and transformation. Cheng states that without an understanding of the Tao, the combination of technology and greed, among other things, will doom humans to self-slavery and eventual self-destruction.

One central question for environmental ethics which must be raised before any other questions is what the term *environment* means or stands for. *Environment* is derived from *environs*, meaning "in circuit" or "turning around in" in Old French.[1] It is apparently a prepositional word, indicating an external relation without a context, also certainly devoid of a relationship of organic interdependence. Yet when we reflect on the experience of environment, we encounter many different things and different processes in the context of organic interdependence. We might say what we experience presupposes the existence of

Reprinted with permission of Chung-ying Cheng and *Environmental Ethics*, from *Environmental Ethics*, Vol. 8, No. 4, 1986. [Edited]

life and the living processes of many forms. This experience of environment is better expressed by the Chinese philosophical paradigm, *sheng-sheng-pu-yi* ("incessant activity of life creativity").[2] We must, therefore, make a distinction between a surface meaning and a depth meaning for environment. Without understanding life and the living process of life, we cannot understand the depth meaning of environment. On the other hand, without understanding the constituents and conditions of life, we cannot understand life and the living process of life. Hence, the very essence of environment requires an understanding of reality and the true identity of life in both its state and process aspects. This means we have to understand the *Tao* content and the *Tao* process in the environment, whereas Tao indicates the way of life-creativity in ceaseless movements and in a multitude of forms.

With the above analysis of the meaning of environment, it is clear that the essential depth meaning of environment was lost in modern man's conception of environment. The modern man's conception of environment is founded on the surface meaning of environment, which is typified by technology and science; with its underlying philosophy of modern-day materialism. Cartesian dualism, and mechanistic naturalism, the concept of environment of modern man was very much objectified, mechanized, rigidified, dehumanized, and possibly even de-enlivened, and so de-environmentalized.[3] Environment is no longer an environment at all; environment becomes simply "the surroundings," the physical periphery, the material conditions and the transient circumstances. The environment is conceived as a passive deadwood, and very often as only visible and tangible externalia. In fact, as the depth meaning of environment suggested above, environment is active life; it is not necessarily visible or tangible, and certainly it cannot be simply a matter of externality. Hence, it cannot be treated as an object, the material conditions, a machine tool, or a transient feature. Environment is more than the visible, more than the tangible, more than the external, more than a matter of quantified period of time or a spread of space. It has a deep structure as well as a deep process, as the concept of *Tao* indicates.

The distinction between the surface meaning and the depth meaning of environment also suggests a distinction between the Western and the Chinese approach to environment. Whereas the West focuses on the external relation of man to his surroundings based upon a qualitative separation and confrontation between the human and nonhuman worlds, the Chinese focus on the internal relation of man to his surroundings based upon an integrative interdependence and a harmony between man and the world. For modern Western man after Descartes, the nonhuman world is to be rationally studied, researched, and then scientifically manipulated and exploited for the maximum utility of serving man. This will to conquer and dominate nature is, of course, premised on the externality of nature to man, but there are two other rational principles or assumptions involved in exercising this will to conquer and dominate.

First, it is assumed that nature is a completed work of mechanical forces with one-dimensional natural laws controlling its workings. The one-dimensional natural laws are revealed in the physical sciences and the reductionistic methodology of physicalism. Hence, biological laws are very often reduced to laws of physics and chemistry; no other laws are permitted to stand on their own. Yet the relationship between various forms of life in the totality of nature cannot be said to be fully captured by physicalistic laws; nor can the relationship between man and the world of things be said to be regulated by these laws. The very fact of the breakdown of the environment in industrialized societies, as reflected, for example, in the problems of water-air-noise pollution, precisely points to the lack of understanding of the relationship between various forms of life and man and his environment by way of modern science and technology.

There is a second assumption of the modern mechanical sciences: everything in the world forms an entity on its own as a closed system, and therefore can be individually and separately dealt with. This isolationist and atomistic assumption in the problem-solving methodology of modern science is strongly reflected in Western medical diagnostics and treatments. It was not until recent times that modern medical and health care researchers became aware of the potential limitations of this isolationist and atomistic approach, and became awakened to a holistic approach.

In contrast with the Western externalistic point of view on environment, the Chinese tradition, as represented by both Confucianism (with the *I Ching* as its metaphysical philosophy) and Taoism (with Chuang Tzu and Lao Tzu as its content), has developed an internalistic point of view on the environment. The internalistic point of view on the environment in Chinese philosophy focuses on man as the *consummator* of nature rather than man as the conqueror of nature, as a participant in nature rather than as a predator of nature. Man as the consummator of nature expresses continuously the beauty, truth, and goodness of nature; and articulates them in a moral or a natural cultivation of human life or human nature. This is paradigmatically well expressed in Confucius' saying "Man can enlarge the Way (*Tao*) rather than the Way enlarging man."[4] It is also expressed in Chuang Tzu's saying, "The *Tao* penetrates and forms a Unity."[5] As part and parcel of nature, man does not stand opposite nature in a hostile way. On the contrary, man has profound concern and care for nature at large, as befitting his own nature. For his own growth and well-being, man has to cultivate the internal link in him between himself and Mother Nature. To conquer nature and exploit it is a form of self-destruction and self-abasement for man. The material consequence of the conquest and exploitation

must be forestalled by an awakening to what man really is or in what his nature really consists.

In contrast with the two Western assumptions about the environment, Chinese philosophy clearly asserts that nature, and therefore man's environment, is not a complete work of production by a transcendent God, but rather is a process of continuous production and reproduction of life. In Bruno's words, nature is *Natura naturans*, not merely *Natura naturata*. In other words, nature is an organism of continuous growth and decay, but never devoid of internal life. With this understanding men cannot treat nature as an isolated and atomic part without regard for the totality involving a past and a future. This leads to the second understanding contrary to the Western methodology of atomism: man has to interact with nature in a totalistic manner, realizing that there is no single linear chain of causality. There is always a many-to-many relationship between cause and effect. Hence, man has to consider a many-to-many level approach to relate the potential needs of man to nature. Man has to naturalize man as well as to humanize nature, treating nature as his equal and as a member within the family of the *Tao*. This approach to nature is reflected in the holistic approach of Chinese medicine in both its diagnostic and medical/health care aspects.

The modern mandarin translation for *environment* is *huan-chin*, meaning "world surroundings." This translation apparently reflects the surface meaning of *environment* correctly. But when embedded in the contexts of Chinese philosophy and Chinese cultural consciousness the "world of surroundings" does not simply denote individual things as entities in a microscopic structure: it also connotes a many-layered reality such as heaven and earth in a macroscopic enfoldment. This "world of surroundings" is generally conceived as something not static but dynamic, something not simply visible but invisible. It is in this sense of environment that we can speak of the *Tao* as the true environment of man: the true environment of man is also the true environment of nature or everything else in nature.

When asked about the presence of the *Tao*, Chuang Tzu had this to say: "(The *Tao* is) nowhere not present." Pressed as to where exactly the *Tao* lies, Chuang Tzu replied that the *Tao* is in the ants, in the weeds, in the ruins, and in the dungs.[6] The import of Chuang Tzu's message is that the *Tao* embraces everything, large or small, in the universe and imparts a unity of relationships in our environment, and that the *Tao* is a totality as well as a part of the totality pervading everything beyond our perception so that we cannot ignore what is hidden in our understanding of the environment. If understanding is the basis for action, this understanding of the environment in terms of the *Tao* is very essential for formulating an ethic of the environment, namely for articulating what human persons should do or attitudinize toward their world of surroundings. Two more observations have to be made in order to explicate the philosophy of the *Tao* for the purpose of the formulating an environmental ethics of the *Tao* or an ethics of the environment based on an understanding of the *Tao*.

The first observation concerns the *Tao* as the *tzu-jan*. *Tzu-jan* means "doing-something-on-its-own-accord," or natural spontaneity. In the *Tao Te Ching* it is said that "Man follows earth; earth follows heaven; heaven follows the *Tao* and the *Tao* follows *tzu-jan*."[7] But *tzu-jan* is not something beyond and above the *Tao*. It is the movement of the *Tao* as the *Tao*, namely as the underlying unity of all things as well as the underlying source of the life of all things. One important aspect of *tzu-jan* is that the movement of things must come from the *internal life** of things and never results from engineering or conditioning by an external power. That is why the life-creativity nature of the *Tao* is the only proper way of describing the nature of the movement of the *Tao*. However, to say this is not to say that only the *Tao* can have the movement of *tzu-jan*. In fact, all things can follow *tzu-jan* insofar as they follow the *Tao*, or in other words, act and move in the manner of the *Tao* and in unison and in accordance with the *Tao*. Perhaps a better way of expressing this is: things will move of their own accord (*tzu-jan*) insofar as they move by way of the *Tao* and the *Tao* moves by way of them. One has to distinguish between, on the one hand, *Tao*-oriented or *Tao*-founded movement and, on the other hand, thing-oriented or thing-founded movement. Only when the movement of a thing comes from the deep source of the thing—the *Tao* and its harmony with the totality of the movements of all other things—will the movement of things be genuinely of its own accord and, therefore, be spontaneous. Spontaneity (*tzu-jan*) is a matter of infinite depth and infinite breadth in an onto-cosmological sense.

One can, of course, speak of different degrees of *tzu-jan* in view of the different degrees of depth and breadth in harmonious relating and self-assertion among things. Just as things have their own histories and defining characteristics in form and substance, things also have their relative freedom of self-movement and life-creativity. Things, in fact, can be considered as conditions or preconditions of various forms of *tzu-jan* (spontaneity): insofar as things preserve their identity without destroying the identities of other things, and insofar as things change and transform without interfering with the process of change and transformation of other things, there is *tzu-jan*. This explains the mutual movement, rise and decline, ebb and flow, in things of nature.

For human beings, *tzu-jan* finds its rationale not only in the internal movement and life-creativity of human activity, but in the principle of least effort with maximum effect.** Whatever produces maximum effect by minimum effort in human activity manifests natural spontaneity. One may, therefore, suggest that only in following natural spontaneity is there least effort and maximum effect. This can be called the *ecological principle of nature*.[8] Using this principle we can correctly interpret the most important point ever made about the nature of the *Tao*: "The *Tao* constantly does nothing and yet everything is being done" (*Tao-chang-wu-wei erh wu-pu-wei*).[9] That the *Tao* constantly does nothing means that the *Tao* does not impose itself on things: the *Tao* only moves of its own accord. This also means that all things come into being on their own accord. The constant nonaction of the *Tao* is the ultimate cosmological principle of life-creativity and the only foundation for the evolution of the variety of life and the multitude of things. The nonaction of the *Tao* in this sense is an intrinsic principle of ultimate creativity; this intrinsic principle of ultimate creativity consists in an unlimitedness and an unlimitation of expression of life forms and life processes in a state of universal harmony and in a process of universal transformation.[10] In this ultimate sense of

creativity, there is no effort made by the *Tao*, and yet there is an infinite effect, achieving life-creativity. The ecological principle reaches its ultimate limit in the principle of *chang-wu-wei*. Hence, we can conceive of the principle of least effort with maximum effect as an approximation to the *tzu-jan* of the *Tao* on the human plane.

With this principle correctly understood, we can resolve the dilemma and predicament arising from civilization and knowledge. The Taoist questions the value of knowledge and civilization, since they lead to greed, lust, and evil (tricks and treachery) in human society. In the same spirit, we can question the value of science and technology. In resolving many problems of man, do science and technology create more problems for man? Do science and technology seem to lead man to a purely pessimistic future? The Taoistic criticism here is that without an understanding of the *Tao* it is indeed possible and necessary that knowledge and civilization, science and technology, will doom man to self-slavery and self-destruction. Man simply falls into the bondage of his own conceptual prison and becomes a victim of his own desires. The Taoistic criticism of *wu-wei* is supposed to awaken man to self-examination and self-doubt; in this way man is awakened to a quest for self-surpassing and self-overcoming in an understanding of the totality of reality and its secret of creativity through *wu-wei* and reversion (*fan*).[11] With this awakening, man can still proceed with his knowledge and civilization, science and technology, if he is able to neutralize and temper his intellectual and intellectualistic efforts with a sense of the *Tao*. This means that man has to develop knowledge and civilization, science and technology, not out of pace with his efforts to relate to things, other humans and himself. His knowledge and civilization, science and technology, have to contribute to his relating to and integrating with the world of his surroundings. To do this he has to keep pace with his own growth as a sentient moral being, having regard and respect for his own identity and dignity as well as the identity and dignity of other beings, including his fellow man. Furthermore, he has to use his knowledge and, hence, science and technology, in keeping with the order of things, with his best interests conceived and deferred in harmony with life and in preservation or promotion of universal creativity. He also has to closely follow the principle of least effort, if not the principle of no effort, with maximum effect, if not infinite effect in terms of life and creativity—preservation and promotion—for his intellectual/scientific/technological/organizational activities.

As man is part and parcel of the *Tao*, it is only when man loses the sense of the *Tao* and respect for the *Tao* in his actual life that man becomes alienated from the *Tao* and his activities become a means of self-alienation which will inevitably result in losing the true identity of man by way of self-destruction. This is the natural and spontaneous reaction of the *Tao* to the self-alienation of man in his intellectual/scientific/exploitative en-grossment and obsession with himself. Hence, the remedy for knowledge and civilization, or for science and technology, is not more knowledge and more civilization, or more science and more technology, but a constant relating and integrating of these with the *Tao*. To do so is to naturalize as well as humanize knowledge and civilization, science and technology. It is to make these a part of the *Tao*. Although knowledge and civilization, science and technology, are man's forms for the appropriation of nature (the *Tao*), these forms

should not remain apart: man should also let nature reappropriate them by integrating them into nature (the *Tao*). This is the essential point of an ethics of man's relation to the environment. To understand the *Tao* and to follow the *Tao* is the essence of the ethics of the environment; it is also the way to transform the artificiality and unnaturalness of knowledge and civilization, science and technology, into the spontaneity and naturalness of the *Tao*.

In light of this understanding, the conflict between the *Tao* and knowledge/civilization/science/technology can be resolved; the true ecology and life-creativity of nature can be restored with knowledge/civilization/science/technology. They can be seen as enhancing rather than obstructing, complementing rather than opposing, the actual spontaneity and harmony of the creativity of the *Tao*. This is the true wisdom of the Taoist critique of knowledge and civilization, science and technology. It is called *hsi-ming*, "hidden light," by Lao Tzu, and *liang-hsing*, "parallel understanding," by Chuang Tzu.[12] In this wisdom lies the most profound principle of both the ecology of nature and the ethics of the environment.

My second observation concerns the *Tao* as a process of the ramification and differentiation of the *ch'i*. Before I explain the meaning and reality of *ch'i* in Chinese philosophy, it is important to appreciate the significance of bringing in *ch'i* as an explanation of the depth structure and depth process of the environment. We have seen that the depth structure and depth process of the environment has been explained in terms of the *Tao* and its life-creativity (*sheng-sheng*). Even though this explanation is necessary in pinpointing the ontological being and becoming of the environment, it is not sufficient, on the one hand, to illuminate the dynamics and dialectics of the differentiation and ramifications of the *Tao* and, on the other hand, to manifest those dynamics and dialectics of the unification and integration of the *Tao*. In other words, there is a gap between the ontology of the *Tao* and the cosmology of the *Tao* which must be bridged.

It is when the *Tao* is seen in the form and activity of *ch'i* that this bridging takes place. It might be suggested that the *Tao* expresses itself in terms of three perspectives which result in three characterizations in the history of Chinese philosophy. The first perspective is derived from understanding the quality of the activity: it is the perspective of life-creativity as clearly formulated in the texts of the *I Ching*. This perspective has already been discussed above. The second perspective is derived from understanding the patterns of the activity: it is the perspective of the movement of internal spontaneity, reversion and return, as clearly formulated in the texts of the *Tao Te Ching* as well as those of the *Chuang Tzu*. In fact, a concentration on the patterns of the movement of the *Tao* may lead one to see the *Tao* in terms of principles and reasons. The Neo-Confucianist metaphysics of *li* ("principle") is a logical result of this development. This development also leads to an epistemology of the *Tao*. In both the ontology of the *Tao* (life-creativity) and epistemology of the *Tao* (principles of nonaction, etc.), the *Tao* is always conceived as a totality and a unity; the nature of the unity and totality of the *Tao* is stressed above all. In fact, the very concept of the *Tao* carries with it a reference to its unity and totality. Yet the *Tao* is as much a distribution and diversification of being and becoming as a unity and totality of being and becoming. Hence, we need another explanation of this former aspect of the *Tao* which will also serve the

purpose of cosmologizing the ontology and epistemology of the *Tao*. This is how the *Tao*-as-the-*ch'i* paradigm comes in. This is also how the concept of *ch'i* based on experience of the *Tao* as *ch'i* develops. We might therefore suggest that to understand environment in its depth meaning, one has to focus on both the totalistic and distributive aspects of the environment. Hence, one must focus on both the *Tao* as *tzu-jan* and the *Tao* as *ch'i*.

Another consideration with regard to the importance of the *Tao* as the *ch'i* is that whereas the *Tao* focuses on reality as a passage of dynamic processes, the *ch'i* focuses on reality as a presence of material—stuff which leads to an actualization of things and the concretization of events. Hence, for understanding the formation and transformation of the environment in its substantive structure, one has to understand *ch'i*. It is in understanding *ch'i* that one can see and grasp the subtleties of the environment *vis-à-vis* human beings. It is only on this basis (i.e., understanding the *Tao* as *ch'i*) that one is capable of formulating an ethics of the environment or an ethics of the *Tao* toward the environment.[13] For this reason, we may consider the discussion of the nature of *ch'i* as constituting a metaphysical inquiry into the depth structure and depth process of the environment. As the goal of an ethics of the environment is to understand how human beings should relate to the environment *via* a true understanding of environment, we may see how a metaphysical inquiry into the structure and process of the environment also constitutes a teleological inquiry into the nature of the environment in relation to man. It is only when we are able to understand the nature of the environment in its true identity that we are able to see what the end-values of our thinking about and acting toward the environment are. The end-values are provided by our understanding of reality: to act in accordance with reality and our true nature will be our end and ultimately will be the criterion of value. . . .

NOTES

1. Cf. Ernest Weekley, *An Etymological Dictionary of Modern English* (New York: Dover, 1967), p. 516 (*environ*), p. 1583 (*veer*).
2. *Sheng-sheng* is derived from the Great Appendix of the *I Ching*, sec. 5, where it is said that "*Sheng-sheng* is called the change." "*Pu-yi*" is derived from the *Book of Poetry* in "Chou Sung," where it is said that "The mandate of Heaven is indeed profound and incessant (*pu-yi*)." This stanza is quoted in *Chung Yung* to describe the depth and width of the reality of Heaven and Earth. It is quite clear that the incessant activity of life-creativity is precisely what the *Tao* is. As a life-experience based concept of reality, *Tao* was universally conceived by ancient philosophers as a universal process of change and transformation as well as the fountainhead of all forms of life in the world. Therefore, *Tao* can be said to be the in-depth foundation, background, and context of the so-called environment for any sentient being. We shall see a more metaphysical consideration of the *Tao* in the writings of Lao Tzu.
3. When I use the word *objectified,* I mean "being treated as an object"; when I use the word *mechanized*, I mean "being used merely as a machine"; when I use the word *rigidified*, I mean "being placed in the state of *rigor mortis*"; and when I use the word *de-enlivened,* I mean "being depleted of life and the living process"; when I use the word *dehumanized*, I mean "being given no consideration of human feeling and care"; finally, when I use the word *de-environmentalized*, I mean "being devalued as environment."
4. *Analects*, 15: 28.
5. *Chuang Tzu*, Chi Wu Lun.
6. See the Chih Pei Yu chapter of *Chuang Tzu*.
7. *Tao Te Ching*, 25.
8. *Ecology* originally meant the economy of nature; when nature acts, it acts ecologically. The production of life and all things in nature can be said to come from the ecological movement of nature. In understanding the ecology of nature, one would naturally understand the *Tao*, but only when one independently sees the universality, unity, and life-creativity of the *Tao*, will one truly understand the ecology of nature. Hence,

the *Tao* can be said to be the metaphysical foundation of the ecology of nature, whereas the ecology of nature is one principle of movement manifesting the *Tao*, corresponding to its spontaneity.

9. Cf. *Tao Te Ching*, 37.
10. This principle can be indeed expressed as the following equivalence: *cheng-wu-wei = tzu-jan = sheng-sheng = wu-pu-wei,* i.e., the constant self-restraining of externality = spontaneity = life-creativity = the natural harmony of all things.
11. *Jan* ("reversion") refers to the fact that the *Tao* reverses what is done against the nature of things. But *jan* is also *fu* ("return"). If things are done according to their nature and of their own accord, things will return to their origin and their identity will be recurrently assured. See the distinction in the context of the *Tao Te Ching*, 40. "Reversion is the movement of the *Tao*," 25, "The distance is the reversion," and 16. "All ten thousand things take place concurrently. I observe their recurrence (*fu*) (*via* their origin)."
12. Cf. *Tao Te Ching* 2; *Chuang Tzu*, Chi W'u Lun.
13. *Tao Te Ching*, 14.

EDITOR'S NOTES

*Internal link or internal life to oneself and Nature (p. 154) Just as the blind person can move about her walking stick as easily as she does other natural parts of the body after some practice, as the cook ceases to handle the ox as a mere object when he grows familiar with the anatomic nuances of the animal, or as the student driver comes to regard the vehicle as his physical extension after he becomes inured to its temper, the same relationship of embodied spontaneity (*tzu-jan*) is expressed in the internal life of *Tao*. There is no grand mastermind (for example, like the Christian God) that deliberately and consciously plants, but, nonetheless, the bees help spread the pollen and initiate new cycles of life. There is no one that deliberately nourishes but yet the carcasses and the excrement of animals provide the necessary nutrients for vegetation which in turn feeds other animate forms of life. The ecology is maintained spontaneously in such manner as manifested in the *Tao*. Unfortunately, however, modern science has wreaked havoc to the human person's spontaneity by instilling a worldview that treats person and nature as objects to be used, mastered, and subdued, and thereby alienates the individual both from himself and nature. Human beings have been made to relate to themselves and nature as awkwardly as the individual who first learns to drive a vehicle or to use a walking stick or to swim. To restore human beings' original spontaneity then, one must get in touch with this internal life of *Tao* as spontaneity.

**The Principle of Least Effort with Maximum Effect (p. 155) Cook Ting's skills best exemplify the principle of least effort with maximum effect operating as *Tao*. By guiding the knife through the most vulnerable parts of the animal's anatomy, Ting is able to conserve his energy as well as minimize the wear and tear on the blade while achieving maximum results. The same is true for *Tao*. Our ecology is maintained in perfect balance without anyone deliberately seeking to maximize the results with the minimum given input, yet it makes use of the bees as medium for pollination and the carcasses of animals as nutrients for other vegetation. Everything is conserved for the maximum benefit of nature. (It must be borne in mind that the principle of least effort with maximum effect must not be equated with the principle of selection advanced by Darwin, the competitive spirit of whose biological framework cannot depart more from the Taoist predisposition for harmony and interdependency. Moreover, it must be remembered that a Taoist is not necessarily opposed to technology, insofar as technology can be reembodied into the human and natural environment to express the original spontaneity as manifested in Tao, for instance designing tools that are more "ergonomically correct.")

Environmental Racism, American Indians, and Monitored Retrievable Storage Sites for Radioactive Waste

Shari Collins-Chobanian

Shari Collins-Chobanian is a professor of philosophy at Arizona State University West in Phoenix. She is coeditor of the first and second editions of this anthology and has written on environmental rights, risk analysis, and harms imposed by technology.

Collins-Chobanian addresses the controversial topic of environmental racism. She provides a brief history of how American Indians have been victims of environmental racism. American Indians have been affected by the generation and handling of radioactive waste and are now targeted for the storage of radioactive waste. She argues that this targeting is ethically unjustified.

> I see no reason why those who use lethal methods of going about their business, who knowingly impose on others significant risk of death by radiation-related cancers—by poisoning from slow-seeping chemical wastes, from poisons emitted into air and water—should not be dealt with in the same way and in the same place as we deal with those who, for gain, send poisoned chocolates to their elderly relatives.
>
> —Annette Baier[1]

Many people have claimed that the poor in general, and minorities in particular are not concerned with the quality of their environment, and will not be until they have achieved a certain economic status after their more basic and pressing needs are met.[2] Recently, many people have challenged this claim, arguing that the polluted environment that many live in is an extension of oppression, and bringing empirical evidence to bear regarding what is known as environmental racism. There is a growing body of evidence that confirms the charge that minority communities are targeted for the location of hazardous waste storage, incinerators, and chemical corporations. There is further evidence that where environmental harm has been established, the federal government does not provide the same protection to minority communities as it does to predominantly white communities.

According to Benjamin F. Chavis, Jr. the term "environmental racism" was coined in 1982 in Warren County, NC, a mostly

African-American community where residents were struggling to prevent a PCB landfill.[3] Environmental racism is defined as

> racial discrimination in environmental policymaking . . . in the enforcement of regulation and laws . . . in the deliberate targeting of communities of color for toxic waste disposal and the siting of polluting industries . . . [and] in the official sanctioning of the life-threatening presence of poisons and pollutants in communities of color.[4]

Awareness of environmental racism has sparked the environmental justice movement. People in this movement are trying to protect areas, especially communities of color, that have become environmental "sacrifice zones." American Indian lands are thought to be one such sacrifice zone. While the phenomenon of environmental racism has recently received much attention within minority, environmental, legal, and academic circles, much of the attention is focused on groups other than American Indians.

The purpose of this paper is to extend the philosophical discussion on environmental racism to include American Indians. American Indians have been harmed by radioactive waste from the generation (mining and milling) and handling of radioactive waste, and have been specifically targeted for the storage of our country's waste via monitored retrievable storage (MRS) site applications. I conclude, especially in light of the past harms in generation and handling of radioactive waste, that the targeting of American Indians for MRS sites is ethically unjustified, even if there is the appearance of consent to the MRS site. Without authentic voluntariness and informedness, this consent to these sites on American Indian land is unjustified.

AMERICAN INDIANS, RADIOACTIVE WASTE, AND THE ENVIRONMENT

The Four Corners region has the largest concentration of American Indians in the United States and includes the Diné (Navajo), and Zuni tribes. Shiprock, New Mexico is in the Four Corners area. In Shiprock, uranium tailings[5] were left from Kerr-McGee's uranium mining. By 1980, 133 of the 150 Navajo uranium miners that worked at the site (beginning in 1952), were either dead or sick from radiation. During operation, Kerr-McGee did not enforce standard safety measures and this resulted in radiation levels in the mining shafts reaching 90 times the level considered "safe."[6] At the Shiprock site, and in the communities downstream along the San Juan watershed, these radiation levels have resulted in an increase in birth defects and disease which result from radiation exposure.[7] Further, seventy-one acres of "raw" tailings were abandoned at the Shiprock site when Kerr-McGee left in 1980, and this waste is 60 feet from the San Juan River, the major water source for people in the area. As has subsequently been established in the Shiprock area, Navajo birth defects were "two to eight times as high as the national average," and "Microcephaly occurred at fifteen times the normal rate."[8] The Shiprock area is now thoroughly contaminated by radiation and sections have been targeted for a national nuclear waste dump.[9]

There is as yet, no permanent storage facility for the disposal of radioactive waste. There is currently a permanent repository being built in Nevada, on seized Western Shoshone land. However, this site is of questionable geologic safety, the facility is over budget, past the projected deadline, and is opposed by the majority of

Nevadans. Meanwhile, the federal government has, for more than a decade, been seeking MRS sites to store high-level radioactive waste until a permanent repository is available. At first this search was not focused on any particular group. Then the search narrowed and the DOE (Department of Energy) targeted American Indian tribes by offering them 100,000 dollars to apply for an MRS site, and claimed among other things that American Indian ties to the land and cultural longevity suited them for the stewardship of this waste. One such claim was made by David H. Leroy, a United States "Nuclear Waste Negotiator" who said, "With atomic facilities designed to safely hold radioactive materials with half-lives of thousands of years, *it is the native American culture and perspective that is best designed to correctly consider and balance the benefits and burdens of these proposals.*"[10] The Council of Energy Resource Tribes has also held joint government, industry, and tribal conference that were designed to identify tribal practices that could be utilized to build consent to MRS sites.[11]

The above cases concerning the nuclear industry and radioactive waste appear to be examples of environmental racism. I see Kerr-McGee's disregard of safety standards for the Navajo miners (the standards were enforced at other facilities) as an illustration of racial discrimination in the enforcement of environmental regulation, and thus as environmental racism. While I also see the federal government's targeting American Indians for waste storage as the "targeting communities of color for toxic waste disposal" as well as "the official sanctioning of the life-threatening presence of poisons and pollutants in communities of color" and thus as environmental racism, this is still being debated.

Regarding this debate, I will consider two possible arguments for defending the tribal MRS site application process. In the first, sovereignty and the tribes' right to consent to MRS sites is the focus. Tribes, as sovereign entities, have the legal and ethical right to make decisions without outside interference, and can therefore consent to MRS facilities, even if these facilities place the tribes and their cultural base, land, at risk. In the second, the MRS applications are seen as offers of economic development extended to groups that are in need of such development, and these groups, in weighing the options, can thus consent to the risks involved in MRS sites. However, before turning to these arguments, I need to address a challenge that is often raised against the general claim of environmental racism. This challenge asserts that what is called environmental racism is, at the most, environmental classism.

WHY ENVIRONMENTAL RACISM IS NOT REDUCIBLE TO CLASSISM

One challenge to the claim of environmental racism is that it is not racism, but classism. The argument proceeds by asserting that polluted communities of color that are provided as examples of environmental racism are, more importantly, poor and politically powerless communities. The reason that these areas are targeted is because the land there is inexpensive and not because the areas are populated by people of color.[12] That is, economic reasons provide the overriding explanation for the dumps and location of manufacturing facilities, not race.

While there is an element of classism in the cases of environmental racism, these cases cannot be reduced to classism.

Racism often persists even when people of color are wealthy. Examples are myriad, from the manner in which African-Americans are treated when buying cars, homes, and insurance (there is a well-known "black tax" that is levied, i.e., a higher price than whites would pay) to the manner in which African-American celebrities are discriminated against even though they have money. That is, racism is not reducible to classism.

Further evidence is provided by the statistical significance of race that has been illuminated in many national reports. The United States General Accounting Office issued a report in 1983 that covered eight Southeastern states. The report found that 75% of offsite commercial hazardous and toxic waste landfills were in African-American and other minority communities, while these minorities make up only 20% of the population there. The report further showed that 60% of Hispanic and African-Americans live in areas with uncontrolled toxic waste sites. Ten years later, in September, 1992, *The National Law Journal* published the results of a special investigation of "the racial divide in environmental law." Their investigation found that:

> Penalties under hazardous waste laws at sites having the greatest white population were about 500 percent higher than penalties at sites with the greatest minority population. . . . The disparity under the toxic waste law occurs by race alone, not income.[13]

Additionally, Superfund cleanup of abandoned sites in minority areas takes 20% longer to be placed on the priority list than those in white neighborhoods, and action at the Superfund sites begins 12%–42% later at minority sites. Given the preceding, the challenge that environmental racism is really a matter of environmental classism will not prevail. Racial bias in environmental policy is not reducible to classism. I now turn to the arguments of sovereignty and economic development that can be advanced against the charge of environmental racism in the MRS sitings.

SOVEREIGNTY AND CONSENT

As established under the Indian Reorganization Act of 1934, American Indian Nations are sovereign. Sovereign status acknowledges a tribe's autonomy, and entails the legal and ethical right to self-determination, and to be free from external control. As discussed above, the government has an interest in acquiring MRS sites until a permanent repository is secured. Although MRS sites are "temporary" in that the waste is to be transferred to a permanent site eventually, once the utilities operating the nuclear power plants transfer the waste, they will be relieved of title and liability for the waste they generated. It will then become the tribes' legal and environmental responsibility. Twenty-nine tribes and counties applied for the grants but most dropped out. Two tribes that did not withdraw are the Mescalero Apache tribe and Ft. McDermitt tribe.[14]

The first argument defends the MRS application process by asserting that while American Indians have been encouraged to apply for MRS sites, it is not because of race. Rather the initial 100,000 dollars, and subsequent increased amounts, constitute offers to apply that were open to any community. Unlike cases of imposed dump sites, the MRS sites will not actualize on tribal land without consent of the tribes. Sovereignty, expressed in voluntary, informed consent, provides a prima facie justification for the tribes assuming the liability of radioactive waste.

Because consent is crucial to the above argument, an analysis of the justification for assuming risk(s) provided by voluntary, informed consent is necessary. The standard justification for a person risking harm to himself or herself is that he or she gives explicit, voluntary, and informed consent to that risk. Informed consent, while derived from medical malpractice caselaw, is a general legal and ethical principle that maintains a person's autonomy in ensuring that she is able to decided what risks she will take, because in deciding, she is able to weigh the risks against the benefits.

The following conditions are necessary for informed consent: all known existing relevant information regarding the risk(s) must be disclosed; the information disclosed must be understood; the risk must be undertaken voluntarily; the risk-taker(s) must be competent to decide; and the risk-taker(s) must consent to the risk.[15] If the above conditions are met, the necessary, although not sufficient, criteria for justifying the explicit assumption of a risk are met. I will briefly address the necessity of each of these criteria, and why they are not sufficient to justify assumption of a risk.

The first criterion, disclosure, places a duty on those seeking consent to provide available information. Without all known existing relevant information, an agent will not have the data necessary to make an authentic choice between accepting or rejecting the action and its risk(s). The second criterion, that the information be understood, also places a duty on those providing the information to ensure that what is provided is understood. This prevents a perfunctory disclosure that meets the first criterion in a legalistic sense, and places a duty on those providing the infor-

mation to impart it in a language and in terms that are understood by the audience. The third criterion of voluntariness is also necessary. For an agent's act to be his own, he must be able to act on his choice, and not be forced to act or restrained from acting by another person, group, or situation. Competence, the fourth criterion, is necessary for it involves the general state of mind of the agent, the ability of that agent to be held responsible for her decisions, and to be able to foresee that responsibility and the risks involved. Competence ensures that a person is not under the influence of a mind-altering substance, under an age competent to make the decision at hand, or unable to understand the issue(s). Competence is necessary for it involves the general state of mind of the agent, the ability of that agent to be held responsible for her decisions, and to be able to forsee that responsibility and risks involved. Consent is the final condition. Without the actual act of consent, the agent has done nothing more than be informed about risks and freely deliberated on them.

Each of the criteria for informed consent will vary along a continuum and need to be considered on a case by case basis. That is, there is not an a priori point at which each criterion can be said to have been fulfilled. However, this variability does not diminish the necessity of each condition being met.

While the above discussion focuses on a single agent giving informed consent, groups can also meet these criteria and give informed consent to an action that risks harm to their group and community. The decision-making procedure will most likely involve group dialogue and an agreed-upon mechanism for making decisions. Issues concerning who will be competent to take part in the dialogue, and issues concerning varying degrees of comprehension within the group will need to be considered on a case by case basis. What will count as consent, whether it is unanimity, majority consent, or some other measure, will also have to be decided in context. What will not vary is that the criteria will need to be met in both individual and group situations. The five conditions remain necessary in order to ensure the autonomy that informed consent is required to secure.

However, authentic informed consent is not sufficient for an agent or a group to undertake a risk, for the conditions of informed consent can be met while violating a more important moral issue. Such issues include harm to others, the degree of harmful effects risked, and whether the risks undertaken are reasonable. While autonomy is an important moral value and is maximized by ensuring informed consent, when there are competing claims of autonomy they cannot be decided by appeal to informed consent, but must be adjudicated in the broader social arena.

In addition, inherent in risk-taking is the notion that there is a benefit from taking the risk.[16] Based on the above discussion, to justify exposure to radioactive waste, those exposed would need to consent freely to the risks after being adequately informed, fully comprehend the risks being taken, be competent to make the decision, and benefit from this risk-taking in a manner that was proportionate to the risk.[17]

The Mescalero Apache tribe, located in Mescalero, New Mexico, has applied for, and received, a final grant of about $3 million to study their land for an MRS site.[18] Wendell Chino, the tribal council president, has tribal constitutional power to negotiate with the federal government on behalf of the tribe without being required to obtain

explicit tribal consent. Thus, there is apparent consent via Chino's pursuit on behalf of the Mescalero Apache tribe to an MRS site. However, there is also opposition in the tribe, although it is subdued. Harlyn Geronimo, a tribal member, claims that 70 percent of the tribe is opposed and that more would be if they understood the issues.[19] Francie Magoosh, also a tribal member, claims that 95% of the tribe is opposed.[20] Another tribe, the Ft. McDermitt tribe, on the Nevada and Oregon border, has also advanced in the site application process and is in the second stage. Their constitution requires more democratic participation, but it has been disregarded by the tribe's chairperson.[21] It is important to remember that as sovereign entities, tribes can adopt their own constitutions, including bestowing power that does not require the tribal leader to obtain informed consent on every issue.

I heartily agree that, given sovereign status, tribes have the legal and ethical right to negotiate with the federal government, to make decisions free from outside interference, and to consent to risks. However, especially in light of harm from the radioactive waste left from mining and milling, it is to necessary ensure that sovereignty does not bypass the process of informed consent. Given the magnitude of risks associated with waste, the justification of informed consent is necessary for the argument advanced in favor of MRS application. Thus, while sovereignty provides a prima facie justification, informed consent may be absent in a sovereign's decision, and if informed consent is absent, the justification is called into question.

Thus, one criterion for informed consent, informedness is called into question by the apparent lack of authentic participation by most of the tribe in the decision-making process. Informedness is further called into question by a lack of tribal education about nuclear waste. A lack of education is relevant to comprehension of the risks at issue, the options available, and the transfer of the responsibility for the waste. There are many points that illustrate the magnitude of the risks from radioactive waste. For example, if the waste is stored at the generation point, it is, compared to alternatives, cost-efficient, has an established record, and does not require the creation of further risks by transporting the waste. Moreover, an MRS facility on American Indian lands exempts waste manufacturers from liability of harm and transfers the burden from those who in some sense benefitted from generation of the waste, to those who did not. It is important to keep in mind that much of this waste has a hazardous life of 240,000 plus years.

The tribes targeted are mostly non-technical communities and lack knowledge of the full range of harms that nuclear technology and its waste impose. On most levels we all do. This lack of technical knowledge is intensified by the fact that many American Indians may be suspicious of what information is presented to them, especially in light of hundreds of years of lies, broken treaties and promises. Although the tribes are sovereign and can justifiably enter into negotiations, consent of tribal members remains crucial to the justification for MRS siting, and consent was compromised by the lack of informedness. In addition, their criterion of voluntariness is also problematic, as I argue below.

ECONOMIC DEVELOPMENT

According to the 1990 United States Census, American Indians constitute less than 1 percent of the population, yet make up 30.9 percent of those who live in poverty. In contrast, whites constitute more than 80 percent of the population, and only have 9.8 percent living at the poverty level. Unemployment is also a serious problem on the reservations. For example, the Ft. McDermitt Tribe had an 80 percent unemployment rate in 1993, and, this is not atypical of reservation statistics.[22] MRS site applications can therefore be defended as offers of economic development extended to groups that are in need of economic benefits that could alleviate poverty. It can be argued that as long as these tribes provide voluntary, informed consent to the risks associated with MRS sites, in exchange for economic benefit, that this is justifiable economic development and not environmental racism. I will first turn to the issue of economic development.

Far from being a self-evident justification for assuming risks, economic duress compromises voluntary consent. Voluntariness is called into question when the lack of money and jobs provides few to no alternatives to the dangerous proposal of storing unwanted waste. The lack of authentic choices is evident in the following quote:

> Garbage and hazardous waste firms are all too aware of the fact that the majority of reservations, which are governed by sovereign tribal leaders, are void of strict environmental regulations and the technical personnel to properly oversee such facilities. They are also keenly aware that many tribes, often faced with unemployment rates of 80 percent or higher, are desperate for both jobs and capital.[23]

The dilemma is that the closer one is to necessity to consent out of duress, the further one is from the voluntary consent being sought to justify the action. The more one does not appear to have a choice and is in a situation where one must "accept the risks associated with this radioactive waste or remain well below the poverty level," the more difficult it will be to arrive at voluntary consent.

As discussed above, the federal government has targeted American Indian communities through national conferences concerning MRS sites held for American Indians, through attempts to foster consent to the sites on tribal land, through the 100,000 dollar application bonuses, and through claims that American Indians are particularly suited for stewardship of the waste. If the sites were to provide economic development, why were other similar groups not courted? For example, Hispanics account for almost one-third of those living at the poverty level in the United States, yet Hispanic communities have not been the target of these applications. Thus, economic need does not appear to be the overarching factor for site applications. In addition, poor, white communities were not encouraged to negotiate for MRS sites. The defense of economic development devoid of environmental racism, like the above claim of sovereignty and consent, therefore will not prevail.

One final note regarding these sites. Even if MRS sites did provide relief from economic duress, they may be a myopic solution since the health risks could preclude all benefits hoped for. Minorities in general, and American Indians in particular (American Indians as a group have the lowest per capita income in the United States) suffer from a lack of iron, calcium, and zinc, among other nutritional deficiencies, and are therefore at a higher risk from exposure to toxic waste, and have less access to health care.[24] Therefore, the risk to these populations is even higher than it is to the majority population. This should, at least, lead to a discussion in the broad-er social area concerning the degree of harm that is risked, as well as the reasonableness of the risks themselves. It may be that there are many options that could be taken to improve the economic situation that do not carry the serious risks that accepting an MRS site entail.

CONCLUSION

The above concerns over voluntariness and informedness call the issue of American Indian consent to MRS sites into question. The racist history of this country, from European contact forward, has firmly established groups that suffer disproportionately from poverty and all of its accompanying ills. The imposition of environmental racism further extends this disproportionate suffering. To further burden American Indians with the "offer" to "benefit" from an MRS site, is unjustified.

Perhaps American Indians accepting MRS sites could be justified if there were truly no other options. However, the lack of options is an empirical question that entails a very broad picture where all possible measure have been taken to ensure the exhaustion of such possibilities. With the inequalities in wealth, nutrition, health care, education, political power, and economic resources that exist between corporate and governmental interests and minorities, advocating a deadly economic "solution" of storing toxic waste to meet needs that have been created through a racist history is unjustifiable.

Rather, the preferred solution is to end the production and resultant dumping of these hazardous wastes. In cases where this is not possible, then those who benefit from the production of this waste should bear the burden of storage and the resultant risks in a nontransferable manner. Furthermore, those who benefited from past generation of hazardous waste, and transferred those burdens, should be required to take responsibility for the harms that have occurred, and those that continue to occur in the communities such as those in the Shiprock area.

NOTES

1. Annette Baier, "Poisoning the Wells," in *Values at Risk*, Douglas MacLean, editor, (Totowa: Rowan & Allanheld, 1986), p. 64.
2. See William K. Reilly, "The Green Thumb of Capitalism: The Environmental Benefits of Sustainable Growth," *Policy Review*, Fall 1990.
3. Five hundred protesters were arrested, and the protesters saw the authorities' behavior as another instance of institutionalized racism many had encountered in the past. The institutional racism many had experienced in the past included discrimination by law enforcement, in housing, in education, and in employment. Benjamin Chavis, Jr., in the foreword to *Confronting Environmental Racism: Voices from the Grassroots*, Robert D. Bullard, editor, (Boston: South End Press, 1993), p. 3.
4. Chavis, from Bullard, 1993, p. 3.
5. "Uranium   tailings—contain   dangerously radioactive radium, radon gases, and 'radon daughters'—short-lived radionuclides produced as the radon in the ore decays into lead. 'Radon daughters' are dangerous because they attach themselves to dust particles which can be inhaled. Once lodged in the lung tissue, these particles emit intense alpha radiation, which can damage the surrounding cells and eventually cause lung cancer and other respiratory disease." Leslie J. Freeman, *Nuclear Witnesses: Insiders Speak Out*, (New York: W. W. Norton & Company, 1981), pp. 140–141. There are over 70,000,000 tons of radioactive tailings in New Mexico alone.
6. In addition, Kerr-McGee paid the Navajo miners 2/3 the standard rate for uranium miners.
7. Ward Churchill and Winona LaDuke, "The Political Economy of Radioactive Colonialism," in *The State of Native America*, M. Annette Jaimes, editor, (Boston: South End Press, 1992), p. 248. See also J. M. Samet, et al., "Uranium Mining and Lung Cancer in Navajo Men," *New England Journal of Medicine*, No. 310, 1984, pp. 1481–1484; and Ward Churchill, *Struggle for the*

Land: Indigenous Resistance to Genocide, Ecocide, and Expropriation in Contemporary North America, (Monroe, ME: Common Courage Press, 1993).
8. Quoted in Churchill and LaDuke, Op. Cit., p. 264. From an unpublished paper presented at the May 25, 1984 American Association of Atomic Scientists symposium in New York, "Outcome of 13,300 Navajo Births from 1964–1981 in the Shiprock Uranium Mining Area," by Laura Mangum Shields and Alan B. Goodman.
9. There are many other examples of environmental racism on American Indian land. The Kerr-McGee Sequoyah Fuels Facility lies within the Cherokee nation in Oklahoma. From accidental leaks, as well as intentional use of radioactive waste for "fertilizer," radioactive contamination has spread into water supplies. See Hans Baer, "Kerr-McGee and the NRC: From Indian Country to Silkwood to Gore," *Soc. Sci. Med.*, Vol. 30, No. 2, 1990, pp. 237–248. In 1991, the *St. Louis Post-Dispatch* reported that in the two previous years, more than 50 tribes had been approached by toxic waste companies. See Bill Lambrecht, "Broken Trust" series, *St. Louis Post-Dispatch*, November, 1991. The fact that these companies approach American Indians for waste sites, and not white communities, (poor or affluent), lends further weight to the intentional racism claimed in cases of environmental racism.
10. David H. Leroy, "Federalism on Your Terms: An Invitation for Dialogue, Government to Government," in a speech given to the National Congress of American Indians, San Francisco, December 4, 1991, quoted in Erickson and Chapman, Op. Cit., 1994, p. 3. (emphasis mine)
11. J. A. A. Hernandez, "How the Feds Push Nuclear Waste onto Indian Lands," *SF Weekly*, September 23, Vol XI, No. 30, 1992, cited in Jon D. Erickson and Duane Chapman, "Sovereignty for Sale: Nuclear Waste in Indian Country," *Akwe:kon Journal: A Journal of Indigenous Issues*, Fall, 1993, pp. 8, 10.
12. Some people further argue that minorities move into these neighborhoods because of lower prices, thus the areas were already polluted, and not targeted because of race. For an excellent analysis of this issue and evidence of targeted expansion, see James T. Hamilton, "Testing for Environmental Racism: Prejudice, Profits, Political Power?," in *Journal of Policy Analysis and Management*, Vol. 14, No. 1, 1995, pp. 107–132. Hamilton argues that the targeting is due to the perception of political powerlessness. However, this is intricately tied to race.
13. "Unequal Protection: The Racial Divide in Environmental Law," *The National Law*

Journal, Vol. 15, No. 3, September 21, 1992, p. S2.

14. See Jon D. Erickson and Duane Chapman, "Sovereignty for Sale: Nuclear Waste in Indian Country," *Akwe:kon Journal: A Journal of Indigenous Issues,* Fall, 1993, pp. 3–10; and Ronald Eagleye Johnny, "Showing Respect for Tribal Law: Siting a Nuclear Waste MRS Facility," *Akwe:kon Journal,* Spring 1994, pp. 16-27.

15. This is drawn from Ruth R. Faden and Tom L. Beauchamp, *A History and Theory of Informed Consent,* (New York: Oxford University Press, 1986).

16. For a discussion of the principle of commensurate burdens and benefit, see Peter Wenz, "Just Garbage," in *Faces of Environmental Racism: Confronting Issues of Global Justice,* Laura Westra and Peter S. Wenz, editors, (Lanham, MD: Rowman & Littlefield Publishers, Inc., 1995), pp. 59–60.

17. Informed consent would provide a justification further assuming that the issue of MRS sites could be justified in broader social arena, as mentioned above.

18. See Matthew L. Wald, "Nuclear Storage Divides Apaches and Neighbors," *The New York Times,* November, 1993, p. 1.

19. Priscilla Feral and Betsy Smart, "Laying Waste: The Future of the Mescalero Apaches," in *Trial Lawyer,* September 1992, pp. 78–82.

20. Jon D. Erickson and Duane Chapman, "Sovereignty for Sale: Nuclear Waste in Indian Country," *Akwe:kon Journal: A Journal of Indigenous Issues,* Fall 1993, p. 8.

21. Ibid.

22. Ibid.

23. Senator Thomas Daschle, "Send Your Poisonous Garbage to the Sioux," *Christian Science Monitor,* February 1991.

24. From discussions with Karen Medville, an American Indian environmental toxicologist who studies environmental toxicology on American Indian lands.

Development, Ecology and Women

Vandana Shiva

Vandana Shiva, a philosopher, physicist, and environmental activist, is director of the Research Foundation for Science, Technology and Natural Resource Policy in Dehradun, India. She is the author of Staying Alive: Women, Ecology and Development *(1988).*

Shiva addresses Western development programs exported to the Third World. She argues from an ecofeminist perspective and contends that these development programs are really "maldevelopment" programs that either worsen, or introduce, patriarchal practices of dominating women and nature. Further, these programs displace people who live sustainably, wreak enormous environmental damage, and risk wholesale destruction of the regenerative abilities of ecosystems. She concludes that the solution is to recover the feminine principle which provides a redefinition of life that is linked to ecological sustainability.

DEVELOPMENT AS A NEW PROJECT OF WESTERN PATRIARCHY

'Development' was to have been a post-colonial project, a choice for accepting a model of progress in which the entire world remade itself on the model of the colonising modern west, without having to undergo the subjugation and exploitation that colonialism entailed. The assumption was that western style progress was possible for all. Development, as the improved well-being of all, was thus equated with the westernisation of economic categories—of needs, of productivity, of growth. Concepts and categories about economic development and natural resource utilisation that had emerged in the specific context of industri-

Reprinted with permission of Zed Books, from *Staying Alive: Women, Ecology and Development*, by Vandana Shiva, 1988.

alisation and capitalist growth in a centre of colonial power, were raised to the level of universal assumptions and applicability in the entirely different context of basic needs satisfaction for the people of the newly independent Third World countries. Yet, as Rosa Luxemberg has pointed out, early industrial development in western Europe necessitated the permanent occupation of the colonies by the colonial powers and the destruction of the local 'natural economy'.[1] According to her, colonialism is a constant necessary condition for capitalist growth: without colonies, capital accumulation would grind to a halt. 'Development' as capital accumulation and the commercialisation of the economy for the generation of 'surplus' and profits thus involved the reproduction not merely of a particular form of creation of wealth, but also of the associated creation of poverty and dispossession. A replication of economic development based on commercialisation of resource use for commodity production in the newly independent countries created the internal colonies.[2] Development was thus reduced to a continuation of the process of colonisation; it became an extension of the project of wealth creation in modern western patriarchy's economic vision, which was based on the exploitation or exclusion of women (of the west and non-west), on the exploitation and degradation of nature, and on the exploitation and erosion of other cultures. 'Development' could not but entail destruction for women, nature and subjugated cultures, which is why, throughout the Third World, women, peasants and tribals are struggling for liberation from 'development' just as they earlier struggled for liberation from colonialism.

The UN Decade for Women was based on the assumption that the improvement of women's economic position would automatically flow from an expansion and diffusion of the development process. Yet, by the end of the Decade, it was becoming clear that development itself was the problem. Insufficient and inadequate 'participation' in 'development' was not the cause for women's increasing underdevelopment; it was rather, their enforced but asymmetric participation in it, by which they bore the costs but were excluded from the benefits, that was responsible. Development exclusivity and dispossession aggravated and deepened the colonial processes of ecological degradation and the loss of political control over nature's sustenance base. Economic growth was a new colonialism, draining resources away from those who needed them most. The discontinuity lay in the fact that it was now new national elites, not colonial powers, that masterminded

the exploitation on grounds of 'national interest' and growing GNPs, and it was accomplished with more powerful technologies of appropriation and destruction.

Ester Boserup[3] has documented how women's impoverishment increased during colonial rule; those rulers who had spent a few centuries in subjugating and crippling their own women into de-skilled, de-intellectualised appendages, disfavoured the women of the colonies on matters of access to land, technology and employment. The economic and political processes of colonial under-development bore the clear mark of modern western patriarchy, and while large numbers of women and men were impoverished by these processes, women tended to lose more. The privatisation of land for revenue generation displaced women more critically, eroding their traditional land use rights. The expansion of cash crops undermined food production, and women were often left with meager resources to feed and care for children, the aged and the infirm, when men migrated or were conscripted into forced labor by the colonisers. As a collective document by women activists, organisers and researchers stated at the end of the UN Decade for Women, 'The almost uniform conclusion of the Decade's research is that with a few exceptions, women's relative access to economic resources, incomes and employment has worsened, their burden of work has increased, and their relative and even absolute health, nutritional and educational status has declined.'[4]

The displacement of women from productive activity by the expansion of development was rooted largely in the manner in which development projects appropriated or destroyed the natural resource base for the production of sustenance and survival. It destroyed women's productivity both by removing land, water and forests from their management and control, as well as through the ecological destruction of soil, water and vegetation systems so that nature's productivity and renewability were impaired. While gender subordination and patriarchy are the oldest of oppressions, they have taken on new and more violent forms through the project of development. Patriarchal categories which understand destruction as 'production' and regeneration of life as 'passivity' have generated a crisis of survival. Passivity, as an assumed category of the 'nature' of nature and of women, denies the activity of nature and life. Fragmentation and uniformity as assumed categories of progress and development destroy the living forces which arise from relationships within the 'web of life' and the diversity in the elements and patterns of these relationships.

The economic biases and values against nature, women and indigenous peoples are captured in this typical analysis of the 'unproductiveness' of traditional natural societies:

> Production is achieved through human and animal, rather than mechanical, power. Most agriculture is unproductive; human or animal manure may be used but chemical fertilizers and pesticides are unknown. . . . For the masses, these conditions mean poverty.[5]

The assumptions are evident: nature is unproductive; organic agriculture based on nature's cycles of renewability spells poverty; women and tribal and peasant societies embedded in nature are similarly unproductive, not because it has been demonstrated that in cooperation they produce *less* goods and services for needs, but because it is assumed that 'production'

takes place only when mediated by technologies for commodity production, even when such technologies destroy life. A stable and clean river is not a productive resource in this view: it needs to be 'developed' with dams in order to become so. Women, sharing the river as a commons to satisfy the water needs of their families and society are not involved in productive labor: when substituted by the engineering man, water management and water use become productive activities. Natural forests remain unproductive till they are developed into monoculture plantations of commercial species. Development thus, is equivalent to maldevelopment, a development bereft of the feminine, the conservation, the ecological principle. The neglect of nature's work in renewing herself, and women's work in producing sustenance in the form of basic, vital needs is an essential part of the paradigm of maldevelopment, which sees all work that does not produce profits and capital as non or unproductive work. As Maria Mies[6] has pointed out, this concept of surplus has a patriarchal bias because, from the point of view of nature and women, it is not based on material surplus produced *over and above* the requirements of the community: it is stolen and appropriated through violent modes from nature (who needs a share of her produce to reproduce herself) and from women (who need a share of nature's produce to produce sustenance and ensure survival).

From the perspective of Third World women, productivity is a measure of producing life and sustenance; that this kind of productivity has been rendered invisible does not reduce its centrality to survival— it merely reflects the domination of modern patriarchal economic categories which see only profits, not life.

MALDEVELOPMENT AS THE DEATH OF THE FEMININE PRINCIPLE

In this analysis, maldevelopment becomes a new source of male-female inequality. 'Modernisation' has been associated with the introduction of new forms of dominance. Alice Schlegel[7] has shown that under conditions of subsistence, the interdependence and complementarity of the separate male and female domains of work is the characteristic mode, based on diversity, not inequality. Maldevelopment militates against this equality in diversity, and superimposes the ideologically constructed category of western technological man as a uniform measure of the worth of classes, cultures and genders. Dominant modes of perception based on reductionism, duality and linearity are unable to cope with equality in diversity, with forms and activities that are significant and valid, even though different. The reductionist mind superimposes the roles and forms of power of western male-oriented concepts on women, all non-western peoples and even on nature, rendering all three 'deficient', and in need of 'development'. Diversity, and unity and harmony in diversity, become epistemologically unattainable in the context of maldevelopment, which then becomes synonymous with women's underdevelopment (increasing sexist domination), and nature's depletion (deepening ecological crises). Commodities have grown, but nature has shrunk. The poverty crisis of the South arises from the growing scarcity of water, food, fodder and fuel, associated with increasing maldevelopment and ecological destruction. This poverty crisis touches women most severely, first because they are the poorest among the poor, and then because, with nature, they are the primary sustainers of society.

Maldevelopment is the violation of the integrity of organic, interconnected and interdependent systems, that sets in motion a process of exploitation, inequality, injustice and violence. It is blind to the fact that a recognition of nature's harmony and action to maintain it are preconditions for distributive justice. This is why Mahatma Gandhi said, 'There is enough in the world for everyone's need, but not for some people's greed.'

Maldevelopment is maldevelopment in thought and action. In practice, this fragmented, reductionist, dualist perspective violates the integrity and harmony of man in nature, and the harmony between men and women. It ruptures the co-operative unity of masculine and feminine, and places man, shorn of the feminine principle, above nature and women, and separated from both. The violence to nature as symptomatised by the ecological crisis, and the violence to women, as symptomatised by their subjugation and exploitation arise from this subjugation of the feminine principle. I want to argue that what is currently called development is essentially maldevelopment, based on the introduction or accentuation of the domination of man over nature and women. In it, both are viewed as the 'other', the passive non-self. Activity, productivity, creativity which were associated with the feminine principle are expropriated as qualities of nature and women, and transformed into the exclusive qualities of man. Nature and women are turned into passive objects, to be used and exploited for the uncontrolled and uncontrollable desires of alienated man. From being the creators and sustainers of life, nature and women are reduced to being 'resources' in the fragmented, anti-life model of maldevelopment.

TWO KINDS OF GROWTH, TWO KINDS OF PRODUCTIVITY

Maldevelopment is usually called 'economic growth', measured by the Gross National Product. Porritt, a leading ecologist has this to say of GNP:

> *Gross* National Product —for once a word is being used correctly. Even conventional economists admit that the hey-day of GNP is over, for the simple reason that as a measure of progress, it's more or less useless. GNP measures the lot, all the goods and services produced in the money economy. Many of these goods and services are not beneficial to people, but rather a measure of just how much is going wrong; increased spending on crime, on pollution, on the many human casualties of our society, increased spending because of waste or planned obsolescence, increased spending because of growing bureaucracies: it's all counted.[8]

The problem with GNP is that it measures some costs as benefits (e.g. pollution control) and fails to measure other costs completely. Among these hidden costs are the new burdens created by ecological devastation, costs that are invariably heavier for women, both in the North and South. It is hardly surprising, therefore, that as GNP rises, it does not necessarily mean that either wealth or welfare increase proportionately. I would argue that GNP is becoming, increasingly, a measure of how real wealth—the wealth of nature and that produced by women for sustaining life—is rapidly decreasing. When commodity production as the prime economic activity is introduced as development, it destroys the potential of nature and women to produce life and goods and services for basic needs. More commodities and more cash mean less life—in nature (through ecological destruction) and in society (through denial of basic needs). Women are devalued first, because their work cooperates with nature's processes, and second, because work which satisfies needs and ensures sustenance is devalued in general. Precisely because more growth in maldevelopment has meant less sustenance of life and life-support systems, it is now imperative to recover the feminine principle as the basis for development which conserves and is ecological. Feminism as ecology, and ecology as the revival of Prakriti, the source of all life, become the decentred powers of political and economic transformation and restructuring.

This involves, first, a recognition that categories of 'productivity' and growth which have been taken to be positive, progressive and universal are, in reality, restricted patriarchal categories. When viewed from the point of view of nature's productivity and growth, and women's production of sustenance, they are found to be ecologically destructive and a source of gender inequality. It is no accident that the modern, efficient and productive technologies created within the context of growth in market economic terms are associated with heavy ecological costs, borne largely by women. The resource and energy intensive production processes they give rise to demand ever increasing resource withdrawals from the ecosystem. These withdrawals disrupt essential ecological processes and convert renewable resources into non-renewable ones. A forest for example, provides inexhaustible supplies of diverse biomass over time if its capital stock is maintained and it is harvested on a sustained yield basis. The heavy and uncontrolled demand for industrial and commercial wood, however, requires the continuous overfelling of trees which exceeds the regenerative capacity of the forest ecosystem, and eventually converts the forests into non-renewable resources. Women's work in the collection of water, fodder and fuel is thus rendered more energy and time-consuming. (In Garhwal, for example, I have seen women who originally collected fodder and fuel in a few hours, now travelling long distances by truck to collect grass and leaves in a task that might take up to two days.) Sometimes the damage to nature's intrinsic regenerative capacity is impaired not by over-exploitation of a particular resource but, indirectly, by damage caused to other related natural resources through ecological processes. Thus the excessive overfelling of trees in the catchment areas of streams and rivers destroys not only forest resources, but also renewable supplies of water, through hydrological destabilisation. Resource intensive industries disrupt essential ecological processes not only by their excessive demands for raw material, but by their pollution of air and water and soil. Often such destruction is caused by the resource demands of non-vital industrial products. Inspite of severe ecological crises, this paradigm continues to operate because for the North and for the elites of the South, resources continue to be available, even now. The lack of recognition of nature's processes for survival *as factors in the process of economic development* shrouds the political issues arising from resource transfer and resource destruction, and creates an ideological weapon for increased control over natural resources in the conventionally employed notion of productivity. All other costs of the economic process consequently become invisible. The forces which contribute to the increased 'productivity' of a modern farmer or factory worker for instance, come from the increased use of natural resources. Lovins has described this as the amount of 'slave' labor presently at work in the world.[9] According to him each person on earth, on an average, possesses the equivalent of about 50 slaves, each working a 40 hour week. Man's global energy conversion from all sources (wood, fossil fuel, hydroelectric power, nuclear) is currently approximately 8×10^{12} watts. This is more than 20 times the energy content of the food necessary to feed the present world population at the FAO standard diet of 3,600 cal/day. The 'productivity' of the western male compared to women or Third World peasants is not intrinsically superior; it is based on inequalities in the distribution of this 'slave' labor. The average inhabitant of the USA for example has 250 times more 'slaves' than the average Nigerian. 'If Americans were short of 249 of those 250 'slaves', one wonders how efficient they would prove themselves to be?'

It is these resource and energy intensive processes of production which divert resources away from survival, and hence from women. What patriarchy sees as productive work, is, in ecological terms highly destructive production. The second law of thermodynamics predicts that resource intensive and resource wasteful economic development must become a threat to the survival of the human species in the long run. Political struggles based on ecology in industrially advanced countries are rooted in this conflict between *long term survival options and short term over-production and over-consumption.* Political struggles of women, peasants and tribals based on ecology in countries like India are far more acute and urgent since they are rooted in the *immediate threat to the options for survival* for the vast majority of the people, *posed by resource intensive and resource wasteful economic growth* for the benefit of a minority.

In the market economy, the organising principle for natural resource use is the maximisation of profits and capital accumulation. Nature and human needs are managed through market mechanisms. Demands for natural resources are restricted to those demands registering on the market; the ideology of development is in large part based on a vision of bringing all natural resources into the market economy for commodity production. When these resources are already being used by nature to maintain her production of renewable resources and by women for sustenance and livelihood, their diversion to the market economy generates a scarcity condition for ecological stability and creates new forms of poverty for women.

TWO KINDS OF POVERTY

In a book entitled *Poverty: the Wealth of the People*[10] an African writer draws a distinction between poverty as subsistence, and misery as deprivation. It is useful to separate a cultural conception of subsistence living as poverty from the material experience of poverty that is a result of dispossession and deprivation. Culturally perceived poverty need not be real material poverty: subsistence economies which satisfy basic needs through self-provisioning are not poor in the sense of being deprived. Yet the ideology of development declares them so because they do not participate overwhelmingly in the market economy, and do not consume commodities produced for and distributed through the market *even though they might be satisfying those needs through self-provisioning mechanisms.* People are perceived as poor if they eat mil-

lets (grown by women) rather than commercially produced and distributed processed foods sold by global agri-business. They are seen as poor if they live in self-built housing made from natural material like bamboo and mud rather than in cement houses. They are seen as poor if they wear handmade garments of natural fibre rather than synthetics. Subsistence, as culturally perceived poverty, does not necessarily imply a low physical quality of life. On the contrary, millets are nutritionally far superior to processed foods, houses built with local materials are far superior, being better adapted to the local climate and ecology, natural fibres are preferable to man-made fibres in most cases, and certainly more affordable. This cultural perception of prudent subsistence living as poverty has provided the legitimisation for the development process as a poverty removal project. As a culturally biased project it destroys wholesome and sustainable lifestyles and creates real material poverty, or misery, by the denial of survival needs themselves, through the diversion of resources to resource intensive commodity production. Cash crop production and food processing take land and water resources away from sustenance needs, and exclude increasingly large numbers of people from their entitlements to food. 'The inexorable processes of agriculture-industrialisation and internationalisation are probably responsible for more hungry people than either cruel or unusual whims of nature. There are several reasons why the high-technology-export-crop model increases hunger. Scarce land, credit, water and technology are pre-empted for the export market. Most hungry people are not affected by the market at all. . . . The profits flow to corporations that have no interest in feeding hungry people without money.'[11]

The Ethiopian famine is in part an example of the creation of real poverty by development aimed at removing culturally perceived poverty. The displacement of nomadic Afars from their traditional pastureland in Awash Valley by commercial agriculture (financed by foreign companies) led to their struggle for survival in the fragile uplands which degraded the ecosystem and led to the starvation of cattle and the nomads.[12] The market economy conflicted with the survival economy in the Valley, thus creating a conflict between the survival economy and nature's economy in the uplands. At no point has the global marketing of agricultural commodities been assessed against the background of the new conditions of scarcity and poverty that it has induced. This new poverty moreover, is no longer cultural and relative: it is absolute, threatening the very survival of millions on this planet.

The economic system based on the patriarchal concept of productivity was created for the very specific historical and political phenomenon of colonialism. In it, the input for which efficiency of use had to be maximised in the production centres of Europe, was industrial labor. For colonial interest therefore, it was rational to improve the labour resource *even at the cost of wasteful use of nature's wealth.* This rationalisation has, however, been illegitimately universalised to all contexts and interest groups and, on the plea of increasing productivity, labour reducing technologies have been introduced in situations where labor is abundant and cheap, and resource demanding technologies have been introduced where resources are scarce and already fully utilised for the production of sustenance. Traditional economies with a stable ecology have shared with industrially advanced affluent economies the ability to use natural resources to satisfy basic vital needs. The former differ from the latter in two essential ways: first, the same needs are satisfied in industrial societies through longer technological chains requiring higher energy and resource inputs and excluding large numbers without purchasing power; and second, affluence generates new and artificial needs requiring the increased production of industrial goods and services. Traditional economies are not advanced in the matter of non-vital needs satisfaction, but as far as the satisfaction of basic and vital needs is concerned, they are often what Marshall Sahlins has called 'the original affluent society'. The needs of the Amazonian tribes are more than satisfied by the rich rainforest; their poverty begins with its destruction. The story is the same for the Gonds of Bastar in India or the Penans of Sarawak in Malaysia.

Thus are economies based on indigenous technologies viewed as 'backward' and 'unproductive'. Poverty, as the denial of basic needs, is not necessarily associated with the existence of traditional technologies, and its removal is not necessarily an outcome of the growth of modern ones. On the contrary, the destruction of ecologically sound traditional technologies, often created and used by women, along with the destruction of their material base is generally believed to be responsible for the 'feminisation' of poverty in societies which have had to bear the costs of resource destruction.

The contemporary poverty of the Afar nomad is not rooted in the inadequacies of traditional nomadic life, but in the *diversion of the productive pastureland of the Awash Valley.* The erosion of the resource base for survival is increasingly being caused by the demand for resources by the market economy, dominated by global forces. The creation of inequality through economic activity which is ecologically disruptive arises in two ways: first, inequalities in the distribution of privileges make for unequal access to natural resources—these include privileges of both a political and economic nature. Second, resource intensive production processes have access to subsidised raw material on which a substantial number of people, especially from the less privileged economic groups, depend for their survival. The consumption of such industrial raw material is determined purely by market forces, and not by considerations of the social or ecological requirements placed on them. The costs of resource destruction are externalised and unequally divided among various economic groups in society, but are borne largely by women and those who satisfy their basic material needs directly from nature, simply because they have no purchasing power to register their demands on the goods and services provided by the modern production system. Gustavo Esteva has called development a permanent war waged by its promoters and suffered by its victims.[13]

The paradox and crisis of development arises from the mistaken identification of culturally perceived poverty with real material poverty, and the mistaken identification of the growth of commodity production as better satisfaction of basic needs. In actual fact, there is less water, less fertile soil, less genetic wealth as a result of the development process. Since these natural resources are the basis of nature's economy and women's survival economy, their scarcity is impoverishing women and marginalised peoples in an unprecedented manner. Their new impoverishment lies in the fact that resources which supported

their survival were absorbed into the market economy while they themselves were excluded and displaced by it.

The old assumption that with the development process the availability of goods and services will automatically be increased and poverty will be removed, is now under serious challenge from women's ecology movements in the Third World, even while it continues to guide development thinking in centres of patriarchal power. Survival is based on the assumption of the sanctity of life; maldevelopment is based on the assumption of the sacredness of 'development'. Gustavo Esteva asserts that the sacredness of development has to be refuted because it threatens survival itself. 'My people are tired of development', he says, 'they just want to live.'[14]

The recovery of the feminine principle allows a transcendance and transformation of these patriarchal foundations of maldevelopment. It allows a redefinition of growth and productivity as categories linked to the production, not the destruction, of life. It is thus simultaneously an ecological and a feminist political project which legitimises the way of knowing and being that create wealth by enhancing life and diversity, and which deligitimises the knowledge and practise of a culture of death as the basis for capital accumulation.

NOTES

1. Rosa Luxemberg, *The Accumulation of Capital*, London: Routledge and Kegan Paul, 1951.
2. An elaboration of how 'development' transfers resources from the poor to the well-endowed is contained in J. Bandyopadhyay and V. Shiva, 'Political Economy of Technological Polarisations,' in *Economic and Political Weekly*, Vol. XVIII.

1982, pp. 1827–32; and J. Bandyopadhyay and V. Shiva, 'Political Economy of Ecology Movements', in *Economic and Political Weekly,* forthcoming.

3. Ester Boserup, *Womens Role in Economic Development*, London: Allen and Unwin, 1970.

4. Dawn, *Development Crisis and Alternative Visions: Third World Women's Perspectives*, Bergen: Christian Michelsen Institute, 1975, p. 21.

5. M. George Foster, *Traditional Societies and Technological Change*, Delhi: Allied Publishers, 1973.

6. Maria Mies, *Patriarchy and Accumulation on a World Scale*, London: Zed Books, 1986.

7. Alice Schlegel (ed.), *Sexual Stratification: A Cross-Cultural Study*, New York: Columbia University Press, 1977.

8. Jonathan Porritt, *Seeing Green*, Oxford: Blackwell, 1984.

9. A. Lovins, cited in S.R. Eyre, *The Real Wealth of Nations*, London: Edward Arnold, 1978.

10. R. Bahro, *From Red to Green*, London: Verso, 1984, p. 211.

11. R.J. Barnet, *The Lean Years*, London: Abacus, 1981, p. 171.

12. U.P. Koehn, 'African Approaches to Environmental Stress: A Focus on Ethiopia and Nigeria' in R.N. Barrett (ed.), *International Dimensions of the Environmental Crisis*, Boulder, CO: Westview, 1982, pp. 253–89.

13. Gustavo Esteva, 'Regenerating People's Space,' in S.N. Mendlowitz and R.B.J. Walker, *Towards a Just World Peace: Perspectives From Social Movements*, London: Butterworths and Committee for a Just World Peace, 1987.

14. G. Esteva, Remarks made at a Conference of the Society for International Development, Rome, 1985.

QUESTIONS: ENVIRONMENTAL ETHICS

1. Leopold poses a challenge to agricultural practices that are considered advances by claiming that these practices are "improvements in the pump, rather than the well." Explain this quote and the cleavage it illustrates. In light of the land ethic, especially the duty to preserve the integrity and stability of the ecosystem, how is this priming of the pump harmful to the environment?

2. Baxter argues that the only normative definition of pollution is in relation to man's needs. Why does he argue that an "optimal state of pollution" and not a clean environment should be our objective? In light of Leopold's essay, can such firm lines be drawn between humans and non-humans?

3. Callicott argues that the American Indian world views hold wisdom relevant to contemporary environmental ethics. Do you agree? How can this wisdom be practical in our society when we hold such radically different values?

4. Cheng discusses how the *Tao* is applicable to our ecological understanding of the environment. How does he advocate that understanding the *Tao* (and living that understanding) will save us from the self-slavery in which our technology and greed have placed us?

5. Collins-Chobanian argues that the targeting of American Indian lands for MRS sites, even if there is apparent consent, is unjustified. Briefly explain her argument. If consent to these sites were not compromised, would the siting be justified?

6. Shiva distinguishes between two kinds of poverty. What are the two types of poverty? Drawing from the entire essay, provide an argument that outlines the benefits of subsistence, especially in relation to how this would avoid harm to women and the environment. Why are people in undeveloped countries, living at subsistence level, perceived as poor?

SUPPLEMENTARY READINGS: ENVIRONMENTAL ETHICS

AMES, ROGER T. "Taoism and the Nature of Nature." *Environmental Ethics,* vol. 8, Winter 1986.

BOOTH, ANNIE, and WAYNE JACOBS. "Ties That Bind: Native American Beliefs as a Foundation for Environmental Consciousness." *Environmental Ethics,* vol. 12. SPRING 1990.

CALLICOTT, J. BAIRD. "Conceptual Resources for Environmental Ethics in Asian Traditions of Thought: A Propaedeutic." *Philosophy East and West,* vol. 37(2), April 1987.

GUHA, RAMACHANDRA. "Radical American Environmentalism and Wilderness Preservation: A Third World Critique." *Environmental Ethics,* vol. 11(1), 1989.

HALL, DAVID L. "On Seeking a Change of Environment. A Quasi-Taoist Proposal." *Philosophy East and West.* vol. 37(2), April 1987.

HARGROVE, EUGENE C. "Anglo-American Land Use Attitudes." *Environmental Ethics,* vol. 2, Summer 1980.

INADA, KENNETH K. "Environmental Problematics in the Buddhist Context." *Philosophy East and West,* vol. 37(2), April 1987.

MAGRAW, DANIEL, and JAMES NICKEL. "Can Today's International System Handle Transboundary Environmental Problems?" In *Upstream/Downstream,* Donald Scherer, editor. Philadelphia: Temple University Press, 1990.

MERCHANT, CAROLYN. "Women of the Progressive Conservation Movement." *Environmental Review,* vol. 8, Spring 1984.

OPHULS, WILLIAM. *Ecology and the Politics of Scarcity.* San Francisco: W. H. Freeman and Company, 1977.

REILLY, WILLIAM K. "The Green Thumb of Capitalism: The Environmental Benefits of Sustainable Growth." *Policy Review,* Fall 1990.

ROLLIN, BERNARD E. "Environmental Ethics and International Justice," in *Problems of International Justice,* Luper-Foy, editor. Boulder, CO: Westview Press, 1988.

SAGOFF, MARK. "Zuckerman's Dilemma: A Plea For Environmental Ethics." *Hastings Center Report,* September–October 1991.

SHRADER-FRECHETTE, KRISTIN. *Nuclear Power and Public Policy.* Dordrecht: D. Reidel Publishing Co., 1980.

WARREN, KAREN J. "The Power and the Promise of Ecological Feminism." *Environmental Ethics,* vol. 12, (2), 1990.

ZAIDI, IQTIDAR H. "On the Ethics of Man's Interaction with the Environment: An Islamic Approach." *Environmental Ethics,* vol. 3, Spring 1980.

III

HUNGER
AND POVERTY

The "philanthropic" food relief programs that have aided many of the neediest countries are experiencing a decline in contributions, known as "famine fatigue." People of means are reportedly getting tired of providing economic assistance to deal with a problem that has not gone away and does not seem to be improving. The economic "famine fatigue" places hungry nations in even more peril.

In addition to giving money, there are other actions that a resident of the United States takes that may have far-reaching global effects. One example is eating beef. Consider:

> For every quarter-pound hamburger that comes from a steer raised in Central or South America, approximately 165 pounds of living matter have been destroyed, including some 20–30 different plant species, perhaps 100 insect species, and dozens of bird, mammal, and reptile species.[1]

Although the United States also has environmental pollution from beef production, the environmental costs of establishing beef production in Central and South America are coupled with human costs, for when cattle ranching is introduced into traditional agricultural societies, humans are also displaced.

> While peasant agriculture can often sustain a hundred people per square mile, the average rainforest cattle ranch "employs one person per 2,000 head of cattle and this . . . amounts at best to one person per twelve square miles." It has been the decision to use the land to create an artificial food chain, the most inequitable in history, that has resulted in misery for hundreds of millions of human beings around the world.[2]

As Jeremy Rifkin points out, the carrying capacity (or amount of life a specific area can sustain) of a square mile in the rain forest is drastically lessened when traditional agriculture is replaced with a cattle ranch. Where one square mile in the rain forest had previously sustained 100 people, after the intervention of cattle ranching, 12 square miles sustains one person. Considering that most of this beef is exported, local hunger is being *created* and the displaced 1,199 people must now find sustenance elsewhere. Those displaced may end up in cities with high unemployment, contributing to a cycle of poverty all too common in undeveloped countries. If this is the case, then a United States citizen's consumption of rain forest beef has many effects on people and the environment in areas far removed from that citizen.

Various situations in the Third World concerning hunger and poverty are affected by our actions, whether it be from our consumption habits or monetary donations (or lack thereof) to relief organizations. Some people assert that we have a *duty* to share with those in need. One example of people who assert that we have a duty to share are those in the Gabra tribe.

The Gabra are nomadic camel herders in Kenya's Chalbi Desert, who have adapted and survived for generations in their arid climate. The Gabra do not share Western assumptions about property and do not even consider the milk from the animals they care for to "belong" to them. Furthermore, they lend camels to both their own people and outsiders, a practice that has strengthened their community. The Gabra recognize that they must (that is, they have a moral obligation to) share such milk and camels with those who are in need. According to the Gabra perspective, a poor person shames them all.

What, then, are the limitations of our moral duties concerning situations such as hunger and poverty, both of particular urgency in the Third World? One could agree with William K. Reilly's assumptions that education, proper economic growth, and population control are what is needed to change the situation. Or perhaps one believes there is a need for a more immediate answer and agrees with the Gabra of Kenya that we must share what we have with those in need. Of concern in this chapter are the moral duties those of the developed nations have to those in the undeveloped nations concerning hunger and poverty, especially in light of the role the developed nations have played and continue to play in creating these problems.

Thomas Malthus (1766–1834) has long been cited as a voice of forewarning in the debate concerning population and food supplies. Malthus warned that because population grows geometrically and food production only increases arithmetically, the human race is endangered since population growth will always outrun food supplies. The only checks on this "law of population" are birth control and death. War, disease, and famine check the population by death, but to control birth, we must actively intervene. Although Malthus was mistaken on the *necessity* (at least in the short run in the "developed" countries) of population *always* outstripping food supplies, many still hold to his view that continued population growth cannot be sustained. Those who hold to his views concerning overpopulation and world hunger are called "neo-Malthusians," and they argue that overpopulation is the cause of world hunger. Garrett Hardin advocates this view.

According to Hardin, the problems encountered in countries such as India are the result of overpopulation. Overpopulation outruns the land's carrying capacity, and the end result is the *complete* inability to sustain life. Hardin points out that if we persist in feeding an overpopulated country, the results will be even more harmful than allowing those who are starving now to do so. Citing empirical evidence of the destruction that a minimally fed and overpopulated country wreaks on the land in the search for energy, he concludes that in order to provide adequate help, along with food we must send sufficient fuel (for warmth and cooking). Since this is nearly impossible, he argues that food-only policies must be abandoned. Hardin's moral argument is consequentialist and asserts that in looking to the most likely future, food-only programs do more harm than good, and our moral obligation is to refrain from causing harm.

Amartya Sen challenges Malthus' and neo-Malthusians' (such as Hardin) predictions concerning the global food supply and population via statistics and empirical evidence. Sen discusses two forms of population control. The first form of population control is "override" where a family's reproductive wishes are overridden by an outside agency. Examples of override policies include China's one-child policy and the practice of withholding aid to countries that do not adhere to population policies. The second approach is the collaborative approach. Collaboration relies on education about population issues and allows men and women to make rational decisions. Sen points out that the latter is very effective, especially when it includes the improvement of women's status, political participation, health care, and a secure economy. However the collaborative approach, which is indicative of a higher standard of living than currently exists in the Third World, does not come without some high costs. Some of the costs of that higher standard of living include wholesale threats to the environment that are worse than those from the threat of overpopulation. Although Sen illuminates this paradox from the higher standard of living, he still sees development as the solution to overpopulation.

Concerning those who are starving and those who are affluent, Peter Singer asserts a principle that states that if we can prevent suffering without sacrificing anything of comparable moral importance, then we are morally obligated to do so. Those with affluent lifestyles spend money on nonessential goods, and Singer finds this practice morally indefensible in view of the good the money could do when spent to alleviate suffering caused by starvation. Singer looks at the immediate consequences of suffering and does not focus on the long-range scenario that Hardin does. Singer makes a valuable contribution to the debate by considering the roles of the affluent nations in causing hunger in poverty-stricken nations. He argues that almost everyone is equally involved in the problems of overpopulation, pollution, and poverty, and hence moral obligations cannot be compartmentalized. Singer also points out that with our communications systems, we have become a "global village," and people may no longer justifiably claim ignorance of distant atrocities. Additionally, Singer argues, the principle of equality requires that we do not discriminate based on distance. In a later essay in this section Carlo Filice addresses this issue, including our duty to remain informed on distant atrocities.

John Arthur disagrees with Singer's conclusion that the affluent are morally obligated to give money, up to the point of sacrificing something of comparable moral importance. Arthur denies that Singer establishes that the affluent "few" have obligations to feed starving people. He argues that theories like Singer's fail to take into account the rights of the affluent. He states that there are cases where obligations of benevolence can override property rights; however, the fact that some are starving and some are affluent is not decisive in and of itself in settling the clash of rights. Arthur suggests that there is a duty of benevolence which *may* obligate those who are affluent not to exercise their consumption rights. Arthur further considers it a moral right to be able to pursue one's goals as one sees fit, as long as the rights of others are not violated. It is crucial, however, to determine precisely when our actions can be carried out without violating another's rights, in order to determine when we are obliged to act or not act.

In order to determine how our actions affect others we need to become informed. What are our obligations for keeping informed, especially about distant atrocities? Carlo Filice addresses this question in his essay. As discussed above, Singer asserts that the fact that a starving person is in a distant part of the world does not excuse us from our moral duty to aid him or her. Filice agrees, especially for the "average" United States citizen. Filice reports the situation in East Timor as an example of a typical moral atrocity, particularly relevant because of the role the United States played. Most United States citizens are unaware of both the situation and the United States' role, although there is information (which must generally be sought out) in the public arena. Filice argues that most citizens are under a *prima facie* obligation (an authentic moral claim that may occasionally be overridden by another stronger moral claim) to keep informed of such distant atrocities. Indeed, Filice argues that being informed is a necessary condition for being able to fulfill one's moral obligation to help prevent a harm.

Concerning starvation, what models might we apply in order to help end current famines and prevent future occurrences? The green revolution is generally regarded as a beneficial program and has been unquestionably accepted as a better means than prerevolution agricultural practices to feed growing, and often starving, populations. Deane Curtin challenges the assumption that the green revolution has been beneficial. Curtin argues that the green revolution, rather than alleviating hunger through more productive yields, displaces traditional, organic agriculture (largely a women's practice) that is often more productive. Further, the green revolution's pesticides and herbicides, valued for their "kill ratios," include Agent Orange, and are far from the peaceful intentions claimed. Curtin challenges the oft-touted peaceful means and ends of the green revolution. He argues that the green revolution is not peaceful but is warist and is an example of developmentalism, a form of domination.

Following Filice, we have an obligation to become informed about United States' practices and programs that we "export," especially to be informed about the harmful results of these activities. Much of the information Curtin, Filice, and others in this chapter provide concerns issues of which the average citizen is unaware. However, much like our laws, ignorance is not an excuse.

—Shari Collins-Chobanian

NOTES

1. Julie Denslow and Christine Padoch, *People of the Tropical Rainforest* (Berkeley: University of California Press, 1988), p. 169.
2. Jeremy Rifkin, *Beyond Beef: The Rise and Fall of the Cattle Culture* (New York: Dutton, 1992), p. 153.

Carrying Capacity
as an Ethical Concept

Garrett Hardin

Garrett Hardin is a professor of biology at the University of California, Santa Barbara. His books include Population, Evolution, and Birth Control *(1969).* The Limits of Altruism: An Ecologist's View of Survival *(1977), and* Promethean Ethics: Living with Death, Competition, and Triage *(1980).*

Hardin supports a "lifeboat ethics" that is adapted from the notion of the tragedy of the commons. He argues that the developed countries should not help countries with starving people, such as those in India, by sending only food. He explains that the notion that those who are starving can be helped by food-only shipments is ill-founded because it assumes a fixed amount of people, and progress in conquering starvation. Hardin asserts that in sending food we are seriously harming countries like India. He emphasizes that we can "never merely do one thing," and that supplying only food worsens political and economic strife, agricultural dependency, overpopulation, and environmental degradation.

Lifeboat Ethics is merely a special application of the logic of the commons.[1] The classic paradigm is that of a pasture held as common property by a community and governed by the following rules: first, each herdsman may pasture as many cattle as he wishes on the commons; and second, the gain from the growth of cattle accrues to the individual owners of the cattle. In an underpopulated world the system of the commons may do no harm and may even be the most economic way to manage things, since management costs are kept to a minimum. In an overpopulated (or overexploited) world a system of the commons leads to ruin, because each herdsman has more to gain individually by increasing the size of his herd than he has to lose as a single member of the community guilty of lowering the carrying capacity of the environment. Consequently he (with others) overloads the commons.

Even if an individual fully perceives the ultimate consequences of his actions he is most unlikely to act in any other way, for he cannot count on the restraint *his* conscience might dictate being matched by a similar restraint on the part of *all* the others. (Anything less than all is not enough.) Since mutual ruin is inevitable, it is quite proper to speak of the *tragedy* of the commons.

Tragedy is the price of freedom in the commons. Only by changing to some other system (socialism or private enterprise, for example) can ruin be averted. In other

Reprinted by permission of *Soundings: An Interdisciplinary Journal,* Volume 59, No. 1, © 1976. [Edited]

words, in a crowded world survival requires that some freedom be given up. (We have, however, a choice in the freedom to be sacrificed.) Survival is possible under several different politico-economic systems—but not under the system of the commons. When we understand this point, we reject the ideal of distributive justice stated by Karl Marx a century ago. "From each according to his ability, to each according to his needs."[2] This ideal might be defensible if "needs" were defined by the larger community rather than by the individual (or individual political unit) *and if "needs" were static.*[3] But in the past quarter-century, with the best will in the world, some humanitarians have been asserting that rich populations must supply the needs of poor populations even though the recipient populations increase without restraint. At the United Nations conference on population in Bucharest in 1973 spokesmen for the poor nations repeatedly said in effect: "We poor people have the right to reproduce as much as we want to: you in the rich world have the responsibility of keeping us alive."

Such a Marxian disjunction of rights and responsibilities inevitably tends toward tragic ruin for all. It is almost incredible that this position is supported by thoughtful persons, but it is. How does this come about? In part, I think, because language deceives us. When a disastrous loss of life threatens, people speak of a "crisis," implying that the threat is temporary. More subtle is the implication of quantitative stability built into the pronoun "they" and its relatives. Let me illustrate this point with quantified prototype statements based on two different points of view.

Crisis analysis: "These poor people (1,000,000) are starving, because of a crisis (flood, drought, or the like). How can we

refuse *them* (1,000,000)? Let us feed *them* (1,000,000). Once the crisis is past those who are still hungry are few (say 1,000) and there is no further need for our intervention."

Crunch analysis: "Those (1,000,000) who are hungry are reproducing. We send food to *them* (1,010,000). *Their* lives (1,020,000) are saved. But since the environment is still essentially the same, the next year *they* (1,030,000) ask for more food. We send it to them (1,045,000); and the next year *they* (1,068,000) ask for still more. Since the need has not gone away, it is a mistake to speak of a passing crisis: it is evidently a permanent crunch that this growing 'they' face—a growing disaster, not a passing state of affairs."

"They" increases in size. Rhetoric makes no allowance for a ballooning pronoun. Thus we can easily be deceived by language. We cannot deal adequately with ethical questions if we ignore quantitative matters. This attitude has been rejected by James Sellers, who dismisses prophets of doom from Malthus[4] to Meadows[5] as "chiliasts." Chiliasts (or millenialists, to use the Latin-derived equivalent of the Greek term) predict a catastrophic end of things a thousand years from some reference point. The classic example is the prediction of Judgment Day in the year 1000 anno Domini. Those who predicted it were wrong, of course; but the fact that this specific prediction was wrong is no valid criticism of the use of numbers in thinking. Millenialism is numerology, not science.

In science, most of the time, it is not so much exact numbers that are important as it is the relative size of numbers and the direction of change in the magnitude of them. Much productive analysis is accomplished with only the crude quantification of "order of magnitude" thinking. First and second derivatives are often calculated with no finer aim than to find out if they are positive or negative. Survival can hinge on the crude issue of the sign of change, regardless of number. This is a far cry from the spurious precision of numerology. Unfortunately the chasm between the "two cultures," as C.P. Snow called them,[6] keeps many in the nonscientific culture from understanding the significance of the quantitative approach. One is tempted to wonder also whether an additional impediment to understanding may not be the mortal sin called Pride, which some theologians regard as the mother of all sins.

Returning to Marx, it is obvious that the *each* in "to each according to his needs" is not—despite the grammar—a unitary, stable entity: "each" is a place holder for a ballooning variable. Before we commit ourselves to saving the life of *each* and every person in need we had better ask this question: *"And then what?"* That is, what about tomorrow, what about posterity? As Hans Jonas has pointed out,[7] traditional ethics has almost entirely ignored the claims of posterity. In an overpopulated world humanity cannot long endure under a regime governed by posterity-blind ethics. It is the essence of ecological ethics that it pays attention to posterity.

Since "helping" starving people requires that we who are rich give up some of our wealth, any refusal to do so is almost sure to be attributed to selfishness. Selfishness there may be, but focusing on selfishness is likely to be non-productive. In truth, a selfish motive can be found in all policy proposals. The selfishness of *not* giving is obvious and need not be elaborated. But the selfishness of giving is no less real, though more subtle.[8] Consider the sources of support for Public Law 480, the act of Congress under which surplus foods were given to poor countries, or sold to them at bargain prices ("concessionary terms" is the euphemism). Why did we give food away? Conventional wisdom says it was because we momentarily transcended our normal selfishness. Is that the whole story?

It is not. The "we" of the above sentence needs to be subdivided. The farmers who grew the grain did not give it away. They sold it to the government (which then gave it away). Farmers received selfish benefits in two ways: the direct sale of grain, and the economic support to farm prices given by this governmental purchase in an otherwise free market. The operation of P.L. 480 during the past quarter-century brought American farmers to a level of prosperity never known before.

Who else benefited—in a selfish way? The stockholders and employees of the railroads that moved grain to seaports benefited. So also did freight-boat operators (U.S. "bottoms" were specified by law). So also did grain elevator operators. So also did agricultural research scientists who were financially supported in a burgeoning but futile effort "to feed a hungry world."[9] And so also did the large bureaucracy required to keep the P.L. 480 system working. In toto, probably several million people personally benefited from the P.L. 480 program. Their labors cannot be called wholly selfless.

Who *did* make a sacrifice for P.L. 480? The citizens generally, nearly two hundred million of them, paying directly or indirectly through taxes. But each of these many millions lost only a little: whereas each of the million or so gainers gained a great deal. The blunt truth is that *philanthropy pays*—if you are hired as a philanthropist. Those on the gaining side of P.L. 480 made a great deal of money and could afford to spend lavishly to persuade

Congress to continue the program. Those on the sacrificing side sacrificed only a little bit per capita and could not afford to spend much protecting their pocketbooks against philanthropic inroads. And so P.L. 480 continued, year after year.

Should we condemn philanthropy when we discover that some of its roots are selfish? I think not, otherwise probably no philanthropy would be possible. The secret of practical success in large-scale public philanthropy is this: see to it that the losses are widely distributed so that the per capita loss is small, but concentrate the gains in a relatively few people so that these few will have the economic power needed to pressure the legislature into supporting the program.

I have spent some time on this issue because I would like to dispose once and for all of condemnatory arguments based on "selfishness." As a matter of principle we should always assume that selfishness is *part* of the motivation of every action. But what of it? If Smith proposes a certain public policy, it is far more important to know whether the policy will do public harm or public good than it is to know whether Smith's motives are selfish or selfless. Consequences ("ends") can be more objectively determined than motivations ("means"). Situational ethics wisely uses consequences as the measure of morality. "If the end does not justify the means, what does?" asked Joseph Fletcher.[10] The obsession of older ethical systems with means and motives is no doubt in part a consequence of envy, which has a thousand disguises.[11] (Though I am sure this is true, the situationist should not dwell on envy very long, for it is after all only a motive, and as such not directly verifiable. In any case public policy must be primarily concerned with consequences.)

Even judging an act by its consequences is not easy. We are limited by the basic theorem of ecology, "We can never do merely one thing."[12] The fact that an act has many consequences is all the more reason for deemphasizing motives as we carry out our ethical analyses. Motives by definition apply only to intended consequences. The multitudinous unintended ones are commonly denigrated by the term "side effects." But "The road to hell is paved with good intentions," so let's have done with motivational evaluations of public policy.

Even after we have agreed to eschew motivational analysis, foreign aid is a tough nut to crack. The literature is large and contradictory, but it all points to the inescapable conclusion that a quarter of a century of earnest effort has not conquered world poverty. To many observers the threat of future disasters is more convincing now than it was a quarter of a century ago—and the disasters are not all in the future either.[13] Where have we gone wrong in foreign aid?

We wanted to do good, of course. The question, "How can we help a poor country?" seems like a simple question, one that should have a simple answer. Our failure to answer it suggests that the question is not as simple as we thought. The variety of contradictory answers offered is disheartening.

How can we find our way through this thicket? I suggest we take a cue from a mathematician. The great algebraist Karl Jacobi (1804–1851) had a simple stratagem that he recommended to students who found themselves butting their heads against a stone wall. *Umkehren, immer umkehren*—"Invert, always invert." Don't just keep asking the same old question over and over: turn it upside down and ask the opposite question. The answer you get then may not be the one you want, but it may throw useful light on the question you started with.

Let's try a Jacobian inversion of the food/population problem. To sharpen the issue, let us take a particular example, say India. The question we want to answer is, "How can we help India?" But since that approach has repeatedly thrust us against a stone wall, let's pose the Jacobian invert, "How can we *harm* India?" After we've answered this perverse question we will return to the original (and proper) one.

As a matter of method, let us grant ourselves the most malevolent of motives: let us ask, "How can we harm India—*really* harm her?" Of course we might plaster the country with thermonuclear bombs, speedily wiping out most of the 600 million people. But, to the truly malevolent mind, that's not much fun: a dead man is beyond harming. Bacterial warfare could be a bit "better," but not much. No: we want something that will really make India suffer, not merely for a day or a week, but on and on and on. How can we achieve this inhumane goal?

Quite simply: by sending India a bounty of food, year after year. The United States exports about 80 million tons of grain a year. Most of it we sell: the foreign exchange it yields we use for such needed imports as petroleum (38 percent of our oil consumption in 1974), iron ore, bauxite, chromium, tin, etc. But in the pursuit of our malevolent goal let us "unselfishly" tighten our belts, make sacrifices, and do without that foreign exchange. Let us *give* all 80 million tons of grain to the Indians each year.

On a purely vegetable diet it takes about 400 pounds of grain to keep one person alive and healthy for a year. The 600 million Indians need 120 million tons per year; since their nutrition is less than ade-

quate presumably they are getting a bit less than that now. So the 80 million tons we give them will almost double India's per capita supply of food. With a surplus, Indians can afford to vary their diet by growing some less efficient crops; they can also convert some of the grain into meat (pork and chickens for the Hindus, beef and chickens for the Moslems). The entire nation can then be supplied not only with plenty of calories, but also with an adequate supply of high quality protein. The people's eyes will sparkle, their steps will become more elastic; and they will be capable of more work. "Fatalism" will no doubt diminish. (Much so-called fatalism is merely a consequence of malnutrition.) Indians may even become a bit overweight, though they will still be getting only two-thirds as much food as the average inhabitant of a rich country. Surely—we think—surely a well-fed India would be better off?

Not so: *ceteris paribus*, they will ultimately be worse off. Remember, "We can never do merely one thing." A generous gift of food would have not only nutritional consequences: it would also have political and economic consequences. The difficulty of distributing free food to a poor people is well known. Harbor, storage, and transport inadequacies result in great losses of grain to rats and fungi. Political corruption diverts food from those who need it most to those who are more powerful. More abundant supplies depress free market prices and discourage native farmers from growing food in subsequent years. Research into better ways of agriculture is also discouraged. Why look for better ways to grow food when there is food enough already?

There are replies, of sorts, to all the above points. It may be maintained that all these evils are only temporary ones; in time, organizational sense will be brought into the distributional system and the government will crack down on corruption. Realizing the desirability of producing more food, for export if nothing else, a wise government will subsidize agricultural research in spite of an apparent surplus. Experience does not give much support to this optimistic view, but let us grant the conclusions for the sake of getting on to more important matters. Worse is to come.

The Indian unemployment rate is commonly reckoned at 30 percent, but it is acknowledged that this is a minimum figure. *Under*employment is rife. Check into a hotel in Calcutta with four small bags and four bearers will carry your luggage to the room—with another man to carry the key. Custom, and a knowledge of what the traffic will bear, decree this practice. In addition malnutrition justifies it in part. Adequately fed, half as many men would suffice. So one of the early consequences of achieving a higher level of nutrition in the Indian population would be to increase the number of unemployed.

India needs many things that food will not buy. Food will not diminish the unemployment rate (quite the contrary); nor will it increase the supply of minerals, bicycles, clothes, automobiles, gasoline, schools, books, movies, or television. All these things require energy for their manufacture and maintenance.

Of course, food is a form of energy, but it is convertible to other forms only with great loss; so we are practically justified in considering energy and food as mutually exclusive goods. On this basis the most striking difference between poor and rich countries is not in the food they eat but in the energy they use. On a per capita basis rich countries use about three times as much of the primary foods—grains and the like—as do poor countries. (To a large

extent this is because the rich convert much of the grain to more "wasteful" animal meat.) But when it comes to energy, rich countries use ten times as much per capita. (Near the extremes Americans use 60 times as much per person as Indians.) By reasonable standards much of this energy may be wasted (e.g., in the manufacture of "exercycles" for sweating the fat off people who have eaten too much), but a large share of this energy supplies the goods we regard as civilized: effortless transportation, some luxury foods, a variety of sports, clean space-heating, more than adequate clothing, and energy-consuming arts—music, visual arts, electronic auxiliaries, etc. Merely giving food to a people does almost nothing to satisfy the appetite for any of these other goods.

But a well-nourished people is better fitted to try to wrest more energy from its environment. The question then is this: Is the native environment able to furnish more energy? And at what cost?

In India energy is already being gotten from the environment at a fearful cost. In the past two centuries millions of acres of India have been deforested in the struggle for fuel, with the usual environmental degradation. The Vale of Kashmir, once one of the garden spots of the world, has been denuded to such an extent that the hills no longer hold water as they once did, and the springs supplying the famous gardens are drying up. So desperate is the need for charcoal for fuel that the Kashmiri now make it out of tree leaves. This wasteful practice denies the soil of needed organic mulch.

Throughout India, as is well known, cow dung is burned to cook food. The minerals of the dung are not thereby lost, but the ability of dung to improve soil tilth is. Some of the nitrogen in the dung goes off into the air and does not return to Indian soil. Here we see a classic example of the "vicious circle": because Indians are poor they burn dung, depriving the soil of nitrogen and make themselves still poorer the following year. If we give them plenty of food, as they cook this food with cow dung they will lower still more the ability of their land to produce food.

Let us look at another example of this counter-productive behavior. Twenty-five years ago western countries brought food and medicine to Nepal. In the summer of 1974 a disastrous flood struck Bangladesh, killing tens of thousands of people, by government admission. (True losses in that part of the world are always greater than admitted losses.) Was there any connection between feeding Nepal and flooding Bangladesh? Indeed there was, and is.[14]

Nepal nestles amongst the Himalayas. Much of its land is precipitous, and winters are cold. The Nepalese need fuel, which they get from trees. Because more Nepalese are being kept alive now, the demand for timber is escalating. As trees are cut down, the soil under them is washed down the slopes into the rivers that run through India and Bangladesh. Once the absorption capacity of forest soil is gone, floods rise faster and to higher maxima. The flood of 1974 covered two-thirds of Bangladesh, twice the area of "normal" floods—which themselves are the consequence of deforestation in preceding centuries.

By bringing food and medicine to Nepal we intend only to save lives. But we can never do merely one thing, and the Nepalese lives we saved created a Nepalese energy-famine. The lives we saved from starvation in Nepal a quarter of a century ago were paid for in our time by lives lost to flooding and its attendant evils in Bangladesh. The saying, "Man does not live by bread alone," takes on new meaning.

Still we have not described what may be the worst consequence of a food-only policy: revolution and civil disorder. Many kindhearted people who support food aid programs solicit the cooperation of "hard-nosed" doubters by arguing that good nutrition is needed for world peace. Starving people will attack others, they say. Nothing could be further from the truth. The monumental studies of Ancel Keys and others have shown that starving people are completely selfish.[15] They are incapable of cooperating with others; and they are incapable of laying plans for tomorrow and carrying them out. Moreover, modern war is so expensive that even the richest countries can hardly afford it.

The thought that starving people can forcefully wrest subsistence from their richer brothers may appeal to our sense of justice, *but it just ain't so.* Starving people fight only among themselves, and that inefficiently.

So what would happen if we brought ample supplies of food to a population that was still poor in everything else? They would still be incapable of waging war at a distance, but their ability to fight among themselves would be vastly increased. With vigorous, well-nourished bodies and a keen sense of their impoverishment in other things, they would no doubt soon create massive disorder in their own land. Of course, they might create a strong and united country, but what is the probability of that? Remember how much trouble the thirteen colonies had in forming themselves into a United States. Then remember that India is divided by two major religions, many castes, fourteen major languages and a hundred dialects. A partial separation of peoples along religious lines in 1947, at the time of the formation of Pakistan and of independent India, cost untold millions of lives. The budding off of Bangladesh (formerly East Pakistan) from the rest of Pakistan in 1971 cost several million more. All these losses were achieved on a low level of nutrition. The possibilities of blood-letting in a population of 600 million well-nourished people of many languages and religions and no appreciable tradition of cooperation stagger the imagination. Philanthropists with any imagination at all should be stunned by the thought of 600 million well-fed Indians seeking to meet their energy needs from their own resources.

So the answer to our Jacobian questions, "How can we harm India?" is clear: send food *only.* Escaping the Jacobian by reinverting the question we now ask, "How can we *help* India?" Immediately we see that we must *never* send food without a matching gift of non-food energy; but before we go careening off on an intoxicating new program we had better look at some more quantities.

On a per capita basis, India uses the energy equivalent of one barrel of oil per year; the U.S. uses sixty. The world average of all countries, rich and poor, is ten. If we want to bring India only up to the present world average, we would have to send India about 9 x 600 million bbl. of oil per year (or its equivalent in coal, timber, gas or whatever). That would be more than five billion barrels of oil equivalent. What is the chance that we will make such a gift?

Surely it is nearly zero. For scale, note that our total yearly petroleum use is seven billion barrels (of which we import three billion). Of course we use (and have)

a great deal of coal too. But these figures should suffice to give a feeling of scale.

More important is the undoubted psychological fact that a fall in income tends to dry up the springs of philanthropy. Despite wide disagreements about the future of energy it is obvious that from now on, for at least the next twenty years and possibly for centuries, our per capita supply of energy is going to fall, year after year. The food we gave in the past was "surplus." By no accounting do we have an energy surplus. In fact, the perceived deficit is rising year by year.

India has about one-third as much land as the United States. She has about three times as much population. If her people-to-land ratio were the same as ours she would have only about seventy million people (instead of 600 million). With the forested and relatively unspoiled farmlands of four centuries ago, seventy million people was probably well within the carrying capacity of the land. Even in today's India, seventy million people could probably make it in comfort and dignity—provided they didn't increase!

To send food only to a country already populated beyond the carrying capacity of its land is to collaborate in the further destruction of the land and the further impoverishment of its people.

Food plus energy is a recommendable policy; but for a large population under today's conditions this policy is defensible only by the logic of the old saying, "If wishes were horses, beggars would ride." The fantastic amount of energy needed for such a program is simply not in view. (We have mentioned nothing of the equally monumental "infrastructure" of political, technological, and educational machinery needed to handle unfamiliar forms and quantities of energy in the poor countries.

In a short span of time this infrastructure is as difficult to bring into being as is an abundant supply of energy.)

In summary, then, here are the major foreign-aid possibilities that tender minds are willing to entertain:

a. Food plus energy—a conceivable, but practically impossible program.

b. Food alone—a conceivable and possible program, but one which would destroy the recipient.

In the light of this analysis the question of triage shrinks to negligible importance. If any gift of food to overpopulated countries does more harm than good, it is not necessary to decide which countries get the gift and which do not. For posterity's sake we should never send food to any population that is beyond the realistic carrying capacity of its land. The question of triage does not even arise . . .

NOTES

1. Garrett Hardin, 1968. "The Tragedy of the Commons," *Science*, 162: 1243–48.
2. Karl Marx, 1875: "Critique of the Gotha program." (Reprinted in *The Marx-Engels Reader*, Robert C. Tucker, editor. New York: Norton, 1972).
3. Garrett Hardin and John Baden, 1977. *Managing the Commons.* (San Francisco: W.H. Freeman.)
4. Thomas Robert Malthus, 1798: *An Essay on the Principle of Population, as It Affects the Future Improvement of Society.* (Reprinted, inter alia, by the University of Michigan Press, 1959, and The Modern Library, 1960).
5. Donella H. Meadows, Dennis L. Meadows, Jorgen Randers, and William H. Behrens, 1972: *The Limits to Growth* (New York: Universe Books).
6. C.P. Snow, 1963: *The Two Cultures; and a Second Look.* (New York: Mentor).
7. Hans Jonas, 1973: "Technology and Responsibility: Reflections on the New Task of Ethics," *Social Research*, 40:31–54.
8. William and Paul Paddock, 1967: *Famine—1975* (Boston: Little, Brown & Co.).
9. Garrett Hardin, 1975: "Gregg's Law," *BioScience*, 25:415.
10. Joseph Fletcher, 1966: *Situation Ethics* (Philadelphia: Westminster Press)
11. Helmut Schoeck, 1969: *Envy* (New York: Harcourt, Brace & World).
12. Garrert Hardin, 1972: *Exploring New Ethics for Survival* (New York: Viking).
13. Nicholas Wade, 1974: "Sahelian Drought: No Victory for Western Aid," *Science,* 185:234–37.
14. Erik P. Eckholm, 1375: "The Deterioration of Mountain Environments," *Science,* 189:764–70.
15. Ancel Keys, et al., 150: *The Biology of Human Starvation.* 2 vols. (Minneapolis: University of Minnesota Press).

Population:
Delusion and Reality

Amartya Sen

Amartya Sen is a professor of philosophy at Harvard University. Sen is the author of numerous books on hunger and poverty, including Inequality Reexamined *(1992),* On Ethics and Economics *(1987), and* Resources, Values, and Development *(1984).*

Drawing from extensive empirical evidence, Sen counters Malthus' predictions concerning population growth and food supply. Sen argues that not only have Malthus' predictions not materialized, but the global food supply is relatively more plentiful than population demand. Sen defines two approaches to population control, override and collaboration, and argues that current conditions do not justify override. Rather, he advocates that our global efforts should focus on the collaborative approach.

1.

Few issues today are as divisive as what is called the "world population problem." With the approach this autumn of the International Conference on Population and Development in Cairo, organized by the United Nations, these divisions among experts are receiving enormous attention and generating considerable heat. There is a danger that in the confrontation between apocalyptic pessimism, on the one hand, and a dismissive smugness, on the other, a genuine understanding of the nature of the population problem may be lost.[1]

Visions of impending doom have been increasingly aired in recent years, often presenting the population problem as a "bomb" that has been planted and is about

to "go off." These catastrophic images have encouraged a tendency to search for emergency solutions which treat the people involved not as reasonable beings, allies facing a common problem, but as impulsive and uncontrolled sources of great social harm, in need of strong discipline.

Such views have received serious attention in public discussions, not just in sensational headlines in the popular press, but also in seriously argued and widely read books. One of the most influential examples was Paul Ehrlich's *The Population Bomb*, the first three sections of which were headed "Too Many People," "Too Little Food," and "A Dying Planet."[2] A more recent example of a chilling diagnosis of imminent calamity is Garrett Hardin's *Living within Limits*.[3] The arguments on which these pessimistic visions are based deserve serious scrutiny.

If the propensity to foresee impending disaster from overpopulation is strong in some circles, so is the tendency, in others, to dismiss all worries about population size. Just as alarmism builds on the recognition of a real problem and then magnifies it, complacency may also start off from a reasonable belief about the history of population problems and fail to see how they may have changed by now. It is often pointed out, for example, that the world has coped well enough with fast increases in population in the past, even though alarmists had expected otherwise. Malthus anticipated terrible disasters resulting from population growth and a consequent imbalance in "the proportion between the natural increase of population and food."[4] At a time when there were fewer than a billion people, he was quite convinced that "the period when the number of men surpass their means of subsistence has long since arrived." However, since Malthus first published his famous *Essay on Population* in 1798, the world population has grown nearly six times larger, while food output and consumption per person are considerably higher now, and there has been an unprecedented increase both in life expectancies and in general living standards.[5]

The fact that Malthus was mistaken in his diagnosis as well as his prognosis two hundred years ago does not, however, indicate that contemporary fears about population growth must be similarly erroneous. The increase in the world population has vastly accelerated over the last century. It took the world population millions of years to reach the first billion, then 123 years to get to the second, 33 years to the third, 14 years to the fourth, 13 years to the fifth billion, with a sixth billion to come, according to one UN projection, in another 11 years.[6] During the last decade, between 1980 and 1990, the number of people on earth grew by about 923 million, an increase nearly the

size of the total world population in Malthus's time. Whatever may be the proper response to alarmism about the future, complacency based on past success is no response at all.

Immigration and Population

One current worry concerns the regional distribution of the increase in world population, about 90 percent of which is taking place in the developing countries. The percentage rate of population growth is fastest in Africa—3.1 percent per year over the last decade. But most of the large increases in population occur in regions other than Africa. The largest absolute increases in numbers are taking place in Asia, which is where most of the world's poorer people live, even though the rate of increase in population has been slowing significantly there. Of the worldwide increase of 923 million people in the 1980s, well over half occurred in Asia—517 million in fact (including 146 million in China and 166 million in India).

Beyond concerns about the well-being of these poor countries themselves, a more self-regarding worry causes panic in the richer countries of the world and has much to do with the current anxiety in the West about the "world population problem." This is founded on the belief that destitution caused by fast population growth in the third world is responsible for the severe pressure to emigrate to the developed countries of Europe and North America. In this view, people impoverished by overpopulation in the "South" flee to the "North." Some have claimed to find empirical support for this thesis in the fact that pressure to emigrate from the South has accelerated in recent decades, along with a rapid increase in the population there.

There are two distinct questions here: first, how great a threat of intolerable immigration pressure does the North face from the South, and second, is that pressure closely related to population growth in the South, rather than to other social and economic factors? There are reasons to doubt that population growth is the major force behind migratory pressures, and I shall concentrate here on that question. But I should note in passing that immigration is now severely controlled in Europe and North America, and insofar as Europe is concerned, most of the current immigrants from the third world are not "primary" immigrants but dependent relatives—mainly spouses and young children—of those who had come and settled earlier. The United States remains relatively more open to fresh immigration, but the requirements of "labor certification" as a necessary part of the immigration procedure tend to guarantee that the new entrants are relatively better educated and more skilled. There are, however, sizable flows of illegal immigrants, especially to the United States and to a lesser extent to southern Europe, though the numbers are hard to estimate.

What causes the current pressures to emigrate? The "job-worthy" people who get through the immigration process are hardly to be seen as impoverished and destitute migrants created by the sheer pressure of population. Even the illegal immigrants who manage to evade the rigors of border control are typically not starving wretches but those who can make use of work prospects in the North.

The explanation for the increased migratory pressure over the decades owes more to the dynamism of international capitalism than to just the growing size of the population of the third world countries.

The immigrants have allies in potential employers, and this applies as much to illegal farm laborers in California as to the legally authorized "guest workers" in automobile factories in Germany. The economic incentive to emigrate to the North from the poorer Southern economies may well depend on differences in real income. But this gap is very large anyway, and even if it is presumed that population growth in the South is increasing the disparity with the North—a thesis I shall presently consider—it seems unlikely that this incentive would significantly change if the Northern income level were, say, twenty times that of the Southern as opposed to twenty-five times.

The growing demands for immigration to the North from the South is related to the "shrinking" of the world (through revolutions in communication and transport), reduction in economic obstacles to labor movements (despite the increase in political barriers), and the growing reach and absorptive power of international capitalism (even as domestic politics in the North has turned more inward-looking and nationalistic). To try to explain the increase in immigration pressure by the growth rate of total population in the third world is to close one's eyes to the deep changes that have occurred—and are occurring—in the world in which we live, and the rapid internationalization of its cultures and economies that accompanies these changes.

Fears of Being Engulfed

A closely related issue concerns what is perceived as a growing "imbalance" in the division of the world population, with a rapidly rising share belonging to the third world. That fear translates into worries of various kinds in the North, especially the sense of being overrun by the South. Many Northerners fear being engulfed by people from Asia and Africa, whose share of the world population increased from 63.7 percent in 1950 to 71.2 percent by 1990, and is expected, according to the estimates of the United Nations, to rise to 78.5 percent by 2050 A.D.

It is easy to understand the fears of relatively well-off people at the thought of being surrounded by a fast growing and increasingly impoverished Southern population. As I shall argue, the thesis of growing impoverishment does not stand up to much scrutiny; but it is important to address first the psychologically tense issue of racial balance in the world (even though racial composition as a consideration has only as much importance as we choose to give it). Here it is worth recollecting that the third world is right now going through the same kind of demographic shift—a rapid expansion of population for a temporary but long stretch—that Europe and North America experienced during their industrial revolution. In 1650 the share of Asia and Africa in the world population is estimated to have been 78.4 percent, and it stayed around there even in 1750.[7] With the industrial revolution, the share of Asia and Africa diminished because of the rapid rise of population in Europe and North America; for example, during the nineteenth century while the inhabitants of Asia and Africa grew by about 4 percent per decade or less, the population of "the area of European settlement" grew by around 10 percent every decade.

Even now the combined share of Asia and Africa (71.2 percent) is considerably *below* what its share was in 1650 or 1750. If the United Nations' prediction that this share will rise to 78.5 percent by 2050 comes true, then the Asians and the Africans would return to being proportionately almost exactly as numerous as they were before the European industrial revolution. There is, of course, nothing sacrosanct about the distributions of population in the past; but the sense of a growing "imbalance" in the world, based only on recent trends, ignores history and implicitly presumes that the expansion of Europeans earlier on was natural, whereas the same process happening now to other populations unnaturally disturbs the "balance."

Collaboration versus Override

Other worries involving the relation of population growth to food supplies, income levels, and the environment reflect more serious matters.[8] Before I take up those questions, a brief comment on the distinction between two rival approaches to dealing with the population problem may be useful. One involves voluntary choice and a collaborative solution, and the other overrides voluntarism through legal or economic coercion.

Alarmist views of impending crises tend to produce a willingness to consider forceful measures for coercing people to have fewer children in the third word. Imposing birth control on unwilling people is no longer rejected as readily as it was until quite recently, and some activists have pointed to the ambiguities that exist in determining what is or is not "coercion."[9] Those who are willing to consider—or at least not fully reject—programs that would use some measure of force to reduce population growth often point to the success of China's "one child policy" in cutting down the national birth rate. Force can also take an indirect form, as when economic opportunities are changed so radically by government regulations that people are left with very little choice except to behave in ways the government would approve. In China's case, the government may refuse to offer housing to families with too many children—thus penalizing the children as well as the dissenting adults.

In India the policy of compulsory birth control that was initiated during the "emergency period" declared by Mrs. Gandhi in the 1970s was decisively rejected by the voters in the general election in which it—along with civil rights—was a major issue. Even so, some public health clinics in the northern states (such as Uttar Pradesh) insist, in practice, on sterilization before providing normal medical attention to women and men beyond a certain age. The pressures to move in that direction seem to be strong, and they are reinforced by the rhetoric of "the population bomb."

I shall call this general approach the "override" view, since the family's personal decisions are overridden by some agency outside the family—typically by the government of the country in question (whether or not it has been pressed to do so by "outside" agencies, such as international organizations and pressure groups). In fact, overriding is not limited to an explicit use of legal coercion or economic compulsion, since people's own choices can also be effectively overridden by simply not offering them the opportunities for jobs or welfare that they can expect to get from a responsible government. Override can take many different forms and can be of varying intensity (with the Chinese "one child policy" being something of an extreme case of a more general approach).

A central issue here is the increasingly vocal demand by some activists concerned with population growth that the highest "priority" should be given in third world countries to family planning over other public commitments. This demand goes much beyond supporting family planning as a part of development. In fact, proposals for shifting international aid away from development in general to family planning in particular have lately been increasingly frequent. Such policies fit into the general approach of "override" as well, since they try to rely on manipulating people's choices through offering them only some opportunities (the means of family planning) while denying others, no matter what they would have themselves preferred. Insofar as they would have the effect of reducing health care and educational services, such shifts in public commitments will not only add to the misery of human lives, they may also have, I shall argue, exactly the opposite effect on family planning than the one intended, since education and health care have a significant part in the *voluntary* reduction of the birth rate.

The "override" approach contrasts with another, the "collaborative" approach, that relies not on legal or economic restrictions but on rational decisions of women and men, based on expanded choices and enhanced security, and encouraged by open dialogue and extensive public discussions. The difference between the two approaches does not lie in government's activism in the first case as opposed to passivity in the second. Even if solutions are sought through the decisions and actions of people themselves, the chance to take reasoned decisions with more knowledge and a greater sense of personal security can be increased by public policies, for example, through expanding educational facilities, health care, and economic well-being, along with providing better access to family planning. The central political and ethical issue concerning the "override" approach does not lie in its insistence on the need for public policy but in the ways it significantly reduces the choices open to parents.

The Malthus–Condorcet Debate

Thomas Robert Malthus forcefully argued for a version of the "override" view. In fact, it was precisely this preference that distinguished Malthus from Condorcet, the eighteenth-century French mathematician and social scientist from whom Malthus had actually derived the analysis of how population could outgrow the means of living. The debate between Condorcet and Malthus in some ways marks the origin of the distinction between the "collaborative" and the "override" approaches, which still compete for attention.[10]

In his *Essay on Population,* published in 1798, Malthus quoted—extensively and with approval—Condorcet's discussion, in 1795, of the possibility of overpopulation. However, true to the Enlightenment tradition, Condorcet was confident that this problem would be solved by reasoned human action: through increases in productivity, through better conservation and prevention of waste, and through education (especially female education) which would contribute to reducing the birth rate.[11] Voluntary family planning would be encouraged, in Condorcet's analysis, by increased understanding that if people "have a duty toward those who are not yet born, that duty is not to give them existence but to give them happiness." They would see the value of limiting family size "rather than foolishly . . . encumber the world with useless and wretched beings."[12]

Even though Malthus borrowed from Condorcet his diagnosis of the possibility of overpopulation, he refused to accept Condorcet's solution. Indeed, Malthus's essay on population was partly a criticism of Condorcet's enlightenment reasoning, and even the full title of Malthus's famous essay specifically mentioned Condorcet. Malthus argued that

> there is no reason whatever to suppose that anything beside the difficulty of procuring in adequate plenty the necessaries of life should either *indispose* this greater number of persons to marry early, or *disable* them from rearing in health the largest families.[13]

Malthus thus opposed public relief of poverty: he saw the "poor laws" in particular as contributing greatly to population growth.[14]

Malthus was not sure that any public policy would work, and whether "overriding" would in fact be possible: "The perpetual tendency in the race of man to increase beyond the means of subsistence is one of the great general laws of animated nature which we can have no reason to expect will change."[15] But insofar as any solution would be possible, it could not come from voluntary decisions of the people involved, or acting from a position of strength and economic security. It must come from overriding their preferences through the compulsions of economic necessity, since their poverty was the only thing that could "indispose the greater number of persons to marry early, or disable them from rearing in health the largest families."

Development and Increased Choice

The distinction between the "collaborative" approach and the "override" approach thus tends to correspond closely to the contrast between, on the one hand, treating economic and social development as the way to solve the population problem and, on the other, expecting little from development and using, instead, legal and economic pressures to reduce birth rates. Among recent writers, those such as Gerard Piel[16] who have persuasively emphasized our ability to solve problems through reasoned decisions and actions have tended—like Condorcet—to find the solution of the population problem in economic and social development. They advocate a broadly collaborative approach, in which governments and citizens would together produce economic and social conditions favoring slower population growth. In contrast, those who have been thoroughly skeptical of reasoned human action to limit population growth have tended to go in the direction of "override" in one form or another, rather than concentrate on development and voluntarism.

Has development, in fact, done much to reduce population growth? There can be little doubt that economic and social development, in general, has been associated with major reductions in birth rates and the emergence of smaller families as the norm. This is a pattern that was, of course, clearly observed in Europe and North America as they underwent industrialization, but that experience has been repeated in many other parts of the world.

In particular, conditions of economic security and affluence, wider availability of contraceptive methods, expansion of education (particularly female education), and lower mortality rates have had—and are currently having—quite substantial effects in reducing birth rates in different parts of the world.[17] The rate of world population growth is certainly declining, and even over the last two decades its percentage growth rate has fallen from 2.2 percent

per year between 1970 and 1980 to 1.7 percent between 1980 and 1992. This rate is expected to go steadily down until the size of the world's population becomes nearly stationary.[18]

There are important regional differences in demographic behavior: for example, the population growth rate in India peaked at 2.2 percent a year (in the 1970s) and has since started to diminish, whereas most Latin American countries peaked at much higher rates before coming down sharply, while many countries in Africa currently have growth rates between 3 and 4 percent, with an average for sub-Saharan Africa of 3.1 percent. Similarly, the different factors have varied in their respective influence from region to region. But there can be little dispute that economic and social development tends to reduce fertility rates. The regions of the third world that lag most in achieving economic and social development, such as many countries in Africa, are, in general, also the ones that have failed to reduce birth rates significantly. Malthus's fear that economic and social development could only encourage people to have more children has certainly proved to be radically wrong, and so have all the painful policy implications drawn from it.

This raises the following question: in view of the clear connection between development and lower fertility, why isn't the dispute over how to deal with population growth fully resolved already? Why don't we reinterpret the population problem simply as a problem of underdevelopment and seek a solution by encouraging economic and social development (even if we reject the oversimple slogan "development is the most reliable contraceptive")?

In the long run, this may indeed be exactly the right approach. The problem is more complex, however, because a "contraceptive" that is "reliable" in the long run may not act fast enough to meet the present threat. Even though development may dependably work to stabilize population if it is given enough time, there may not be, it is argued, time enough to give. The death rate often falls very fast with more widely available health care, better sanitation, and improved nutrition, while the birth rate may fall rather slowly. Much growth of population may meanwhile occur.

This is exactly the point at which apocalyptic prophecies add force to the "override" view. One claim, then, that needs examination is that the world is facing an imminent crisis, one so urgent that development is just too slow a process to deal with it. We must try right now, the argument goes, to cut down population growth by drastic and forceful means if necessary. The second claim that also needs scrutiny is the actual feasibility of adequately reducing population growth through these drastic means, without fostering social and economic development.

2.

Population and Income

It is sometimes argued that signs of an imminent crisis can be found in the growing impoverishment of the South, with falling income per capita accompanying high population growth. In general, there is little evidence for this. As a matter of fact, the average population of "low-income" countries (as defined by the World Bank) has been not only enjoying a rising gross national product (GNP) per head, but a growth rate of GNP per capita (3.9 percent per year for 1980–1992) that is much faster than those for the "high-income" countries (2.4 percent) and for the "middle-income" ones (0 percent).[19]

The growth of per capita GNP of the population of low-income countries would have been even higher had it not been for the negative growth rates of many countries in sub-Saharan Africa, one region in which a number of countries have been experiencing economic decline. But the main culprit causing this state of affairs is the terrible failure of economic production in sub-Saharan Africa (connected particularly with political disruption, including wars and military rule), rather than population growth, which is only a subsidiary factor. Sub-Saharan Africa does have high population growth, but its economic stagnation has contributed much more to the fall in its per-capita income.

With its average population growth rate of 3.1 percent per year, had sub-Saharan Africa suddenly matched China's low population growth of 1.4 percent (the lowest among the low-income countries), it would have gained roughly 1.7 percent in per-capita GNP growth. The real income per person would still have fallen, even with that minimal population growth, for many countries in the region. The growth of GNP per capita is *minus* 1.9 percent for Ethiopia, *minus* 1.8 percent for Togo, *minus* 3.6 percent for Mozambique, *minus* 4.3 percent for Niger, *minus* 4.7 percent for Ivory Coast, not to mention Somalia, Sudan, and Angola, where the political disruption has been so serious that no reliable GNP estimates even exist. A lower population growth rate could have reduced the magnitude of the fall in per capita GNP, but the main roots of Africa's economic decline lie elsewhere. The complex political factors underlying the troubles of Africa include, among other things, the subversion of democracy and the rise of combative military rulers, often encouraged by the cold war (with Africa providing "client states"—from Somalia and Ethiopia to Angola and Zaire—for the superpowers, particularly from the 1960s onward). The explanation of sub-Saharan Africa's problems has to be sought in these political troubles, which affect economic stability, agricultural and industrial incentives, public health arrangements, and social services—even family planning and population policy.[20]

There is indeed a very powerful case for reducing the rate of growth of population in Africa, but this problem cannot be dissociated from the rest of the continent's woes. Sub-Saharan Africa lags behind the developing regions in economic security, in health care, in life expectancy, in basic education, and in political and economic stability. It should be no great surprise that it lags behind in family planning as well. To dissociate the task of population control from the politics and economics of Africa would be a great mistake and would seriously mislead public policy.

Population and Food

Malthus's exact thesis cannot, however, be disputed by quoting statistics of income per capita, for he was concerned specifically with food supply per capita, and he had concentrated on "the proportion between the natural increase of population and food." Many modern commentators, including Paul Ehrlich and Garrett Hardin, have said much about this, too. When Ehrlich says, in his *Population Bomb*, "too little food," he does not mean "too little income," but specifically a growing shortage of food.

Is population beginning to outrun food production? Even though such an impression is often given in public discussions, there is, in fact, no serious evidence that

this is happening. While there are some year-to-year fluctuations in the growth of food output (typically inducing, whenever things slacken a bit, some excited remarks by those who anticipate an impending doom), the worldwide trend of food output per person has been firmly upward. Not only over the two centuries since Malthus's time, but also during recent decades, the rise in food output has been significantly and consistently outpacing the expansion of world population.[21]

But the total food supply in the world as a whole is not the only issue. What about the regional distribution of food? If it were to turn out that the rising ratio of food to population is mainly caused by increased production in richer countries (for example, if it appeared that US wheat output was feeding the third world, in which much of the population expansion is taking place), then the neo-Malthusian fears about "too many people" and "too little food" may have some plausibility. Is this what is happening?

In fact, with one substantial exception, exactly the opposite is true. The largest increases in the production of food—not just in the aggregate but also per person—are actually taking place in the third world, particularly in the region that is having the largest absolute increases in the world population, that is, in Asia. The many millions of people who are added to the population of India and China may be constantly cited by the terrorized—and terrorizing—advocates of the apocalyptic view, but it is precisely in these countries that the most rapid rates of growth in food output per capita are to be observed. For example, between the three-year averages of 1979–1981 and 1991–1993, food production per head in the world moved up by 3 percent, while it went up by only 2 percent in Europe and went down by nearly 5 percent in North America. In contrast, per capita food production jumped up by 22 percent in Asia generally, including 23 percent in India and 39 percent in China.[22] (See Table 1.)

During the same period, however, food production per capita went down by 6 percent in Africa, and even the absolute size of food output fell in some countries (such as Malawi and Somalia). Of course, many countries in the world—from Syria, Italy, and Sweden to Botswana in Africa—have had declining food production per head without experiencing hunger or starvation since their economies have prospered and grown; when the means are available, food can be easily bought in the international market if it is necessary to do so. For many countries in sub-Saharan Africa the problem arises from the fact that the decline in food production is an integral part of the story of overall economic decline, which I have discussed earlier.

Difficulties of food production in sub-Saharan Africa, like other problems of the national economy, are not only linked to wars, dictatorships, and political chaos. In addition, there is some evidence that climatic shifts have had unfavorable effects on parts of that continent. While some of the climatic problems may be caused partly by increases in human settlement and environmental neglect, that neglect is not unrelated to the political and economic chaos that has characterized sub-Saharan Africa during the last few decades. The food problem of Africa must be seen as one part of a wider political and economic problem of the region.[23]

The Price of Food

To return to "the balance between food and population," the rising food production per capita in the world as a whole, and in the third world in general, contradicts some of the pessimism that characterized the gloomy predictions of the past. Prophecies of imminent disaster during the last few decades have not proved any more accurate than Malthus's prognostication nearly two hundred years ago. As for new prophecies of doom, they cannot, of course, be contradicted until the future arrives. There was no way of refuting the thesis of W. Paddock and P. Paddock's popular book *Famine—1975!*, published in 1968, which predicted a terrible cataclysm for the world as a whole by 1975 (writing off India, in particular, as a basket case), until 1975 actually arrived. The new prophets have learned not to attach specific dates to the crises they foresee, and past failures do not seem to have reduced the popular appetite for this creative genre.

However, after noting the rather dismal forecasting record of doomsayers, we must also accept the general methodological point that present trends in output do not necessarily tell us much about the prospects of further expansion in the future. It could, for example, be argued that maintaining growth in food production may require proportionately increas-

Table 1 Indices of Food Production per Capita

	1979–1981 Base Period	1991–1993
World	100	103
Europe	100	102
North America	100	95
Africa	100	94
Asia	100	122
including		
India	100	123
China	100	139

Source: FAO Quarterly Bulletin of Statistics.

ing investments of capital, drawing them away from other kinds of production. This would tend to make food progressively more expensive if there are "diminishing returns" in shifting resources from other fields into food production. And, ultimately, further expansion of food production may become so expensive that it would be hard to maintain the trend of increasing food production without reducing other outputs drastically.

But is food production really getting more and more expensive? There is, in fact, no evidence for that conclusion either. In fact, quite the contrary. Not only is food generally much cheaper to buy today, in constant dollars, than it was in Malthus's time, but it also has become cheaper during recent decades. As a matter of fact, there have been increasing complaints among food exporters, especially in the third world, that food prices have fallen in relation to other commodities. For example, in 1992 a United Nations report recorded a 38 percent fall in the relative prices of "basic foods" over the last decade.[24] This is entirely in line with the trend, during the last three decades, toward declining relative prices of particular food items, in relation to the prices of manufactured goods. The World Bank's adjusted estimates of the prices of particular food crops, between 1953–1955 and 1983–1985, show similarly steep declines for such staples as rice (42 percent), wheat (57 percent), sorghum (39 percent), and maize (37 percent).[25]

Not only is food getting less expensive, but we also have to bear in mind that the current increase in food production (substantial and well ahead of population growth, as it is) is itself being kept in check by the difficulties in selling food profitably, as the relative prices of food have fallen. Those neo-Malthusians who concede that food production is now growing faster than population often point out that it is growing "only a little faster than population," and they are inclined to interpret this as evidence that we are reaching the limits of what we can produce to keep pace with population growth.

But that is surely the wrong conclusion to draw in view of the falling relative prices of food, and the current difficulties in selling food, since it ignores the effects of economic incentives that govern production. When we take into account the persistent cheapening of food prices, we have good grounds to suggest that food output is being held back by a lack of effective demand in the market. The imaginary crisis in food production, contradicted as it is by the upward trends of total and regional food output per head, is thus further debunked by an analysis of the economic incentives to produce more food.

Deprived Lives and Slums

I have examined the alleged "food problem" associated with population growth in some detail because it has received so much attention both in the traditional Malthusian literature and in the recent writings of neo-Malthusians. In concentrating on his claim that growing populations would not have enough food, Malthus differed from Condorcet's broader presentation of the population question. Condorcet's own emphasis was on the possibility of "a continual diminution of happiness" as a result of population growth, a diminution that could occur in many different ways—not just through the deprivation of food, but through a decline in living conditions generally. That more extensive worry can remain even when Malthus's analysis of the food supply is rejected.

Indeed, average income and food production per head can go on increasing even as the wretchedly deprived living conditions of particular sections of the population get worse, as they have in many parts of the third world. The living conditions of backward regions and deprived classes can decline even when a country's economic growth is very rapid on the average. Brazil during the 1960s and 1970s provided an extreme example of this. The sense that there are just "too many people" around often arises from seeing the desperate lives of people in the large and rapidly growing urban slums—*bidonvilles*—in poor countries, sobering reminders that we should not take too much comfort from aggregate statistics of economic progress.

But in an essay addressed mainly to the population problem, what we have to ask is not whether things are just fine in the third world (they obviously are not), but whether population growth is the root cause of the deprivations that people suffer. The question is whether the particular instances of deep poverty we observe derive mainly from population growth rather than from other factors that lead to unshared prosperity and persistent and possibly growing inequality. The tendency to see in population growth an explanation for every calamity that afflicts poor people is now fairly well established in some circles, and the message that gets transmitted constantly is the opposite of the old picture postcard: "Wish you weren't here."

To see in population growth the main reason for the growth of overcrowded and very poor slums in large cities, for example, is not empirically convincing. It does not help to explain why the slums of Calcutta and Bombay have grown worse at a faster rate than those of Karachi and Islamabad (India's population growth rate is 2.1 percent per year, Pakistan's 3.1), or why Jakarta has deteriorated faster than Ankara or Istanbul (Indonesian population growth is 1.8 percent, Turkey's 2.3), or why the slums of Mexico City have become worse more rapidly than those of San José (Mexico's population growth rate is 2.0, Costa Rica's 2.8), or why Harlem can seem more and more deprived when compared with the poorer districts of Singapore (US population growth rate is 1.0, Singapore's is 1.8). Many causal factors affect the degree of deprivation in particular parts of a country—rural as well as urban—and to try to see them all as resulting from overpopulation is the negation of social analysis.

This is not to deny that population growth may well have an effect on deprivation, but only to insist that any investigation of the effects of population growth must be part of the analysis of economic and political processes, including the effects of other variables. It is the isolationist view of population growth that should be rejected.

Threats to the Environment

In his concern about "a continual diminution of happiness" from population growth, Condorcet was a pioneer in considering the possibility that natural raw materials might be used up, thereby making living conditions worse. In his characteristically rationalist solution, which relied partly on voluntary and reasoned measures to reduce the birth rate, Condorcet also envisaged the development of less improvident technology: "The manufacture of articles will be achieved with less wastage in raw materials and will make better use of them."[26]

The effects of a growing population on the environment could be a good deal more serious than the food problems that have received so much attention in the literature inspired by Malthus. If the environment is damaged by population pressures this obviously affects the kind of life we lead, and the possibilities of a "diminution in happiness" can be quite considerable. In dealing with this problem, we have to distinguish once again between the long and the short run. The short-run picture tends to be dominated by the fact that the per-capita consumption of food, fuel, and other goods by people in third world countries is often relatively low; consequently the impact of population growth in these countries is not, in relative terms, so damaging to the global environment. But the problems of the local environment can, of course, be serious in many developing economies. They vary from the "neighborhood pollution" created by unregulated industries to the pressure of denser populations on rural resources such as fields and woods.[27] (The Indian authorities had to close down several factories in and around Agra, since the façade of the Taj Mahal was turning pale as a result of chemical pollution from local factories.) But it remains true that one additional American typically has a larger negative impact on the ozone layer, global warmth, and other elements of the earth's environment than dozens of Indians and Zimbabweans put together. Those who argue for the immediate need for forceful population control in the third world to preserve the global environment must first recognize this elementary fact.

This does not imply, as is sometimes suggested, that as far as the global environment is concerned, population growth in the third world is nothing to worry about. The long-run impact on the global environment of population growth in the develop-ing countries can be expected to be large. As the Indians and the Zimbabweans develop economically, they too will consume a great deal more, and they will pose, in the future, a threat to the earth's environment similar to that of people in the rich countries today. The long-run threat of population to the environment is a real one.

3.

Women's Deprivation and Power

Since reducing the birth rate can be slow, this and other long-run problems should be addressed right now. Solutions will no doubt have to be found in the two directions to which, as it happens, Condorcet pointed: (1) developing new technology and new behavior patterns that would waste little and pollute less, and (2) fostering social and economic changes that would gradually bring down the growth rate of population.

On reducing birth rates, Condorcet's own solution not only included enhancing economic opportunity and security, but also stressed the importance of education, particularly female education. A better-educated population could have a more informed discussion of the kind of life we have reason to value; in particular it would reject the drudgery of a life of continuous child bearing and rearing that is routinely forced on many third world women. That drudgery, in some ways, is the most immediately adverse consequence of high fertility rates.

Central to reducing birth rates, then, is a close connection between women's well-being and their power to make their own decisions and bring about changes in the fertility pattern. Women in many third world countries are deprived by high birth frequency of the freedom to do other things in life, not to mention the medical dangers of repeated pregnancy and high maternal mortality, which are both characteristic of many developing countries. It is thus not surprising that reductions in birth rates have been typically associated with improvement of women's status and their ability to make their voices heard—often the result of expanded opportunities for schooling and political activity.[28]

There is nothing particularly exotic about declines in the birth rate occurring through a process of voluntary rational assessment, of which Condorcet spoke. It is what people do when they have some basic education, know about family planning methods and have access to them, do not readily accept a life of persistent drugery, and are not deeply anxious about their economic security. It is also what they do when they are not forced by high infant and child mortality rates to be so worried that no child will survive to support them in their old age that they try to have many children. In country after country the birth rate has come down with more female education, the reduction of mortality rates, the expansion of economic means and security, and greater public discussion of ways of living.

Development versus Coercion

There is little doubt that this process of social and economic change will over time cut down the birth rate. Indeed the growth rate of world population is already firmly declining—it came down from 2.2 percent in the 1970s to 1.7 percent between 1980 and 1992. Had imminent cataclysm been threatening, we might have had good reason to reject such gradual progress and consider more drastic means of population control, as some have advocated. But that apocalyptic view is empirically baseless. There is no imminent emergency that calls for a breathless response. What is called for is systematic support for people's own decisions to reduce family size through expanding education and health care, and through economic and social development.

It is often asked where the money needed for expanding education, health care, etc., would be found. Education, health services, and many other means of improving the quality of life are typically highly labor-intensive and are thus relatively inexpensive in poor countries (because of low wages).[29] While poor countries have less money to spend, they also need less money to provide these services. For this reason many poor countries have indeed been able to expand educational and health services widely without waiting to become prosperous through the process of economic growth. Sri Lanka, Costa Rica, Indonesia, and Thailand are good examples, and there are many others. While the impact of these social services on the quality and length of life have been much studied, they are also major means of reducing the birth rate.

By contrast with such open and voluntary developments, coercive methods, such as the "one child policy" in some regions, have been tried in China, particularly since the reforms of 1979. Many commentators have pointed out that by 1992 the Chinese birth rate has fallen to 19 per 1,000, compared with 29 per 1,000 in India, and 37 per 1,000 for the average of poor countries other than China and India. China's total fertility rate (reflecting the number of children born per woman) is now at "the replacement level" of 2.0, compared with India's 3.6 and the weighted average of 4.9 for low-income countries other than China and India.[30] Hasn't

China shown the way to "solve" the population problem in other developing countries as well?

4.

China's Population Policies

The difficulties with this "solution" are of several kinds. First, if freedom is valued at all, the lack of freedom associated with this approach must be seen to be a social loss in itself. The importance of reproductive freedom has been persuasively emphasized by women's groups throughout the world.[31]

The loss of freedom is often dismissed on the grounds that because of cultural differences, authoritarian policies that would not be tolerated in the West are acceptable to Asians. While we often hear references to "despotic" Oriental traditions, such arguments are no more convincing than a claim that compulsion in the West is justified by the traditions of the Spanish Inquisition or of the Nazi concentration camps. Frequent references are also made to the emphasis on discipline in the "Confucian tradition"; but that is not the only tradition in the "East," nor is it easy to assess the implications of that tradition for modern Asia (even if we were able to show that discipline is more important for Confucius than it is for, say, Plato or Saint Augustine).

Only a democratic expression of opinion could reveal whether citizens would find a compulsory system acceptable. While such a test has not occurred in China, one did in fact take place in India during "the emergency period" in the 1970s, when Indira Gandhi's government imposed compulsory birth control and suspended various legal freedoms. In the general elections that followed, the politicians favoring the policy of coercion were overwhelmingly defeated. Furthermore, family planning experts in India have observed how the briefly applied programs of compulsory sterilization tended to discredit voluntary birth control programs generally, since people became deeply suspicious of the entire movement to control fertility.

Second, apart from the fundamental issue of whether people are willing to accept compulsory birth control, its specific consequences must also be considered. Insofar as coercion is effective, it works by making people do things they would not freely do. The social consequences of such compulsion, including the ways in which an unwilling population tends to react when it is coerced, can be appalling. For example, the demands of a "one-child family" can lead to the neglect—or worse—of a second child, thereby increasing the infant mortality rate. Moreover, in a country with a strong preference for male children—a preference shared by China and many other countries in Asia and North Africa—a policy of allowing only one child per family can easily lead to the fatal neglect of a female child. There is much evidence that this is fairly widespread in China, with very adverse effects on infant mortality rates. There are reports that female children have been severely neglected as well as suggestions that female infanticide occurs with considerable frequency. Such consequences are hard to tolerate morally, and perhaps politically also, in the long run.

Third, what is also not clear is exactly how much additional reduction in the birth rate has been achieved through these coercive methods. Many of China's longstanding social and economic programs have been valuable in reducing fertility, including those that have expanded education for women as well as men, made health care more generally available, provided more job opportunities for women, and stimulated rapid economic growth. These factors would themselves have reduced the birth rates, and it is not clear how much "extra lowering" of fertility rates has been achieved in China through compulsion.

For example, we can determine whether many of the countries that match (or outmatch) China in life expectancy, female literacy rates, and female participation in the labor force actually have a higher fertility rate than China. Of all the countries in the world for which data are given in the *World Development Report 1994*, there are only three such countries: Jamaica (2.7), Thailand (2.2), and Sweden (2.1)—and the fertility rates of two of these are close to China's (2.0). Thus the additional contribution of coercion to reducing fertility in China is by no means clear, since compulsion was superimposed on a society that was already reducing its birth rate and in which education and jobs outside the home were available to large numbers of women. In some regions of China the compulsory program needed little enforcement, whereas in other—more backward—regions, it had to be applied with much severity, with terrible consequences in infant mortality and discrimination against female children. While China may get too much credit for its authoritarian measures, it gets far too little credit for the other, more collaborative and participatory, policies it has followed, which have themselves helped to cut down the birth rate.

China and India

A useful contrast can be drawn between China and India, the two most populous countries in the world. If we look only at the national averages, it is easy to see that China with its low fertility rate of 2.0 has achieved much more than India has with its average fertility rate of 3.6. To what extent this contrast can be attributed to the effectiveness of the coercive policies used in China is not clear, since we would expect the fertility rate to be much lower in China in view of its higher percentage of female literacy (almost twice as high), higher life expectancy (almost ten years more), larger female involvement (by three quarters) in the labor force, and so on. But India is a country of great diversity, whose different states have very unequal achievements in literacy, health care, and economic and social development. Most states in India are far behind the Chinese provinces in educational achievement (with the exception of Tibet, which has the lowest literacy rate of any Chinese or Indian state), and the same applies to other factors that affect fertility. However, the state of Kerala in southern India provides an interesting comparison with China, since it too has high levels of basic education, health care, and so on. Kerala is a state within a country, but with its 29 million people, it is larger than most countries in the world (including Canada). Kerala's birth rate of 18 per 1,000 is actually lower than China's 19 per 1,000, and its fertility rate is 1.8 for 1991, compared with China's 2.0 for 1992. These low rates have been achieved without any state coercion.[32]

The roots of Kerala's success are to be found in the kinds of social progress Condorcet hoped for, including among others, a high female literacy rate (86 percent, which is substantially higher than China's 68 percent). The rural literacy rate is in fact higher in Kerala—for women as well as men—than in every single province in China. Male and female life expectancies at birth in China are respectively 67 and 71 years; the provisional 1991 figures for men and women in Kerala are 71 and 74 years. Women have been active in Kerala's economic and political life for a long time. A high proportion do skilled and semi-skilled work and a large number have taken part in educational movements.[33] It is perhaps of symbolic importance that the first public pronouncement of the need for widespread elementary education in any part of India was made in 1817 by Rani Gouri Parvathi Bai, the young queen of the princely state of Travancore, which makes up a substantial part of modern Kerala. For a long time public discussions in Kerala have centered on women's rights and the undesirability of couples marrying when very young.

This political process has been voluntary and collaborative, rather than coercive, and the adverse reactions that have been observed in China, such as infant mortality, have not occurred in Kerala. Kerala's low fertility rate has been achieved along with an infant mortality rate of 16.5 per 1,000 live births (17 for boys and 16 for girls), compared with China's 31 (28 for boys and 33 for girls). And as a result of greater gender equality in Kerala, women have not suffered from higher mortality rates than men in Kerala, as they have in the rest of India and in China. Even the ratio of females to males in the total population in Kerala (above 1.03) is quite close to that of the current ratios in Europe and America (reflecting the usual pattern of lower female mortality whenever women and men receive similar care). By contrast, the average female to male ratio in China is 0.94 and in India as a whole 0.93.[34] Anyone drawn to the Chinese experience of compulsory birth control must take note of these facts.

The temptation to use the "override" approach arises at least partly from impatience with the allegedly slow process of fertility reduction through collaborative, rather than coercive, attempts. Yet Kerala's birth rate has fallen from 44 per 1,000 in the 1950s to 18 by 1991—not a sluggish decline. Nor is Kerala unique in this respect. Other societies, such as those of Sri Lanka, South Korea, and Thailand, which have relied on expanding education and reducing mortality rates—instead of on coercion—have also achieved sharp declines in fertility and birth rates.

It is also interesting to compare the time required for reducing fertility in China with that in the two states in India, Kerala and Tamil Nadu, which have done most to encourage voluntary and collaborative reduction in birth rates (even though Tamil Nadu is well behind Kerala in each respect).[35] Table 2 shows the fertility rates both in 1979, when the one-child policy and related programs were introduced in China, and in 1991. Despite China's one-child policy and other coercive measures, its fertility rate seems to have fallen much less sharply than those of Kerala and Tamil Nadu. The "override"

Table 2 Fertility Rates in China, Kerala, and Tamil Nadu

	1979	1991
China	2.8	2.0
Kerala	3.0	1.8
Tamil Nadu	3.5	2.2

Sources: For China, Xizhe Peng, *Demographic Transition in China* (Oxford University Press, 1991), Li Chengrui, *A Study of China's Population* (Beijing: Foreign Language Press, 1992), and *World Development Report 1994.* For India, *Sample Registration System 1979–80* (New Dehli: Ministry of Home Affairs, 1982) and *Sample Registration System: Fertility and Mortality Indicators 1991* (New Delhi: Ministry of Home Affairs, 1993).

view is very hard to defend on the basis of the Chinese experience, the only systematic and sustained attempt to impose such a policy that has so far been made.

Family Planning

Even those who do not advocate legal or economic coercion sometimes suggest a variant of the "override" approach—the view, which has been getting increasing support, that the highest priority should be given simply to family planning, even if this means diverting resources from education and health care as well as other activities associated with development. We often hear claims that enormous declines in birth rates have been accomplished through making family planning services available, without waiting for improvements in education and health care.

The experience of Bangladesh is sometimes cited as an example of such success. Indeed, even though the female literacy rate in Bangladesh is only around 22 percent and life expectancy at birth no higher than 55 years, fertility rates have been substantially reduced there through the greater availability of family planning services, including counseling.[36] We have to examine carefully what lessons can, in fact, be drawn from this evidence.

First, it is certainly significant that Bangladesh has been able to cut its fertility rate from 7.0 to 4.5 during the short period between 1975 and 1990, an achievement that discredits the view that people will not voluntarily embrace family planning in the poorest countries. But we have to ask further whether family planning efforts may themselves be sufficient to make fertility come down to really low levels, without providing for female education and the other features of a fuller collaborative approach. The fertility rate of 4.5 in Bangladesh is still quite high—considerably higher than even India's average rate of 3.6. To begin stabilizing the population, the fertility rates would have to come down closer to the "replacement level" of 2.0, as has happened in Kerala and Tamil Nadu, and in many other places outside the Indian subcontinent. Female education and the other social developments connected with lowering the birth rate would still be much needed.

Contrasts between the records of Indian states offer some substantial lessons here. While Kerala, and to a smaller extent Tamil Nadu, have surged ahead in achieving radically reduced fertility rates, other states in India in the so-called "northern heartland" (such as Uttar Pradesh, Bihar, Madhya Pradesh, and Rajasthan), have very low levels of education, especially female education, and of general health care (often combined with pressure on the poor to accept birth control measures, including sterilization, as a qualifying condition for medical attention and other public services). These states all have high fertility rates—between 4.4 and 5.1. The regional contrasts within India strongly argue for the collaborative approach, including active and educated participation of women.

The threat of an impending population crisis tempts many international observers to suggest that priority be given to family planning arrangements in the third world countries over other commitments such as education and health care, a redirection of public efforts that is often recommended by policy-makers and at international conferences. Not only will this shift have negative effects on people's well-being and reduce their freedoms, it can also be self-defeating if the goal is to stabilize population.

The appeal of such slogans as "family planning first" rests partly on misconceptions about what is needed to reduce fertility rates, but also on mistaken beliefs about the excessive costs of social development, including education and health care. As has been discussed, both these activities are highly labor intensive, and thus relatively inexpensive even in very poor economies. In fact, Kerala, India's star performer in expanding education and reducing both death rates and birth rates, is among the poorer Indian states. Its domestically produced income is quite low—lower indeed in per capita terms than even the Indian average—even if this is somewhat deceptive, for the greatest expansion of Kerala's earnings derives from citizens who work outside the state. Kerala's ability to finance adequately both educational expansion and health coverage depends on both activities being labor-intensive; they can be made available even in a low-income economy when there is the political will to use them. Despite its economic backwardness, an issue which Kerala will undoubtedly have to address before long (perhaps by reducing bureaucratic controls over agriculture and industry, which have stagnated), its level of social development has been remarkable, and that has turned out to be crucial in reducing fertility rates. Kerala's fertility rate of 1.8 not only compares well with China's 2.0, but also with the US's and Sweden's 2.1, Canada's 1.9, and Britain's and France's 1.8.

The population problem is serious, certainly, but neither because of "the proportion between the natural increase of population and food" nor because of some impending apocalypse. There are reasons for worry about the long-term effects of population growth on the environment; and there are strong reasons for concern about the adverse effects of high birth rates on the quality of life, especially of women. With greater opportunities for education (especially female education), reduction of mortality rates (especially of children), improvement in economic security (especially in old age), and greater participation of women in employment and in political action, fast reductions in birth rates can be expected to result through the decisions and actions of those whose lives depend on them.

This is happening right now in many parts of the world, and the result has been a considerable slowing down of world population growth. The best way of dealing with the population problem is to help to spread these processes elsewhere. In contrast, the emergency mentality based on false beliefs in imminent cataclysms leads to breathless responses that are deeply counterproductive, preventing the development of rational and sustainable family planning. Coercive policies of forced birth control involve terrible social sacrifices, and there is little evidence that they are more effective in reducing birth rates than serious programs of collaborative action.

NOTES

1. This paper draws on my lecture arranged by the "Eminent Citizens Committee for Cairo '94" at the United Nations in New York on April 18, 1994, and also on research supported by the National Science Foundation.
2. Paul Ehrlich, *The Population Bomb* (Ballantine, 1968). More recently Paul Ehrlich and Anne H. Ehrlich have written *The Population Explosion* (Simon and Schuster, 1990).
3. Garrett Hardin, *Living within Limits* (Oxford University Press, 1993).
4. Thomas Robert Malthus, *Essay on the Principle of Population As It Affects the Future Improvement of Society with Remarks on the Speculation of Mr. Godwin, M. Condorcet, and Other Writers* (London: J. Johnson, 1798), Chapter 8; in the Penguin classics edition, *An Essay on the Principle of Population* (1982), p. 123.

5. See Simon Kuznets, *Modern Economic Growth* (Yale University Press, 1966).

6. Note by the Secretary-General of the United Nations to the Preparatory Committee for the International Conference on Population and Development, Third Session, A/Conf.171/PC/5, February 18, 1994, p. 30.

7. Philip Morris Hauser's estimates are presented in the National Academy of Sciences publication *Rapid Population Growth: Consequences and Policy Implications,* Vol. 1 (Johns Hopkins University Press, 1971). See also Simon Kuznets, *Modern Economic Growth*, Chapter 2.

8. For an important collection of papers on these and related issues see Sir Francis Graham-Smith, F.R.S., editor, *Population—The Complex Reality: A Report of the Population Summit of the World's Scientific Academies*, issued by the Royal Society and published in the US by North American Press, Golden, Colorado. See also D. Gale Johnson and Ronald D. Lee, editors, *Population Growth and Economic Development, Issues and Evidence* (University of Wisconsin Press, 1987).

9. Garrett Hardin, *Living within Limits*, p. 274.

10. Paul Kennedy, who has discussed important problems in the distinctly "social" aspects of population growth, has pointed out that this debate "has, in one form or another, been with us since then," and "it is even more pertinent today than when Malthus composed his *Essay*," in *Preparing for the Twenty-first Century* (Random House, 1993), pp. 5–6.

11. On the importance of "enlightenment" traditions in Condorcet's thinking, see Emma Rothschild, "Condorcet and the Conflict of Values," forthcoming in *The Historical Journal*.

12. Marie Jean Antoine Nicholas de Caritat Marquis de Condorcet's *Esquisse d'un Tableau Historique des Progrès de l'Esprit Humain, Xe Epoque* (1795). English translation by June Barraclough, *Sketch for a Historical Picture of the Progress of the Human Mind*, with an introduction by Stuart Hampshire (Weidenfeld and Nicholson, 1955), pp. 187–192.

13. T. R. Malthus, *A Summary View of the Principle of Population* (London: John Murray, 1830); in the Penguin classics edition (1982), p. 243; italics added.

14. On practical policies, including criticism of poverty relief and charitable hospitals, advocated for Britain by Malthus and his followers, see William St. Clair, *The Godwins and the Shelleys: A Biography of a Family* (Norton, 1989).

15. Malthus, *Essay on the Principle of Population*, Chapter 17; in the Penguin classics edition, *An Essay on the Principle of Population*, pp. 198–199. Malthus showed some signs of weakening in this belief as he grew older.

16. Gerard Piel, *Only One World: Our Own to Make and to Keep* (Freeman, 1992).

17. For discussions of these empirical connections, see R. A. Easterlin, editor, *Population and Economic Change in Developing Countries* (University of Chicago Press, 1980): T. P. Schultz, *Economics of Population* (Addison-Wesley, 1981); J. C. Caldwell, *Theory of Fertility Decline* (Academic Press, 1982); E. King and M. A. Hill, editors, *Women's Education in Developing Countries* (Johns Hopkins University Press, 1992); Nancy Birdsall, "Economic Approaches to Population Growth" in *The Handbook of Development Economics*, edited by H. B. Chenery and T. N. Srinivasan (Amsterdam: North Holland, 1988); Robert Cassen et al., *Population and Development: Old Debates, New Conclusions* (New Brunswick: Overseas Development Council/Transaction Publishers, 1994).

18. World Bank, *World Development Report 1994* (Oxford University Press, 1994), Table 25. pp. 210–211.

19. World Bank, *World Development Report 1994*, Table 2.

20. These issues are discussed in my joint book with Jean Drèze, *Hunger and Public Action* (Oxford University Press, 1989), and the three volumes edited by us, *The Political Economy of Hunger* (Oxford University Press, 1990), and also in my paper "Economic Regress: Concepts and Features," *Proceedings of the World Bank Annual Conference on Development Economics 1993* (World Bank, 1994).

21. This is confirmed by, among other statistics, the food production figures regularly presented by the United Nations Food and Agricultural Organization (see the *FAO Quarterly Bulletin of Statistics*, and also the *FAO Monthly Bulletins*).

22. For a more detailed picture and reference to data sources, see my "Population and Reasoned Agency: Food, Fertility and Economic Development," in *Population, Economic Development, and the Environment*, edited by Kerstin Lindahl-Kiessling and Hans Landberg (Oxford University Press, 1994); see also the other contributions in this volume. The data presented here have been slightly updated from later publications of the FAO.

23. On this see my *Poverty and Famines* (Oxford University Press, 1981).

24. See UNCTAD VIII, Analytical Report by the UNCTAD Secretariat to the Conference (United Nations, 1992). Table V-S, p. 235. The period covered is between 1979–1981 to 1988–1990. These figures and related ones are discussed in greater detail in my paper "Population and Reasoned Agency," cited earlier.

25. World Bank, *Price Prospects for Major Primary Commodities*, Vol. II (World Bank, March 1993). Annex Tables 6, 12, and 18.

26. Condorcet, *Esquisse d'un Tableau Historique des Progrès de l'Esprit Humain*; in the 1968 reprint, p. 187.

27. The importance of "local" environmental issues is stressed and particularly explored by Partha Dasgupta in *An Inquiry into Well-Being and Destitution* (Oxford University Press, 1993).

28. In a forthcoming monograph by Jean Drèze and myself tentatively called "India: Economic Development and Social Opportunities," we discuss the importance of women's political agency in rectifying some of the more serious lapses in Indian economic and social performance—not just pertaining to the deprivation of women themselves.

29. See Jean Drèze and Amartya Sen, *Hunger and Public Action* (Oxford University Press, 1989), which also investigates the remarkable success of some poor countries in providing widespread educational and health services.

30. World Bank, *World Development Report 1994*, p. 212; and *Sample Registration System: Fertility and Mortality Indicators 1991* (New Delhi: Ministry of Home Affairs, 1993).

31. See the discussions, and the literature cited, in Gita Sen. Adrienne German, and Lincoln Chen, editors, *Population Policies Reconsidered: Health, Empowerment, and Rights* (Harvard Center for Population and Development Studies/International Women's Health Coalition, 1994).

32. On the actual processes involved, see T. N. Krishnan, "Demographic Transition in Kerala: Facts and Factors," in *Economic and Political Weekly*, Vol. 11 (1976), and P. N. Mari Bhat and S. I. Rajan, "Demographic Transition in Kerala Revisited," in *Economic and Political Weekly*, Vol. 25 (1990).

33. See, for example, Robin Jeffrey, "Culture and Governments: How Women Made Kerala Literate," in *Pacific Affairs*, Vol. 60 (1987).

34. On this see my "More Than 100 Million Women Are Missing," *New York Review of Books*, December 20, 1990; Ansley J. Coale, "Excess Female Mortality and the Balance of the Sexes: An Estimate of the Number of 'Missing Females'," *Population and Development Review*, No. 17 (1991); Amartya Sen, "Missing Women," *British Medical Journal*, No. 304 (March 1992); Stephan Klasen, "'Missing Women' Reconsidered," *World Development*, forthcoming.

35. Tamil Nadu has benefited from an active and efficient voluntary program of family planning, but these efforts have been helped by favorable social conditions as well, such as a high literacy rate (the second highest among the sixteen major states), a high rate of female participation in work outside the home (the third highest), a relatively low infant mortality rate (the third lowest), and a traditionally higher age of marriage. See also T. V. Antony, "The Family Planning Programme—Lessons from Tamil Nadu's Experience," *Indian Journal of Social Science*, Volume 5 (1992).

36. World Bank and Population Reference Bureau, *Success in a Challenging Environment: Fertility Decline in Bangladesh* (World Bank, 1993).

Famine, Affluence, and Morality

Peter Singer

Peter Singer is a professor of philosophy and director of the Centre for Human Bioethics at Monash University, in Victoria, Australia. He is the author of Animal Liberation *(1975) and* Practical Ethics *(1980) and the editor of* Applied Ethics *(1986).*

 Singer considers it morally wrong for affluent people to spend money on nonessential goods while others are starving. Concerning the suffering of others, Singer asserts a principle we are morally obligated to follow. The principle states that if we can prevent suffering without sacrificing anything of comparable moral importance, then we ought to do it. Giving monetary assistance to aid the starving is one way to prevent suffering. Those people who have the means are morally obligated to give money away until they sacrifice something of comparable moral importance, even if it requires them to radically alter and drastically reduce their standard of living.

As I write this, in November 1971, people are dying in East Bengal from lack of food, shelter, and medical care. The suffering and death that are occurring there now are not inevitable, not unavoidable in any fatalistic sense of the term. Constant poverty, a cyclone, and a civil war have turned at least nine million people into destitute refugees; nevertheless, it is not beyond the capacity of the richer nations to give enough assistance to reduce any further suffering to very small proportions. The decisions and actions of human beings can prevent this kind of suffering. Unfortunately, human beings have not made the necessary decisions. At the individual level, people have, with very few exceptions, not responded to the situation in any signifi-

Singer, Peter; "Famine, Affluence, and Morality." *Philosophy and Public Affairs*, Vol. 1, No. 3, Spring 1972. Reprinted by permission of Princeton University Press.

cant way. Generally speaking, people have not given large sums to relief funds; they have not written to their parliamentary representatives demanding increased government assistance; they have not demonstrated in the streets, held symbolic fasts, or done anything else directed toward providing the refugees with the means to satisfy their essential needs. At the government level, no government has given the sort of massive aid that would enable the refugees to survive for more than a few days. Britain, for instance, has given rather more than most countries. It has, to date, given £14,750,000. For comparative purposes, Britain's share of the nonrecoverable development costs of the Anglo-French Concorde project is already in excess of £275,000,000, and on present estimates will reach £440,000,000. The implication is that the British government values a supersonic transport more than thirty times as highly as it values the lives of the nine million refugees. Australia is another country which, on a per capita basis, is well up in the "aid to Bengal" table. Australia's aid, however, amounts to less than one-twelfth of the cost of Sydney's new opera house. The total amount given, from all sources, now stands at about £65,000,000. The estimated cost of keeping the refugees alive for one year is £464,000,000. Most of the refugees have now been in the camps for more than six months. The World Bank has said that India needs a minimum of £300,000,000 in assistance from other countries before the end of the year. It seems obvious that assistance on this scale will not be forthcoming. India will be forced to choose between letting the refugees starve or diverting funds from her own development program, which will mean that more of her own people will starve in the future.[1]

These are the essential facts about the present situation in Bengal. So far as it concerns us here, there is nothing unique about this situation except its magnitude. The Bengal emergency is just the latest and most acute of a series of major emergencies in various parts of the world, arising both from natural and from man-made causes. There are also many parts of the world in which people die from malnutrition and lack of food independent of any special emergency. I take Bengal as my example only because it is the present concern, and because the size of the problem has ensured that it has been given adequate publicity. Neither individuals nor governments can claim to be unaware of what is happening there.

What are the moral implications of a situation like this? In what follows, I shall argue that the way people in relatively affluent countries react to a situation like that in Bengal cannot be justified; indeed, the whole way we look at moral issues— our moral conceptual scheme—needs to be altered, and with it, the way of life that has come to be taken for granted in our society.

In arguing for this conclusion I will not, of course, claim to be morally neutral. I shall, however, try to argue for the moral position that I take, so that anyone who accepts certain assumptions, to be made explicit, will, I hope, accept my conclusion.

I begin with the assumption that suffering and death from lack of food, shelter, and medical care are bad. I think most people will agree about this, although one may reach the same view by different routes. I shall not argue for this view. People can hold all sorts of eccentric positions, and perhaps for some of them it would not follow that death by starvation is in itself bad. It is difficult, perhaps impossible, to refute such positions, and so for brevity I will henceforth take this assumption as accepted. Those who disagree need read no further.

My next point is this: if it is in our power to prevent something bad from happening, without thereby sacrificing anything of comparable moral importance, we ought, morally, to do it. By "without sacrificing anything of comparable moral importance" I mean without causing anything else comparably bad to happen, or doing something that is wrong in itself, or failing to promote some moral good, comparable in significance to the bad thing that we can prevent. This principle seems almost as uncontroversial as the last one. It requires us only to prevent what is bad, and not to promote what is good, and it requires this of us only when we can do it without sacrificing anything that is, from the moral point of view, comparably important. I could even, as far as the application of my argument to the Bengal emergency is concerned, qualify the point so as to make it: if it is in our power to prevent something very bad from happening, without thereby sacrificing anything morally significant, we ought, morally, to do it. An application of this principle would be as follows: if I am walking past a shallow pond and see a child drowning in it, I ought to wade in and pull the child out. This will mean getting my clothes muddy, but this is insignificant, while the death of the child would presumably be a very bad thing.

The uncontroversial appearance of the principle just stated is deceptive. If it were acted upon, even in its qualified form, our lives, our society, and our world would be fundamentally changed. For the principle takes, firstly, no account of proximity or distance. It makes no moral difference whether the person I can help is a neighbor's child ten yards from me or a Bengali whose name I shall never know, ten thousand miles away. Secondly, the principle makes no distinction between cases in which I am the only person who could possibly do anything and cases in which I am just one among millions in the same position.

I do not think I need to say much in defense of the refusal to take proximity and distance into account. The fact that a person is physically near to us, so that we have personal contact with him, may make it more likely that we *shall* assist him, but this does not show that we *ought* to help him rather than another who happens to be further away. If we accept any principle of impartiality, universalizability, equality, or whatever, we cannot discriminate against someone merely because he is far away from us (or we are far away from him). Admittedly, it is possible that we are in a better position to judge what needs to be done to help a person near to us than one far away, and perhaps also to provide the assistance we judge to be necessary. If this were the case, it would be a reason for helping those near to us first. This may once have been a justification for being more concerned with the poor in one's own town than with famine victims in India. Unfortunately for those who like to keep their moral responsibilities limited, instant communication and swift transportation have changed the situation. From the moral point of view, the development of the world into a "global village" has made an important, though still unrecognized, difference to our moral situation. Expert observers and supervisors, sent out by famine relief organizations or permanently stationed in famine-prone areas, can direct our aid to a refugee in Bengal almost as effectively as we could get it to someone in our own block. There would seem, therefore, to be no possible justification for discriminating on geographical grounds.

There may be greater need to defend the second implication of my principle—that the fact that there are millions of other people in the same position, in respect to the Bengali refugees, as I am, does not make the situation significantly different from a situation in which I am the only person who can prevent something very bad from occurring. Again, of course, I admit that there is a psychological difference between the cases: one feels less guilty about doing nothing if one can point to others, similarly placed, who have also done nothing. Yet this can make no real difference to our moral obligations.[2] Should I consider that I am less obliged to pull the drowning child out of the pond if on looking around I see other people, no further away than I am, who have also noticed the child but are doing nothing? One has only to ask this question to see the absurdity of the view that numbers lessen obligation. It is a view that is an ideal excuse for inactivity; unfortunately most of the major evils—poverty, overpopulation, pollution—are problems in which everyone is almost equally involved.

The view that numbers do make a difference can be made plausible if stated in this way: if everyone in circumstances like mine gave £5 to the Bengal Relief Fund, there would be enough to provide food, shelter, and medical care for the refugees; there is no reason why I should give more than anyone else in the same circumstances as I am; therefore I have no obligation to give more than £5. Each premise in this argument is true, and the argument looks sound. It may convince us, unless we notice that it is based on a hypothetical premise, although the conclusion is not stated hypothetically. The argument would be sound if the conclusion were: if everyone in circumstances like mine were to give £5, I would have no obligation to give more than £5. If the conclusion were so stated, however, it would be obvious that the argument has no bearing on a situation in which it is not the case that everyone else gives £5. This, of course, is the actual situation. It is more or less certain that not everyone in circumstances like mine will give £5. So there will not be enough to provide the needed food, shelter, and medical care. Therefore by giving more than £5 I will prevent more suffering than I would if I gave just £5.

It might be thought that this argument has an absurd consequence. Since the situation appears to be that very few people are likely to give substantial amounts, it follows that I and everyone else in similar circumstances ought to give as much as possible, that is, at least up to the point at which by giving more one would begin to cause serious suffering for oneself and one's dependents—perhaps even beyond this point to the point of marginal utility, at which by giving more one would cause oneself and one's dependents as much suffering as one would prevent in Bengal. If everyone does this, however, there will be more than can be used for the benefit of the refugees, and some of the sacrifice will have been unnecessary. Thus, if everyone does what he ought to do, the result will not be as good as it would be if everyone did a little less than he ought to do, or if only some do all that they ought to do.

The paradox here arises only if we assume that the actions in question—sending money to the relief funds—are performed more or less simultaneously, and are also unexpected. For if it is to be expected that everyone is going to contribute something, then clearly each is not obliged to give as much as he would have been obliged to had others not been giving too. And if everyone is not acting more or less simultaneously, then those giving later will know how much more is needed, and will have no obligation to give more than is necessary to reach this amount. To say this is not to deny the principle that people in the same circumstances have the same obligations, but to point out that the fact that others have given or may be expected to give, is a relevant circumstance: those giving after it has become known that many others are giving and those giving before are not in the same circumstances. So the seemingly absurd consequence of the principle I have put forward can occur only if people are in error about the actual circumstances—that is, if they think they are giving when others are not, but in fact they are giving when others are. The result of everyone doing what he really ought to do cannot be worse than the result of everyone doing less than he ought to do, although the result of everyone doing what he reasonably believes he ought to do could be.

If my argument so far has been sound, neither our distance from a preventable evil nor the number of other people who, in respect to that evil, are in the same situation as we are, lessens our obligation to mitigate or prevent that evil. I shall therefore take as established the principle I asserted earlier. As I have already said, I need to assert it only in its qualified form: if it is in our power to prevent something very bad from happening, without thereby sacrificing anything else morally significant, we ought, morally, to do it.

The outcome of this argument is that our traditional moral categories are upset. The traditional distinction between duty and charity cannot be drawn, or at least, not in the place we normally draw it. Giving money to the Bengal Relief Fund is regarded as an act of charity in our society. The bodies which collect money are known as "charities." These organizations see themselves in this way—if you send them a check, you will be thanked for your "generosity." Because giving money is regarded as an act of charity, it is not thought that there is anything wrong with not giving. The charitable man may be praised, but the man who is not charitable is not condemned. People do not feel in any way ashamed or guilty about spending money on new clothes or a new car instead of giving it to famine relief. (Indeed, the alternative does not occur to them.) This way of looking at the matter cannot be justified. When we buy new clothes not to keep ourselves warm but to look "well-dressed" we are not providing for any important need. We would not be sacrificing anything significant if we were to continue to wear our old clothes, and give the money to famine relief. By doing so, we would be preventing another person from starving. It follows from what I have said earlier that we ought to give money away, rather than spend it on clothes which we do not need to keep us warm. To do so is not charitable, or generous. Nor is it the kind of act which philosophers and theologians have called "supererogatory"—an act which it would be good to do, but not wrong not to do. On the contrary, we ought to give the money away, and it is wrong not to do so.

I am not maintaining that there are no acts which are charitable, or that there are no acts which it would be good to do but not wrong not to do. It may be possible to redraw the distinction between duty and charity in some other place. All I am arguing here is that the present way of drawing the distinction, which makes it an act of charity for a man living at the level of affluence which most people in the "developed nations" enjoy to give money to save someone else from starvation, cannot be supported. It is beyond the scope of my argument to consider whether the distinction should be redrawn or abolished altogether. There would be many other possible ways of drawing the distinction—for instance, one might decide that it is good to make other people as happy as possible, but not wrong not to do so.

Despite the limited nature of the revision in our moral conceptual scheme which I am proposing, the revision would, given the extent of both affluence and famine in the world today, have radical implications. These implications may lead to further objections, distinct from those I have already considered. I shall discuss two of these.

One objection to the position I have taken might be simply that it is too drastic a revision of our moral scheme. People do not ordinarily judge in the way I have suggested they should. Most people reserve their moral condemnation for those who violate some moral norm, such as the norm against taking another person's property. They do not condemn those who indulge in luxury instead of giving to famine relief. But given that I did not set out to present a morally neutral description of the way people make moral judgments, the way people do in fact judge has nothing to do with the validity of my conclusion. My conclusion follows from the principle which I advanced earlier, and unless that principle is rejected, or the arguments shown to be unsound, I think the conclusion must stand, however strange it appears.

It might, nevertheless, be interesting to consider why our society, and most other societies, do judge differently from the way I have suggested they should. In a well-known article, J.O. Urmson suggests that the imperatives of duty, which tell us what we must do, as distinct from what it would be good to do but not wrong not to do, function so as to prohibit behavior that is intolerable if men are to live together in society.[3] This may explain the origin and continued existence of the present division between acts of duty and acts of charity. Moral attitudes are shaped by the needs of society, and no doubt society needs people who will observe the rules that make social existence tolerable. From the point of view of a particular society, it is essential to prevent violations of norms against killing, stealing, and so on. It is quite inessential, however, to help people outside one's own society.

If this is an explanation of our common distinction between duty and supererogation, however, it is not a justification of it. The moral point of view requires us to look beyond the interests of our own society. Previously, as I have already mentioned, this may hardly have been feasible, but it is quite feasible now. From the moral point of view, the prevention of the starvation of millions of people outside our society must be considered at least as pressing as the upholding of property norms within our society.

It has been argued by some writers, among them Sidgwick and Urmson, that we need to have a basic moral code which is not too far beyond the capacities of the ordinary man, for otherwise there will be a general breakdown of compliance with the moral code. Crudely stated, this argument suggests that if we tell people that they ought to refrain from murder and give everything they do not really need to famine relief, they will do neither, whereas if we tell them that they ought to refrain from murder and that it is good to give to famine relief but not wrong not to do so, they will at least refrain from murder. The issue here is: Where should we draw the line between conduct that is required and conduct that is good although not required, so as to get the best possible result? This would seem to be an empirical question, although a very difficult one. One objection to the Sidgwick-Urmson line of argument is that it takes insufficient account of the effect that moral standards can have on the decisions we make. Given a society in which a wealthy man who gives five percent of his income to famine relief is regarded as most generous, it is not surprising that a proposal that we all ought to give away half our incomes will be thought to be absurdly unrealistic. In a society which held that no man should have more than enough while others have less than they need, such a proposal might seem narrow-minded. What is it possible for a man to do and what he is likely to do are both, I think, very greatly influenced by what people around him are doing and expecting him to do. In any case, the possibility that by spreading the idea that we ought to be doing very much more than we are to relieve famine we shall bring about a general breakdown of moral behavior seems remote. If the stakes are an end to widespread starvation, it is worth the risk. Finally, it should be emphasized that these considerations are relevant only to the issue of what we should require from others, and not to what we ourselves ought to do.

The second objection to my attack on the present distinction between duty and charity is one which has from time to time been made against utilitarianism. It follows from some forms of utilitarian theory that we all ought, morally, to be working full time to increase the balance of happiness over misery. The position I have taken here would not lead to this conclusion in all circumstances, for if there were no bad occurrences that we could prevent without sacrificing something of comparable moral importance, my argument would have no application. Given the present conditions in many parts of the world, however, it does follow from my argument that we ought, morally, to be working full time to relieve great suffering of the sort that occurs as a result of famine or other disasters. Of course, mitigating circumstances can be adduced—for instance, that if we wear ourselves out through overwork, we shall be less effective than we would otherwise have been. Nevertheless, when all considerations of this sort have been taken

into account, the conclusion remains: we ought to be preventing as much suffering as we can without sacrificing something else of comparable moral importance. This conclusion is one which we may be reluctant to face. I cannot see, though, why it should be regarded as a criticism of the position for which I have argued, rather than a criticism of our ordinary standards of behavior. Since most people are self-interested to some degree, very few of us are likely to do everything that we ought to do. It would, however, hardly be honest to take this as evidence that it is not the case that we ought to do it.

It may still be thought that my conclusions are so wildly out of line with what everyone else thinks and has always thought that there must be something wrong with the argument somewhere. In order to show that my conclusions, while certainly contrary to contemporary Western moral standards, would not have seemed so extraordinary at other times and in other places, I would like to quote a passage from a writer not normally thought of as a way-out radical, Thomas Aquinas.

> Now, according to the natural order instituted by divine providence, material goods are provided for the satisfaction of human needs. Therefore the division and appropriation of property, which proceeds from human law, must not hinder the satisfaction of man's necessity from such goods. Equally, whatever a man has in superabundance is owed, of natural right, to the poor for their sustenance. So Ambrosius says, and it is also to be found in the *Decretum Gratiani*: "The bread which you withhold belongs to the hungry; the clothing you shut away, to the naked; and the money you bury in the earth is the redemption and freedom of the penniless."[4]

I now want to consider a number of points, more practical than philosophical, which are relevant to the application of the moral conclusion we have reached. These points challenge not the idea that we ought to be doing all we can to prevent starvation, but the idea that giving away a great deal of money is the best means to this end.

It is sometimes said that overseas aid should be a government responsibility, and that therefore one ought not to give to privately run charities. Giving privately, it is said, allows the government and the non-contributing members of society to escape their responsibilities.

This argument seems to assume that the more people there are who give to privately organized famine relief funds, the less likely it is that the government will take over full responsibility for such aid. This assumption is unsupported, and does not strike me as at all plausible. The opposite view—that if no one gives voluntarily, a government will assume that its citizens are uninterested in famine relief and would not wish to be forced into giving aid—seems more plausible. In any case, unless there were a definite probability that by refusing to give one would be helping to bring about massive government assistance, people who do refuse to make voluntary contributions are refusing to prevent a certain amount of suffering without being able to point to any tangible beneficial consequence of their refusal. So the onus of showing how their refusal will bring about government action is on those who refuse to give.

I do not, of course, want to dispute the contention that governments of affluent nations should be giving many times the amount of genuine, no-strings-attached aid that they are giving now. I agree, too, that giving privately is not enough, and that we ought to be campaigning actively for entirely new standards for both public and private contributions to famine relief. Indeed, I would sympathize with someone who thought that campaigning was more important than giving oneself, although I doubt whether preaching what one does not practice would be very effective. Unfortunately, for many people the idea that "it's the government's responsibility" is a reason for not giving which does not appear to entail any political action either.

Another, more serious reason for not giving to famine relief funds is that until there is effective population control, relieving famine merely postpones starvation. If we save the Bengal refugees now, others, perhaps the children of these refugees, will face starvation in a few years' time. In support of this, one may cite the now well-known facts about the population explosion and the relatively limited scope for expanded production.

This point, like the previous one, is an argument against relieving suffering that is happening now, because of a belief about what might happen in the future; it is unlike the previous point in that very good evidence can be adduced in support of their belief about the future. I will not go into the evidence here. I accept that the earth cannot support indefinitely a population rising at the present rate. This certainly poses a problem for anyone who thinks it important to prevent famine. Again, however, one could accept the argument without drawing the conclusion that it absolves one from any obligation to do anything to prevent famine. The conclusion that should be drawn is that the best means of preventing famine, in the long run, is population control. It would then follow from the position reached earlier that one ought to be doing all one can to promote population control (unless one held that all forms of population control were wrong in themselves, or would have significantly bad consequences). Since there are organizations working specifically for population control, one would then support them rather than more orthodox methods of preventing famine.

A third point raised by the conclusion reached earlier relates to the question of just how much we all ought to be giving away. One possibility, which has already been mentioned, is that we ought to give until we reach the level of marginal utility—that is, the level at which, by giving more, I would cause as much suffering to myself or my dependents as I would relieve by my gift. This would mean, of course, that one would reduce oneself to very near the material circumstances of a Bengali refugee. It will be recalled that earlier I put forward both a strong and a moderate version of the principle of preventing bad occurrences. The strong version, which required us to prevent bad things from happening unless in doing so we would be sacrificing something of comparable moral significance, does seem to require reducing ourselves to the level of marginal utility. I should also say that the strong version seems to me to be the correct one. I proposed the more moderate version—that we should prevent bad occurrences unless to do so, we had to sacrifice something morally significant—only in order to show that even on this surely undeniable principle a great change in our way of life is required. On the more moderate principle, it may not follow that we ought to reduce ourselves to the level of marginal utility, for one might hold that to reduce oneself and one's family to this level is to cause something significantly bad to happen. Whether this is so I shall not discuss, since, as I have said, I can see no good reason for

holding the moderate version of the principle rather than the strong version. Even if we accepted the principle only in its moderate form, however, it should be clear that we would have to give away enough to ensure that the consumer society, dependent as it is on people spending on trivia rather than giving famine relief, would slow down and perhaps disappear entirely. There are several reasons why this would be desirable in itself. The value and necessity of economic growth are now being questioned not only by conservationists, but by economists as well.[5] There is no doubt, too, that the consumer society has had a distorting effect on the goals and purposes of its members. Yet looking at the matter purely from the point of view of overseas aid, there must be a limit to the extent to which we should deliberately slow down our economy; for it might be the case that if we gave away, say forty percent of our Gross National Product, we would slow down the economy so much that in absolute terms we would be giving less than if we gave twenty-five percent of the much larger GNP that we would have if we limited our contribution to this smaller percentage.

I mention this only as an indication of the sort of factor that one would have to take into account in working out an ideal. Since Western societies generally consider one percent of the GNP an acceptable level for overseas aid, the matter is entirely academic. Nor does it affect the question of how much an individual should give in a society in which very few are giving substantial amounts.

It is sometimes said, though less often now than it used to be, that philosophers have no special role to play in public affairs, since most public issues depend primarily on an assessment of facts. On questions of fact, it is said, philosophers as such have no special expertise, and so it has been possible to engage in philosophy without committing oneself to any position on major public issues. No doubt there are some issues of social policy and foreign policy about which it can truly be said that a really expert assessment of the facts is required before taking sides or acting, but the issue of famine is surely not one of these. The facts about the existence of suffering are beyond dispute. Nor, I think, is it disputed that we can do something about it, either through orthodox methods of famine relief or through population control or both. This is therefore an issue on which philosophers are competent to take a position. The issue is one which faces everyone who has more money than he needs to support himself and his dependents, or who is in a position to take some sort of political action. These categories must include practically every teacher and student of philosophy in the universities of the Western world. If philosophy is to deal with matters that are relevant to both teachers and students, this is an issue that philosophers should discuss.

Discussion, though, is not enough. What is the point of relating philosophy to public (and personal) affairs if we do not take our conclusions seriously? In this instance, taking our conclusion seriously means acting upon it. The philosopher will not find it any easier than anyone else to alter his attitudes and way of life to the extent that, if I am right, is involved in doing everything that we ought to be doing. At the very least, though, one can make a start. The philosopher who does so will have to sacrifice some of the benefits of the consumer society, but he can find compensation in the satisfaction of a way of life in which theory and practice, if not yet in harmony, are at least coming together.

NOTES

1. There was also a third possibility: that India would go to war to enable the refugees to return to their lands. Since I wrote this paper, India has taken this way out. The situation is no longer that described above, but this does not affect my argument, as the next paragraph indicates.
2. In view of the special sense philosophers often give to the term, I should say that I use "obligation" simply as the abstract noun derived from "ought," so that "I have an obligation to" means no more, and no less, than "I ought to." This usage is in accordance with the definition of "ought" given by the *Shorter Oxford English Dictionary*: "the general verb to express duty or obligation." I do not think any issue of substance hangs on the way the term is used; sentences in which I use "obligation" could all be rewritten, although somewhat clumsily, as sentences in which a clause containing "ought" replaces the term "obligation."
3. J. O. Urmson, "Saints and Heroes," in *Essays in Moral Philosophy*, ed. Abraham I. Melden (Seattle and London, 1958), p. 214. For a related but significantly different view see also Henry Sidgwick *The Methods of Ethics*, 7th ed. (London. 1907) pp. 220–221, 492–493.
4. *Summa Theologica*, II–II, Question 66. Article 7, in *Aquinas, Selected Political Writings*, ed. A. P. d'Entreves, trans J. G. Dawson (Oxford, 1948), p. 171.
5. See, for instance. John Kenneth Galbraith, *The New Industrial State* (Boston, 1967); and E. J. Mishan, *The Cost of Economic Growth* (London, 1967).

Rights and the Duty
to Bring Aid

John Arthur

John Arthur is a professor of philosophy at State University of New York, Binghamton. He is the author of Justice and Economic Distribution (1978) and The Unfinished Constitution (1989).

Arthur asserts that views which are utilitarian in nature and hold that the affluent are morally obligated to help prevent starvation do not give the rights of the affluent adequate weight. Arthur takes issue with Peter Singer's principle which mandates that those who are affluent have a moral duty to give aid to the suffering if this aid does not cost the affluent anything of comparable moral importance. He places much weight on the importance of rights and denies that the rights of those suffering from starvation automatically outweigh the rights of the affluent in their quest for satisfaction of their interests. He argues instead for a duty of benevolence that may at times obligate the affluent to refrain from exercising their right to consume.

I

There is no doubt that the large and growing incidence of world hunger constitutes a major problem, both moral and practical, for the fortunate few who have surpluses of cheap food. Our habits regarding meat consumption exemplify the magnitude of the moral issue. Americans now consume about two and one-half times the meat they did in 1950 (currently about 125 lbs. per capita per year). Yet, meat is extremely inefficient as a source of food. Only a small portion of the total calories consumed by the animal remains to be eaten in the meat. As much as 35 percent of the food is lost by feeding and eating cattle rather than producing the grain for direct human consumption. Thus, the same amount of food consumed by Americans largely indirectly in meat form could feed one and a half billion persons on a (relatively meatless) Chinese diet. Much, if not all, of the world's food crisis could be resolved if Americans were simply to change their eating habits by moving toward direct consumption of grain and at the same time providing the surpluses for the hungry. Given this, plus the serious moral problems associated with animal suffering,[1] the overall case for vegetarianism seems strong.

I want to discuss here only one of these two related problems, the obligations of the affluent few to starving people. I begin by considering a recent article on the subject by Peter Singer, entitled "Famine, Affluence, and Morality."[2] I argue that Singer fails to establish the claim that such an obligation exists. This is the case for both the strong and weak interpretations of his view. I then go on to show that the role of rights needs to be given greater weight than utilitarian theories like Singer's allow. The rights of both the affluent and the starving are shown to be morally significant but not in themselves decisive, since obligations of benevolence can and often do override rights of others (e.g., property rights). Finally, I argue that under specific conditions the affluent are obligated not to exercise their rights to consume at the expense of others' lives.

II

Singer's argument is in two stages. First, he argues that two general moral principles are and ought to be accepted. Then he claims that the principles imply an obligation to eliminate starvation. The first principle is simply that "suffering and death from lack of food, shelter and medical care are bad."[3] This principle seems obviously true and I will have little to say about it. Some may be inclined to think that the existence of an evil in itself places an obligation on others, but that is, of course, the problem which Singer addresses. I take it that he is not begging the question in this obvious way and will argue from the existence of evil to the obligation of others to eliminate it. But how, exactly, does he establish the connection? It is the second principle which he thinks shows that connection.

The necessary link is provided by either of two versions of this principle. The first (strong) formulation which Singer offers of the second principle is as follows:

> if it is in our power to prevent something bad from happening, without thereby sacrificing anything of comparable moral importance, we ought, morally, to do it.[4]

The weaker principle simply substitutes for "comparable moral importance" the phrase "any moral significance." He goes on to develop these notions, saying that:

> By "without sacrificing anything of comparable moral importance" I mean without causing anything else comparably bad to happen, or doing something that is wrong in itself, or failing to promote some moral good, comparable in significance to the bad thing we can prevent.[5]

These remarks can be interpreted for the weaker principle by simply eliminating "comparable" in the statement.

One question is, of course, whether either of these two principles ought to be accepted. There are two ways in which this could be established. First, they could be shown, by philosophical argument, to follow from reasonably well established premises or from a general theory. Second, they might be justified because they are principles which underlie particular moral judgments the truth of which is accepted. Singer doesn't do either of these explicitly, although he seems to have the second in mind. He first speaks of what he takes to be the "uncontroversial appearance" of the principles. He then applies the principles to a similar case in which a drowning child requires help. Singer argues, in essence, that since the drowning is bad and it can be avoided without sacrificing something of moral significance, it is obligatory that the child be saved. He claims further that both the strong and weak versions are sufficient to establish the duty. Dirtying one's clothes, for example, is not of "moral significance" and so does not justify failure to act. The last part of his paper is devoted to the claim that the analogy between the case of the child and starving people is apt in that geographical distance and others' willingness to act are not acceptable excuses for inaction.

III

My concern here is not with these latter issues. Rather, I want to focus on the two versions of the second principle, discussing each in terms of (1) whether it is plausible, and (2) if true, whether it establishes the duty to provide aid. I will deal with the weak version first, arguing that it fails at step (2) in the argument.

This version reads, "if it is in our power to prevent something bad from happening without thereby sacrificing *anything* morally significant we ought morally to do it." Singer later claims that:

> Even if we accept the principle in its moderate form, however, it should be clear that we would have to give away enough to ensure that the consumer society, dependent as it is on people spending on trivia rather than giving to famine relief, would slow down and perhaps disappear entirely.[6]

The crucial idea of "morally significant" is left largely unanalyzed. Two examples are given: dirtying one's clothes and being "well dressed." Both are taken to be morally *in*significant.

It could perhaps be argued against Singer that these things *are* morally significant. Both, for example, would be cases of decreasing aesthetic value, and if you think aesthetic values are intrinsic you might well dispute the claim that being "well dressed" is without moral significance. There is, however, a more serious objection to be raised. To see this, we need to distinguish between the possible value of the *fact* of being "well dressed" and the value of the *enjoyment* some persons receive and create by being "well dressed" (and, of course, the unhappiness avoided by being "badly dressed").

That such enjoyment and unhappiness are of some moral significance can be seen by the following case. Suppose it were possible that, by simply singing a chorus of "Dixie" you could eliminate all the unhappiness and embarrassment that some people experience at being badly dressed. Surely, doing that would be an act of moral significance. It would be good for you to do so, perhaps even wrong not to. Similarly, throwing mud on people's clothes, though not a great wrong, is surely not "without *any* moral significance."

It seems then, that the weak principle (while perhaps true) does not generally establish a duty to provide aid to starving people. Whether it does in specific instances depends on the nature of the cost to the person providing the aid. If *either* the loss to the giver is in itself valuable or the loss results in increased unhappiness or decreased happiness to someone, then the principle does not require that the burden be accepted.

(It is interesting to ask just how much giving *would* be required by this principle. If we can assume that givers would benefit in some minimal way by giving—and that they are reasonable—then perhaps the best answer is that the level of giving required is the level that is actually given. Otherwise, why would people *not* give more if there is no value to them in things they choose to keep?)

In addition to the moral significance of the costs that I just described, there is a further problem which will become particularly significant in considering the strong principle. For many people it is part of their moral sense that they and others have a special relationship to their own goals or projects. That is, in making one's choices a person may properly weigh the outcome that one desires more heavily than the goals that others may have. Often this is expressed as a right or entitlement.[7]

Thus, for example, if P acquires some good (x) in a just social arrangement without violating others' rights, then P has a special title to x that P is entitled to weigh against the desires of others. P need not, in determining whether he ought to give x to another, overlook the fact that x is his; he acquired it fairly, and so has special say in what happens to it. If this is correct, it is a fact of some moral significance and thus would also block the inference from the weak principle to the obligation to give what one has to others. I will pursue this line of argument in the following section while considering the strong version of the principle.

IV

Many people, especially those inclined toward utilitarianism, would probably accept the preceding, believing that it is the stronger of the two principles that should be used. "After all," they might argue, "the real issue is the great *disparity* between the amount of good which could be produced by resources of the rich if applied to problems of starvation as against the small amount of good produced by the resources if spent on second cars and houses, fancy clothes etc." I will assume that the facts are just as the claim suggests. That is, I will assume that it can *not* be plausibly argued that there are, for example, artistic or cultural values which (1) would be lost by such redistribution of wealth and (2) are equal in value to the starvation which would be eliminated. Thus, if the strong principle is true, then it (unlike the weak version) would require radical changes in our common understanding of the duties of the wealthy to starving people.

But is it true, as Singer suggests, that "if it is in our power to prevent something bad from happening without thereby sacrificing something of comparable moral significance we ought morally to do it"? Here the problem with the meaning of "moral significance" is even more acute than in the weak version. All that was required for the weak principle was that we be able to distinguish courses of action that have moral significance from those that do not. Here, however, the moral significance of alternative acts must be both *recognized* and *weighed*. And how is this to be done, according to Singer? Unfortunately, he provides little help here, though this is crucial in evaluating his argument.

I will discuss one obvious interpretation of "comparable moral significance," argue it is inadequate, and then suggest what I take to be some of the factors an adequate theory would consider.

Assuming that giving aid is not "bad in itself," the only other facts which Singer sees as morally significant in evaluating obligations are the good or bad consequences of actions. Singer's strong version obviously resembles the act utilitarian principle. With respect to starvation, this interpretation is open to the objection raised at the end of part III above, since it takes no account of a variety of important factors, such as the apparent right to give added weight to one's own choices and interests, and to ownership. I now wish to look at this claim in more detail.

Consider the following examples of moral problems which I take to be fairly common. One obvious means by which you could aid others is with your body. Many of your extra organs (eye, kidney) could be given to another with the result that there is more good than if you kept both. You wouldn't see as well or live as long, perhaps, but that is not of comparable significance to the benefit others would receive. Yet, surely the fact that it is your eye and you need it is not insignificant. Perhaps there could be cases where one is obligated to sacrifice one's health or sight, but what seems clear is that this is not true in every case where (slightly) more good would come of your doing so. Second, suppose a woman has a choice between remaining with her husband or leaving. As best she can determine, the morally relevant factors do not indicate which she should do (the consequences of each seem about equally good and there is no question of broken promises, deception, or whatever). But, suppose in addition to these facts, it is the case that by remaining with her husband the woman will be unable to pursue important aspects of the plan of life she has set for herself. Perhaps by remaining she will be forced to sacrifice a career which she wishes to pursue. If the *only* facts that are of moral significance are the consequences of her choice, then she ought, presumably, to flip a coin (assuming there is some feature of her staying that is of equal importance to the unhappiness at the loss of the career *she* will experience). Surely, though, the fact that some goals are ones *she* chooses for herself (assuming she doesn't violate the others' rights) is of significance. It is, after all, *her* life and *her* future and she is entitled to treat it that way. In neither of these cases is the person required to accept as equal to his or her own goals and well-being the welfare of even his or her family, much less the whole world. The fact that others may benefit even slightly more from their pursuing another course is not in itself sufficient to show they ought to act other than they choose. Servility, though perhaps not a vice, is certainly not an obligation that all must fulfill.[8]

The above goes part way, I think, in explaining the importance we place on allowing people maximal latitude in pursuing their goals. Rights or entitlements to things that are our own reflect important facts about people. Each of us has only one life and it is uniquely valuable to each of us. Your choices do not constitute my life, nor do mine yours. The purely utilitarian interpretation of "moral significance" provides for assigning no special weight to the goals and interests of individuals in making their choices. It provides no basis for saying that though there may be greater total good done by one course, still a person could be entitled for some reason to pursue another.

It seems, then, that determining whether giving aid to starving persons would be sacrificing something of comparable moral significance demands weighing the fact that the persons are entitled to give special weight to their own interests where their future or (fairly acquired) property is at issue. Exactly *how much* weight may be given is a question that I will consider shortly. The point here is that the question of the extent of the obligation to eliminate starvation has not been answered. My argument was that however "moral significance" is best understood, it is far too simple to suggest that *only* the total good produced is relevant. If providing quality education for one's children is a goal, then (assuming the resources were acquired fairly) the fact that it is a goal *itself* provides additional weight against other ways the resources might be used, including the one that maximizes the total good. Further, if the resources to be used for the purpose are legitimately owned, then that too is something that the parent is entitled to consider.

Returning to the case of the drowning child, the same point may be made. Suppose it is an important part of a person's way of life that he not interfere. Perhaps the passer-by believes God's will is being manifested in this particular incident and strongly values noninterference with God's working out of His plan. Surely, this is especially relevant to the question of whether the person is obligated to intervene, even when the greatest good would be promoted by intervention. When saying that a person is obligated to act in some way, the significance *to the person* of the act must not only be considered along with all the other features of the act, but is also of special moral significance in determining that person's duty. More, however, needs to be said here.

Suppose, for instance, that the case were like this: A passer-by sees a child drowning but fails to help, not for the sake of another important goal but rather out of lack of interest. Such situations are not at all uncommon, as when people fail to report violent crimes they observe in progress. I assume that anyone who fails to act in such circumstances is acting wrongly. As with the case of the utilitarian principle discussed earlier, the drowning child also represents a limiting case. In the former, *no* significance is assigned to the woman's choice by virtue of its being *hers*. Here, however, the interests of *others* are not weighed. An acceptable principle of benevolence would fall between the two limiting cases. The relative moral significance of alternative acts could then be determined by applying the principle, distinguishing acts which are obligatory from charitable ones.

In summary, I have argued that neither the strong nor the weak principle advanced by Singer provides an adequate solution to the issue of affluence and hunger. The essential problem is with his notion of "moral significance." I argued that the weak principle fails to show any obliga-tions, given the normal conception of factors which possess such significance. I then argued that the strong principle (which is close to act utilitarianism) is mistaken. The basic objection to this principle is that it fails to take account of certain aspects of the situation which must be considered in any adequate formulation of the principle.

V

As I suggested earlier, a fully adequate formulation of the principle of benevolence depends on a general theory of right. Such a theory would not only include a principle of benevolence but also give account of the whole range of rights and duties and a means to weigh conflicting claims. In this section, I discuss some of the various problems associated with benevolence, obligation, and rights. In the final section, I offer what I believe to be an adequate principle of benevolence.

One view, which has been criticized recently by Judith Thomson,[9] suggests that whenever there is a duty or obligation there must be a corresponding right. I presume we want to say that in some cases (e.g., the drowning child) there is an obligation to benevolence, but does this also mean that the child has a *right* to be aided? Perhaps there is only a semantic point here regarding "right," but perhaps also there is a deeper disagreement.

I suggest that, whether we call it a "right" or not, there are important differences between obligations based on benevolence and other obligations. Two differences are significant. First, the person who has the obligation to save the drowning child did not *do anything* that created the situation. But, compare this case with a similar one of a lifeguard who fails to save someone.

Here there is a clear sense in which the drowning victim may claim a right to have another do his utmost to save him. An agreement was reached whereby the lifeguard *accepted* the responsibility for the victim's welfare. The guard, in a sense, took on the goals of the swimmers as his own. To fail to aid is a special sort of injustice that the passer-by does not do. It seems clearly appropriate to speak of the lifeguard's failure to act as a case of a right being violated.

A second important point regarding the drowning child example and rights is that the passer-by is not *taking positive steps* in reference to the child. This can be contrasted with an action that might be taken to drown a child who would not otherwise die. Here, again, it is appropriate to describe this act as a violation of a right (to life). Other violations of rights also seem to require that one act, not merely fail to take action—for example, property rights (theft) and privacy rights (listening without leave). The drowning child and starvation cases are wrong not because of acts but the failure to act.

Thus, there are important differences between duties of benevolence and others where a right is obviously at issue. Cases of failing to aid are not (unlike right violations) either instances of positive actions that are taken or ones in which the rich or the passer-by has taken responsibility by a previous act. It does not follow from this, however, that strong obligations are not present to save other persons. Obviously, one ought to aid a drowning child (at least) in cases where there is no serious risk or cost to the passer-by. This is true even though there is no obvious right that the child has to be aided.

Furthermore, if saving a drowning child requires using someone's boat without their permission (a violation of proper-

ty right), then it still ought to be done. Duties to bring aid can override duties not to violate rights. The best thing to say here is that, depending on the circumstances, duties to aid and not to violate rights can each outweigh the other. Where actions involve both violation of rights and failing to meet duties to aid (the lifeguard's failing to save), the obligation is stronger than either would be by itself. Describing the situation in this way implies that although there is a sense in which the boat owner, the affluent spender, and the passer-by have a right to fail to act, still they are obligated not to exercise that right because there is a stronger duty to give aid.

Some may be inclined to say, against this, that in fact the passer-by does not have such a right not to help. But this claim is ambiguous. If what is meant is that they ought to help, then I agree. There is, however, still a point in saying owners of food have the right to use the food as they see fit. It serves to emphasize that there is a moral difference between these cases and ones where the object of need is *not* legitimately owned by anyone (as, for example, if it's not another's boat but a log that the drowning child needs). To say that the property right is *lost* where the principle of benevolence overrides is to hide this difference, though it is morally significant.

Other people might be inclined to say about these situations that the point of saying someone has a right to their food, time, boat or whatever is that others ought not to intervene to force them to bring aid. A person defending this view might accept my claim that in fact the person ought to help. It might then be argued that because they are not violating a right of another (to be saved) and they have a (property) right to the good, others can't, through state authority, force them to bring aid.

This claim obviously raises a variety of questions in legal and political philosophy, and is outside the scope of the present paper. My position does not preclude good samaritan laws, nor are they implied. This is a further question which requires further argument. That one has a moral right to x, but is obligated for other reasons not to exercise the right, leaves open the issue of whether others either can or should make that person fulfill the obligation.

If what I have said is correct, two general points should be made about starvation. First, even though it may be that the affluent have a right to use resources to pursue their own goals, and not provide aid, they may also be strongly obligated not to exercise the right. This is because, in the circumstances, the duty to benevolence is overriding. The existence and extent of such an obligation can be determined only by discovering the relative weight of these conflicting principles. In the final section, I consider how this should be done.

Second, even if it is also true that the passer-by and the affluent do not violate a right of another in failing to help, it may still be the case that they strongly ought not do so. Of course, their behavior could also be even worse than it is (by drowning the child or sending poisoned food to the hungry and thus violating their rights). All that shows, however, is that the failure to help is not the *most* morally objectionable course that can be imagined in the circumstances. This point hardly constitutes justification for failing to act.

VI

I argued earlier that neither Singer's weak principle nor the utilitarian one is what we are after. The former would imply (wrongly) little or no duty of benevolence, and the latter does not take seriously enough the rights and interests of the affluent. What is needed is a principle which we may use to determine the circumstances in which the needs of others create a duty to bring aid which is more stringent than the rights of the affluent to pursue their own interests and use their property as they desire.

The following principle, while similar to the utilitarian one, seems to be most adequate: "If it is in our power to prevent death of an innocent without sacrificing anything of *substantial* significance then we ought morally to do it." The problem, of course, is to determine exactly what is meant by "substantial significance." I assume there are no duties present that arise out of others' rights, as, for example, those of one's children to be provided for. Considerations of that sort would lead beyond the present paper. My concern here is limited to instances in which there is a question of bringing aid (where no obvious right to the aid is present) or using resources for other (preferred) ends.

There are two questions which are important in deciding whether what is being given up by the affluent is of substantial significance. First, we might specify *objectively* the needs which people have, and grant that the duty to bring aid is not present unless these needs have already been met. Included among the needs which are of substantial significance would be those things without which a person cannot continue to function physically—for example, food, clothing, health care, housing, and sufficient training to provide these for oneself.

It also, however, seems reasonable that certain psychological facts ought to be weighed before a person is obligated to help others meet their needs. For example, if you cannot have an even modestly happy life without some further good, then surely that, too, is something to which you are entitled. This suggests a second, *subjective* standard that should also be employed to determine whether something is of no substantial significance and so ought not be consumed at the expense of others' basic needs. The best way to put this, I believe, is to say that "if the lack of x would not affect the long-term happiness of a person, then x is of no substantial significance." By "long-term happiness" I mean to include anything which, if not acquired, will result in unhappiness over an extended period of one's life, not just something the lack of which is a source of momentary loss but soon forgotten. Thus, in a normal case, dirtying one's clothes to save a drowning child is of no substantial significance and so the duty of benevolence is overriding. If, however, selling some possession for famine relief would mean the person's life *really is* (for a long period) less happy, then the possessions are of substantial significance and so the person is not wrong in exercising the right of ownership instead of providing aid. If the possessions had been sold, it would have been an act of charity, not fulfillment of a duty. The same analysis can be provided for other choices we make—for example, how our time is spent and whether to donate organs. If doing so would result in your not seeing well and this would make your life less happy over time, then you are not obligated to do so.

If what I have said is correct, then duties of benevolence increase as one's dependence on possessions for living a happy life decreases. If a person's long-term happiness does not depend on (second?) cars and fancy clothes, then that

person ought not to purchase those goods at the expense of others' basic needs being unfulfilled. Thus, depending on the psychological nature of persons, their duties of benevolence will vary.

The question of the actual effect of not buying a new car, house, clothes, or whatever on one's long-term happiness is of course a difficult one. My own feeling is that if the principle were to be applied honestly, those of us who are relatively affluent would discover that a substantial part of the resources and time we expend should be used to bring aid. The extent of the obligation must, finally, be determined by asking whether the lack of some good *really would* result in a need not being met or in a less happy life for its owner, and that is a question between each of us and our conscience.

In summary, I have argued that Singer's utilitarian principle is inadequate to establish the claim that acts to eliminate starvation are obligatory, but that such an obligation still exists. The rights of both the affluent and the hungry are considered, and a principle is defended which clarifies the circumstances in which it is a duty and not merely charitable to provide aid to others whose basic needs are not being met.

NOTES

1. Peter Singer, Animal Liberation, *New York Review of Books* (New York: Random House, 1975).
2. Peter Singer, "Famine, Affluence, and Morality," *Philosophy and Public Affairs*. I, no. 3 (Spring 1972).
3. Ibid., p. 149.
4. Ibid.
5. Ibid. I assume "importance" and "significance" are synonymous.
6. Ibid., p. 156.

7. In a recent book (*Anarchy, State, and Utopia,* New York: Basic Books, 1974), Robert Nozick argues that such rights are extensive against state authority.

8. For an argument that servility is wrong, see Thomas Hill, "Servility and Self-Respect," *The Monist,* VII, no. 4 (January 1973).

9. Judith Jarvis Thomson, "The Right to Privacy," *Philosophy and Public Affairs,* IV, no. 4 (Summer 1975).

On the Obligation
to Keep Informed
about Distant Atrocities

Carlo Filice

Carlo Filice is a professor of philosophy at the College at Geneseo, State University of New York. Filice has published essays on pacifism, theories of agency and of the self, and value inquiry.

Filice argues that we have a prima facie *duty to remain informed about distant atrocities. This duty is connected to our duty to help prevent major, avoidable harms such as suffering and death, whenever helping only requires us to make trivial sacrifices. He argues that in order for one to be truly helpful, one also has an obligation to place oneself in a position to be able to help prevent the harm. Filice states that the information necessary to judge one's ability to help end or prevent major harms is available to most people in developed countries and can be had without making major sacrifices. Given the conditions and guidelines Filice sets out, he concludes that it is morally wrong not to keep informed and not to help prevent all major, avoidable harm.*

One must know about faraway moral atrocities if one is to attempt to remedy them. Ignorance of these atrocities is at times a legitimate excuse for failure to make such attempts but not generally. It certainly is not a legitimate excuse when one deliberately keeps oneself uninformed of major atrocities; an example of such a person would be the well-educated, refined hedonist whose world revolves, by conscious choice, around private pleasure. On the other hand, it is a legitimate excuse in many cases when one simply lacks the means for being informed; an example of such would be the seriously underprivileged, culturally deprived, illiterate person.

But what about the cases of those people who fall somewhere between these two extremes? What about the single mother, working full-time as a nurse, who takes care of her children's needs most of the remainder of her hours? What about the young businessman almost wholly preoccupied with his struggle to make it in the business world? What about the medical student whose workload saps her of all desire to look at additional printed pages? What about the secretary whose after-work life is dedicated to cultivating her interest in French literature? What about the real estate agent in constant pursuit of new listings and loan agreements, who finds barely enough time to spend with her family? What about the small farmer in whose circle of friends and relatives questions about what might be happening in

Reprinted by permission of *Human Rights Quarterly,* Vol. 12, No. 3; August 1900. [Edited]

China, Brazil, or Mozambique do not come up? Is their relative ignorance of major moral atrocities excusable? Is their consequent inaction excusable?

This is the issue I would like to explore in this essay. My claim will be that this type of ignorance is not excusable in most cases of "average" Westerners and of "average" U.S. citizens in particular. Consequently this ignorance does not excuse their doing nothing about large-scale abuses.

Consider the events in East Timor during the last fifteen years. They constitute a typical major moral atrocity. The choice of this example is recommended by a number of factors: (1) the relative magnitude of the evil; (2) the supportive (military, economic, diplomatic) role played by the U.S. government and others in this bloody episode; (3) the fact that most of us are unaware of this atrocity; (4) the fact that some sources of information concerning it can be found in the public arena, though they generally must be sought out.

The following are the basic facts of the East Timor situation as reported by Noam Chomsky and Edward S. Herman who gathered them from various uncontestable sources:

> On December 7, 1975 Indonesian armed forces invaded the former Portuguese colony of East Timor, only a few hours after the departure of President Gerald Ford and Henry Kissinger from a visit to Jakarta. Although Indonesia has effectively sealed off East Timor from the outside world, reports have filtered through indicating that there have been massive atrocities, with estimates running to 100,000 killed, about one-sixth of the population. An assessment by the Legislative Research Service of the Australian Parliament concluded that there is "mounting evidence that the Indonesians have been carrying out a brutal operation in East Timor," involving "indiscriminate killing

on a scale unprecedented in post-World War II history."[1]

The above account reflects the number of dead as of 1979. A 1987 estimate as reported by the *New York Times* is 150,000. The entire population of East Timor was estimated by the *New York Times* in 1974 to be 620,000. That means that by now nearly one fourth of the population of this tiny, backward area has been killed. The main reason for the Indonesian invasion was the 1975 popular victory in East Timor (one year after East Timor was granted independence from Portugal) of a party named FRETILIN and the defeat of more conservative parties. FRETILIN's character is summarized by Chomsky and Herman on the basis of independent reports:

> FRETILIN was a moderate reformist national front, headed by a Catholic seminarian and initially involving largely urban intellectuals, among them young Lisbon-educated radical Timorese who "were most eager to search for their cultural origins" and who were "to lead the FRETILIN drive into the villages initiating consumer and agricultural cooperatives, and a literary campaign conducted in (the native language) along the lines used by Paulo Freire in Brazil. . . . It was "more reformist than revolutionary," calling for gradual steps towards complete independence, agrarian reform, transformation of uncultivated land and large farms to people's cooperatives, educational programs, steps towards producer-consumer cooperatives supplementing existing Chinese economic enterprises "for the purposes of supplying basic goods to the poor at low prices, controlled foreign aid and investment, and a foreign policy of non-alignment."[2]

This victorious party's platform did not please the Indonesian leadership which ten years earlier had carried out an internal purge of half a million suspected "communists." Thus, under a pretext to end a civil war in East Timor (there had in fact been some fighting between followers of FRETILIN and of UDT that had, however, quickly come to an end due to the former's preponderance of public support), Indonesia invaded and sealed the area from international observers and organizations, including the International Red Cross, and finding widespread indigenous resistance, proceeded to carry out the slaughter.

It is important to note that between 1973 and 1977 Indonesia received $254 million of military aid (in arms, military aid grants, and military sales credit), and $634 million in economic aid from the U.S.[3] Moreover, during this time 1,272 Indonesian military officers received U.S. military training.[4] These facts, together with the timing of the invasion, (just after high-level consultations with Ford and Kissinger), the traditionally close ties between the Indonesian and the U.S. governments, and the lack of serious protests by the United States in the years since the invasion, show complicity on the part of the U.S. government and establishment, which included the media and the intellectual community.

The attempt by Indonesia to "pacify" East Timor has continued during the last thirteen years. While this was happening, the few books and reports on the massacre have generally escaped wide public attention in both the United States and in Europe. When mainstream publications such as the *New York Times* and *Newsweek* have reported on the invasion, they have generally distorted what actually occurred, by relying upon official Indonesian accounts, by ignoring reports offered by refugees in Portugal, and at least on one occasion, by deliberately altering the published version of events given by an Australian reporter who was

in East Timor during the early weeks of the invasion.[5]

One could go on with such depressing details. One could also tell similar stories about other states within the U.S. sphere of influence such as Guatemala, Thailand, El Salvador, and Brazil. The point is that the case of East Timor is not an anomaly. The factors which make it an example of a slaughter relevant for the present essay apply to many other cases. In nearby El Salvador, for example, we find a regime which has permitted, or perhaps sponsored, the death-squad killing of tens of thousands during the last twelve years.[6] That same regime has received consistent U.S. economic, military, and diplomatic aid. Again, despite the magnitude of the evil, its proximity to the United States, and its greater news coverage, most of us are unable to locate El Salvador on a world map.

Because the "average" U.S. citizen does not know these massacres occur, nor of the government's relatively close ties to the regimes perpetrating them, the average citizen does nothing to help end the slaughters. Is this ignorance and resulting inaction morally excusable? The following is one line of argument in favor of a "no" answer. It tries to establish that most of us are under a prima facie obligation to keep informed about cases such as East Timor. What it maintains about U.S. citizens would also apply to citizens of other major powers whose governments play supportive roles in the atrocities of other governments.

1. One has a prima facie obligation to help prevent harm, especially major, avoidable suffering and death, whenever helping to do so requires only trivial sacrifices, such as buying fewer or no luxury items, spending less time watching television, etc., and whenever there is some chance that one's efforts will produce at least some success.[7]

2. One will not be in a position to help prevent harm if one is unaware of the occurrence of this harm.

3. One who has a prima facie obligation to help prevent X also has a prima facie obligation to attempt to position oneself so as to be able to help prevent X, particularly if these positional attempts are likely to be successful (e.g., if A has a prima facie duty to prevent his own violent behavior, A also has a prima facie duty to attempt to remain sober if drunkenness tends to make A violent, and if A's attempts to remain sober are not absolutely hopeless).

4. Therefore, each of us has a prima facie obligation to make serious attempts to become and remain informed about the occurrence of major, avoidable harm whenever these attempts at gaining the necessary information are likely to succeed and require small sacrifices, and whenever there is some chance for the prevention of at least some harm.

5. Major moral atrocities, such as the systematic and large-scale torture and killing by a government for political reasons, constitute one class of major avoidable harm.

6. Therefore, each of us has a prima facie obligation to make serious attempts to be informed about the occurrence of major moral atrocities (whenever the conditions in 4 above obtain).

7. Most people in developed countries who attempt to gain the necessary information are likely to succeed.

8. Most people in developed countries can make serious attempts to gain the necessary information about current moral atrocities without such attempts resulting in major sacrifices.

9. The preventive actions based on such information have some likelihood of leading to the prevention of at least some harm resulting from major moral atrocities.

10. Therefore, most people in developed countries have a prima facie obligation to make serious attempts to become informed about the current major moral atrocities, especially those occurring within their country's sphere of influence.

I will enlarge on this argument by considering a number of likely objections.

OBJECTION I: CITIZENS ARE POLITICALLY TOO NAIVE.

Attempting to seek information about ongoing atrocities taking place outside the sphere of most mainstream news coverage requires a prior decision to do so. This decision, in turn, cannot come about unless one has a considerable awareness of history and global politics. For example, one must know that mainstream national news services, even in "open" societies, tend to have blind spots concerning stories that would embarrass the fatherland and harm its perceived interests. One must know that there is a vast and complex world outside of one's own borders and that simple characterizations of this world, such as "Free World" versus "Communist World," are quite misleading. The avenge U.S. citizen, however, lacks this necessary historical and political astuteness, arguably through no fault of his or her own. Thus, since "ought" implies "can," and the average U.S. citizen lacks the cultural-motivational prerequisites to decide to seek information, he or she cannot really make such decisions, and thus cannot be morally obligated to seek such information. Similarly, naive creatures like young children cannot be under a moral obligation to decide to learn how to read so as to become responsible citizens.

This seems plausible, but consider a parallel argument. Johnny has grown up amidst people who perceive women as subservient to men. This assessment is reinforced by his sincere religious beliefs, which are also shared by his family and friends. It never occurs to Johnny to examine the validity of his view of women. Upon marrying, he bullies his wife into a subservient role, often through physical threats. He construes her complaints as symptoms of her rebellious and spoiled character. Shall we say that because Johnny is motivationally incapable of questioning his own assumptions about gender roles, he has no obligation to do so and consequently no obligation to change?[8]

Surely such an assertion would be problematic. There may be some extreme cases where a person, for example, a child, is absolutely incapable of examining his own morally dubious beliefs. In most cases, however, a person has some moments of doubt, even if briefly and rarely. At such times there is at least the possibility of serious probing. If most individuals who have such momentary doubts choose not to probe and instead slide back into blind self-righteousness, this does not show an absolute incapacity for change. It does show how difficult change is in these circumstances. Needless to say, however, fulfilling moral obligations is often quite difficult. While failure to do what one should may be understood and perhaps even forgiven, this does not lessen one's duty.

Similar things can be said about the alleged incapacity to decide to seek information about massive atrocities generally ignored or downplayed by mainstream media. Most people on at least some occasion do get hints that not all that is important is reported on television or in the local paper. These hints may come from some unusual public broadcasting program; or from one's own or an acquaintance's overseas trip which exposes one to slightly different and more skeptical points of view; or from one too many public confessions by

government spokespersons about official lies; or from newsworthy events like Watergate and the Iran-contra affair. These occasional doubts concerning one's ordinary sources of information constitute tiny motivational openings which can lead to decisions to seek further and to see what additional matters are regularly being kept from one. The fact that on these occasions of doubt most individuals choose not to probe further does not show an absolute incapacity to do so. The additional fact that one's failing to do so can be understood and perhaps even forgiven does not lessen one's obligation to make such decisions.

OBJECTION II: CITIZENS ARE TOO POWERLESS TO FIND OUT.

Should the average U.S. citizen decide to seek the relevant information, are there not a number of factors which show that he or she most likely will not succeed in finding out about affairs such as the East Timor or the El Salvador bloodshed? Consider the following: large numbers of people are only semi-literate and would not walk into a library or bookstore or even read a newspaper. Others more literate lack knowledge of geography, history, international affairs, economics, and political and religious ideologies. They lack the general intellectual sophistication to know where to start looking and how to interpret what they find. Should this large majority of people not be exempt from the obligation to seek knowledge of matters beyond their intellectual reach?

My answer to this second objection is similar to my preceding reply. This second objection shows how difficult it is for most people to become informed about atrocities. Most people would first, or in the process, have to broaden themselves on many different fronts before they would be armed to do the requisite research. This intellectual broadening most people will choose not to do. However, I find it excessive to say that most people cannot do it.[9] Help can always be found, whether from the parish priest, the local librarian, or the college educated daughter-in-law. Naturally, sacrifices would have to be made.

But, our opponent might continue, most parish priests, librarians, and college educated daughters-in-law have never even heard of places like East Timor, and they may barely recognize names such as El Salvador, Indonesia, Guatemala, and Paraguay. How can they be counted on to inform the rest of us about what is going on there? If such information is available mainly in relatively obscure publications such as *The Nation* or Amnesty International reports which are not found in most libraries and bookstores, and they are not mentioned in most university courses, how can the average citizen be held morally accountable for being unaware of it? Should the blame not go to the mainstream press and to mainstream educators instead?

Undoubtedly, the press and the intellectual corps are preeminent bearers of moral responsibility for not taking sufficient measures to inform themselves and the public of various moral atrocities. But given that there are publications, albeit off the main media routes, which do report on these matters, is this responsibility not shared also by average middle-class literate citizens? Perhaps their responsibility is diminished due to their greater difficulty in attaining access to this information. But clearly one would not want to accept the principle that major wrongdoing can be ignored whenever information about it is hard to obtain, since such ignorance would

have justified ignoring Nazi atrocities during the 1930s and 1940s.

The fact that difficulty of access can be overcome is shown by the success average citizens have had in pursuing their family "roots." The ingenuity in overcoming language, culture, and time barriers demonstrated by those seeking genealogical data belies attestations concerning the average person's research impotence. While one should not press the "roots" analogy too much, it is noteworthy that it, too, requires some prior preparatory work before the actual research can be undertaken. It may require learning to use libraries, to seek assistance, to consult with experts, and so on. The key point is that one does find ways when pursuing what is close to one's heart. The essential step, therefore, consists in bringing important moral matters close to one's heart. Failure to do so is not a failure due to research impotence. It is more like the unwillingness to take the moral point of view and thereby recognize "that objectively no one matters more than anyone else."[10]

OBJECTION III: HELP ONLY THOSE YOU CAN, I.E., YOUR NEIGHBORS.

The average individual's attempt to influence matters like the Indonesian policy vis-à-vis East Timor, runs this objection, is not likely to lead to the prevention of any harm. Perhaps if most individuals acted collectively the likelihood of harm-prevention would be quite significant. But the effort of a lone individual is completely negligible, especially if one sets aside drastic options such as a public hunger strike. Would one not be more effectively beneficent by helping instead local charities, an alcoholic relative, or the neighborhood stray cats? And if so, why waste time and effort in trying to become informed about distant atrocities?

Naturally, there is some validity to this line of thinking. One's replies might include the following observations. First, one must concede that an individual alone will not generally accomplish visible results when speaking out on distant occurrences about which officialdom—government, educational institutions, the press—is silent. But surely there are exceptions to this. If nothing else, the average individual may be heard by a few other individuals, each of whom, in turn, might reach a few others, generating a significant ripple effect. Perhaps, someone will be reached who has considerable power or access to the public ear.

Second, if likelihood of impact were an absolute moral prerequisite for action, then one could argue that a person should also not invest any effort in speaking out on those matters on which many others are already speaking out. Why? Because to add one more voice to a chorus of thousands would make no noticeable difference. Hence, the principle here presumed—i.e., that one should speak out only when one's voice is likely to have some nonnegligible effect—will justify a policy of almost never speaking out on large-scale affairs. Surely this consequence is objectionable, since such affairs are not what they could and should be. At the very least the magnitude of the preventable evil is an additional factor one should consider in deciding what to do.

Third, the ideal conditions for "local morality" cannot be obtained in the actual world. Perhaps in an ideal world where power and resources are somewhat equitably distributed, if each tends only to her own locality where a noticeable difference can be affected, the global result would probably be morally acceptable (though protection of common resources, such as the ozone layer, would require global and collective attention). But in a world like ours, where resources and power are disproportionately distributed, often through past and present injustice, the policy of each tending to her own property and community will not lead to morally acceptable global results. In this askew world, pursuing one's personal interests and community interests may mean keeping those in Timor or Brazil dispossessed; and one's power to do so is likely to more than offset another's power to improve his or her position. Any view that justifies the pursuit of ends benefiting only oneself and one's own, and that neglects to consider seriously the implications of such pursuits for "others," does not deserve the appellation "moral." Impartiality must be one of the essential features of the moral viewpoint. One aim of this viewpoint is the transcendence of the "one's own/others" dichotomy, hard as this may be.[11] Impartiality in an interconnected world implies a cosmopolitan outlook.

Thus, the principle at issue—only speak out on those issues where one's voice is *likely* to have a noticeable effect—must be rejected on moral grounds. It may be necessary, of course, to choose those ways of speaking out that are most likely to be productive, since the goal is not to attain some empty psychological and moral purity. Thus, one should, perhaps, write to those legislators, newspapers, and organizations which are most likely to listen and which can help publicize one's cause. There is no point in sending letters or articles to *The National Review* about East Timor or El Salvador and then expressing outrage when this material is not printed. As I have argued, however, the need for intelligence in one's efforts must not collapse into the need to limit one's focus to parochial matters.

Needless to say, having an obligation to find out about, and speak out on, distant matters does not exempt one from obligations to help the local indigent, alcoholic, or cat. Many of us can do both. In fact, since parochial and distant matters often causally interact, one may need to do both. But, one might ask, where does one *find* the line? And where does one *draw* the time? One does have to earn a living so as to be in a position to help both the local and the distant needy. One does have to fulfill one's family obligations. And one needs to take care of oneself, to do things for sheer pleasure, or to develop artistic and other skills, and not out of moral considerations.

Obviously these questions lead to immense complexities. One suggestion may be that in the interest of time and effectiveness what each individual should devote herself to, in addition to providing for self, family, and friends, depends on the individual's circumstances and expertise. For instance, the lawyer might most effectively use some of her time to defend the interests of the local disenfranchised and speak out about the misuses of the legal system in South Africa or about the U.S. government's selective and self-serving compliance with World Court decisions; the local radio announcer might best use her position to insert unusual and personally researched news items into ordinary broadcasts; the corporate employee might best explore the policies of the firm's international division, and if necessary blow the whistle on ethically dubious practices. Despite countless idiosyncrasies and com-

plications, it remains a fact that most (or at least many) individuals can afford to sacrifice some of the time and resources ordinarily allotted for personal pleasure for the sake of those less fortunate.

These sacrifices need not result in significant "losses." One might, in fact, find that these "moral" pursuits will turn into creative and satisfying projects. These projects may even become replacements for some of one's more mindless leisure activities. Perhaps this is hoping for too much. At any rate, being embattled by myriad prima facie moral obligations, as well as by various practical exigencies, psychological addictions, and other demands, need not paralyze a person. To be sure, juggling all of these interests is quite a challenge; yet, given our present global interdependency and our wide informational access, it must be part of the condition of the average Westerner. As Sartre might say, choose one must. Such choices can be made intelligently and consciously, or nonreflectively and haphazardly. Morally speaking, there is no dilemma here. . . .

OBJECTION IV: IT WOULD BE GREAT TO HELP, BUT IS IT WRONG NOT TO HELP?

Philosophers of ethics distinguish between acts that are morally required and acts that, while commendable if done, are not obligatory, called "supererogatory" acts. Sharing one's salary with some group of destitute strangers constitutes a commendable but not an obligatory act. What about taking steps to broaden oneself culturally and intellectually in order to be able to keep abreast of foreign developments so as to help fight against major moral abuses? Wouldn't this also be a commendable but not required course of action? If so, the average citizen is not under any compelling obligation to engage in this course of action.

Let us assume that the commendable/obligatory distinction is valid. Even so, by appealing to certain considerations of compensatory justice it can be shown that the information-seeking course of action is obligatory. Consider the salary sharing example. While generally your sharing your salary with some poor strangers is not morally required (though some historical figures, like Jesus, have thought otherwise), what if you have contributed—even if only to a tiny degree—to their systematic impoverishment and have done so in some unfair way? One would think then that by way of compensation you owe them at least some help or some fraction of your possessions.

Has the average citizen contributed to a tiny degree, and in an unfair way, to the moral atrocities committed by foreign governments and the U.S. government in Vietnam? Those who would answer "yes" can advance the following argument:

1. In a democratic country, the government speaks for citizens and invests some of their tax money in foreign affairs. It performs this general function with their knowledge and approval. It is, thus, their agent or broker.
2. The U.S. government has helped, and continues to help, many brutal foreign regimes, often with some of its citizens' tax money.
3. Therefore, U.S. citizens' agent has clearly supported brutal foreign regimes.
4. A person shares responsibility with the agent for what the latter does while carrying out the duties with which it is charged; and the responsibility is shared even when the agent's actions are taken without the person's knowledge, so long as that agent is granted broad powers of action.
5. The U.S. government is given broad powers of action, especially in foreign affairs, and

often does not fully inform the citizens about its foreign policies.
6. Therefore, the average U.S. citizen shares responsibility with the government for its foreign affairs policies which often support brutal foreign regimes.

Having thus contributed to moral atrocities, U.S. citizens are morally obligated to help the victims of such atrocities by way of compensation, if nothing else.[12]

But what about the case of those citizens who oppose the government's policies and vote for or otherwise support candidates and parties who call for an end to support to brutal regimes? Are these citizens not exempt from any complicity in these atrocities? Must they take further and more drastic actions, such as not paying a proportional share of their income taxes, in order to satisfy their moral obligations? Considered in its own right, this is a very difficult issue. For our purposes it suffices to say that this group constitutes a very small minority (most people, again, do not cast their votes and support on the basis of a candidate's position on foreign policy issues). Moreover, the type of person who is aware of and opposes these immoral foreign policies has thereby shown currency with the relevant world events and has already taken steps to help alleviate the atrocities. For most of the rest of us, the argument still stands.

But what if the government, as our agent, conceals from us or at least fails to explicitly inform us about its activities in other parts of the world? Would this not relieve us of the responsibility for the related atrocities despite our contribution to these atrocities through, for example. unwitting financial support? To answer this, we would have to know how actively we tend to seek the relevant information from our agent; how willing we are to close our eyes to its practices; and whether there are sources which can, if necessary, provide us with the relevant information. What has already been said on these issues shows that we can uncover our government's role in foreign atrocities.[13] In that case we, the citizens, remain partially responsible for its foreign deeds, and our compensatory obligation stands. In fact, once the moral obligation is seen as deriving from the principle of compensatory justice, our duty to help alleviate systematic human rights abuses becomes much stronger than would be the case if it derived merely from a general obligation to prevent harm to people we have in no way affected. Our actions and omissions have affected and do affect distant people, however unwitting we may be in this.

Because of this contribution to the harm, we have a particularly compelling duty to inform ourselves about these distant atrocities. Indeed, there are many other major sources of harm in our world, such as famines, diseases, environmental destruction, and the nuclear arms threat. My earlier argument, based on a general obligation to prevent harm, can also be used to spur us into keeping informed about these other evils. But if the demands upon our personal time and energy become too burdensome, and we must choose among subjects about which to keep informed, then we ought to inform ourselves first about those major evils to which we contribute directly, through our actions, and indirectly, through the actions of our representative government. And while such major evils will not be confined to distant atrocities, some of these atrocities will surely fall under this most stringent category.

One must add that this argument has made no mention of the economic benefits that accrue to us through big business' exploitation of favorable foreign conditions (e.g., cheap labor, cheap resources, lenient safety regulations, low taxes, etc.). These favorable investment conditions are often systematically maintained by repressive regimes at steep human rights costs. Most of us benefit considerably from the success of these multinational firms. We benefit as consumers through cheaper products. We benefit as investors in stocks, banks, pension funds, and through greater dividends. And we benefit many other ways, given the support by multinationals for media organizations, hospitals, universities, and the arts. Accordingly, are we not obligated to compensate those who are violently repressed so that such benefits will continue to flow our way? . . .

The victims in El Salvador, East Timor, and elsewhere are not simply children, and perhaps they are not our "neighbors," but in our current global village, their cries can be heard by most of us, if we are willing to listen. And many of us unwittingly benefit from and contribute to their suffering. In such circumstances, one would think that the distance of the victims would not lessen our obligation to pay attention and take action.

NOTES

1. Noam Chomsky and Edward S. Herman, *The Washington Connection and Third World Fascism*, vol. 1 of *The Political Economy of Human Rights* (Boston: South End Press, 1979), 130.
2. Ibid., 134. The internal quotation quotes Jill Joliffe, *East Timor: Nationalism and Colonialism* (Australia: University of Queensland Press, 1978), 79.
3. Ibid., 45. The original sources of these data are the following: United States Department of Defense, *Foreign Military Sales and Military Assistance Facts* (Washington, 1976); U.S. Department of Defense, *Security Assistance*

Program, Presentation to Congress, F.Y. 1978 (Washington, 1977); U.S. Agency for International Development, *U.S. Overseas Loans and Grants,* 1 July 1945–30 June 1975 (Washington, 1976).

4. Chomsky and Herman, 45.

5. Ibid., 136–38.

6. According to a 1985 Americas Watch Report these were the relevant statistics: "more than 40,000 civilian noncombatants killed—murdered by government forces and 'death squads' allied to them; another 3,000 disappeared; 750,000 or so (15 percent of the population) . . . homeless or 'displaced' within its borders." "With Friends Like These," in Cynthia Brown, ed., *Americas Watch Report on Human Rights and U.S. Policy in Latin America* (New York: Pantheon Books, 1985), 115.

   According to *New York Times* reporter James LeMoyne, "The Civil War has killed more than 70,000 people, most of them civilians shot by the army during the early 1980's." The victims have included nuns, priests, and an archbishop. No one has been successfully prosecuted and arrested for any of these thousands of killings. James LeMoyne, "The Guns of Salvador," *New York Times Magazine,* 5 Feb. 1989, 20.

7. The notion of "prima facie obligation" employed in this argument is most naturally derivative from consequentialist moral theories. However, I believe that it can also be grounded on deontological theories of rights and obligations. I would think that victims of torture and killing are entitled, by virtue of having basic "negative" rights, to receiving our help in avoiding being tortured and killed. However, this topic is too vast for it to be properly addressed here. I choose not to rely on the notion of rights generally, because I find rights to be metaphysically suspect unless they are taken as derived from more basic values such as harm and benefit.

8. Michael Slote correctly observes that the principle of "ought implies can" is vague because "(s)omeone might, for example, argue that since (a rich person), because of his given nature, is so selfish that he can not bring himself to give away his money, he has no obligation to do so." The principle "claims the right to be as one oneself is because of one's nature . . ." Presumably these implications are quite objectionable. M. Slote, "The Morality of Wealth," in *World Hunger and Moral Obligations,* W. Aiken and H. LaFollette, eds. (Englewood Cliffs, New Jersey: Prentice Hall, 1977), 138.

9. Whether one has the right not to change and improve oneself is a complex issue. At the very least, however, such a right may conflict with the rights of others (to be given help in preventing their being tortured and killed) which may

generate a duty that one keep informed on the condition of these others. I discuss this issue more fully in non-rights terms below. See note 11.

10. Recognizing this value parity constitutes the "basic moral insight," according to Thomas Nagel. T. Nagel, *The View From Nowhere* (New York, Oxford University Press, 1986, 205).

11. This claim has been contested by a number of contemporary philosophers: Philippa Foot, *Virtues and Vices and Other Essays in Moral Philosophy* (Berkeley: University of California Press, 1978); Bernard Williams, *Moral Luck* (Cambridge: Cambridge University Press, 1981); Susan Wolf, "Moral Saints," *Journal of Philosophy* 79 (1982); 419–31; Michael Slote, *Goods and Virtues* (Oxford: Clarendon Press, 1983); and Thomas Nagel, *The View From Nowhere.* In different ways each argues that it is not necessarily immoral to pursue personal, familial, or local goals at the expense of "common good" goals. The personal vs. impersonal dilemma is at the center of Nagel's moral and general philosophy. His opinion is that "the impartial standpoint of morality . . . will give to everyone a dispensation for a certain degree of partiality—in recognition of the fact that it is one aspect of the human perspective." In other words, an objective moral theory, in acknowledging all the facts in our universe, must take into account the fact that humans encounter the world from the subjective perspective of self, family, race, and nationality. The theory's moral demands cannot ignore this human fact. Consequently, an objective moral theory, such as utilitarianism, cannot be strictly impartial. I admit that the issue is profound and fascinating. But I would lean toward the hard line considered, but finally rejected, by Nagel: "One might take the severe line that moral requirements result from a correct assessment of the weight of good and evil, impersonally revealed, that it is our job to bring our motives into line with this, and that if we cannot do it because of personal weakness, this shows not that the requirements are excessive but that we are bad—though one might refrain from being too censorious about it." This view strikes me as rationally unavoidable once one grants the equal moral value of virtually every human. The partiality toward self that the above-mentioned philosophers defend goes directly against this moral axiom, particularly in a world of limited resources where my having x often deprives another or others. Were each of us insulated from others, the case might be different. Thomas Nagel, *The View From Nowhere,* 202–05.

12. A similar point is made by Slote in discussing whether wealthy individuals and nations who

omit to share some of their wealth with the poor are justified in this omission. He observes that "(o)missions may not be permissible . . . if they in some sense preserve or perpetuate commissive wrongdoings." And since he thinks that in fact most wealthy individuals and nations become and remain wealthy by immoral means, they are obligated to share their wealth with those at whose expense this wealth becomes accumulated. M. Slote, "The Morality of Wealth," 141–45.

13. Note that here I am not relying on the conclusion of my earlier argument based on the general obligation to prevent harm. I am merely borrowing one premise from that argument.

Making Peace with the Earth: Indigenous Agriculture and the Green Revolution

Deane Curtin

Deane Curtin is a professor of philosophy and Sponberg Chair of Ethics at Gustavus Adolphus College in St. Peter, Minnesota. He is co-editor of Cooking, Eating, Thinking: Transformative Philosophies of Food *(1992), author of* Resisting Development: Global Environmental Conflict and the Future of Traditional Communities *(forthcoming), and has authored essays on Deep Ecology and an Ecological Ethic of Care.*

Curtin challenges the widespread assumption that the green revolution is a moral program designed to address world hunger and to promote peace. Curtin argues that not only does the green revolution fail to meet these goals, but that it also does violence to the environment and indigenous women's agriculture. Curtin illuminates the environmental costs of the green revolution, including increased water use, vulnerable monoculture agriculture, pollution, loss of ecosystem integrity, and further dependence on the "First World." Thus, far from being a solution to world hunger, the green revolution is a harmful and environmentally costly program.

1. "DEVELOPMENTALISM" AS THE IDEOLOGY OF PROGRESS

In 1970 Norman Borlaug won the Nobel Prize recognizing his role as father of the green revolution. While Borlaug's work was on plant genetics, he did not win for biology. He won the prize for *peace*. Thus culminated the effort of two decades and more to represent the green revolution as a peace program.

It is often said that this "peace agenda" began precisely on Thursday, January 20,

1949 when President Harry S. Truman announced in his inaugural address a new American vision for the post-war world. "The supreme need of our time," Truman proclaimed, "is for men to learn to live together in peace and harmony" based on the foundation of inalienable human rights granted by God. The chief threat to Truman's vision was communism. Thus, almost as an afterthought, the post-war conflict between the "First World" (The United States and its allies) and the "Second World" (The Soviet Union and its allies) created the "Third World": half the world's people whose "food is inadequate," who are "victims of disease," and whose "economic life is primitive and stagnant." Truman proposed, not the "old imperial-

An earlier version of this paper appeared in *Environmental Ethics*, Vol. 17, No. 1, 1995. Printed with permission of Deane Curtin and *Environmental Ethics*.

ism—exploitation for foreign profit," but a new, ethical "program of development based on the concepts of democratic fair-dealing."[1]

According to narrowly defined criteria, the green revolution has been proclaimed a success: yields on all the major seeds it produced have at least doubled in annual production since World War II. Yet, its claim to a peace agenda, its explicit claim to a moral justification, demand a broader assessment. It is striking, for example, how different Truman's vision of "progress" was from Mahatma Gandhi's vision for a newly independent India. Gandhi had recently called for village "swaraj": small-scale, decentralized, village-based development using technologies appropriate to the village and communalistic lifestyles. Such deep conflict over what counts as progress surely demands moral scrutiny.

The assessment I propose here has two dimensions, both intended to understand the characteristic *violence* of the green revolution despite its explicit peace agenda. The green revolution's violence is, I believe, enabled by a set of "First World" attitudes toward the so-called "Third World" that puts the First World at the center ethically and conceptually, spinning out other "worlds" from that center to ethical and conceptual margins. This system of marginalization, which I call "developmentalism," is a system of domination that connects with, and benefits from, other forms of domination such as racism, sexism, classism, and naturism. Any analysis of domination that is not linked to developmentism risks a conceptual bias toward the First World.

Second, to address the peace claims of the green revolution specifically, I characterize developmentalism as an ideology that is akin to what Duane Cady has called warism.[2] It is structurally committed to violence in its treatment of indigenous communities and the earth, violence that is justified as a moral good. If the green revolution is a peace program, therefore, it must defend the claim that peace comes through violence. This, I believe confuses peace with pacification.

Since women have been the Third World's principal food producers, the green revolution was designed to displace women's agriculture. These agricultural practices, ironically, tend to be forms of ecological peacemaking, akin to pacifism. I do not intend to romanticize indigenous women's agriculture. Women are not inherently closer to nature than men. Men are not the sole perpetrators of environmental violence. For complex reasons, however, women's agricultural practices do tend toward peacemaking with the earth.

This article focuses on the effects of the green revolution in India because, as one of the two original test sites for the new technologies, its effects can most clearly be seen there. Even within India, however, generalization can be difficult. The state of Kerala, for example, has a matrilineal social structure, high literacy rates, and a stable system of small subsistence farms that make it an exception to developmental change that occurred elsewhere in India. Nevertheless, from the very fact that the green revolution was a *global* plan whose purpose was to effect a revolutionary change in traditional relationships to land it is a powerful vehicle for understanding global change despite otherwise culturally diverse contexts.

2. THE VIOLENCE OF THE GREEN REVOLUTION

In *Principles of Political Economy* John Stuart Mill, champion of political liberty in

Europe and Examiner of Indian Correspondence for the East India Company, described the British Empire's colonies as,

> . . . hardly to be looked upon as countries, . . . but more properly as outlying agricultural or manufacturing estates belonging to a larger community. Our West Indian colonies, for example, cannot be regarded as countries with a productive capital of their own . . . [but are rather] the place where England finds it convenient to carry on the production of sugar, coffee and a few other tropical commodities.[3]

Mill's "liberalism for the center/colonialism for the periphery," the sense that what we now call the Third World is "outlying," distant from, dependent on, and defined by, the center, is at the heart of contemporary developmentalism.

Richard Levins captures the dynamic of center and margin through "seven developmentalist myths in agriculture":

(1) *Backward is labor-intensive, modern is capital intensive agriculture.*
(2) *Diversity is backward, uniform monoculture is modern.*
(3) *Small scale is backward, large scale is modern.*
(4) *Backward is subjection to nature, modern implies increasingly complete control over everything that happens in the field or orchard or pasture.*
(5) *Folk knowledge is backward, scientific knowledge is modern.*
(6) *Specialists are modern, generalists backward.*
(7) *The smaller the object of study, the more modern.*[4]

Developmentalism is defined by a complex set of attitudes including issues of economic scale, reductionism, relationship of the person and community to the land, and the epistemic status of the outside expert as against the insider to a practice. In this section I characterize the green revolution historically as a form of developmentalism.

The green revolution began in 1944 when the Rockefeller Foundation invited Borlaug to leave his wartime job in a Dupont laboratory to direct the wheat breeding program at the International Maize and Wheat Improvement Center in Mexico. Under Borlaug's direction, the Center produced the so-called High Yielding Variety (HYV) of wheat that was initially targeted for two areas, northwest Mexico, and the Punjab region of India and Pakistan.

In principle, Borlaug's accomplishment was simple. Inorganic nitrogen fertilizer, when applied to traditional varieties of wheat, made the whole plant grow larger. Tall varieties, top-heavy with grain, had the tendency to topple over (called "lodging"), thus reducing the yield. Borlaug genetically engineered a dwarf variety of wheat to concentrate fertilizer in the grain (and profit) producing part of the plant. The green revolution was possible because HYVs can accept very high doses of fertilizer.

While the core of the green revolution is simple, the broader impact is complex. As Borlaug himself explained, a whole package of technologies was transferred to the Punjab, including ". . . seeds, fertilizers, insecticides, weed killers, and machinery—and the credit with which to buy them."[5]

High doses of fertilizer require much greater reserves of water to be effective. Green revolution crops therefore require massive irrigation.[6] In contrast to traditional agriculture, which is based on crop rotation, the green revolution involves plant monoculture. This makes HYVs especially susceptible to pests and diseases, thus the green revolution's dependence on pesticides.[7] In contrast to agriculture based on the principle of recycling inputs, the green revolution depends on external sources for seeds, chemicals, and machinery. Green revolution hybrid seeds are not self-pollinating, so they must be purchased each year from a seed company. The biotechnology revolution now occurring in agriculture carries plant monoculture further, to the level of individual brand names. Agrochemical companies are now engineering seeds to respond (or not respond) only to their particular commercial brand of fertilizer, herbicide, or pesticide.[8]

Though brief, this summary of green revolution technology is sufficient to illustrate the impact it has had on indigenous women's agriculture. The green revolution does not depend on replenishing the soil, the peasant's traditional source of security. It does not depend on conserving water, but on the assumption that access to water is unlimited. It demands political and economic dependence on a small number of seed and agrochemical companies rather than building in Gandhian fashion on local self-reliance. Since its economy of scale depends on the ideology of "bigger is better," it depends on loans—and the ability to repay loans—from Western dominated international agencies, such as the World Bank.

3. INDIGENOUS WOMEN'S AGRICULTURE

What were the agricultural practices that needed "development" by the green revolution? Anthropological research helps to explain the gendered roles of traditional farmers. The hunter/gatherer paradigm, according to which the hunters provide most of the food, has been dismissed as a sexist myth. In such societies, up to eighty percent of food is gathered by women. Women's roles as gatherers, in turn, led to the invention of agriculture as predominantly a women's practice. On the assumption that "the workers invented their tools" most anthropologists now agree that women invented the important agricultural tools. Because women have also been the traditional plant breeders, they bred most of the world's grains including wheat, rice, maize, barley, oats, sorghum, millet, and rye. These cereals still supply 75% of all human food energy.[9]

In Africa and many parts of Asia, agriculture is still disproportionately women's work. According to a recent Worldwatch Paper, "Gender Bias: Roadblock to Sustainable Development," women in sub-Saharan Africa grow 80 percent of household food. Women's labor produces 70 to 80 percent of food on the Indian subcontinent, and 50 percent of food consumed in Latin America and the Caribbean.[10]

This is much the situation Sir Albert Howard encountered in the late 1800's when he was dispatched to India by the British government to investigate methods of improving Indian agriculture. He found, much to his surprise, that their crops were free of pests, and that insecticides and fungicides had no place in their system of agriculture. Impressed, he decided ". . . I could not do better than watch the operations of these peasants, and acquire their traditional knowledge as rapidly as possible. For the time being, therefore, I regarded them as my professor of agriculture."[11]

The best agriculture, Howard would later write, is modeled on "nature's agriculture":

> The main characteristic of Nature's farming can therefore be summed up in a few words. Mother earth never attempts to farm without live stock: she always raises

mixed crops; great pains are taken to preserve the soil and to prevent erosion; the mixed vegetable and animal wastes are converted into humus; there is no waste; the processes of growth and the processes of decay balance one another; ample provision is made to maintain large reserves of fertility; the greatest care is taken to store the rainfall; both plants and animals are left to protect themselves against disease.[12]

The cyclical principle made Howard's book, *An Agricultural Testament*, a classic in the organic, sustainable agriculture movement. It is not often recognized that this movement owes a great debt to Third World women's agricultural knowledge.[13]

The foremost commitment of cyclical agriculture is to biological diversity. In a healthy ecosystem, decay balances growth. Soil regenerates through recycling plant and animal matter. Plant agriculture, therefore, requires animals for fertilizer. Crops that use nitrogen, such as wheat and rice, must rotate with plants that return nitrogen to the soil, such as pulses (beans, peas and lentils).

The cyclical principle also embraces water conservation, which begins with healthy soil that retains moisture. Water depends on mixed land use as well. Agricultural land must be mixed with forested land. Trees prevent flooding, and are a self-regenerating resource for fodder that retains water. Forests are also necessary for food, building materials, and traditional medicines.

Traditional agriculture does not depend on pesticides. It lets biological diversity do the work. As any agriculturist knows, it is not true that everything is connected in nature. If that were the case, Dutch Elm disease would have wiped out oak and other species. Traditional agriculture takes advantage of the disjunctions in nature to control pests. Corn rootworm

will not eat soybean roots, for example, so crop rotation removes the rootworm's source of food.

Traditional agriculture is also cyclical and localized in the genetics of its seeds. It is typical for each family to maintain its own stock of seeds from year to year. Women usually are responsible for selecting the best seeds for cultivation the next season. Village-based genetic breeding means that seeds are developed to meet the needs of widely diverse growing conditions. Seeds are bred to "meet the expectations of the land," in the words of Wes Jackson;[14] land is not altered to meet the demands of the seed. The genetic diversity of traditional agriculture is a safeguard against widespread devastation of crops due to climatic change or pests. Village plant breeding is also a political issue. When women control plant breeding, they are at the nexus of activities that most determine family and community survival. It is just this sense of what is appropriate to a place, the refusal to dominate a place, I will contend, that developmentalism reads as backward.

4. WARISM, WOMEN, AND THE ENVIRONMENT

I will not argue directly against warism. Rather, my purpose here is to clarify what would have to go into a defense of a warist environmental ideology. In keeping the argument "close to the ground," in focusing, that is, on the actual impact of the green revolution on Third World peoples, I hope to show how *difficult* it would be to defend the violence of the green revolution as moral.

Duane Cady coined the term "warism" as a parallel term to "pacifism." Warism is the view ". . . that war is both morally justifiable in principle and often morally justified in fact." Pacifism holds that, ". . . war, by its very nature, is morally wrong and . . . humans should work for peaceful resolution of conflict." Cady was thinking in terms of explicit military violence rather than the covert political violence of the green revolution. Recently, however, Cady has connected warism with other forms of domination: sexism, racism, and classism.[15] As a reminder that I am stretching Cady's meaning beyond military violence, I say that the ideology of the green revolution is *akin* to warism, that developmentalism is warist.

In connecting warism with other forms of domination, Cady draws on Marilyn Frye's insight that "arrogant perception" underlies the structures of oppression. According to Frye, Western civilization's answer to the question of man's place in nature is ". . . everything that is is resource for man's exploitation. With this world view, men see with arrogant eyes which organize everything seen with reference to themselves and their own interests."[16] Developmentalism and warism both perceive the world arrogantly. Like racism, sexism, classism, and naturism, they construct a moral pecking order. Those at the top "know," "act," "develop," and enjoy the moral prerogative. Those at the bottom are ignorant, passive (and deserving) recipients of the actions of others.

While the dominations of women and nature are connected in the green revolution, they are not identical. Nature is entirely outside the moral sphere for the developmentalist; it is something to be controlled as a "resource for man's exploitation." Since it lacks moral standing, the developmentalist's impact on nature is regarded as nonmoral. While developmentalism itself is a moral crusade, applications of science to nature are understood as morally neutral technical improvements.

Women and indigenous cultures are morally unlike nature in this respect. They do have moral standing for the developmentalist. We see this in the very fact that they are constructed as needing "development." While different, the connection between the domination of women and the domination of nature is that developmentalism operates in the mode of "control over" indigenous communities through controlling their natural "resources." I will consider, first, the warist domination of women and indigenous communities in the green revolution, then the warist domination of nature.

Warism and Indigenous Peoples. It would be inviting to think that the effects of the green revolution on women, their communities, and their environments, were unfortunate side effects of well-intentioned development programs. However, that is not true. Before the green revolution, there were important research programs in both Mexico[17] and India on a wide variety of self-pollinating seeds traditionally cultivated by peasants. These programs were consciously undermined by the politics of the green revolution.

In India, the Cuttack Institute was investigating techniques to increase yields on traditional varieties of rice based on the indigenous knowledge of tribal peoples. The Institute had collected and preserved 20,000 indigenous varieties of rice, a storehouse of genetic information patiently developed over centuries by village women. Unlike the genetically uniform rice developed by the IRRI in the Philippines—another Rockefeller/Ford food for peace program—these indigenous species were genetically diverse, having been bred over the entire Indian subcontinent. Nevertheless, for political reasons, the Indian minister of agriculture, who had been trained in Mexico, demanded to have the Cuttack Institute's germplasm turned over to IRRI. When the director resisted, he was fired.[18]

There were elements in Mexico and India that resisted the green revolution as an assault against national autonomy. They were often silenced when food was used as a political weapon. In 1966, for example, Lyndon Johnson refused to commit food aid to India until it adopted the green revolution as national agricultural policy.[19]

There was no scientific reason for directing research exclusively toward improving seeds that undercut the political control of the world's poor. Such programs already existed, as I have noted; Richard Lewontin has argued that open-pollinated varieties of seed could have been as productive as HYV hybrids.[20] In fact, under less than ideal conditions, traditional seeds are often *more* productive than HYVs. Since most Third World farmers work small plots of marginal land with irregular access to water, less than ideal conditions are the norm, not the exception. The fact that HYVs were chosen for development, therefore, while programs on open-pollinated varieties were forcibly shut down, reflects the class and gender interests of the green revolution. HYVs are genetically engineered to be a privately owned commodity.

In addition to the attempt by multinationals to control indigenous communities through genetic research, control is also increasing as courts in the United States and its industrialized allies are now recognizing the legal right to patent genetic information, thus privatizing the seed. American companies often claim that the Third World steals intellectual property from the First World. However, this conveniently narrow argument only applies to items that are defined by the First World as commodities. Resources taken from the Third World are defined (by the First World) as "the common heritage of mankind."

Most of the world's sources of genetic diversity, upon which First World research depends, are in the Third World. Colonialism has always depended on exploitation of this diversity to produce commodities that are sold back to the Third World on credit provided by the First World. As early as 1848, for example, the East India Company was collecting plant species in India. In 1853, when Admiral Perry colonized Japan, he collected plant species, including rice.[21] That this kind of treatment is warist is not news to many residents of the Third World. Recently, for example, five hundred farmers in Bangalore, India, stormed and ransacked the office of Cargill, Inc. to protest the intellectual property provisions of the General Agreement on Tariffs and Trades.[22]

The effects of this "top-down" ideology on indigenous people are both predictable and tragic. Vandana Shiva and Maria Mies have challenged the claim that so-called "ethnic violence" is responsible for increasing violence in India's Punjab region.[23] Religious conflict, they argue, is the effect. The cause is the green revolution. The same system of irrigation that caused the Punjab to be chosen in the first place as the test site for green revolution techniques, is now causing violence over water rights. Farmers who had the means to mechanize and repay foreign loans have benefited, their acreages increasing rapidly as small farmers are driven out of business. Small farmers— women and men—have been displaced, cut off from their traditional source of security. Men who are displaced by this process seek wage-labor jobs on the large farms, or they migrate to the cities leaving their families behind. Women who are displaced often are expected to work as an unpaid adjunct to their husband's wage-labor. As is almost always the case in such situations, violence against women has increased in the form of sati, "kitchen accidents," and female infanticide.[24] In many cultures, the same women who grow and prepare the food are the last to eat, even in the best of times.

Warism and Nature. The green revolution's vision of agriculture is the violent conquest of nature. This begins with a reductionist, non-contextual conception of science. A Harvard botanist said, "We now operationally have a kind of world gene pool . . . Darwin aside, speciation aside, we can now envision moving any gene, in principle at least, out of any organism and into any organism." Nobel laureate David Baltimore put it even more succinctly. He said, "We can outdo evolution."[25] The desire to outdo evolution in the control of nature reveals the dualistic intentions of green revolution ideology. Science is not a romance *with* nature, it is a race *against* nature, and science is winning.

Most revealing are the conceptual and empirical connections between green revolution techniques and the technology of war. Vandana Shiva has pointed out that, "Violence was part of the very context of discovery of pesticides during World War I. The manufacture of explosives had a direct spin-off on the development of synthetic insecticides. The tear gas, chloropicrin, was found to be insecticidal in 1916 and thus changed from a wartime product to a peacetime one."[26] Organophosphates, such as malathion, are designed to destroy the central nervous system. Insecticides and herbicides are tested by their "kill ratios." Broad spectrum herbicides kill all vegetation leaving the earth biologically neutral. Agent Orange, used as a defoliant during the war in Vietnam, is one such product.

It is often claimed that science and technology are morally neutral, and that only political judgments about the applications of science are open to moral scrutiny. The green revolution makes this distinction between technology and gender bias difficult to sustain. Class, race, and gender biases have been genetically engineered into the "miracle seeds" of the green revolution. Research such as the Cuttack Institute's that is sensitive to local traditions shows that women's agriculture is not at all opposed, in principle, to culturally sensitive development or to scientific research. It is opposed to the political genetics of the green revolution.

I do not doubt the moral integrity of Borlaug and others who sincerely believed that the green revolution would bring world peace. Nevertheless, the green revolution succeeded to a much greater degree than any overt form of militarism in reducing Third World peasants to political and economic dependence on Northern industrial and scientific powers. A recent survey of sustainable Third World development concluded that, "There is much merit to the argument that if given the choice between the present system of international assistance and no assistance at all, the Third World's poor would be better off with none."[27]

5. WOMEN'S AGRICULTURE AS ECOLOGICAL PACIFISM

In stark contrast to the ideology of the green revolution, Third World women's agriculture is structurally akin to pacifism in its commitment to ecological peacemaking. Its mode is "collaboration with" nature. Unlike the universalism of the developmentalist, which regards everything that is different as needing "development" in its own image, women's cyclical practices reveal a sense of what is appropriate to and sustainable in a particular place. Nature is not on the far side of the moral divide. The community includes the land as much as its people. Treatment of the land, therefore, reveals the moral self.

The sense of the deep relation of person and place is often expressed in moral or mythological terms. Consider, for example, the arrogant perception in the following passage from the *Journal of the Indian Pesticide Industry* as the author struggles to explain the peasant's relationship to the land:

> [A] more important [difficulty in marketing products in India] is the mental attitude of the agriculturalist about killing. Pesticides spell killing, maybe small and perhaps invisible insects. But it is killing that they are used for. This killing is anathema to the majority of the agriculturalist, be they Hindu, Jain or others. By nature, the agriculturalist is generous, wanting to bestow on others what he reaps out of Mother Earth. He [sic] does not think that he alone should enjoy the fruits of his labor . . . to kill those unseen and unknown lives, though they were thriving on what Mother Earth yields, is foreign to his nature . . . . It takes some time for the simple folk to get acclimatized to the very conception of killing tiny helpless and unarmed creatures.[28]

The Indian idea of "ahimsa," or nonharming, puts the violence of the green revolu-tion, and its cultural specificity, into sharp relief. Ahimsa requires a moral universe that includes insects in the moral cycle of life and death. Nature is seen in moral relationship to human beings. We are defined morally by our conduct with nature.

It is telling how often, in practice, development experts fail to perceive this deep relationship between women, indigenous cultures, and place. Third World women, for example, have long depended on grasses that grow along the borders of fields to make baskets and mats. When development experts decide that these grasses have no market value and plan programs that kill them with herbicide, this is arrogant perception. When these same experts decide that public, forested land is "undeveloped," and only has value when it is privatized and "developed" for profit, this too is arrogant perception.

Of Richard Levins' seven developmentalist myths, one seems most powerful in explaining the developmentalist's inability to appreciate place: "Backward is subjection to nature, modern implies increasingly complete control over everything that happens in the field or orchard or pasture." In the developmentalist's moral pecking order, one is either dominant over nature, or subject to it, either master or slave. The sense of living with nature in a particular place, which is neither subjugation nor dominance, is misread by the developmentalist as backwardness, as a life fit for a slave.

Far from defending the world's poor, the green revolution sought to defeat communism by destroying the world's peasant class. It did this by dividing the peasant economically, politically and spiritually from the sense of place. Conversely, one could understand much about peasant resistance movements by considering them to be localized defenses of the connection between person and place.[29] It is no accident that Liberation Theology in Central America, or Dalit Theology[30] in India are perspectives that express the particular conditions of peoples. They reject the universalizing tendencies of traditional theology in favor of a theology of place.

Finally, it cannot be insisted often enough that pacifism is not passivism. Characterizing typically women's farming as pacifist does not mean that women must simply accept the violence perpetrated against them and their communities. On the contrary, pacifism is a form of resistance. The Chipko Movement in India, the green Belt Movement in Africa,[31] and countless other small scale women's movements the world over testify to the fact that women are not passive in defending the integrity of their communities and their environments.

6. INSTITUTIONAL VIOLENCE

This article began by contrasting President Truman's developmentalist vision for the Third World with Mahatma Gandhi's ideal of village *swaraj*. A great puzzle remains: how could Truman and Gandhi look at the same world and come to such profoundly different conclusions about the meaning of "progress"? This deep dislocation between basic moral attitudes, I believe, provides us with a final opportunity to understand the nature of violence.

We in the "First World" are very good at recognizing *individual violence*. Individual violence is one-on-one violence, and it can be either overt or covert. For example, child abuse can be either overt and physical, resulting in broken bones and bruised faces, or it can be more subtle, covert violence, as in a parent's pattern of psychological abuse that robs a child of self-esteem. We are good at recognizing individual violence, I suggest, because we[32] are the heirs of political liberalism one of whose defining beliefs is in the primacy of the individual. The utilitarian philosophers of colonialism in India regarded community as a "fictitious *body*" whose interests were nothing more than the sum of the interests of individual members.[33]

Political liberalism makes it difficult to recognize two other forms of violence, *systemic* and *institutional violence*. By systemic violence I mean a pervasive, hierarchical pattern of thinking, a form of "arrogant perception" that privileges some groups and marginalizes others, for no morally justifiable reason. By institutional violence I mean violence facilitated by well organized cultural institutions. Racism and sexism, therefore, are forms of systemic violence. These violent patterns of thought may, however, necessitate the creation of violent institutions. Racism may necessitate the creation of racist schools, police forces, and legal systems.

Unlike individual violence, systemic and institutional violence are rarely the result of any individual's conscious intentions. If I am guilty of mugging or murdering another person it is likely that I will be able to introspect and find myself responsible for these acts of individual violence. However, it is very unlikely that we could say that any individual is responsible for creation of institutional forms of violence. A racist police officer may be "part of the system" of institutional violence, but it is unlikely that we could hold any individual responsible for the system or the institution. In opposition to affirmative action programs in the United States, for example, we often hear people say "I didn't personally endorse past injustices so I can't be held responsible for contemporary inequalities." Such a view makes sense in the context of liberal individualism where only culpability for individual violence counts. However, it fails to recognize institutional and systemic forms of violence. There are forms of violence that *no individual intended*. If we are benefited by these systems of exclusion, we are likely to think such systems are just. Those who are excluded know better.

My conclusion is probably obvious: developmentalism is a form of systemic violence that facilitated the creation of violent institutions: the political, scientific, and economic institutions of the green revolution. Those in the First World who have benefited from this system of marginalization are likely to think of the green revolution as progress. Those who experience the green revolution from the other side know better.

NOTES

1. Harry S Truman. "Inaugural Address" in *Inaugural Addresses of the Presidents of the United States* (Washington, D.C.: U.S. Government Printing Office), pp. 286–90.
2. See Duane Cady, *From Warism to Pacifism: A Moral Continuum* (Philadelphia: Temple University Press, 1989).
3. John Stuart Mill, *Principles of Political Economy*, Vol. 3, ed. J. M. Robson (Toronto: University of Toronto Press, 1965), p. 693.
4. Richard Levins, "Science and Progress: Seven Developmentalist Myths in Agriculture," *Monthly Review* 38(3 1986): 13–20.
5. Norman Borlaug, "The Green Revolution, Peace, and Humanity," in *Les Prix Nobel en 1970*, ed. anon. (Stockholm: Imprimerieal Royal P.A Norstedt & Söner, 1971), p. 231.
6. One reason the Punjab was chosen as the site for transfer of green revolution technology is that it already had a system of irrigation based on partial diversion of rivers. See Shiva, *The Violence of the Green Revolution*, p. 122.
7. F. Chabousson. "How Pesticides Increase Pests," *Ecologist* 16(1 1986): 29–36.
8. See Jack Ralph Kloppenburg, *First the Seed: The Political Economy of Plant Biotechnology: 1492–2000* (Cambridge: Cambridge University Press, 1988). The impact of these technologies is indicated by the juxtaposition of two facts: in the latter half of the 1960's, consumption of inorganic nitrogen fertilizer in India increased from 58,000 metric tons to 1.2 million metric tons. During that decade, India's currency was devalued by 37.5 percent as a result of its rising foreign debt. See Borlaug, "The Green Revolution, Peace, and Humanity," p. 233 and Shiva, *The Violence of the Green Revolution*, p. 30.
9. Autumn Stanley, "Daughters of Isis, Daughters of Demeter: When Women Sowed and Reaped," in *Women, Technology and Innovation*, ed. Joan Rothschild (New York: Pergamon, 1982), pp. 293–94.
10. Jodi L. Jacobson, *Gender Bias: Roadblock to Sustainable Development*, Vol. 110 (Washington, D.C.: Worldwatch Institute, 1992), p. 19. Also see J.B. Bhati and D.V. Singh, "Women's Contribution to Agricultural Economy in Hill Regions of Northwest India," *Economic and Political Weekly* 22 (17 1987); Ester Boserup, *Woman's Role in Economic Development* (London: Allen and Unwin, 1970); Lynne Brydon and Sylvia Chant, *Women in the Third World: Gender Issues in Rural and Urban Areas* (New Brunswick, N.J.: Rutgers University Press, 1989); Sue Ellen Charlton, *Women in Third World Development* (Boulder, CO: Westview Press, 1984); Irene Dankelman and Joan Davidson, eds. *Women and Environment in the Third World* (London: Earthscan, 1988); Donald Michelwait, Mary Ann Riegelman, and Charles Sweet, eds. *Women in Rural Development* (Boulder, CO: Westview, 1976); Maria Mies, "The Dynamics of the Sexual Division of Labor and Integration of Rural Women into the World Market," in *Women and Development*, ed. Lourdes Benería (New York: Praeger, 1982): Ingrid Palmer, "New Official Ideas on Women and Development," *Bulletin Institute of Development Studies, University of Sussex* 10 (3 1979): 42–52; Vandana Shiva, *Staying Alive: Women, Ecology and Development* (London: Zed Books, 1988).
11. Sir Albert Howard, *An Agricultural Testament*, Rodale Press Edition. 1972 ed. (London: Oxford University Press, 1943), p. 160. It is clear from the history of Indian agriculture that Howard had placed his education primarily in the hands of Indian peasant women.
12. Ibid., pp. 23 and 14.
13. The Rodale system of organic gardening is a direct result of peasant women's farming. Rodale was a student of Howard's.
14. Wes Jackson, "Meeting the Expectations of the Land," in *Altars of Unhewn Stone: Science and the Earth* (San Francisco: North Point Press, 1987).
15. Cady, *From Warism to Pacifism*, pp. 3–4, and Cady, "War, Gender, Race & Class," *Concerned*

Philosophers for Peace Newsletter 11 (2 1991): 4–10.

16. Marilyn Frye, *The Politics of Reality: Essays in Feminist Theory* (Trumansburg, NY: Crossings Press, 1983), p. 67.

17. For the history of the issue in Mexico, see Frances Moore Lappé and Joseph Collins, *Food First: Beyond the Myth of Scarcity* (New York: Ballantine, 1978), pp. 112–116, and Andrew Pearse, *Seeds of Plenty, Seeds of Want: Social and Economic Implication of the green revolution* (Oxford: Oxford University Press, 1980), pp. 33–37.

18. Shiva, *The Violence of the Green Revolution,* pp. 43–44. The fragility of such genetic information cannot be overstated. As one observer commented, "The genetic heritage of a millennium in a particular valley can disappear in a single bowl of porridge." Once lost, it is lost forever. This has, in fact, happened. A cache of wheat germplasm 'stored at the Maize and Wheat Institute in Mexico was destroyed when an Institute refrigerator shut down during a power outage. (Lappé and Collins., p. 174.)

19. Lappé and Collins, *Food First,* pp. 357–360.

20. Richard Lewontin, "Agricultural Research and the Penetration of Capital," *Science for the People* 14(1 1982): 16.

21. Kloppenburg, *First the Seed,* pp. 14, 55.

22. *Minneapolis Star Tribune,* January 1, 1993.

23. Maria Mies, Veronika Bennholdt-Thomsen, and Claudia von Werlhof, *Women: The Last Colony* (London: Zed Books Ltd., 1988), p. 134, and Shiva, *The Violence of the Green Revolution,* pp. 189–192. See also Maria Mies, *Patriarchy and Accumulation on a World Scale* (London: Zed Books, 1986).

24. Sati is the practice of burning the widow on the husband's funeral pyre. The euphemism "kitchen accident" refers to situations in which women are doused with kerosene in the family kitchen and burned to death, often by the husband's relatives. The cause is often disappointment over a dowry. Female infanticide has become a subject of national debate in India with the advent of genetic testing for gender before birth.

25. Quoted in Kloppenburg, p. 3.

26. Shiva, *Staying Alive* (London: Zed Books, 1988), p. 156. At a political level, green revolution techniques marginalize Third World countries in other ways. Products, such as DDT that have long been banned in the First World because of their known damage to human health and the environment, are still widely sold in the Third World. Pesticide accidents among people who are illiterate and cannot read directions for recommended use are responsible for 40,000 deaths each year.

27. David C. Korten, "Sustainable Development," *World Policy Journal* (1991): 177.

28. Quoted in Lappé and Collins, *Food First,* p. 61.

29. See Ramachandra Guha, *The Unquiet Woods: Ecological Change and Peasant Resistance in the Himalaya* (Berkeley: University of California Press, 1989) for a detailed account of the relation of person and place in the Himalaya foothills.

30. Dalit means "the oppressed." It is often preferred as more descriptive term than either Untouchable or Harajin (Gandhi's term meaning "children of God").

31. Founded by Wangari Maathi, the Green Belt Movement is run by women. It provides tree seedlings for planting in green belts in rural and urban areas. The women who plant the trees receive 25 cents for each tree that survives for at least three months. This generates income for women, who are generally excluded from the wage labor market. It also generates self-esteem: these plantings have a success rate of over 80 percent. Fifty thousand women and children have planted over 10 million trees since the movement began. Maathi recently won the alternative Nobel Prize.

The Chipko Movement is a movement of indigenous women in the Himalayan foothills which began when they hugged trees to prevent deforestation at the hands of lumber companies. The movement has grown into a comprehensive development program that addresses the environment, health, education, and political justice.

32. We should be cautious in using words like "we." Not all residents of the "First World" have enjoyed the benefits of political liberalism. This is part of the problem with understanding the distinction between First and Third geographically.

33. Jeremy Bentham, *The Principles of Morals and Legislation* (Prometheus Books, 1988), p. 3.

QUESTIONS: HUNGER AND POVERTY

1. Do you consider it ethically problematic that Hardin bases his conclusion concerning providing aid to countries like India on an assumption of what will happen in the future rather than being concerned with ending immediate suffering? Provide a utilitarian, Kantian, or rights-based justification for the position you take,

2. Sen discusses two approaches to population control. Explain both of these approaches and why he advocates the collaborative approach. If this approach

results in a higher standard of living with its accompanying higher levels of consumption and increased threats to the environment, how does Sen justify its advocacy?

3. In his essay, Singer quotes Thomas Aquinas from *Summa Theologica:* "Whatever a man has in superabundance is owed, of natural right, to the poor for their sustenance." Explain this quote and which of Singer's principles this best illustrates (the strong or the weak version). Why do you think that most people do not live according to this principle?

4. Arthur denies that the rights of starving people to be fed automatically outweigh the rights of affluent people to purchase things that affect their happiness. Explain why he argues this. Do people have a duty to reeducate themselves so that they do not depend on second cars and bigger homes for happiness?

5. Why do we, as Filice argues, have a duty to keep informed about distant atrocities? How can Filice answer challenges, such as Arthur might pose, concerning our right to pursue happiness, if our becoming informed threatens our pursuit of happiness? (In answering, be sure to address the nature of a prima facie duty, and the balance Filice advocates concerning other duties and interests.)

6. How has the green revolution harmed indigenous cultures, the environment, and furthered dependence on the "First World"? In light of the evidence that Curtin presents, and drawing from the first chapter, *Human Rights and Justice*, provide an ethical critique of the green revolution. (Is this program justified? Do the benefits outweigh the harm?)

SUPPLEMENTARY READINGS: HUNGER AND POVERTY

AIKEN, WILLIAM. "The 'Carrying Capacity' Equivocation." *Social Theory and Practice*, vol. 6(1), Spring 1980.

CHEN, MARTHA. "A Matter of Survival: Women's Right to Employment in India and Bangladesh." In *Women, Culture, and Development*, Nussbaum and Glover, editors. Clarendon Press, 1995.

DONNELLY, JACK. "Satisfying Basic Needs in Africa: Human Rights, Markets and the State." *Africa Today*, vol. 32(1 & 2), 1985.

EMMANUEL, ARGHIRI. "The Multinational Corporations and Inequality of Development." In *Multi-National Corporations and Third World Development*, Ghosh, editor. New York: Greenwood Press, 1984.

HARDIN, GARRETT. "Living on a Lifeboat." *BioScience* 24, October 1974.

HERNANDEZ, DONALD. "Fertility Reduction Policies and Poverty in Third World Countries: Ethical Issues." *Journal of Applied Behavioral Science*, vol. 20(4), 1984.

KAHN, HERMAN. "The Confucian Ethic and Economic Growth." In *The Gap Between Rich and Poor*, Seligson, editor. Boulder, CO: Westview Press, 1984.

LAFOLLETE, HUGH, and LARRY MAY. "Suffer the Little Children." In *World Hunger and Morality*, second edition, LaFollette and Aiken, editors. Englewood Cliffs, NJ: Prentice Hall, 1996.

Li, Lillian M. "Famine and Famine Relief: Viewing Africa in the 1980s from China in the 1920s." In *Drought and Hunger in Africa*, Glantz, editor. New York, NY: Cambridge University Press, 1987.

May, Larry. "Minimal Justice and the World Hunger Problem." In *Agriculture, Change and Human Values*. Gainesville, FL: University of Florida, 1982.

Nagel, Thomas. "Poverty and Food: Why Charity Is Not Enough." In *Food Policy*. New York: The Free Press, 1977.

O'Neill, Onora. "Rights, Obligations and Needs." *Logos*, 1985.

Parpart, Jane L. "Women's Rights and the Lagos Plan of Action." *Human Rights Quarterly*, vol. 8(2), May 1986.

Sen, Amartya. "The Great Bengal Famine." In *Poverty and Famine*. London, England: Oxford University Press, 1981.

Sethi, J.D. "Human Rights and Development." *Human Rights Quarterly*, vol. 3 (3), 1981.

Simon, Laurence. "Social Ethics and Land Reform: The Case of El Salvador." *Agriculture and Human Values*, Summer 1984.

IV

WAR
AND VIOLENCE

I observed that men rushed to arms for slight causes, or no cause at all, and that when arms have once been taken up there is no longer any respect for law, divine or human: it is as if in accordance with a general decree, frenzy had openly been let loose for the committing of all crimes. Confronted with such utter ruthlessness, many men who are the very furthest from being bad men, have come to the point of forbidding all use of arms . . . .

—Hugo Grotius[1]

Most justifications for war begin with some reference to the principle of self-defense. Just as it is nearly uncontroversial that a person is morally justified in defending himself or herself from attack, so it is thought that nations are justified in defending themselves from attack by the use of violent force. Recourse is often made to another principle as well, namely, that we are all required to go to the aid of suffering innocent persons. As in the case of self-defense, it is often necessary to use violence to thwart an attack upon an innocent person. Finally, many people believe that it is justified to use force to prevent a greater evil than is had by the use of violence. This final view, much more controversial than the first two, is an important element in what has come to be known as the "just war" doctrine.

In sharp contrast to the just war doctrine is the doctrine called pacifism. Pacifists believe that all, or almost all, uses of violence are morally unjustified, especially in relations between nations. This doctrine often starts, as in our quotation from Grotius (who was not a pacifist), with the claim that individuals are corrupted by engaging in war and violence. In addition, violence is considered a direct affront to the humanity of the person against whom violence is used. The use of violence, even to thwart violence, is always a form of disrespect which fails to treat the other as possessing intrinsic value and as having a life worthy of respect. Most pacifists believe that one need not be passive to be nonviolent; indeed the most famous pacifists of recent times have also developed strategies of collective action and resistance, as we will see in several of the readings of this section.

Those who believe that war can be morally justified usually point to a paradigmatic case of a war waged for a just cause. Typically the Second World War is cited as an example of a war which no reasonable person could have opposed since it had the highest of moral aims, namely, ending the Nazi attempt to exterminate all Jews and subjugate all of Europe. Indeed, some suggest that not only was it morally justified, but there was also a strong moral obligation to fight in the Second World War. But even in such wars, pacifists will ask whether there were no other alternative nonviolent courses of action that could have been pursued.

Just as the case for the moral justifiability of some wars is buttressed by the facts of the Second World War, so the case for pacifism is tremendously buttressed by the facts concerning the struggle for India's liberation from British colonial rule. Mohandas K. Gandhi led a successful mass revolution without the use of military arms or violence. And in more recent times, Martin Luther King, Jr., led very successful nonviolent confrontations with state governments that engaged in unjust discriminatory practices against Blacks. In both cases, the leaders of these movements were philosophically committed to nonviolence and through their own successful efforts showed the effectiveness of collective political efforts that stop short of war.

There also are moral issues raised by the manner in which war is conducted. A controversy has raged about whether the United States used more bombing runs than it needed to use in order to achieve their military objectives in the Gulf War. And, even more people have claimed that the Iraqis engaged in immoral tactics in using Kuwaiti and American civilian hostages as shields to protect military targets during the same Gulf War. Indeed, many argue that the taking of hostages is always immoral, although it has been a tactic employed by both sides in most of the major wars of the last few hundred years. Even more persuasive arguments are made against the use of nuclear or chemical weapons.

One strand of revolutionary literature argues that most tactics, no matter how violent, are justifiable as long as the cause for which one fights is sufficiently honorable. Indeed, there is a long tradition of important political theorists, from Machiavelli through Lenin, who have argued that the goodness of the cause for which one fights justifies nearly any means one may employ to achieve that end. Such a position, sometimes referred to as "the ends justify the means" has also been roundly criticized for a similarly long period of time.

Our readings begin with an essay by Douglas Lackey who provides a very careful summary of the main elements and problems of the traditional just war theory. The first part of his essay is devoted to the doctrine of *jus ad bellum*, the principles justifying engaging in war. The two most important considerations are whether the war is planned in defense of a just cause, and whether that war is planned for good intentions. The second half of the essay concerns the doctrine of *jus in bello*, the principles governing justified practices in wars. Here the two most important considerations are whether the violence inflicted is proportional to the just objective of the war, and whether the violent instruments of war are directed only at enemy soldiers, rather than at noncombattant civilians.

Mohandas K. Gandhi attempts to respond to some of the main critics of pacifism, especially those who criticized his own refusal to consider a resort to violence in the seemingly just cause of confronting British oppression in India. Gandhi sets out his own views in the context of the principle of mutual love which most of the great religions of the East espouse. It is a violation of this principle, he argues, to use violence even to counter violence directed at oneself. But Gandhi was not an advocate of passive inaction. Rather he points us toward a form of nonviolent noncooperation that he has good reason to believe can be effective, especially when it is mounted on a very large scale. At the end of this selection, Gandhi attempts to explain why it was not morally justifiable for the British to go to war to stop Hitler, perhaps one of the most controversial of pacifist claims.

Haig Khatchadourian argues that terrorist violence is not justified because of the destruction of innocent life that inevitably occurs when terrorists strike. In the just war tradition, it is considered important that the violence used must not be directed at innocent civilians. Also within that tradition, the principle of proportion is a key limiting ingredient in any justification of violence. The evil of the violence used must be in proportion to the evil which the violence alleviates. When innocent lives are taken by a terrorist's act, indeed when they are the goal of the terrorist's act, moral justification is blocked. Respect for the human rights of the innocent victims demands this much.

Burleigh Wilkins provides a basis for countering Khatchadourian's critique of terrrorism and also Gandhi's claim that even a violent confrontation of Hitler would be unjustified on pacifist grounds. Drawing on the work of Karl Jaspers, Wilkins argues that many of us are responsible for great tragedies in the world, such as the Holocaust. If the only means that could have brought down Hitler's regime, and could have alleviated the collective guilt of peoples throughout the world, was a terrorist act, then that act can be morally justified. Just as it is often justified to kill in self-defense, so it may be justified to kill so as to protect the innocent lives of those threatened by political regimes such as that of Nazi Germany.

Some feminists have pointed out that they share in common with pacifists a condemnation of a predominantly male-aggressive manner of confronting instances of social injustice. Sara Ruddick sketches several cases of mass movements of resistance inspired by the values which have been traditionally cherished in women's lives. The traditional role of mother as maintainer of love and protector of the innocent has been used, she argues, to combat potentially harmful situations concerning war, state terrorism, and environmental destruction. The efforts of women's groups have resulted, she concludes, in new ways to invent peace.

Martin Luther King, Jr., defends a version of nonviolent civil disobedience by reference to several of the main principles of Judeo-Christian morality. Like Gandhi, King sees nonviolence as the expression of love, especially the biblical doctrine of "love thy neighbor as thyself." King outlines a strategy for confronting injustice which has proven to be the blueprint for many social movements of the last 25 years in the United States and Europe. He takes great pains to argue that there is nothing unpatriotic about civil disobedience. Indeed he argues that civil disobedience can be one of the greatest expressions of concern for the laws of a nation.

—Larry May

NOTE

1. Hugo Grotius, *Prolegomena to the Law of War and Peace*, 1625, translated by Francis Kelsey, Indianapolis, IN: Library of Liberal Arts, 1957, p. 21.

Just War Theory

Douglas P. Lackey

Douglas P. Lackey is a professor of philosophy at Baruch College and the Graduate Center of the City University of New York. He is the author of Moral Principles and Nuclear Weapons (1984) and The Ethics of War and Peace (1989). He is the editor of Ethics and Strategic Defense (1989).

Lackey surveys most of the important moral issues involved in the just war tradition. In addition to setting out the traditional justifications for engaging in war and the justifications for various forms of conduct during war, he focuses on several issues that have been quite problematic. For example, he points out that certain practices in the Vietnam War involved terrorist tactics but, according to the traditional doctrine of just war, these practices are justifiable. He also argues that attacks on a nation's citizens living abroad, or the seizure of their property, would not normally count as a just cause that would justify going to war.

WHEN TO FIGHT

Introduction

Rightly or wrongly, pacifism has always been a minority view. Most people believe that *some* wars are morally justifiable; the majority of Americans believe that World War II was a moral war. But though most people have clear-cut intuitions about the moral acceptability of World War II, the Vietnam War, and so forth, few people have a theory that justifies and organizes their intuitive judgments. If morally concerned nonpacifists are to defeat the pacifists to their moral left and the cynics to their moral right, they must develop a theory that will distinguish justifiable wars from unjustifiable wars, using a set of consistent and consistently applied rules.

The work of specifying these rules, which dates at least from Aristotle's *Politics*, traditionally goes under the heading of "just war theory." The name is slightly misleading, since justice is only one of several primary moral concepts, all of which must be consulted in a complete moral evaluation of war. A just war—a morally good war—is not merely a war dictated by principles of justice. A just war is a morally justifiable war after justice, human rights, the common good, and all other relevant moral concepts have been consulted and weighed against the facts and against each other.

Just war theorists sometimes fail to notice that just war theory describes two sorts of just wars: wars that are morally permissible and wars that are morally obligatory. The distinction between the permissible and the obligatory is persuasively demonstrable at the personal level.

From Douglas P. Lackey, *The Ethics of War and Peace*, ©1989, pp. 28–35 and 58–61. Reprinted by permission of Prentice Hall, Englewood Cliffs, NJ. [Edited]

268

If I am unjustly attacked, I have a right to use force in my own defense—assuming that I have no other recourse. But since it is always open for the holder of a right to waive that right, I am not *obliged* to use force in my own defense. But suppose that I have promised to defend Jones, that Jones is now exposed to unjust attack, and that Jones calls for my help. In such a case I am obliged to defend Jones. At the level of nations, the distinction between permissible war and obligatory war has important consequences for policy. Frequently policy analysts demonstrate that a certain use of force passes the tests of just war, and then infer that the war is obligatory, that "justice demands it." But it may well be that the use of force is merely permissible, in which case it is also permissible to forgo the use of force. Indeed, there may be powerful prudential considerations why such a merely permissible just war should not be fought.

Another little point in the logic of just war theory deserves attention. In just war theory, the terms "just" and "unjust" are logical contraries. It follows that in war one side at most can be the just side. But it is possible that both sides may be unjust, and it is fallacious to think that if one side is provably unjust, the other side must be provably just. If your enemy is evil, it does not follow that you are good.

In undertaking the moral evaluation of war, it is natural to distinguish rules that determine *when* it is permissible or obligatory to begin a war (*jus ad bellum*) from rules that determine *how* a war should be fought once it has begun (*jus in bello*). *Jus ad bellum* rules apply principally to political leaders; *jus in bello* rules apply principally to soldiers and their officers. The distinction is not ironclad, since there may be situations in which there is no morally

permissible way to wage war, in which case it follows that the war should not be waged in the first place. (Some believe that American intervention in Vietnam was such a case.) In this section we take up *jus ad bellum*; the next section is devoted to *jus in bello*.

Competent Authority

From the time of Augustine, theorists have maintained that a just war can be prosecuted only by a "competent authority." Augustine . . . considered the use of force by private persons to be immoral; consequently the only permissible uses of force were those sanctioned by public authorities. Medieval authors, with a watchful eye for peasant revolts, followed Augustine in confining the just use of force to princes, whose authority and patronage were divinely sanctioned. Given these scholastic roots, considerations of competent authority might appear archaic, but it is still helpful for purposes of moral judgment to distinguish wars from spontaneous uprisings, and soldiers and officers from pirates and brigands. Just war must, first of all, be war.

To begin, most scholars agree that war is a controlled use of force, undertaken by persons organized in a functioning chain of command. An isolated assassin cannot wage war; New York City's Mad Bomber in the 1950s only metaphorically waged war against Con Edison. In some sense, then, war is the contrary of violence. Second, the use of force in war must be directed to an identifiable political result, a requirement forever associated with the Prussian theorist Karl von Clauswitz. An "identifiable political result" is some change in a government's policy, some alteration in a form of government, or some extension or limitation of the scope of its authority. Since the extermination of a people is not an identifiable political result, most acts of genocide are not acts of war: the Turks did not wage war against the Armenians, nor did Hitler wage war on the Jews. (The American frontier cliché, "the only good Indian is a dead Indian" expresses the hopes of murderers, not soldiers.) And since the religious conversion of people is, in most cases, not a political result, many holy wars, by this definition, have not been wars.

Our definition of war as the controlled use of force for political purposes does not imply that wars can be waged only by the governments of nation-states. Many rebels and revolutionaries have used controlled force through a chain of command for political purposes, and there have been at least as many wars within states as there have been wars between states. If civil wars are genuine wars, the scope of "competent authority" must be extended from princes and political leaders to rebels and revolutionaries as well. But, as the case of Pancho Villa perhaps indicates, it is sometimes difficult to distinguish revolutionaries from bandits. In international law, this difficulty is described as the problem of determining when a rebel movement has obtained "belligerent status."

In the most recent international discussion of this issue, at the Geneva Conference of 1974–1977, delegates agreed that in the case of conflicts arising within a single nation-state between the government and "dissident armed forces or other organized groups," a state of war shall exist, provided the dissident forces are

> . . . under responsible command, exercise such control over part of its territory as to enable them to carry out sustained and concerted military operations and [to imple-

ment the laws of war]. (Protocol II, Article 1.1)

This recognition of belligerent status, however,

> shall not apply to situations of internal disturbances and tensions, such as riots, isolated and sporadic acts of violence, and other acts of similar nature, as not being armed conflicts. (Protocol I, Article 1.2)

According to these rules, the American Confederacy in 1860, by virtue of its military organization and control of territory, qualifies for belligerent status, whereas the Symbionese Liberation Army, which controlled no territory, and the Newark rioters of 1967, who obeyed no commands, fail to qualify. By this standard, the American Civil War was war but the Patty Hearst kidnapping was crime, verdicts with which most people would agree.

But the new Geneva standard does not always yield satisfactory results. The partisan movements in World War II—the resistance movements in France, Italy, and the Ukraine, and Tito's great movement in Yugoslavia—rarely could claim specific territory as their own, yet their struggles can hardly be dismissed as unjust on grounds of absence of competent authority. Different perplexities arise in the case of peasant movements, where frequently territory is controlled from the capital by day and by the revolutionaries at night. Perhaps the requirement of "territorial control" is too strong.

The new Geneva standard also requires that genuine belligerents must be capable of carrying out "sustained and concerted military operations." This proviso would deny belligerent status to revolutionary groups that engage primarily in terrorist attacks against civilians, and most people would happily classify such terrorists as international outlaws. But what of revolutionary groups that do not engage in "sustained and concerted military operations"—which, in many cases, would be suicidal for the revolutionaries— but engage in sustained acts of terror against government buildings and officials of the incumbent regime? The campaign of assassination directed by the National Liberation Front (NLF) in Vietnam against village chiefs and other officials siding with the Saigon government was, at one point, the main form of its revolutionary struggle, and it seems pointless to deny the NLF belligerent status on the ground that its members were not engaging in sustained and concerted military operations. Though it might be criticized on other grounds, the NLF assassination campaign was controlled use of force directed to political ends, not a riot and not sporadic violence. It was dirty, but it was war.

Right Intention

One can imagine cases in which a use of military force might satisfy all the external standards of just war while those who order this use of force have no concern for justice. Unpopular political leaders, for example, might choose to make war in order to stifle domestic dissent and win the next election. The traditional theory of just war insists that a just war be a war for the right, fought for the sake of the right.

In the modern climate of political realism, many authors are inclined to treat the standard of right intention as a quaint relic of a more idealistic age, either on the grounds that moral motives produce disastrous results in international politics or on the grounds that motives are subjective and unobservable. ("I will not speculate on the motives of the North Vietnamese," Henry Kissinger once remarked, "I have too much difficulty understanding our own.") But it is unfair to dismiss idealistic motives on the grounds that they produce disaster in international politics, since realistic motives have produced their own fair share of disasters. It is a mistake to dismiss motives as unobservable, when they are so often clearly exhibited in behavior. The real difficulty with the demand for idealistic motives is that people usually have more than one motive for each of their actions, which makes it difficult or impossible to specify *the* motive for the act

Despite the difficulty of multiple motives, it is important to retain some version of the rule of right intention as part of the theory of just war. No thoughtful person can fail to be disturbed by current international practice, in which leaders make policy decisions without regard for moral considerations and then have their staffs cook up moral rationalizations after the fact. If it is too much to insist that political leaders make decisions solely on moral grounds or even primarily on moral grounds, we can insist that desire for what is morally right be at least *one* of their motives.

It follows from this qualified insistence on moral motivation in the political leadership that political leaders must be able to justify their decisions on moral grounds. They may not act primarily or solely for the right, but they must have some reason, producible on request, for thinking that they are acting for the right, among other things. For those who let slip the dogs of war, it is not sufficient that things turn out for the best. The evils of even a just war are sufficiently great that we can demand of leaders who initiate war that they understand the moral character of the results they seek.

If desire for the right must be included as one of the motives for just war, are there any motives that must be *excluded*? Various authors have insisted that a just war cannot be motivated by love of violence or hatred of the enemy. Even in the fifth century Augustine wrote, "The real evils in war are love of violence, vengeful cruelty, fierce and implacable enmity, wild resistance, lust for power, and the like" (*Contra Faustum*, XXII.75). Most people will agree that a leader who has love of violence or hatred of the enemy as his sole or chief motivation for war has a bad intention. But Augustine and other authors go further and argue that it is immoral to make war if hatred is just one of the many motivations one has for fighting. The rule is severe, but worth considering.

Consider the American campaign against Japan in World War II. By the usual standards, the American decision to fight against Japan satisfied the rules of just war. But as the war proceeded, many Americans, stirred up by wartime propaganda, were seized with racial animosity and came to hate all Japanese as such. The 4-year internment of 180,000 innocent Japanese Americans, the campaign of extermination against Japanese cities, and the attack on Hiroshima were all caused or rendered tolerable by this atmosphere of hate. Observing this, Augustine would condemn this hatred of the Japanese as sin and the war against Japan as unjust. Nevertheless, it would be unreasonable to tell the relatives of those who died at Pearl Harbor or on Bataan that they should not feel hatred toward those whose acts and decisions took the lives of those they loved.

The difficulties concerning hatred can perhaps be resolved by distinguishing jus-tifiable from unjustifiable hatred. Hatred of leaders who choose to wage unjust war is justifiable; hatred of their compatriots and coracialists is not, since hatred of human beings as such—apart from their voluntary acts—is not a morally acceptable emotion. By this standard, American leaders who chose wartime policies as a result of race hatred toward the Japanese were not engaged in just war, even if their policies were acceptable by all other moral tests.

Just Cause

The most important of the *jus ad bellum* rules is the rule that the moral use of military force requires a just cause. From the earliest writings, just war theorists rejected love of war and love of conquest as morally acceptable causes for war: "We [should] wage war," Aristotle wrote, "for the sake of peace" (*Politics*, 1333A). Likewise, the seizure of plunder was always rejected as an acceptable cause for war. Beyond these elementary restrictions, however, a wide variety of "just causes" were recognized. The history of the subject is the history of how this repertoire of just causes was progressively cut down to the modern standard, which accepts only the single cause of self-defense.

As early as Cicero in the first century B.C., analysts of just war recognized that the only proper occasion for the use of force was a "wrong received." It follows from this that the condition or characteristics of potential enemies, apart from their actions, cannot supply a just cause for war. Aristotle's suggestion that a war is justified to enslave those who naturally deserve to be slaves, John Stuart Mill's claim that military intervention is justified in order to bestow the benefits of Western civilization on less advanced peoples, and the historically common view that forcible conversion to some true faith is justified as obedience to divine command are all invalidated by the absence of a "wrong received."

Obviously, the concept of a "wrong received" stands in need of considerable analysis. In the eighteenth century, the notion of wrong included the notion of insult, and sovereigns considered it legitimate to initiate war in response to verbal disrespect, desecrations of national symbols, and so forth. The nineteenth century, which saw the abolition of private duels, likewise saw national honor reduced to a secondary role in the moral justification of war. For most nineteenth century theorists, the primary wrongs were not insults, but acts or policies of a government resulting in violations of the rights of the nation waging just war.

By twentieth-century standards, this definition of international wrongs providing conditions of just war was both too restrictive and too loose. It was too restrictive in that it failed to recognize any rights of *peoples,* as opposed to *states:* rights to cultural integrity, national self-determination, and so forth. It was too loose in that it sanctioned the use of military force in response to wrongs the commission of which may not have involved military force, thus condoning, on occasion, the first use of arms.

These two excesses were abolished in twentieth-century international law. The right to national self-determination was a prevailing theme at the Versailles conference in 1919 and was repeatedly invoked in the period of decolonization following World War II. Prohibition of first use of force was attempted in drafting of the U.N. Charter in 1945:

Article 2(4): All Members shall refrain in their international relations from the

threat or use of force against the territorial integrity or political independence of any state or in any other manner inconsistent with the Purposes of the United Nations.

Article 51: Nothing in the present Charter shall impair the inherent right of individual or collective self-defense if an armed attack occurs against a member of the United Nations, until the Security Council has taken the measures necessary to maintain international peace and security.

Strictly speaking, Article 51 does not prohibit first use of military force: to say that explicitly, the phrase "if an armed attack occurs" would have to be replaced by "if and only if an armed attack occurs." Nevertheless, Article 51, coupled with article 2(4), rules out anticipatory self-defense. Legitimate self-defense must be self-defense against an actual attack.

The U.N. Charter represents the most restrictive analysis of just cause in the history of the subject. In discussions since, members of the United Nations have continued to assume that just cause consists only in self-defense, but "self-defense" has come to be understood as a response to aggression. The definition of "aggression" thus becomes central to the analysis of just cause. In the United Nations, a special committee established to analyze the concept of aggression produced a definition adopted by the General Assembly on 14 December 1974:

Article 1. Aggression is the use of armed force by a State against the sovereignty, territorial integrity, or political independence of another State, or in any other manner inconsistent with the Charter of the United Nations. . . .

Article 2. The first use of armed force by a State in contravention of the Charter shall constitute *prima facie* evidence of an act of aggression [although the Security Council may come to determine that an act of aggression has not in fact been committed]. . . .

Article 3. Any of the following acts regardless of a declaration of war shall . . . qualify as an act of aggression:

(a) The invasion or attack by the armed force of a State on the territory of another State, or any military occupation, however temporary;

(b) Bombardment by the armed forces of a State against the territory of another State;

(c) The blockade of the ports or coasts of a State by the armed forces of another State;

(d) An attack by the armed forces of a State on the land, sea, air, or marine and air fleets of another State; . . .

(g) The sending by or on behalf of a State of armed bands, groups, irregulars, or mercenaries, which carry out acts of armed force against another State of such gravity as to amount to the acts listed above. . . .

Article 4. The acts enumerated are not exhaustive.

Article 5. No consideration of whatever nature, whether political, economic, military, or otherwise, may serve as a justification for aggression. . . .

Article 7. Nothing in this definition . . . could in any way prejudice the right to self-determination, freedom, and independence, as derived from the Charter, of peoples forcibly deprived of that right . . . particularly peoples under colonial and racist regimes or other forms of alien domination; nor the right of these peoples to struggle to that end and to seek and receive support. . . .

By reading between the lines, the intent of the special committee can be easily discerned. In failing to enumerate under "acts of aggression" such traditional causes of war as attacks on citizens abroad, assaults on nonmilitary ships and aircraft on the high seas, and the seizure of property of aliens, the committee counted as aggression only military acts that might substantially affect the physical security of the nation suffering aggression. The only violation of rights that merits the unilateral use of force by nations is the physically threatening use of force by another state. . . .

The Rule of Proportionality

It is a superficially paradoxical feature of just war theory that a just cause need not make for a just war. If the just cause can be achieved by some means other than war, then war for that just cause is not morally justified. If the just cause *might* be achieved by other means that have not been attempted, then war for that just cause is not just war. If the cause is just but cannot be achieved by war, then war for that cause is not just war. These rules, sometimes called the rule of necessity, the rule of last resort, or the "chance of victory" requirement, are part of that section of just war theory which acknowledges that some just causes are not sufficiently weighty, on the moral scales, to justify the evils that war for those just causes might produce. The rule of proportionality states that a war cannot be just unless the evil that can reasonably be expected to ensue from the war is less than the evil that can reasonably be expected to ensue if the war is not fought.

The rule of proportionality is easy to state but hard to interpret, since there are no guidelines as to what counts as an "evil" when the rule is applied. Suppose that we interpret an "evil" as a loss of value, that is, as death, injury, physical and psychological suffering, misery, and so forth. On this view of evil, the rule of proportionality implies that a war is just only if there will be more death, suffering, and so forth if the war is not fought than if the war is fought: a just and proportionate war does more good than harm. Given the destructiveness of war, the rule of proportionality, on this interpretation would declare that almost all wars, even wars with just causes, have been unjust wars.

Suppose that we count as "evils" not merely losses of welfare but also losses that are violations of someone's rights. Then the rule of proportionality implies that a war is just if more rights would be violated if the war is not fought than if the war is fought. Since we have defined a just cause as a cause that seeks to prevent violations of rights, on this interpretation of the rule of proportionality, almost all wars with just causes have been proportionate wars.

Which interpretation of "evil" is the most appropriate for the moral analysis of war? If we interpret "evil" as "violation of rights," then the rule of proportionality, which was supposed to provide an additional and independent check on the moral permissiblity of war, is subsumed into the requirement of just cause. If the rule of proportionality is to do any work, we must consider an "evil" to be the destruction of a value. But then the problem arises that the rule condemns almost all wars and reduces just war theory to antiwar pacifism. Some revision of the rule is in order.

From the standpoint of theories of moral rights, a rule which says that war is unjust unless it does more good than harm is far too restrictive. If a war has a just cause, then it is a war in defense of rights and, according to most theories of rights, the maintenance and protection of rights is morally permissible unless the defense of rights causes a *great deal* more harm than good. Accordingly, in just war theory, we can replace the traditional principle—a just war must cause more good than harm—with the less restrictive rule that a war for a just cause passes the test of proportionality unless it produces a *great deal* more harm than good. Even this greatly liberalized rule of proportionality will declare that many wars fought for just causes have been unjust wars, since many wars for just causes have

in fact produced a great deal more harm than good. On the other hand, if a war is fought for a just cause and produces only slightly more harm than good, the liberalized rule of proportionality will not judge that war to be unjust. . . .

HOW TO FIGHT

Introduction

People who believe that there are moral limits defining *when* wars should be fought naturally believe that there are moral limits defining *how* they should be fought. The idea that there are right and wrong ways to conduct war is an ancient one. In the Hebrew Bible, God states that though it may be necessary to kill one's enemy, it is never permissible to cut down his fruit trees (Deut. 20:19). In the sixth century B.C. the Hindu Laws of Manu specified, "When the King fights with his foes in battle, let him not strike with weapons concealed in wood, nor with barbed, poisoned, or flaming arrows."

Over the centuries, a vast array of rules and customs constituting *jus in bello* have been elaborated. There are rules that specify proper behavior toward neutral countries, toward the citizens of neutral countries, and toward neutral ships. There are rules governing what can and cannot be done to enemy civilians, to enemy soldiers on the battlefield, and to enemy soldiers when they are wounded and when they have surrendered. There are rules concerning proper and improper weapons of war, and proper and improper tactics on the battlefield.

In the late nineteenth and twentieth centuries, many of these "laws of war" were codified in a series of treaties, conventions, and protocols, signed and ratified by most of the principal nations of the world. Nations ratifying these sets of rules undertook to impose them on their own military establishments, pledging to prosecute violations and punish wrongdoers. When domestic enforcements have fallen short, nations victorious in war have undertaken the prosecution of violations perpetrated by defeated enemies. (Victorious nations are rarely prosecuted.)

With the exceptions of the Geneva Convention banning chemical warfare (1925) and the Second Protocol to the Fourth Geneva Convention (1977), the United States has ratified most of the principal international conventions regarding the laws of war. In their field manuals, the various military services of the United States consider themselves bound by the Hague Conventions of 1899 and 1907, by the Geneva Conventions of 1929, and by the four Geneva Conventions of 1949, which govern the sick and wounded on the battlefield (I), the sick and wounded at sea (II), prisoners of war (III), and the protection of civilian persons in time of war (IV).

Necessity, Proportionality, and Discrimination

For the student approaching the laws of war for the first time, the profusion of covenants, treaties, customs, and precedents can be bewildering. But fortunately there are a few leading ideas that have governed the development of the laws of war. The first is that the destruction of life and property, even enemy life and property, is inherently bad. It follows that military forces should cause no more destruction than is strictly necessary to achieve their objectives. (Notice that the principle does not say that whatever is necessary is permissible, but that every-

thing permissible must be necessary.) This is the principle of necessity: that *wanton destruction is forbidden*. More precisely, the principle of necessity specifies that a military operation is forbidden if there is some alternative operation that causes less destruction but has the same probability of producing a successful military result.

The second leading idea is that the amount of destruction permitted in pursuit of a military objective must be proportionate to the importance of the objective. This is the *military* principle of proportionality (which must be distinguished from the *political* principle of proportionality in the *jus ad bellum*). It follows from the military principle of proportionality that certain objectives should be ruled out of consideration on the grounds that too much destruction would be caused in obtaining them.

The third leading idea, the principle of noncombatant immunity, is that civilian life and property should not be subjected to military force: military force must be directed only at military objectives. Obviously, the principle of noncombatant immunity is useful only if there is a consensus about what counts as "civilian" and what counts as "military." In the older Hague Conventions, a list of explicit nonmilitary targets is developed: "buildings dedicated to religion, art, science, or charitable purposes, historic monuments, hospitals . . . undefended towns, buildings, or dwellings." Anything that is not explicitly mentioned qualifies as a military target. But this list is overly restrictive, and the consensus of modern thought takes "military" targets to include servicemen, weapons, and supplies; the ships and vehicles that transport them; and the factories and workers that produce them. Anything that is not "military" is "civilian." Since, on either definition, the principle of noncombatant immunity distinguishes acceptable military objectives from unacceptable civilian objectives, it is often referred to as the principle of discrimination. (In the morality of war, discrimination is good, not evil.)

There is an objective and subjective version of the principle of noncombatant immunity. The objective version holds that if civilians are killed as a result of military operations, the principle is violated. The subjective version holds that if civilians are *intentionally* killed as a result of military operations, the principle is violated. The interpretation of "intentional" in the subjective version is disputed, but the general idea is that the killing of civilians is intentional if, and only if, they are the chosen *targets* of military force. It follows, on the subjective version, that if civilians are killed in the course of a military operation directed at a military target, the principle of discrimination has *not* been violated. Obviously, the objective version of the principle of discrimination is far more restrictive than the subjective.

The earlier Hague Conventions leaned toward the objective version of the principle of discrimination. The later Geneva Convention (IV), as interpreted in the Second Protocol of 1977, leans toward the subjective version:

> The civilian population as such, as well as individual civilians, shall not be the object of attack. . . . Indiscriminate attacks are prohibited, [including] those which are not directed at a specific military objective, those which employ a method or means which cannot be directed at a specific objective, or those which employ a method or means the effects of which cannot be limited or which are of a nature to strike military objectives and civilians or civilian objects without distinction.

If we adopt the subjective version of the principle of discrimination, it does not follow that any number of civilians may be permissibly killed so long as they are killed in pursuit of military objectives. The number of civilian deaths resulting from a military operation remains limited by the principle of proportionality. In sum,

> In all military operations, civilians should not be the target of attack. The deaths of civilians or damage to their property which are side-effects of military operations must be necessary for the achievement of the objective and proportionate to its importance.

The principles of necessity, proportionality, and discrimination apply with equal force to all sides in war. Violation of the rules cannot be justified or excused on the grounds that one is fighting on the side of justice. Those who developed the laws of war learned through experience that just causes must have moral limits.

The Practice of Satyagraha

Mohandas K. Gandhi

Mohandas K. Gandhi was a revolutionary political leader in India. He led a successful nonviolent revolt against British colonial rule that resulted in the creation of the independent state of India. He was the author of over 20 books, including The India of My Dreams (1947), Delhi Diary (1948), Satyagraha in South Africa (1950), and Women and Social Injustice (1954).

Gandhi presents the "classical" argument in favor of nonviolent resistance for a just cause. Gandhi argues that morality requires that all available means be attempted before recourse to violence can ever be justified. Nonviolent resistance must be attempted, he argues, and it can be such a successful alternative to violent war that its methods need to be taught to everyone. The main features of Gandhi's version of nonviolent resistance include respect for law; humility and lack of anger toward one's opponents; restraint not retaliation; and noncooperation rather than aggression. Gandhi justifies his views by reference to Hindu and Islamic traditions.

For the past thirty years, I have been preaching and practicing *satyagraha.* The principles of *satyagraha,* as I know it today, constitute a gradual evolution.[1]

Satyagraha differs from Passive Resistance as the North Pole from the South. The latter has been conceived as a weapon of the weak and does not exclude the use of physical force or violence for the purpose of gaining one's end, whereas the former has been conceived as a weapon of the strongest and excludes the use of violence in any shape or form.

The term *satyagraha* was coined by me in South Africa to express the force that the Indians there used for a full eight years, and it was coined in order to distinguish it from the movement then going on in the United Kingdom and South Africa under the name of Passive Resistance.

On the political field, the struggle on behalf of the people mostly consists in opposing error in the shape of unjust laws. When you have failed to bring the error home to the law-giver by way of petitions and the like, the only remedy open to you, if you do not wish to submit to error, is to compel him by physical force to yield to you or by suffering in your own person by inviting the penalty for the breach of the law. Hence *satyagraha* largely appears to the public as Civil Disobedience or Civil Resistance. It is civil in the sense that it is not criminal.

The law-breaker breaks the law surreptitiously and tries to avoid the penalty; not so the civil resister. He ever obeys the laws of the state to which he belongs, not out of fear of the sanctions, but because he considers them to be good for the welfare of society. But there come occasions, generally rare, when he considers certain laws to

Mohandas K. Gandhi, "The Practice of Satyagraha," from *Gandhi: Selected Writings,* Ronald Duncan, editor (New York: Harper & Row, 1971). Reprinted with permission of the Navajivan Trust. [Edited]

be so unjust as to render obedience to them a dishonor. He then openly and civilly breaks them and quietly suffers the penalty for their breach. And in order to register his protest against the action of the lawgivers, it is open to him to withdraw his cooperation from the state by disobeying such other laws whose breach does not involve moral turpitude.

In my opinion, the beauty and efficacy of *satyagraha* are so great and the doctrine so simple that it can be preached even to children. It was preached by me to thousands of men, women, and children commonly called indentured Indians with excellent results.

> The spirit of non-violence necessarily leads to humility. Non-violence means reliance on God, the Rock of Ages. If we would seek His aid, we must approach Him with a humble and a contrite heart. Non-cooperationists may not trade upon their amazing success at the Congress. We must act, even as the mango tree which droops as it bears fruit. Its grandeur lies in its majestic lowliness.

Non-cooperation is not a movement of brag, bluster, or bluff. It is a test of our sincerity. It requires solid and silent self-sacrifice. It challenges our honesty and our capacity for national work. It is a movement that aims at translating ideas into action. And the more we do, the more we find that much more must be done than we had expected. And this thought of our imperfection must make us humble.

A non-cooperationist strives to compel attention and to set an example not by his violence, but by his unobtrusive humility. He allows his solid action to speak for his creed. His strength lies in his reliance upon the correctness of his position. And the conviction of it grows most in his opponent when he least interposes his speech between his action and his opponent.

Speech, especially when it is haughty, betrays want of confidence and it makes one's opponent skeptical about the reality of the act itself. Humility therefore is the key to quick success. I hope that every non-cooperationist will recognize the necessity of being humble and self-restrained. It is because so little is really required to be done and because all of that little depends entirely upon ourselves that I have ventured the belief that Swaraj is attainable in less than one year.

I am sorry that I find a nervous fear among some Hindus and Mohammedans that I am undermining their faith, and that I am even doing irreparable harm to India by my uncompromising preaching of non-violence. They seem almost to imply that violence is their creed. I touch a tender spot if I talk about extreme non-violence in their presence. They confound me with texts from the Mahabharata and the Koran eulogizing or permitting violence. Of the Mahabharata I can write without restraint, but the most devoted Mohammedan will not, I hope, deny me the privilege of understanding the message of the Prophet. I make bold to say that violence is the creed of no religion and that, whereas non-violence in most cases is obligatory in all, violence is merely permissible in some cases. But I have not put before India the final form of non-violence. The non-violence that I have preached from Congress platforms is non-violence as a policy. But even policies require honest adherence in thought, word and deed. If I believe that honesty is the best policy, surely whilst I so believe, I must be honest in thought, word and deed; otherwise I become an imposter. Non-violence being a policy means that it can upon due notice be given up when it proves unsuccessful or ineffective. But simple morality demands that, whilst a particular policy is pursued, it must be pursued with all one's heart. It is simple policy to march along a certain route, but the soldier who marches with an unsteady step along that route is liable to be summarily dismissed. I become therefore incredulous when people talk to me skeptically about non-violence or are seized with fright at the very mention of the word non-violence. If they do not believe in the expedient of nonviolence, they must denounce it but not claim to believe in the expedient when their heart resists it. How disastrous it would be, if, not believing in violence even as an expedient, I joined, say a violence party and approached a gun with a perturbed heart! The reader will believe me when I say that I have the capacity for killing a fly. But I do not believe in killing even flies. Now suppose I joined an expedition for fly-killing as an expedient. Will I not be expected, before being permitted to join the expedition, to use all the available engines of destruction, whilst I remained in the army of fly-killers? If those who are in the Congress and the Khilafat committees will perceive this simple truth, we shall certainly either finish the struggle this year to a successful end, or be so sick of non-violence as to give up the pretension and set about devising some other program.

I hold that Swami Shraddhanandji has been needlessly criticized for the proposition he intended to move. His argument is absolutely honest. He thinks that we, as a body, do not really believe in non-violence even as a policy. Therefore, we shall never fulfill the program of non-violence. Therefore, he says, let us go to the councils and get what crumbs we may. He was trying to show the unreality of the position of those who believe in the policy with their lips, whereas they are looking forward to

violence for final deliverance. I do say that, if Congressmen do not fully believe in the policy, they are doing an injury to the country by pretending to follow it. If violence is to be the basis of future government, the councillors are undoubtedly the wisest. For it is through the councils that, by the same devices by which the present administrators rule us, the councillors hope to seize power from the former's hands. I have little doubt that those who nurse violence in their bosoms will find no benefit from the lip-profession of non-violence. I urge, therefore, with all the vehemence at my command, that those who do not believe in non-violence should secede from the Congress and from noncooperation and prepare to seek election or rejoin law courts or Government colleges as the case may be. Let there be no manner of doubt that Swaraj established by non-violent means will be different in kind from the Swaraj that can be established by armed rebellion. Police and punishments there will be, even under such Swaraj. But there would be no room for brutalities such as we witness today both on the part of the people and the Government. And those, whether they call themselves Hindus or Mussulmans, who do not fully believe in the policy of non-violence, should abandon both noncooperation and non-violence.

For me, I am positive that neither in the Koran nor in the Mahabharata is there any sanction for and approval of the triumph of violence. Though there is repulsion enough in Nature, she lives by attraction. Mutual love enables Nature to persist. Man does not live by destruction. Self-love compels regard for others. Nations cohere, because there is mutual regard among the individuals composing them. Some day we must extend the national law to the universe, even as we have extended the family law to form nations—a larger family. God had ordained that India should be such a nation. For so far as reason can perceive, India cannot become free by armed rebellion for generations. India can become free by refraining from national violence. India has now become tired of rule based upon violence. That to me is the message of the plains. The people of the plains do not know what it is to put up an organized armed fight. And they must become free, for they want freedom. They have realized that power seized by violence will only result in their greater grinding.

Such, at any rate, is the reasoning that has given birth to the policy, not the *dharma*, of non-violence. And even as a Mussulman or a Hindu, believing in violence, applies the creed of non-violence in his family, so are both called upon without question to apply the policy of non-violence in their mutual relations and in their relation to other races and classes, not excluding Englishmen. Those who do not believe in this policy and do not wish to live up to it in full, retard the movement by remaining in it.

When a person claims to be non-violent, he is expected not to be angry with one who has injured him. He will not wish him harm; he will wish him well; he will not swear at him; he will not cause him any physical hurt. He will put up with all the injury to which he is subjected by the wrong-doer. Thus non-violence is complete innocence. Complete non-violence is complete absence of ill-will against all that lives. It therefore embraces even sub-human life, not excluding noxious insects or beasts. They have not been created to feed our destructive propensities. If we only knew the mind of the Creator, we should find their proper place in His creation. Non-violence is therefore in its active form good will towards all life. It is pure Love. I read it in the Hindu scriptures, in the Bible, in the Koran.

Non-violence is a perfect state. It is a goal towards which all mankind moves naturally though unconsciously. Man does not become divine when he personifies innocence in himself. Only then does he become truly man. In our present state, we are partly men and partly beasts and in our ignorance and even arrogance say that we truly fulfill the purpose of our species, when we deliver blow for blow and develop the measure of anger required for the purpose. We pretend to believe that retaliation is the law of our being, whereas in every scripture we find that retaliation is nowhere obligatory. Retaliation is indulgence requiring elaborate regulating. Restraint is the law of our being. For highest perfection is unattainable without highest restraint. Suffering is thus the badge of the human tribe.

The goal ever recedes from us. The greater the progress, the greater the recognition of our unworthiness. Satisfaction lies in the effort, not in the attainment. Full effort is full victory. . . .

AN APPEAL TO EVERY BRITON

In 1896 I addressed an appeal to every Briton in South Africa on behalf of my countrymen who had gone there as laborers or traders and their assistants. It had its effect. However important it was from my viewpoint, the cause which I pleaded then was insignificant compared with the cause which prompts this appeal. I appeal to every Briton, wherever he may be now, to accept the method of non-violence instead of that of war, for the adjustment of relations between nations and other matters. Your statesmen have declared that this is a war on behalf of democracy. There are many other reasons given in justification. You know them all by heart. I suggest that, at the end of the war, whichever way it ends, there will be no democracy left to represent democracy. This war has descended upon mankind as a curse and a warning. It is a curse inasmuch as it is brutalizing man on a scale hitherto unknown. All distinctions between combatants and non-combatants have been abolished. No one and nothing is to be spared. Lying has been reduced to an art. Britain was to defend small nationalities. One by one they have vanished, at least for the time being. It is also a warning. It is a warning that, if nobody reads the writing on the wall, man will be reduced to the state of the beast, whom he is shaming by his manners. I read the writing when the hostilities broke out. But I had not the courage to say the word. God has given me the courage to say it before it is too late.

I appeal for cessation of hostilities, not because you are too exhausted to fight, but because war is bad in essence. You want to kill Nazism. You will never kill it by its indifferent adoption. Your soldiers are doing the same work of destruction as the Germans. The only difference is that perhaps yours are not as thorough as the Germans. If that be so, yours will soon acquire the same thoroughness as theirs, if not much greater. On no other condition can you win the war. In other words, you will have to be more ruthless than the Nazis. No cause, however just, can warrant the indiscriminate slaughter that is going on minute by minute. I suggest that a cause that demands the inhumanities that are being perpetrated today cannot be called just.

I do not want Britain to be defeated, nor do I want her to be victorious in a trial of brute strength, whether expressed through the muscle or the brain. Your muscular bravery is an established fact. Need you demonstrate that your brain is also as unrivaled in destructive power as your muscle? I hope you do not wish to enter into such an undignified competition with the Nazis. I venture to present you with a nobler and braver way, worthy of the bravest soldier. I want you to fight Nazism without arms, or, if I am to retain the military terminology, with nonviolent arms. I would like you to lay down the arms you have as being useless for saving you or humanity. You will invite Herr Hitler and Signor Mussolini to take what they want of your beautiful island, with your many beautiful buildings. You will give all these but neither your souls, nor your minds. If these gentlemen choose to occupy your homes, you will vacate them. If they do not give you free passage out, you will allow yourselves man, woman, and child, to be slaughtered, but you will refuse to owe allegiance to them.

This process or method, which I have called non-violent non-cooperation, is not without considerable success in its use in India. Your representatives in India may deny my claim. If they do, I shall feel sorry for them. They may tell you that our non-cooperation was not wholly non-violent, that it was born of hatred. If they give that testimony, I will not deny it. Had it been wholly non-violent, if all the non-cooperators had been filled with goodwill towards you, I make bold to say that you who are India's masters would have become her pupils and, with much greater skill than we have, perfected this matchless weapon and met the German and Italian friends' menace with it. Indeed the history of Europe during the past few months would then have been written differently. Europe would have been spared seas of innocent blood, the rape of so many small nations, and the orgy of hatred.

This is no appeal made by a man who does not know his business. I have been practicing with scientific precision non-violence and its possibilities for an unbroken period of over fifty years. I have applied it in every walk of life, domestic, institutional, economic and political. I know of no single case in which it has failed. Where it has seemed sometimes to have failed, I have ascribed it to my imperfections. I claim no perfection for myself. But I do claim to be a passionate seeker after Truth, which is but another name for God. In the course of that search the discovery of non-violence came to me. Its spread is my life mission. I have no interest in living except for the prosecution of that mission.

I claim to have been a lifelong and wholly disinterested friend of the British people. At one time I used to be also a lover of your empire. I thought that it was doing good to India. When I saw that in the nature of things it could do no good, I used, and am still using, the non-violent method to fight imperialism. Whatever the ultimate fate of my country, my love for you remains, and will remain, undiminished. My non-violence demands universal love, and you are not a small part of it. It is that love which has prompted my appeal to you.

May God give power to every word of mine. In His name I began to write this, and in His name I close it. May your statesmen have the wisdom and courage to respond to my appeal. I am telling His Excellency the Viceroy that my services are at the disposal of His Majesty's Government, should they consider them of any practical use in advancing the object of my appeal.

(*Harijan*, 6th July 1940)

12th September 1947

Anger breeds revenge and the spirit of revenge is today responsible for all the horrible happenings here and elsewhere. What good will it do the Muslims to avenge the happenings in Delhi or for the Sikhs and the Hindus to avenge cruelties on our co-religionists in the Frontier and West Punjab? If a man or a group of men go mad, should everyone follow suit? I warn the Hindus and Sikhs that by killing and loot and arson they are destroying their own religions. I claim to be a student of religion and I know that no religion teaches madness. Islam is no exception. I implore you all to stop your insane actions at once. Let not future generations say that we lost the sweet bread of freedom because we could not digest it. Remember that unless we stop this madness the name of India will be mud in the eyes of the world.

21st October 1947

I have heard of another sad incident. It is not a communal murder. The victim is a Hindu government officer. A soldier shot him dead, because he would not act as he was directed. This tendency to use a gun on the slightest pretext is a grave portent. There are barbarous people in the world, to whom life has no value. They shoot dead human beings as they would shoot down birds or beasts. Is free India to be in this category? Man has not the power to create life, hence he has no right to take it. Yet the Muslims murder the Hindus and Sikhs and vice versa. When this cruel game is finished, the blood lust is bound to result in the Muslims slaughtering the Muslims, and the Hindus and Sikhs slaughtering themselves. I hope they will never reach that savage state. That is their fate unless both the states pull themselves together and set things right before it is too late.

NOTE

1. Extract from *Young India,* Vol. 1 by M.K. Gandhi, Madras, Ganesan Ltd. 1922.

Terrorism and Morality

Haig Khatchadourian

Haig Khatchadourian is a professor of philosophy at the University of Wisconsin at Milwaukee. He is the author of A Critical Study in Method (1971) and The Concept of Art (1971).

Khatchadourian argues that terrorism is always morally wrong, even revolutionary forms of terrorism that are aimed at the seemingly just cause of bringing down a despotic regime. He appeals to traditional just war doctrine and to the principles of human rights to justify his claims. He focuses throughout on the loss of life to innocent people by terrorist acts and contends that such loss of life is virtually impossible to justify.

I

Terrorism, in all its types and forms, is always wrong; that is the claim I shall try to establish in this paper. A sequel will deal with the question of deterring and, more importantly, addressing the root causes of political terrorism and moralistic terrorism—terrorism aiming at a moral end. Although the claim that terrorism is always wrong is very widely held in the world today, some practitioners of terrorism and those who support them or sympathise with their goals believe that it is morally justifiable, at least in the form in which they practise or support it. Other practitioners or supporters of terrorism vehemently deny that they are terrorists or supporters of terrorism; implying that they too believe that terrorism is morally wrong. They argue that they are 'freedom fighters' or supporters of 'freedom fighting'. What terror-

From "Terrorism and Morality" by Haig Khatchadourian, in *Applied Philosophy*, eds B. Arnold and D. Hill. London: Routledge 1991.

ism therefore is or how the word should be employed is a much vexed question, and adds greatly to the confusion and divergence of views on the morality of terrorism. The practical importance of what people understand by the word is never greater than in the case of heads of state and governments that either support terrorism or attempt to fight it. For instance, President Reagan's characterisation of terrorism as the deliberate maiming or killing of innocent people, and of terrorists as 'base criminals,' reflects and at the same time shapes his administration's avowed condemnation of terrorism, and the diplomatic and military steps it has so far taken to fight terrorism.[1]

Some moral philosophers argue on ethical grounds that certain types or species of terrorism (e.g. revolutionary terrorism) are morally justifiable: a view I shall consider in this paper.

In the following section I shall deal with the problem of defining 'terrorism,' and in Section III I shall consider the possible application of 'just war' theory to it. I shall argue that the relevant conditions of a 'just war,' duly modified, support this paper's overall contention. A consideration of human rights will provide additional support for my thesis. . . .

II

An adequate description of any type, species or form of terrorism must minimally include a description of the following five aspects or elements of terrorism in general: (1) the socioeconomic or historical and cultural root causes of its incidence (e.g. homelessness); (2) its immediate, intermediate and long-range or ultimate goals, e.g. retaliation, publicity, and the regaining of a lost homeland, respectively and (3) the forms and methods of coercion and force[2] generally used to terrorise the immediate victims and those the terrorists coerce or hope to coerce as a result (the 'patients' or 'sufferers'[3]). The forms and methods of coercion and force used define the different *species* or *forms* of terrorism of any given *type*. Another aspect of terrorism is (4) the nature or kinds of organisations and institutions, or the political systems, supporting or sponsoring the terrorism. In 'international terrorism' and 'state terrorism' the support is provided by one or more nation states. The final aspect of terrorism that must be considered is (5) the social, political, economic or military circumstances in which the terrorism occurs; e.g. whether it occurs in time of peace or in wartime.

Defining 'Terrorism': What's in a Name

For the purposes of this paper, an adequate definition of 'terrorism' in general, besides reflecting the preceding five aspects or dimensions of terrorism, must be neutral, nonevaluative. It must not beg the issue of the morality of any type or form of terrorism, or of terrorism in general; though as I noted, the word is generally if not universally used as a highly condemnatory term at present. Like 'murder' it is generally used to designate a highly reprehensible act or series of acts. The strongly negative connotations of the word are not only reflected in the characterisation of terrorism by heads of governments and other politicians, and by the average person, but also in some purportedly objective, philosophical definitions of the term. A good example occurs in Burton M. Leiser's *Liberty, Justice, and Morals*.[4] According to the latter,

> *Terrorism* is any organized set of acts of violence designed to create an atmosphere of despair or fear, to shake the faith of ordinary citizens in their government and its representatives, to destroy the structure of authority which normally stands for security, or to reinforce and perpetuate a governmental regime whose popular support is shaky. It is a policy of seemingly senseless, irrational, and arbitrary murder, assassination, sabotage, subversion, robbery and other forms of violence, all committed with dedicated indifference to existing legal and moral codes or with claims to special exemption from conventional social norms.[5]

This characterisation too makes all terrorism morally unjustifiable by definition. The link between terrorism and murder in Reagan's or Leiser's conception is immediately established if we add Elizabeth Anscombe's proposition that the deliberate killing of the innocent is, by definition, murder.[6] Apart from morally dismissing terrorism out of hand, both Reagan's and Leiser's characterisations are too broad; while Reagan's characterisation is also woefully incomplete. Leiser's definition does incorporate several of the aspects of terrorism I have mentioned, but fails to spell out the various sorts of causes of terrorism and makes only passing mention of what it calls the terrorists' 'political ends.'[7] In short, it is too narrow as well as too broad.

The two aforementioned characterisations share a significant element; viz. that terrorism *always* involves the maiming, killing or coercion of innocent—and only innocent—persons; where 'innocent persons' is defined by Leiser as ". . . persons who have little or no direct connection with the causes to which the terrorists are dedicated . . . ."[8] Although his definition of 'terrorism' is not quite clear on this point, Leiser sharply distinguishes terrorism from political assassination later in the chapter on terrorism, and appears to equate terrorism with "the victimisation of defenseless, innocent persons" as opposed to ". . . the assassination of political and military leaders."[9] His dismissal of all Palestinian armed resistance to Israel as terrorism, naturally follows.[10]

The question of whether non-innocents can be included among the possible targets of terrorism, in the current uses of 'terrorism' in the media and in everyday discourse, e.g. in Europe and the United States, is an unsettled and moot question. The absence of clarity and fixity—indeed, the ambivalence and uncertainty in the current employments of the word—reflect the particular users' stand on the morality of terrorism, and the more general morality of the use of force. It is also intimately connected with the distinction between terrorism and 'freedom fighting,' including 'guerilla warfare.' Those who consider the harming of innocents alone as an essential feature of terrorism would tend to define 'freedom fighting' as involving (together with other elements analogous to the elements of 'terrorism' I listed earlier) the maiming, killing or coercing of non-innocents. That would permit considering 'political assassination' as a species of 'freedom fighting.' Leiser states that 'guerilla warfare' is characterised by small-scale, unconventional, limited actions carried out by irregular forces *"against regular military forces, their supply lines, and communications."*[11] That definition (which aptly characterises the Afghan rebels as they are commonly called) would be perfectly in order if we include in it the notion that all the targeted soldiers are in the army of their own free will.

The preceding discussion indicates that the current concepts of terrorism, like other evaluative concepts, are what W. B. Gallie calls 'essentially contested,'[12] as well as open textured and vague. Yet like most or all vague and unsettled terms, 'terrorism' has a 'common core of meaning' in its different usages. This 'core of meaning' includes the notion that terrorist acts are acts of coercion or of force,[13] aiming at monetary gain (*predatory terrorism*), revenge (*retaliatory terrorism*), a political end (*political terrorism*), or a moral end (*moralistic terrorism*).[14] It also includes the notion that all terrorism involves a crucial distinction between 'immediate victims' and 'sufferers.'

The *causes* and the *goals* of terrorism differ with the different types of terrorism: predatory, retaliatory, etc. The *methods* used by the terrorists also vary depending on these and other factors.

So-called 'state protected,' 'state sponsored' or 'state' terrorism is not (*pace* Edel) a distinct type of terrorism but only a special form of political terrorism. Instances of state terrorism may therefore also be instances of moralistic terrorism. Political terrorism, including state terrorism, is often international in character—so-called 'international terrorism'—as defined by the U.S. House Resolution 2781, 99th Congress, 1st Session, pp. 1–3. Among other things the Resolution states that an act of terror is an act of international terror if it transcends the national boundaries of the perpetrators or is directed against foreign nationals within the perpetrators' national boundaries. The act also falls within this definition if it violates any of the provisions set under the *Convention for the Suppression of Unlawful Seizures of Aircraft* (The Hague, 16 December 1970).[15]

All types of terrorism may be terrorism either in time of peace or in wartime. In the latter moralistic terrorism may be in the service of a putatively legitimate cause such as national self-defence (in general, as part of a putatively just war). On the other hand predatory and retaliatory terrorism may thrive in time of war, revolution or civil war, as in many instances of Lebanese terrorism during the past decade. Terrorism in war involves special complexities whenever it is practised by or on behalf of one or more of the belligerents, who may or may not be fighting a just war.

The foregoing discussion of the current uses of 'terrorism' bears out Edel's observation that terrorism ". . . is an emerging concept rather than one endowed with an established essence, and what will emerge will be a quasi-technical usage on which will hang a variety of legal and moral consequences."[16] The definitions of 'international terrorism' I noted are examples of emerging quasi-technical legal usages; though, understandably, they are or will be mainly concerned with political terrorism.

In light of the complexity, diversity and variability of the activities and actions currently covered by the term 'terrorism' and reflected in the five aspects of terrorism I noted, an adequate *essentialist* definition of what is now usually called terrorism appears to me to be undesirable as well as impossible. Rather, a 'range definition' expressing a certain kind of 'family resemblance' concept would avoid the two opposite problems that plague essentialist definitions or concepts in such cases: narrowness and over-inclusiveness. Leiser's definition has the merit of characterising terrorism in terms of a set of disjunctions reflecting the diversity of the goals, hence the different types, of terrorism. But since there exist some very general features *common* to all acts of terrorism as generally understood (the 'common core of meaning' noted earlier), though neither peculiar to them nor exhaustive of their features as acts of terrorism, *terrorism* as we now have it and as I hope it will continue to be, is a 'quasi-essentialist' concept. Such a concept is logically intermediate between an essentialist concept, defined in terms of a set of necessary and sufficient conditions or a set of common and peculiar features, and a 'pure' 'family resemblance' concept,[17] wholly and solely delimited in terms of crisscrossing resemblances of different degrees of generality or specificity.

III

Terrorism and Just-war Theory

The traditional conditions of a just war are of two sorts: conditions of *jus ad bellum* or conditions of a morally justified launching of a war, and conditions of *jus in bello* or conditions of the just prosecution of a war in progress. One of the fundamental conditions of the latter sort is the Principle of Discrimination, which prohibits the deliberate harming—above all the killing—of innocent persons. In *Just-war Theory* William O'Brien defines it as the principle that "prohibits direct intentional attacks on non-combatants and nonmilitary targets."[18] Another fundamental condition is the Principle of Proportion, as "applied to discrete military ends."[19] That condition is defined by O'Brien as "requiring proportionality of means to political and military ends."[20] My contention is that these two principles, duly modified or adapted to terrorism, are applicable to all the types of terrorism I distinguished in Section II, and that they are flagrantly violated by them.

The Principle of Discrimination and Terrorism

Let us start with the Principle of Discrimination. It is a patent fact that in many acts of terrorism some or all of the immediate victims and/or the sufferers are innocent persons, in no way—morally or even causally—connected with or responsible in any degree for the physical or mental harm inflicted on them. Indeed, in predatory terrorism the immediate victims and sufferers are, almost without exception, innocent persons. In all other types of terrorism, whether in peacetime or in time of war, some of the immediate victims or sufferers tend to be innocent persons; though some may be non-innocents, such as high-ranking members or representatives of the governments or the military morally responsible for the real or imagined wrong that triggers the terrorism.

The problem of distinguishing innocent and non-innocent persons in relation to the different types and forms of terrorism, except terrorism in war, is generally less difficult than the much-vexed corresponding problem in relation to war. My position here, as, *mutatis mutandis,* in relation to war, stated briefly and simply, is this. (a) 'Innocence' and 'non-innocence' consist in *moral* innocence and non-innocence respectively, relative to the particular acts, types or forms of terrorism *T*; (b) they are a matter of degree; and (c) a perfectly innocent person is one who has no share in the moral responsibility, a *fortiori,* no causal responsibility at all, for any wrong, if any, that gives or gave rise to *T*. A paradigmatically non-innocent person is someone who has an appreciable degree of moral (hence direct or indirect causal) responsibility[21] for some real wrong triggering *T*. Between that extreme and paradigmatic non-innocents we find possible cases of decreasing moral responsibility corresponding to decreasing degrees of causal responsibility. Here the targets are to some extent non-innocent but less so than in paradigmatic cases. (d) Moral responsibility may be direct or indirect by virtue of a person's direct or indirect role in *T*'s causation—where *T* is caused by some real injustice or wrong. The degree of a person's innocence may therefore also vary in that way. A person whose actions are a proximate cause of the wrong is non-innocent in a higher degree than someone who has only indirect responsibility for it. *In principle* it is always possible to ascertain in particular cases whether a given individual is (causally) directly involved. Generally, it is also actually possible though often quite difficult to do so. Ascertaining who is indirectly involved and who is not involved at all is another matter. That is not too disquieting for our purposes, in so far as we are mainly concerned with the theoretical problem of the morality of terrorism. But it is of the essence from the would-be terrorists' as well as the law's point of view, unless the terrorists happen to be deranged, and target individuals or groups they imagine to be morally responsible for the grievances they are out to avenge, redress, etc. Further, the very life of some individuals may depend on the potential terrorists' ability to distinguish innocent from non-innocent persons or groups. Political, retaliatory or moralistic terrorists, driven by passion or paranoia, often baselessly enlarge, sometimes to a tragically absurd extent, the circle of alleged non-innocents. They sometimes target individuals, groups or whole nations having only a tenuous relation, often of a completely innocent kind, to those who have wronged their compatriots or ancestors, stolen their land, etc. The example I gave earlier of terrorists striking at the high-ranking officials of governments whose predecessors committed crimes against their people, illustrates this. Another example is the terrorists' targeting innocent persons they presume to be guilty by association; because they happen to be of the same race, ethnic heritage, nationality or religion as those they deem responsible for their hurt.

An extreme and horrifying type of justification of the targeting of completely innocent persons was brought to my attention by Anthony O'Hear in a private communication. It involves the justification one sometimes hears, of the killing of holidaymakers, travellers and others, in Israel and other terrorist targets, in O'Hear's words, "on the ground that . . . the very fact that they were contributing to the economy and morale of the targeted country [unwittingly] implicated them". As O'Hear commented, that defence is "a disgusting piece of casuistry". Its implications, I might add, are so far-reaching as to be positively frightening. If the travellers or holiday-

makers were guilty of a crime against, say, the Palestinian people, as is claimed, then by parity of reasoning all individuals, institutions, groups or peoples, all countries or nations that have any kind of economic dealings with Israel and so contribute to its economy would likewise be guilty of a crime against the Palestinian people and so may be justifiably targeted! But then why exempt those *Arabs* who live in Israel and even those *Palestinians* residing on the West Bank or in the Gaza Strip who are employed in Israel—indeed, all those who spend any amount of money there—from guilt? The absurdity of all this needs no further elaboration.

Finally, law enforcement agencies as well as governments in general, to be able to protect individuals against terrorism, need to make reliable predictions about who is a likely target of known terrorist organisations. Yet in few other kinds of coercion or the use of force is the element of unpredictability and surprise greater or the strikes more impelled by emotion and passion than in terrorism.

The Principle of Proportion and Terrorism

In his discussion of the principle of proportion William O'Brien observes that "One of the criteria [of just war] requires that the good to be achieved by the realisation of the war aims be proportionate to the evil resulting from the war."[22] And "the calculus of proportionality in just cause [that is, the political purpose, *raison d'état*, 'the high interests of the state'] is the total good to be expected if the war is successful balanced against the total evil the war is likely to cause."[23] As in the case of war, formidable problems face the attempt to reach even the roughest estimates of the total expected good *vis-à-vis* the total evil likely to be caused by a particular act, and more so by a series of connected acts, of *political* or *moralistic* terrorism. The crudest estimates of the expected good of some political cause against the suffering or death of even one victim or patient of terrorism are exceedingly difficult. And if we turn from isolated acts of political terror to a whole series of such acts extending over a period of years or decades, as with Arab or IRA terrorism, the task becomes utterly hopeless. For how can we possibly measure the expected good resulting from the creation of e.g. an independent Catholic Northern Ireland or a Catholic Northern Ireland united with the Irish Republic, and compare it with the overall evil likely to be the lot of the Ulster Protestants in such an eventuality or on different scenarios of their eventual fate—then add the latter evil to the evils consisting in and consequent upon all the acts of terrorism that are supposed to help realise the desired good end? I see no possible way in which these factors can be quantified, hence added or subtracted.[24]

The conclusion to which we are driven is that the Principle of Proportion in the present sense does not enable us to ascertain the rightness *or* wrongness of political or moralistic terrorism. The same conclusion can be similarly shown to follow from the Principle of Proportion as understood by Donald Wells in *The 'Just War' Justifies Too Much*[25] or in my *Self-defense and the Just War*,[26] respectively.

In addition to stipulating the proportionality of the *raison d'état* and the evil resulting from a war as a whole, O'Brien rightly stipulates that "a discrete military means . . . when viewed independently on the basis of its intermediate military end (*raison de guerre*), must . . . be proportion-

ate . . . to that military end for which it was used, irrespective of the ultimate end of the war at the level of *raison d'état.*"[27] Barring that, it would be an immoral act. This principle, applied to discrete military means, O'Brien observes, is in line with the law of Nuremberg, which judged the "legitimacy of discrete acts of the German forces, . . . inter alia, in terms of their proportionality to intermediate military goals, *raison de guerre* . . . It was . . . a reasonable way to evaluate the substance of the allegations that war crimes had occurred."[28]

The present, second form of the Principle of Proportion *can* be applied, *mutatis mutandis,* to discrete acts of terrorism; provided that their probable intermediate results can be roughly assessed. For example, in evaluating the morality of the Achille Lauro seajacking, the short-term and intermediate "political" gains the terrorists expected to receive from it must be weighed, if possible, against the killing of an innocent passenger and the terrors visited on the other passengers on board. It can be safely said that wholly apart from the damage the seajacking did to the PLO and to the Middle East peace process as a whole, whatever short term and intermediate benefit the seajackers expected to reap from their acts,[29] such as publicity and the dramatisation of the plight of the Palestinians under Israeli military rule in the occupied territories, was vastly outweighed by the evils the seajacking resulted in.[30] More important still, the actual and not (as in O'Brien's formulation of the principle) merely the expected outcome of acts of terrorism, good and bad, must be weighed if possible, against each other. That is, actual proportionality must obtain if, in retrospect, the acts are to be objectively evaluated. But to do so is precisely to assess the consequences of the acts in terms of a consequentialist criterion, and so will be left for later consideration.

IV

Terrorism and Human Rights

If one believes that human beings have a (an equal) human right to life, one can argue that acts of terrorism are wrong whenever they threaten the lives of, and, especially, kill, their immediate victims; on the ground that acts that violate a human right are morally wrong. Unfortunately this way of making short shrift with terrorism in general is not open to those who, like myself, do not believe that a human right to life *as such* ought to be acknowledged.[31] Elsewhere I have argued that we must acknowledge that all human beings have a fundamental human right to be treated as moral persons. Further, that that right includes an equal right of all to be free to satisfy their needs and interests,[32] and to actualise their potentials: that is, to seek to realise themselves and their wellbeing.[33] In addition to that right, I contended, human beings have an equal human right to equal opportunity and treatment to help them realize the aforementioned values, and that that right is either part of or is implied by the right to be treated as a moral person.

The rights in question do not entail a moral right to life. But his/her being alive is obviously necessary for an individual's having the possibility of realising the preceding and other values. Consequently the protective umbrella of these rights must be extended to it;[34] except when that protection is overridden by strong moral or other axiological claims. These may include the protection of the equal rights of others; or

situations where taking a human life or letting nature take its course is (1) the lesser of two evils and (2) the action violates no one's equal human rights or other moral rights.

From the above it follows that acts of terrorism that cause the immediate or delayed death of their victims—unless they satisfy e.g. conditions (1) and (2)—are morally wrong. Condition (1) may perhaps be sometimes satisfied; but condition (2) cannot ever be satisfied. In fact all forms of terrorism I have distinguished seriously violate their immediate victims' and the sufferers' human rights as moral persons. Treating people as moral persons means treating them with consideration, in two closely related ways. First, it means respecting their autonomy. That autonomy is clearly violated if they are humiliated, coerced and terrorised, taken hostage or kidnapped, and, above all, killed. Second, consideration involves "a certain cluster of attitudes, hence certain ways of acting toward, reacting to and thinking about"[35] people. Part of that lies in sensitivity to and consideration of their feelings and desires, aspirations, projects and goals. That in turn is an integral part of treating their life as a whole—including their relationships and memories—as a thing of value. In fact, it also includes respecting their "culture or ethnic, religious or racial identity or heritage."[36] These things are the very antithesis of what terrorism does to its victims and sufferers.

In sum, terrorism in general violates both aspects of its targets' right to be treated as moral persons. In retaliatory and moralistic terrorism that is no less true of those victims or those sufferers who are morally responsible, in some degree, for the wrong that precipitates the terrorist strike than of those who are completely innocent of that wrong. In predatory terrorism the terrorism violates the human right of everyone directly or indirectly hurt by it. For the terrorists the life of the immediate victims and their human rights matter not in the least. Similarly with the sufferers they terrorise. The terrorists use both groups, against their will, simply as instruments[37] for their own ends.

The matter can also be looked upon in terms of the ordinary concepts of *justice* and *injustice*. Terror directed against innocent persons is a grave injustice against them. In no case is this truer than when terrorists impute to their immediate victims or to the sufferers guilt by association. It is equally true when the victims are representatives of a government one or more of whose predecessors committed large-scale atrocities, such as attempted genocide, against the terrorists' compatriots or ancestors. True, the present government would be tainted by the original crimes if, to cite an actual case, it categorically refuses to acknowledge its predecessors' guilt and take any steps to redress the grievous wrongs. Similarly if it verbally acknowledges its predecessors' guilt but washes its hands of all moral or legal responsibility to make amends to the survivors of the atrocities or to their families, on the ground that it is a new government, existing decades later than the perpetrators. Yet only if the targeted representatives of the present government themselves are in some way responsible for their government's stand would they be non-innocent in some degree. Otherwise targeting them from a desire for revenge would be sheer murder or attempted murder.

Whenever the victims or sufferers are innocent persons terrorism directed against them constitutes a very grave injustice, just like 'punishing' an innocent person for a crime he or she has not committed. For in the present sense justice consists in one's receiving what one merits or deserves, determined by what one has done or refrained from doing.

It may be argued that some terrorist acts *may* be just punishment for wrongs committed by the immediate victims or the sufferers themselves, against the terrorists or persons close to them. But first, punishment cannot be just if founded on a denial of the wrongdoer's human rights. Second, a vast difference exists between terrorist 'punishment' and just legal punishment, which presupposes the establishment of guilt by a preponderance of the evidence. By definition terrorists do not and cannot respect the victims' and the sufferers' legal protections and rights, but erect themselves both as judges and jury—and executioners—giving the 'accused' no opportunity to defend themselves or be defended by counsel against the terrorists' allegations; let alone the possibility of defending themselves physically against their assailants.[38] This is a further corollary of the terrorists' denial of the moral and legal rights of the victims and sufferers. . . .

NOTES

1. Cf. also Secretary of State George Schulz's characterisation of terrorism as "murderous adventures" ('Small Wins in a Long War,' *Newsweek*, May 26, 1986, p. 34). Israel's and the U.S.'s branding of the PLO as a terrorist organization is part of the grave and complex problem facing the quest for a negotiated settlement of the Palestine Problem.

   It is noteworthy that up to this moment, in the aftermath of the Iran arms scandal, the Reagan administration continues to insist that there was no swap of arms for U.S. hostages of Lebanese terrorists; and that its policy toward terrorism and states that support it has not changed.
2. I use 'force' rather than the more common 'violence' since it is morally neutral or near-neutral, unlike the latter expression.

3. I borrow these terms as well as 'immediate victim' from Abraham Edel, 'Notes on terrorism,' *Values in Conflict*, edited by Burton M. Leiser (New York, 1981), p. 458.
4. Second Edition (New York, [1979]), 13, pp. 375–397.
5. Ibid., p. 375. Italics in original.
6. 'War and murder,' *War and Morality*, edited by Richard A. Wasserstrom (Belmont, CA, 1970), p. 45.
7. Op. cit., p. 375.
8. Ibid., p. 375. For a more precise characterization see later.
9. Ibid., p. 379. Leiser's view of terrorism is crystalized in the section on pp. 389–391, entitled 'Terrorists: enemies of mankind'.
10. Ibid., pp. 386ff. Leiser's whole discussion of Palestinian armed resistance is conceived from a pro-Israeli, Zionist point of view.
11. Ibid., p. 381. Italics in original.
12. 'Essentially Contested Concepts,' *Proceedings of the Aristotelian Society*, N.S. vol. LVI (March, 1956), pp. 180ff. But Gallie maintains that a concept must have certain characteristics in addition to appraisiveness (enumerated in ibid., pp. 171–172; p. 180) in order to be 'essentially contested' in his sense.
13. Those who use 'terrorism' in general as a condemnatory term would substitute 'violence' for 'force', since the former is generally used to mean morally (or legally) unjustified use of force.
14. I borrow the categories 'predatory' and 'moralistic' from Edel, Leiser (op. cit., p. 453). Some but not all moralistic terrorism is political terrorism, or vice versa.
15. See also the CIA's definition, in: Allan S. Nanes, *International Terrorism* (Congressional Research Service, 1985, p. 1), the *Convention for the Suppression of Unlawful Acts Against the Safety of Civil Aviation* (Montreal, 23 September 1971), and *Convention on the Prevention and Punishment of Crimes Against International Protected Persons, Including Diplomatic Agents*, adopted by the UN General Assembly, 14 December, 1973. See also Harriet Culley, *International Terrorism* (August 1985, Bureau of Public Affairs, Department of State).

   I owe the material on U.S. Resolution 2781, 99th Congress, 1st Session, pp. 1–3, as well as the foregoing references, to the research of a former student of mine, Mr. Thomas Kurzynski.
16. In Leiser, op. cit., p. 458.
17. The type of concept distinguished by Ludwig Wittgenstein in *Philosophical Investigations*.
18. Op. cit., p. 39.
19. Ibid., p. 30.
20. Ibid., p. 37.
21. What constitutes an appreciable degree of moral responsibility would of course be a matter of controversy.
22. Ibid., p. 37.
23. Ibid.
24. For the special significance of this in relation to revolutionary terrorism, see Section V.
25. *Philosophy For a New Generation* (New York. (1970), edited by A.K. Rierman & James A. Gould, pp. 218–230. Wells, following Joseph McKenna ('Ethics and war: a Catholic view,' *America Political Science Review*, September 1960, pp. 647–658) states it as the condition that ". . . the seriousness of the injury inflicted on the enemy must be proportional to the damage sufferrd by the virtuous" (Wells, op. cit., p. 220).
26. As I stated the Principle in relation to morally justified collective self-defense, it stipulates that the defender's military response "must be measured and restrained. That is, as much as circumstances allow, not just the intended but the actual damage it inflicts on . . . the aggressor, during the armed conflict, must be at most roughly proportional to the damage inflicted at the time by . . . the aggressor" (Op. cit., p. 161).
27. Op. cit., p. 37.
28. Ibid., p. 38.
29. One of the seajackers stated after being captured that the seajackers' original objective was a suicidal mission in Israel. That objective, of course, was not realised.
30. Note that the question whether the capture, trial and almost certain punishment of the seajackers and others implicated in the seajacking is to be judged a good or an evil to be added to the one or the other side of the balance sheet, partly depends for its answer on the evaluation of the seajacking itself as morally justified or unjustified. (I say "partly depends" because the legal implications of the act are also relevant.)
31. See my 'Medical ethics and the value of human life,' *Philosophy in Context*, 14, 1984, pp. 42–50.
32. 'Toward a foundation for human rights,' *Man and World*, 18, 1985, pp. 219–240.
33. 'The human right to be treated as a person,' *The Journal of Value Inquiry*, 19, 1985, pp. 183–195.
34. 'Medical ethics and the value of human life,' *passim*.
35. 'The human right to be treated as a person,' p. 21.
36. Ibid., p. 22.
37. Cf. Edel's condemnation of terrorism on Kant's principle ". . . that people ought to be treated as ends in themselves and never as means only. Terrorists necessarily treat human beings as means to the achievement of their political, economic, or social goals" (from Leiser's Introduction to the Section on Terrorism, in *Values in Conflict*, p. 343).
38. See my 'Is political assassination ever morally justified?' in *Assassination* (Boston, [1975]), edited by Harold Zellner, pp. 41–55, for similar criticism of political assassination.

Can Terrorism Be Justified?

Burleigh Wilkins

Burleigh Wilkins is professor of philosophy at the University of California in Santa Barbara. He is the author of The Problem of Burke's Political Philosophy *(1967),* Has History Any Meaning? *(1978), and* Terrorism and Collective Responsibility *(1992).*

Wilkins argues that terrorism can be morally justified. He focuses our attention on situations for which a large number of people share guilt for a tragic situation, such as the rise of Hitler in Nazi Germany. If it makes sense to say that various people share guilt for the tragedy of the Holocaust, then it also makes sense to think that terrorism aimed at bringing Hitler down could also have been justified.

One thing that makes terrorism of interest philosophically is that it compels us to rethink from a somewhat different perspective the question of when, if ever, it is morally justifiable to do violence to another person. The traditional answers, while perhaps valid, will take us only so far. It is generally agreed that it is justifiable to do violence to another person in self-defense; some wars can be accommodated under the category of self-defense where this is construed in terms of a community of persons defending themselves against aggressors. It is also agreed, though less generally, that even violence against an innocent person can be justified in the name of self-defense, in cases where he or she is being used by an aggressor as a hostage or a shield. If in the Second World War the Japanese Army had dispersed

From *Terrorism and Collective Responsibility* by B.T. Wilkins. London: Routledge 1992. [Edited]

crucial weapons and supplies throughout Hiroshima and Nagasaki, and if these weapons and supplies could only have been destroyed by attacks upon the entire cities, then we would, I think, be far less troubled about the moral legitimacy of our attacks upon them. (Here I assume that Japan was the aggressor.) But what about terrorism which seems to be no respector of innocence among persons, and which seems all too willing to sacrifice innocent lives as a means to social or political change? Can we fail to be shocked by the anarchist who justified tossing a bomb into a crowded café in Paris on the ground that there are no innocent bourgeois? (But would it be blasphemous to suggest that we might be somewhat less shocked had he deliberately chosen a café known to be frequented by captains of industry, whom he would have regarded as 'class enemies'?)

Though the victims of terrorist acts may be oppressors or aggressors or tyrants, or their collaborators, often they are not. Often they are innocent, at least as innocent as civilian populations in wartime. If we condemn unjust wars, or unjust acts committed in wartime, are we not also committed to condemning any terrorism in which violence, or the threat of violence, is inflicted upon innocent persons, except in those instances where they are being used as hostages or shields? Terrorism poses this problem: can we ever justify inflicting violence upon innocent persons in circumstances other than self-defense? Will a 'justification' of terrorism succeed only by shrinking the notion of what is to count as innocence and/or by extending the range of activities to be considered as self-defense? Is there such a thing as collective guilt, and if there is can it ever be used to justify acts of violence against persons on the ground that they are members of a certain community or group?

I believe that any adequate answer to the question of when, if ever, terrorism is justified must take into account the problem of collective guilt, which is surely one of the murkiest and least explored topics in moral philosophy and which, to my knowledge, has been entirely neglected by those who have written on terrorism. On the question of whether there is such a thing as collective guilt opinions differ: there are those who believe that we, all of us, are guilty of each and every wrong done by any human being, a view which Mohandas Gandhi seems to have held; there are those who believe that we can be guilty only of those wrongs which we have done in our individual capacity, a view which seems to be lurking just below the surface in the writings of some political libertarians; and there are those of us who are not satisfied with either of these extreme positions and

who are attracted to, but disturbed by, the idea that guilt may be at least in some cases collective. If we are to make sense of the notion of collective guilt, I believe that solidarity in the sense of a shared or common interest is our best guide, and that the absence of wrongdoing by individuals who are nevertheless said to share in some collective guilt remains perhaps the biggest stumbling-block. The reason why humanity at large fails to be a satisfactory basis for pronouncements about collective guilt, except for the Mohandas Gandhis of this world, may be that the interests we share with humanity at large tend to be too slight or fragile, though this shows signs of changing. There are, however, communities of a less extensive and more tangible sort where shared or common interests are already conspicuously present: in families, in neighborhoods, in business or cultural institutions, in political states, and perhaps, if Marxists are correct on this point, in social and economic classes. Pride or shame in what is done in, by, or on behalf of such communities is probably the best phenomenological clue we have to locating the interests, and values we share with others. But where collective guilt is concerned we tend to balk at admitting to guilt for things done in, by, or on behalf of those communities whose interests and values we share, when as individuals we did not actively participate in the doing of the things in question. However, the tie between collective guilt and individual wrongdoing is not a conceptual one; and where collective guilt is concerned we can turn to the law for examples of liability without contributory fault. For example, even if personally entirely innocent of the offense, a bank officer may be held strictly liable for the wrongdoing of a bank employee; and a convincing rationale having to do with the vigilance which society can reasonably expect of bank officers in hiring and management procedures can be given for this practice. In addition, Joel Feinberg, the master taxonomist, has uncovered the following models of liability *with* fault: liability with a fault that is noncontributory; contributory group fault where the fault is collective and distributive; and contributory group fault where the fault is collective but not distributive.[1] I shall return shortly to these three models and to some of Feinberg's examples, but first I wish to consider an example of collective guilt which is, I believe, especially relevant to the question of whether terrorism can ever be justified.

I would suppose that in the history of imperialism, of racial and religious persecutions, and in the economic exploitation of one group by another there are numerous instances of collective guilt, but to my mind the clearest and most indisputable example in recent history is to be found in the persecution of the Jews in Nazi Germany. After the Second World War there was in fact an admission of guilt by the newly established West German government, and Chancellor Adenauer acknowledged an obligation on the part of the German people to make moral and material amends for crimes perpetrated in the name of the German people; through treaty negotiations with Israel, West Germany agreed to pay out some 715 million dollars. As an example of penance this payment of reparations may be lacking somewhat in moral purity: Adenauer was under pressure from the American government and from world opinion, political considerations were obviously much involved, and the negotiations were between a new German government, perhaps even a new German state, and the newly created state

of Israel. Nevertheless the example does fit, however awkwardly, the classic picture of guilt, confession, and repentance in the form of efforts to make amends through reparations.

But what exactly was the nature of the guilt involved in this case? Karl Jaspers in his brilliant book, *The Question of German Guilt*, distinguished four kinds of guilt: criminal guilt, political guilt, moral guilt, and what he called 'metaphysical guilt.' According to Jaspers, criminal guilt involved the violation of national and international laws and would be determined by trials of accused individuals in courts of law, including most conspicuously the Nuremberg trials; political guilt is necessarily collective and involves the liability of the German nation, a liability which, however, does not establish moral guilt; moral guilt concerns individuals who must answer in their own conscience the question of whether they lived in moral disguise, or with a false conscience, or in self-deception, or in a state of inactivity during the Hitler period; metaphysical guilt is defined as the lack of 'absolute solidarity with the human being as such' and found its expression in the feeling of guilt at being alive when one's Jewish neighbors were being taken away. Having made these distinctions, Jaspers warns against their misuse: political liability requires the German nation to make material reparations, but it does not establish moral guilt in the individual; criminal guilt, well, yes, but this affects only a few; moral guilt, here only my conscience can decide, and my conscience won't be too hard on me; metaphysical guilt, well, that's 'a crazy idea of some philosopher'—there's no such thing, or, at least as the philosopher himself admits, no one can charge me with it. Jaspers replies in part that there can be no radical separation of moral and political guilt, the reason for this being that there is no absolute division between politics and human existence: 'There is a sort of collective moral guilt in a people's way of life which I share as an individual, and from which grows political realities.'[2] Jaspers then proceeds to examine various excuses having to do with historical and political circumstances, such as the weaknesses exhibited by the Allies who could surely have stopped Hitler at any of several points, the impotence of the German people in the face of the oppression and terrorism of the Nazi regime, and the ignorance of the German people concerning the cruelties going on in the concentration camps; and for reasons I haven't time to discuss he rejects them all.

Frequently in twentieth-century philosophy, analytic philosophy and existentialism have been at odds, existentialism having been created, or so it seems at times, to provide extravagant hypotheses to be demolished by analytic philosophy. This is not so in the present case, for Jaspers and Feinberg (who makes no mention of Jaspers) appear complementary to one another, and many of the distinctions Jaspers makes can be expressed in terms of a vocabulary familiar to analytic philosophers. Thus, the distinction between moral guilt and metaphysical guilt can be explained partially in terms of the difference between the failure to do one's duty and the failure to perform a supererogatory act: we have a duty of mutual aid to other human beings, to come to their assistance when they are hurt or in trouble, even at the price of considerable inconvenience to ourselves, but the duty of mutual aid does not require us to sacrifice our lives to save the life of another; and obviously nothing requires us to risk our lives in circum-

stances where we know that we cannot save the life of another. Still we can feel quite bad and even guilty in some circumstances where no one has come forward, even if we do not blame ourselves individually for having failed to do so. Metaphysical guilt, far from being a philosopher's invention, seems intelligible along the lines of Feinberg's model of contributory group fault, where the fault is collective but not distributive. Feinberg gives the example of the Jesse James train robbery: one armed man holds up an entire car full of passengers, and only heroes could have been expected to lead a self-sacrificial charge against the robber; however, the whole group could have resisted successfully, but fails to do so. On Feinberg's reading, while we cannot blame any individual passenger for failing to act, there is a flaw in the group. He writes, 'but a whole people can be blamed for not producing a hero when the times require it.'[3] Perhaps the metaphysical guilt which the individual German felt when he stood by helplessly as his Jewish neighbors were taken away, the feeling that he was somehow tainted just by remaining alive under such circumstances, reflects the failure of the community of which he is a member to have produced the hero or heroes which successful resistance to the Nazis would have required.

The persecution of the Jews by the Nazis was so heinous that it seems to me, terrorism on the part of the Jews would have been a morally justifiable response, meeting terrorism with terrorism. What I have in mind is not terrorism thought of in terms of vengeance or even retribution but terrorism regarded as an instrument of self-defense on the part of the Jews. While Jews in Germany did to some extent resist their oppressors, they did not practice terrorism.

Perhaps terrorism by the oppressed was an idea whose time had not come; perhaps the Jews did not want to 'sink to the level' of their persecutors; or perhaps there was a fear of making bad matters worse. Where sinking to the level of their oppressors is concerned, the Jews might have reasoned as follows: they were being persecuted because they were Jews, and if they practiced terrorism in turn, would they not be initiating violence, or threats of violence, against Germans because of their Germanness? There is, however, a crucial disanalogy between the two cases, which is sufficient in my judgment to overcome this objection. The Jews had done no wrong, and the effort to discredit them consisted of a tissue of lies: they had betrayed Germany in the First World War causing its defeat, they were responsible for Germany's post-war economic collapse, and so on. On the other hand, Germans were collectively guilty of the persecution of the Jews—thus, if Germans were the victims of violence, or threats of violence, by the Jews it would not have been because of their 'Germanness' but because of their collective guilt for the persecution of the Jews, for being Jews. As for making bad matters worse, perhaps one could find a point in the history of the persecution of the Jews and say that henceforth it would be difficult to see how anything could have worsened their plight. Perhaps terrorism aimed first against the Nazis and then against other Germans might at least have helped to focus German and especially world attention on what was happening in Germany. Even if terrorism by the Jews had done nothing to improve matters, striking out in self-defense is, I believe, a morally legitimate action on the part of anyone who has been condemned to death. State terrorism was being practiced against the Jews, terrorism not as a species

of coercion but with the aim of the annihilation of the Jews. How much of what the Nazis were doing in this respect was actually sanctioned by German law remains a somewhat controversial topic, but surely whether legally or not the apparatus of the German state was being directed toward the extinction of the Jews. Under such circumstances Jews in Germany were in effect being driven into a Hobbesian state of nature, pursued by a Nazi Leviathan, and this is why I believe that terrorism was a morally acceptable option had the Jews elected to use it.[4]

In summary, my thesis is that in the case of the persecution of the Jews, reparations by the German government for crimes done in the name of the German people was a morally appropriate response *after* the harm was done, but that terrorism as an instrument of self-defense by the Jews would have been a morally appropriate response *while* the harm was in process of being inflicted upon them. But what does this example of a case where terrorism would have been morally justifiable actually show? There is a tendency among some commentators on the topics of terrorism and assassination to maintain that while some instances of terrorism or assassination might be justified, in the name of moral necessity, this is a far cry from our being able to arrive at a moral rule which would justify terrorism or assassination: the thought seems to be that exceptions to a moral rule do not provide the basis for a new moral rule.[5] There are some weighty metaphilosophical and methodological problems involved in all arguments of this kind which I shall, mercifully, not attempt to explore here. Instead, I shall conclude by proposing a rule for your consideration. There may be other rules which would justify terrorism, and the rule I shall propose is couched only in terms of sufficient conditions, although I believe that the first condition laid down by the rule I propose may well be a necessary condition which any justification of terrorism would have to satisfy. Here is the rule: terrorism is justified as a form of self-defense when: (1) all political and legal remedies have been exhausted or are inapplicable (as in emergencies where 'time is of the essence'); and (2) the terrorism will be directed against members of a community or group which is collectively guilty of violence aimed at those individuals who are now considering the use of terrorism as an instrument of self-defense, or at the community or group of which they are members. Perhaps there may be other acceptable moral rules which would justify the use of terrorism, for example in cases where an entire people have been dispossessed of their homeland, or where one part of a country is occupied by a foreign power which prevents its being reunited with the country of which it is historically and culturally a part, or where one economic class or one race systematically exploits another economic class or race. Here the issue would be whether dispossession, separation, or exploitation as contrasted to violence against persons is sufficient to warrant terrorism as a response, and whether the struggle to remedy the wrongs in question could be regarded as falling somehow within the category of self-defense. Perhaps rationales for terrorism which do not depend upon whether self-defense is involved might be constructed, but I shall not explore this possibility here; nor shall I consider whether terrorism in the absence of any collective guilt in the group toward which the terrorism is directed might somehow be justified.

Where the application of the moral rule I have proposed is concerned, I believe that the employment of terrorism against members of a community which is collectively guilty of violence should be subject to certain constraints in which moral and prudential considerations are interwoven. There is no reason why terrorism should necessarily be indiscriminate, and there are good reasons why it should not be. The picture given by the popular press, and R. M. Hare,[6] of the terrorist firing off an automatic weapon in a crowded airport misses the mark: most terrorists are in fact far more selective than this suggests, and even if they were not, there is nothing essential to terrorism which requires that its targets be randomly or indiscriminately selected. Here are the constraints I have in mind. First, the terrorism should be limited to the members of the community which is collectively guilty of violence. (It might be noted that the indiscriminate firing of a weapon in a crowded airport would be disqualified right off, on the ground that members of other communities, tourists and businessmen for example, commonly frequent such places.) Second, as far as possible terrorism should be confined to 'primary targets,' and where this is not possible the terrorist should pick a 'secondary target' who is as guilty or nearly as guilty, in the sense of being responsible for initiating or participating in the violence which can be said to have 'started it all' and which is continuing. An individual who simply shares the beliefs and attitudes of the 'primary target' would not be an acceptable 'secondary target.' (Also, the choice of a morally inappropriate 'secondary target' might backfire tactically in the sense of creating public sympathy for either or both of the targets involved— arguably, something like this may have happened in the Hearst case, which, of course, involved a terrorism different from the kind I am now considering.) Third, the terrorism in question should be directed initially at the perpetrators of violence and then at their accomplices in such a way as to reflect the part they played in the violence. If terrorism still fails to achieve its goal, the successful defense of the terrorists or the community or group to which they belong, then they should proceed to violence against those who, as individuals, are guilty of moral complicity in the violence in question. For example, the editors, the bankers, the university professors and the motion-picture makers who 'knew what was going on'—and were handsomely rewarded for their silence and acquiescence should be the next in line. But what about members of the 'silent majority' who, it would seem, do no evil, see no evil and hear no evil, or if they do hear aren't really listening or dismiss what they hear as rumor? If the terrorists are seeking a change in the policies which have led to the violence directed against themselves or the community or group of which they are members, then perhaps the 'silent majority' was their ultimate addressee all along, i.e. the addressee whose attention they had sought vainly to get by legal or political means and which they now seek by violent means. Certainly it seems reasonable to suppose, again using the German example, that no systematic persecution of significant numbers of innocent persons can continue over long periods of time if the 'silent majority' is awakened from its lethargy or its preoccupation with the details of its daily existence. Terrorists can be pictured as saying, 'We demand your attention.' But what if they fail, in their campaign of violence against the perpetrators of violence and their criminal and

moral accomplices, to awaken the conscience and the voice of the 'silent majority'? Then it would seem that the 'silent majority' itself would become tainted first with moral and perhaps eventually even with criminal complicity in the ongoing violence directed against the terrorists and the community or group they represent. Under these circumstances at least, some judicious, highly selective terrorism aimed at members of the 'silent majority' might become morally appropriate and tactically necessary, as a reminder that no one is safe until the injustice in question is ended.

I shall conclude by giving a brief, explicit statement of how what I have done above relates to the questions I posed earlier. First, can we ever justify inflicting violence upon innocent persons in circumstances other than self-defense? Here my justification of terrorism applies where those who are considering it as an option either have themselves been the actual or intended victims of violence, or are members of a community or group which has been the actual or intended victim of violence. Thus, the terrorism I defend is a species of self-defense, but may it involve inflicting violence upon innocent individuals? Here, the answer is a yes and a no. Yes, it may involve inflicting violence upon those who in their individual capacity may have done or intended no harm to the would be terrorists or to the community or group to which they belong; but no, the individuals in question by virtue of their membership in the community or group which has done or threatened to do violence to the would-be terrorists or the community or group to which they belong are collectively guilty of the violence in question. . . . Will my justification of terrorism succeed only by shrinking the notion of what is to count as innocence and/or by extending the range of activities to be considered as self-defense? The answer to the first part of this question is that no conceptual revision or change in the criteria for the use of the concepts we have is necessary: the concept of collective guilt is already in place in our moral vocabulary, and while my use of collective guilt as part of a justification of terrorism under certain circumstances may be original, I am not using the concept 'collective guilt' in any novel way, as my excursions into Feinberg and Jaspers show. The range of activities to be considered as legitimate self-defense may, however, be extended in the light of my justification of terrorism under certain circumstances. But if individuals and communities may justifiably kill or fight wars in self-defense, I believe that terrorism may also under certain circumstances be considered a legitimate instrument of self-defense. Of course, not all terrorism can be seen as involving self-defense, and I have said nothing to justify any terrorism in which self-defense, and self-defense against actual or intended violence, is not the central moral consideration. Is there such a thing as collective guilt, and if there is can it ever be used to justify acts of violence against persons on the ground that they are members of a certain community or group? Here, of course, my answer is that there is such a thing as collective guilt, but that to justify acts of violence against persons on the ground that they are members of a certain community or group is permissible only when 'membership in a certain community or group' is clearly understood to be elliptical for 'membership in a certain community or group which has done or intended to do violence against the would-be terrorists or the community or group to which they belong.' In other words, it is not member- ship in a particular community *per se* but membership in a community or group which is collectively guilty of wrongdoing that is morally relevant; to regard community membership otherwise would involve a relapse into an unacceptable barbarism.

NOTES

1. Joel Feinberg, 'Collective Responsibility,' *Doing and Deserving*, Princeton, 1970.
2. Karl Jaspers, *The Question of German Guilt*, New York, 1947, p. 76. Earlier Jaspers wrote that 'there can be no collective guilt of a people or a group within a people—except for political liability' (p. 42). But his subsequent judgment that 'there can be no radical separation of moral and political guilt' (p. 77) reflects his awareness of the intimacy of politics and morality and provides a basis for his own pronouncements concerning the collective political and moral guilt of the German people.
3. Feinberg, op. cit., p. 248.
4. It is arguable that state terrorism does not entirely fit my definition of terrorism. While it is aimed at bringing about political, social, economic, or religious change by the use of violence, it does not typically seek publicity for its goals or cause. Stephen Segaller in discussing 'state terror' speaks of acts of 'secret terror' by a government against some of its people, (*Invisible Armies. Terrorism into the 1990's*, New York, 1987, pp. 15–16). In the case of Germany, however, while the *details* of what the Nazis were doing were apparently not in the public domain, the fact that the government was acting against the Jews was not secret, nor was it meant to be. Typically state terrorism does not seek to provoke extreme counter-measures, though it may use such counter-measures to its own advantage, for example as a justification for severe reprisals. Lamentably enough, the practitioners of state terrorism all too often believe in the justice of their cause. On balance, I think we are warranted in classifying 'state terror' as a species of terrorism.
5. Arthur C. Danto, 'A logical portrait of the assassin,' and James Rachel, 'Political assassination,' in Harold Zellner, ed., *Assassination*, Cambridge, MA: 1974.
6. R.M. Hare, 'On Terrorism,' *Journal of Value Inquiry*, XIII (Winter, 1979).

A Women's Politics
of Resistance

Sara Ruddick

Sara Ruddick teaches philosophy and women's studies at the New School for Social Research. She is the author of Maternal Thinking: Towards a Politics of Peace (1989). She has also written a monograph entitled Drafting Women (1982).

Ruddick discusses what she calls "a feminist material peace politics." The key dimension of her pacifist perspective is the use of feminine symbols as a model for organizing politically to resist various state practices and policies. She is especially interested in the symbolic role of the "mother" in providing for sustenance of children and family. Ruddick directly confronts one of the most common criticisms of pacifism, namely that it is unlikely to be effective over the long run. In drawing on examples from Argentina and Chile, Ruddick shows the power of largely nonviolent collective action taken by groups of women to oppose tyranny and military might.

A women's politics of resistance is identified by three characteristics: its participants are women, they explicitly invoke their culture's symbols of femininity, and their purpose is to resist certain practices or policies of their governors.

Women, like men, typically act out of social locations and political allegiances unconnected to their sex; women are socialists or capitalists, patriots or dissidents, colonialists or nationalists. Unlike other politics, a women's politics is organized and acted out by women. Women "riot" for bread, picket against alcohol, form peace camps outside missile bases, protect their schools from government interference, or sit in against nuclear testing. A women's politics often includes men: women call on

men's physical strength or welcome the protection that powerful male allies offer. Nonetheless it is women who organize themselves self-consciously as women. The reasons women give for organizing range from an appreciation of the protection afforded by "womanliness" to men's unwillingness to participate in "sentimental" politics to the difficulty in speaking, much less being taken seriously, with men around. Typically, the point of women's politics is not to claim independence from men but, positively, to organize as women. Whatever the reasons for their separatism, the fact that women organize, direct, and enact a politics enables them to exploit their culture's symbols of femininity.

Women can also organize together without evoking common understandings of femininity. Feminist actions, for example, are often organized by women who explicitly repudiate the roles, behavior, and attitudes expected of "women." What I am calling a women's politics of resistance affirms obligations traditionally assigned to women and calls on the community to respect them. Women are responsible for their children's health; in the name of their maternal duty they call on the government to halt nuclear testing, which, epitomizing a general unhealthiness, leaves strontium-90 in nursing mothers' milk. If women are to be able to feed their families, then the community must produce sufficient food and sell it at prices homemakers can afford. If women are responsible for educating young children, then they resist government efforts to interfere with local schools.

Not all women's politics are politics of resistance. There are politics organized by women that celebrate women's roles and attitudes but that serve rather than resist the state. In almost every war, mothers of heroes and martyrs join together in support of military sons, knitting, writing, and then mourning, in the service of the military state. The best-known instance of women's politics is the organization of Nazi women in praise of *Kinder, Küche, Kirche.*[1] Today in Chile, a women's organization under the direction of the dictator Pinochet's wife celebrates "feminine power" *(el poder femenino),* which expresses itself through loyalty to family and fatherland.

A women's politics of *resistance* is composed of women who take responsibility for the tasks of caring labor and then find themselves confronted with policies or actions that interfere with their right or capacity to do their work. In the name of womanly duties that they have assumed and that their communities expect of them, they resist. This feminine resistance has made some philosophers and feminists uneasy. Much like organized violence,

women's resistance is difficult to predict or control. Women in South Boston resist racial integration; mothers resist the conscription of their children in just wars.

Even where women aim to resist tyranny, their "feminine" protest seems too acceptable to be effective. As Dorothy Dinnerstein eloquently laments, women are *meant* to weep while men rule and fight:

> Women's resigned, implicitly collusive, ventilation of everybody's intuition that the world men rule is murderously crazy is a central theme in folklore, literature, drama [and women's politics of resistance].
>
> Think, for instance, of the proverb that groups woman with wine and song as a necessary counterpoint to battle, a counterpoint that makes it possible for men to draw back from their will to kill just long and far enough so that they can then take it up again with new vigor. Or think of the saying "Men must work and women must weep." Woman's tears over what is lethal in man's work, this saying implies, are part of the world's eternal, unalterable way. . . . [Her] tears serve not to deter man but to help him go on, for she is doing his weeping for him and he is doing what she weeps about for her.[2]

Christa Wolf expresses a related fear that women's resistance is as fragile as their dependence on individual men, loyalty to kin, and privileges of class:

> I was slow on the uptake. My privileges intruded between me and the most necessary insights; so did my attachment to my own family, which did not depend upon the privileges I enjoyed.[3]

For whatever reasons, feminists are apt to be disappointed in the sturdiness and extent of women's resistance. Dorothy Dinnerstein expresses this feminist disappointment:

> The absurd self-importance of his striving has been matched by the abject servility of her derision, which has on the whole been

expressed only with his consent and within boundaries set by him, and which has on the whole worked to support the stability of the realm he rules.[4]

While some people fear that "feminine" resistance is inevitably limited—and their fears seem to me not groundless—I place my hope in its unique potential effectiveness, namely, women's social position makes them inherently "disloyal to the civilization"[5] that depends on them. Thus Hegel worries, and I hope, that ostensibly compliant women are on the edge of dissidence. The state, whose most powerful governors depend on women's work and whose stability rests on the authority of the Fathers, "creates for itself in what it suppresses and what it depends upon an internal enemy—womankind in general."[6] Underlining as Hegel does women's exclusion from power, Julia Kristeva celebrates a woman who is "an eternal dissident in relation to social and political consensus, in exile from power, and therefore always singular, fragmentary, demonic, a witch."[7] Yet like Kristeva, I find that the dissident mother, perhaps unlike other witches, is not only a potential critic of the order that excludes her but also and equally a conserver and legitimator of the order it is her duty to instill in her children. Kristeva expects from this dissident mother an "attentiveness to ethics" rooted in a collective experience and tradition of mothering. And I would expect from her the ambivalence that Jane Lazarre believes keeps the head alive, even as it slows the trigger finger. This attentiveness to ethics can become effectively militant in a women's politics of resistance. Its ambivalence, while a spur to compassion, does not slow action if women are governed by principles of nonviolence that allow them to hate and frustrate oppressors they neither mutilate nor murder.

Women's politics of resistance are as various as the cultures from which they arise. Of the many examples I could choose, I select one, the resistance of Argentinian and Chilean women to military dictatorship, specifically to the policy of kidnapping, imprisonment, torture, and murder of the "disappeared." The resistance of the Madres (mothers) of Argentina to its military regime and the similar, ongoing resistance of Chilean women to the Pinochet dictatorship politically exemplify central maternal concepts such as the primacy of bodily life and the connectedness of self and other. At the same time, these movements politically transform certain tendencies of maternal militarism such as cheery denial and parochialism.

Although women's work is always threatened by violence and although women in war always suffer the hunger, illness, mutilation, and loss of their loved ones, the crime of "disappearance" is especially haunting. Kidnapping and rumors of torture and murder destroy lives and families. Yet because the fate of the disappeared person is unclear, because no one in power acknowledges her or his existence, let alone disappearance, even mourning is impossible:

> *To disappear* means to be snatched off a street corner, or dragged from one's bed, or taken from a movie theater or cafe, either by police, or soldiers, or men in civilian clothes, and from that moment on to disappear from the face of the earth leaving not a single trace. It means that all knowledge of the *disappeared* is totally lost. Absolutely nothing is known about them. What was their fate? If they are alive, where are they? What are they enduring? If they are dead, where are their bones?[8]

Nathan Laks describes the Argentinian protest that began in Buenos Aires in 1976:

> Once in power [in Argentina in 1976], the military systematized and accelerated the

campaign of terror, quickly annihilating the armed organizations of the Left and the unarmed ones, as well as many individuals with little or no connection to either. The indiscriminate nature of the kidnapping campaign and the impunity with which it was carried out spread terror—as intended. Relationships among friends and relatives were shattered by unprecedented fear. Perfectly decent individuals suddenly became afraid even to visit the parents of a kidnap victim, for any such gesture of compassion might condemn the visitor to a terrible fate. In this terrorized society, a small organization of women, mothers and other relatives of kidnapped Argentines staged a stunning act of defiance. One Thursday afternoon they gathered in the Plaza de Mayo, the main square in Buenos Aires and the site of countless historic incidents beginning in 1810 with the events that led to Argentina's separation from the Spanish Empire. In the center of the Plaza de Mayo, within clear sight of the presidential palace, the national cathedral, and several headquarters of ministries and corporations, the Mothers paraded in a closed circle.[9]

The Madres met each other outside hospitals or prisons, where they took food and other provisions and looked for traces of the disappeared, or outside government offices, where they tried, almost invariably without success, to get some accounting of their loved ones' whereabouts. When they marched, the Madres wore white kerchiefs with the names of the disappeared embroidered on them. Often they carried lighted candles and almost always they wore or carried photographs of the disappeared. In Chile, women chained themselves to the steps of the capitol, formed a human chain to a mine, Lonquen, where a mass grave was discovered, and took over a stadium where disappeared people had been rounded up, later to be tortured and killed.

The Latin American women's movements are clearly politics of resistance. The women who engage in them court imprisonment and torture and in some cases have become "disappeared" themselves. Knowing what fearful things could happen to them, women in Chile trained themselves to name and deal with what they feared:

> If they were afraid of facing police, they were told simply to find a policeman and stare at him until they could see him as a man and not as a representative of the state. [They] circled police vans on foot, until these symbols of the regime appeared as just another kind of motor vehicle. . . . The women also instructed one another how to deal with the tear gas . . . to stop eating two hours before demonstrations, to dress in casual clothing, to take off makeup but to put salt on their cheekbones to keep teargas powder from entering their eyes, . . . to carry lemon to avoid teargas sting and to get a jar with homemade smelling salts made up of salt and ammonia.[10]

The women talked among themselves about their terrors, found others who shared their fears, and marched with them in affinity groups. And thus they brought their bodies to bear against the state.

As in many women's politics of resistance, the Argentinian and Chilean women emphasize mothering among women's many relations. They are Madres, whether or not they are biological or adoptive mothers of individual disappeared; a later group is made up of Abuelas (grandmothers). Their presence and the character of their action, as well as the interviews they have given, invariably evoke an experience of mothering that is central to their lives, whatever other home work or wage labor they engage in. Repeatedly they remember and allude to ordinary tasks—clothing, feeding, sheltering, and most of all tending to extensive kin work. All these works, ordinarily taken for granted, are dramatically present just because they are interrupted; they are made starkly visible through the eerie "disappearance," the shattering mockery of a maternal and childlike "unchanging expectation of good in the head."[11]

As these women honor mothering, they honor themselves. The destruction of the lives of their children, often just on the verge of adulthood, destroys years of their work; their loss and the impossibility of mourning it constitutes a violent outrage against them. Yet there is something misleading about this way of talking. The women do not speak of their work but of their children; they carry children's photographs, not their own. The distinctive structuring of the relation between self and other, symbolized in birth and enacted in mothering, is now politicized. The children, the absent ones, are *not* their mothers, who have decidedly *not* disappeared but are bodily present. The singular, irreplaceable children are lost. Yet as the pictures the Madres carry suggest, the children are not, even in disappearance, apart from their mothers but, in their absence, are still inseparable from them.

For these Argentinian and Chilean women, as for women in most cultures, mothering is intuitively or "naturally" connected to giving birth. The Abuelas, especially, have made a political point of the emotional significance of genetic continuity. Since the fall of the military regime, one of their projects has been to form a genetic bank to trace the biological parentage of children adopted by people close to the ruling class at the time the military was in power. The insistence on genetic connection is one aspect of a general affirmation of the body. Indeed, the vulnerability, promise, and power of human bodies is central to this women's politics of resistance, as it is to maternal practice:

> Together with the affirmation of life, the
> human body is a very important reference

for these women. They often speak of physical pain, the wounds caused by the disappearances. It seems that wearing a photograph of the missing one attached to the clothing or in a locket around the neck is a way of feeling closer to them.[12]

Because they have suffered military violence—have been stripped naked, sexually humiliated, and tortured—children's bodies have become a locus of pain. Because the violation of bodies is meant to terrify the body itself becomes a place where terror is wrought. In resistance to this violation mothers' bodies become instruments of nonviolent power. Adorned with representations of bodies loved and violated, they express the necessity of love even amid terror, "in the teeth of all experience of crimes committed, suffered and witnessed."[13]

In their protests, these women fulfill traditional expectations of femininity and at the same time violate them. These are women who may well have expected to live out an ideology of "separate spheres" in which men and women had distinct but complementary tasks. Whatever ideology of the sexual division of labor they may have espoused, their political circumstances, as well as the apparently greater vulnerability and the apparently greater timidity and conventionality of the men they lived among, required that they act publicly as women. Women who bring to the public plazas of a police state pictures of their loved ones, like women who put pillowcases, toys, and other artifacts of attachment against the barbed wire fences of missile bases, translate the symbols of mothering into political speech. Preservative love, singularity in connection, the promise of birth and the resilience of hope, the irreplaceable treasure of vulnerable bodily being—these clichés of maternal work are enacted in public, by women insisting that their governors name and take responsibility for their crimes. They speak a "women's language" of loyalty, love, and outrage; but they speak with a public anger in a public place in ways they were never meant to do.

Although not a "peace politics" in a conventional sense, the Latin American protest undermines tendencies of maternal practice and thinking that are identifiably militarist. To some extent, this is a matter of shifting a balance between tendencies in mothering that support militarism toward tendencies that subvert it. In this case, the balance shifts from denial to truthfulness, from parochialism to solidarity, and from inauthenticity to active responsibility. Writing about André Trocme and his parishioners in the French village of Le Chambon during World War II, Phillip Hallie identified three characteristics that enabled them to penetrate the confusion and misinformation with which Nazis covered their policy and then to act on their knowledge. *"Lucid knowledge, awareness of the pain of others,* and *stubborn decision* dissipated for the Chambonnais the Night and Fog that inhabited the minds of so many people in Europe, and the world at large, in 1942."[14] In the transformed maternal practice of the Argentinian and Chilean women, these same virtues of nonviolent resistance are at work.

Cheery denial is an endemic maternal temptation. A similar "willingness to be self-deceived," as the resistance leader André Trocme called it, also sustains many decent citizens' support of war policy. It is notorious that few people can bear, except very briefly, to acknowledge the dangers of nuclear weapons and the damage they have done and could still do. Similarly, few citizens really look at the political aims and material-emotional lives of people affected by their own country's interventionist war policies. By contrast, the Argentinian and Chilean women insist on, and then disseminate, "lucid knowledge" of military crimes. "What is so profoundly moving about them is their determination to find out the truth."[15] They insist that others, too, hear the truth. They are "ready to talk immediately; they need to talk, to make sure their story, so tragic and so common, . . . be told, be known."[16] In addition to talking, they make tapestries, "arpilleras," that tell stories of daily life including workers' organizing, police brutality, kidnapping, and resistance. The protests, tales, and arpilleras extend the maternal task of storytelling, maintaining ordinary maternal values of realism in the face of temptation to deny or distort. In this context, their ordinary extraordinary work becomes a politics of remembering.

After fighting in World War II the philosopher J. Glenn Gray wrote:

> The great god Mars tries to blind us when we enter his realm, and when we leave he gives us a generous cup of the waters of Lethe to drink. . . . When I consider how easily we forget the millions who suffered unbearably, either permanently maimed in body or mind, or who gave up their lives before they realized their purpose, I rebel at the whole insane spectacle of human existence.[17]

After the junta fell, Argentinian women insisted that violated bodies be *remembered,* which required that crimes be named, the men who committed them be brought to trial, and the bodies themselves, alive or dead, be accounted for and, where possible, returned.

"Awareness of the pain of others." The Argentinian and Chilean Madres spoke first of their own pain and the pain of relatives and friends of others disappeared. Similarly, maternal nonviolence is rooted, and typically limited by, a commitment to one's "own" children and the people they live among. . . . I spoke of this limitation as a principal source of maternal militarism; the parochialism of maternal practice can become the racialism that fuels organized violence. This tribal parochialism was also broken down in the Argentinian and Chilean protests.

As in mothering generally, women found it easiest to extend their concern for their own children to other mothers "like them"; only in this political context likeness had to do not with race or ethnicity but with common suffering. In Argentina, where protests are marked by the "singularity" of photographs, the women came to wear identical masks to mark their commonality. In Chile one woman said:

> Because of all this suffering we are united. I do not ask for justice for my child alone, or the other women just for their children. We are asking for justice for all. All of us are equal. If we find one disappeared one I will rejoice as much as if they had found mine.[18]

Concern for all victims then sometimes extended to collective concern for all the people of the nation:

> We are the women and mothers of this land, of the workers, of the professionals, of the students, and of future generations.[19]

This is still "nationalism," though of a noble sort. Many of the women went further as they explicitly identified with all victims of military or economic violence:

> In the beginning we only wanted to rescue our children. But as time passed we acquired a different comprehension. We understood better what is going on in the world. We know that when babies do not have enough to eat that, too, is a violation of human rights.[20]

We should commit ourselves to make Lonquen [the mine where a mass grave was discovered] a blessed spot. May it be a revered spot, so that never again will a hostile hand be raised against any other person that lives on the earth.[21]

It would be foolish to believe that every woman in the Argentinian and Chilean protest movements extended concern from her own children to all the disappeared then to all of the nation, and finally to all victims everywhere. Why should women whose children and loved ones have been singularly persecuted extend sympathetic protection to all victims, an extension that is extraordinary even among women and men who do not suffer singular assault? Yet many of these women did so extend themselves—intellectually, politically, emotionally. They did not "transcend" their particular loss and love; particularity was the emotional root and source of their protest. It is through acting on that particularity that they extended mothering to include sustaining and protecting any people whose lives are blighted by violence.

"Stubborn decision." As children remind us, stubborn decision is a hallmark of maternity. And mothers reply: what looks like stubborn decision may well be a compound of timidity, vacillation, and desperation. Women in resistance are (almost certainly) not free from ordinary mothers' temptations to inauthenticity, to letting others—teachers, employers, generals, fathers, grandparents—establish standards of acceptability and delegating to them responsibility for children's lives. And like ordinary mothers, women in resistance probably include in their ranks *individuals* who in ordinary times could speak back to the teacher or organize opposition to the local corporate polluter. But "stubborn decision" takes on a new and collective political meaning when women act-

ing together walk out of their homes to appropriate spaces they never were meant to occupy.

Like their counterparts in resistance elsewhere, these stubbornly decisive Argentinian and Chilean women, whatever their personal timidities, publicly announce that they take responsibility for protecting the world in which they and their children must live. These women are the daughters, the heirs, of Kollwitz's *mater dolorosa*. As in Kollwitz's representations, a mother is victimized through the victimization of her children. These women are themselves victims; moreover, they bear witness to victimization first of loved ones, then of strangers; they stand against those in power, in solidarity with those who are hurt. Yet there is also a sense in which, by their active courage, they refuse victimization. More accurately, they mock dichotomies that still riddle political thought. There is no contradiction between "playing the role of victim" and taking responsibility for public policies. It is possible to act powerfully while standing with those who are hurt. It is neither weak nor passive to reveal one's own suffering while refusing to damage or mutilate in return. The Latin American *mater dolorosa* has learned how to fight as a victim for victims, not by joining the strong, but by resisting them.

A women's politics of resistance is not inherently a peace politics. Women can organize to sabotage peace treaties or to celebrate the heroes and martyrs of organized violence. During the Malvinas-Falklands war, Argentinian and English women sought each other out at a women's meeting in New York to denounce together their countries' militarism and imperialism. Yet during that same war, the Argentinian Madres were reported to use patriotic rhetoric to reinforce their own aims: "The Malvinas belong to us and so do our sons."

Nonetheless, in their own contexts, the Argentinian protest had and the Chilean protest still has antimilitarist implications. The regimes against which the women protest were and are militarist; the omnipresence of the soldier as oppressor and the general as the torturers' commander was—and in Chile still is—sufficient to symbolize a contrast between women and war. Moreover, the generals' actions have not been accidentally related to militarism. As Plato saw, when he rejected militarist rule in his totalitarian state, torture, kidnapping and other physical terrorism infect the rule of fearful tyrants, just as atrocities infect the best organized war. In their deliberately and increasingly brutal strategies to ensure absolute control, the generals exemplify the excesses inherent in militarized tyranny. Hence in the women's protests, not only a particular government but military rule is brought to trial.

Whatever their militarist sentiments or rhetoric, the Argentinian and Chilean protests express to the world the ideals of nonviolence. Although effective protest inevitably hurts its opponents and those associated with them, the protesters did not set out to injure but to end injuring. None of their actions even risked serious, lasting physical damage. Their aim was steadfastly one of reconnection and restoration of a just community, even though and because those responsible for violence were held accountable and were punished. By providing an example of persistent, stubborn action, the Argentinian and Chilean women have offered a model of nonviolent resistance to other Latin American countries and to the world. They have therefore contributed to collective efforts to invent peace, whatever their degree of effectiveness within their own countries. Like the maternal practice from which it grows, a women's politics of resistance may remain racial, tribal, or chauvinist; we cannot expect of women in resistance the rare human ability to stand in solidarity with all victims of violence. Yet if these Latin American protests are at all emblematic, they suggest that the peacefulness latent in maternal practice tends to be realized as participants act against, and therefore reflect on, violence itself.

NOTES

1. For a discussion of women's participation in (and occasional resistance to) the Nazi German government, see Claudia Koonz, *Mothers in the Fatherland: Women, the Family, and Nazi Politics* (New York: St. Martin's, 1987). Among the many virtues of this fascinating book is its tracing of the complex interconnections between women's separate spheres, the Nazi and feminist use of women's difference, and women's participation in but also disappointment in the Nazi state.

2. Dorothy Dinnerstein, *The Mermaid and the Minotaur* (New York: Harper & Row, 1976), p. 226.

3. Christa Wolf, *Cassandra* (New York: Farrar Straus & Giroux, 1984), p. 53.

4. Dorothy Dinnerstein, "The Mobilization of Eros," in *Face to Face* (Greenwood Press, 1982). Manuscript courtesy of the author. For an intellectually sophisticated and high-spirited account of an American women's politics of resistance, see Amy Swerdlow's work on Women's Strike for Peace, forthcoming from the University of Chicago Press. For an example of her work, see "Pure Milk, Not Poison: Women's Strike for Peace and the Test Ban Treaty of 1963," in *Rocking the Ship of State: Toward a Feminist Peace Politics,* ed. Adrienne Harris and Ynestra King (Westview Press, 1989).

5. The title of a well-known essay by Adrienne Rich in *Lies, Secrets and Silence* (New York: Norton, 1979), pp. 275–310.

6. Hegel, *The Phenomenology of Mind,* part VI, A, b, "Ethical Action: Knowledge Human and Divine: Guilt and Destiny" (New York: Harper, 1967), p. 496.

7. Julia Kristeva, "Talking about *Polygoue*" (an interview with Francoise van Rossum-Guyon), in *French Feminist Thought,* ed. Toril Moi (Oxford: Basil Blackwell, 1987), p. 113.

8. Marjorie Agosin, "Emerging from the Shadows: Women of Chile," *Barnard Occasional Papers on Women's Issues,* vol. 2, no. 3, Fall 1987, p. 12. I am very grateful to Temma Kaplan, historian and director of the Barnard College Women's Center, whose interest in "motherist" and grass-roots womens' resistance movements inspired this section. Temma Kaplan provided me with material on the Madres and discussed an earlier draft of the chapter.

9. Nathan Laks, cited in Nora Amalia Femenia, "Argentina's Mothers of Plaza de Mayo: The Mourning Process from Junta to Democracy," *Feminist Studies,* vol. 13, no. 1, p. 10. The Argentinian Madres protested until the fall of the military regime and still exist today, though they are now divided in their political aims.

10. Marjorie Agosin, Temma Kaplan, Teresa Valduz, "The Politics of Spectacle in Chile," *Barnard Occasional Papers on Women's Issues,* vol. 2, no. 3, Fall 1987, p. 6.

11. Simone Weil, "Human Personality," in *Simone Weil Reader,* p. 315.

12. Agosin, "Emerging," p. 18.

13. Simone Weil, "Human Personality," in *Simone Weil Reader* p. 315.

14. Phillip Hallie, *Lest Innocent Blood Be Shed* (New York: Harper & Row, 1979), p. 104. (Italics added.)

15. Agosin, "Emerging," p. 16.

16. Agosin, "Emerging," p. 14.

17. J. Glenn Gray, *The Warriors* (New York: Harper & Row, 1970), pp. 21, 23.

18. Agosin, "Emerging," p. 21.

19. Patricia M. Chuchryk, "Subversive Mothers: The Women's Opposition to the Military Regime in Chile," paper presented at the International Congress of the Latin American Studies Association, Boston, 1986, p. 9.

20. Rene Epelbaum, member of the Argentinian protest, in an interview with Jean Bethke Elshtain, personal communication.

21. Agosin, "Emerging," p. 18.

Letter from the
Birmingham City Jail

Martin Luther King, Jr.

Martin Luther King, Jr. was a minister and one of the most important leaders of the civil rights movement in the United States. He was awarded the Nobel Peace Prize in 1964. He was the author of Strive Toward Freedom *(1958),* Why We Can't Wait *(1964), and* The Trumpet of Conscience *(1968).*

King provides another extremely influential account of nonviolent civil disobedience. He defines a nonviolent campaign as one that has four stages: (a) a determination that injustice is occurring; (b) negotiation to try to end the injustice; (c) a cleansing process that steels one against hatred and revenge; (d) nonviolent direct action. He offers a defense of this strategy, as opposed to a strategy of violence, by reference to traditional Judeo-Christian moral principles. Of central concern to King is the contention that we all share in responsibility for stopping injustice wherever it occurs. This contention is supported by reference to the principle of "love your neighbor," a principle which King believed to be strongly opposed to violence.

My dear Fellow Clergymen,

While confined here in the Birmingham City Jail, I came across your recent statement calling our present activities "unwise and untimely." Seldom, if ever, do I pause to answer criticisms of my work and ideas. If I sought to answer all of the criticisms that cross my desk, my secretaries would be engaged in little else in the course of the day, and I would have no time for constructive work. But since I feel that you are men of genuine goodwill and your criticisms are sincerely set forth, I would like

to answer your statement in what I hope will be patient and reasonable terms.

I think I should give the reason for my being in Birmingham, since you have been influenced by the argument of "outsiders coming in." I have the honor of serving as president of the Southern Christian Leadership Conference, an organization operating in every Southern state, with headquarters in Atlanta, Georgia. We have some eighty-five affiliate organizations all across the South—one being the Alabama Christian Movement for Human Rights. Whenever necessary and possible we share staff, educational and financial resources with our affiliates. Several months ago our local affiliate here in Birmingham invited us to be on call to engage in a nonviolent direct action program if such were deemed necessary. We readily consented and when the hour came we lived up to our promises. So I am here, along with several members of my staff, because we were invited here. I am here because I have basic organizational ties here.

Beyond this, I am in Birmingham because injustice is here. Just as the eighth century prophets left their little villages and carried their "thus saith the Lord" far beyond the boundaries of their home towns; and just as the Apostle Paul left his little village of Tarsus and carried the gospel of Jesus Christ to practically every hamlet and city of the Greco-Roman world, I too am compelled to carry the gospel of freedom beyond my particular home town. Like Paul, I must constantly respond to the Macedonian call for aid.

Moreover, I am cognizant of the interrelatedness of all communities and states. I cannot sit idly by in Atlanta and not be concerned about what happens in Birmingham. Injustice anywhere is a threat to justice everywhere. We are caught in an inescapable network of mutuality, tied in a single garment of destiny. Whatever affects one directly affects all indirectly. Never again can we afford to live with the narrow, provincial "outside agitator" idea. Anyone who lives inside the United States can never be considered an outsider anywhere in this country.

You deplore the demonstrations that are presently taking place in Birmingham. But I am sorry your statement did not express a similar concern for the conditions that brought the demonstrations into being. I am sure that each of you would want to go beyond the superficial social analyst who looks merely at effects, and does not grapple with underlying causes. I would not hesitate to say that it is unfortunate that so-called demonstrations are taking place in Birmingham at this time, but I would say in more emphatic terms that it is even more unfortunate that the white power structure of this city left the Negro community with no other alternative.

In any nonviolent campaign there are four basic steps: (1) Collection of the facts to determine whether injustices are alive, (2) Negotiation, (3) Self-purification and (4) Direct Action. We have gone through all of these steps in Birmingham. There can be no gainsaying of the fact that racial injustice engulfs this community.

Birmingham is probably the most thoroughly segregated city in the United States. Its ugly record of police brutality is known in every section of this country. Its unjust treatment of Negroes in the courts is a notorious reality. There have been more unsolved bombings of Negro homes and churches in Birmingham than any city in this nation. These are hard, brutal and unbelievable facts. On the basis of these conditions Negro leaders sought to negotiate with the city fathers. But the political leaders consistently refused to engage in good faith negotiation.

Then came the opportunity last September to talk with some of these leaders of the economic community. In the negotiating sessions certain promises were made by the merchants—such as the promise to remove the humiliating racial signs from the stores. On the basis of these promises Rev. Shuttlesworth and the leaders of the Alabama Christian Movement for Human Rights agreed to call a moratorium on any type of demonstrations. As the weeks and months unfolded we realized that we were the victims of a broken promise. The signs remained. Like so many experiences of the past we were confronted with blasted hopes, and the dark shadow of a deep disappointment settled upon us. So we had no alternative except that of preparing for direct action, whereby we would present our very bodies as a means of laying our case before the conscience of the local and national community. We were not unmindful of the difficulties involved. So we decided to go through a process of self-purification. We started having workshops on nonviolence and repeatedly asked ourselves the questions, "Are you able to accept blows without retaliating?" "Are you able to endure the ordeals of jail?" We decided to set our direct action program around the Easter season, realizing that with the exception of Christmas, this was the largest shopping period of the year. Knowing that a strong economic withdrawal program would be the by-product of direct action, we felt that this was the best time to bring pressure on the merchants for the needed changes. Then it occurred to us that the March election was ahead and so we speedily decided to postpone action until after election day. When we discovered that Mr. Connor was in the run-off, we decided again to postpone action so that the demonstrations could not be used to cloud the issues. At this time we agreed to begin our nonviolent witness the day after the run-off.

This reveals that we did not move irresponsibly into direct action. We too wanted to see Mr. Connor defeated; so we went through postponement after postponement to aid in this community need. After this we felt that direct action could be delayed no longer.

You may well ask, "Why direct action? Why sit-ins, marches etc.? Isn't negotiation a better path?" You are exactly right in your call for negotiation. Indeed, this is the purpose of direct action. Nonviolent direct action seeks to create such a crisis and establish such creative tension that a community that has constantly refused to negotiate is forced to confront the issue. It seeks so to dramatize the issue that it can no longer be ignored. I just referred to the creation of tension as a part of the work of the nonviolent resister. This may sound rather shocking. But I must confess that I am not afraid of the word tension. I have earnestly worked and preached against violent tension, but there is a type of constructive nonviolent tension that is necessary for growth. Just as Socrates felt that it was necessary to create a tension in the mind so that individuals could rise from the bondage of myths and half-truths to the unfettered realm of creative analysis and objective appraisal, we must see the need of having nonviolent gadflies to create the kind of tension in society that will help men to rise from the dark depths of prejudice and racism to the majestic heights of understanding and brotherhood. So the purpose of the direct action is to create a situation so crisis-packed that it will inevitably open the door to negotiation. We, therefore, concur with you in your call for negotiation. Too long has our beloved Southland been bogged down in the tragic attempt to live in monologue rather than dialogue.

One of the basic points in your statement is that our acts are untimely. Some have asked, "Why didn't you give the new administration time to act?" The only answer I can give to this inquiry is that the new administration must be prodded about as much as the outgoing one before it acts. We will be sadly mistaken if we feel the election of Mr. Boutwell will bring the millenium to Birmingham. While Mr. Boutwell is much more articulate and gentle than Mr. Connor, they are both segregationists, dedicated to the task of maintaining the status quo. The hope I see in Mr. Boutwell is that he will be reasonable enough to see the futility of massive resistance to desegregation. But he will not see this without pressure from the devotees of civil rights. My friends, I must say to you that we have not made a single gain in civil rights without determined legal and nonviolent pressure. History is the long and tragic story of the fact that privileged groups seldom give up their privileges voluntarily. Individuals may see the moral light and voluntarily give up this unjust posture; but as Reinhold Niebuhr has reminded us, groups are more immoral than individuals.

We know through painful experience that freedom is never voluntarily given by the oppressor; it must be demanded by the oppressed. Frankly, I have never yet engaged in a direct action movement that was "well timed," according to the timetable of those who have not suffered unduly from the disease of segregation. For years now I have heard the word "Wait!" It rings in the ear of every Negro with piercing familiarity. This "Wait" has almost always meant "Never." It has been a tranquilizing thalidomide, relieving the emotional stress for a moment, only to give birth to an ill-formed infant of frustration. We must come to see with the distinguished jurist of yesterday that "justice too long delayed is justice denied." We have waited for more that three hundred and forty years for our constitutional and God-given rights. The nations of Asia and Africa are moving with jet-like speed toward the goal of political independence, and we still creep at horse and buggy pace toward the gaining of a cup of coffee at a lunch counter. I guess it is easy for those who have never felt the stinging darts of segregation to say, "Wait." But when you have seen vicious mobs lynch your mothers and fathers at will and drown your sisters and brothers at whim; when you have seen hate-filled policemen curse, kick, brutalize and even kill your black brothers and sisters with impunity; when you see the vast majority of your twenty million Negro brothers smoldering in an air-tight cage of poverty in the midst of an affluent society; when you suddenly find your tongue twisted and your speech stammering as you seek to explain to your six-year-old daughter why she can't go to the public amusement park that has just been advertised on television, and see tears welling up in her little eyes when she is told that Funtown is closed to colored children, and see the depressing clouds of inferiority begin to form in her little mental sky, and see her begin to distort her little personality by unconsciously developing a bitterness toward white people; when you have to concoct an answer for a five-year-old son asking in agonizing pathos: "Daddy, why do white people treat colored people so mean?"; when you take a cross country drive and find it necessary to sleep night after night in the uncomfortable corners of your automobile because no motel will accept you; when you are humiliated day in and day out by nagging signs reading "white" and "colored"; when your first name becomes "nigger" and your middle name becomes "boy" (however old you are) and your last name becomes "John," and when your wife and mother are never given the respected title "Mrs."; when you are harried by day and haunted at night by the fact that you are a Negro, living constantly at tip-toe stance never quite knowing what to expect next, and plagued with inner fears and outer resentments; when you are forever fighting a degenerating sense of "nobodiness"; then you will understand why we find it difficult to wait.

There comes a time when the cup of endurance runs over, and men are no longer willing to be plunged into an abyss of injustice where they experience the blackness of corroding despair. I hope, sirs, you can understand our legitimate and unavoidable impatience.

You express a great deal of anxiety over our willingness to break laws. This is certainly a legitimate concern. Since we so diligently urge people to obey the Supreme Court's decision of 1954 outlawing segregation in the public schools, it is rather strange and paradoxical to find us consciously breaking laws. One may well ask, "How can you advocate breaking some laws and obeying others?" The answer is found in the fact that there are two types of laws: There are *just* and there are *unjust* laws. I would agree with Saint Augustine that "An unjust law is no law at all."

Now what is the difference between the two? How does one determine when a law is just or unjust? A just law is a man-made code that squares with the moral law or the law of God. An unjust law is a code that is out of harmony with the moral law. To put it in the terms of Saint Thomas Aquinas, an unjust law is a human law that is not rooted in eternal and natural law. Any law that uplifts human personality is just. Any law that degrades human personality is unjust. All segregation statutes are unjust because segregation distorts the soul and damages the personality. It gives the segregator a false sense of superiority, and the segregated a false sense of inferiority. To use the words of Martin Buber, the great Jewish philosopher, segregation substitutes an "I-it" relationship for the "I-thou" relationship, and ends up relegating persons to the status of things. So segregation is not only politically, economically and sociologically

unsound, but it is morally wrong and sinful. Paul Tillich has said that sin is separation. Isn't segregation an existential expression of man's tragic separation, an expression of his awful estrangement, his terrible sinfulness? So I can urge men to disobey segregation ordinances because they are morally wrong.

Let us turn to a more concrete example of just and unjust laws. An unjust law is a code that a majority inflicts on a minority that is not binding on itself. This is difference made legal. On the other hand a just law is a code that a majority compels a minority to follow that it is willing to follow itself. This is sameness made legal.

Let me give you another explanation. An unjust law is a code inflicted upon a minority which that minority had no part in enacting or creating because they did not have the unhampered right to vote. Who can say that the legislature of Alabama which set up the segregation laws was democratically elected? Throughout the state of Alabama all types of conniving methods are used to prevent Negroes from becoming registered voters and there are some counties without a single Negro registered to vote despite the fact that the Negro constitutes a majority of the population. Can any law set up in such a state be considered democratically structured?

These are just a few examples of unjust and just laws. There are some instances when a law is just on its face and unjust in its application. For instance, I was arrested Friday on a charge of parading without a permit. Now there is nothing wrong with an ordinance which requires a permit for a parade, but when the ordinance is used to preserve segregation and to deny citizens the First Amendment privilege of peaceful assembly and peaceful protest, then it becomes unjust.

I hope you can see the distinction I am trying to point out. In no sense do I advocate evading or defying the law as the rabid segregationist would do. This would lead to anarchy. One who breaks an unjust law must do it *openly, lovingly* (not hatefully as the white mothers did in New Orleans when they were seen on television screaming "nigger, nigger, nigger"), and with a willingness to accept the penalty. I submit that an individual who breaks a law that conscience tells him is unjust, and willingly accepts the penalty by staying in jail to arouse the conscience of the community over its injustice, is in reality expressing the very highest respect for law.

Of course, there is nothing new about this kind of civil disobedience. It was seen sublimely in the refusal of Shadrach, Meshach and Abednego to obey the laws of Nebuchadnezzar because a higher moral law was involved. It was practiced superbly by the early Christians who were willing to face hungry lions and the excruciating pain of chopping blocks, before submitting to certain unjust laws of the Roman empire. To a degree academic freedom is a reality today because Socrates practiced civil disobedience.

We can never forget that everything Hitler did in Germany was "legal" and everything the Hungarian freedom fighters did in Hungary was "illegal". It was "illegal" to aid and comfort a Jew in Hitler's Germany. But I am sure that if I had lived in Germany during that time I would have aided and comforted my Jewish brothers even though it was illegal. If I lived in a Communist country today where certain principles dear to the Christian faith are suppressed, I believe I would openly advocate disobeying these antireligious laws. I must make two honest confessions to you, my Christian and Jewish brothers. First, I must confess that over the last few years I have been gravely disappointed with the white moderate. I have almost reached the regrettable conclusion that the Negro's great stumbling block in the stride toward freedom is not the White Citizen's Council-er or the Ku Klux Klanner, but the white moderate who is more devoted to "order" than to justice; who prefers a negative peace which is the absence of tension to a positive peace which is the presence of justice; who constantly says, "I agree with you in the goal you seek, but I can't agree with your methods of direct action"; who paternalistically feels that he can set the timetable for another man's freedom; who lives by the myth of time and who constantly advises the Negro to wait until a "more convenient season." Shallow understanding from people of goodwill is more frustrating than absolute misunderstanding from people of ill will. Lukewarm acceptance is much more bewildering than outright rejection.

I had hoped that the white moderate would understand that law and order exist for the purpose of establishing justice, and that when they fail to do this they become dangerously structured dams that block the flow of social progress. I had hoped that the white moderate would understand that the present tension of the South is merely a necessary phase of the transition from an obnoxious negative peace, where the Negro passively accepted his unjust plight, to a substance-filled positive peace, where all men will respect the dignity and worth of human personality. Actually, we who engage in nonviolent direct action are not the creators of tension. We merely bring to the surface the hidden tension that is already alive. We bring it out in the open where it can be seen and dealt with. Like a boil that can never be cured as long as it is covered up but must be opened with all its pus-flowing ugliness to the natural medicines of air and light, injustice must likewise be exposed, with all of the tension its exposing creates, to the light of human conscience and the air of national opinion before it can be cured.

In your statement you asserted that our actions, even though peaceful, must be condemned because they precipitate violence. But can this assertion be logically made? Isn't this like condemning the robbed man because his possession of money precipitated the evil act of robbery? Isn't this like condemning Socrates because his unswerving commitment to truth and his philosophical delvings precipitated the misguided popular mind to make him drink the hemlock? Isn't this like condemning Jesus because His unique God-Consciousness and never-ceasing devotion to His will precipitated the evil act of crucifixion? We must come to see, as federal courts have consistently affirmed, that it is immoral to urge an individual to withdraw his efforts to gain his basic constitutional rights because the quest precipitates violence. Society must protect the robbed and punish the robber.

I had also hoped that the white moderate would reject the myth of time. I received a letter this morning from a white brother in Texas which said: "All Christians know that the colored people will receive equal rights eventually, but it is possible that you are in too great of a religious hurry. It has taken Christianity almost 2000 years to accomplish what it has. The teachings of Christ take time to come to earth." All that is said here grows out of a tragic misconception of time. It is the strangely irrational notion that there is something in the flow of time that will inevitably cure all ills. Actually time is neutral. It can be used either destructively or constructively. I am coming to feel that the people of ill will have used time much more effectively than the people of goodwill. We will have to repent in this generation not merely for the vitriolic words and actions of the bad people, but for the appalling silence of the good people. We must come to see that human progress never rolls in on wheels of inevitability. It comes through the tireless efforts and persistent work of men willing to be co-workers with God, and without this hard work time itself becomes an ally of the forces of social stagnation. We must use time creatively, and forever realize that the time is always ripe to do right. Now is the time to make real the promise of democracy, and transform our pending national elegy into a creative psalm of brotherhood. Now is the time to lift our national policy from the quicksand of racial injustice to the solid rock of human dignity.

You spoke of our activity in Birmingham as extreme. At first I was rather disappointed that fellow clergymen would see my nonviolent efforts as those of an extremist. I started thinking about the fact that I stand in the middle of two opposing forces in the Negro community. One is a force of complacency made up of Negroes who, as a result of long years of oppression, have been so completely drained of self-respect and a sense of "somebodiness" that they have adjusted to segregation, and, of a few Negroes in the middle class who, because of a degree of academic and economic security, and because at points they profit by segregation, have unconsciously become insensitive to the problems of the masses. The other force is one of bitterness and hatred, and comes perilously close to advocating violence. It is expressed in the various black nationalist groups that are springing up over the nation, the largest and best known being Elijah Muhammad's Muslim movement. This movement is nourished by the contemporary frustration over the continued existence of racial discrimination. It is made up of people who have lost faith in America, who have absolutely repudiated Christianity, and who have concluded that the white man is an incurable "devil." I have tried to stand between these two forces, saying that we need not follow the "do-nothingism" of the complacent or the hatred and despair of the black nationalist. There is the more excellent way of love and nonviolent protest. I'm grateful to God that, through the Negro church, the dimension of nonviolence entered our struggle. If this philosophy had not emerged, I am convinced that by now many streets in the South would be flowing with floods of blood. And I am further convinced that if our white brothers dismiss as "rabble rousers" and "outside agitators" those of us who are working through the channels of nonviolent direct action and refuse to support our nonviolent efforts, millions of Negroes, out of frustration and despair, will seek solace and security in black nationalist ideologies, a development that will inevitably lead to a frightening racial nightmare.

Oppressed people cannot remain oppressed forever. The urge for freedom will eventually come. This is what happened to the American Negro. Something within has reminded him of his birthright of freedom; something without has reminded him that he can gain it. Consciously and unconsciously, he has been swept in by what the Germans called the *Zeitgeist,* and with his black brothers of Africa, and his brown and yellow brothers of Asia, South America and the Caribbean, he is moving with a sense of cosmic urgency toward the promised land of racial justice. Recognizing this vital urge that has engulfed the Negro community, one should readily understand public demonstrations. The Negro has many pent-up resentments and latent frustrations. He has to get them out. So let him march sometime; let him have his prayer pilgrimages to the city hall; understand why he must have sit-ins and freedom rides. If his repressed emotions do not come out in these nonviolent ways, they will come out in ominous expressions of violence. This is not a threat; it is a fact of history. So I have not said to my people "get rid of your discontent." But I have tried to say that this normal and healthy discontent can be channelized through the creative outlet of nonviolent direct action. Now this approach is being dismissed as extremist. I must admit that I was initially disappointed in being so categorized.

But as I continued to think about the matter I gradually gained a bit of satisfaction from being considered an extremist. Was not Jesus an extremist in love—"Love your enemies, bless them that curse you, pray for them that despitefully use you." Was not Amos an extremist for justice— "Let justice roll down like waters and righteousness like a mighty stream." Was not Paul an extremist for the gospel of Jesus Christ—"I bear in my body the marks of the Lord Jesus." Was not Martin Luther an extremist—"Here I stand; I can do none other so help me God." Was not John Bunyan an extremist—"I will stay in jail to the end of my days before I make a butchery of my conscience." Was not Abraham Lincoln an extremist—"This nation cannot survive half slave and half free." Was not Thomas Jefferson an extremist—"We hold these truths to be self-evident, that all men are created equal." So the question is not whether we will be extremist but what kind of extremist will we be. Will we be extremists for hate or will we be extremists for love? Will we be extremists for the preservation of injustice—or will we be extremists for the cause of justice? In that dramatic scene on Calvary's hill, three men were crucified. We must not forget that all three men were crucified for the same crime—the crime of extremism. Two were extremists for immorality, and thusly fell below their environment. The other, Jesus Christ, was an extremist for love, truth and goodness, and thereby rose above his environment. So, after all, maybe the South, the nation and the world are in dire need of creative extremists.

I had hoped that the white moderate would see this. Maybe I was too optimistic. Maybe I expected too much. I guess I should have realized that few members of a race that has oppressed another race can understand or appreciate the deep groans and passionate yearnings of those that have been oppressed and still fewer have the vision to see that injustice must be rooted out by strong, persistent and determined action. I am thankful, however, that some of our white brothers have grasped the meaning of this social revolution and committed themselves to it. They are still all too small in quantity, but they are big in quality. Some like Ralph McGill, Lillian Smith, Harry Golden and James Dabbs have written about our struggle in eloquent, prophetic and understanding terms. Others have marched with us down nameless streets of the South. They have languished in filthy roach-infested jails, suffering the abuse and brutality of angry policemen who see them as "dirty nigger lovers." They, unlike so many of their moderate brothers and sisters, have recognized

the urgency of the moment and sensed the need for powerful "action" antidotes to combat the disease of segregation.

Let me rush on to mention my other disappointment. I have been so greatly disappointed with the white church and its leadership. Of course, there are some notable exceptions. I am not unmindful of the fact that each of you has taken some significant stands on this issue. I commend you, Rev. Stallings, for your Christian stand on this past Sunday, in welcoming Negroes to your worship service on a non-segregated basis. I commend the Catholic leaders of this state for integrating Springhill College several years ago.

But despite these notable exceptions I must honestly reiterate that I have been disappointed with the church. I do not say that as one of the negative critics who can always find something wrong with the church. I say it as a minister of the gospel, who loves the church; who was nurtured in its bosom; who has been sustained by its spiritual blessings and who will remain true to it as long as the cord of life shall lengthen.

I had the strange feeling when I was suddenly catapulted into the leadership of the bus protest in Montgomery several years ago that we would have the support of the white church. I felt that the white ministers, priests and rabbis of the South would be some of our strongest allies. Instead, some have been outright opponents, refusing to understand the freedom movement and misrepresenting its leaders; all too many others have been more cautious than courageous and have remained silent behind the anesthetizing security of the stained-glass windows.

In spite of my shattered dreams of the past, I came to Birmingham with the hope that the white religious leadership of this community would see the justice of our cause, and with deep moral concern, serve as the channel through which our just grievances would get to the power structure. I had hoped that each of you would understand. But again I have been disappointed. I have heard numerous religious leaders of the South call upon their worshippers to comply with a desegregation decision because it is the *law,* but I have longed to hear white ministers say, "Follow this decree because integration is morally *right* and the Negro is your brother." In the midst of blatant injustices inflicted upon the Negro, I have watched white churches stand on the sideline and merely mouth pious irrelevancies and sanctimonious trivialities. In the midst of a mighty struggle to rid our nation of racial and economic injustice, I have heard so many ministers say "Those are social issues with which the gospel has no real concern," and I have watched so many churches commit themselves to a completely other-worldly religion which made a strange distinction between the body and soul, the sacred and the secular.

So here we are moving toward the exit of the twentieth century with a religious community largely adjusted to the status quo, standing as a tail-light behind other community agencies rather than a headlight leading men to higher levels of justice.

I have traveled the length and breadth of Alabama, Mississippi, and all the other southern states. On sweltering summer days and crisp autumn mornings I have looked at her beautiful churches with their lofty spires pointing heavenward. I have beheld the impressive outlay of her massive religious education buildings. Over and over again I have found myself asking: "What kind of people worship here? Who is their God? Where were their voices when the lips of Governor Barnett dripped the words of interposition and nullification? Where were they when Governor Wallace gave the clarion call for defiance and hatred? Where were their voices of support when tired, bruised and weary Negro men and women decided to rise from the dark dungeons of complacency to the bright hills of creative protest?"

Yes, these questions are still in my mind. In deep disappointment, I have swept over the laxity of the church. But be assured that my tears have been tears of love. There can be no deep disappointment where there is not deep love. Yes, I love the church; I love her sacred walls. How could I do otherwise? I am in the rather unique position of being the son, the grandson and the great-grandson of preachers. Yes, I see the church as the body of Christ. But, oh! How we have blemished and scarred that body through social neglect and fear of being nonconformists.

There was a time when the church was very powerful. It was during that period when the early Christians rejoiced when they were deemed worthy to suffer for what they believed. In those days the church was not merely a thermometer that recorded the ideas and principles of popular opinion; it was a thermostat that transformed the mores of society. Wherever the early Christians entered a town the power structure got disturbed and immediately sought to convict them for being "disturbers of the peace" and "outside agitators." But they went on with the conviction that they were "a colony of heaven," and had to obey God rather than man. They were small in number but big in commitment. They were too God-intoxicated to be "astronomically intimidated." They brought an end to such ancient evils as infanticide and gladiatorial contest.

Things are different now. The contemporary church is often a weak, ineffectual voice with an uncertain sound. It is so often the arch supporter of the status quo. Far from being disturbed by the presence of the church the power structure of the average community is consoled by the church's silent and often vocal sanction of things as they are.

But the judgment of God is upon the church as never before. If the church of today does not recapture the sacrificial spirit of the early church, it will lose its authentic ring, forfeit the loyalty of millions, and be dismissed as an irrelevant social club with no meaning for the twentieth century. I am meeting young people every day whose disappointment with the church has risen to outright disgust.

Maybe again, I have been too optimistic. Is organized religion too inextricably bound to the status quo to save our nation and the world? Maybe I must turn my faith to the inner spiritual church, the church within the church, as the true *ecclesia* and the hope of the world. But again I am thankful to God that some noble souls from the ranks of organized religion have broken loose from the paralyzing chains of conformity and joined us as active partners in the struggle for freedom. They have left their secure congregations and walked the streets of Albany, Georgia, with us. They have gone through the highways of the South in tortuous rides for freedom. Yes, they have gone to jail with us. Some have been kicked out of their churches, and lost support of their bishops and fellow ministers. But they have gone with the faith that right defeated is stronger than evil triumphant. These men have been the leaven in the lump of the race. Their witness has been the spiritual salt that has preserved the true meaning of the Gospel in these troubled times. They have carved a tunnel of hope through the dark mountain of disappointment.

I hope the church as a whole will meet the challenge of this decisive hour. But even if the church does not come to the aid of justice, I have no despair about the future. I have no fear about the outcome of our struggle in Birmingham, even if our motives are presently misunderstood. We will reach the goal of freedom in Birmingham and all over the nation, because the goal of America is freedom. Abused and scorned though we may be, our destiny is tied up with the destiny of America. Before the pilgrims landed at Plymouth we were here. Before the pen of Jefferson etched across the pages of history the majestic words of the Declaration of Independence, we were here. For more than two centuries our foreparents labored in this country without wages; they made cotton king; and they built the homes of their masters in the midst of brutal injustice and shameful humiliation—and yet out of a bottomless vitality they continued to thrive and develop. If the inexpressible cruelties of slavery did not stop us, the opposition we now face will surely fail. We will win our freedom because the sacred heritage of our nation and the eternal will of God are embodied in our echoing demands.

I must close now. But before closing I am impelled to mention one other point in your statement that troubled me profoundly. You warmly commended the Birmingham police for keeping "order" and "preventing violence." I don't believe you would have so warmly commended the police force if you had seen its angry violent dogs literally biting six unarmed, nonviolent Negroes. I don't believe you would so quickly commend the policemen if you would observe their ugly and inhuman treatment of Negroes here in the city jail; if you would watch them push and curse old Negro women and young Negro girls; if you would see them slap and kick old Negro men and young boys; if you will observe them, as they did on two occasions, refuse to give us food because we wanted to sing our grace together. I'm sorry that I can't join you in your praise for the police department.

It is true that they have been rather disciplined in their public handling of the demonstrators. In this sense they have been rather publicly "nonviolent." But for what purpose? To preserve the evil system of segregation. Over the last few years I have consistently preached that nonviolence demands that the means we use must be as pure as the ends we seek. So I have tried to make it clear that it is wrong to use immoral means to attain moral ends. But now I must affirm that it is just as wrong or even more so, to use moral means to provide immoral ends. Maybe Mr. Connor and his policemen have been rather publicly nonviolent, as Chief Pritchett was in Albany, Georgia, but they have used the moral means of nonviolence to maintain the immoral end of flagrant racial injustice. T.S. Eliot has said that there is no greater treason than to do the right deed for the wrong reason.

I wish you had commended the Negro sit-inners and demonstrators of Birmingham for their sublime courage, their willingness to suffer and their amazing discipline in the midst of the most inhuman provocation. One day the South will recognize its real heroes. They will be the James Merediths, courageously and with a majestic sense of purpose facing jeering and hostile mobs and the agonizing loneliness that characterizes the life of the pioneer. They will be old, oppressed, battered Negro women, symbolized in a seventy-two year old woman of Montgomery, Alabama, who rose up with a sense of dignity and with her people decided not to ride the segregated buses, and responded to one who inquired about her tiredness with ungrammatical profundity: "My feet is tired, but my soul is rested." They will be the young high school and college students, young ministers of the Gospel and a host of their elders courageously and nonviolently sitting-in at lunch counters and willingly going to jail for conscience's sake. One day the South will know that when these disinherited children of God sat down at lunch counters they were in reality standing up for the best in the American dream and the most sacred values in our Judeo-Christian heritage, and thusly, carrying our whole nation back to those great wells of democracy which were dug deep by the founding fathers in the formulation of the Constitution and the Declaration of Independence.

Never before have I written a letter this long (or should I say a book?). I'm afraid that it is much too long to take your precious time. I can assure you that it would have been much shorter if I had been writing from a comfortable desk, but what else is there to do when you are alone for days in the dull monotony of a narrow jail cell other than to write long letters, think strange thoughts, and pray long prayers?

If I have said anything in this letter that is an overstatement of the truth and is indicative of an unreasonable impatience, I beg you to forgive me. If I have said anything in this letter that is an understatement of the truth and is indicative of my having a patience that makes me patient with anything less than brotherhood, I beg God to forgive me.

I hope this letter finds you strong in the faith. I also hope that circumstances will soon make it possible for me to meet each of you, not as an integrationist or a civil-rights leader, but as a fellow clergyman and a Christian brother. Let us all hope that the dark clouds of racial prejudice will soon pass away and the deep fog of misunderstanding will be lifted from our fear-drenched communities and in some not too distant tomorrow the radiant stars of love and brotherhood will shine over our great nation with all their scintillating beauty.

Yours for the cause of Peace and Brotherhood,

Martin Luther King, Jr.

STUDY QUESTIONS

1. Apply the criteria Douglas P. Lackey discusses in his essay to the Gulf War, the action taken by the United States in Somalia, and the inaction taken in Bosnia. Do these criteria justify the actions and inaction, or not?
2. Gandhi claims that when the British engaged in World War II, they were "doing the same work of destruction as the Germans" and that no matter how just the cause, it will not justify the means. Drawing from one of the other essays in this section, how would you justify or discredit his claim?
3. According to Khatchadourian, is it ever justified to use terrorism against innocent civilians? What reasons does he develop for this position? Construct the best counterargument that you can to this position. Which of these two positions do you find most plausible?
4. Burleigh Wilkins argues that employing the notion of collective responsibility could allow us to justify some terrorist acts. What is collective responsibility and how does this notion help him justify terrorism? Do you agree with his reasoning? Why or why not?
5. Sara Ruddick discusses the Madres of Argentina and the Chilean women and their emphases on the "primacy of bodily life and the connectedness of self and others." Discuss the implications of these emphases for obtaining peace, in environmental ethics, and as an overall approach in ethics.
6. What does King mean by saying that injustice anywhere is a threat to justice everywhere? If the injustice is extreme enough, why wouldn't violence be justified to confront it so that it does not threaten justice everywhere? Construct an argument both pro and con.

SUPPLEMENTARY READINGS: WAR AND VIOLENCE

BACK, ALLAN, and DAESHIK KIM. "Pacifism and the Eastern Martial Arts." *Philosophy East and West,* April 1982.

BELLIOTTI, RAYMOND. "Are All Modern Wars Morally Wrong?" *Journal of Social Philosophy,* vol. 26 (2), Fall 1995.

CHILDRESS, JAMES F. "Just War Theories." *Theological Studies* 1978.

DOMBROWSKI, DANIEL M. "Gandhi, Sainthood, and Nuclear Weapons." *Philosophy East and West,* vol. 33 (4), October 1983.

FASHINA, OLADIPO. "Frantz Fanon and the Ethical Justification of Anti-Colonial Violence." *Social Theory and Practice,* Summer 1989.

GRAY, J. GLENN. "The Enduring Appeals of Battle." In *The Warriors.* New York: Harcourt Brace, 1959.

HAJJAR, SAMI G., and R. KIERON SWAINE. "Social Justice: The Philosophical Justifications of Qadhafi's Construction." *Africa Today,* vol. 31 (3), 1984.

HOLMES, ROBERT L. "Violence and the Perspective of Morality." In *On War and Morality.* Princeton, NJ: Princeton University Press, 1989.

IHARA, CRAIG K. "Pacifism as a Moral Ideal." *Journal of Value Inquiry,* vol. 22, 1988.

KAINZ, HOWARD. "Is Just War Theory Justifiable?" *Journal of Social Philosophy,* vol. 27 (2), Fall 1996.

LLOYD, GENEVIEVE. "Selfhood, War and Masculinity." In *Feminist Challenges,* Pateman and Gross, editors. Boston: Northeastern University Press, 1986.

MAGNO, JOSEPH A. "Hinduism on the Morality of Violence." *International Philosophical Quarterly,* vol. 28 (1), March 1988.

NICKEL, JAMES W. "Ethnocide and Indigenous Peoples." *Journal of Social Philosophy,* vol. 25, special issue, June 1994.

NIELSEN, KAI. "Violence and Terrorism: Its Uses and Abuses." In *Values in Conflict,* Leiser, editor. New York: Macmillan, 1981.

NNOLI, OKWUDIBIA. "Revolutionary Violence, Development, Equality, and Justice in South Africa." In *Emerging Human Rights,* Shephard and Anikpo, editors. New York: Greenwood Press, 1990.

O'BRIEN, WILLIAM. "Just-War Theory." *The Conduct of Just and Limited War.* New York: Praeger, 1981.

RICHARDS, GLYN. *The Philosophy of Gandhi.* Atlantic Highlands, NJ: Humanities Press, 1991.

RUESGA, G. ALBERT. "Selective Conscientious Objection and the Right Not to Kill." *Social Theory and Practice,* vol. 21 (1), Spring 1995.

SONN, TAMARA. "Irregular Warfare and Terrorism in Islam: Asking the Right Questions." In *Cross, Crescent, and Sword: The Justification and Limitation of War in Western and Islamic Tradition,* Johnson and Kelsay, editors. New York: Greenwood Press, 1990.

WALZER, MICHAEL. "War Crimes: Soldiers and Their Officers." In *Just and Unjust Wars.* New York: Harper Torchbooks, 1977.

V

GENDER ROLES AND MORALITY

T raditionally in many societies being male or female meant that one had different moral obligations and a different moral status. In the West, women were thought to be more emotional and less rational than men, and so women were assigned the task of primary child-raisers and not given much of a voice in the political affairs of their societies. In most societies, women are considered weak and in need of protection by a man. As women have become increasingly involved in public affairs, they have been subjected to discriminatory treatment of various forms, often explicitly rationalized by reference to the fact that they have different natures from men.

There are indeed biological differences between men and women. Women menstruate, gestate, and lactate, whereas men do not. Men ejaculate, whereas women do not. Beyond these differences, it is true that in general women as a group differ from men as a group. Men have greater upper-body strength than women. Women in the West score more highly on verbal tests than men, and men score more highly in mathematical tests than women. Here though the differences are statistical, not natural, for there are some women who have greater upper-body strength than most men. The question to be raised is this: Do these natural and statistical differences between males and females call for differences in moral obligation or moral status? This is the topic of this chapter.

In many societies, natural and statistical differences between men and women are indeed thought to justify differential treatment of the sexes. In some Islamic societies, it is considered immoral for women to appear in public without being veiled, whereas this is not true for men. In many societies, especially in Asia, there is a strong preference for male children over female children, which has resulted in the commonly accepted practice of neglect of female newborns. Such practices have led to a disproportionate female mortality rate. In the United States, parents continue to voice a similarly strong preference for male over female children, and they spend a disproportionate amount of money educating their sons. Until quite recently the term "lady lawyer" was a commonly accepted term of derision.

Crimes which are gender-linked have also not been given the same status in many societies. Rape and sexual harassment in the United States are often not taken as seriously as are similar assault crimes that are not predominantly directed against women. The public humiliation of Anita Hill who accused Clarence Thomas of sexually harassing her when he was her supervisor at the Equal Employment Opportunity Commission is only the most recent example. Sexual harassment and even sexual slavery are severe problems in many parts of the world and are generally not considered as important as other crimes. In what follows we will survey some of the main viewpoints on the moral justifiability of differential treatment based on gender.

We begin this chapter with a selection from Carol Gilligan. Gilligan is the best-known person doing empirical work on gender and morality. In this early piece of hers, we find a discussion of two children, one male and one female, who interpret a moral dilemma in very different ways, illustrating what Gilligan thinks are different moral voices which correlate with different genders. Amy is concerned about maintaining relationships, while Jake is concerned with rules and fairness. Jake sees people standing alone whereas Amy sees them as always situated in relationships of interdependence. From these different conceptions of self emerge very different orientations toward morality, an appreciation of which helps us understand differences between what has been considered appropriate ways for men and women to treat each other.

Marilyn Friedman discusses the ways that traditional male roles have contributed to harms against women. Friedman begins by discussing how traditional family roles contribute to male dominance and female dependency. While traditional families have encouraged women to be devoted to their families, there is nothing especially honorable about women being subordinated to men, since this often harms a woman's moral integrity and "threatens her own well-being and that of her children." In addition, traditional gender roles in sexual relationships have further contributed to women's loss of control over their lives, where women are "coerced, pressured, or seduced into sexual encounters over which they exercise no control." The feminist project of reshaping gender roles is aimed at empowering women to diminish their subordination to men.

Contrary to Friedman's views, David Blankenhorn argues that traditional gender roles in the family served quite a useful purpose. Blankenhorn focuses on the traditional male role of breadwinner and economic supporter of the family. When such a role is called into question, men are left at sea as to what their role should be in the family, encouraging men to think of themselves as dispensable and encouraging the abandonment of families by men, a phenomenon America has experienced in the last few decades. Breaking down gender roles in the family, espousing "genderless parenting," and encouraging men to take on traditional female roles in childrearing will simply further their insecurity and sense of inadequacy. What we need instead, he argues, is gender complementarity, where men can return to traditional roles now somewhat reconceptualized so that they are not so harmful.

Joel Anderson counters Blankenhorn's arguments by pointing out that "genderless parenting" need not lead to a problematic "decline of the family," since it demands only that we open up access to the social roles of father and mother on an equal basis. Like Friedman, Anderson argues that traditional assumptions about gendered roles have violated women's claim to equal treatment. Against neo-traditionalists he argues that promoting family stability is compatible with a commitment to gender equality, even when that is seen to require promoting equal power between spouses and expanding job opportunities for women.

Lila Abu-Lughod discusses rather traditional gender roles in Islamic societies, especially among Bedouins, a seminomadic people who believe in maintenance of separate societies for women and men. While such societies limit women's freedom in significant ways, there is also significant room in such societies for women to develop a sense of autonomy and responsibility unaffected by pressure from males to be more like them. The positive effects of gender isolation are mirrored in recent studies that Carol Gilligan has done of American girls who go to all-female high schools or colleges. The sense of self-esteem of these girls is greater than it is for those girls who remain in gender mixed schools.

M. Annette Jaimes and Theresa Halsey address the myth that American Indian women were always subordinate to the males in their tribes. Some have insisted that the divisions of moral labor were necessitated by our physiological nature. Halsey and Jaimes challenge this and present examples of different American Indian tribal cultures in which power was shared and was not gender-defined. They argue that the sterotype of women, particularly American Indian women, as docile, meek, and subordinate to males, is incorrect. They cite numerous tribal examples of women in key decision-making positions, and of women involved in all aspects of tribal culture, from war to economics to spirtual leadership. Halsey and Jaimes argue that the subsequent divestiture of American Indian women's status and power within the cultures was intentional, and was forced upon the tribes by the European colonizers.

As will become evident in the next section, many of the issues facing women overlap with those of racial and ethnic minorities, as both groups have been systematically denied economic, social, and political power.

—Larry May

Images of Relationship

Carol Gilligan

Carol Gilligan is a developmental psychologist and professor of education at Harvard University. She is the author of In a Different Voice (1982), Remapping the Moral Domain (1988), and many articles.

Gilligan focuses on different responses by males and females to the Heinz dilemma. Heinz is faced with either breaking into a drug store and stealing a drug his sick wife needs to live, or watching his wife die. Boys tend to see the problem as a self-contained problem in "moral logic" involving a reconciliation of conflict factors. Girls tend to see the problem as one of relationships. These different approaches correlate with different, gendered approaches to morality.

In 1914, with his essay "On Narcissism,"[1] Freud swallows his distaste at the thought of "abandoning observation for barren theoretical controversy" and extends his map of the psychological domain. Tracing the development of the capacity to love, which he equates with maturity and psychic health, he locates its origins in the contrast between love for the mother and love for the self. But in thus dividing the world of love into narcissism and "object" relationships, he finds that while men's development becomes clearer, women's becomes increasingly opaque. The problem arises because the contrast between mother and self yields two different images of relationships. Relying on the imagery of men's lives in charting the course of human growth, Freud is unable to trace in women the development of relationships, morality, or a clear sense of self. This difficulty in fit-ting the logic of his theory to women's experience leads him in the end to set women apart, marking their relationships, like their sexual life, as "a 'dark continent' for psychology" (1926, p. 212).

Thus the problem of interpretation that shadows the understanding of women's development arises from the differences observed in their experience of relationships. To Freud, though living surrounded by women and otherwise seeing so much and so well, women's relationships seemed increasingly mysterious, difficult to discern, and hard to describe. While this mystery indicates how theory can blind observation, it also suggests that development in women is masked by a particular conception of human relationships. Since the imagery of relationships shapes the narrative of human development, the inclusion of women, by changing that imagery, implies a change in the entire account.

The shift in imagery that creates the problem in interpreting women's development is elucidated by the moral judgments of two eleven-year-old children, a boy and a girl, who see, in the same dilemma, two very different moral problems. While current theory brightly illuminates the line and the logic of the boy's thought, it casts scant light on that of the girl. The choice of a girl whose moral judgments elude existing categories of developmental assessment is meant to highlight the issue of interpretation rather than to exemplify sex differences per se. Adding a new line of interpretation, based on the imagery of the girl's thought, makes it possible not only to see development where previously development was not discerned but also to consider differences in the understanding of relationships without scaling these differences from better to worse.

The two children were in the same sixth-grade class at school and were participants in the rights and responsibilities study, designed to explore different conceptions of morality and self. The sample selected for this study was chosen to focus the variables of gender and age while maximizing developmental potential by holding constant, at a high level, the factors of intelligence, education, and social class that have been associated with moral development, at least as measured by existing scales. The two children in question, Amy and Jake, were both bright and articulate and, at least in their eleven-year-old aspirations, resisted easy categories of sex-role stereotyping, since Amy aspired to become a scientist while Jake preferred English to math. Yet their moral judgments seem initially to confirm familiar notions about differences between the sexes, suggesting that the edge girls have on moral development during the early school years gives way at puberty with the ascendance of formal logical thought in boys.

The dilemma that these eleven-year-olds were asked to resolve was one in the series devised by Kohlberg to measure moral development in adolescence by presenting a conflict between moral norms and exploring the logic of its resolution. In this particular dilemma, a man named Heinz considers whether or not to steal a drug which he cannot afford to buy in order to save the life of his wife. In the standard format of Kohlberg's interviewing procedure, the description of the dilemma itself—Heinz's predicament, the wife's disease, the druggist's refusal to lower his price—is followed by the question, "Should Heinz steal the drug?" The reasons for and against stealing are then explored through a series of questions that vary and extend the parameters of the dilemma in a way designed to reveal the underlying structure of moral thought.

Jake, at eleven, is clear from the outset that Heinz should steal the drug. Constructing the dilemma, as Kohlberg did, as a conflict between the values of property and life, he discerns the logical priority of life and uses that logic to justify his choice:

> For one thing, a human life is worth more than money, and if the druggist only makes $1,000, he is still going to live, but if Heinz doesn't steal the drug, his wife is going to die. (*Why is life worth more than money?*) Because the druggist can get a thousand dollars later from rich people with cancer, but Heinz can't get his wife again. (*Why not?*) Because people are all different and so you couldn't get Heinz's wife again.

Asked whether Heinz should steal the drug if he does not love his wife, Jake replies that he should, saying that not only is there "a difference between hating and killing," but also, if Heinz were caught, "the judge would probably think it was the right thing to do." Asked about the fact that, in stealing, Heinz would be breaking the law, he says that "the laws have mistakes, and you can't go writing up a law for everything that you can imagine."

Thus, while taking the law into account and recognizing its function in maintaining social order (the judge, Jake says, "should give Heinz the lightest possible sentence"), he also sees the law as manmade and therefore subject to error and change. Yet his judgment that Heinz should steal the drug, like his view of the law as having mistakes, rests on the assumption of agreement, a societal consensus around moral values that allows one to know and expect others to recognize what is "the right thing to do."

Fascinated by the power of logic, this eleven-year-old boy locates truth in math, which, he says, is "the only thing that is totally logical." Considering the moral dilemma to be "sort of like a math problem with humans," he sets it up as an equation and proceeds to work out the solution. Since his solution is rationally derived, he assumes that anyone following reason would arrive at the same conclusion and thus that a judge would also consider stealing to be the right thing for Heinz to do. Yet he is also aware of the limits of logic. Asked whether there is a right answer to moral problems, Jake replies that "there can only be right and wrong in judgment," since the parameters of action are variable and complex. Illustrating how actions undertaken with the best of intentions can eventuate in the most disastrous of consequences, he says, "like if you give an old lady your seat on the trolley, if you are in a trolley crash and that seat goes through the window, it might be that reason that the old lady dies."

Theories of developmental psychology illuminate well the position of this child, standing at the juncture of childhood and adolescence, at what Piaget describes as the pinnacle of childhood intelligence, and beginning through thought to discover a wider universe of possibility. The moment of preadolescence is caught by the conjunction of formal operational thought with a description of self still anchored in the factual parameters of his childhood world—his age, his town, his father's occupation, the substance of his likes, dislikes, and beliefs. Yet as his self-description radiates the self-confidence of a child who has arrived, in Erikson's terms, at a favorable balance of industry over inferiority—competent, sure of himself, and knowing well the rules of the game—so his emergent capacity for formal thought, his ability to think about thinking and to reason things out in a logical way, frees him from dependence on authority and allows him to find solutions to problems by himself.

This emergent autonomy follows the trajectory that Kohlberg's six stages of moral development trace, a three-level progression from an egocentric understanding of fairness based on individual need (stages one and two), to a conception of fairness anchored in the shared conventions of societal agreement (stages three and four), and finally to a principled understanding of fairness that rests on the free-standing logic of equality and reciprocity (stages five and six). While this boy's judgments at eleven are scored as conventional on Kohlberg's scale, a mixture of stages three and four, his ability to bring deductive logic to bear on the solution of moral dilemmas, to differentiate morality from law, and to see how laws can be considered to have mistakes points toward the principled conception of justice that Kohlberg equates with moral maturity.

In contrast, Amy's response to the dilemma conveys a very different impression, an image of development stunted by a failure of logic, an inability to think for herself. Asked if Heinz should steal the drug, she replies in a way that seems evasive and unsure:

> Well, I don't think so. I think there might be other ways besides stealing it, like if he could borrow the money or make a loan or something, but he really shouldn't steal the drug—but his wife shouldn't die either.

Asked why he should not steal the drug, she considers neither property nor law but rather the effect that theft could have on the relationship between Heinz and his wife:

> If he stole the drug, he might save his wife then, but if he did, he might have to go to jail, and then his wife might get sicker again, and he couldn't get more of the drug, and it might not be good. So, they should really just talk it out and find some other way to make the money.

Seeing in the dilemma not a math problem with humans but a narrative of relationships that extends over time, Amy envisions the wife's continuing need for her husband and the husband's continuing concern for his wife and seeks to respond to the druggist's need in a way that would sustain rather than sever connection. Just as she ties the wife's survival to the preservation of relationships, so she considers the value of the wife's life in a context of relationships, saying that it would be wrong to let her die because, "if she died, it hurts a lot of people and it hurts her." Since Amy's moral judgment is grounded in the belief that, "if somebody has something that would keep somebody alive, then it's not right not to give it to them," she considers the problem in the dilemma to arise not from the druggist's assertion of rights but from his failure of response.

As the interviewer proceeds with the series of questions that follow from Kohlberg's construction of the dilemma, Amy's answers remain essentially unchanged, the various probes serving neither to elucidate nor to modify her initial response. Whether or not Heinz loves his wife, he still shouldn't steal or let her die; if it were a stranger dying instead, Amy says that "if the stranger didn't have anybody near or anyone she knew," then Heinz should try to save her life, but he should not steal the drug. But as the interviewer conveys through the repetition of questions that the answers she gave were not heard or not right, Amy's confidence begins to diminish, and her replies become more constrained and unsure. Asked again why Heinz should not steal the drug, she simply repeats, "Because it's not right." Asked again to explain why, she states again that theft would not be a good solution, adding lamely, "if he took it, he might not know how to give it to his wife, and so his wife might still die." Failing to see the dilemma as a self-contained problem in moral logic, she does not discern the internal structure of its resolution; as she constructs the problem differently herself, Kohlberg's conception completely evades her.

Instead, seeing a world comprised of relationships rather than of people standing alone, a world that coheres through human connection rather than through systems of rules, she finds the puzzle in the dilemma to lie in the failure of the druggist to respond to the wife. Saying that "it is not right for someone to die when their life could be saved," she assumes that if the druggist were to see the consequences of his refusal to lower his price, he would realize that "he should just give it to the wife and then have the husband pay back the money later." Thus she considers the solution to the dilemma to lie in making the wife's condition more salient to the druggist or, that failing, in appealing to others who are in a position to help.

Just as Jake is confident the judge would agree that stealing is the right thing for Heinz to do, so Amy is confident that, "if Heinz and the druggest had talked it out long enough, they could reach something besides stealing." As he considers the law to "have mistakes," so she sees this drama as a mistake, believing that the world should just share things more and then people wouldn't have to steal." Both children thus recognize the need for agreement but see it as mediated in different ways—he impersonally through systems of logic and law, she personally through communication in relationship. Just as he relies on the conventions of logic to deduce the solution to this dilemma, assuming these conventions to be shared, so she relies on a process of communication, assuming connection and believing that her voice will be heard. Yet while his assumptions about agreement are confirmed by the convergence in logic between his answers and the questions posed, her assumptions are belied by the failure of communication, the interviewer's inability to understand her response.

Although the frustration of the interview with Amy is apparent in the repetition of questions and its ultimate circularity, the problem of interpretation is focused by the assessment of her response. When considered in the light of Kohlberg's definition of the stages and sequence of moral development, her moral judgments appear to be a full stage lower in maturity than those of the boy. Scored as a mixture of stages two and three, her responses seem to reveal a feeling of powerlessness in the world, an inability to think systematically about the concepts of morality or law, a reluctance to challenge authority or to examine the logic of received moral truths, a failure even to conceive of acting directly to save a life or to consider that such action, if taken, could possibly have an effect. As her reliance on relationships seems to reveal a continuing dependence and vulnerability, so her belief in communication as the mode through which to resolve moral dilemmas appears naive and cognitively immature.

Yet Amy's description of herself conveys a markedly different impression. Once again, the hallmarks of the preadolescent child depict a child secure in her sense of herself, confident in the substance of her beliefs, and sure of her ability to do something of value in the world. Describing herself at eleven as "growing and changing," she says that she "sees some things differently now, just because I know myself really well now, and I know a lot more about the world." Yet the world she knows is a different world from that refracted by Kohlberg's construction of Heinz's dilemma. Her world is a world of relationships and psychological truths where an awareness of the connection between people gives rise to a recognition of responsibility for one another, a perception of the need for response. Seen in this light, her understanding of morality as arising from the recognition of relationship, her belief in communication as the mode of conflict resolution, and her conviction that the solution to the dilemma will follow from its compelling representation seem far from naive or cognitively immature. Instead, Amy's judgments contain the insights central to an ethic of care, just as Jake's judgments reflect the logic of the justice approach. Her incipient awareness of the "method of truth," the central tenet of nonviolent conflict resolution, and her belief in the restorative activity of care, lead her to see the actors in the dilemma arrayed not as opponents in a contest of rights but as members of a network of relationships on whose continuation they all depend. Consequently her solution to the dilemma lies in activating the network by communication, securing the inclusion of the wife by strengthening rather than severing connections.

But the different logic of Amy's response calls attention to the interpretation of the interview itself. Conceived as an interrogation, it appears instead as a dialogue, which takes on moral dimensions of its own, pertaining to the interviewer's uses of power and to the manifestations of respect. With this shift in the conception of the interview, it immediately becomes clear that the interviewer's problem in understanding Amy's response stems from the fact that Amy is answering a different question from the one the interviewer thought had been posed. Amy is considering not *whether* Heinz should act in this situation ("*should* Heinz steal the drug?") but rather *how* Heinz should act in response to his awareness of his wife's need ("Should Heinz *steal* the drug?"). The interviewer takes the mode of action for granted, presuming it to be a matter of fact; Amy assumes the necessity for action and considers what form it should take. In the interviewer's failure to imagine a response not dreamt of in Kohlberg's moral philosophy lies the failure to hear Amy's question and to see the logic in her response, to discern that what appears, from one perspective, to be an evasion of the dilemma signifies in other terms a recognition of the problem and a search for a more adequate solution.

Thus in Heinz's dilemma these two children see two very different moral problems—Jake a conflict between life and property that can be resolved by logical deduction, Amy a fracture of human relationship that must be mended with its own thread. Asking different questions that arise from different conceptions of the moral domain, the children arrive at answers that fundamentally diverge, and the arrangement of these answers as successive stages on a scale of increasing moral maturity calibrated by the logic of the boy's response misses the different truth revealed in the judgment of the girl. To the question, "What does he see that she does not?" Kohlberg's theory provides a ready response, manifest in the scoring of Jake's judgments a full stage higher than Amy's in moral maturity; to the question, "What does she see that he does not?" Kohlberg's theory has nothing to say. Since most of her responses fall through the sieve of Kohlberg's scoring system, her responses appear from his perspective to lie outside the moral domain.

Yet just as Jake reveals a sophisticated understanding of the logic of justification, so Amy is equally sophisticated in her understanding of the nature of choice. Recognizing that "if both the roads went in totally separate ways, if you pick one, you'll never know what would happen if you went the other way," she explains that "that's the chance you have to take, and like I said, it's just really a guess." To illustrate her point "in a simple way," she describes her choice to spend the summer at camp:

> I will never know what would have happened if I had stayed here, and if something goes wrong at camp, I'll never know if I stayed here if it would have been better. There's really no way around it because

there's no way you can do both at once, so you've got to decide, but you'll never know.

In this way, these two eleven-year-old children, both highly intelligent and perceptive about life, though in different ways, display different modes of moral understanding, different ways of thinking about conflict and choice. In resolving Heinz's dilemma, Jake relies on theft to avoid confrontation and turns to the law to mediate the dispute. Transposing a hierarchy of power into a hierarchy of values, he defuses a potentially explosive conflict between people by casting it as an impersonal conflict of claims. In this way, he abstracts the moral problem from the interpersonal situation, finding in the Logic of fairness an objective way to decide who will win the dispute. But this hierarchical ordering, with its imagery of winning and losing and the potential for violence which it contains, gives way in Amy's construction of the dilemma to a network of connection, a web of relationships that is sustained by a process of communication. With this shift, the moral problem changes from one of unfair domination, the imposition of property over life, to one of unnecessary exclusion, the failure of the druggist to respond to the wife.

This shift in the formulation of the moral problem and the concomitant change in the imagery of relationships appear in the responses of two eight-year-old children, Jeffrey and Karen, asked to describe a situation in which they were not sure what was the right thing to do:

JEFFREY   When I really want to go to my friends and my mother is cleaning the cellar, I think about my friends, and then I think about my mother, and then I think about the right thing to do. (*But how do you know it's the right thing to do?*)

Because some things go before other things.

KAREN   I have a lot of friends, and I can't always play with all of them, so everybody's going to have to take a turn, because they're all my friends. But like if someone's all alone, I'll play with them. (*What kinds of things do you think about when you are trying to make that decision?*) Um, someone all alone, loneliness.

While Jeffrey sets up a hierarchical ordering to resolve a conflict between desire and duty, Karen describes a network of relationships that includes all of her friends. Both children deal with the issues of exclusion and priority created by choice, but while Jeffrey thinks about what goes first, Karen focuses on who is left out.

The contrasting images of hierarchy and network in children's thinking about moral conflict and choice illuminate two views of morality which are complementary rather than sequential or opposed. But this construction of differences goes against the bias of developmental theory toward ordering differences in a hierarchical mode. The correspondence between the order of developmental theory and the structure of the boys' thought contrasts with the disparity between existing theory and the structure manifest in the thought of the girls. Yet in neither comparison does one child's judgment appear as a precursor of the other's position. Thus, questions arise concerning the relation between these perspectives: what is the significance of this difference, and how do these two modes of thinking connect? These questions are elucidated by considering the relationship between the eleven-year-old children's understanding of morality and their descriptions of themselves:

(How would you describe yourself to yourself?)

JAKE Perfect. That's my conceited side. What do you want—any way that I choose to describe myself?

AMY You mean my character? (*What do you think?*) Well, I don't know. I'd describe myself as, well, what do you mean?

(If you had to describe the person you are in a way that you yourself would know it was you, what would you say?)

JAKE I'd start off with eleven years old. Jake [last name]. I'd have to add that I live in [town], because that is a big part of me, and also that my father is a doctor, because I think that does change me a little bit, and that I don't believe in crime, except for when your name is Heinz; think school is boring, because I think that kind of changes your character a little bit. I don't sort of know how to describe myself, because I don't know how to read my personality. (*If you had to describe the way you actually would describe yourself what would you say?*) I like corny jokes. I don't really like to get down to work, but I can do all the stuff in school. Every single problem that I have seen in school I have been able to do, except for ones that take knowledge, and after I do the reading, I have been able to do them, but sometimes I don't want to waste my time on easy homework. And also I'm crazy about sports. I think, unlike a lot of people, that the world still has hope . . . Most people that I know I like, and I have the good life, pretty much as good as any I have seen, and I am tall for my age.

AMY Well, I'd say that I was someone who likes school and studying, and that's what I want to do with my life. I want to be some kind of a scientist or something, and I want to do things, and I want to help people. And I think that's what kind of person I am, or what kind of person I try to be. And that's probably how I'd describe myself. And I want to do something to help other people. (*Why is that?*) Well, because I think that this world has a lot of problems, and I think that everybody should try to help somebody else in some way, and the way I'm choosing is through science.

In the voice of the eleven-year-old boy, a familiar form of self-definition appears, resonating to the inscription of the young Stephen Daedalus in his geography book: "himself, his name and where he was," and echoing the descriptions that appear in *Our Town*, laying out across the coordinates of time and space a hierarchical order in which to define one's place. Describing himself as distinct by locating his particular position in the world, Jake sets himself apart from that world by his abilities, his beliefs, and his height. Although Amy also enumerates her likes, her wants, and her beliefs, she locates herself in relation to the world, describing herself through actions that bring her into connection with others, elaborating ties through her ability to provide help. To Jake's ideal of perfection, against which he measures the worth of himself, Amy counterposes an ideal of care, against which she measures the worth of her activity. While she places herself in relation to the world and chooses to help others through science, he places the world in relation to himself as it defines his character, his position, and the quality of his life.

The contrast between a self defined through separation and a self delineated through connection, between a self measured against an abstract ideal of perfection and a self assessed through particular activities of care, becomes clearer and the implications of this contrast extend by considering the different ways these children resolve a conflict between responsibility to others and responsibility to self. The question about responsibility followed a dilemma posed by a woman's conflict between her commitments to work and to family relationships. While the details of this conflict color the text of Amy's response, Jake abstracts the problem of responsibility from the context in which it appears, replacing the themes of intimate relationship with his own imagery of explosive connection:

(When responsibility to oneself and responsibility to others conflict, how should one choose?)

JAKE   You go about one-fourth to the others and three-fourths to yourself.

AMY   Well, it really depends on the situation. If you have a responsibility with somebody else, then you should keep it to a certain extent, but to the extent that it is really going to hurt you or stop you from doing something that you really, really want, then I think maybe you should put yourself first. But if it is your responsibility to somebody really close to you, you've just got to decide in that situation which is more important, yourself or that person, and like I said, it really depends on what kind of person you are and how you feel about the other person or persons involved.

(Why?)

JAKE   Because the most important thing in your decision should be yourself, don't let yourself be guided totally by other people, but you have to take them into consideration. So, if what you want to do is blow yourself up with an atom bomb, you should maybe blow yourself up with a hand grenade because you are thinking about your neighbors who would die also.

AMY   Well, like some people put themselves and things for themselves before they put other people, and some people really care about other people. Like, I don't think your job is as important as somebody that you really love, like your husband or your parents or a very close friend. Somebody that you really care for—or if it's just your responsibility to your job or somebody that you barely know, then maybe you go first—but if it's somebody that you really love and love as much or even more than you love yourself, you've got to decide what you really love more, that person, or that thing, or yourself. (*And how do you do that?*) Well, you've got to think about it, and you've got to think about both sides, and you've got to think which would be better for everybody or better for yourself, which is more important, and which will make everybody happier. Like if the other people can get somebody else to do it, whatever it is, or don't really need you specifically, maybe it's better to do what you want, because the other people will be just fine with somebody else so they'll still be happy, and then you'll be happy too because you'll do what you want.

(What does responsibility mean?)

JAKE   It means pretty much thinking of others when I do something, and like if I want to throw a rock, not throwing it at a window, because I thought of the people who would have to pay for that window, not doing it just for yourself, because you have to live with other people and live with your community, and if you do something that hurts them all, a lot of people will end up suffering, and that is sort of the wrong thing to do.

AMY That other people are counting on you to do something, and you can't just decide, "Well, I'd rather do this or that." (*Are there other kinds of responsibility?*) Well, to yourself. If something looks really fun but you might hurt yourself doing it because you don't really know how to do it and your friends say, "Well, come on, you can do it, don't worry," if you're really scared to do it, it's your responsibility to yourself that if you think you might hurt yourself, you shouldn't do it, because you have to take care of yourself and that's your responsibility to yourself.

Again Jake constructs the dilemma as a mathematical equation, deriving a formula that guides the solution: one-fourth to others, three-fourths to yourself. Beginning with his responsibility to himself, a responsibility that he takes for granted, he then considers the extent to which he is responsible to others as well. Proceeding from a premise of separation but recognizing that "you have to live with other people," he seeks rules to limit interference and thus to minimize hurt. Responsibility in his construction pertains to a limitation of action, a restraint of aggression, guided by the recognition that his actions can have effects on others, just as theirs can interfere with him. Thus rules, by limiting interference, make life in community safe, protecting autonomy through reciprocity, extending the same consideration to others and self.

To the question about conflicting responsibilities, Amy again responds contextually rather than categorically, saying "it depends" and indicating how choice would be affected by variations in character and circumstance. Proceeding from a premise of connection, that "if you have a responsibility *with* somebody else, you

should keep it," she then considers the extent to which she has a responsibility to herself. Exploring the parameters of separation, she imagines situations where, by doing what you want, you would avoid hurting yourself or where, in doing so, you would not thereby diminish the happiness of others. To her, responsibility signifies response, an extension rather than a limitation of action. Thus it connotes an act of care rather than the restraint of aggression. Again seeking the solution that would be most inclusive of everyone's needs, she strives to resolve the dilemma in a way that "will make everybody happier." Since Jake is concerned with limiting interference, while Amy focuses on the need for response, for him the limiting condition is, "Don't let yourself be guided totally by others," but for her it arises when "other people are counting on you," in which case "you can't just decide, 'Well, I'd rather do this or that.'" The interplay between these responses is clear in that she, assuming connection, begins to explore the parameters of separation, while he, assuming separation, begins to explore the parameters of connection. But the primacy of separation or connection leads to different images of self and of relationships.

Most striking among these differences is the imagery of violence in the boy's response, depicting a world of dangerous confrontation and explosive connection, where she sees a world of care and protection, a life lived with others whom "you may love as much or even more than you love yourself." Since the conception of morality reflects the understanding of social relationships, this difference in the imagery of relationships gives rise to a change in the moral injunction itself. To Jake, responsibility means *not doing* what he wants because he is thinking of others;

to Amy, it means *doing* what others are counting on her to do regardless of what she herself wants. Both children are concerned with avoiding hurt but construe the problem in different ways—he seeing hurt to arise from the expression of aggression, she from a failure of response.

NOTE

1. Sigmund Freud, "On Narcissism: An Introduction," 1914, in Vol. XIV of *The Standard Edition of the Complete Psychological Writings of Sigmund Freud*, trans. and ed. James Strachey, London: The Hogarth Press, 1961.

Of Mothers and Families, Men and Sex

Marilyn Friedman

Marilyn Friedman is a professor of philosophy at Washington University in St. Louis. She is the author of What Are Friends For? *(1993), and co-author of* Political Correctness: For and Against *(1995). She is also the co-editor of* Feminism and Community *(1995), and* Mind and Morals *(1996).*

Friedman presents an argument against traditional male roles in marriage, family, and heterosexual relations. She presents a feminist response to these traditional gender roles that is supportive of mothers and not opposed to sex, contrary to the way that feminism is often portrayed. She concludes with an explanation of why men are in many ways morally responsible for harms to women.

A sex/gender system, in general, comprises the many aspects of a social system that differentiate persons based on their sex or gender. The differentiations, in turn, bear significantly on the identities, roles, norms, ideals, expectations, opportunities and constraints that pertain to people.

There is no doubt that all human societies feature a sex/gender system of some sort. The institutions of sexuality, marriage, child rearing, productive activity, military defense, and governing, in most human societies, allocate roles partly according to gender. In addition, most human societies sustain these wide-ranging roles with a host of child rearing and

From *Political Correctness: For and Against.* Reprinted with permission of Rowan & Littlefield.

other practices that promote in females and males the personality traits and identifications appropriate to their assigned gender roles and that discourage or forbid outright their participation in the roles of the *other* gender. The real issue is not *whether* we have a sex/gender system; *obviously* we have one.[1] The real controversies have to do with its nature and origin and the extent to which it benefits or harms women.

Feminists generally believe that the sex/gender system of the United States involves widespread male dominance and female subordination. This particular view is one that we can debate. To argue intelligently against this view, however, calls for careful reconsideration of a good deal of evidence in its favor.[2] It should be debated on both moral and empirical grounds.

I. MOTHERS AND FAMILIES

Social commentators who praise "family values" usually have in mind the values of the so-called "traditional family." The traditional family is a nuclear family consisting of a legally married heterosexual couple and their children, in which the man is the principal breadwinner and head of the household and the woman is responsible for all, or nearly all, the domestic work and child care. As early as 1977, however, this family form comprised only 16 percent of all U.S. households, according to the U.S. Census Bureau.[3]

A family is, generically speaking, any group of persons who together form a household based at least partly on some sort of enduring interpersonal commitment. Legally or religiously sanctioned marriage is one example of such a commitment but it is hardly the only one. The concept of an enduring household captures the core idea of family life, and it has the credibility of having appeared in dictionary definitions of "family" even before the recent wave of the feminist movement.[4]

The notion of an enduring household does not resonate with greeting card sentimentality, however—and that is its distinct theoretical advantage. The point of the conception is to serve as an analytical category to enable understanding of the institution. To understand contemporary families in their diversity, we need a generic concept of family life that does not presuppose any norms about who is supposed to do what. Family norms should be debated as separately as possible from the relevant descriptive categories.[5]

Defining family generically as any enduring household based on interpersonal commitment allows us to acknowledge the familyness of all sorts of domestic relationships. We already know (although some of us mindlessly forget) that families by *adoption* are genuine families and, thus, that biological links between parents and children are not necessary for family life. It is now high time to give social recognition and support to families comprised of heterosexual couples who are not married (with or without children), heterosexual couples who do not abide by traditional gender roles in domestic tasks or child rearing, lesbian and gay couples (with or without children), and single parents with children.

Any stable and nonoppressive domestic relationship will constitute a better family environment if it is, in turn, sustained by a respectful and supportive community that grants it all the privileges of family life. Feminists work to support nontraditional families, which sadly still receive substantially fewer of the privileges reserved for traditionally correct families (privileges such as inheritance rights and family health insurance) and which suffer a great deal of social stigma instead. In supporting nontraditional families, feminists promote family life more extensively and more thoroughly than our opponents who otherwise intone family values. Feminists, thus, do not oppose family life as such. Far from it. We are just as concerned as anyone else that the familial dimensions of our lives and our various enduring domestic relationships satisfy the needs and promote the flourishing of their participants—all of their participants. It is society at large, not feminists, that, by neglecting or denying the needs of *nontraditional* families, is currently forsaking family life.

When feminists criticize family life, our targets are usually male family dominance and the female dependency that it promotes and enforces. It is patently obvious that to criticize this form of family life is not to oppose family life as such.

The notion of the traditional family is ambiguous. Heterosexual marriages are traditional in one respect when the husband is the sole income provider and the wife is responsible for the domestic work and primary parenting. A woman who participates in this sort of relationship is not necessarily dominated by her husband. Heterosexual marriages, however, are traditional in a different, and objectionable, manner when husbands make all the major decisions for their family units, exercise ultimate control over the spending of money, and generally hold topmost authority and power in their homes.

In the mildest forms of male dominance, husband/fathers love and protect their wives and children with wisdom and kindness. Mild male dominance is benevolent paternalism.[6] In the most virulent forms of male dominance, husbands beat up their wives and children and generally tyrannize over their households. Many people will concede that tyrannical husbands are a nasty lot. Despite this concession, however, traditional social practices and institutions have often shamefully tolerated such men.[7] Part of the feminist fight against male family domination has been the uphill struggle to make social institutions more punitive toward such abuses as wife-battering, marital rape, and incest. Feminists have also argued that even seemingly *benevolent* male family paternalism is a problem for women in traditional family roles.

A woman who creates a loving and supportive home life for her family members gives them a moral as well as a material gift; such activities can be the source of deep and justified satisfaction for her.

Child rearing, even more so, is a domain of breathtaking challenges and transcendent rewards. Child rearing is also a paramount social necessity; when done well, it is a veritable public service. A woman who chooses full-time homemaking and mothering is choosing one of the various honorable vocations now available to women.

There is nothing particularly honorable, however, about the subordination of women to men. There is no reason why a woman who chooses full-time homemaking and mothering should therefore relinquish to her husband her own autonomous selfhood or an equal share of legitimate control over the home *she makes* or the family *she is raising*. The philosophical tradition is rich with praise for self-determination and the importance of being a "free man." Until the recent decades of contemporary feminism, however, the ideals of liberty and autonomy were *never* applied by conventional (usually male) philosophers to traditional female roles.

To be sure, the concern for self-determination can devolve into a narrow moral obsession that obscures the self-enlarging values of community and relationships with others. Nevertheless, substantial self-determination is an important counterbalance to the requirements of endless service and self-sacrifice that threaten to deplete the moral resources of the traditional wife/mother role. At stake is the legitimacy of women following our own considered judgments about what is worth valuing and pursuing in the lives we make for ourselves and our families. It is no less than a question of women's moral integrity.

Male family dominance threatens more than a woman's moral integrity; it also threatens her own material well-being and that of her children. A woman who is a full-time homemaker and mother in a heterosexual marriage is economically dependent on, and therefore vulnerable to, her husband in a variety of ways.[8] For financial reasons alone, she much more than he needs the marriage to persist. Her financial standard of living would likely plummet after divorce while his would almost certainly rise. Because her income-earning husband can profitably leave the marriage at any time if he does not get his way, she has more need to please and defer to him than vice versa in those inevitable situations in which their desires or values conflict.[9] One overriding concern that keeps many battered women tied to their violent husbands is the fear of losing financial support, a paramount consideration when children are involved.

A woman who chooses life as a full-time homemaker and mother surely does not choose, *for its own sake*, the subordination and excessive vulnerability that she risks by her financial dependence on her husband. These hazards, however, inhere in the nature of financial dependence. Add to that the cultural ideals of masculinity with their incessant pressure on men to be strong, decisive, aggressive, and forceful—and the risks for women only intensify.

To be sure, there have always been some women who were strong and independent enough to stand up to their husbands for the views and values to which they were committed. There have also, fortunately, been men who did not avail themselves of the power provided by their breadwinning status and legitimized by masculine ideals. There are, in other words, genuinely good men.[10] Such men, however, run the risk of being socially stigmatized as wimps. The comic, though often sympathetic, figure of the "henpecked husband" only makes sense against a background presumption that men ought to

prevail in their marriages. "Taming" the "shrew" is, after all, part of the Western canon. The rooster-pecked wife, by contrast, is not even a recognized category. Remember that it was *his* castle, not hers, the place where he was supposed to rule supreme.

If women are to choose their ways of life with some measure of autonomy and wisdom, then they should be informed about the risks inherent in the available options. To criticize male-dominant families for the risks and oppressions that they pose for women is not to criticize the women who choose such arrangements. Rather, it is to challenge uncritical and overly romantic cultural images of those male-dominant marriage and family forms. Women, depending on their circumstances, might well derive satisfactions within male-dominated marriages and families—but at what cost? The fact that some people are content with certain social arrangements is hardly a conclusive reason to avoid questioning those arrangements.

Some critics have, nevertheless, tried to undermine feminist challenges to *male-dominated* family life by claiming that such families are beneficial for women and that women secretly recognize this. The philosopher and social critic, Alan Bloom, has argued this line.

Bloom has the candor to admit that the "old family arrangements" were not entirely good for women. He concedes that because of economic changes and the recognition of injustices, "the feminist case [against the old family arrangements] is very strong indeed." The problem, in Bloom's view, is that there are no "viable substitutes." Macho men can be "softened" but they cannot be made caring, sensitive, or nurturant. Men will make positive contributions to family life only in the old-fashioned families in which they can exercise power and protectiveness over "weak," "modest," "blushing" women (Bloom's words). Women's independence, however, diminishes men's motivations for staying thus married and providing for children. And women' s premarital sexual independence reduces men's motivations for getting married in the first place. "Women can say they do not care," about this loss of men's interest in them, warns Bloom, "but everyone, and they best of all, knows that they are being, at most, only half truthful with themselves."[11]

This antifeminist theme has a cunning seductiveness to it. It avoids the argument that feminism is bad because it hurts men, an argument that, we must admit, will not necessarily deter women from joining the ranks. Bloom argues instead that feminism *hurts women*. If the very people who might be attracted to feminism can be convinced that feminism is bad *for them*, then there is some chance of stopping the spread of this contagion. The argument hinges on two claims: first, by becoming feminist (too independent, too self-reliant), women will lose male love and male commitment to marriage and family; and second, women *really* want male love and commitment more than we want independence—*regardless of what we might think*.

This message evokes the age-old genre of cliches that warn women not to be too sensible or too self-reliant in our habits. Not too long ago, women were routinely admonished: "men don't make tracks for girls who wear slacks," and "men don't make passes at girls who wear glasses."[12] (In the days before contact lenses, the latter meant giving up clear sightedness in order to please men.) Since our cultural traditions give so little public recognition or esteem to love and friendship among women ourselves, the threat of a woman's being unloved by a man has the public meaning of being unloved period. What women, other than lesbians, would not be made a little anxious by these sorts of messages?

II. SEX

Unfortunately, sexual libertinism has yet to face the sexual crises of the 1990s. We are a culture deeply confused about sex. We live in a world so burgeoning with population that some commentators already warn of imminent brutal, militaristic, global anarchy.[13] We live in an era when individual sexual contact can be a death-defying act. Eros has become Thanatos. We bemoan, in one breath, the problems of rampant teenage pregnancy, global overcrowding, and sexually transmitted diseases, yet, in the next breath, scold feminists for their prudery. Go figure.

Amidst all this sexual chaos, the antiseptic and well-worn notion of informed consent offers some individual and local guidance to women. Informed consent is a person's right of self-protection against the serious risks posed by sexual contact. Informed consent, however, must be genuine. Despite her raptures the next morning, Scarlett O'Hara never did consent to Rhett Butler dragging her up the stairs for some sexual brutality at his but not her instigation.[14] Even when no coercion or pressure are involved, a woman has not given informed consent unless she has both a clear understanding of the risks involved and the genuine option throughout her sexual encounters of protecting herself against those risks with contraception and prophylaxis—or refusal. If it is sex-phobic to say so, then perhaps our culture needs more sex-phobia.

We can no longer afford to view with tolerant amusement the glorification of male sexual aggression or the myth that women in general enjoy it. Apart from the question of women's right to protect ourselves against risky sexual contact, the idea that we enjoy sexual domination is, to say the least, perplexing. It is an odd psychology that would see no need to explain why someone enjoyed being dominated or humiliated, sexually or otherwise, and a still odder sociology that would unquestioningly attribute this phenomenon to whole groups.

The societal conditions that could promote and explain female sexual masochism are not hard to find. Typical patterns of gender socialization combine with mass media, advertising, and other cultural institutions to feed us a steady diet of messages that glorify and eroticize male sexual aggression and male sexual domination of women. Mass media and advertising compound the problem by relentlessly urging women to shape our sexuality around pleasing men—in our appearance, behavior, and sexual responses.

Critics of feminism might charge that this analysis is patronizing (matronizing?) toward women. That facile response, however, would miss the mark. For one thing, it is not only women, but men as well, whose desires are affected by socialization and cultural images. For another thing, an entire advertising industry is built on the conviction that media images and messages do significantly impinge on human desires. Are advertisers really just wasting our time and their financial millions? While the research is often inconclusive and the notion of strict determination overstates the case, nevertheless, many studies reveal complex effects of mass media on people's attitudes.[15] Why suppose that women would be immune to these influences or that it would not affect one of the most plastic of human passions, sexual desire?

Media portrayals of heterosexuality that endorse, routinize, and eroticize men's domination of women and women's deference to men are the key problem. How we solve the problem is, of course, an open question. Nothing about feminist critiques of those media entails the view that individual women—or even, with more reason, men—should be "forced to be free."[16] I am not, that is, advocating that anyone be legally denied her pound of pornography or put through nonconsensual sex sensitivity training. Cultural dialogue about the issues is the approach that I and most other feminists seek. The cultural dialogue about sexuality is obstructed, however, when feminists who criticize male-dominant heterosexuality are condemned, for example, by Camille Paglia as "sex-phobic" or by Christina Sommers as totalitarian "Big Sisters" out to enforce "boring" "sexual correctness" on innocent women.

When sex can lead to unwanted pregnancy or a fatal disease, it ought to be obvious to everyone that no one should be pressured to engage in it and no one should be denied an informed understanding of what is going on. Women should have full and genuine control over our sexuality. This has been a feminist credo from the start. Media representations of male sexual conquest, no matter how titillating to some consumers, glorify nothing less than women's loss of sexual control and consequent inability to protect ourselves in a crucial realm of our lives. "Sexual correctness," or, more perspicuously, *heterosexuality without male domination*, may offend the sensibilities of some, but the gain in women's control is well worth the cost. And when it comes to sexual pleasure, only a sadly limited range of experience or a failure of imagination could underlie the insistence that sex minus male domination is "boring."

When a woman is "locked" in a man's embrace, she may become aroused by the "bonds" of love and want the sexual contact to continue. Her compliance under those conditions, however, is hardly the sort of self-protective, informed consent that she needs these days for her own safety. The precipitous urgency of sexual arousal does not by itself provide any reason to trust a man's assurance *at the time* that, yes, he had a vasectomy and, of course, he is HIV-negative.[17] The possibility that some women like male-dominated sex should not undercut our critical reflection on it. We, as a community, can still ask ourselves whether we want to continue supporting cultural glorifications of women being coerced, pressured, or seduced into sexual encounters over which they exercise no control.

Sex is no longer just a playful pastime and the means of reproduction; sex has become a matter of life and death. *It ain't the '60s anymore.* Sexual (as well as nonsexual) images of men dominating women and women submitting to men have always been demeaning to women. In the 1990s, they represent a dangerous frivolity we cannot afford.

III. RESENTMENT AGAINST MEN

In order for women to focus their energies, loves, and loyalties on other women, they must usually redirect some of their attention and support away from men.[18] As women begin to value and cherish each other more, their interest in men in gener-al, and most men in the particular, inevitably declines. Women who are intensely focused on other women might ignore men altogether. Women also sometimes get angry at men who oppose the improvements that women seek for their own lives. In addition, women who spend time challenging male-dominated social institutions often become less reverent toward, even overtly critical of, the male achievements and authority buttressed by those institutions. At what costs were they achieved? To what ends have they been put? Whose domestic service made them possible?, and so on.

When women grow indifferent or angry toward men, criticize male-domination, or challenge male authority and power, it is not surprising that men will feel this reaction as hostility and resentment directed at them. Those masculine feelings, however, are *not* the right measure for understanding women's attitudes. To think so perpetuates the very problem at issue by interpreting women's behavior and attitudes exclusively in terms of how they make men feel.[19] My point, to the contrary, is that an attitude that might appear to some people to be antimale is really *pro-female*, a very different attitude—and one that our culture at large still widely misunderstands.

Even if feminism does foster genuine and positive resentment against men, this attitude is only a problem if it is unjustified. Is it unjustified? Is it *false* that many women are significantly exploited, abused, or subordinated either by individual men or by male-dominated social practices or institutions?

My dictionary defines resentment as "anger and ill will in view of real or fancied wrong or injury."[20] Ill will is often a useless emotion, like spite or malicious envy, and may hurt most the one who feels it. No feminist wants women merely to reverberate with feelings of useless malice. Anger, however, can empower someone to harness her energies into positive action against the constraints that harm or oppress her. It is scarcely improper for feminists to want women to harness their energies into constructive action against the wrongs that are inflicted on us.

John Stuart Mill regarded as natural the feeling of resentment and the desire to retaliate against those who harm us. This attitude, in Mill's view, becomes properly moral when imbued with social concern, that is, when we thereby take ourselves to be standing up for the interests of society and "asserting a rule which is for the benefit of others," and not simply ourselves. It is this complex sentiment that, in Mill's view, sanctions no less than the rule of justice.[21]

Whether or not resentment toward men is justified depends in part on whether or not the wrongs or injuries that feminists think men have inflicted on women are real or merely fancied. This issue is not settled simply by complaining that resentment is not a nice attitude. To decide whether or not women are justified in resenting men, we would have to consider a wide array of social practices: unwanted male sexual aggression (rape, incest, sexual harassment, and the rest), male violence against women, male power strongholds that minimize female participation, and so on.

Even if some women are now directing negative, nasty, useless resentment toward men, that issue would be trivial in comparison to the gender-related difficulties still facing women, difficulties ranging from economic disadvantages to sexual violence. Women who express resentment toward individual and, admittedly, some-times nonsexist men have probably suffered their share of male catcalls, gropes, putdowns, and worse, and just gotten fed up with it. While two wrongs seldom make a right, a second wrong can sometimes bring the first one into clearer view.

I am far less worried about women's hostility to men than I am about the attitudes of those boys in my daughter's kindergarten class who keep telling her that girls can't be scientists, girls can't be heroes, who bully or demean the girls on the schoolyard and, occasionally, try to pull up their skirts. (Yes, it still goes on.) Women's hostility toward men has no enforcement mechanism behind it; it will scarcely make a dent in cultural practices. Men's derogatory view of women, by contrast, has been buttressed by all forms of social power and authority. One is merely an annoyance; the other has fostered historic injustice and oppression.

It does not require much perceptiveness to see that women are at least *sometimes* wronged by men. It also does not require much historical knowledge to see that complacency has not helped women to end or to rectify those wrongs. In the United States, prior to the days of recent feminist anger, there were few places of refuge or support for battered women or rape victims; sexual harassment was not even a named problem; unwanted pregnancies could not be ended except by criminal means which threatened the lives of the pregnant women and girls; government and economy were overwhelmingly male-dominated domains, and on and on. The recent gains in women's social conditions have depended heavily on feminist activism. Feminist activism, in turn, has been energized by a variety of attitudes, among which anger figures prominently. Resentment against men would not be too high a social price to pay if it empowered some women to diminish their subordination to men and to promote their own well-being at long last.

NOTES

1. More probably, we have a number of sex/gender systems, reflecting the privileges and constraints of other overlapping social groupings such as race, class, religion, and so on. Men of a socially subordinated ethnic group, for example, might be just as unlikely to hold the reins of governmental power as women of the same ethnic group. Interrelationships between those women and men might show less, or merely differently distributed patterns of, male domination than is found in white, middle-class U. S. culture.
2. Deborah Rhode has carefully documented numerous areas of male abuse or domination of women that have figured prominently in law; cf. her *Justice and Gender* (Cambridge, Mass.: Harvard Univ. Press, 1989).
3. Cited in Barrie Thorne with Marilyn Yalom, eds., *Rethinking the Family* (New York: Longman, 1982), p. 5. It is important to note that the so-called traditional family has never been traditional for all social groups in our culture. Women from low-income households often worked outside the home long before the current wave of the feminist movement.
4. I have previously discussed this issue of definition in "They Lived Happily Ever After: Sommers on Women and Marriage," *Journal of Social Philosophy* 21, nos. 2 & 3 (1990), p. 57. Some scholars have recently challenged the presumption that the "traditional family" was *ever* as widespread as family nostalgia buffs would have us believe. See, for example, Stephanie Coontz, *The Way We Never Were: American Families and the Nostalgia Trap* (New York: Basic Books, 1992).
5. See, for example, definition #3 of "family" in the Funk & Wagnalls *Standard Dictionary of the English Language*, International Edition (Chicago: Encyclopaedia Brittanica, Inc., 1965), p. 457. I have added "enduringness" to the dictionary definition in order to exclude transitory cohabitation arrangements.
6. It is curious that philosophers who, in the current lingo, "go ballistic" over the thought of paternalism by governments or between co-equal citizens should be so unconcerned about the widespread paternalism of husbands toward wives in traditional marriages.

7. See, for example, Dorie Klein, "The Dark Side of Marriage: Battered Wives and the Domination of Women," "in *Judge, Lawyer, Victim, Thief: Women, Gender Roles, and Criminal Justice*, ed. Nicole Hahn Rafter and Elizabeth Anne Stanko (Boston: Northeastern University Press, 1982), pp. 83–107.
8. This discussion is based on Susan Moller Okin's well-documented study, *Justice, Gender, and the Family* (New York: Basic Books, 1989), especially chap. 7, "Vulnerability by Marriage."
9. Anyone who really thinks that this is an overly adversarial view of marriage and that marriage is a blissful harmony of two concordant hearts, minds, and wills has not been married for any length of time, and has certainly not raised children with a spouse.
10. Said in memory of my father, whose ways of goodness I grow to appreciate more and more with time.
11. Alan Bloom, The *Closing of the American Mind* (New York: Simon & Schuster, 1987), pp. 129–32.
12. The asymmetric parlance of "men" and "girls" has still not disappeared.
13. See, for example, Robert D. Kaplan, "The Coming Anarchy," *Atlantic Monthly*, February 1994, pp. 44–46, 48–49, 52, 54, 58–60, 62–63, 66, 68–70, 72–76. Kaplan believes that the contemporary U.S. emphasis on multiculturalism is weakening the ability of the United States to withstand the impending militaristic disasters (p. 76). An alternative view, however, is equally compelling, namely, that genuine multicultural (including cross-cultural) dialogue is our only hope of forestalling mass global destruction.
14. According to Margaret Mitchell's own narrative wording, Rhett was "bullying and breaking" Scarlett in the scene in question; he "humbled her, hurt her, used her brutally" (*Gone with the Wind* [New York: Macmillan, 1936], p. 940). For my more extended discussion of this scene and the novel in general, see "Does Sommers Like Women?: More on Liberalism, Gender Hierarchy, and Scarlett O'Hara," *Journal of Social Philosophy* 21, nos. 2 & 3 (1990), pp. 85–88.

Sommers rejects the word "rape" and resists even the somewhat milder notion of sexual domination ("Argumentam ad Feminam," *Journal of Social Philosophy*, vol. 22, no. 1 (1991), p. 15). The producer of the movie version of *Gone with the Wind* was not so shy. David O. Selznick referred frankly to this scene as the "Row and Rape." See Helen Taylor, *Scarlett's Women: Gone with the Wind and its Female Fans* (New Brunswick, N.J.: Rutgers Univ. Press, 1991), p. 130.
15. See, for example, Jennings Bryant and Dolf Zillmann, eds., *Perspectives on Media Effects* (Hillsdale, N.J.: Lawrence Erlbaum Associates,

1986); and Doris A. Graber, *Mass Media and American Politics*, 4th ed. (Washington, D.C.: CQ Press, 1993).

16. Sommers tries to convince her readers that feminists are out to impose totalitarian reconditioning on women, so as to make women's sexual desires conform to feminist blueprints ("Argumentam," pp. 11–17). To correct such distortions, it is necessary to state clearly that: (1) I criticize not the women (if any there be) who enjoy images of men dominating women, but rather the cultural endorsements and glorifications of male-dominated heterosexuality; (2) criticizing a type of cultural representation is obviously not the same as forcing one's values and ideals on other people; and most importantly, (3) I do not seek to impose my values or ideals on anyone, but rather to share my views with others through dialogue and debate. Sommers's caricatures of feminist views threaten to shut down genuine dialogue altogether. By contrast, I offer reasons to support my conviction that male-dominated heterosexuality is disrespectful to women at best, and, at worst in the 1990s, positively fatal. My hope is that we, as bearers of culture, will alter our predominant values and diminish our production and consumption of those potentially disastrous images.

17. After intravenous drug use, women's second most likely source of contracting AIDS is heterosexual contact with men who already have it. Furthermore, women are at much greater risk than men of getting AIDS through heterosexual contact alone. See Nora Kizer Bell, "Women and AIDS: Too Little, Too Late?," *Hypatia* 4, no. 3 (1989): p. 5. As ever, heterosexuality poses far greater risks for women than it does for men, at the same time providing insufficient intrinsic deterrents to male sexual aggression.

18. Marilyn Frye articulates this notion well in *The Politics of Reality: Essays in Feminist Theory* (Trumansburg, N.Y.: The Crossing Press, 1983), see esp. pp. 72–82 and 162–73.

19. Rush Limbaugh, invoking the common stereotype, brands "many" leading feminists as "man-haters" (*The Way Things Ought to Be* (New York: Simon & Schuster, 1993), p. 188). For him, this stance was exemplified in the controversial episode of the television series *Murphy Brown*, in which the lead character, Murphy Brown, a single woman, gives birth to a child and decides to raise it on her own. According to Limbaugh, "The real message of that *Murphy Brown* episode was that women don't need men, shouldn't desire them, and that total fulfillment and happiness can be achieved without men or husbands" (p. 189). To equate such a message with hatred of men is an example of the error I am highlighting.

Limbaugh offers no arguments against the view that he derides, but it is obvious that some women indeed do not need men (or any particular man), should not desire them, and can very well achieve fulfillment and happiness without them.

20. Funk & Wagnall's *Standard Dictionary of the English Language* (Chicago: Encyclopedia Britannica, 1965), p. 1071.

21. John Stuart Mill, *Utilitarianism*, ed. George Sher (Indianapolis: Hackett, 1979), pp. 50–52.

The Unnecessary Father

David Blankenhorn

David Blankenhorn is president of the Instutute for American Values in New York. He is the author of Fatherless America (1995) and the editor of Rebuilding the Nest: A New Commitment to the American Family (1990).

   Blankenhorn argues that fathers should not think of themselves as pale reflections of mothers. Men should continue to see themselves as providers for their families, as they have traditionally viewed themselves. Only in this way will men stop fleeing from their familial responsibilities. Men, as traditional men, can contribute richly to family life and should not be pushed out of the family in favor of women-dominated families or single-mother families.

For some social tasks, individual volunteers will suffice. But effective fatherhood requires cultural conscription. As a social role, the deepest purpose of fatherhood is to socialize men by obligating them to their children. In turn, the success of fatherhood depends fundamentally upon the success of its cultural story.

For obligating fathers to their children is less a matter of biology than of culture. Compared to mothers, fathers are less born than made. As a social role, fatherhood is less the inelastic result of sexual embodiment than the fragile creation of cultural norms.

It is almost impossible to find a culture in which large numbers of mothers voluntarily abandon their children. Yet to find a culture in which large numbers of fathers voluntarily abandon their children, all we need to do is look around. For this reason

alone, a society's fatherhood story—the shared understanding of what it means for a man to have a child—is almost certainly that society's primary indicator of how many children will grow up with fathers, and also, therefore, probably that society's most important determinant of overall child well-being.

In a larger sense, the fatherhood story is the irreplaceable basis of a culture's most urgent imperative: the socialization of males. More than any other cultural invention, fatherhood guides men away from violence by fastening their behavior to a fundamental social purpose. By enjoining men to care for their children and for the mothers of their children, the fatherhood story is society's important contrivance for shaping male identity. . . .

An essential claim of the script is that there are not—and ought not to be—any key parental tasks that belong essentially and primary to fathers. In this view, society no longer requires, or can afford to recognize, any meaningful difference between norms of fatherhood and norms of parenthood.

This conception of fatherhood, now widespread, constitutes a unifying philosophical premise of almost all currently fashionable arguments about men, masculinity, and fatherhood. Its ideologically diverse proponents justify it on grounds that are both societal and personal, pragmatic and utopian.

Intellectually, the ideal of superfluous fatherhood rests on three propositions. The first is that fatherhood as a gender-based social role is literally what the dictionary defines as superfluous: exceeding what is necessary. The second proposition is that men in general, and fathers in particular, are part of the problem. The third is that social progress depends largely upon a transformation of fatherhood based on the ideal of gender role convergence. Accordingly, this final proposition urges that fathers, for their own good and for the sake of women and society as a whole, transcend gender-specific male roles in favor of essentially gender-neutral human values. These three propositions order the plot and prompt the characters of our contemporary fatherhood story.

Heidi Brennen is a co-director of Mothers at Home, a volunteer-run national support group for mothers. She summarizes the type of letter that she often receives from new members.

> I am on maternity leave from a good job. I have a six-month-old baby. We could afford to live on his salary, but my husband is pressuring me to return to work. He thinks it is a waste of time for me to stay home because we could afford decent day care and get ahead financially with my income. It is hard for him to understand how I feel or what I do all day—he can't really see the results in the way that I do. How do other mothers handle this?

In her talks and correspondence with new mothers on this subject, Brennen, a mother of four young children, has arrived at this view:

> Now, when I hear a mother sigh that she would like to be at home but that they can't afford it, and I know that her husband's income is possible to live on, I begin to wonder if there isn't this tension going on between them. I especially question it when I hear the husband rave about the child-care arrangements while the wife remains silent. . . . It seems that many of today's fathers no longer have any pride in, and willingness to accept responsibility for, breadwinning. . . . We have received letters from women [at home] who say that their husbands are sometimes mocked at work for "having a wife that lives off them." Today it seems that men are congratulated for finding a high- or consistently income-earning wife.[1]

A generation ago, a man might brag to other men: "I would never let my wife work." But today, it seems, due in part to the New Father idea, a much more typical boast might be: "I would never let my wife not work." Both views, of course, veer toward a form of sexism and male coercion. But only one—the New Father view of who should win bread and why—repudiates the notion that fathers have a special, unequal obligation to provide for their families.

Does paternal breadwinning burden men? In some ways, of course, yes. A man who embraces the New Father philosophy of employment does indeed unburden himself. He frees himself up to make more choices, perhaps to express more emotions, certainly to discover himself apart from externally defined "roles." Certainly there is much to commend in this aspiration. Freedom is good. Especially in America, freedom is hard to argue against. But in this case, let me try.

For in liberating fathers from the breadwinner role, the New Father model also seeks to liberate fathers from widely held norms of masculinity. At the same time, our elite cultural script notwithstanding, most men in our society simply do not wish to be liberated from their masculinity. This viewpoint is a key to understanding their unprogressive, lopsided commitment to the provider role.

Paternal attachment to breadwinning is neither arbitrary nor anachronistic. Historically and currently, the breadwinner role matches quite well with core aspects of masculine identity. Especially compared to other parental activities, breadwinning is objective, rule-oriented, and easily measurable. It is an instrumental, goal-driven activity in which success derives, at least in part, from aggression. Most important, the provider role permits men to serve their families through competition with other men.[2] In this sense, the ideal of paternal breadwinning encultures male aggression by directing it toward a prosocial purpose.

For these reasons, the breadwinner role has always been, and remains, a basic cultural device for integrating masculinity into familism—the clearest, simplest means for men to act out their obligations to their children. Faced with these stubborn facts, our society can respond in one of two ways. We can, through the New Father model, continue to assault male breadwinning in a root-and-branch attempt to reinvent men and deconstruct traditional masculinity. Or we can endeavor, however imperfectly, to incorporate men as they are into family life, in part by giving them distinctive, gendered roles that reflect, rather than reject, inherited masculine norms—such as, for example, the breadwinner role.

The New Father model does not merely unburden men of breadwinning as a special obligation. Ultimately, it unburdens them of fatherhood itself. For, as the example of breadwinning demonstrates, the essence of the New Father model is a repudiation of gendered social roles. But fatherhood, by definition, is a gendered social role. To ungender fatherhood—to deny males any gender-based role in family life—is to deny fatherhood as a social activity. What remains may be New. But there is no more Father.

WHY CAN'T A MAN BE MORE LIKE A WOMAN?

Ultimately, the ideal of androgynous fatherhood—fatherhood without the masculinity—emerges as the animating principle of the contemporary New Father model. Michael Lamb roots his advocacy of the New Father model in the basic premise that "very little about the gender of the parent seems to be distinctly important. The characteristics of the father as a parent rather than the characteristics of the father as a man appear to influence child development."[3] Similarly, Andrew M. Greeley urges society to administer a "dose of androgyny" to men. We should "insist that men become more like women."[4]

This view is widely shared among the experts. In *Fathers and Families,* Henry B. Biller urges basic changes in gender identity for fathers. They must become more sensitive, less rigid, much more flexible. They must "broaden their personal identities." They must avoid "rigid conceptions of masculinity." They must "defuse gender stereotypes." They must "overcome some entrenched misconceptions about fatherhood." Only if they implement these identity changes will they be able to "equitably share child-rearing responsibilities."[5]

Diane Ehrensaft agrees. In *Parenting Together,* she asks: "Can a man and woman mother together?" Her basic answer is, Yes, if they try very hard. Her book investigates co-ed mothering, or "men and women who have embarked on the project of 'mothering' their children jointly."[6]

For her study, Ehrensaft interviewed forty fathers dedicated to "equal parenting" or "co-ed mothering." Her conclusions about these fathers are remarkable. "Central to their own childrearing philosophy," she finds, "was a disavowal of gender expectations." Why? Because these men, above all, "did not feel comfortable with the male culture they grew up in or had to live in now." These fathers, she finds, "grimace about maleness." She reports: "If being male meant fathering as their fathers had done, they wanted nothing of it. They would instead be 'mothering' men." As a result of this view of paternity, "the fathers in this sample did not express the desire for a same-sex child; there was not the same longing to re-create the self." Thus, "many of the fathers wished for a girl so as to avoid having a boy."[7] Ehrensaft strongly endorses this model of fatherhood.

Her approving portrayal of fathers who hope not to have sons is revealing, since it highlights a larger ethos that is impossible to ignore in so much of the contemporary literature on fatherhood: the ethos of malevolence toward men. Some of this malevolence is implicit; much of it is overt and perfervid.

Consider, in this regard, both the Old Father and the New Father. In the case of the Old Father—the fathers of those who are writing—the malevolence toward men is direct. They are the victimizers, the rapists, the oppressors. In the case of the New Father—either the writers as they see themselves or the desired partners of the writers—the animus toward men is more indirect. New Fathers are the last,

best hope for rerigging men. In both cases, males are clearly defined as the problem to be overcome. The solution desired by Ehrensaft's new fathers—do not conceive male offspring—is extreme, but consistent with this larger ethos and the overall perception of the problem.

Closely related to the desire to avoid male offspring is the desire to remove masculine traits from male offspring. In one case, the goal is to eliminate the problem of maleness by avoiding the birth of males. In the other, the goal is to minimize the problem of maleness by transforming the sexual identity of male children.

Consequently, a prominent theme throughout the New Father literature is the urgent need to resocialize boys. As Letty Cottin Pogrebin succinctly puts it: "Childhood is where fatherhood must be changed."[8] The logic is simple: Rewire masculinity by rewiring little boys. The New Child is parent of the New Father. This logic informs a cascade of New Father recommendations. Mandate child-rearing classes for boys in the schools. Replace their toys. Rewrite their books.[9] Offer them nontraditional role models. Teach them that aggression is bad, gentleness is good. Discourage competitive sports. Discourage hunting. Discourage traditional gender roles. Teach them how to change. Teach them how to transcend masculinity.[10]

A third revealing aspect of the New Father ethos is the tolerant and even celebratory view of mother-headed homes embraced by many proponents of the New Father model. One might expect these fatherhood advocates to worry about, perhaps even criticize, the steady growth of fatherless homes in our society. But most do not. Many of the strongest advocates of the New Father model are also the strongest defenders of the viability of single-parent homes. Dorothy Dinnerstein of Rutgers University succinctly summarizes this viewpoint:

> we should be less concerned about the growing number of single-parent households in our society—as long as they can provide the child with an involved parenting figure of the missing sex—and more concerned about our many "traditional" families which dump all the child-rearing responsibilities on the mother.[11]

Let's see, now. Single-parent homes are just fine, thank you. But we desperately need the New Father model. What unites these two seemingly contradictory ideas in the head of one person? It is the belief that there is nothing special about a father, that there are no fundamental tasks in family life that are properly and necessarily his work. In short, what unites these two ideas is the belief that fatherhood is superfluous.

If fathers are superfluous, fatherless homes do not alarm us. And if fathers are superfluous, the main project for men in two-parent homes is to prevent things from being "dumped" on women, primarily by mimicking femininity and overcoming masculinity. In one instance, the final result is a fatherless home. No big deal. In the other, the final result is an extra set of hands via genderless paternity. Much to be desired.

At bottom, the New Father idea presupposes the larger thesis that fatherhood is superfluous. In this respect, the New Father is indistinguishable from the Unnecessary Father. In our current cultural discourse, the two are usually understood as opposites: one good, one bad. But in this larger sense, they are interchangeable characters in a single cultural narrative. Whether we look at the New Father or the Unnecessary Father, the underlying theme is the same: the irrelevance of fatherhood as a distinct male activity.

For this reason, undergirding the entire New Father model is the imperative of gender role convergence. The essence of this imperative is the removal of socially defined male and female roles from family life. Such roles should be replaced by two ideas. The first is the moral importance of personal choice—the belief that choosing freely among family behaviors is not simply a possible means to something good but is itself something good.[12]

The second is an ideal of human development based on a rejection of gendered values—especially those associated with traditional masculinity—and an embrace of gender-neutral human values. In part, the imperative of role convergence simply urges the reduction or elimination of sex specialization within the family. But in a larger sense, the imperative warns that any notion of socially defined roles for human beings constitutes an oppressive and socially unnecessary restriction on the full emergence of human potentiality.

Benjamin Spock, who has probably had more influence on American parents than any other person in this century, substantially revised his famous book, *Baby and Child Care*, in 1985 to incorporate this imperative of gender role convergence. Women, he tells us in the updated version,

> in trying to liberate themselves have realized that men, too, are victims of sexist assumptions—sexual stereotyping. . . . When individuals feel obliged to conform to a conventional male or female sex stereotype, they are all cramped to a degree, depending on how much each has to deny and suppress his or her natural inclinations.[13]

More poetically but in exactly this vein, Mark Gerzon celebrates the new cultural narrative of family life:

Couples may write their own scripts, construct their own plots, with unprecedented freedom. Whether the encounter is between strangers on a bus, colleagues in a meeting, or lovers in bed, a man and a woman are free to find the fullest range of possibilities. Neither needs to act in certain ways because of preordained cross-sexual codes of conduct.[14]

This is a vision, ultimately, of freedom. In many ways, it is a bracing, exhilarating vision, bravely contemptuous of boundaries and inherited limitations, distinctly American in its radical insistence on self-created identity. It draws upon the American myth, the nation's founding ideals; it echoes much of what is best in the American character. It is the vision of Whitman in his "Song of the Open Road":

> From this hour I ordain myself loos'd of
>   limits and imaginary lines,
> Going where I list, my own master total and
>   absolute.[15]

There is so much to commend in this vision. It is the reigning ethos of much of contemporary American culture. But as a social ethic for fatherhood, I dispute it.

I dispute it because it demands the obliteration of precisely those cultural boundaries, limitations, and behavioral norms that valorize paternal altruism and therefore favor the well-being of the human infant. I dispute it because it denies the necessity, and even repudiates the existence, of fathers' work: irreplaceable work in behalf of family that is essentially and primarily the work of fathers. I dispute it because it tells an untrue story of what a good man is, and of what a good marriage is.[16] In addition, I dispute it because it rests upon a narcissistic and ultimately self-defeating conception of male happiness and human completion. Thus it cannot be, at bottom, the vision of

the good father. It is finally the vision of Huckleberry Finn, the boy who ran away from society, and of Peter Pan, the boy who would never grow up.[17]

Fundamentally, the New Father's imperative of role convergence is based on the sexual equivalent of what some political scientists term the "end of history."[18] Politically, the end of history refers to the ending of the historical contest between communism and capitalism, between the two political ideologies whose struggle, now over, shaped the politics of the modern era. The struggle is over because one side won everything. The losing side not only lost but now seeks to emulate the victor. Thus, in world political terms, consensus replaces conflict; sameness replaces difference; universalism replaces particularism.

Sexually, the end of history would refer to the ending of any historically inherited and socially important differences between males and females. Unlike past sexual history, which was based on differences and complementarities, the end of sexual history would denote the fundamental social irrelevance of sexual roles—a new fusion of previously divided components of humanity.

Moreover, the end of sexual history also suggests the end of a tension or struggle. As in the political analogue, the struggle ends because, at least within the home, one side wins everything. The losing side not only loses but also seeks to emulate the winning side. Sexually, the losing side is aggression, instrumentalism, competition, toughness, and other historically masculine norms. The winning side is nurture, cooperation, empathy, and other historically feminine norms. Accordingly, in the realm of domestic life—in public life, the trend is the same but the other side wins—the historical tensions rooted in sexual complementarities are replaced by a new consensus rooted in sexual universalities. Independence replaces dependency. Sameness replaces difference. Particularisms evaporate into the whole. History ends.

I will leave it to others to debate the end of political history. But I decline to accept the end of sexual history, either as an empirical fact or as a utopian goal.

For as David Gutmann and Alice Rossi remind us, the sexual division of labor within the family is a common trait in human societies, occurring across history and cultures, precisely because it is integral to the survival and reproduction of the society. The parental emergency requires—indeed, is defined by—the adoption of gendered parental roles. The human child does not know or care about some disembodied abstraction called "parent." What it needs is a mother and a father who will work together, in overlapping but different ways, in its behalf.

The sexual division of labor is not, at bottom, the result of social conditioning or cultural values. Nor does it have anything to do with fostering the desire for omnipotentiality that is present in all humans. As Gutmann pointedly insists: "the parental transformation is not aimed at forging the adult self but is instead aimed at bringing about the psychological formation, the selfhood, of the offspring."[19] Ultimately, the division of parental labor is the consequence of our biological embodiment as sexual beings and of the inherent requirements of effective parenthood.

These basic facts have not disappeared and will not disappear. History continues. Moreover, the necessity and irreplaceability of a father's work have not disappeared and will not disappear. In service to the child and to the social good, fathers do certain things that other people, including mothers, do not do as often, as naturally, or as well. When fathers do not do this work—as is increasingly the case in our society—child and societal well-being decline.

Historically, the good father protects his family, provides for its material needs, devotes himself to the education of his children, and represents his family's interests in the larger world. This work is necessarily rooted in a repertoire of inherited male values: historically and socially mediated understandings of what it means to be a good father. These values are not limited to toughness, competition, instrumentalism, and aggression—but they certainly include them. These "hard" male values have changed and will continue to change. But they will not disappear or turn into their opposites. Nor should we wish them to.

Finally, I dispute the New Father's imperative of gender role convergence because I do not credit its promise of greater human happiness. The desire for omnipotentiality—including the wish to be both sexes at once—is part of the human condition. Indeed, Lawrence Kubie calls this infantile desire "one of the deepest tendencies in human nature."[20] But as a governing ideal of human completion, androgyny and gender role convergence reflect the ultimate triumph of radical individualism as a philosophy of life.

Indeed, androgyny constitutes the most radical conception of expressive individualism that a society can imagine. It is the belief, quite simply, that human completion is a solo act. It is the insistence that the pathway to human happiness lies in transcending the old polarities of sexual embodiment in order for each individual man and woman to embrace and express all of human potentiality within his or her self. No longer, in this view, do we accept otherness as a biosocial fact. Instead, we appropriate otherness into the self. No longer would a man alone consider himself in some way to be incomplete. The fractured moieties of male and female, child and adult, reside together as part of the omnipotentiality of the individual man. Now each man, within the cell of himself, can be complete.

This idea, so deeply a part of our culture, is fool's gold. It is a denial of sexual complementarity and ultimately a denial of generativity—particularly male generativity, which is, much more than the female's, largely a social construction. Especially for men, this particular promise of happiness is a cruel hoax. Like all forms of narcissism, its final product is not fulfillment but emptiness. If fatherhood has anything to say to men, it is that human completion is not a solo act.

NOTES

1. Interview with Heidi Brennen on May 17, 1993. Mothers at Home, headquartered in Vienna, Virginia, has 14,000 subscribers to its monthly publication, *Welcome Home.*
2. Why do men and women work? Of course, at the most basic level, both men and women work to earn money and support their families. But there are also important gender differences in the motivation to work and in styles of work. Compared to men, for example, women frequently value achievement more than money at work. Opinion poll data suggest that employed women are also substantially more likely than men to place a high priority on having lots of contact with coworkers, doing work that can help others, having flexible and limited work hours, and having jobs with limited amounts of stress. See "Relations Between the Sexes," *The American Enterprise* 4, no. 5 (September/October 1993): 89–90, 94.

   Moreover, and more central to an exploration of paternal breadwinning, men at work, more than women, are typically motivated in large part by the need to compete with other men and to establish hierarchical relationships of power. Of course, since this gender-related goal is increasingly criticized and denied in our culture, many men now refrain from talking about it, but it remains at the center of male motivation in the workplace. Turning this motivation toward the support of children and child rearing is the cultural basis of the breadwinner role for men.
3. Michael E. Lamb, "The Changing Role of Fathers," in Lamb, *The Father's Role*, 14. Kyle D. Pruett stresses virtually the same point: "Nurturing fathers do not treat their sons much differently from their daughters. In fact, these particular fathers resemble traditional mothers, in that they seem less occupied with shaping gender-appropriate behavior and beliefs in their children than are traditional fathers." See Kyle D. Pruett, *The Nurturing Father: Journey Toward the Complete Man* (New York: Warner, 1987), 37.
4. Andrew M. Greeley, "Necessity of Feminism," *Society* 30, no. 6 (September 1993): 13–14.
5. Henry Biller, *Fathers and Families*, (Westport: Greenwood Publishing, 1993), 28, 35, 48, 60.
6. Diane Ehrensaft, *Parenting Together: Men and Women Sharing the Care of Their Children* (Urbana: University of Illinois Press, 1990), x, 13, 35.
7. Ibid., 78–79, 85, 139.
8. Letty Pogrebin, *Family Politics*, (New York: McGraw-Hill, 1984), 211.
9. Gayle Kimball similarly believes that fathers must "move in an androgynous direction." To help them, she recommends certain children's books "that show boys and men in nurturing roles [that] provide useful role models. Examples of such books are *The Daddy Book*, *George the Babysitter*, and *My Daddy Is a Nurse*." See Gayl Kimball, *50-50 Parenting*, (Boston: Beacon Press, 1983), 142–43.
10. In endorsing this idea, Andrienne Rich does admit that such rewired little boys—those who "grow up unmutilated by gender roles"—are apt to be lonely: "We also have to face the fact that in the present stage of history our sons may feel profoundly alone in the masculine world, with few if any close relationships with other men." Arguably a small price to pay for such progress. And presumably we may take comfort in the fact that this suffering will not occur in future stages of history. See Adrienne Rich, *Of Women Born* (New York: Bantam, 1977), 206.
11. Cited in Phil Donahue, *The Human Animal* (New York: Simon & Schuster, 1985), 308–9.
12. This idea—that moral import lies not primarily in what I do, or even in what I choose, but instead in the act of choosing freely—has become a defining norm of contemporary elite discourse, not only regarding fatherhood, but also regarding our culture as a whole. This reg-

nant idea carries particularly important social consequences for fatherhood. As Joseph Veroff, Elizabeth Douvan, and Richard A. Kulka put it in their important 1981 book, *The Inner American:* "While earlier generations took marriage and parenthood for granted as necessary parts of adulthood, such unconsidered assumptions now gave way to processes of choice, deliberation, and decision. Once parenthood is cast as a choice, the experience is compared to the outcomes of other possible choices and some metric (personal satisfaction, cost-benefit, etc.) must be found on which alternative outcomes can be scaled."

Yet fatherhood, much more than motherhood, depends for its very existence on shared cultural norms. Social paternity is largely the fragile result of applying effective cultural pressures on males. The current transformation of fatherhood from cultural expectation to personal option must powerfully contribute to the decline of fatherhood in our society—especially since the transformation is occurring in the context of widespread cultural ambivalence, and even hostility, toward most forms of authority, including paternal authority. Despite these facts, the valorization of personal choice and the denigration of social roles remain almost universally celebrated ideals in our elite discourse on fatherhood. Pepper Schwartz, for example, warns us against allowing "nostalgia for the institution of the past" to obscure the new reality (for which she offers at least two cheers), namely, that "the contemporary family is composed of voluntary associations" in which "all family actors are essentially using individual rather than group welfare as their basis for everyday action." More poetically, Charles Scull offers this appreciation: "Fathers come in varied guises. We live in a time of many options as to the form fathering can take—divorced, single fathers, stepfathers, gay fathers. . . . There are as many ways of fathering as their are fathers." See Joseph Veroff, Elizabeth Douvan, and Richard A. Kulka, *The Inner American: A Self-Portrait from 1957 to 1976* (New York: Basic Books, 1981), 239; Pepper Schwartz, "The Family as a Changed Institution," *Journal of Family Issues* 8, no. 4 (December 1987): 455; and Charles S. Scull, ed., *Fathers, Sons, and Daughters: Exploring Fatherhood, Renewing the Bond* (Los Angeles: Jeremy P. Tarcher, 1992), xvii, 1.

13. Benjamin Spock and Michael B. Rothenberg, *Baby and Child Care* (New York: Pocket Books, 1985), 38.
14. Mark Gerzon, *A Choice of Heroes* (Boston: Houghton Mifflin, 1982), 237.
15. Walt Whitman, "Song of the Open Road," in *Leaves of Grass* (New York: New American Library, 1958), 138.

16. Clearly, proposals for androgynous parenthood spring not primarily from the timeless needs of children but rather from the modern desires of adults. At the same time, ironically, considerable evidence now suggests that the pursuit of androgyny actually undermines, rather than fosters, the modern adult pursuit of intimacy, particularly sexual intimacy, and therefore reduces the likelihood of adult marital satisfaction.

Most scholars agree that the current drift toward parental androgyny is occurring during a period of declining levels of marital satisfaction. More important, however, some recent research concludes that the growing espousal of androgynous parental norms directly contributes to this increase in marital unhappiness. For example, Jay Belsky, Mary Lang, and Ted L. Huston find that, particularly among couples espousing androgynous norms, marital happiness drops with the arrival of children, since the transition to parenthood is typically, almost regardless of parental attitudes, accompanied by greater gender-role divergence. Similarly, Judith Wallerstein finds that first-time fathers who are committed to "co-parenting" frequently cause marital strain by misunderstanding what their wives need from them. The hardest challenge for these fathers, Wallerstein observes, is less to nurture the infant than to love and support the new mother, including supporting her decision to focus primarily on the needs of the newborn child rather than on his needs, including his desire for sex. Yet, nothing in the androgynous ideal is likely to prepare the male co-parent for these challenges, or even alert him to their likely existence.

Recent research from Sweden and Norway—two cultures deeply influenced by androgynous parental norms—confirms these trends. Marriage counselors from Sweden, for example, report that increasing numbers of divorcing wives attribute their decision to divorce to sheer boredom with their husbands, including loss of sexual interest. Why? One reason, surely, is that sexual attraction between men and women is based not on sameness but on differences. As Marianne Gullestad, an anthropologist from Norway, has summarized the problem: "There is a contradiction between romantic love and the desired equality in the division of tasks, because romantic love implies imagination and mystery, and therefore, some cultivation of otherness. Romantic love implies imagination, adventure, excitement, that the two genders are able to be a little secretive to each other, and that is doubtless difficult if they strive to define their relationship in terms of being more and more similar, more and more the same."

Closer to home, Suzanne Fields puts it less delicately. Recalling a woman who complained that her "husband suffers from premature emasculation," Fields reasons: "When men pursue a feminine sensibility, women are inevitably shortchanged in their own fundamental psychic and sensual needs. 'In my practice,' says F. Joseph Whelan . . . 'I have noted that today's women want to have a placid, pliable man to deal with most of the time. However, they also want a virile, aggressive male when it comes to bedroom activities . . . a tiger in bed and a lamb in the living room. Such a creature is hard to find.' "

See Norval D. Glenn, "The Recent Trend in Marital Success in the United States," *Journal of Marriage and the Family* 53, no. 2 (May 1991): 261–70; Diane N. Lye and Timothy J. Biblarz, "The Effects of Attitudes Toward Family Life and Gender Roles on Marital Satisfaction," *Journal of Family Issues* 14, no. 2 (June 1993): 157–88; Jay Belsky, Mary Lang, and Ted L. Huston, "Sex Typing and Division of Labor as Determinants of Marital Change Across the Transition to Parenthood," *Journal of Personality and Social Psychology* 50, no. 3 (March 1986): 517–22; David Popenoe, "Parental Androgyny," *Society* 30, no. 6 (September/October 1993): 5–11; Suzanne Fields, *Like Father, Like Daughter: How Father Shapes the Woman His Daughter Becomes* (Boston: Little, Brown, 1983), 273. Comments from Judith Wallerstein are from an interview on June 4, 1993. Relevant to the consideration of androgyny and the pursuit of intimacy is Milton C. Regan, Jr., *Family Law and the Pursuit of Intimacy* (New York: New York University Press, 1993). For a criticism of measuring fathers according to a "deficit model" of parenthood—that is, a model that posits maternity as the standard—see Ronald D. Day and Wade C. Mackey, "An Alternative Standard for Evaluating American Fathers," *Journal of Family Issues* 10, no. 3 (September 1989): 401–8; and Wade C. Mackey, *Fathering Behaviors: The dynamics of the Man-Child Bond* (New York: Planum, 1985), especially 149–66.

17. The archetypal male hero in American literature is frequently identified with freedom from civilization, especially as represented by women and children. From Natty Bumpo to Sam Spade to Travis McGee, this hero is the man who got away—the man who lives in what R. W. B. Lewis calls "the area of total possibility." Yet this understanding of masculinity as juvenility and the escape from adulthood—so ubiquitous in American culture—directly challenges the ideal of responsible fatherhood. See R. W. B. Lewis, *The American Adam: Innocence, Tragedy and Tradition in the Nineteenth Century* (Chicago: University of Chicago Press, 1955), 91 passim. See also Leslie Fielder, "Adolescence and Maturity in the American Novel," in Fielder, *An End to Innocence* (Boston: Beacon Press, 1955), 191–210; and Ann Swidler, "Love and Adulthood in American Culture," in Neil J. Smelzer and Erik H. Erikson, eds., *Themes of Work and Love in Adulthood* (Cambridge, Mass.: Harvard University Press, 1980), 120–47.

18. See Francis Fukuyama, "The End of History?" *The National Interest* 16 (summer 1989): 3–18.

19. David Gutmann, *Reclaimed Powers*, (Evanston: Northwestern Univ. Press, 1994), 198.

20. Lawrence Kubie, "The Desire to Become Both Sexes," *Psychoanalytic Quarterly* 43, no. 3 (July 1974): 370. See also Robert May, *Sex and Fantasy: Patterns of Male and Female Development* (New York: Norton, 1980), 163–77.

Is Equality Tearing
Families Apart?

Joel Anderson

Joel Anderson teaches philosophy at Washington University in St. Louis. He has written articles on autonomy, value pluralism, practical reasoning, and contemporary German social theory.

Anderson defends the principle of gender equality against the charge that it leads to a decline of the family. In his criticism of neotraditionalist approaches such as that of Blankenhorn, he argues that stable, rewarding family life is perfectly compatible with egalitarian feminists' demands for genderless parenting, equal power, and freedom of opportunity. He concludes that the perceived conflict between pro-family and pro-equality positions is an illusion.

Let me begin with what I take to be two basic truths. First, social inequality between the sexes should be eliminated. Second, anything that systematically undermines the possibility for healthy, stable, fulfilling family life should be eliminated as well. Put positively, a good society must be *both* pro-equality and pro-family.

On its own, neither position is particularly controversial. Treating women as inferior to men clearly denies them their dignity and moral worth. Insofar as the majority of society's rewards go to men solely because of their sex, women are victims of injustice. Similarly clear intuitions hold with regard to the importance of stable, caring, mutually rewarding marriages and families. Assuming (as I do here) that "married couple" and "family" are understood broadly, as including both traditional and nontraditional household

arrangements,[1] what is at issue is one of the most basic forms of social relationships around which individuals build their understanding of the good life. A society that denied its members something that is so widely held to be an essential component of a life worth living would be gravely depriving them. Properly understood, then, a "decline of the family" would pose a genuine threat to human well-being.

My concern here is with the perceived conflict between pro-equality and pro-family approaches. Those who have fought hardest for gender equality often view "pro-family" rhetoric with suspicion and even hostility. And those who have worried most about the decline of the family often view campaigns for gender equality with a similar degree of suspicion and hostility. In this essay, I examine this second set of worries, put forward by a range of social critics and philosophers whom I will label "neotraditionalists."[2] I shall be focusing on three ways in which promoting equality is

Not previously published. Used by permission of Joel Anderson.

thought to contribute to the disintegration of families. In each case, these neotraditionalist critics argue that the egalitarian policies of feminists entail further social developments—specifically, genderless parenting, selfish individualism, and competing agendas—that are tearing families apart. I shall be arguing that this entailment is rarely plausible, and that even when it is, the risks of social fragmentation should not overshadow the importance of gender equality.

Before continuing, a brief clarification is in order with regard to what it means to say that the family is "in decline" or is being "torn apart." I do not mean this as simply a matter of a demographic shift from "intact" families (a couple in their first marriage plus their children) to single-parent families and "step-families." Unless one assumes that particular structures for living together are ordained by God or biology, it is an open question whether the increase in single-parent households or common-law marriages represents a problem. What clearly would represent a problem, however, are developments that threaten to rob family life of its meaning and purpose. If, for example, the very point of families is to provide a context in which family members are nurtured, cared for, socialized, etc., then a lack of contact between family members represents a decline of the family. In this sense, a family can be torn apart even without a divorce. Being torn apart is thus also a matter of degree. Again, however, what would be problematic is not that a particular form of household is on the decline,[3] but that people are having trouble maintaining the interpersonal commitments about which they care deeply. On the broad understanding assumed here, the break-up of an unmarried couple can be an instance of family disintegration.

There is mounting evidence that the family is suffering from social fragmentation: half of all marriages end in divorce; "in disrupted families, only one child in six, on average, saw his or her father as often as once a week in the past year";[4] and "parents had roughly 10 fewer hours per week for their children in 1986 than in 1960."[5] None of this demonstrates that we should return to the past, but if some degree of stability and integration is a necessary condition for the sort of family life that so many people deeply value, then the criticisms raised by neotraditionalists must be taken seriously.

EQUALITY AND GENDERLESS PARENTING

Neotraditionalist critics of egalitarian feminism sometimes claim that promoting equality involves endorsing the idea of a genderless family in which breadwinning, homemaking, and childrearing are divided evenly between husband and wife.[6] Neotraditionalists then argue that eliminating distinctions between the role of father and mother forces both men and women to deny essential components of their identity as parents, which is not only bad in itself but also denies families the much-needed stability and complementarity provided by the male breadwinner/ female homemaker model.

Arguments for this position come from a wide range of viewpoints. The most familiar neotraditionalist arguments in this connection focus on women's "natural" role as nurturers and their greater suitability for the role of primary care-giver.[7] But neotraditionalists such as David Blankenhorn also argue that the role of fathers has been unduly neglected and that men have a special contribution to make in the distinctive role of "father."[8] I shall focus on this latter discussion.

Neotraditionalists have taken issue with the ideal of the sensitive, caring, supportive "New Father" who changes half the diapers and whose sense of self-worth depends as much on his homemaking as his breadwinning.[9] Against this ideal, they argue that it is vitally important to recognize the distinctiveness of a father's contribution to the family, especially as a good provider and a strong protector. According to these critics of egalitarian feminism, recognizing this is important for three reasons.

First, if we eliminate the differences between what it means to be a father and what it means to be a mother, we will lose the benefits of diverse role models within the family. For example, Blankenhorn cites studies that have shown that men tend to inspire adventurousness, assertiveness, and risk-taking in their children, whereas women tend to be more risk-averse and protective. If, as seems plausible, children need to learn to balance these two modes of behavior, then it would be a genuine loss if this diversity were eliminated.

Second, as with many social organizations, the family benefits from functional differentiation, that is, from having a diversity of roles and functions that complement one another, rather than having everyone performing the same roles. On these grounds, neotraditionalists hold, for example, that children do best in a situation in which the authority figure of the father contrasts with the sympathetic ear of a mother.

Third, neotraditionalists argue that by telling men that they must think of themselves as homemakers, proponents of gender equality exacerbate family disintegration by leaving men feeling that they have nothing special to contribute.[10] Without the feeling of masculine pride that comes from being a good provider and a role model of strength in the family, it is argued, men's attachment to the responsibilities of fatherhood is diminished. Thus genderless parenting denies men this feeling of pride.

These neotraditionalist arguments all attempt to link genderless parenting to the depletion of crucial resources for healthy families. Though some critics might go so far as to claim that this means we should reinstate the traditional, male-breadwinner/female-homemaker family as the normative model, the more moderate position is that the differences between men and women should be accepted, thereby "allowing" women to choose full-time homemaking without guilt and men to focus on breadwinning without shame.

There are several difficulties with this line of argument. To begin with, it is not entirely clear that promoting equality between men and women requires eliminating the distinctive roles of mothers and fathers. "Genderless" parenting does not deny that there will be role differences ("father" and "mother") but only that parents should not be trapped in one role or the other. Thus one can maintain the diversity of roles on which neotraditionalists insist, while keeping open the question of *who* must fill the roles. Neither of the first two arguments has given us reason to think that men should not occupy the socio-cultural role of "mothers" nor women that of "fathers."

The third argument does aim to provide such reasons. At this point, neotraditionalists often appeal to claims about what is "natural." They reject the idea that men can be "mothers" and women can be "fathers." Given how much of what gives humans their dignity is the ability to refrain from doing "what comes naturally," such direct appeals to nature are generally dubious. Even so, many people are impressed with the purported "brute fact" that women are more emotionally attached to their children, so that they have a much harder time leaving them in the care of others, and are much more reluctant to put young children in child care.[11] Assuming, charitably, that there is empirical evidence for a persistent and fairly general trend, would this show what the neotraditionalists want it to show? Not necessarily. For it might turn out that the persistence of this phenomenon may be traceable to inequalities that are the result of socialization rather than chromosomes.

Consider, for example, Rhona Mahony's suggestion that women's "headstart effect" can be overcome through the use of "affirmative action for fathers."[12] Mahony acknowledges that pregnancy often gives mothers an inevitable "headstart" over fathers when it comes to their emotional attachment and sensitive attunement to the infant, but she stresses that what happens after the birth is not biologically predetermined. Typically, of course, mothers' headstart leads to quicker and more successful responses. Even without the greater degree of coaching and encouragement women generally receive from female friends and relatives, the headstart effect can quickly lead to a situation in which mothers are able to quiet a child quickly and generally set a standard of care that fathers have difficulty living up to. Even when a couple is resolved to share the parenting, Mahony argues, there are unintentional mechanisms that tend to snowball, so that after only a few months it becomes much more efficient for mothers to take over the greater share of the childcare. She

gets exasperated, and he gets frustrated. This may look like a "natural" outcome, but biology does not determine this outcome beyond the "headstart effect." In fact, if fathers are given significant periods of time in which they have sole responsibility for the young infant, there is every reason to expect that such "affirmative action" will correct the balance. Before large numbers of fathers have had the opportunity to become equally expert with their children, speculation about what men and women "naturally" want is a poor basis for legitimating practices that perpetuate the unequal status of women.

In this connection, we must be very clear about what is at stake for women in the present discussion. Neotraditionalist attempts to restore the idea that women and men have specific roles to play as mothers and fathers threaten to re-entrench the situation in which women who have the primary childcare responsibilities see their chances diminished of later returning to interesting jobs. As recent discussions of "mommy tracks" and "glass ceilings" have made clear, being the primary caregiver for their children often hinders women on the job front, both by restricting the amount of time they can devote to their work and by making them less attractive candidates for being promoted to positions of responsibility.[13] I shall return to this point below.

EQUAL NEGOTIATING POSITIONS

A second set of neotraditionalist suspicions about the egalitarian agenda has to do with the destabilizing effects of a focus on equal power. Here the argument is that, although some equality of power in the family is probably a good thing, a concern with it should not become a dominant principle. The family, it is argued, follows a different logic than that of politics or business. It is a place of unconditional love and fidelity, a "haven in a heartless world."[14] This climate of love and trust can easily be destroyed by a focus on equal power and equal negotiating positions.

Neotraditionalists do not advocate inequality. They agree with egalitarians that wives should be equal before the law, should be able to own and inherit property, and (for the most part) should not be required to submit to the wishes of their husbands. What they object to is the stronger position taken by egalitarians.

According to this egalitarian position, genuine equality demands both a commitment to equalizing power imbalances as much as possible and an adequate awareness of one's relative power in the relationship. If they care about equality, couples must be concerned with how the choices they make are shaped in subtle ways. Unless the negotiating positions are equal, the appearance of fair decision-making may be easily misleading. Furthermore, and this is the importance of *awareness*, even if neither spouse perceives a problematic imbalance, that may simply be because some spouses may be in such a vulnerable position that they cannot *afford* to think about their inequalities.[15]

To understand the egalitarian position, it is best to focus on the difficult decisions that families inevitably face, because it is there that subtle differences on a person's negotiating position can have a huge impact. Take the case of young parents making decisions about who will cut back on his or her hours at work (or quit altogether) in order to care for the newborn, when both spouses are in careers that they love but that will be jeopardized if they cut back on work. Equality demands that the interests of each spouse should weigh as much as those of the other (which is not to say that the only fair outcome is a 50/50 split). That requires, in turn, that it is a genuinely open question whether the mother or the father will go part-time to take care of the babies. But if, as is very often the case, the husband's more established career provides a better income, or if he has little idea how to take care of children by himself, then the wife's negotiating position is seriously weakened. Whether the mother wants to or not, the "obvious" thing to do will be for her to cut back on her hours and thereby jeopardize her career. In this way, even among spouses who love each other, an unequal negotiating position can deny women the opportunity to have their career plans adequately considered.

In a similar way, ensuring equal negotiating positions requires guaranteeing that divorce is not available to one spouse on more advantageous terms. This point is important, because when family conflicts arise, they are played out against the background of the possibility of that the marriage may break down. The possibility of divorce gives partners not only a way of escaping an unacceptable position—not insignificant in a world of marital rape and spousal abuse—but also a way of increasing the chances of their criticism being taken seriously. As Albert O. Hirschman observes, "The chances for voice to function effectively as a recuperation mechanism are appreciably strengthened if voice is backed up by the *threat of exit*, whether it is made openly or whether the possibility of exit is merely well understood to be an element in the situation by all concerned."[16] Thus, the equal availability of an "exit option" may actually serve to pre-

vent divorce by ensuring that both men and women have a threat at their disposal that will ensure that their voice gets heard.

Beyond formal access to divorce, it is crucially important that the consequences of divorce are equally costly. Otherwise, the negotiating position of one spouse will be stronger. Currently, men's exit options are generally better than those of women: "income for mothers and children declines on average about 30 percent, while fathers experience a 10 to 15 percent increase in their incomes in the year following the separation."[17] The causes of this disparity are complex, but they surely include not only lax enforcement of child support payments but also the fact that while fathers were improving their employment position, mothers have often focused on childcare and housekeeping rather than job experience and networking. Whatever the reasons, however, in this situation of unequal negotiating positions, when the disagreements are intense or the decisions of great consequence, women's awareness that they will be the bigger losers in a divorce can make them willing to tolerate treatment that their husbands would not tolerate. Eliminating these forms of inequality is a major task. It calls for significant changes in family law, public policy, and business practices. But it also calls for spouses to be vigilant about their relative negotiating positions.

For neotraditionalists, this vigilant attitude threatens to increase marital instability, for the more a couple focuses on the equality of their negotiating positions, the more they are likely to undermine the climate of trust, commitment, and self-sacrifice that makes families both stable and worthwhile. From this perspective, when spouses start closely monitoring who is taking advantage of whom or thinking about who will lose out in a divorce, they introduce ways of relating to each other that are antithetical to good marriages (as well as being symptomatic of deeper problems). This is often expressed by saying that the culture of the public world of contracts and self-interest has invaded the private domain of the family, where a distinctive culture is to be cherished.

> The goals of women (and of men, too) in the workplace are primarily individualistic: social recognition, wages, opportunities for advancement, and self-fulfillment. But the family is about collective goals that by definition extend beyond individuals: procreation, socializing the young, caring for the old, and building life's most enduring bonds of affection, nurturance, mutual support, and long-term commitment.[18]

Without this commitment to the larger whole, it is argued, families lack the glue that holds them together, and they tend to disintegrate as soon as sacrifices are required. On this view, if family members are focused on making sure that they get their share, they will have trouble weathering the short-term conflicts that inevitably arise.

But does equalizing negotiating positions between spouses really lead to the sort of self-interested culture that tears families apart? Ultimately, this is an empirical question, but given the complexity of the issue and the sort of data needed, some philosophical analysis may help to clarify which hypotheses are most plausible. Where we should come down on this issue will certainly depend, in part, on the sorts of families that one has in mind. Here we can distinguish three different cases.

(1) In some families, the negotiating positions will be roughly equal. When spouses must make choices that jeopardize their chances of career advancement

and financial independence in the future, the sacrifices are made equally; various arrangements are in place to ensure that neither spouse will end up benefiting financially from a divorce; furthermore, when applicable, childcare responsibilities are distributed in such a way that parents' emotional investment in the children and expertise in childcare is likely to be fairly decided on an equal basis. In such cases, an awareness of their equal negotiating positions seems likely to strengthen the stability of the family, for spouses will know that *even when they are not getting along,* they are not in a position to take advantage of the other. Of course, equality of negotiating positions is not sufficient to hold a marriage together. My point is simply that there is no reason to think that if a couple knows that their interests are balanced, this will threaten their mutual love.

(2) In families where inequalities of power are actually exploited, the different issue arises as to whether keeping the family together is really the best option. I said at the outset that family disintegration is *usually* something that no one wants, and it is bad for that reason—but not always. If we care about human dignity and autonomy, we must recognize that only if people are aware of the possibility of inequality arising in a relationship will they have any chance of correcting a situation in which someone is taking advantage of them. In a family with young children, of course, the choice to end a marriage often represents a tragic situation, and neotraditionalists are right to point out that parents may have an obligation to accept some sacrifices for the sake of a maintaining a tense but stable situation at home. But a situation in which it was typically *women* who made the sacrifices would be a situation of (at

least) indirect sexism and would deserve moral condemnation.

(3) The neotraditionalist objection is perhaps on its best footing in cases in which there are unequal negotiating positions, but the more powerful spouse does not exploit the other. If the power imbalance is *temporary*—say, if one parent loses a job—then it may well be just a matter of family members needing to take the long view and to trust that advantages will balance out over time. In a situation of lasting and structural inequality, matters may also seem benign, as long as both spouses feel that they have an equal say. An insistence that spouses be aware of the imbalance may then seem unnecessarily risky to the relationship. As long as we are talking about *adequate* and not *maximal* awareness of relative negotiating positions, however, the greater danger, I would suggest, lies in being blind to the presence of serious inequality. For an awareness of it allows both spouses to be attentive to the ways in which they may inadvertently slide into patterns that they would not have accepted if their negotiating positions had been equal. Furthermore, only with an awareness of such imbalances is it possible for spouses to make a moral appeal to each other based on a special vulnerability, which itself can contribute to marital stability.

This last point can be generalized. If neotraditionalists are concerned with genuine stability in a relationship, they would do well to acknowledge the ways in which genuine equality provides a basis that is at least as stable as the reliance on traditional family models. To ensure that the stability is more than skin-deep conventionalism, some awareness of and concern with spouses relative negotiating positions is vitally important.

EQUALITY OF INDIVIDUAL OPPORTUNITY

The third neotraditionalist criticism that I wish to consider focuses, like the one just discussed, on the threat that increasing individualism poses to the family. The central suspicion is that feminist egalitarianism undermines the stability of families by allowing the centrifugal forces of the labor market to affect the family more brutally than ever before. Neotraditionalists suggest that, in the push for women's equality, traditional assumptions about the family have been dismantled, taking with them one of the best bulwarks against the divisive demands of the labor market.

In order to examine this claim, we need to understand something of the importance of freedom of choice, especially with regard to the choice of occupation. Historically, the process of industrialization has led to fundamental transformations of family life, for example, in nineteenth-century Europe.[19] Whereas the vast majority of people in pre-industrial societies had no choice of occupation (to the point that their role, usually as peasant, was prescribed by the metaphysical world order), in modern industrial societies the possibilities for choice expanded both in scope and significance. The modern view emerged that free choice of occupation is an important basic liberty, one that guaranteed the opportunity for self-realization. Freedom of choice—and particularly freedom to choose one's occupation—thus became a fundamentally important moral claim of modern individuals, for it affects the very possibility of leading one's life as one's own. Only if people could choose their line of work could they truly be free to develop their own sense of individual identity and self-worth.

Women were, of course, long denied this freedom. Men planned their careers, and women planned their weddings. Insofar as that is still the case, promoting equality will indeed demand that the roles available to women be expanded so as to be equal with that of men. As a general proposition, few would deny that women have an equal moral claim to opportunities for self-determination and self-realization. What feminists have shown, however, is that developing the social conditions under which women have *real* opportunities requires significant transformations. In particular, it involves eliminating the automatic assumption that women will be the ones staying home to care for small children. For as long as employers have reason to believe that young women are more likely to leave the work force, request a shift to a part-time position, decline positions that require overtime or travel, and take time off to care for a sick relative, employers have significant economic incentives to invest in training and promoting men rather than women, thus reducing women's opportunities for self-realization.[20] Rectifying this situation is not, it should be noted, a matter of making special accommodations to women but of realizing more consistently the principles of a free and fair labor market.[21]

As neotraditionalists point out, however, the labor market does not operate on the basis of family-friendly principles.[22] Especially in a world in which global competition is intense and labor unions are relatively weak, the labor market often demands, for example, that workers relocate to find work and that they put in extra hours if they are to remain competitive. The German sociologist Ulrich Beck follows out this line of thought to its logical extreme:

> Ultimately, the market model of modernity presupposes a society without families or

marriages. Everyone must be free and independent for the requirements of the market, in order to secure his or her existence. . . . Accordingly, a fully realized market society is also a society without children—unless the children grow up with mobile, single-parent fathers and mothers.[23]

Given this, even some feminists have recently discussed the costs to women (and their families) of their entry into the labor market, even if it is something that equality demands.[24] Neotraditionalists tend to blame these costs on feminists' campaign for equal opportunity. But it seems far more accurate to say, as Beck does, that this transformation was a matter of artificial barriers to womens' participation in the workplace finally being removed.

Whatever the cause, having both men and women in the labor market has added strains on the family as a result of the increasing number of difficult decisions that must be made. The more options people have, the more complicated the task becomes of trying to coordinate cooperative relationships. As a result of the constant demands to communicate needs and arrive at agreements, the potential for conflict rises dramatically. Take the case of being relocated for a job. In a world in which tradition clearly dictates that the family will move wherever the father's job takes him, no decision really needs to be made. There may still be unhappiness and conflict about the move, but the source of the conflict is situated outside the family. As those traditional assumptions crumble, it becomes a contingent matter how families should resolve such situations. Simple appeals to "how we have always done things" must be replaced by the hard work of finding a way to take everyone's needs into consideration. As a result, to quote Beck again, "The family becomes a constant juggling act of dis-

parate multiple ambitions among careers and their requirements for mobility, educational demands, conflicting parental obligations, and bothersome housework."[25] If this is what women's equality of opportunity brings us, neotraditionalists ask, is it really worth it?

With regard to what women's full participation in the labor market has *taken away*, the critics argue that given how promoting equality involves challenging traditional assumptions about how parental responsibilities will be divided, the egalitarian agenda may be undermining the very bulwark that it needs against the centrifugal pressures of the labor market. When women did not insist on working outside the home, they argue, family stability was less threatened by employers demands for mobility, because the pressures were again construed as lying *outside the private sphere of the family*. On this view, the head of household faced the competitive, interest-based public world, but came home to a world free of competing agendas. Furthermore, the traditional family model also provided clear roles and expectations, such that much less was open to the sort of debates that can tear families apart.

The difficulties with this neotraditionalist line of argument lie both in what it advocates and what it fails to advocate. On the first count, the neotraditionalist proposal that we restore our faith in certain traditional assumptions about the family—such as the model of men as family providers—is not really an option available in modern industrial societies, even if we could afford it. Aside from the fact that returning to more traditional approaches would involve unconscionably disproportionate sacrifices from women, it would not actually eliminate the need to make complex and conflict-ridden decisions. Once "how we do things" has become a contingent matter, every form of traditionalism is a *neo*traditionalism. You have to argue for it, or at least choose it. Today, when a couple picks the traditional male-breadwinner/female-homemaker pattern, the modern understanding of mutual and just respect demands that it be a *choice* made by *equals*—and that it be done in a way that does not jeopardize future possibilities for self-determination.

What neotraditionalists overlook are the posttraditional alternatives. Since industrial societies have been based on the assumption that only half of the potential work force would participate, it is not really all that surprising that fundamental changes are needed as part of the shift to genuinely full employment (that is, of both men and women). There are numerous proposals regarding *structural changes* that can be made in the way in which homemaking and breadwinning are distributed.[26] For example, some have proposed policies that would enable couples to participate effectively in the labor market *as couples*.[27]

Much of the appeal of the call for retraditionalization is based on the assumption that people will necessarily be overwhelmed by the complexities of a world without traditional gender roles. Talk of "disorientation" is common here. Such talk is premature, however. With the appropriate support, there is clearly room to increase people's capacities to handle these complex new decisions, not simply as individuals but also as families, concerned with their well-being as families. This will involve developing, for example, capacities to listen sympathetically and express oneself clearly, commitments to ensuring that no one is inadvertently silenced and that even unconventional solutions are given

due consideration, and clearly established (but revisable) procedures for family deliberations. Developing and maintaining these capacities can empower individuals to build and maintain their families amidst growing complexity.

Although providing a full blueprint for change is beyond the scope of the present essay, these brief sketches serve to highlight the possibilities for responding effectively to contemporary challenges to family stability without having to follow the neotraditionalists in compromising a commitment to equality.

There is no denying the difficulties involved in keeping a family together today, and many of these challenges result partly from the increasing equality of men and women. But it would be a narrow-minded mistake to say that the current challenges are generated by demands for gender equality. Rather, they are part of the larger challenge posed by living in a world in which the artificial constraints of tradition and conventions are increasingly dissolving. What I have argued here is that neotraditionalism presents us with a false dichotomy between genuine gender equality and a supportive climate for stable family life. These critics of feminist egalitarianism would have us choose between pro-family and pro-equality positions. Fortunately, even in complex modern societies, that is one decision that no one has to make.[28]

NOTES

1. In "Of Mothers and Families, Men and Sex" (in the present anthology), Marilyn Friedman provides a suitably broad definition of "family" as an "enduring household based on interpersonal commitment," which rightly includes homosexual couples. I shall focus on heterosexual couples, however, since I am concerned with gender equality and thus on relations between men and women.

2. In this essay, "neotraditionalism" represents a composite portrait of positions defended by a wide range of authors, most typically by the members of The Council on Families in America and the Institute for American Values. See the essays collected in *Rebuilding the Nest: A New Commitment to the American Family*, ed. David Blankenhorn, Steven Bayme, and Jean Bethke Elshtain (Milwaukee, WI: Family Service America, 1990); and *Promises to Keep: Decline and Renewal of Marriage in America*, ed. David Popenoe, Jean Bethke Elshtain, and David Blankenhorn (Lanham, MD: Rowman and Littlefield, 1996). Although the positions I outline are typical of this approach, my concern here is with widely held viewpoints rather than the claims of particular authors.

3. After all, social critics in the past decried the breakdown of the extended family and the rise of the nuclear family.

4. Barbara Defoe Whitehead, "Dan Quayle was Right," *The Atlantic Monthly* (April 1993), 65.

5. Janet Z. Giele, "Decline of the Family: Conservative, Liberal, and Feminist Views," in Popenoe (ed.), *Promises to Keep*, 91.

6. E.g., Susan Moller Okin, *Justice, Gender, and the Family* (New York: Basic Books, 1989).

7. Similar views are defended by some feminists, e.g., Nel Noddings, *Caring: A Feminine Approach to Ethics and Moral Education* (Berkeley: University of California Press, 1984) and Virginia Held, "Feminism and Moral Theory," in *Women and Moral Theory*, ed. Eva Feder Kittay and Diana T. Meyers (Totowa, NJ: Rowman and Littlefield, 1987), 111–28.

8. David Blankenhorn, *Fatherless America: Confronting Our Most Urgent Social Problem* (New York: Basic Books, 1995).

9. In addition to Blankenhorn's *Fatherless America*, see Bruno Bettleheim's earlier piece, "Fathers Shouldn't Try to Be Mothers," *Parents Magazine*, October, 1956.

10. This is the main theme of Blankenhorn's *Fatherless America*. It is also a prominent message in various recent "men's movements," including the "Promise-Keepers" and the Nation of Islam's "Million Man March."

11. A recent *New York Times* op-ed presents the greater attachment of mothers as a fact of "genetic wiring" (see Danielle Crittenden, "Yes, Motherhood Lowers Pay," *The New York Times*, op. ed. page, August 22, 1995).

12. Rhona Mahony, *Kidding Ourselves: Bread-winning, Babies, and Bargaining Power* (New York: Basic Books, 1995), 102–6. It should be noted that the biological headstart effect may be absent in the case of adoptive mothers.

13. See, e.g., Mahony, *Kidding Ourselves*, 14–17.

14. Christopher Lasch, *Haven in a Heartless World* (New York: Basic Books, 1977).

15. See Okin, *Justice, Gender, and the Family*, ch. 7; and Laura Sanchez and Emily W. Kane, "Women's and Men's Constructions of Perceptions of Housework Fairness," *Journal of Family Issues* 17 (1996): 358–87.

16. *Exit, Voice, and Loyalty.: Responses to Decline in Firms, Organization, and States* (Cambridge, MA: Harvard University Press, 1970), p. 82.

17. Whitehead, "Dan Quayle Was Right," 62. See also Lenore J. Weitzman, *The Divorce Revolution: The Unexpected Social and Economic Consequences for Women and Children in America* (New York: The Free Press, 1985). For a discussion of how this affects women's negotiating position, see Mahony, *Kidding Ourselves*, ch. 3. It should be noted that different issues affect the very poor: insofar as welfare assistance is restricted to unmarried mothers, the breakdown of a marriage may leave men with even fewer resources than women (with custody).

18. David Blankenhorn, "American Family Dilemmas," in Blankenhorn (ed.), *Rebuilding the Nest*, 10f.

19. For an excellent analysis of this development, see Elisabeth Beck-Gernsheim, "Auf dem Weg in die postfamiliale Familie: Von der Notgemeinschaft zur Wahlverwandtschaft," in *Riskante Freiheiten: Individualisierung in modernen Gesellschaften*, ed. Ulrich Beck and Elisabeth Beck-Gernsheim (Frankfurt: Suhrkamp, 1994), 115–38.

20. Felice N. Schwartz makes clear what it currently costs companies to ensure that mothers make their way into the executive ranks in "Management Women and the New Facts of Life," *Harvard Business Review* (Jan./Feb. 1989).

21. Ulrich Beck, *Risk Society: Toward a New Modernity* (London: Sage, 1992), 176–81.

22. Robert N. Bellah, "The Invasion of the Money World," in *Rebuilding the Nest*, 227.

23. Beck, *Risk Society*, 191.

24. Judith Stacey, *Brave New Families: Stories of Domestic Upheaval in Late Twentieth Century* (New York: Basic Books, 1990).

25. Beck, *Risk Society*, 184.

26. E.g., Okin, *Justice, Gender, and the Family*, ch. 8; and Mahony, *Kidding Ourselves*, ch. 9–10. Neotraditionailsts make some of these proposals themselves but see structural change as far from sufficient to counter the pressures towards social fragmentation: see, esp., The Council on Families in America, "Marriage in America: A Report to the Nation," in Popenoe (ed.), *Promises to Keep*, 310.

27. Beck, *Risk Society*, 194–204.

28. I would like to thank Larry May, Herbert Anderson, and Pauline Kleingeld for comments on earlier drafts.

A Community of Secrets:
The Separate World
of Bedouin Women

Lila Abu-Lughod

Lila Abu-Lughod teaches anthropology at New York University. She is the author of Veiled
Sentiments: Honor and Poetry in a Bedouin Society *(1986) and* Language and the Politics of
Emotion *(1988).*

*Abu-Lughod argues that even though Bedouin women lead strikingly restricted lives behind the
veil of Islam, they manage to create a community of women where autonomy and personal responsibility are stressed. Men continue to arrange the marriages and provide financial support for these
women, yet, she contends, the women are in control of their own sphere and by and large comfortable with this arrangement.*

The terms "harem" and "seclusion," so intertwined with popular and scholarly conceptions of Arab women, are in most respects grossly misleading. Conjuring up provocative images of groups of idle women imprisoned in sumptuous quarters awaiting the attentions of their master, or submissive veiled shadows scurrying down alleys, confined behind high walls. and excluded from the bustle of the public male world, these terms suggest the nadir of women's status and autonomy. They also suggest male initiative in the creation of separate worlds and direct male control over groups of women. Although these interpretations misrepresent reality, the images evoked by the terms, which indicate that women spend much of their time apart from men living in a separate world and form some sort of community within the larger society, capture an essential truth of social life in the Arab world, if not in other Muslim societies as well. By shifting our gaze and assuming the perspective of those for whom this community of women is the primary arena of social life, we get a more accurate and nuanced view not only of its connection to the men's world, but of the nature of women's experiences and relationships within the community.

Although the generalized principle of mutual avoidance applies in many traditional Middle Eastern societies,[1] the degree to which sexual segregation structures people's lives and the actual patterns it creates vary considerably depending on how it articulates with social and economic organization and historical circumstances. Lumping rural arid urban groups; pastoral, peasant, and mercantile economies; or different geographic and cultural areas only confuses the issue. Thus I confine my description to one society in the Middle East, that of the Awlad 'Ali Bedouins of the Egyptian Western Desert.[2] I know this case intimately because I lived in an Awlad 'Ali camp made up of the households of my host, his brothers and cousins, some distant relatives, and some clients. The role of adoptive daughter within the household was open to me because of my Arab and Muslim background and the circumstances of my introduction to the families,[3] and I embraced it for the acceptance it provided in a society in which, first, kinship defines relationships and, second, young women never live alone. Thus I traded access to a wide network for the advantages of close relationships within the smaller community in which most people lived their lives. Although in the first phase of my fieldwork I moved back and forth from the men's world to the women's, I soon realized that my contact with men—boring and frustrating because of barriers to conversation about personal matters created by the rules of propriety and the formality of men's gatherings—also foreclosed the possibility that the women would trust me. Since I wished to study interpersonal relations (those between men and women in particular) and the ideology of social life, topics that could not be studied without people's willingness to talk openly about their personal lives and feelings, I chose to declare my loyalty to the women.

In this article I explore in detail the sense in which the Bedouin women with whom I spent nearly two years live in a separate community—a community that could also be considered a subsociety: separate from and parallel to the men's, yet cross-cut by ties to men and encompassed in the larger world defined by kinship in a tribal structure; characterized by complex and intense interpersonal relations; and maintained by shared secrets, conveyed most poignantly through poetry. More importantly, I consider the women's attitudes about this community and about their separation from men, and the apparent consequences of such arrangements with regard to women's autonomy, personal development, and interpersonal relations. This study will also contribute to our general understanding of the forces that create and shape communities of women and the advantages and dilemmas that face women who live in separate communities.

SEXUAL SEGREGATION AMONG AWLAD 'ALI

Living in camps and towns scattered throughout the coastal region of the Egyptian Western Desert, the Bedouins known collectively as Awlad 'Ali are semi-nomadic pastoralists in the process of sedentarization. Their traditional economy was based on sheep and camel herding, supplemented by rain-fed barley cultivation and trade (recently replaced by smuggling and legal commercial ventures). Arabic speakers and Muslims who migrated from Cyrenaica (Eastern Libya) at least two hundred years ago, they proudly differentiate themselves from the peasants and urbanites of the Nile Valley by the tribal ideology that shapes their social and political organization, not to mention their interpersonal relations, and by their stricter adherence to a moral code of honor and modesty. A key entailment of this code is sexual propriety facilitated by sexual segregation.[4]

The Bedouins' everyday social world is divided in two. In one half are adult men, in the other are women and children. The division does not take the form of a rigidly demarcated ecological separation between home, or the private sphere, and public space, as it does in other parts of the Middle East, particularly in urban areas. The locus of most activities for both men and women was, until recently, the camp and its environs. The division of space is relatively informal and flexible, segregation depending on mutual avoidance and the separation of activities that results from the sexual division of labor.[5] Yet even when they are not working, men and women rarely socialize together. Indeed, my host's senior wife confessed to me that before I had come to live with them and to spend time chatting with my host in her room, she had never spent an entire evening in his company.

The two worlds coexist side by side, a function not of the wishes and power of particular men, but of the sexual division of labor and a social system structured by the primacy of agnatic bonds (those between male and female paternal kin) and the authority of senior kinsmen, and maintained by individuals whose attitudes and actions are guided by a shared moral ideology. This code of honor and modesty discourages expression of sexuality because it constructs a set of personal ideals revolving around notions of independence and autonomy in which a person's status depends on his or her distance from social and natural sources of weakness and lack of control.[6] The denial of sexuality is best expressed by avoiding members of the opposite sex with whom one might have a sexual relationship, and deferring, through modest avoidance, to those senior kinsmen who embody and represent the social ideals of independence and the triumph of agnation.[7] Hence develops the system of sexual segregation, upheld equally by men and women who

wish to be respectable members of their communities and who derive their social positions and support through family and tribe.

The degree to which contact between men and women is determined by their social categories is evidence that this separation of the sexes has to do with the avoidance of sexuality and deference to senior kinsmen. The boundaries between the men's and women's worlds are no more impermeable than the woven blanket that in the past used to divide the Bedouin tent into women's and men's sections. Men may more easily enter the women's world than vice versa, but the men who do so are those considered neither sexual threats nor authority figures. They are young kinsmen or household members and low-status men of the community. In fact, interactions between individual men and women range from relaxed familiarity to extremely formal avoidance, marked by women's veiling and men's aversion of gaze. Kinship relation, relative age, and social status determine the types of interaction. Sons, nephews, and younger kinsmen are greeted warmly and engaged in lively conversation. Fathers, paternal uncles, or fathers-in-law radically transform the atmosphere of the women's world; their intrusions bring a sudden hush to a roomful of garrulous women and boisterous children. Men who are not kin, especially those of high status, would not even come close to an area where a group of women was gathered.

STRUCTURAL DEPENDENCE AND CROSS-CUTTING TIES

The character of the community of women is shaped by the same social system whose by-product it is. Kinship is the primary idiom of social, political, and economic relationships in this tribal society, and the women's community is embedded in that society and cross-cut by numerous ties. Structurally, the community is by no means autonomous; it is neither self-contained nor economically self-sufficient. It controls no particular property or space, has no formal political presence or representation within the larger system, nor even an informal means of acting as an interest group. It is fragmented because its members define their primary ties and allegiances not to one another but to their kin groups.

The community is composed of individual women, all of whom are economically dependent and each of whom derives her right to support through links to kinsmen or husbands or both. In this, women are not much different from other dependent persons, including poor and young men. Among Awlad 'Ali, senior men of each lineage control the resources and are responsible for supporting kin, male and female. Dependents face serious restrictions on their autonomy in decision making. Senior kinsmen arrange marriages for daughters (and sons) and can order a young kinswoman to abandon a marriage, for example, if her own lineage and that of her husband have a serious fight. A woman who wants a divorce depends on the cooperation of senior male kin or senior males forced to take on the role of kin.[8] Given these facts, it should not be surprising that kinship bonds are affectively charged. In a very real sense, a woman's interests are one with those of her kin group, as her reputation and status are linked to theirs.

Thus kinship creates structural pulls that divide the women's community. Solidarity and identification with agnatic kin override bonds based on gender, common experience, or a shared daily life. One of the first questions asked of any stranger is "Where are you from?" The answer is not, as one would expect, a geographic area, but rather a tribal or lineage affiliation. Women retain their tribal identity even after marriage, although their children belong to the husband's tribe. More importantly, the ideology of the unbreakable and special bond among patrikin pervades the Awlad 'Ali's vision of their social relations. This is as true for women as for men, which means that women conceive of their primary bonds as those to kin, not to one another. In short, the women's community is encompassed and penetrated; it has no structural independence, and its members have their primary structural ties to those outside the community. . . .

AUTONOMY AND THE WOMEN'S WORLD

When one turns one's attention from structural concerns to women's day-to-day activities and their experiences of living together within Awlad 'Ali female society, the women's community takes on a more independent appearance. The community regulates its internal affairs free from the interference and often the knowledge of men. Sexual segregation is also a source of personal autonomy for women. Rather than feeling deprived or excluded from the men's world, women are oriented toward each other and concerned to guard the boundaries of their exclusive world.[9] Adult men's intrusions are infrequent and for the most part unwelcome; women are always anxious to shake off husbands and their male guests. When men are about, an often-heard question among the women is, "Have they gone?" The relief at their departure is palpable. One of the complaints I most frequently heard from a particular group of women concerned the layout of their new house. They thought the men's and women's sections were not sufficiently far apart, and they resented the way this interfered with their privacy.

Bedouin women collude to erect a barrier of silence about their world. Information flows unidirectionally from the men's arena into the women's and not vice versa. Since women become deferentially silent in the presence of most adult men, men generally do not overhear the natural conversations of women.[10] Young and low-status men have easy access to the women's community, and they bring information to the women about what goes on in the male world. But such men, because they are circumspect in their own community and must be deferential to senior males, do not report back about what goes on among women. The extent to which women collude to keep men out of their world is apparent from the reaction of one Bedouin woman who discovered that her brother-in-law had gotten wind of something she had said about him. She guessed that the comment must have been passed on to him by his new bride. She fumed: "We [the women in the core community] have lived together for seventeen years and never has any woman brought women's talk to the men! In our community we have one way. Women don't tell the men what goes on between women. Even the old women—why, they talk to the men, but they don't expose the secrets."

In her analysis of urban Moroccan women, Daisy Dwyer notes that women support men's avoidance of them in part because it offers the women opportunity for independence and defiance.[11] Bedouin women appreciate this aspect of sexual segregation as well. When men are absent, women can engage in activities that are forbidden in men's presence. Smoking, for example, is considered improper for women, but most Bedouin women like to smoke cigarettes and do so whenever they can. When a child or someone's loud throat clearing warns them of a man's approach, they hide the cigarettes. Similarly, when men are not around, women go places without permission. Often they visit local healers to get treatments or holy men to get amulets and charms. Other women cover for them if spouses or male kinsmen return unexpectedly.

SOCIAL RESPONSIBILITY

The separation of male and female worlds grants women more than freedom to indulge in minor defiances of the system and the men in control. It allows for the development of social responsibility. Within their community, women run their own daily affairs. They manage their households with little interference from men, dividing up the tasks and seeing to it that the necessary work that is women's province gets done each day. During slack periods, women occupy themselves as they wish, weaving, paying visits to neighbors, or just sitting around. Since men are gone for much of the day, seeing to the sheep and to business concerns, they impose themselves on women only rarely, usually at mealtimes.

More importantly, women are the arbiters of women's morality. Social control over women is in the hands of other women and is guided by a set of moral ideals that girls learn as they grow up in the women's community. Women correct one another well into adulthood through gossip, teasing, and other forms of indirect criticism, even poetry. Men interfere only when serious infractions of basic norms occur—particularly those of sexual propriety. They have no direct authority over the community as a whole, and their legitimate control over individual women derives from their kinship ties. Husbands have limited authority because wives have recourse to kin for protection. And because the worlds are so separate, men are generally ignorant of what women do, which also effectively restricts male control.

Children are socialized into Bedouin society by women. Women teach children to be modest or deferential in the proper situations. Girls are more harshly criticized for immodesty and insubordination, and heavy pressure begins to fall on them as they reach puberty. Girls watch and listen, learning a great deal about moral standards from women's conversations. Neither punishment nor force is used, although threats abound. Often, older women show their disapproval in a humorous way. The following incident illustrates such indirect social control. Female peddlers in the desert areas had just begun to carry western-style negligées. The adolescent girls were enthralled and, in one camp, two of them had bought negligées for their trousseaus. Their grandmothers were outraged. As she sat with a group of women, one grandmother demanded that the negligée be brought to her. She showed it to the other women, asking if indeed this wasn't the most shameless thing they had ever seen. She then pulled the sheer lime-green nightgown over her bulky dresses and danced provocatively around the room, threatening to go outside and show it to the men. The women wailed with laughter and dragged her away from the doorway. The other grandmother then

threatened to take a match to the negligées and suggested that the girls return them to the peddler. . . .

When someone has actually done something wrong, the women of the community let her know that they disapprove, often through oblique references. On one occasion a new bride ran away from her husband without complaining first to her husband's kin or returning directly to her family; instead she took refuge among some neighbors of a different tribe. Everyone disapproved. After she was persuaded to return to her husband, each of the women in the community came to see her. They recounted stories about their own and others' experiences of running away in the proper manner. With a kind smile and a twinkle in her eyes, an older woman in the bride's household told the young woman she deserved a good beating. The women joked about "evil spirits" a good deal, because the bride had claimed that her husband suddenly looked like an evil spirit and frightened her.

The assumption of social control by women, particularly senior women, could be viewed as an expression of false consciousness. One could argue that when women enforce societal standards that support the male-dominant status quo, they help to maintain the system that keeps them subordinate. On the other hand, by regulating their own affairs rather than letting men do so, they avoid direct experiences of their own subordination and dependency. By participating equally in the maintenance of cultural ideals and social standards, women can come to see themselves as responsible moral beings, not powerless pawns whose only hope for gain lies in manipulation and subversion. They can have honor and command respect just as men do. And within their own unsupervised and autonomous arena, managing their own affairs allows women to develop both competence and dignity.

PERSONAL DEVELOPMENT

These observations regarding the effects of women's social responsibility raise other questions about the relationship between sexual segregation and female "personality" or the cultural construction of the ideal woman. Perhaps most critical to Bedouin women's personal development are their minimal interaction with those to whom they are subordinate and the de-emphasis of sexuality as an orientation in social life. These two circumstances encourage women to develop in terms of the cultural ideals of pride and independence.

The ideals of feminine personality are context dependent in Bedouin culture. Both men and women agree that women should be "modest," but this only applies in certain social situations. Modesty is a complex cultural concept that refers to both an internal state of embarrassment and shyness, and a repertoire of behaviors indicative of this state, including downcast eyes, silence, and a general self-effacement, made literal among married women by use of the veil. It relates in a sense to sexual propriety in that it indicates respect for a social system threatened by sexual bonds and for those who are most responsible for upholding such a system (kinsmen and elders). Modesty is thus the spontaneous and appropriate response to encounters with status superiors and is the path to honor for the socially weak.

In interactions among women, modesty is not an issue since neither sexuality nor hierarchy (except in the most under-

stated form) are relevant. There is another set of standards at work in the separate women's world. The attributes Bedouin women value in one another are not those of passivity or delicacy often associated with the feminine ideal in the West, but rather those of energy, industry, enterprise, and emotional and physical toughness. Wisdom, intelligence, and verbal skill, exemplified in storytelling and singing, are also much admired. The active capabilities of women are even celebrated in the ideals of feminine beauty. For the Bedouins a beautiful woman has a robust build and shines with the rosy glow of good health. They abhor slenderness, weakness, or sickliness as much in women as in men. . . .

CONCLUSION

Awlad 'Ali women live neither in harems nor in seclusion. But like their sisters in societies or classes that can afford to keep women indoors, they live in a world where the general principle of sexual segregation structures social life. Rather than assuming the male perspective and viewing one-half of the bifurcated world as residual or even excluded, we saw, by looking closely at actual lives, that two coexisting communities are created when persons associate primarily with members of their own sex. Even if cross-cut by various ties, each has its integrity and must be examined in its own right. Among Bedouins, the ideological predominance of patrilateral, patrilineal kinship in economic and social relationships and its impact on identity and identification necessarily preclude the structural independence of the women's community. Further, a woman's economic and social dependency severely curtails her autonomy, particularly in making major life decisions.

Yet sexual segregation is not inherently bad for women. In this case, it seems clear that the separation of the worlds mitigates the negative effects of sexual inequality and women's dependence. By taking responsibility for regulating their own conformity to social norms and by avoiding encounters with men who have authority over them, women escape the direct experience of their subordination and gain the respect accorded those who do their share to uphold the social order. Women enthusiastically support the segregation that allows them to carve out significant fields for autonomous action in their relatively unsupervised and egalitarian world. In the women's community, they have an arena for self-assertion. Individual development among women does not occur in opposition to male development; indeed cultural ideals of the feminine "personality" resemble the masculine and include enterprise, boldness, pride, and independence. Because of the denial of sexuality among Awlad 'Ali, women do not orient themselves toward men or try to please them. Instead they value competence, self-sufficiency, and respectful distance. They orient themselves toward other women.

The community of Bedouin women is, above all, a rich world of close ties, intimacy, and shared experience. Because power and authority are hardly at issue in the relations among women, their world is one of relaxed informality, familiarity, and a certain honesty. Although not the result of a self-conscious feminist separatism or a deliberate fostering of bonds of sisterhood, the tone, intensity, and closeness of relations within the Bedouin women's community approach those idealized by feminists. Yet the poems through which women share

many of their most intimate sentiments reveal another dimension of experience. Not all women's poems describe love and attachment or concern relationships with men. . . . But enough of them revolve around such themes to suggest that women develop deep affective bonds with men— lovers and husbands as well as kin. For the Awlad 'Ali Bedouins, the bonds of womanhood that integrate the world of women have much to do with shared suffering and longing for those outside their community.

NOTES

Acknowledgments: The research on which this essay is based was conducted in Egypt between October 1978 and May 1980. I am grateful to many who facilitated my research there but most of all to the community of Awlad 'Ali Bedouins with whom I lived. For financial support for my research in Egypt and writing at Harvard, I am grateful to the National Institute of Mental Health and the American Association of University Women. For encouragement, comments, and help in preparing this essay for presentation at the conference "Communities of Women" I want to thank Barb Smuts and John Watanabe. For inspiration and critical response I must thank the organizers of and participants in that conference sponsored by *Signs* and the Center for Research on Women at Stanford University, and for thought-provoking comments, the anonymous readers of the manuscript for *Signs.*

1. On sexual segregation outside the Middle East, see Janet Bujra, "Introductory: Female Solidarity and the Sexual Division of Labour," in *Women United, Women Divided,* ed. Patricia Caplan and Janet Bujra (Bloomington: Indiana University Press, 1979), pp. 13–45, esp. p. 31; Ursula Sharma, "Segregation and Its Consequences in India: Rural Women in Himachal Pradesh," in the same volume, pp. 259–82.
2. This is an anglicized version of the name by which these tribes are collectively known. The correct Arabic transcription is *Awlaad 'Alii.* For ethnographic material, see Ahmed H. Abou-Zeid, "Honour and Shame among the Bedouins of Egypt," in *Honour and Shame: The Values of Mediterranean Society,* ed. Jean Peristiany (Chicago: University of Chicago Press, 1966), pp. 243–59; Abdalla Bujra, "The Social Implications

of Development Policies: A Case Study from Egypt," in *The Desert and the Sown: Nomads in the Wider Society,* ed. Cynthia Nelson (Berkeley: University of California, Institute of International Studies, 1973), pp. 143–57; Safia Mohsen, "Legal Status of Women among the Awlad 'Ali," *Anthropological Quarterly* 40, no. 3 (July 1967): 153–66.

3. These circumstances and the consequences of having been accompanied initially by my father are detailed in the first chapter of Lila Abu-Lughod, *Veiled Sentiments: Honor and Poetry in a Bedouin Society* (Berkeley: University of California Press, 1986).

4. The analysis of the code of honor and modesty on which the arguments of this article hinge is far too complex to present here. For elaboration, see ibid.

5. In the traditional economy, subsistence depended on the joint labor of all members of one or more households. Men now travel a great deal and much of their work takes them outside the camp. What may have been a more informal separation of men and women on the basis of separate tasks has become rigid and extreme. For a similar case, see Lois Beck, "Women among Qashqa'i Nomadic Pastoralists in Iran," in *Women in the Muslim World,* ed. Lois Beck and Nikki Keddie (Cambridge, Mass.: Harvard University Press, 1978), pp. 351–73.

6. In this article references to sexuality are to heterosexuality, which is in keeping with Awlad 'Ali ways of thinking about sexuality.

7. See Abu-Lughod, *Veiled Sentiments.*

8. The customary procedure for obtaining a divorce is either to return to one's natal home and have one's father or older male kin negotiate the divorce, or to "throw oneself" at the mercy of a tribal leader or religious figure. See Mohsen (n. 2 above, esp. pp. 163–65).

9. For a similar observation regarding urban Yemen, see Carla Makhlouf, *Changing Veils: Women and Modernisation in North Yemen* (London: Croom Helm, 1979), p. 28.

10. For a similar situation among peasants in southern France, see Susan Carol Rogers, "Female Forms of Power and the Myth of Male Dominance: A Model of Female/Male Interaction in a Peasant Society," *American Ethnologist* 2, no. 4 (November 1975): 727–56, esp. 741.

11. Daisy Hilse Dwyer, *Images and Self-Images: Male amd Female in Morocco* (New York: Columbia University Press, 1978), p. 163.

American Indian Women
at the Center of
Indigenous Resistance
in Contemporary North America

M. Annette Jaimes with Theresa Halsey

M. Annette Jaimes (Juaneño/Yaqui), is a lecturer in American Indian studies with the Center for Studies of Ethnicity and Race in America (CESRA). Jaimes has edited The State of Native America: Genocide, Colonization and Resistance *(1992), and* Fantasies of the Master Race *(1992). Theresa Halsey (Standing Rock Sioux) is the director of the Title V American Indian Education Program of the Boulder Valley School District in Colorado. A longtime activist, she works primarily on community educational issues.*

Jaimes and Halsey argue that historically, American Indian women were not meek, docile and subordinate to males, as they have often been portrayed. Furthermore, American Indian women formed, and continue to form, the core of resistance in the conflict between tribal peoples and Euro-Americans. Citing many historically documented examples, they argue that traditional American Indian societies were not male-dominated. Indeed, female "warriors" were not uncommon, women held key decision-making positions concerning all aspects of socioeconomic existence, and most tribal cultures were matrilineal, placing property ownership in women. Jaimes and Halsey attribute the changes in women's tribal status to the European colonizers' direct intervention in indigenous cultures.

A people is not defeated until the hearts of its women are on the ground.

> Traditional Cheyenne Saying

The United States has not shown me the terms of my surrender.

> Marie Lego
> Pit River Nation, 1970

Reprinted by permission of the South End Press, 116 St. Botolph Street, Boston, MA 02115, from *The State of Native America* by M. Annette Jaimes with Theresa Halsey, 1992. [Edited]

The two brief quotations forming the epigraph of this chapter were selected to represent a constant pattern of reality within Native North American life from the earliest times. This is that women have always formed the backbone of indigenous nations on this continent. Contrary to those images of meekness, docility, and subordination to males with which we women typically have been portrayed by the dominant culture's books and movies, anthropology, and political ideologues of both rightist and leftist persuasions, it is women who have formed the very core of indigenous resistance to genocide and colonization since the first moment of conflict between Indians and invaders. . . .

MYTHS OF MALE DOMINANCE

A significant factor militating against fruitful alliances—or even dialogue—between Indians and non-Indians is the vast and complex set of myths imposed and stubbornly defended by the dominant culture as a means of "understanding" Native America both historically and topically. . . . As concerns indigenous women in particular, this fantastical lexicon includes what anthropologist Eleanor Burke Leacock has termed the "myths of male dominance."[1] Adherence to its main tenets of the stereotypes involved seems to be entirely trans-ideological within the "mainstream" of American life, a matter readily witnessed by recent offerings in the mass media by Paul Valentine, a remarkably reactionary critic for the *Washington Post,* and Barbara Ehrenreich, an ostensibly socialist-feminist columnist for *Time* Magazine and several more progressive publications.

In a hostile review of the film *Dances with Wolves* published in April 1991, Valentine denounces producer-director Kevin Costner for having "romanticized" American Indians.[2] He then sets forth a series of outlandish contentions designed to show how nasty things really were in North America before Europeans came along to set things right. An example of the sheer absurdity with which his polemic is laced is a passage in which he has "the Arapaho of eastern Colorado . . . igniting uncontrolled grass fires on the prairies" which remained barren of grass "for many years afterward," causing mass starvation

among the buffalo (as any high school botany student might have pointed out, a fall burn-off actually *stimulates* spring growth of most grasses, prairie grasses included). He then proceeds to explain the lot of native women in precontact times as being the haulers of "the clumsy two stick travois used to transport a family's belongings on the nomadic seasonal treks" (there were virtually no precontact "nomads" in North America, and dogs were used to drag travois prior to the advent of horses).[3]

Ehrenreich, for her part, had earlier adopted a similar posture in a *Time* Magazine column arguing against the rampant militarism engulfing the United States during the fall of 1990. In her first paragraph, while taking a couple of gratuitous and utterly uninformed shots at the culture of the southeast African Masai and indigenous Solomon Islanders, she implies America's jingoist policies in the Persian Gulf had "descended" to the level of such "primitive"—and male dominated—"warrior cultures" as "the Plains Indian societies," where "the passage to manhood allowing young males to marry required the blooding of the spear, the taking of a scalp or head."[4] Ehrenreich's thoroughly arrogant use of indigenous cultures as a springboard upon which to launch into the imagined superiority of her own culture and views is no more factually supportable than Valentine's, and is every bit as degrading to native people of *both* genders. Worse, she extends her "analysis" as a self-proclaimed "friend of the oppressed" rather than as an unabashed apologist for the status quo.

The truth of things was, of course, rather different. Contra Ehrenreich's thesis, the Salish/Kootenai scholar D'Arcy McNickle long ago published the results of lengthy and painstaking research which showed that 70 percent or more of all pre-contact societies in North America practiced no form of warfare at all. . . .[5] This may have been due in part to the fact that, as Laguna researcher Paula Gunn Allen has compellingly demonstrated in her recent book, *The Sacred Hoop*, traditional native societies were never "male dominated" and there were likely no "warrior cultures" worthy of the name before the European invasion.[6] There is no record of *any* American Indian society, even after the invasion, requiring a man to kill in war before he could marry. To the contrary, military activity—including being a literal warrior—was never an exclusively male sphere of endeavor.

Although it is true that women were typically accorded a greater social value in indigenous tradition—both because of their biological ability to bear children, and for reasons which will be discussed below—and therefore tended to be noncombatant to a much greater degree than men, female fighters were never uncommon once the necessity of real warfare was imposed by Euroamericans.[7] These included military commanders like Cousaponakeesa—Mary Matthews Musgrove Bosomworth, the "Creek Mary" of Dee Brown's 1981 novel—who led her people in a successful campaign against the British at Savannah during the 1750s.[8] Lakota women traditionally maintained at least four warrior societies of their own, entities which are presently being resurrected.[9] Among the Cherokees, there was Da'nawa-gasta, or "Sharp War," an especially tough warrior and head of a women's military society.[10] The Piegans maintained what has been mistranslated as "Manly-Headed Women," more accurately understood as being "Strong-Headed Women," a permanent warrior society.[11] The Cheyennes in partic-

ular fielded a number of strong women fighters, such as Buffalo Calf Road (who distinguished herself at both the Battle of the Rosebud in 1876 and during the 1878 "Cheyenne Breakout"), amidst the worst period of the wars of annihilation waged against them by the United States.[12] Many other native cultures produced comparable figures, a tradition into which the women of the preceding section fit well, and which serves to debunk the tidy (if grossly misleading and divisive) male/female, warlike/peaceful dichotomies deployed by such Euroamerican feminist thinkers as Ehrenreich and Robin Morgan.[13]

More important than their direct participation in military activities was native women's role in making key decisions, not only about matters of peace and war, but in all other aspects of socioeconomic existence. Although Gunn Allen's conclusion that traditional indigenous societies added up to "gynocracies" is undoubtedly overstated and misleading, this is not to say that Native American women were not politically powerful. Creek Mary was not a general *per se,* but essentially head of state within the Creek Confederacy. Her status was that of "Beloved Woman," a position better recorded with regard to the system of governance developed among the Cherokees slightly to the north of Creek domain:

> Cherokee women had the right to decide the fate of captives, decisions that were made by vote of the Women's Council and relayed to the district at large by the War Woman or Pretty Woman. The decisions had to be made by female clan heads because a captive who was to live would be adopted into one of the families whose affairs were directed by the clan-mothers. The clan-mothers also had the right to wage war, and as Henry Timberlake wrote, the stories about Amazon women warriors were not so farfetched considering how many Indian women were famous warriors

and powerful voices in the councils. . . . The war women carried the titled Beloved Women, and their power was great. . . . The Women's Council, as distinguished from the District, village, or Confederacy councils, was powerful in a number of political and socio-spiritual ways, and may have had the deciding voice on which males would serve on the Councils. . . . Certainly the Women's Council was influential in tribal decisions, and its spokeswomen served as War Women and Peace Women, presumably holding offices in the towns designated as red towns and white towns, respectively. Their other powers included the right to speak in the men's Council [although men lacked a reciprocal right, under most circumstances], the right to choose whom and whether to marry, the right to bear arms, and the right to choose their extramarital occupations.[14]

While Creek and Cherokee women "may" have held the right to select which males assumed positions of political responsibility, this was unquestionably the case within the Haudenosaunee (Six Nations Iroquois Confederacy) of New York state. Among the "Sixers," each of the fifty extended families (clans) was headed by a clan mother. These women formed a council within the confederacy which selected the males who would hold positions on a second council, composed of men, representing the confederacy's interests, both in formulation of internal policies and in conduct of external relations. If at any time, particular male council members adopted positions or undertook policies perceived by the women's council as being contrary to the people's interests, their respective clan mothers retained the right to replace them. Although much diminished after two centuries of U.S. colonial domination, this "Longhouse" form of government is ongoing today.[15]

The Haudenosaunee were hardly alone among northeastern peoples in according women such a measure of power. At the time of the European arrival in North America, the Narragansett of what is now Rhode Island were headed by a "sunksquaw," or female chief. The last of these, a woman named Magnus, was executed along with ninety other members of the Narragansett government after their defeat by English Major James Talcot in 1675.[16] During the same period, the Esopus Confederacy was led, at least in part, by a woman named Mamanuchqua (also known as Mamareoktwe, Mamaroch, and Mamaprocht).[17] The Delawares *generically* referred to themselves as "women," considering the term to be supremely complementary.[18] Among other Algonquin peoples of the Atlantic Coast region—e.g., the Wampanoag and Massachusetts Confederacies, and the Niaticks, Scaticooks, Niantics, Pictaways, Powhatans, and Caconnets—much the same pattern prevailed:

> From before 1620 until her death in 1677, a squaw-sachem known as the "Massachusetts Queen" by the Virginia colonizers governed the Massachusetts Confederacy. It was her fortune to preside over the Confederacy's destruction as the people were decimated by disease, war, and colonial manipulations. . . . Others include the Pocasett sunksquaw Weetamoo, who was King Philip's ally and "served as a war chief commanding over 300 warriors" during his war with the British. . . . Awashonks, another [woman head of state] of the Mid-Atlantic region, was squaw-sachem of the Sakonnet, a [nation] allied with the Wampanoag Confederacy. She [held her office] in the latter part of the seventeenth century. After fighting for a time against the British during King Philip's War, she was forced to surrender. Because she then convinced her warriors to fight with the British, she was able to save them from enslavement in the West Indies.[19]

Women's power within traditional Indian societies was also grounded in other ways. While patrilineal/patrilocal cultures did exist, most precontact North American civilizations functioned on the basis of matrilineage and matrilocality. Insofar as family structures centered upon the identities of wives rather than husbands—men joined women's families, not the other way around—and because men were usually expected to relocate to join the women they married, the context of native social life was radically different from that which prevailed (and prevails) in European and Euro-derived cultures.[20]

> Many of the largest and most important Indian peoples were matrilineal. . . . Among these were: in the East, the Iroquois, the Siouan [nations] of the Piedmont and Atlantic coastal plain, the Mohegan, the Delaware, various other [nations] of southern New England, and the divisions of the Powhatan Confederacy in Virginia; in the South, the Creek, the Choctaw, the Chickasaw, the Seminole, and the [nations] of the Caddoan linguistic family; in the Great Plains, the Pawnee, the Hidatsa, the Mandan, the Oto, the Missouri, and the Crow and other Siouan [nations]; in the southwest, the Navajo, and the numerous so-called Pueblo [nations], including the well known Hopi, Laguna, Acoma, and Zuñi.[21]

In many indigenous societies, the position of women was further strengthened economically, by virtue of their owning all or most property. Haudenosaunee women, for example, owned the fields which produced about two-thirds of their people's diet.[22] Among the Lakota, men owned nothing but their clothing, a horse for hunting, weapons and spiritual items; homes, furnishings, and the like were the property of their wives. All a Lakota woman needed to do in order to divorce her husband was to set his meager personal possessions outside the door of their lodge, an action against which he had no appeal under traditional law.[23] Much the same

system prevailed among the Anishinabé and numerous other native cultures. As Mary Oshana, an Anishinabé activist, has explained it:

> Matrilineal [nations] provided the greatest opportunities for women: women in these [nations] owned houses, furnishings, fields, gardens, agricultural tools, art objects, livestock and horses. Furthermore, these items were passed down through female lines. Regardless of their marital status, women had the right to own and control property. The woman had control of the children and if marital problems developed the man would leave the home.[24]

Additional reinforcement of native women's status accrues from the spiritual traditions of most of North America's indigenous cultures. First, contrary to the Euroamerican myth that American Indian spiritual leaders are invariably something called "medicine men," women have always held important positions in this regard. Prime examples include Coocoochee of the Mohawks, Sanapia of the Comanches, and Pretty Shield of the Crows.[25] Among the Zuñi and other Puebloan cultures, women were members of the Rain Priesthood, the most important of that society's religious entities.[26] Women are also known to have played crucial leadership roles within Anishinabé, Blackfeet, Chilula, and Diné spiritual practices, as well as those of many other native societies.[27]

More important in some ways, virtually all indigenous religions on this continent exhibit an abundant presence of feminine elements within their cosmologies.[28] When contrasted to the hegemonic masculinity of the deities embraced by such "world religions" as Judaism, Christianity, and Islam—and the corresponding male supremacism marking those societies which adhere to them—the real significance of concepts like Mother

Earth (universal), Spider woman (Hopi and Diné), White Buffalo Calf Woman (Lakota), Grandmother Turtle (Iroquois), Sky Woman (Iroquois), Hard Beings Woman and Sand Altar Woman (Hopi), First Woman (Abanaki), Thought Woman (Laguna), Corn Woman (Cherokee), and Changing Woman (Diné) becomes rather obvious.[29] So too does the real rather than the mythical status of women in traditional Native American life. Indeed, as Diné artist Mary Morez has put it, "In [our] society, the woman is the dominant figure who becomes the wise one with old age. It's a [matrilineal/matrilocal] society, you know. But the Navajo woman never demands her status. She achieves, earns, accomplishes it through maturity. That maturing process is psychological. It has to do with one's feelings for the land and being part of the whole cycle of nature. It's difficult to-describe to a non-Indian."[30]

Bea Medicine, a Hunkpapa Lakota scholar, concurs, noting that "Our power is obvious. [Women] are primary socializers of our children. Culture is transmitted primarily through the mother. The mother teaches languages, attitudes, beliefs, behavior patterns, etc."[31] Anishinabé writer and activist Winona LaDuke concludes, "Traditionally, American Indian women were never subordinate to men. Or vice versa, for that matter. What native societies have always been about is achieving balance in all things, gender relations no less than any other. Nobody needs to tell us how to do it. We've had that all worked out for thousands of years. And, left to our own devices, that's exactly how we'd be living right now."[32] Or, as Priscilla K. Buffalohead, another Anishinabé scholar, has put it, "[We] stem from egalitarian cultural traditions. These traditions are concerned less with equality of the sexes and more with the dignity of the individual and their inherent right—whether they be women, men or children—to make their own choices and decisions."[33]

DISEMPOWERMENT

The reduction of the status held by women within indigenous nations was a first priority for European colonizers eager to weaken and destabilize target societies. With regard to the Montagnais and Naskapi of the St. Lawrence River Valley, for example, the French, who first entered the area in the 1550s, encountered a people among whom "women have great power. . . . A man may promise you something and if he does not keep his promise, he thinks he is sufficiently excused when he tells you that his wife did not wish him to do it."[34] They responded, beginning in 1633, by sending Jesuit missionaries to show the natives a "better and more enlightened way" of comporting themselves, a matter well-chronicled by the priest, Paul Le Jeune:

> Though some observers saw women as drudges, Le Jeune saw women as holding "great power" and having "in every instance . . . the choice of plans, of undertakings, of journeys, of winterings." Indeed, independence of women was considered a problem by the Jesuits, who lectured the men about "allowing" their wives sexual and other freedom and sought to introduce European principles of obedience.[35]

Most likely, the Jesuit program would have gone nowhere had the sharp end of colonization not undercut the Montagnais-Naskapi traditional economy, replacing it with a system far more reliant upon fur trapping and traders by the latter part of the 17th century.[36] As their dependence upon their colonizers increased, the

Indians were compelled to accept more and more of the European brand of "morality." The Jesuits imposed a form of monogamy in which divorce was forbidden, implemented a system of compulsory Catholic education, and refused to deal with anyone other than selected male "representatives" of the Montagnais and Naskapi in political or economic affairs (thus deforming the Indian structure of governance beyond recognition).[37]

> Positions of formal power such as political leadership, [spiritual leadership], and matrilocality, which placed the economic dependence of a woman with children in the hands of her mother's family . . . shifted. [Spiritual and political leadership were male [by 1750], and matrilocality had become patrilocality. This is not so strange given the economics of the situation and the fact that over the years the Montagnais became entirely Catholicized.[38]

Among the Haudenosaunee, who were not militarily defeated until after the American Revolution, such changes took much longer. It was not until the early 19th century that, in an attempt to adjust to the new circumstances of subordination to the United States, the Seneca prophet Handsome Lake promulgated a new code of law and social organization which replaced their old "petticoat government" with a male-centered model more acceptable to the colonizers.[39] In attempting to shift power from "the meddling old women" of Iroquois society,

> Handsome Lake advocated that young women cleave to their husbands rather than to their mothers and abandon the man-mother controlled Longhouse in favor of a patriarchal, nuclear family arrangement. . . . While the shift was never complete, it was sufficient. Under the Code of Handsome Lake, which was the tribal version of the white man's way, the Longhouse declined in importance, and eventually

Iroquois women were firmly under the thumb of Christian patriarchy.[40]

To the south, the British worked hard to lessen the power of women in Cherokee affairs. They took Cherokee men to England and educated them in European ways. These men returned to Cherokee country and exerted great influence on behalf of the British in the region.[41] Intermarriage was also encouraged, with markedly privileged treatment accorded mixed-blood offspring of such unions with English colonialists. In time, when combined with increasing Cherokee dependence on the British trade economy, these advantages resulted in a situation where "men with little Cherokee blood [and even less loyalty] wielded considerable power over the nation's policies."[42] Aping the English, this new male leadership set out to establish a plantation economy devoted to the growing of cotton and tobacco.

> The male leadership bought and sold not only black men and women but men and women from neighboring tribes, the women of the leadership retreated to Bible classes, sewing circles, and petticoats that rivaled those of their white sisters. Many of these upper-strata Cherokee women married white ministers and other opportunists, as the men of their class married white women, often the daughters of white ministers. . . . Cherokee society became rigid and modeled on Christian white social organization of upper, middle, and impoverished classes usually composed of very traditional clans.[43]

This situation, of course, greatly weakened the Cherokee Nation, creating sharp divisions within it which have not completely healed even to the present day. Moreover, it caused Euroamericans in surrounding areas to covet not only Cherokee land *per se,* but the lucrative farming enterprises built up by the mixed-blood male caste. This was a powerful incentive for the U.S. to undertake the compulsory removal of the Cherokees and other indigenous nations from east of the Mississippi to points west during the first half of the 19th century.[44] The reaction of assimilated Cherokees was an attempt to show their "worth" by becoming even more ostentatiously Europeanized.

> In an effort to stave off removal, the Cherokee in the early 1800s, under the leadership of men such as Elias Boudinot, Major Ridge, and John Ross (later Principal Chief of the Cherokee in Oklahoma Territory), and others, drafted a constitution that disenfranchised women and blacks. Modeled after the Constitution of the United Sates, whose favor they were attempting to curry, and in conjunction with Christian sympathizers to the Cherokee cause, the new Cherokee constitution relegated women to the position of chattel. . . . [Under such conditions], the last Beloved Woman, Nancy Ward, resigned her office in 1817, sending her cane and her vote on important questions to the Cherokee Council.[45]

Despite much groveling by the "sell-outs," Andrew Jackson ordered removal of the Cherokees—as well as the Creeks, Choctaws, Chickasaws, and Seminoles—to begin in 1832.[46] By 1839, the "Trail of Tears" was complete, with catastrophic population loss for the indigenous nations involved.[47] By the latter stage, traditionalist Cherokees had overcome sanctions against killing other tribal members in a desperate attempt to restore some semblance of order within their nation: Major Ridge, his eldest son, John, and Elias Boudinot were assassinated on June 22, 1839.[48] Attempts were made to eliminate other members of the "Ridge Faction" such as Stand Watie, John A. Bell, James Starr, and George W. Adair, but these failed, and the assimilationist faction continued to do substantial damage to Cherokee sovereignty.[49] Although John Rollin Ridge, the Major's grandson, was forced to flee to California in 1850 and was unable to return to Cherokee Country until after the Civil War,[50] Stand Watie (Boudinot's younger brother) managed to lead a portion of the Cherokees into a disastrous alliance with the Confederacy from which the nation never recovered.[51]

Across the continent, the story was the same in every case. In *not one* of the more than 370 ratified and perhaps 300 unratified treaties negotiated by the United States with indigenous nations was the federal government willing to allow participation by native women. In *none* of the several thousand non-treaty agreements reached between the United States and these same nations were federal representatives prepared to discuss anything at all with women. In *no* instance was the United States open to recognizing a female as representing her people's interests when it came to administering the reservations onto which American Indians were ultimately forced; always, men were required to do what was necessary to secure delivery of rations, argue for water rights, and all the rest.[52] Meanwhile, . . . the best and most patriotic of the indigenous male leadership—men like Tecumseh, Osceola, Crazy Horse, and Sitting Bull—were systematically assassinated or sent to faraway prisons for extended periods. The male leadership of the native resistance was then replaced with men selected on the basis of their willingness to cooperate with their oppressors. Exactly how native women coped with this vast alteration of their circumstances, and those of their people more generally, is a bit mysterious:

> If a generalization may be made, it is that female roles of mother, sister, and wife were ongoing because of the continued care

they were supposed to provide for the family. But what of the role of women in relationship to agents, to soldiers guarding the "hostiles," and to their general physical deprivation in societies whose livelihood and way of life had been destroyed along with the bison? We are very nearly bereft of data and statements which could clarify the transitional status of women during this period. The strategies adopted for cultural survival and the means of transmitting these to daughters and nieces are valuable adaptive mechanisms which cannot be even partially reconstructed.[53]

These practical realities, imposed quite uniformly by the conquerors, were steadily reinforced by officially sponsored missionizing and mandatory education in boarding schools, processes designed to inculcate the notion that such disempowerment of Indian women and liquidation of "recalcitrant" males was "natural, right, and inevitable."[54] . . .

NOTES

1. Burke Leacock, Eleanor, *Myths of Male Dominance: Collected Articles on Women Cross-Culturally,* Monthly Review Press, New York, 1981.
2. Valentine, Paul, "Dances with Myths," *Washington Post;* reprinted in the *Boulder* [Colorado] *Daily Camera,* April 7, 1991.
3. Valentine also informs us that these "nomadic hunters and gatherers moved from spot to spot, strewing refuse in their wake" (What sort of "refuse"? Plastic? Aluminum cans? Polyvinyl Chlorides?) before running down the usual litany of imagined native defects: "[Indians] were totalitarian, warlike and extremely brutal. Some practiced slavery, torture, human sacrifice and cannibalism, and imposed rigid social dictatorships." That there is not one shred of solid evidence supporting *any* of this is no bother. Valentine and his ilk simply condemn anyone bothering with the facts as a "politically correct . . . revisionist." Left unexplained is why anyone might deliberately seek to be politically *incorrect,* or why blatant inaccuracies or lies—such as those in which they trade—shouldn't be revised and corrected.
4. Ehrenreich, Barbara, "The Warrior Culture," *Time,* October 15, 1990. It should be noted that the practice of scalping, derived from the taking of heads, was introduced to North America by the British, who had earlier developed the technique during the conquest and colonization of Ireland (see Canny, Nicholas P., "The Ideology of English Colonization: From Ireland to America," *William and Mary Quarterly,* 3rd Ser., No. 30, 1973, pp. 575–98). For a more detailed response, see Ward Churchill's letter on the article (frozen out of *Time*) in *Z Magazine,* November 1990.
5. McNickle, D'Arcy, *The Surrounded,* University of New Mexico Press, Albuquerque (2nd edition), 1978.
6. Gunn Allen, Paula, *The Sacred Hoop: Recovering the Feminine in American Indian Traditions,* Beacon Press, Boston, 1986, p. 266.
7. Indication of the relatively higher valuation placed upon women may be found in the fact that among the Iroquois, Susquehannahs, and Abenakis ("Hurons"), for example, the penalty for killing a woman was double that for killing a man (see Thomas Foreman, Caroline, *American Indian Women Chiefs,* Hoffman Printing Co., Muskogee, OK (1954, p. 9). On the diversity of native women's social functions and activities, see Shirer Mathes, Valerie, "A New Look at the Role of Women in Indian Societies," *American Indian Quarterly,* Vol. 2, No. 2, 1975, pp. 131–39.
8. See Thomas Foreman, op. cit., pp. 85–7. Also see Coulter, E. Merton, "Mary Musgrove, Queen of the Creeks; A Chapter of the Early Georgia Troubles," *Georgia Historical Quarterly,* Vol. 11, no. 1, 1927, pp. 1–30, and Corry, John Pitts, "Some New Light on the Bosworth Claims," *Georgia Historical Quarterly,* No. 25, 1941, pp. 195–224 The novel in question is Brown, Dee, *Creek Mary's Blood,* Simon and Schuster Publishers, New York, 1981.
9. Discussion with Madonna Thunderhawk (Hunkpapa Lakota), April 1985; discussion with Robert Grey Eagle (Oglala Lakota), July 1991.
10. Thomas Foreman, op. cit., p. 85.
11. See Lewis, Oscar, "Manly-Hearted Women Among the Northern Piegan," *American Anthropologist,* No. 43, 1941, pp. 173–87.
12. On Buffalo Calf Road, see Agonito, Rosemary, and Joseph Agonito, "Resurrecting History's Forgotten Women: A Case Study from the Cheyenne Indians," *Frontiers: A Journal of Women's Studies,* No. 6, Fall 1981, pp. 8–9; and Sandoz, Mari, *Cheyenne Autumn,* Avon Books, New York, 1964). Information on four other 19th-century warrior women may be found in Ewers, John C., "Deadlier than the Male," *American Heritage,* No. 16, 1965, pp. 10–13. More generally, see Medicine, Bea, "'Warrier Women': Sex Role Alternatives for Plains Indian Women," in Patricia Albers and Beatrice Medicine, eds., *The Hidden Half: Studies of*

Plains Indian Women, University Press of America, Lanham, MD, 1983, pp. 267–80.

13. Robin Morgan's *The Demon Lover: On the Sexuality of Terrorism* (W.W. Norton Publishers, New York, 1989), in which any female engaged in physical combat is found to be the mere pawn of some man (or at least "male energy") is the most extraordinarily insulting and demeaning treatise possible, not only for Native American women, but for African Americans like Assata Shakur, Latinas like Lolita Labron and Alejandrina Tones, Europeans like Ingrid Barabass and Monica Helbing, Euroamericans like Susan Rosenberg and Linda Evans, and perhaps a quarter of the female populations of Africa, Asia, and Palestine.

14. Gunn Allen, op. cit., pp. 36-37. She is drawing on Timberlake, Lt. Henry, *Lieutenant Henry Timberlake's Memoirs,* Marietta, GA, 1948, p. 94.

15. Concerning the ongoing nature of the Longhouse government, and women's role in it, see Anonymous, "A Woman's Ways: An Interview with Judy Swamp," *Parabola,* Vol. 5, No. 4, 1980, pp. 52–61. Also see Cook, Katsi, "The Women's Dance: Reclaiming Our Powers on the Women's Side of Life," *Native Self-Sufficiency,* No. 6, 1981, pp. 17–19.

16. See Grumet, Robert Steven, "Sunksquaws, Shamans, and Tradeswomen: Middle-Atlantic Coastal Algonkian Women During the 17th and 18th Centuries," in Mona Etienne and Eleanor Burke Leacock, eds., *Women and Colonization: Anthropological Perspectives,* Praeger Publishers, New York, 1980.

17. Ibid., pp. 51-2.

18. See Wallace, Anthony F.C., "Women, Land, and Society: Three Aspects of Aboriginal Delaware Life," *Pennsylvania Archaeologist,* No. 17, 1947, pp. 1–35; and Weslager, C.S., "The Delaware Indians as Women," *Journal of the Washington Academy of Science,* No. 37, September 15, 1947, pp. 298–304.

19. Gunn Allen, op. cit., p. 35. She relies heavily on Grumet, op. cit.

20. For further information on these customs, see Niethammer, Carolyn, *Daughters of the Earth: The Lives and Legends of Native American Women,* Macmillan Publishers, New York, 1977. Also see Kidwell, Clara Sue, "The Power of Women in Three American Indian Societies," *Journal of Ethnic Studies,* Vol. 6, No. 3, 1979, pp. 113–21. An overview of the extent to which matrilineal/matrilocal societies predominated in precontact Native North America, see Lowie, Robert H., "The Matrilineal Complex," *University of California Publications in Archaeology and Ethnology,* No. 16, 1919-1920, pp. 29–45.

21 Terrell, John Upton, and Donna M. Terrell, *Indian Women of the Western Morning: Their Life in Early America,* Anchor Books, New York, 1974, p. 24.

22. See Brown, Judith K., "Economic Organization and the Position of Women Among the Iroquois," *Ethnohistory,* Vol. 17, Nos. 3–4, Summer–Fall 1970, pp. 151–67. Also see Trigger, Bruce G. "Iroquoian Matriliny," *Pennsylvania Archaeologist,* No. 48, 1978, pp. 55–65.

23. See Powers, Marla N., *Oglala Women: Myth, Ritual and Reality,* University of Chicago Press, Chicago, 1986, p. 89.

24. Oshana, Mary, "Native American Women in Westerns: Reality and Myth," *Frontiers. A Journal of Women's Studies,* No. 6, Fall 1981, p. 46.

25. See Hornbeck Tanner, Helen, "Coocoochee: Mohawk Medicine Woman," *American Indian Culture and Research Journal,* Vol. 3, No. 3, 1979, pp. 23–42; Jones, David, *Sanapia: A Comanche Medicine Woman,* Holt, Rinehart and Winston Publishers, New York, 1968; and Linderman, Frank, *Pretty Shield: Medicine Woman of the Crows,* John Day Publishers, New York, 1932; reprinted 1974.

26. Terrell and Terrell, op. cit., p. 25.

27. See Landes, Ruth, *The Ojibwa Religion and the Midewiwin,* University of Wisconsin Press, Madison, 1968; Kent, Susan, "Hogans, Sacred Circles and Symbols: The Navajo Use of Space," in David Brugge and Charlotte J. Frisbie, eds., *Essays in Honor of Leland Wyman,* Museum of New Mexico Press, Santa Fe, 1982; Lake, Robert G., "Chilula Religion and Ideology: A Discussion of Native American Humanistic Concepts and Processes," *Humbolt Journal of Social Relations,* Vol. 7, No. 2, 1980, pp. 113–34; and Kehoe, Alice, "Old Woman Had Great Power," *Western Canadian Journal of Anthropology,* Vol. 6, No. 3, 1976, pp. 68–76. Also see Thrift Nelson, Ann, "Native American Women's Ritual Sodalities in Native North America," *Western Canadian Journal of Anthropology,* Vol. 6, No. 3, 1976, pp. 29–67.

28. For a thorough analysis of the metatheological precepts embodied in indigenous American spirituality, see Deloria, Vine Jr., *God Is Red,* Grossett and Dunlap Publishers, New York, 1973. reprinted by Dell Books, New York, 1983. Further elaboration is provided in his *Metaphysics of Modern Existence,* Harper and Row Publishers, New York, 1979.

29. Contrary to the contentions of University of Colorado Professor of Religious Studies Sam Gill, the idea of Mother Earth—which is quite universal among Native North Americans—was not imported from Europe (Gill, Sam D., *Mother Earth: An American Story,* University of Chicago Press, Chicago, 1987). For detailed refutation, see the special section of *Bloomsbury Review,* (Vol. 8, No. 5, September–October 1988) edited

by M. Annette Jaimes and devoted to critique of Gill's thesis and methods.

30. Quoted in Katz, op. cit., p. 126. For further background on the status of Diné women, see Stewart, Irene, *A Voice in Her Tribe: A Navajo Woman's Own Story,* Ballena Press, Socorro, NM, 1980; and Roessel, Ruth, *Women in Navajo Society,* Navajo Resource Center, Rough Rock, AZ, 1981.

31. Quoted in Katz, op. cit., p. 123.

32. From a talk delivered during International Women's Week, University of Colorado at Boulder, April 1985 (tape on file).

33. Buffalohead, Priscilla K., "Farmers, Warriors, Traders: A Fresh Look at Ojibway Women," *Minnesota History,* No. 48, Summer 1983, p. 236.

34. Thwaites, Rubin Gold, ed., *The Jesuit Relations and Allied Documents,* Vol. 5 (of 71 Volumes), Burrow Brothers Publishers, Cleveland, 1906, p. 179.

35. Leacock, op. cit., p. 35.

36. For a broader examination of the impact of the fur trade upon the internal structures of indigenous societies, see Van Kirk, Sylvia, *Many Tender Ties: Women in Fur-Trade Society, 1670–1870,* University of Oklahoma Press, Norman, 1980.

37. Leacock, "Montagnais Women and the Jesuit Program for Colonization," in ibid., pp. 43–62.

38. Gunn Allen, op. cit., p. 40.

39. The expression "petticoat government" comes from the British colonialist John Adair in regard to the Cherokee Nation. See Brown, John P., *Old Frontiers,* State Historical Society of Wisconsin, Madison, 1938, p. 20.

40. Gunn Allen, op. cit., p. 33. She relies upon Brandon, William, *The Last Americans: The Indian in American Culture,* McGraw-Hill Publishers, New York, 1974, p. 214.

41. Gunn Allen, op. cit., p. 37.

42. Ibid. It should be noted that this calculated and vicious colonialist use of mixed-bloods as a means to undercut traditional societies, a tactic which is ongoing in the present day, is a primary cause of the sort of racially-oriented infighting among Indians which continues to confuse the questions of Indian identity addressed in Chapter Four.

43. Ibid.

44. For a solid sample of the avaricious sentiments involved in this federal policy, see U.S. Congress, *Speeches on the Passage of the Bill for Removal of the Indians, Delivered in the Congress of the United States, April and May, 1830,* Perkins and Marvin Publishers, Boston, 1830; Kraus Reprint Co., Millwood, NY, 1973.

45. Gunn Allen, op. cit., pp. 37–8. It should be noted that the three men named did not share the same position on Cherokee removal. John Ross, "despite his large degree of white blood," was an ardent Cherokee patriot and fought mightily against U.S. policy (see Eaton, Rachel E., *John Ross and the Cherokee People,* Cherokee National Museum, Muskogee, OK, 1921). Boudinot and Major Ridge (or "The Ridge"), were devout assimilationists who worked—for a fee— to further U.S. interests by engineering an appearance of acceptance of removal among their own people (see Wilkins, Thurman, *Cherokee Tragedy: The Ridge Family and the Decimation of a People,* University of Oklahoma Press, Norman [2nd edition, revised], 1986). On Nancy Ward, see Tucker, Norma, "Nancy Ward: Gighau of the Cherokees," *Georgia Historical Quarterly,* No. 53, June 1969, pp. 192–200.

46. On the forced relocation, see Pirtle, Caleb III, *The Trail of Broken Promises: Removal of the Five Civilized Tribes to Oklahoma,* Eakin Press, Austin, TX, 1987.

47. Cherokee demographer Russell Thornton estimates that about 10,000 Cherokees—approximately half the nation's population—perished as a result of the Trail of Tears. See Thornton, Russell, *The Cherokees.: A Population History,* University of Nebraska Press, Lincoln, 1990, pp. 73–7.

48. Starr, Emmet McDonald, *Starr's History of the Cherokee Indians,* Indian Heritage Association, Fayetteville, AK, 1922; reprinted 1967, p. 113.

49. Wardell, Morris L., *A Political History of the Cherokee Nation 1838–1907,* University of Oklahoma Press, Norman, 1938; reprinted 1977, p. 17.

50. See Parins, James W., *John Rollin Ridge: His Life and Works,* University of Nebraska Press, Lincoln, 1991.

51. See Franks, Kenny A., *Stand Watie and the Agony of the Cherokee Nation,* Memphis State University Press, Memphis, TN, 1979.

52. The author has been through hundreds of the relevant documents—all of them engineered in Washingon, D.C.—without ever coming across a single reference to federal negotiators dealing with a native woman responsibly. Instead, they appear to have been quite uniformly barred from meetings and other proceedings, these being "men's work" in the Euroamerican view. Early reservation records are replete with the same attitude.

53. Medicine, Bea, "The Interaction of Culture and Sex Roles in Schools," in U.S. Department of Education, Office of Educational Research and Development. National Institute of Education, *Conference on Educational and Occupational Needs of Amencan Indian Women,* October 1976, U.S. Government Printing Office, Washington, D.C., 1980, p. 149.

54. For an excellent first-hand recounting of the process, see Lindsey, Lilah Denton, "Memories of the Indian Territory Mission Field," *Chronicles of Oklahoma,* No. 36, Summer 1958, p. 181–98.

STUDY QUESTIONS: GENDER ROLES AND MORALITY

1. According to Gilligan what is the difference between care reasoning and justice reasoning? Provide two different arguments, one from the care perspective and one from the justice perspective, in favor of Heinz stealing the drug from the pharmacist. Which argument do you find most plausible? Why?

2. Friedman argues that even seemingly benevolent male paternalism is a problem for women in traditional families. What is meant by benevolent paternalism? According to Friedman why is it a problem for women? From Blankenhorn's perspective, provide a counterargument to Friedman's view.

3. Anderson argues that gender equality in the home does not necessarily lead to the "decline of the family." Set out some of his reasons in support of this claim. Then provide a sustained counterargument to his view by referring to Blankenhorn's essay. Which view do you find most plausible? Why?

4. The gender roles in Islamic societies are very different from Western gender roles. For example, women in some Islamic societies must wear veils to cover their faces and must cover the rest of their bodies when they leave the house. First, provide an argument showing that this policy creates inequality between men and women. Then provide a counterargument showing that policies like this that respect the differences between men and women can actually create equality. Which argument do you find most plausible? Why?

5. In 1991, Antioch College in Ohio instituted a Sexual Offense Policy. In part it required that
   (a) consent must be obtained verbally before there is any sexual contact or conduct;
   (b) if the level of sexual intimacy increases during an interaction (e.g., if two people move from kissing while fully clothed—which is one level— to undressing for direct physical contact, which is another level), the people involved need to express their clear verbal consent before moving to that new level.
   First, offer arguments defending such a policy. Second mount a counterargument to this policy.

6. In their essay, M. Annette Jaimes and Theresa Haisey quote Mary Morez, "In [our] society, the woman is the dominant figure who becomes the wise one with old age. It's a (matrilineal/matrilocal] society . . . the Navajo woman never demands her status. She achieves, earns, accomplishes it . . . . It has to do with one's feelings for the land and being part of the whole cycle of nature. It's difficult to describe to a non-Indian." Discuss the emphasis on responsibility over rights, interconnection with all of nature, respect for women, and the type of culture and society that result from these emphases. What advantages do you see in this representation of women's status in society over the dominant one in our society?

SUPPLEMENTARY READINGS: GENDER ROLES AND MORALITY

ACCAD, EVELYNE. "Sexuality and Sexual Politics: Conflicts and Contradictions for Contemporary Women in the Middle East." In *Third World Women and the Politics of Feminism,* Mohanty, Russo, and Torres, editors. Bloomington, IN: Indiana University Press, 1991.

ALEXANDER, M. JACQUI. "Redrafting Morality: The Postcolonial State and the Sexual Offenses Bill of Trinidad and Tobago." In *Third World Women and the Politics of Feminism,* Mohanty, Russo, and Torres, editors. Bloomington, IN: Indiana University Press, 1991.

ANAGOL-McGINN, PADMA. "Sexual Harassment in India: A Case Study of Eve-teasing in Historical Perspective." In *Rethinking Sexual Harassment*, Brant and Too, editors. London: Pluto Press, 1994.

BAIER, ANNETTE. "Whom Can Women Trust." In *Feminist Ethics,* Card, editor. Lawrence, KS: University of Kansas Press, 1991.

BARRY, KATHLEEN. "Female Sexual Slavery: Understanding the International Dimensions of Women's Oppression." *Human Rights Quarterly,* vol. 3(2), Spring 1981.

CHEN, MARTHA. "A Matter of Survival: Women's Right to Employment in India and Bangladesh." In *Women, Culture, and Development,* Nussbaum and Glover, editors. Oxford: Clarendon Press, 1995.

CHOW, ESTHER NGAN-LING. "The Feminist Movement: Where Are All the Asian American Women?" In *From Different Shores: Perspectives on Race and Ethnicity in America,* second edition, Takaki, editor. New York: Oxford University Press, 1994.

DILLON, ROBIN S. "Care and Respect." In *Explorations in Feminist Ethics,* Cole and Coultrap-McQuin, editors. Bloomington, IN: Indiana University Press, 1992.

EL MERNISSI, FATIMA. "Democracy as Moral Disintegration: The Contradiction Between Religious Belief and Citizenship as a Manifestation of the Ahistoricity of the Arab Identity." In *Women of the Arab World,* Toubia, editor. London: Zed Books, 1988.

HARDING, SANDRA. "The Curious Coincidence of Feminine and African Moralities." In *Women and Moral Theory,* Kittay and Meyers, editors. Totowa, NJ: Rowman & Littlefield, 1987.

HOAGLAND, SARAH LUCIA. "Lesbian Ethics and Female Agency." In *Explorations in Feminist Ethics,* Cole and Coultrap-McQuin, editors. Bloomington, IN: Indiana University Press, 1992.

JAGGAR, ALISON. "On Sexual Equality." *Ethics,* 1974.

LEVIN, MICHAEL. "Sex, The Family, and the Liberal Order." In *Feminism and Freedom.* New Brunswick, NJ: Transaction Books, 1987.

MacKINNON, CATHERINE. "Racial and Sexual Harassment." In *Only Words.* Cambridge, MA: Harvard University Press, 1993.

MAJOR, BRENDA. "Gender, Entitlement, and the Distribution of Family Labor." *Journal of Social Issues,* vol. 49 (3), 1993.

MOODY-ADAMS, MICHELLE. "Gender and the Complexity of Moral Voices." In *Feminist Ethics,* Card, editor. Lawrence, KS: University of Kansas Press, 1991.

STEVENS, EVELYN P. "*Marianismo*: The Other Face of *Machismo* in Latin America." In *Female and Male in Latin America*, edited by Pascatello. Pittsburgh, PA: University of Pittsburgh Press, 1973.

SWANTON, CHRISTINE, VIVIANE ROBINSON, and JAN CROSTHWAITE. "Treating Women as Sex-Objects." *Journal of Social Philosophy,* vol. 20(3), Winter 1989.

TONG, ROSEMARY. "Sexual Harassment." In *Women, Sex and the Law.* Totowa, NJ: Rowman and Allenheld, 1984.

VI

RACIAL AND ETHNIC DISCRIMINATION

Prejudice is the reason of fools.

—Voltaire

Racial and ethnic discrimination is a fact of life for many people. Although the more blatant forms may have declined in certain countries within the last 30 years or so, discrimination persists in many areas of life. Economically, in the United States, there is still unequal pay. In 1992, women and minorities earned an average of 75 cents for every dollar earned by white men for the same job. Furthermore, many desirable jobs are still without any minority or women employees. This situation is referred to as the "glass ceiling" and is an invisible barrier in the job market which keeps women and minorities "in their place" on the job. Low pay is a particularly effective tool for keeping groups of people fixed at a lower societal position and precluding their equal access to political, social, and economic power.

There is far-reaching agreement that discrimination against women and minorities, based on the trait of gender or ethnic origin, is morally wrong. These practices of discrimination violate the *principle of equality*. Although not universally accepted, this principle mandates that equals be treated equally, and that unequals be treated unequally. The treatment should be based on relevant similarities or differences among individuals. Relevant differences in job hiring are those that have to do with job performance. For example, for a mechanic's position, one needs proper training and education to meet the requirements for certification. Sex and race are not relevant traits for the job, and to deny anyone a job based on these traits is to violate the principle of equality. Normally, the principle of equality is not violated when discrimination is based on relevant differences such as training or ability. Furthermore, it does not always violate the principle of equality to discriminate based on race—as, for example, only auditioning a black man to play Othello, since the part calls for a black man. What is morally objectionable is to discriminate based on irrelevant traits.

However, there is no such far-reaching agreement on how to correct past and present practices that systematically discriminate against women and minorities. The principle of equality requires that equals be treated equally in the matters of hiring, promotion, and pay. If the principle of equality entails a moral right, employers are morally obligated not to violate this principle. Furthermore, there is a legal obligation in the United States not to discriminate based on irrelevant traits such as racial or ethnic origin. However, it is controversial whether or not a business must go beyond this obligation and adopt a policy actively favoring minorities or women. Affirmative action is one such policy.

Affirmative action programs range from actively recruiting qualified minorities and women, to favoring qualified, though unequally qualified minority and women applicants, to establishing quota systems whereby a certain number of minorities or women *must* be hired. Although all three are preferential treatment programs, the last two provoke the most controversy. Affirmative action is often criticized as perpetuating the harms which it hopes to cure, and for this reason some of its opponents call affirmative action "reverse discrimination." They argue that affirmative action uses the same morally irrelevant traits used in unjust racial discrimination, and thus it is inconsistent and not morally justifiable. Proponents of affirmative action argue that it is fair and consistent, as well as necessary to correct past injustices. Proponents also argue that without active intervention, minority applicants will not have access to their fair share of the prized jobs in society. In the United States, hard quotas have been ruled unconstitutional; however, the shortage of minorities in some professions may constitute a "compelling state interest," and active recruitment to correct this imbalance would then be legally acceptable.

Bernard Boxill addresses such a compelling interest and argues in favor of color-conscious policies such as affirmative action. Boxill addresses the need of minorities to have representation in the professions, such as the need for Black attorneys. Boxill asserts that a doctor or lawyer with black skin is more likely to provide services to those who otherwise would not have access to them. He contends that colorblind policies involve a grave cost to self-esteem, as they imply that people should not be treated differently just because they are born with qualities such as dark skin color. However, society does not value dark skin and discriminates accordingly, further aggravating the shortage of Black professionals. Concerned that Blacks receive fair consideration, he argues for a type of merit in color-conscious policies wherein differences in color and talent are equally weighted. He concludes that color-conscious policies can be justifiable in the same way that talent-based policies can be.

Shelby Steele argues that affirmative action is unjustified because it harms the people that it was designed to help. Steele focuses on affirmative action as a form of reparation. Regarding reparations, he argues that affirmative action is a form of repayment for past discrimination against minorities and women. Steele points out that this requires recipients of affirmative action to not only see themselves as victims but also to become invested in their victim status in order to receive certain positions. This investment results in their being rewarded for their victim status rather than moving beyond that status and becoming self-reliant. In addition, he argues that affirmative action's preferences for Blacks implies that they are only given the positions because of color, and not ability. This perception further marks Blacks with the stamp of inferiority and whites with the stamp of superiority. Finally, Steele argues that affirmative action avoids the expensive, difficult, and morally necessary work of providing authentic equal opportunity through educational and economic development, and ending all racial, gender, and ethnic discrimination.

Kwame Anthony Appiah addresses the concept of racism. Appiah distinguishes between racialism, intrinsic racism, and extrinsic racism. Racialism, he states, is the belief that there are intrinsic and specific characteristics of the races which are not shared among the races. These characteristics allow races to be distinguished from one another. Extrinsic racism asserts that the races warrant morally different treatment because of their inherent traits. Intrinsic racism is the belief that each race has a different moral status, regardless of the characteristics of the race. Intrinsic racism is often associated with partiality for those of one's own race. Appiah asserts that holding racist dispositions involves self-deception, for it requires that one believe that there are morally relevant differences between the races. Appiah denounces all forms of racism as morally wrong, because racism violates the imperative to utilize only morally relevant bases in making moral distinctions, and allows one to escape universal moral demands.

Laurence Thomas questions the commonly held assumption that racism and sexism are similar. Although women and minorities have been treated similarly, he states that there are fundamental conceptual differences between racism and sexism. One example Thomas raises is that since women are required for the perpetuation of the species, men will not completely exclude themselves from women, but there is no such natural basis for whites to keep Blacks around.

Thomas argues that the identity of men is fundamentally tied to their sexist views of women, while the identity of whites has no fundamental tie to being racists. For example, Thomas claims that the women's movement has led men to form groups to deal with the challenges to their masculine identities, while the civil rights movement did not result in a similar action by whites. Thomas labels his thesis—that sexism is more central to identity than racism—the Racial and Sexual Identity thesis (RSI thesis). Thomas concludes that racism and sexism are two different and distinct social aberrations, and that in light of the RSI thesis, racist views are easier to eliminate than sexist views. While acknowledging that racism does not exclusively apply to blacks, Thomas limits his discussion of racism to that against Blacks. Thomas thus epitomizes the traditional approach to racism that Vine Deloria, Jr., brings into question.

Deloria asserts that racism is much more than a matter of white–Black relations. He charges that the forms of racism against African Americans and American Indians are very different. African Americans were ignored and systematically kept out of the dominant society, while American Indians were forced to assimilate. One such example is that Blacks did not have their children taken from their homes and sent to white schools where they were forced to learn the white culture, as Indian children were. American Indians are still being forced to assimilate, as is exemplified in the recent Supreme Court ruling denying the use of peyote in American Indian religion, and the continuing refusal to honor the sanctity of burial grounds. Furthermore, black–white segregation is still very much a part of our experience. Deloria asserts that solving the racial problem requires that the white man (his words) must understand and take responsibility for the past by facing racism as a problem he has created within himself and others.

Taking responsibility for one's racist attitudes is one such starting point in understanding the racial question. Larry May argues for such a moral accountability. He addresses the role racist attitudes play in facilitating racially motivated harms. May asserts that a racist climate increases the likelihood of racially motivated harm. This climate is produced by people who share racist attitudes, and even though these people may not directly cause racial harms, their attitudes often contribute to a type of joint venture in which all members share in moral responsibility for that harm. May argues that continuing to hold racist attitudes that are known to contribute to a moral climate that permits racial harms is a form of reckless behavior. People who exhibit reckless behavior share responsibility for the risk for and the actual harm. Although those who actually cause the harm are legally culpable, the moral responsibility does not lie with them alone. To begin to understand one's share in responsibility for racism requires one to take steps to eliminate one's racist attitudes and to refuse to contribute to a racist climate.

—Shari Collins-Chobanian

The Color-Blind Principle

Bernard Boxill

Bernard Boxill is a professor of philosophy at the University of North Carolina at Chapel Hill. He is the author of Blacks and Social Justice *(1984).*

Boxill attempts to defend affirmative action plans by arguing that there is no reason for selection plans to be strictly colorblind, that is, for race never to be a criterion of selection. He asserts that some theorists misinterpret the reasons why it is unjust to discriminate based on race. Although he acknowledges that color-conscious policies, such as Jim Crow laws, can be heinous, he contends that it may be perfectly justified to discriminate among people according to traits or skills they are not responsible for possessing. He argues that it is just as bad to completely ignore race as it is to completely ignore talent. He concludes that either color or talent may be the foundation of just discrimination.

PLESSY

In 1892, Homer Plessy, an octoroon, was arrested in Louisiana for taking a seat in a train car reserved for whites. He was testing a state law which required the "white and colored races" to ride in "equal but separate" accommodations, and his case eventually reached the Supreme Court.

Part of Plessy's defense, though it must be considered mainly a snare for the opposition, was that he was "seven-eighths Caucasian and one-eighth African blood," and that the "mixture of colored blood was not discernible in him." The bulwark of his argument was, however, that he was "entitled to every right, privilege and immunity secured to citizens of the white race," and that the law violated the Fourteenth Amendment's prohibition against unequal protection of the laws.[1] Cannily, the court

refused the snare. Perhaps it feared—and with reason—that the ancestry of too many white Louisianans held dark secrets. But it attacked boldly enough Plessy's main argument that the Louisiana law was unconstitutional. That argument, Justice Henry Billings Brown wrote for the majority, was unsound. "Its underlying fallacy," he averred, was its "assumption that the enforced separation of the two races stamps the colored race with a badge of inferiority." "If this be so," Brown concluded, "it is not by reason of anything found in the act, but solely because the colored race chooses to put that construction upon it."[2]

Only one judge dissented from the court majority—Justice John Marshall Harlan. It was the occasion on which he pronounced his famous maxim: "Our Constitution is color-blind." In opposition to Justice Brown, Justice Harlan found that the "separation of citizens on the basis of race [was a] badge of servitude . . . wholly inconsistent [with] equality before the law."[3]

Plessy's is the kind of case which makes the color-blind principle seem indubitably right as a basis for action and policy, and its contemporary opponents appear unprincipled, motivated by expediency, and opportunistic. This impression is only strengthened by a reading of Justice Brown's tortuously preposterous defense of the "equal but separate" doctrine. It should make every advocate of color-conscious policy wary of the power of arguments of expediency to beguile moral sense and subvert logic. Yet I argue that color-conscious policy can still be justified. The belief that it cannot is the result of a mistaken generalization from *Plessy*. There is no warrant for the idea that the color-blind principle should hold in some general and absolute way.

"I DIDN'T NOTICE" LIBERALS

In his book *Second Wind,* Bill Russell recalls how amazed he used to be by the behavior of what he called "I didn't notice" liberals. These were individuals who claimed not to notice people's color. If they mentioned someone Russell could not place, and Russell asked whether she was black or white, they would answer, "I didn't notice." "Sweet and innocent," Russell recalls, "sometimes a little proud."[4] Now, the kind of color-blindness the "I didn't notice" liberals claim to have may be a worthy ideal—Richard Wasserstrom, for example, argues that society should aim toward it—but it is absolutely different from the color-blind principle which functions as a basis for policy.[5] Thus, while Wasserstrom supports color-conscious policies to secure the ideal of people not noticing each others' color, the principle of color-blindness in the law opposes color-conscious policies and

does not necessarily involve any hope that people will not notice each others' color. Its thesis is simple: that no *law* or *public policy* be designed to treat people differently because they are of a different color.

COLOR-BLIND AND COLOR-CONSCIOUS POLICIES

The essential thing about a color-conscious policy is that it is designed to treat people differently because of their race. But there are many different kinds of color-conscious policies. Some, for example the Jim Crow policies now in the main abolished, aim to subordinate blacks, while others, such as busing and preferential treatment, aim at elevating blacks.

Some color-conscious policies explicitly state that persons should be treated differently because of their race, for example the segregation laws at issue in *Plessy;* others make no mention of race, but are still designed so that blacks and whites are treated differently, for example, the "grandfather clauses" in voting laws that many states adopted at the turn of the century. To give one instance, in Louisiana this clause stated that those who had had the right to vote before or on 1 January 1867, or their lineal descendants, did not have to meet the educational, property, or tax requirements for voting. Since no blacks had had the right to vote by that time, this law worked effectively to keep blacks from voting while at the same time allowing many impoverished and illiterate whites to vote—yet it made no mention of race.

My object in this chapter is to demonstrate that the color-blind principle, which considers all color-conscious policies to be invalid, is mistaken. I do not deny that many color-conscious policies are wrong. Jim Crow was certainly wrong, and, for different reasons, proposals for black control of inner cities and inner city schools are probably wrong. But this is not because they are color-conscious, but for reasons which indicate that color-conscious policies like busing and affirmative action could be correct.

Advocates of the belief that the law should be color-blind often argue that this would be the best means to an ideal state in which people are color-blind. They appeal to the notion that, only if people notice each other's color can they discriminate on the basis of color and, with considerable plausibility, they argue that color-conscious laws and policies can only heighten people's awareness of each other's color, and exacerbate racial conflict. They maintain that only if the law, with all its weight and influence, sets the example of color-blindness, can there be a realistic hope that people will see through the superficial distinctions of color and become themselves color-blind.

But this argument is not the main thesis of the advocates of legal color-blindness. Generally, they eschew it because of its dependency on the empirical. Their favorite argument, one that is more direct and intuitively appealing, is simply that it is wicked, unfair, and unreasonable to penalize a person for what he cannot help being. Not only does this seem undeniably true, but it can be immediately applied to the issue of race. No one can help being white or being black, and so it seems to follow that it is wicked, unfair, and unreasonable to disqualify a person from any consideration just because he is white or black. This, the advocates of color-blindness declare, is what made Jim Crow law heinous, and it is what makes affirmative action just as heinous.

The force of this consideration is enhanced because it seems to account for one peculiar harmfulness of racial discrimination—its effect on self-respect and self-esteem. For racial discrimination makes some black people hate their color, and succeeds in doing so because color cannot be changed. Furthermore, a racially conscious society has made color seem an important part of the individual's very essence, and since color is immutable it is easily susceptible to this approach. As a result, the black individual may come, in the end, to hate even himself. Even religion is here a dubious consolation. For if God makes us black or white, to the religious black that by which he is marked may come to seem a curse by the Almighty, and he himself therefore essentially evil.

Of course, there are strategies that attempt to circumvent these effects of racial discrimination, but their weaknesses seem to confirm the need for color-blindness. For example, some black people concede that black is bad and ugly, but attempt to soften the effects of this concession by insisting that black is only "skin deep," we are all brothers beneath the skin, and the body, which is black and ugly, is no part of and does not sully the soul, which is the real self and is good. Thus, black people sometimes protested that although their skins were black, their souls were white, which is to say, good. There is truth to this feeling, in that nothing is more certain than that neither a black nor a white skin can make a person good or bad.Yet it is not a wholly successful approach to the problem of color. It requires that the black person believe that he is in some sense a ghost, which he can believe only if he is a lunatic. Another strategy is put forth by Black Nationalism. The black nationalist agrees with the racists' view that his color is an important and integral part of his self, but affirms, in opposition to the racists, that it has value. This strategy, which is exemplified by the slogans "black is beautiful" and "black and proud," has the obvious advantage of stimulating pride and self-confidence. Nevertheless, it is no panacea. For one thing, it has to contend with the powerful propaganda stating that black is *not* beautiful. And there is a more subtle problem. Since the black cannot choose *not* to be black, he cannot be altogether confident that he would choose to *be* black, nor, consequently, does he really place a special value in being black. Thus, some people, black and white, have expressed the suspicion that the slogan "black is beautiful" rings hollow, like the words of the man who protests too loudly that he loves the chains he cannot escape. In this respect the black who can pass as white has an advantage over the black who cannot. For, though he cannot choose not to be black, he can choose not to be *known* to be black.

THE RESPONSIBILITY CRITERION

A final argument in favor of legal color-blindness is related to, and further develops, the point that people do not choose to be, and cannot avoid being, black or white. This links the question of color-blindness to the protean idea of individual responsibility. Thus, William Frankena writes, that to use color as a fundamental basis for distributing "opportunities, offices, etc." to persons is "unjust in itself," because it is to distribute goods on the basis of a feature "which the individual has not done, and can do nothing about; we are treating people differently in ways that profoundly affect their lives because of differences for which they have no responsibility."[6] Since

this argument requires that people be treated differently in ways which profoundly affect their lives only on the basis of features for which they are responsible, I call it the responsibility criterion.

The responsibility criterion also seems to make the principle of color-blindness follow from principles of equal opportunity. Joel Feinberg takes it to be equivalent to the claim that "properties can be the grounds of just discrimination between persons only if those persons had a fair opportunity to acquire or avoid them."[7] This implies that to discriminate between persons on the basis of a feature for which they can have no responsibility is to violate the principle of fair opportunity. But color (or sex) is a feature of persons for which they can have no responsibility.

The responsibility criterion may seem innocuous because, though, strictly interpreted it supports the case for color-blindness, loosely interpreted it leaves open the possibility that color-conscious policies are justifiable. Thus, Frankena himself allows that color could be an important basis of distribution of goods and offices if it served "as [a] reliable sign[s] of some Q, like ability or merit, which is more justly employed as a touchstone for the treatment of individuals."[8] This sounds like a reasonable compromise and is enough to support some arguments for color-conscious policies. For example, it could support the argument that black and white children should go to the same schools because being white is a reliable sign of being middle-class, and black children, who are often lower-class, learn better when their peers are middle-class. Similarly, it might support the argument that preferential hiring is compensation for the harm of being discriminated against on the basis of color, and that being black is a reliable sign of having been harmed by that discrimination.

But however loosely it is interpreted, the responsibility criterion cannot be adduced in support of all reasons behind color-conscious policies. It cannot, for example, sustain the following argument, sketched by Ronald Dworkin, for preferential admission of blacks to medical school. "If quick hands count as 'merit' in the case of a prospective surgeon this is because quick hands will enable him to serve the public better and for no other reason. If a black skin will, as a matter of regrettable fact, enable another doctor to do a different medical job better, then that black skin is by the same token 'merit' as well."[9] What is proposed here is not that a black skin is a justifiable basis of discrimination because it is a reliable sign of merit or some other factor Q. A closely related argument does make such a proposal, viz., that blacks should be preferentially admitted to medical school because being black is a reliable sign of a desire to serve the black community. But this is not the argument that Dworkin poses. In the example quoted above what he suggests is that being black is in *itself* merit, or, at least, something very like merit.

According to the responsibility criterion, we ought not to give A a job in surgery rather than B, if A is a better surgeon than B only because he was born with quicker hands. For if we do, we treat A and B "differently in ways that profoundly affect their lives because of differences for which they have no responsibility." This is the kind of result which puts egalitarianism in disrepute. It entails the idea that we might be required to let fumblers do surgery and in general give jobs and offices to incompetents, and this is surely intolerable. But, as I plan to show, true egalitarianism has

no such consequences. They are the result of applying the responsibility criterion, not egalitarian principles. Indeed, egalitarianism must scout the responsibility criterion as false and confused.

Egalitarians should notice first, that, while it invalidates the merit-based theories of distribution that they oppose, it also invalidates the need-based theories of distribution they favor. For, if people are born with special talents for which they are not responsible, they are also born with special needs for which they are not responsible. Consequently, if the responsibility criterion forbids choosing A over B to do surgery because A is a better surgeon because he was born with quicker hands, it also forbids choosing C rather than D for remedial education because C needs it more than D only because he was born with a learning disability and D was not.

At this point there may be objections. First, that the responsibility criterion was intended to govern only the distribution of income, not jobs and offices—in Feinberg's discussion, for example, this is made explicit. Second, that it does not mean that people should not be treated differently because of differences, good or bad, which they cannot help, but rather that people should not get less just because they are born without the qualities their society prizes or finds useful. This seems to be implied in Frankena's claim that justice should make the "same proportionate contribution to the best life for everyone" and that this may require spending more on those who are "harder to help"—probably the untalented—than on others. Qualified in these ways, the responsibility criterion becomes more plausible. It no longer implies, for example, that fumblers should be allowed to practice surgery, or that the blind be treated just like the sighted. But with these qualifications it also becomes almost irrelevant to the color-blind issue. For that issue is not only about how income should be distributed. It is also about how jobs and offices should be distributed.

Most jobs and offices are distributed to people in order to produce goods and services to a larger public. To that end, the responsibility criterion is irrelevant. For example, the purpose of admitting people to medical schools and law schools is to provide the community with good medical and legal service. It does not matter whether those who provide them are responsible for having the skills by virtue of which they provide the goods, or whether the positions they occupy are "goods" to them. No just society makes a person a surgeon just because he is responsible for his skills or because making him a surgeon will be good for him. It makes him a surgeon because he will do good surgery.

Accordingly, it may be perfectly just to discriminate between persons on the basis of distinctions they are not responsible for having. It depends on whether or not the discrimination serves a worthy end. It may be permissible for the admissions policies of professional schools to give preference to those with higher scores, even if their scores are higher than others only because they have higher native ability (for which they cannot, of course, be considered responsible), if the object is to provide the community with good professional service. And, given the same object, if for some reason a black skin, whether or not it can be defined as merit, helps a black lawyer or doctor to provide good legal or medical service to black people who would otherwise not have access to it, or avail themselves of it, it is difficult to see how there can be a principled objection to admissions policies which prefer people with black skins—though, again, they are not responsible for the quality by virtue of which they are preferred.

JUSTICE AND THE RESPONSIBILITY CRITERION

A further point needs to be made in order to vindicate color-conscious policies. The principles of justice are distributive: Justice is concerned not only with increasing the total amount of a good a society enjoys, but also with how that good should be distributed among individuals. Generally, judicial principles dictate that people who are similar in ways deemed relevant to the issue of justice, such as in needs or rights, should get equal amounts of a good, and people who are dissimilar in these regards should get unequal amounts of the good. In terms of these principles certain laws and rules must be considered unjust which would not otherwise be thought unjust. Consider, for example, a policy for admitting persons to medical school which resulted in better and better medical service for white people, but worse and worse medical service for black people. This policy would be unjust, however great the medical expertise—certainly a good—it produced, unless color is relevant to the receiving of good medical attention.

In a case like this, where it is not, the theoretical circumstance outlined by Dworkin, in which black skin might be considered a "merit," becomes viable. It is true, of course, that color is not, precisely, merit. But to insist on strict definition in this context is to cavil. The point is that if black clients tend to trust and confide more in black lawyers and doctors, then color—functioning as merit—enables a good to be produced and distributed according to some principle of justice.

If these considerations are sound, then the responsibility criterion thoroughly misconstrues the reasons for which racial discrimination is unjust. Racial discrimination against blacks is unjust because it does not enable goods to be produced and distributed according to principles of justice. It is not unjust because black people do not choose to be black, cannot *not* be black, or are not responsible for being black. This is completely irrelevant. For example, a policy denying university admission to people who parted their hair on the right side would be unjust because the way in which people part their hair is irrelevant to a just policy of school admission. It does not matter in the least, in relation to the nature and object of education, that they choose how they part their hair. Similarly, even if black people could choose to become white, or could all easily pass as white, a law school or medical school that excluded blacks because they were black would still act unjustly. Nothing would have changed.

The arguments in support of colorblindness tend to make the harmfulness of discrimination depend on the difficulty of avoiding it. This is misleading. It diverts attention from the potential harmfulness of discrimination that *can* be avoided and brings the specious responsibility criterion into play. Suppose again, for example, that a person is denied admission to law school because he parts his hair on the right side. Though he, far more easily than the black person, can avoid being unfairly discriminated *against,* he does not thereby more easily avoid being the object, indeed, in a deeper sense, the victim, of unfair discrimination. If he parts his hair on the left side he will presumably be admitted to law school. But then he will have knowingly complied with a foolish and unjust rule and this may well make him expedient and servile. Of course, he will not be harmed to the same extent and in the same way as the victim of racial discrimination. For example, he probably will not hate himself. Unlike color, the cause of his ill-treatment is too easily changed for him to conceive of it as essential to himself. Moreover, if he chooses to keep his hair parted on the right side and thus to forego law school, he *knows* that he is not going to law school because he freely chose to place a greater value on his integrity or on his taste in hairstyles than on a legal education. He knows this because he knows he could have chosen to change his hairstyle. As I noted earlier, this opportunity for self-assertion, and thus for self-knowledge and self-confidence, is denied the black who is discriminated against on the basis of his color.

Nevertheless, as I stated earlier, the considerations that stem from applying the responsibility criterion to a judgment of racial discrimination are secondary to understanding its peculiar harmfulness. Suppose, for example, that a person is not admitted to medical school to train to be a surgeon because he was born without fingers. If all the things he wants require that he have fingers, he may conceivably come to suffer the same self-hatred and self-doubt as the victim of racial discrimination. Yet his case is different, and if he attends to the difference, he will not suffer as the victim of racial discrimination suffers. The discrimination that excludes him from the practice of surgery is not denigrating his interests because they are his. It is a policy that takes into account a just object—the needs of others in the community for competent surgery. Allowing him to be a surgeon would rate other, equally important, interests below his. But racial discrimination excludes its victims from opportunities on the basis of a belief that their interests are ipso facto less important than the interests of whites. The man without fingers may regret not being born differently, but he cannot resent how he is treated. Though his ambitions may be thwarted, he himself is still treated as a moral equal. There is no attack on his self-respect. Racial discrimination, however, undermines its victims' self-respect through their awareness that they are considered morally inferior. The fact that racial discrimination, or any color-conscious policy, is difficult to avoid through personal choice merely adds to its basic harmfulness if it is in the first place unjust, but is not the *reason* for its being unjust.

It remains to consider Feinberg's claim that if people are discriminated for or against on the basis of factors for which they are not responsible the equal opportunity principle is contravened. This I concede. In particular, I concede that color-conscious policies giving preference to blacks place an insurmountable obstacle in the path of whites, and since such obstacles reduce opportunities, such policies may make opportunities unequal. But this gives no advantage to the advocates of color-blind policies. For giving preference to the competent has exactly the same implications as giving preference to blacks. It, too, places obstacles in the paths of some people, this time the untalented, and just as surely makes opportunities unequal. Consequently, an advocate of color-blindness cannot consistently oppose color-conscious policies on the grounds that they contravene equal opportunity and at the same time support talent-conscious policies. Nor, finally, does my concession raise any further difficulty with the issue of equal opportunity. As I argue later, equal opportunity is not a fundamental principle of justice, but is derived from its basic principles. Often these basic principles require that opportunities be made more equal. Invariably, however, these same principles require that the process of equalization stop before a condition of perfect equality of opportunity is reached.

To conclude, adopting a color-blind principle entails adopting a talent-blind principle, and since the latter is absurd, so also is the former. Or, in other words, differences in talent, and differences in color, are, from the point of view of justice, on a par. Either, with equal propriety, can be the basis of a just discrimination. Consequently, the color-blind principle is not as simple, straightforward, or self-evident as many of its advocates seem to feel it is. Color-conscious policies can conceivably be just, just as talent-conscious policies can conceivably be—and often are—just. It depends on the circumstances.

NOTES

1. Derrick A. Bell, Jr., ed., *Plessy v. Ferguson* in *Civil Rights: Leading Cases* (Boston: Little, Brown, 1980), 64–77.
2. Ibid., 71.
3. Ibid., 71–77.
4. Bill Russell and Taylor Brand, *Second Wind* (New York: Random House, 1979), 187.
5. Richard A. Wasserstrom, "Racism and Sexism," in Richard A. Wasserstrom, *Philosophy and Social Issues* (Notre Dame, Ind.: University of Notre Dame Press, 1980), 24, 25.
6. William Frankena, "Some Beliefs About Justice," in *Justice*, ed. Joel Feinberg and Hyman Gross (Encino, Calif.: Dickenson, 1977), 49.
7. Joel Feinberg, *Social Philosophy* (Englewood Cliffs. N.J.: Prentice Hall, 1973), 49.
8. Frankena, "Some Beliefs About Justice," 49.
9. Ronald Dworkin, "Why Bakke Has No Case," *New York Review of Books*, 10 Nov. 1977, 14.

Affirmative Action:
The Price of Preference

Shelby Steele

Shelby Steele is a professor of English, currently on leave, at San Jose State University. He is the author of numerous essays on Blacks, race and blame, and white guilt, as well as the author of The Content of Our Character *(1990).*

Steele argues that affirmative action, as it is currently practiced, perpetuates, rather than alleviates, the harm it was meant to address. Steele states that affirmative action policies' emphasis on color has the result of further stereotyping a group that is already perceived as inferior. Steele further argues that affirmative action is a type of shortcut to the goal of equality. Affirmative action is a shortcut because it does not provide educational and economic development and does not provide sanctions for racial, ethnic, and sexual discrimination, which are the real means necessary for overcoming discrimination and inequality.

In a few short years, when my two children will be applying to college, the affirmative action policies by which most universities offer black students some form of preferential treatment will present me with a dilemma. I am a middle-class black, a college professor, far from wealthy, but also well-removed from the kind of deprivation that would qualify my children for the label "disadvantaged." Both of them have endured racial insensitivity from whites. They have been called names, have suffered slights, and have experienced firsthand the peculiar malevolence that racism brings out in people. Yet, they have never experienced racial discrimination, have never been stopped by their race on any path they have chosen to follow. Still, their society now tells them that if they will only designate themselves as black on their college applications, they will likely do better in the college lottery than if they conceal this fact. I think there is something of a Faustian bargain in this.

Of course, many blacks and a considerable number of whites would say that I was sanctimoniously making affirmative action into a test of character. They would say that this small preference is the meagerest recompense for centuries of unrelieved oppression. And to these arguments other very obvious facts must be added. In America, many marginally competent or flatly incompetent whites are hired everyday—some because their white skin suits the conscious or unconscious racial preference of their employer. The white children of alumni are often grandfathered into elite universities in what can only be seen as a residual benefit of historic white privilege. Worse, white incompetence is always an individual matter, while for blacks it is often confirmation of ugly stereotypes. The Peter Principle was not conceived with only blacks in mind. Given that unfairness cuts both ways, doesn't it only balance the scales of history that my children now receive a slight preference over whites? Doesn't this repay, in a small way, the systematic denial under which their grandfather lived out his days?

So, in theory, affirmative action certainly has all the moral symmetry that fairness requires—the injustice of historical and even contemporary white advantage is offset with black advantage; preference replaces prejudice, inclusion answers exclusion. It is reformist and corrective, even repentant and redemptive. And I would never sneer at these good intentions. Born in the late forties in Chicago, I started my education (a charitable term in this case) in a segregated school and suffered all the indignities that come to blacks in a segregated society. My father, born in the South, only made it to the third grade before the white man's fields took permanent priority over his formal education. And though he educated himself into an advanced reader with an almost professional authority, he could only drive a truck for a living and never earned more than ninety dollars a week in his entire life. So, yes, it is crucial to my sense of citizenship, to my ability to identify with the spirit and the interests of America, to know that this country, however imperfectly, recognizes its past sins and wishes to correct them.

Yet good intentions, because of the opportunity for innocence they offer us, are very seductive and can blind us to the effects they generate when implemented.

In our society, affirmative action is, among other things, a testament to white goodwill and to black power, and in the midst of these heavy investments, its effects can be hard to see. But after twenty years of implementation, I think affirmative action has shown itself to be more bad than good and that blacks—whom I will focus on in this essay—now stand to lose more from it than they gain.

In talking with affirmative action administrators and with blacks and whites in general, it is clear that supporters of affirmative action focus on its good intentions while detractors emphasize its negative effects. Proponents talk about "diversity" and "pluralism"; opponents speak of "reverse discrimination," the unfairness of quotas and set-asides. It was virtually impossible to find people outside either camp. The closest I came was a white male manager at a large computer company who said, "I think it amounts to reverse discrimination, but I'll put up with a little of that for a little more diversity." I'll live with a little of the effect to gain a little of the intention, he seemed to be saying. But this only makes him a halfhearted supporter of affirmative action. I think many people who don't really like affirmative action support it to one degree or another anyway.

I believe they do this because of what happened to white and black Americans in the crucible of the sixties when whites were confronted with their racial guilt and blacks tasted their first real power. In this stormy time white absolution and black power coalesced into virtual mandates for society. Affirmative action became a meeting ground for these mandates in the law, and in the late sixties and early seventies it underwent a remarkable escalation of its mission from simple anti-discrimination enforcement to social engineering by means of quotas, goals, timetables, set-asides, and other forms of preferential treatment.

Legally, this was achieved through a series of executive orders and EEOC guidelines that allowed racial imbalances in the workplace to stand as proof of racial discrimination. Once it could be assumed that discrimination explained racial imbalances, it became easy to justify group remedies to presumed discrimination, rather than the normal case-by-case redress for proven discrimination. Preferential treatment through quotas, goals, and so on is designed to correct imbalances based on the assumption that they always indicate discrimination. This expansion of what constitutes discrimination allowed affirmative action to escalate into the business of social engineering in the name of anti-discrimination, to push society toward statistically proportionate racial representation, without any obligation of proving actual discrimination.

What accounted for this shift, I believe, was the white mandate to achieve a new racial innocence and the black mandate to gain power. Even though blacks had made great advances during the sixties without quotas, these mandates, which came to a head in the very late sixties, could no longer be satisfied by anything less than racial preferences. I don't think these mandates in themselves were wrong, since whites clearly needed to do better by blacks and blacks needed more real power in society. But, as they came together in affirmative action, their effect was to distort our understanding of racial discrimination in a way that allowed us to offer the remediation of preference on the basis of mere color rather than actual injury. By making black the color of prefer-

ence, these mandates have reburdened society with the very marriage of color and preference (in reverse) that we set out to eradicate. The old sin is reaffirmed in a new guise.

But the essential problem with this form of affirmative action is the way it leaps over the hard business of developing a formerly oppressed people to the point where they can achieve proportionate representation on their own (given equal opportunity) and goes straight for the proportionate representation. This may satisfy some whites of their innocence and some blacks of their power, but it does very little to truly uplift blacks.

A white female affirmative action officer at an Ivy League university told me what many supporters of affirmative action now say: "We're after diversity. We ideally want a student body where racial and ethnic groups are represented according to their proportion in society." When affirmative action escalated into social engineering, diversity became a golden word. It grants whites an egalitarian fairness (innocence) and blacks an entitlement to proportionate representation (power). *Diversity* is a term that applies democratic principles to races and cultures rather than to citizens, despite the fact that there is nothing to indicate that real diversity is the same thing as proportionate representation. Too often the result of this on campus (for example) has been a democracy of colors rather than of people, an artificial diversity that gives the appearance of an educational parity between black and white students that has not yet been achieved in reality. Here again, racial preferences allow society to leapfrog over the difficult problem of developing blacks to parity with whites and into a cosmetic diversity that covers the blemish of disparity—a full six years after admission, only about 26 percent of black students graduate from college.

Racial representation is not the same thing as racial development, yet affirmative action fosters a confusion of these very difficult needs. Representation can be manufactured; development is always hard-earned. However, it is the music of innocence and power that we hear in affirmative action that causes us to cling to it and to its distracting emphasis on representation. The fact is that after twenty years of racial preferences, the gap between white and black median income is greater than it was in the seventies. None of this is to say that blacks don't need policies that ensure our right to equal opportunity, but what we need more is the development that will let us take advantage of society's efforts to include us.

I think that one of the most troubling effects of racial preferences for blacks is a kind of demoralization, or put another way, an enlargement of self-doubt. Under affirmative action the quality that earns us preferential treatment is an implied inferiority. However this inferiority is explained—it is still inferiority. There are explanations, and then there is the fact. And the fact must be borne by the individual as a condition apart from the explanation, apart even from the fact that others like himself also bear this condition. In integrated situations where blacks must compete with whites who may be better prepared these explanations may quickly wear thin and expose the individual to racial as well as personal self-doubt.

All of this is compounded by the cultural myth of black inferiority that blacks have always lived with. What this means in practical terms is that when blacks deliver themselves into integrated situations, they encounter a nasty little reflex in whites, a mindless, atavistic reflex that responds to the color black with alarm. Attributions may follow this alarm if the white cares to indulge them, and if they do, they will most likely be negative—one such attribution is intellectual ineptness. I think this reflex and the attributions that may follow it embarrass most whites today; therefore, it is usually quickly repressed. Nevertheless, on an equally atavistic level, the black will be aware of the reflex his color triggers and will feel a stab of horror at seeing himself reflected in this way. He, too, will do a quick repression, but a lifetime of such stabbings is what constitutes his inner realm of racial doubt.

The effects of this may be a subject for another essay. The point here is that the implication of inferiority that racial preferences engender in both the white and black mind expands rather than contracts this doubt. Even when the black sees no implication of inferiority in racial preferences, he knows that whites do, so that—consciously or unconsciously—the result is virtually the same. The effects of preferential treatment—the lowering of normal standards to increase black representation—puts blacks at war with an expanded realm of debilitating doubt, so that the doubt itself becomes an unrecognized preoccupation that undermines their ability to perform, especially in integrated situations. On largely white campuses, blacks are five times more likely to drop out than whites. Preferential treatment, no matter how it is justified in the light of day, subjects blacks to a midnight of self-doubt, and so often transforms their advantage into a revolving door.

Another liability of affirmative action comes from the fact that it indirectly encourages blacks to exploit their own past victimization as a source of power and privilege. Victimization, like implied inferiority, is what justifies preference, so that to receive the benefits of preferential treatment one must, to some extent, become invested in the view of one's self as a victim. In this way, affirmative action nurtures a victim-focused identity in blacks. The obvious irony here is that we become inadvertently invested in the very condition we are trying to overcome. Racial preferences send us the message that there is more power in our past suffering than our present achievements—none of which could bring us a *preference* over others.

When power itself grows out of suffering, then blacks are encouraged to expand the boundaries of what qualifies as racial oppression, a situation that can lead us to paint our victimization in vivid colors, even as we receive the benefits of preference. The same corporations and institutions that give us preference are also seen as our oppressors. At Stanford University minority students—some of whom enjoy as much as $15,000 a year in financial aid—recently took over the president's office demanding, among other things, more financial aid. The power to be found in victimization, like any power, is intoxicating and can lend itself to the creation of a new class of super-victims who can feel the pea of victimization under twenty mattresses. Preferential treatment rewards us for being underdogs rather than for moving beyond that status—a misplacement of incentives that, along with its deepening of our doubt, is more a yoke than a spur.

But, I think, one of the worst prices that blacks pay for preference has to do with an illusion. I saw this illusion at work recently in the mother of a middle-class black student who was going off to his first semester of college. "They owe us this, so don't think for a minute that you don't belong there." This is the logic by which many blacks, and some whites, justify affirmative action—it is something "owed," a form of reparation. But this logic overlooks a much harder and less digestible reality, that it is impossible to repay blacks living today for the historic suffering of the race. If all blacks were given a million dollars tomorrow morning it would not amount to a dime on the dollar of three centuries of oppression, nor would it obviate the residues of that oppression that we still carry today. The concept of historic reparation grows out of man's need to impose a degree of justice on the world that simply does not exist. Suffering can be endured and overcome; it cannot be repaid. Blacks cannot be repaid for the injustice done to the race, but we can be corrupted by society's guilty gestures of repayment.

Affirmative action is such a gesture. It tells us that racial preferences can do for us what we cannot do for ourselves. The corruption here is in the hidden incentive *not* to do what we believe preferences will do. This is an incentive to be reliant on others just as we are struggling for self-reliance. And it keeps alive the illusion that we can find some deliverance in repayment. The hardest thing for any sufferer to accept is that his suffering excuses him from very little and never has enough currency to restore him. To think otherwise is to prolong the suffering.

Several blacks I spoke with said they were still in favor of affirmative action because of the "subtle" discrimination blacks were subject to once on the job. One photojournalist said, "They have ways of ignoring you." A black female television producer said, "You can't file a lawsuit when your boss doesn't invite you to the insider meetings without ruining your career. So we still need affirmative action." Others mentioned the infamous "glass ceiling" through which blacks can see the top positions of authority but never reach them. But I don't think racial preferences are a protection against this subtle discrimination; I think they contribute to it.

In any workplace, racial preferences will always create two-tiered populations composed of preferreds and unpreferreds. This division makes automatic a perception of enhanced competence for the unpreferreds and of questionable competence for the preferreds—the former earned his way, even though others were given preference, while the latter made it by color as much as by competence. Racial preferences implicitly mark whites with an exaggerated superiority just as they mark blacks with an exaggerated inferiority. They not only reinforce America's oldest racial myth but, for blacks, they have the effect of stigmatizing the already stigmatized.

I think that much of the "subtle" discrimination that blacks talk about is often (not always) discrimination against the stigma of questionable competence that affirmative action delivers to blacks. In this sense, preferences scapegoat the very people they seek to help. And it may be that at a certain level employers impose a glass ceiling, but this may not be against the race so much as against the race's reputation for having advanced by color as much as by competence. Affirmative action makes a glass ceiling virtually necessary as a protection against the corruptions of preferential treatment. This ceiling is the point at which corporations shift the emphasis from color to competency and stop playing the affirmative action game. Here preference backfires for blacks and becomes a taint that holds them back. Of course, one could argue that this taint,

which is, after all, in the minds of whites, becomes nothing more than an excuse to discriminate against blacks. And certainly the result is the same in either case— blacks don't get past the glass ceiling. But this argument does not get around the fact that racial preferences now taint this color with a new theme of suspicion that makes it even more vulnerable to the impulse in others to discriminate. In this crucial yet gray area of perceived competence, preferences make whites look better than they are and blacks worse, while doing nothing whatever to stop the very real discrimination that blacks may encounter. I don't wish to justify the glass ceiling here, but only to suggest the very subtle ways that affirmative action revives rather than exinguishes the old rationalizations for racial discrimination.

In education, a revolving door; in employment, a glass ceiling.

I believe affirmative action is problematic in our society because it tries to function like a social program. Rather than ask it to ensure equal opportunity we have demanded that it create parity between the races. But preferential treatment does not teach skills, or educate, or instill motivation. It only passes out entitlement by color, a situation that in my profession has created an unrealistically high demand for black professors. The social engineer's assumption is that this high demand will inspire more blacks to earn Ph.D.'s and join the profession. In fact, the number of blacks earning Ph.D.'s has declined in recent years. A Ph.D. must be developed from preschool on. He requires family and community support. He must acquire an entire system of values that enables him to work hard while delaying gratification. There are social programs, I believe, that can (and should) help blacks *develop* in all these areas, but entitlement by color is not a social program; it is a dubious reward for being black . . .

I would also like to see affirmative action go back to its original purpose of enforcing equal opportunity—a purpose that in itself disallows racial preferences. We cannot be sure that the discriminatory impulse in America has yet been shamed into extinction, and I believe affirmative action can make its greatest contribution by providing a rigorous vigilance in this area. It can guard constitutional rather than racial rights, and help institutions evolve standards of merit and selecting that are appropriate to the institution's needs yet as free of racial bias as possible (again, with the understanding that racial imbalances are not always an indication of racial bias). One of the most important things affirmative action can do is to define exactly what racial discrimination is and how it might manifest itself within a specific institution. The impulse to discriminate *is* subtle and cannot be ferreted out unless its many guises are made clear to people. Along with this there should be monitoring of institutions and heavy sanctions brought to bear when actual discrimination is found. This is the sort of affirmative action that America owes to blacks and to itself. It goes after the evil of discrimination itself, while preferences only sidestep the evil and grant entitlement to its *presumed* victims.

But if not preferences, then what? I think we need social policies that are committed to two goals: the educational and economic development of disadvantaged people, regardless of race, and the eradication from our society—through close monitoring and severe sanctions—of racial, ethnic, or gender discrimination. Preferences will not deliver us to either of these goals, since they tend to benefit those who are not disadvantaged—middle-class blacks—and attack one form of discrimination with another. Preferences are inexpensive and carry the glamour of good intentions—change the numbers and the good deed is done. To be against them is to be unkind. But I think the unkindest cut is to bestow on children like my own an undeserved advantage while neglecting the development of those disadvantaged children on the East Side of my city who will likely never be in a position to benefit from a preference. Give my children fairness; give disadvantaged children a better shot at development—better elementary and secondary schools, job training, safer neighborhoods, better financial assistance for college, and so on. Fewer blacks go to college today than ten years ago; more black males of college age are in prison or under the control of the criminal justice system than in college. This despite racial preferences.

The mandates of black power and white absolution out of which preferences emerged were not wrong in themselves. What was wrong was that both races focused more on the goals of these mandates than on the means to the goals. Blacks can have no real power without taking responsibility for their own educational and economic development. Whites can have no racial innocence without earning it by eradicating discrimination and helping the disadvantaged to develop. Because we ignored the means, the goals have not been reached, and the real work remains to be done.

Racisms

Kwame Anthony Appiah

Kwame Anthony Appiah was raised in Ghana and is a professor of philosophy and African-American studies at Harvard University. He is the author of several books, including In My Father's House *(1992). He is currently editing* The Oxford Book of African Literature.

Appiah distinguishes various aspects of racism, including racialism, as well as intrinsic and extrinsic racism. Racialism is the view that there are inherent traits and tendencies of each race that are not shared with members of other races, and which allow us to divide people into distinct races. Extrinsic racism is the view that the races inherently have different essences that entail different morally relevant traits. Intrinsic racism is the view that moral differentiation between races is justified because each race has a different moral status, irrespective of its racial essence. The disposition he calls "racial prejudice" is the tendency to subscribe to false moral and theoretical propositions about races. Appiah asserts that racialism is false, and that both kinds of racism are theoretically and morally wrong.

If the people I talk to and the newspapers I read are representative and reliable, there is a good deal of racism about. People and policies in the United States, in Eastern and Western Europe, in Asia and Africa and Latin America are regularly described as "racist." Australia had, until recently, a racist immigration policy; Britain still has one; racism is on the rise in France; many Israelis support Meir Kahane, an anti-Arab racist; many Arabs, according to a leading authority, are anti-Semitic racists;[1] and the movement to establish English as the "official language" of the United States is motivated by racism. Or, at least, so many of the people I talk to and many of the journalists with the newspapers I read believe.

But visitors from Mars—or from Malawi—unfamiliar with the Western concept of racism could be excused if they had some difficulty in identifying what exactly racism was. We see it everywhere, but rarely does anyone stop to say what it is, or to explain what is wrong with it. Our visitors from Mars would soon grasp that it had become at least conventional in recent years to express abhorrence for racism. They might even notice that those most often accused of it—members of the South African Nationalist party, for example—may officially abhor it also. But if they sought in the popular media of our day—in newspapers and magazines, on television or radio, in novels or films—for an explicit definition of this thing "we" all abhor, they would very likely be disappointed.

Kwame Anthony Appiah, "Racisms," in *Anatomy of Racism*, edited by David Theo Goldberg (Minneapolis, MN: University of Minnesota Press, 1990). Reprinted with permission of The University of Minnesota Press and Kwame Anthony Appiah.

Now, of course, this would be true of many of our most familiar concepts. *Sister, chair, tomato*—none of these gets defined in the course of our daily business. But the concept of racism is in worse shape than these. For much of what we say about it is, on the face of it, inconsistent.

It is, for example, held by many to be racist to refuse entry to a university to an otherwise qualified "Negro" candidate, but not to be so to refuse entry to an equally qualified "Caucasian" one. But "Negro" and "Caucasian" are both alleged to be names of races, and invidious discrimination on the basis of race is usually held to be a paradigm case of racism. Or, to take another example, it is widely believed to be evidence of an unacceptable racism to exclude people from clubs on the basis of race; yet most people, even those who think of "Jewish" as a racial term, seem to think that there is nothing wrong with Jewish clubs, whose members do not share any particular religious beliefs, or Afro-American societies, whose members share the juridical characteristic of American citizenship and the "racial" characteristic of being black.

I say that these are inconsistencies "on the face of it," because, for example, affirmative action in university admissions is importantly different from the earlier refusal to admit blacks or Jews (or other "Others") that it is meant, in part, to correct. Deep enough analysis may reveal it to be quite consistent with the abhorrence of racism; even a shallow analysis suggests that it is intended to be so. Similarly, justifications can be offered for "racial" associations in a plural society that are not available for the racial exclusivism of the country club. But if we take racism seriously we ought to be concerned about the adequacy of these justifications.

In this essay, then, I propose to take our ordinary ways of thinking about race and racism and point up some of their presuppositions. And since popular concepts are, of course, usually fairly fuzzily and untheoretically conceived, much of what I have to say will seem to be both more theoretically and more precisely committed than the talk of racism and racists in our newspapers and on television. My claim is that these theoretical claims are required to make sense of racism as the practice of reasoning human beings. If anyone were to suggest that much, perhaps most, of what goes under the name "racism" in our world cannot be given such a rationalized foundation, I should not disagree; but to the extent that a practice cannot be rationally reconstructed it ought, surely, to be given up by reasonable people. The right tactic with racism, if you really want to oppose it, is to object to it rationally in the form in which it stands the best chance of meeting objections. The doctrines I want to discuss can be rationally articulated: and they are worth articulating rationally in order that we can rationally say what we object to in them.

RACIST PROPOSITIONS

There are at least three distinct doctrines that might be held to express the theoretical content of what we call "racism." One is the view—which I shall call *racialism*[2]—that there are heritable characteristics, possessed by members of our species, that allow us to divide them into a small set of races, in such a way that all the members of these races share certain traits and tendencies with each other that they do not share with members of any other race. These traits and tendencies characteristic of a race constitute, on the racialist view, a sort of racial essence; and it is part of the content of racialism that the essential heritable characteristics of what the nineteenth century called the "Races of Man" account for more than the visible morphological characteristics—skin color, hair type, facial features—on the basis of which we make our informal classifications. Racialism is at the heart of nineteenth-century Western attempts to develop a science of racial difference; but it appears to have been believed by others—for example, Hegel, before then, and many in other parts of the non-Western world since—who have had no interest in developing scientific theories.

Racialism is not, in itself, a doctrine that must be dangerous, even if the racial essence is thought to entail moral and intellectual dispositions. Provided positive moral qualities are distributed across the races, each can be respected, can have its "separate but equal" place. Unlike most Western-educated people, I believe—and I have argued elsewhere[3]—that racialism is false; but by itself, it seems to be a cognitive rather than a moral problem. The issue is how the world is, not how we would want it to be.

Racialism is, however, a presupposition of other doctrines that have been called "racism," and these other doctrines have been, in the last few centuries, the basis of a great deal of human suffering and the source of a great deal of moral error.

One such doctrine we might call "extrinsic racism": extrinsic racists make moral distinctions between members of different races because they believe that the racial essence entails certain morally relevant qualities. The basis for the extrinsic racists' discrimination between people is their belief that members of different races differ in respects that *warrant* the differential treatment, respects—such as honesty or courage or intelligence—that are uncontroversially held (at least in most contemporary cultures) to be acceptable as a basis for treating people differently. Evidence that there are no such differences in morally relevant characteristics—that Negroes do not necessarily lack intellectual capacities, that Jews are not especially avaricious—should thus lead people out of their racism if it is purely extrinsic. As we know, such evidence often fails to change an extrinsic racist's attitudes substantially, for some of the extrinsic racist's best friends have always been Jewish. But at this point—if the racist is sincere—what we have is no longer a false doctrine but a cognitive incapacity, one whose significance I shall discuss later in this essay.

I say that the *sincere* extrinsic racist may suffer from a cognitive incapacity. But some who espouse extrinsic racist doctrines are simply insincere intrinsic racists. For *intrinsic racists*, on my definition, are people who differentiate morally between members of different races because they believe that each race has a different moral status, quite independent of the moral characteristics entailed by its racial essence. Just as, for example, many people assume that the fact that they are biologically related to another person—a brother, an aunt, a cousin—gives them a moral interest in that person,[4] so an intrinsic racist holds that the bare fact of being of the same race is a reason for preferring one person to another. (I shall return to this parallel later as well.)

For an intrinsic racist, no amount of evidence that a member of another race is capable of great moral, intellectual, or cultural achievements, or has characteristics that, in members of one's own race, would make them admirable or attractive, offers any ground for treating that person as he or she would treat similarly endowed members of his or her own race. Just so, some sexists are "intrinsic sexists," holding that the bare fact that someone is a woman (or man) is a reason for treating her (or him) in certain ways.

There are interesting possibilities for complicating these distinctions: some racists, for example, claim, as the Mormons once did, that they discriminate between people because they believe that God requires them to do so. Is this an extrinsic racism, predicated on the combination of God's being an intrinsic racist and the belief that it is right to do what God wills? Or is it intrinsic racism because it is based on the belief that God requires these discriminations because they are right? (Is an act pious because the gods love it, or do they love it because it is pious?) Nevertheless, the distinctions between racialism and racism and between two potentially overlapping kinds of racism provide us with the skeleton of an anatomy of the propositional contents of racial attitudes.

RACIST DISPOSITIONS

Most people will want to object already that this discussion of the propositional content of racist moral and factual beliefs misses something absolutely crucial to the character of the psychological and sociological reality of racism, something I touched on when I mentioned that extrinsic racist utterances are often made by people who suffer from what I called a "cognitive incapacity." Part of the standard force of accusations of racism is that their objects are in

some way *irrational*. The objection to Professor Shockley's claims about the intelligence of blacks is not just that they are false; it is rather that Professor Shockley seems, like many people we call "racist," to be unable to see that the evidence does not support his factual claims and that the connection between his factual claims and his policy prescriptions involves a series of non sequiturs.

What makes these cognitive incapacities especially troubling—something we should respond to with more than a recommendation that the individual, Professor Shockley, be offered psychotherapy—is that they conform to a certain pattern: namely, that it is especially where beliefs and policies are to the disadvantage of nonwhite people that he shows the sorts of disturbing failure that have made his views both notorious and notoriously unreliable. Indeed, Professor Shockley's reasoning works extremely well in some other areas: that he is a Nobel Laureate in physics is part of what makes him so interesting an example.

This cognitive incapacity is not, of course, a rare one. Many of us are unable to give up beliefs that play a part in justifying the special advantages we gain (or hope to gain) from our positions in the social order—in particular, beliefs about the positive characters of the class of people who share that position. Many people who express extrinsic racist beliefs—many white South Africans, for example—are beneficiaries of social orders that deliver advantages to them by virtue of their "race," so that their disinclination to accept evidence that would deprive them of a justification for those advantages is just an instance of this general phenomenon.

So too, evidence that access to higher education is as largely determined by the quality of our earlier educations as by our own innate talents, does not, on the whole, undermine the confidence of college entrants from private schools in England or the United States or Ghana. Many of them continue to believe in the face of this evidence that their acceptance at "good" universities shows them to be intellectually better endowed (and not just better prepared) than those who are rejected. It is facts such as these that give sense to the notion of false consciousness, the idea that an ideology can prevent us from acknowledging facts that would threaten our position.

The most interesting cases of this sort of ideological resistance to the truth are not, perhaps, the ones I have just mentioned. On the whole, it is less surprising, once we accept the admittedly problematic notion of self-deception, that people who think that certain attitudes or beliefs advantage them or those they care about should be able, as we say, to "persuade" themselves to ignore evidence that undermines those beliefs or attitudes. What is more interesting is the existence of people who resist the truth of a proposition while thinking that its wider acceptance would in no way disadvantage them or those individuals about whom they care—this might be thought to describe Professor Shockley; or who resist the truth when they recognize that its acceptance would actually advantage them—this might be the case with some black people who have internalized negative racist stereotypes; or who fail, by virtue of their ideological attachments, to recognize what is in their own best interests at all.

My business here is not with the psychological or social processes by which these forms of ideological resistance operate, but it is important, I think, to see the refusal on the part of some extrinsic racists

to accept evidence against the beliefs as an instance of a widespread phenomenon in human affairs. It is a plain fact, to which theories of ideology must address themselves, that our species is prone both morally and intellectually to such distortions of judgment, in particular to distortions of judgment that reflect partiality. An inability to change your mind in the face of appropriate[5] evidence is a cognitive incapacity; but it is one that all of us surely suffer from in some areas of belief; especially in areas where our own interests or self-images are (or seem to be) at stake.

It is not, however, as some have held, a tendency that we are powerless to resist. No one, no doubt, can be impartial about everything—even about everything to which the notion of partiality applies; but there is no subject matter about which most sane people cannot, in the end, be persuaded to avoid partiality in judgment. And it may help to shake the convictions of those whose incapacity derives from this sort of ideological defense if we show them how their reaction fits into this general pattern. It is, indeed, because it generally *does* fit this pattern that we call such views "racism"—the suffix "-ism" indicating that what we have in mind is not simply a theory but an ideology. It would be odd to call someone brought up in a remote corner of the world with false and demeaning views about white people a "racist" if that person gave up these beliefs quite easily in the face of appropriate evidence.

Real live racists, then, exhibit a systematically distorted rationality, the kind of systematically distorted rationality that we are likely to call "ideological." And it is a distortion that is especially striking in the cognitive domain: extrinsic racists, as I said earlier, however intelligent or otherwise well informed, often fail to treat evidence against the theoretical propositions of extrinsic racism dispassionately. Like extrinsic racism, intrinsic racism can also often be seen as ideological; but since scientific evidence is not going to settle the issue, a failure to see that it is wrong represents a cognitive incapacity only on controversially realist views about morality. What makes intrinsic racism similarly ideological is not so much the failure of inductive or deductive rationality that is so striking in someone like Professor Shockley but rather the connection that it, like extrinsic racism, has with the interests— real or perceived—of the dominant group.[6] Shockley's racism is in a certain sense directed *against* nonwhite people: many believe that his views would, if accepted, operate against their objective interests, and he certainly presents the black "race" in a less than flattering light.

I propose to use the old-fashioned term "racial prejudice" in the rest of this essay to refer to the deformation of rationality in judgment that characterizes those whose racism is more than a theoretical attachment to certain propositions about race.

RACIAL PREJUDICE

It is hardly necessary to raise objections to what I am calling "racial prejudice"; someone who exhibits such deformations of rationality is plainly in trouble. But it is important to remember that propositional racists in a racist culture have false moral beliefs but may not suffer from racial prejudice. Once we show them how society has enforced extrinsic racist stereotypes; once we ask them whether they really believe that race in itself, independently of those extrinsic racist beliefs, justifies differential treatment, many will come to give up racist

propositions, although we must remember how powerful a weight of authority our arguments have to overcome. Reasonable people may insist on substantial evidence if they are to give up beliefs that are central to their cultures.

Still, in the end, many will resist such reasoning; and to the extent that their prejudices are really not subject to any kind of rational control, we may wonder whether it is right to treat such people as morally responsible for the acts their racial prejudice motivates, or morally reprehensible for holding the views to which their prejudice leads them. It is a bad thing that such people exist; they are, in a certain sense, bad people. But it is not clear to me that they are responsible for the fact that they are bad. Racial prejudice, like prejudice generally, may threaten an agent's autonomy, making it appropriate to treat or train rather than to reason with them.

But once someone has been offered evidence both (1) that their reasoning in a certain domain is distorted by prejudice, and (2) that the distortions conform to a pattern that suggests a lack of impartiality, they ought to take special care in articulating views and proposing policies in that domain. They ought to do so because, as I have already said, the phenomenon of partiality in judgment is well attested in human affairs. Even if you are not immediately persuaded that you are yourself a victim of such a distorted rationality in a certain domain, you should keep in mind always that this is the usual position of those who suffer from such prejudices. To the extent that this line of thought is not one that itself falls within the domain in question, one can be held responsible for not subjecting judgments that *are* within that domain to an especially extended scrutiny; and this is a fortiori true if the policies one is recommending are plainly of enormous consequence.

If it is clear that racial prejudice is regrettable, it is also clear in the nature of the case that providing even a superabundance of reasons and evidence will often not be a successful way of removing it. Nevertheless, the racist's prejudice will be articulated through the sorts of theoretical propositions I dubbed extrinsic and intrinsic racism. And we should certainly be able to say something reasonable about why these theoretical propositions should be rejected.

Part of the reason that this is worth doing is precisely the fact that many of those who assent to the propositional content of racism do not suffer from racial prejudice. In a country like the United States, where racist propositions were once part of the national ideology, there will be many who assent to racist propositions simply because they were raised to do so. Rational objection to racist propositions has a fair chance of changing such people's beliefs.

EXTRINSIC AND INTRINSIC RACISM

It is not always clear whether someone's theoretical racism is intrinsic or extrinsic, and there is certainly no reason why we should expect to be able to settle the question. Since the issue probably never occurs to most people in these terms, we cannot suppose that they must have an answer. In fact, given the definition of the terms I offered, there is nothing barring someone from being both an intrinsic and an extrinsic racist, holding both that the bare fact of race provides a basis for treating members of his or her own race differently from others and that there are morally relevant characteristics that are differentially distributed among the races. Indeed, for reasons I shall discuss in a moment, *most* intrinsic racists are likely to express extrinsic racist beliefs, so that we should not be surprised that many people seem, in fact, to be committed to both forms of racism.

The Holocaust made unreservedly clear the threat that racism poses to human decency. But it also blurred our thinking because in focusing our attention on the racist character of the Nazi atrocities, it obscured their character as atrocities. What is appalling about Nazi racism is not just that it presupposes, as all racism does, false (racialist) beliefs—not simply that it involves a moral incapacity (the inability to extend our moral sentiments to all our fellow creatures) and a moral failing (the making of moral distinctions without moral differences)—but that it leads, first, to oppression and then to mass slaughter. In recent years, South African racism has had a similar distorting effect. For although South African racism has not led to killings on the scale of the Holocaust—even if it has both left South Africa judicially executing more (mostly black) people per head of population than most other countries and led to massive differences between the life chances of white and nonwhite South Africans—it *has* led to the systematic oppression and economic exploitation of people who are not classified as "white," and to the infliction of suffering on citizens of all racial classifications, not least by the police state that is required to maintain that exploitation and oppression.

Part of our resistance, therefore, to calling the racial ideas of those, such as the Black Nationalists of the 1960s, who advocate racial solidarity, by the same term that we use to describe the attitudes of Nazis or of members of the South African Nationalist party, surely resides in the fact that they largely did not contemplate using race as a basis for inflicting harm. Indeed, it seems to me that there is a significant pattern in the modern rhetoric of race, such that the discourse of racial solidarity is usually expressed through the language of *intrinsic* racism, while those who have used race as the basis for oppression and hatred have appealed to *extrinsic* racist ideas. This point is important for understanding the character of contemporary racial attitudes.

The two major uses of race as a basis for moral solidarity that are most familiar in the West are varieties of Pan-Africanism and Zionism. In each case it is presupposed that a "people," Negroes or Jews, has the basis for shared political life in the fact of being of the same race. There are varieties of each form of "nationalism" that make the basis lie in shared traditions; but however plausible this may be in the case of Zionism, which has in Judaism, the religion, a realistic candidate for a common and nonracial focus for nationality, the peoples of Africa have a good deal less in common culturally than is usually assumed. I discuss this issue at length in *In My Father's House: Essays in the Philosophy of African Culture,* but let me say here that I believe the central fact is this: what blacks in the West, like secularized Jews, have mostly in common is that they are perceived—both by themselves and by others—as belonging to the same race, and that this common race is used by others as the basis for discriminating against them. "If you ever forget you're a Jew, a goy will remind you." The Black Nationalists, like some Zionists, responded to their experience of racial discrimination by accepting the racialism it presupposed.[7]

Although race is indeed at the heart of Black Nationalism, however, it seems that it is the fact of a shared race, not the fact of a shared racial character, that provides the basis for solidarity. Where racism is implicated in the basis for national solidarity, it is intrinsic, not (or not only) extrinsic. It is this that makes the idea of fraternity one that is naturally applied in nationalist discourse. For, as I have already observed, the moral status of close family members is not normally thought of in most cultures as depending on qualities of character; we are supposed to love our brothers and sisters in spite of their faults and not because of their virtues. Alexander Crummell, one of the founding fathers of Black Nationalism, literalizes the metaphor of family in these startling words:

> Races, like families, are the organisms and ordinances of God; and race feeling, like family feeling, is of divine origin. The extinction of race feeling is just as possible as the extinction of family feeling. Indeed, a race *is* a family.[8]

It is the assimilation of "race feeling" to "family feeling" that makes intrinsic racism seem so much less objectionable than extrinsic racism. For this metaphorical identification reflects the fact that, in the modern world (unlike the nineteenth century), intrinsic racism is acknowledged almost exclusively as the basis of feelings of community. We can surely, then, share a sense of what Crummell's friend and coworker Edward Blyden called "the poetry of politics," that is, "the feeling of race," the feeling of "people with whom we are connected."[9] The racism here is the basis of acts of supererogation, the treatment of others better than we otherwise might, better than moral duty demands of us.

This is a contingent fact. There is no logical impossibility in the idea of racialists whose moral beliefs lead them to feelings of hatred for other races while leaving no room for love of members of their own. Nevertheless most racial hatred is in fact expressed through extrinsic racism: most people who have used race as the basis for causing harm to others have felt the need to see the others as independently morally flawed. It is one thing to espouse fraternity without claiming that your brothers and sisters have any special qualities that deserve recognition, and another to espouse hatred of others who have done nothing to deserve it.[10]

Many Afrikaners—like many in the American South until recently—have a long list of extrinsic racist answers to the question why blacks should not have full civil rights. Extrinsic racism has usually been the basis for treating people worse than we otherwise might, for giving them less than their humanity entitles them to. But this too is a contingent fact. Indeed, Crummell's guarded respect for white people derived from a belief in the superior moral qualities of the Anglo-Saxon race.

Intrinsic racism is, in my view, a moral error. Even if racialism were correct, the bare fact that someone was of another race would be no reason to treat them worse—or better—than someone of my race. In our public lives, people are owed treatment independently of their biological characters: if they are to be differently treated there must be some morally relevant difference between them. In our private lives, we are morally free to have aesthetic preferences between people, but once our treatment of people raises moral issues, we may not make arbitrary distinctions. Using race in itself as a morally relevant distinction strikes most of us as obviously arbitrary. Without associated moral characteristics, why should race provide a bet-

ter basis than hair color or height or timbre of voice? And if two people share all the properties morally relevant to some action we ought to do, it will be an error—a failure to apply the Kantian injunction to universalize our moral judgments—to use the bare facts of race as the basis for treating them differently. No one should deny that a common ancestry might, in particular cases, account for similarities in moral character. But then it would be the moral similarities that justified the different treatment.

It is presumably because most people—outside the South African Nationalist party and the Ku Klux Klan—share the sense that intrinsic racism requires arbitrary distinctions that they are largely unwilling to express it in situations that invite moral criticism. But I do not know how I would argue with someone who was willing to announce an intrinsic racism as a basic moral idea; the best one can do, perhaps, is to provide objections to possible lines of defense of it.

DE GUSTIBUS

It might be thought that intrinsic racism should be regarded not so much as an adherence to a (moral) proposition as the expression of a taste, analogous, say, to the food prejudice that makes most English people unwilling to eat horse meat, and most Westerners unwilling to eat the insect grubs that the !Kung people find so appetizing. The analogy does at least this much for us, namely, to provide a model of the way that *extrinsic* racist propositions can be a reflection of an underlying prejudice. For, of course, in most cultures food prejudices are rationalized: we say insects are unhygienic and cats taste horrible. Yet a cooked insect is no more health-threatening than a cooked carrot, and the unpleasant taste of cat meat, far from justifying our prejudice against it, probably derives from that prejudice.

But there the usefulness of the analogy ends. For intrinsic racism, as I have defined it, is not simply a taste for the company of one's "own kind," but a moral doctrine, one that is supposed to underlie differences in the treatment of people in contexts where moral evaluation is appropriate. And for moral distinctions we cannot accept that "de gustibus non est disputandum." We do not need the full apparatus of Kantian ethics to require that public morality be constrained by reason.

A proper analogy would be with someone who thought that we could continue to kill cattle for beef, even if cattle exercised all the complex cultural skills of human beings. I think it is obvious that creatures that shared our capacity for understanding as well as our capacity for pain should not be treated the way we actually treat cattle—that "intrinsic speciesism" would be as wrong as racism. And the fact that most people think it is worse to be cruel to chimpanzees than to frogs suggests that they may agree with me. The distinction in attitudes surely reflects a belief in the greater richness of the mental life of chimps. Still, I do not know how I would *argue* against someone who could not see this; someone who continued to act on the contrary belief might, in the end, simply have to be locked up.

THE FAMILY MODEL

I have suggested that intrinsic racism is, at least sometimes, a metaphorical extension of the moral priority of one's family; it

might, therefore, be suggested that a defense of intrinsic racism could proceed along the same lines as a defense of the family as a center of moral interest. The possibility of a defense of family relations as morally relevant—or, more precisely, of the claim that one may be morally entitled (or even obliged) to make distinctions between two otherwise morally indistinguishable people because one is related to one and not to the other—is theoretically important for the prospects of a philosophical defense of intrinsic racism. This is because such a defense of the family involves—like intrinsic racism—a denial of the basic claim, expressed so clearly by Kant, that from the perspective of morality, it is as rational agents *simpliciter* that we are to assess and be assessed. For anyone who follows Kant in this, what matters, as we might say, is not who you are but how you try to live. Intrinsic racism denies this fundamental claim also. And, in so doing, as I have argued elsewhere, it runs against the mainstream of the history of Western moral theory.[11]

The importance of drawing attention to the similarities between the defense of the family and the defense of the race, then, is not merely that the metaphor of family is often invoked by racism; it is that each of them offers the same general challenge to the Kantian stream of our moral thought. And the parallel with the defense of the family should be especially appealing to an intrinsic racist, since many of us who have little time for racism would hope that the family is susceptible to some such defense.

The problem in generalizing the defense of the family, however, is that such defenses standardly begin at a point that makes the argument for intrinsic racism immediately implausible: namely, with the family as the unit through which we live what is most intimate, as the center of private life. If we distinguish, with Bernard Williams, between ethical thought, which takes seriously "the demands, needs, claims, desires, and generally, the lives of other people,"[12] and morality, which focuses more narrowly on obligation, it may well be that private life matters to us precisely because it is altogether unsuited to the universalizing tendencies of morality.

The functioning family unit has contracted substantially with industrialization, the disappearance of the family as the unit of production, and the increasing mobility of labor, but there remains that irreducible minimum: the parent or parents with the child or children. In this "nuclear" family, there is, of course, a substantial body of shared experience, shared attitudes, shared knowledge and beliefs; and the mutual psychological investment that exists within this group is, for most of us, one of the things that gives meaning to our lives. It is a natural enough confusion—which we find again and again in discussions of adoption in the popular media—that identifies the relevant group with the biological unit of *genitor, genetrix,* and *offspring* rather than with the social unit of those who share a common domestic life.

The relations of parent and their biological children are of moral importance, of course, in part because children are standardly the product of behavior voluntarily undertaken by their biological parents. But the moral relations between biological siblings and half-siblings cannot, as I have already pointed out, be accounted for in such terms. A rational defense of the family ought to appeal to the causal responsibility of the biological parent and the common life of the domestic unit, and not

to the brute fact of biological relatedness, even if the former pair of considerations defines groups that are often coextensive with the groups generated by the latter. For brute biological relatedness bears no necessary connection to the sorts of human purposes that seem likely to be relevant at the most basic level of ethical thought.

An argument that such a central group is bound to be crucially important in the lives of most human beings in societies like ours is not, of course, an argument for any specific mode of organization of the "family": feminism and the gay liberation movement have offered candidate groups that could (and sometimes do) occupy the same sort of role in the lives of those whose sexualities or whose dispositions otherwise make the nuclear family uncongenial; and these candidates have been offered specifically in the course of defenses of a move toward societies that are agreeably beyond patriarchy and homophobia. The central thought of these feminist and gay critiques of the nuclear family is that we cannot continue to view any one organization of private life as "natural," once we have seen even the broadest outlines of the archaeology of the family concept.

If that is right, then the argument for the family must be an argument for a mode of organization of life and feeling that subserves certain positive functions; and however the details of such an argument would proceed it is highly unlikely that the same functions could be served by groups on the scale of races, simply because, as I say, the family is attractive in part exactly for reasons of its personal scale.

I need hardly say that rational defenses of intrinsic racism along the lines I have been considering are not easily found. In the absence of detailed defenses to consider, I can only offer these general reasons for doubting that they can succeed: the generally Kantian tenor of much of our moral thought threatens the project from the start; and the essentially unintimate nature of relations within "races" suggests that there is little prospect that the defense of the family—which seems an attractive and plausible project that extends ethical life beyond the narrow range of a universalizing morality—can be applied to a defense of races.

CONCLUSIONS

I have suggested that what we call "racism" involves both propositions and dispositions.

The propositions were, first, that there are races (this was *racialism*) and, second, that these races are morally significant either (a) because they are contingently correlated with morally relevant properties (this was *extrinsic racism*) or (b) because they are intrinsically morally significant (this was *intrinsic racism*).

The disposition was a tendency to assent to false propositions, both moral and theoretical, about races—propositions that support policies or beliefs that are to the disadvantage of some race (or races) as opposed to others, and to do so even in the face of evidence and argument that should appropriately lead to giving those propositions up. This disposition I called "racial prejudice."

I suggested that intrinsic racism had tended in our own time to be the natural expression of feelings of community, and this is, of course, one of the reasons why we are not inclined to call it racist. For, to the extent that a theoretical position is not associated with irrationally held beliefs

that tend to the *dis*advantage of some group, it fails to display the *directedness* of the distortions of rationality characteristic of racial prejudice. Intrinsic racism may be as irrationally held as any other view, but it does not *have* to be directed *against* anyone.

So far as theory is concerned I believe racialism to be false: since theoretical racism of both kinds presupposes racialism, I could not logically support racism of either variety. But even if racialism were true, both forms of theoretical racism would be incorrect. Extrinsic racism is false because the genes that account for the gross morphological differences that underlie our standard racial categories are not linked to those genes that determine, to whatever degree such matters are determined genetically, our moral and intellectual characters. Intrinsic racism is mistaken because it breaches the Kantian imperative to make moral distinctions only on morally relevant grounds—granted that there is no reason to believe that race, *in se,* is morally relevant, and also no reason to suppose that races are like families in providing a sphere of ethical life that legitimately escapes the demands of a universalizing morality.

NOTES

1. Bernard Lewis, *Semites and Anti-Semites* (New York: Norton, 1986).
2. I shall be using the words "racism" and "racialism" with the meanings I stipulate: in some dialects of English they are synonyms, and in most dialects their definition is less than precise. For discussion of recent biological evidence see M. Nei and A. K. Roychoudhury, "Genetic Relationship and Evolution of Human Races," *Evolutionary Biology,* vol. 14 (New York: Plenum, 1983) pp. 1–59; for useful background see also M. Nei and A.K. Roychoudhury, "Gene Differences between Caucasian, Negro, and

Japanese Populations," *Science,* 177 (August 1972), pp. 434–35.

3. See my "The Uncompleted Argument: Du Bois and the Illusion of Race," *Critical Inquiry,* 12 (Autumn 1985); reprinted in Henry Louis Gates (ed.), *"Race," Writing, and Difference* (Chicago: University of Chicago Press, 1986), pp. 21–37.

4. This fact shows up most obviously in the assumption that adopted children intelligibly make claims against their natural siblings: natural parents are, of course, causally responsible for their child's existence and that could be the basis of moral claims, without any sense that biological relatedness entailed rights or responsibilities. But no such basis exists for an interest in natural *siblings;* my sisters are not causally responsible for my existence. See "The Family Model," later in this essay.

5. Obviously what evidence should *appropriately* change your beliefs is not independent of your social or historical situation. In mid-nineteenth-century America, in New England quite as much as in the heart of Dixie, the pervasiveness of the institutional support for the prevailing system of racist belief—the fact that it was reinforced by religion and state, and defended by people in the universities and colleges, who had the greatest cognitive authority—meant that it would have been appropriate to insist on a substantial body of evidence and argument before giving up assent to racist propositions. In California in the 1980s, of course, matters stand rather differently. To acknowledge this is not to admit to a cognitive relativism; rather, it is to hold that, at least in some domains, the fact that a belief is widely held—and especially by people in positions of cognitive authority—may be a good prima facie reason for believing it.

6. Ideologies, as most theorists of ideology have admitted, standardly outlive the period in which they conform to the objective interests of the dominant group in a society, so even someone who thinks that the dominant group in our society no longer needs racism to buttress its position can see racism as the persisting ideology of an earlier phase of society. (I say "group" to keep the claim appropriately general; it seems to me a substantial further claim that the dominant group whose interests an ideology serves is

always a class.) I have argued, however, in "The Conservation of 'Race'" that racism continues to serve the interests of the ruling classes in the West; in *Black American Literature Forum,* 23 (Spring 1989), pp. 37–60.

7. As I argued in "The Uncompleted Argument: Du Bois and the Illusion of Race." The reactive (or dialectical) character of this move explains why Sartre calls its manifestations in Négritude an "antiracist racism"; see "Orphée Noir," his preface to Senghor's *Anthologie de la nouvelle poeésie nègre et malagache de langue française* (Paris: PUF, 1948). Sartre believed, of course, that the synthesis of this dialectic would be transcendence of racism; and it was his view of it as a stage—the antithesis—in that process that allowed him to see it as a positive advance over the original "thesis" of European racism. I suspect that the reactive character of antiracist racism accounts for the tolerance that is regularly extended to it in liberal circles; but this tolerance is surely hard to justify unless one shares Sartre's optimistic interpretation of it as a stage in a process that leads to the end of all racisms. (And unless your view of this dialectic is deterministic, you should in any case want to play an argumentative role in moving to this next stage.)

   For a similar Zionist response see Horace Kallen's "The Ethics of Zionism," *Maccabean,* August 1906.

8. "The Race Problem in America," in Brotz's *Negro Social and Political Thought* (New York: Basic Books 1966), p. 184.

9. *Christianity, Islam and the Negro Race* (1887; reprinted Edinburgh: Edinburgh University Press, 1967), p. 197.

10. This is in part a reflection of an important asymmetry: loathing, unlike love, needs justifying; and this, I would argue, is because loathing usually leads to acts that are *in se* undesirable, whereas love leads to acts that are largely *in se* desirable—indeed, supererogatorily so.

11. See my "Racism and Moral Pollution," *Philosophical Forum,* 18 (Winter–Spring 1986–87), pp. 185–202.

12. *Ethics and the Limits of Philosophy* (Cambridge, Mass.: Harvard University Press, 1985). p. 12. I do not, as is obvious, share Williams's skepticism about morality.

Sexism and Racism:
Some Conceptual Differences

Laurence Thomas

Laurence Thomas is a professor of philosophy at Syracuse University in New York. He is the author of Living Morally: A Psychology of Moral Character *(1989).*

Thomas addresses what he considers to be conceptual differences between sexism and racism. He argues that the positive self-concept of men is chiefly tied to their being sexists, and thus is central to their being, while the self-concept of being white is not inextricably tied to being racist. Thomas asserts that the way men perceive women is fundamental to men's conception of who they are, while the way whites conceive of blacks is not fundamental to their identity as whites. He therefore concludes that sexism is more difficult to end than racism.

How should we understand the difference between sexism and racism? Is the difference merely that we have women as victims of the former and blacks (or some other minority group) as victims of the latter? Or, are there differences of a deeper sort?

Consider: If a black were to report to his colleagues (all of whom are white) that he had just been called a "nigger," one could be reasonably certain that, since he is black, his colleagues would convey considerable sympathy toward him for having been subjected to such extreme verbal abuse. But if a woman were to report to her colleagues (all of whom are male) that she had just been called a "chick," "fox," or even a "dumb

broad," I suspect that her colleagues—and it is the reaction of her male colleagues which should concern us—would not be likely to suppose that she had been subjected to equally extreme verbal abuse;[1] and, therefore, they would be less inclined to view her as deserving of or in need of sympathy, let alone considerable sympathy. I believe that the different reactions that we would get here are indicative of some fundamental differences between sexism and racism. In this essay, I shall argue that the following are two such differences: *(a)* Sexism, unlike racism, readily lends itself to morally unobjectionable description. *(b)* The positive self-concept of men has been more centrally tied to their being sexists than has been the positive self-concept of whites to their being racists. An unfortunate consequence of *a* and *b,* I am afraid, is that racist attitudes are relatively easier to give up than sexist ones. This perhaps is what one would expect given the different

Laurence Thomas, "Sexism and Racism: Some Conceptual Differences" in *Ethics,* Vol. 90. January 1980, Published by the University of Chicago Press. Reprinted by permission of the University of Chicago Press and Laurence Thomas.

reactions that we would get from the two parallel situations which I have just described. Before getting underway, though, I want to make a few preliminary remarks.

1. Sexism and racism are obviously very large topics to try to cover in a single essay. My discussion, therefore, will be extremely one sided in that I shall be concerned with the attitude of the sexist and the racist qua perpetrator only and not qua victim. This, of course, is not to say that a person cannot be on both sides of the fence.[2] Thus, I shall make no attempt, except in passing, to give an account of the self-concept which a victim of either sexism or racism has. It seems to be a fact that women are less likely to see themselves as victims of sexism than blacks (say) are to see themselves as victims of racism.[3] I believe that what I shall have to say on these two topics will be compatible with this fact.

2. Undoubtedly, there are different conceptions of sexism and racism, just as there are different conceptions of justice.[4] However, my aim is not to defend a particular conception of either social phenomenon; instead, I shall offer only a skeletal account of both which others, no doubt, will flesh out in different ways.

3. I mean only to be explaining the difference between sexism and racism. I do not in any way suppose that either can be morally justified. Moreover, I shall not be concerned with whether one is more morally objectionable than the other. For both are sufficiently objectionable, on moral grounds, that everyone should be equally concerned to perpetuate neither.

4. Finally, although I hardly think that blacks constitute the only ethnic group which has been the victim of racism, I am going to limit the discussion to blacks nonetheless. Not only will this make the discussion more manageable; I am, for the most part, concerned with racism (and sexism) in the United States—and it is fair to say that, because of both their physical features and numbers, blacks have been the primary target of racism in the United States.

I

Obviously enough, if *a* and *b* are true, then sexism and racism must differ in the way in which each views its victims. The following social phenomenon sheds some light on the matter. In response to the demands of liberated women, men are forming groups in order to come to grips with their conception of themselves as men, that is, in order to understand what the male role comes to.[5] However, whereas the struggle against sexism has sent men back to the drawing board, as it were, in order to redefine their maleness, the struggle against racism has not resulted in a similar reaction on the part of whites. Whites have not found themselves at a loss to understand themselves qua white persons. The point here is not that the lives of whites have gone unaffected in this regard. Rather, it is that, although men often perceive the women's movement as an affront to their masculinity, the black movement has not been perceived in a similar vein by whites. Whites have not taken being less of a racist to mean being less of a white in the way that men have taken being less of a sexist to mean being less of a man (see Section III). Why is this? The answer which readily recommends itself is that the conception which men have of women is much more central to the conception which men have of themselves than is the case for whites with respect to blacks. I shall refer to this view as the racial and sexual identity (RSI) thesis. Lest there be any misunderstanding, I should note that it no more follows from the truth of this thesis that sexism exists than it does that racism does not.

The truth of the RSI thesis is, I believe, well supported by the following considerations: (1) Since the beginning of humanity, women and men have had to interact for the purpose of procreation in order for the human species to survive. (2) There are male and female members of every race; hence, no race is dependent upon the members of any other race for its survival. (3) Any male and female member of any race can have offspring. (4) Whereas one can be racially mixed, one's gender is an all-or-nothing matter. A person is either male or female, taking the sexual organs to be the determining factor.[6] (5) The races are not regarded as biological complementaries of one another, but the two sexes are. Thus, it suffices that there exists some race or other which is different from a person's own race in order for it to be possible for that person to have a racial identity; such identity does not require the existence of a particular race. Our sexual identity, however, is clearly predicated upon the existence of a particular sex, namely, the opposite one. I shall assume that the RSI thesis is well supported by these five considerations. The thesis will be central to the account which I shall give of the way in which sexism and racism each conceives of its object: women and blacks, respectively.

Now, I should note that sexism and racism are commonly taken to be quite similar. This is because both racist and sexist attitudes rest upon the view that, respectively, there are innate differences between whites and blacks, on the one hand, and men and women, on the other, which in each case make it natural for the latter to be subordinate to the former.[7] For instance, blacks and women have been stereotyped as being both intellectually and emotionally inferior to whites and men, respectively. But closer inspection reveals that even this similarity is not without a fundamental difference. For whereas the woman's lack turns out to

make her naturally suited for the home and raising children and, therefore, natural for her to be around, the conclusion that it is natural for blacks to be around is not forthcoming. Indeed, it has been said by blacks and whites alike that things would be better if all blacks were back in Africa.[8] So we encounter a difference between sexism and racism even in the respect in which they are thought to be most similar. It takes only a moment of reflection to see that this difference can be explained by reference to the considerations offered in support of the RSI thesis. There is no biological role for blacks to play in the reproduction of white offspring, however much whites may find it desirable to have blacks around for other reasons. It is in this light that the remarks of this paragraph must be understood.

Taking my cue from the preceding discussion, the way in which sexism and racism each conceives of its object can be put as follows: Sexism entails the view that, although (a) women are inferior to men in some sense, (b) biological considerations dictate that women ought to be around in order to insure the survival of the human species. Moreover, in view of a and b, (c) it is appropriate for women to cater to the wants and needs of men; indeed, women are understood as complementing men. Racism entails the view that (a) blacks are in some sense inferior to whites and that, in view of this, (b) it is appropriate for blacks to cater to the wants and needs of whites, but not the view that (c) biological considerations dictate that blacks ought to be around whites and, therefore, that blacks complement whites. It goes without saying that I am merely stating what I take to be the core of a sexist conception of women and a racist conception of blacks; in no way do I mean to be endorsing either.

Some explanatory remarks are in order. What I mean by the claim that women complement men is aptly expressed by the saying, "Behind every man there is a good woman." Women are supposed to possess or excel at those virtues which make them naturally suited for being supportive of and bringing out the best in men.[9] For instance, women are supposed to possess a greater capacity than men for being understanding, encouraging, and sympathetic. (The first capacity, which has to do with patience and tolerance, is not to be confused with the capacity to understand, which has to do with intellectual ability.) Thus, it is thought to be to a man's benefit to associate himself with the right woman, since the right woman, so the view goes, will be a man's constant source of support and encouragement, thereby enabling him to excel at what he does. Women, then, are thought to play a central role in the self-development of men and, thus, in men having a positive conception of themselves. Nothing of the sort is thought to be true of blacks vis-à-vis whites. There are no time-honored sayings to the effect that "behind every white there is a good black." It has not been thought that by associating with the right black whites will enhance their chances of excelling at whatever they do, of being their best as whites.[10]

We now have before us a skeletal account of the way in which sexism and racism construe women and blacks, respectively. As I have remarked, others may wish to flesh out these accounts in different ways. In any event, we are in the position to make good the claim that the following are two of the fundamental differences between sexism and racism: *(a)* Sexism, unlike racism, readily lends itself to a morally unobjectionable description. *(b)* The positive self-concept of men has been more centrally

tied to their being sexists than has been the positive self-concept of whites to their being racists. In the order mentioned, I turn to these two claims in the sections which follow.

II

I shall proceed in this section by arguing first that sexism readily lends itself to a morally unobjectionable description and then for the claim that racism does not.

A major aspect of the traditional male role is what I shall call the benefactor role. It is the role of men to protect women and to provide them with the comforts of life. That men should be the benefactors of women (in the sense described) is, it should be observed, a natural outcome of a sexist conception of women. For it will be recalled that, according to that conception, women play a central role in the self-development of men. And, of course, any person has good reasons to protect and provide for that which plays a central role in her or his self-development. But it goes without saying that this aspect of the traditional male role hardly seems morally objectionable.[11] For we do not normally suppose that a person does that which is morally wrong in benefiting someone. And on the face of it, surely, providing a person with the comforts of life would hardly seem to be a morally objectionable thing to do. After all, are they not desired by nearly everyone? At first blush, then, the traditional male role seems quite immune to moral criticism, which explains why the charge of sexism often seems to be lacking in moral force. Indeed, it is not uncommon to hear a man boast of being a sexist—even nowadays!

Now, of course, an arrangement where men benefit women is not morally objectionable—in and of itself, that is. What is morally objectionable, though, are the presuppositions behind it, one of the most important of them being that this sort of arrangement is ordained by nature.[12] From this presupposition, a number of things are thought to follow, such as that men should earn more money than women (period) and that the work which women do around the home is not as important as the work which men do on the job. These matters could be pursued at length, but I shall not do so here. For my concern has been to show that sexism, readily lends itself to a morally unobjectionable description. And to show that it is a natural outcome of a sexist conception of women that men should be the benefactors of women (in the sense described) is to show this much.

Let us now look at racism. The first thing we should observe is that a racist conception of blacks does not naturally give rise to the view that whites should be the benefactors of blacks. This should come as no surprise, for it will be remembered (a) that blacks and whites alike have thought that things would be better if all blacks were back in Africa and (b) that blacks have not been thought to play a central role in the self-development of whites. For blacks were thought to be too inferior for that. Whites, then, have never conceived of it as their role qua whites to be the benefactor of blacks. And, as history shows,[13] the benefit of blacks has hardly been the concern of racist arrangements. For the most part, the benefit of blacks was incidental to (an unintended side effect of) such arrangements or, in any case, up to the whim of those responsible for such arrangements. These facts, alone, make it very difficult for racism to be viewed in a morally unobjectionable light.

Now it might be objected that racism can be so viewed if we suppose that whites held blacks to be inferior in their moral status to whites.[14] But not so. For one thing, the case of women shows that persons can have what I called the benefactor role even with respect to living things presumed to be of inferior moral status. After all, it is impossible to understand the doctrine of coverture (e.g.) without supposing that according to it women are inferior in their moral status to men.[15] For another, the cruel treatment of living things of inferior moral status is morally wrong in any event, as the case of animals shows. Racism, though, has often called for the cruel treatment of blacks, whose moral status has most certainly not been thought to be inferior to the moral status of animals. So the objection fails.

A satisfactory case, I believe, has been made for the claims that sexism unlike racism, readily admits of a morally unobjectionable description.

III

The task of this section is to show that the positive self-concept of men has been more centrally tied to their being sexists than has been the positive self-concept of whites to their being racists. I shall first say a few words about what a person's positive self-concept comes to.

There are various aspects of a person's positive self-concept. However, the one which is germane to our discussion is what is called self-esteem.[16] It is the attitude which we have toward ourselves regarding our ability to interact effectively with our social environment, to achieve the goals which we set for ourselves. Respectively, our self-esteem is positive or negative if we have a reasonably favorable or unfavorable attitude toward ourselves in this regard. No person without deep psychological problems desires to have a negative conception of her- or himself. Thus, those activities which we believe will enhance our self-esteem have a natural attraction for us. So we are disinclined to give up those activities the successful pursuit of which enhances our self-esteem unless we have reason to believe that we can maintain our self-esteem by engaging in other activities. Obviously enough, the range of our abilities is very relevant here. The wider it is the more options there are that are open to us.

But now it is our values which determine the sorts of activities whose successful pursuit will enhance our self-esteem. Hence, having an excellent voice for classical music will do little to enhance our self-esteem if we have no interest in such music. On the other hand, if being able to sing classical music well is very important to us, then our self-esteem will suffer a severe blow if we are told by someone whose opinion we highly respect that this is an end which is beyond our reach. In large measure the social institutions among which we live determine the sorts of values which we come to have. And those values which have been instilled in us since childhood by our familial, educational, and religious institutions may have such a tenacious hold upon us that we find ourselves unable to give them up even when the ends which they call for prove to be beyond our reach. These few remarks about self-esteem, as sketchy as they are, should give us enough of a handle on the concept to permit us to proceed with the task of showing that the positive self-concept (self-esteem) of sexists is more centrally tied to the fact that they are sexists

than is the positive self-concept (self-esteem) of racists to the fact that they are racists. (Throughout the remainder of this essay, I shall use the term "self-esteem" instead of "self-concept.")

If the RSI thesis is sound, then our sexual identity is clearly central to the conception which we have of ourselves. As things stand, though, while our gender is clearly relevant to our sexual identity, it is far from being the sole determiner of it.[17] Our beliefs about the sorts of roles we should play have a most powerful influence in this regard. There is, we might say, as much a social sense of the terms "woman" and "man" as there is a biological one. A person is a woman or man in the biological sense merely in virtue of having the appropriate biological properties. But to be a woman or man in the social sense not only must one have the appropriate biological properties; one must also have the appropriate aspirations and social behavior. The traditional female and male roles define a social sense of the terms "woman" and "man." Hence, a woman's self-esteem can turn upon the fact that she measures up to the traditional female role; a man's self-esteem can turn upon the fact that he measures up to the traditional male role.

Now we have seen that, according to the traditional male role, men have what I have called the benefactor role with respect to women: they are supposed to protect women and provide them with the comforts of life. That men should have this role with respect to women is, without a doubt, one of the most deeply entrenched views of our society. A "real" man is one who "wears the pants around the house." He is the breadwinner. Indeed, the benefactor role is not an optional feature of the traditional male role—something which a man may take or leave as it pleases him. For it will be remembered that it is supposedly ordained by nature that men should have the benefactor role with respect to women, Unless there is some excuse, such as that of being a priest, it follows, according to the traditional male role, that men ought to be the benefactors of women. Thus, men believe that it is appropriate for their conception of themselves to turn upon how well they live up to the benefactor role. And, in the cases of those men who do so reasonably well, their self-esteem is enhanced precisely because their success in this regard constitutes an affirmation of their ability to be men in the social sense of the term. In view of the considerations advanced in this and the preceding paragraph, there is no getting around the fact that the positive self-esteem of men has been centrally tied to their being sexists.

We do not encounter an analogous situation between the black and white races. One very important reason why this is so is that there is only a biological sense of the races and, so, the black and white races. Thus, racial identity for whites, and any other race, is something which has been more or less entirely settled by biological considerations. To be a full-fledged white person one has never had to own black slaves or even to hate blacks. This latter point is well illustrated by the case of the nigger lover. To be sure, many whites looked rather disparagingly upon the nigger lover. But this is not because whites considered her or him to be a white person *manqué*. The nigger lover was not a mulatto! A mulatto can no more be a nigger lover than a male a tomboy or a female a sissy. As for the first point, suffice it to say that American slaveowners were hardly of the opinion that European whites were less than full-fledged whites on account of the fact that black slavery was

not a very prominent feature of European white societies.

Of course, I do not mean to deny the obvious fact that whites have perceived there to be fundamental differences among themselves, as, for example, class differences.[18] Nor do I mean to deny that whites have thought certain forms of conduct to be inappropriate for them, as, for example, the conduct of a nigger lover. What I do mean to deny, however, is that the racial identity of whites turned upon any of these differences. And if I am right about this, then it follows with impeccable logic that the racial identity of whites has not turned upon their being racists.

Now, to be sure, there have been many whites whose self-esteem has been enhanced by the fact that they were racists. At one point in his life George Wallace was certainly such an individual. It is significant to note, though, that the word "racist" is not the name of an institutional role, as are, say, the words "teacher," "governor," and "spouse."[19] Moreover, the definitions of such roles do not make any reference to the sorts of activities which, under some description or other, are properly characterized as racist. No one, for instance, supposes that a person cannot be a teacher, governor, or spouse unless she or he is a racist,[20] though, to be sure, many may think that only racists should occupy such roles. If, therefore, it is true that for any institutional role K a person S can perform K without being a racist, under some description or other, then it has to be equally true that, if S were a racist, then S could cease to be one without S's self-esteem being jeopardized with respect to the performance of K. When this consideration is coupled with the fact that the racial identity of whites has not turned upon their being racists, what follows most straightforwardly is that the self-esteem of whites has not been centrally tied to their being racists.

Now, the word "sexist" is not the name of an institutional role either. However, there is at least one institutional role, namely that of being a spouse (traditionally understood), which by definition makes reference to the sorts of activities which are sexist under at least some description. For the attitudes which the traditional male spouse has toward women (his wife, in particular) are, needless to say, dictated by the traditional male role, as what I have called the benefactor role should make clear. And, as we have seen, in their endeavors to measure up to the benefactor role, the self-esteem of men has been centrally tied to their being sexists.

I should conclude this section by noting that nothing I have said implies that the self-esteem of slavemasters did not or could not have turned upon their owning slaves. For their slaves were their property; and one's self-esteem can turn upon how much property one owns, whether that property is land, cattle, houses, or black slaves. Thus, it would be a mistake to suppose that the fact that the self-esteem of slaveowners turned upon their owning slaves militates against the arguments of this section. For being a slave holder was not, surely, a defining characteristic of either a racist or a white person during the times of slavery; and so, a fortiori, it has not been since the passing of slavery.

IV

Throughout this essay, I have assumed that the traditional male role can be described in a morally objectionable way. I do not now want to argue the case. Rather, I would like for the reader to engage in a brief thought experiment with me. Suppose that men were the victims of sexism and that

> [everything a man] wore, said, or did had to be justified by reference to female approval; if he were compelled to regard himself, day in day out, not as a member of society, but merely . . . as a virile member of society. If the center of his dress-consciousness were the cod-piece, his education directed to making him a spirited lover and meek paterfamilias; his interests held to be natural only in so far as they were sexual. If from school and lecture-room, press and pulpit, he heard the persistent outpouring of a shrill and scolding voice, bidding him remember his biological function. If he were vexed by continual advice how to add a rough male touch to his typing, how to be learned without losing his masculine appeal, how to combine chemical research with education, how to play bridge without incurring the suspicion of impotence. If, instead of allowing with a smile that "women prefer cavemen," he felt the unrelenting pressure of a whole social structure forcing him to order all his goings in conformity with that pronouncement.[21]

I have no doubt that most men would find a world thus described quite objectionable—and on moral grounds. If so, then there is indeed a morally objectionable way of describing the traditional male role in this world.

The differences between sexism and racism go much deeper than, as is commonly supposed, the fact that women are victims of the former and blacks of the latter. If I have argued soundly in this essay, then we have seen that sexism and racism are not two ways of referring to the same social monster, but two rather different ones.

V

My objective in this essay has been to show that there are at least two fundamental differences between sexism and racism: *(a)* Sexism, unlike racism, readily lends itself to a morally unobjectionable description. *(b)* The positive self-concept of men has been more centrally tied to their being sexists than has been the positive self-concept of whites to their being racists. As I said at the outset of this essay, it is, I believe, a consequence of the truth of *a* and *b* that racist attitudes are relatively easier to give up than sexist ones. I shall not attempt a defense of this claim at this point. Suffice to say, first of all, that persons must see that something is morally objectionable before they take themselves to have a moral reason for giving it up. We have seen that sexism presents a greater difficulty than racism in this regard. Second, it is a fact that people are disinclined to alter their behavior if they have reason to believe that in doing so they would jeopardize their self-esteem.[22] And we have seen that sexism presents a greater difficulty than racism in this regard as well.

In this essay, I have argued that there are some fundamental differences between sexism and racism. I have not denied that there are any similarities between the two; nor have I meant to do so.

ACKNOWLEDGMENT

I was first prompted to think about the topic of this paper in the fall of 1976 when I received an invitation from Stanley M. Browne, on behalf of Talladega College (Alabama), to give a talk on it. Versions of this paper have since been read at Georgia State University, Tuskegee Institute, Union College, Western Michigan University, and the American Philosophical Association meetings (Pacific Division). Lawrence Alexander saved me from a number of slips and stylistic infelicities. Lyla H. O'Driscoll and Alison M. Jagger forced me to be more careful than I would have been in my remarks about the sexual identity of men. Section III of this paper was extensively revised in the light of the very forthright criticisms of my APA commentator, Robert C. Williams. Among others who have been kind enough to offer extensive comments are: C. Freeland, D. Jamieson. H. McGary, J. Narveson, J. Nickel, and A. Soble. A special word of thanks goes to Sandra Bartky and Connie Price for their encouragement in writing this paper from the very start. The completion of later drafts of this paper was facilitated by my having an A. W. Mellon Faculty Fellowship at Harvard University for the 1978-79 academic year.

NOTES

1. A sexual parallel here would have to be denigrating, but not vulgar. Thus, words such as "bitch" and "cunt" do not parallel the racial epithet "nigger." Indeed, in certain contexts, the word "nigger" is not even denigrating: a black woman may call a black man with whom she is in love her "sweet nigger." Of the three expressions mentioned in the text, I suspect that "dumb broad," suggested to me by A. Soble, is the closest parallel to "nigger," though it still misses the mark.

2 Marabel Morgan, it would seem, is a woman who is on both sides of the fence. The "total woman" classes organized by her are based on the view that for a married woman "love is *unconditional* acceptance of him [her husband] and his feelings" (emphasis added) (see *The Total Woman* [New York; Pocket Books, 1975], p. 161).

3. See Eugene D. Genovese, *Roll, Jordan, Roll: The World Slaves Made* (New York: Pantheon Books, 1974).

4. On the difference between the concept and a conception of justice, see John Rawls, *A Theory of Justice* (Cambridge, Mass.: Harvard University Press, 1971), pp. 5–11.

5. Cf. David Gelman et al., "How Men Are Changing," *Newsweek* (January 16, 1978), and Peter Knobler, "Is It More Difficult to Be a Man Today?" *New York Times* (May 27, 1978). Also, there is Gene Marine, *A Male Guide to Women's*

Liberation (New York: Avon Books, 1972), and many other books of this genre.

6. Among persons and other higher animals, there can only be what is called pseudohermaphroditism, i.e., genetic abnormalities or hormonal imbalances (see *The Encyclopedia Americana*, international ed., s.v. "hermaphrodite").

7. In connection with sexism, two of the most sophisticated writers whom I have come across are Mary Wollstonecraft, *A Vindication of the Rights of Women* (first published in 1792), and Dorothy L. Sayers, *Unpopular Opinions* (New York: Harcourt Brace & Co., 1947).

8. Among blacks who have held this view, Marcus Garvey comes foremost to mind (see Edmund David Cronon, *Black Moses: The Story of Marcus Garvey and the Universal Negro Improvement Association* [Madison: University of Wisconsin Press. 1969]).

9. Cf Morgan. Wollstonecraft speaks of men having the pleasure of commanding flattering sycophants (see p. 13 of the edition of *A Vindication of the Rights of Women* edited by Carol H. Post [New York: W.W. Norton & Co., 1975]). Wollstonecraft's point is developed in a contemporary vein by L. Blum et al., "Altruism and Women's Oppression," *Philosophical Forum* 5 (1973): 196–221.

10. During the times of slavery American whites did not think that European whites needed to find themselves the right black in order to better themselves.

11. In order to keep down the length of this essay, I have deliberately not said anything about the traditional male role in connection with sex. The sexual exploitation of women is surely one of the worst aspects of the traditional male role. In the work compiled by the Sex Information and Educational Council of the United States, *Sexuality and Man* (New York: Charles Scribner's Sons, 1970), we find the following remarks: "Four major premarital sexual standards exist today: Abstinence, the formal standard of forbidding intercourse to both sexes; the Double Standard, the Western world's oldest standard, which allows males to have greater access to coitus than females; Permissiveness with Affection . . .; and Permissiveness without Affection . . . " (p. 40). And this is to say nothing of the humiliation to which women have been subjected in connection with rape. It was once common practice for men to sexually abuse the women they captured. And, even today, many rapes go unreported because of the humiliation to which the victims are subjected (See Gerda Lerna, *The Female Experience: An American Documentary* [Indianapolis: Bobbs-Merrill Co., 1977], pp. 433 ff). It goes without saying that I have also left aside the traditional female role in

connection with sex and childbearing. For an excellent discussion in connection with the former, see Christopher Lasch, "The Flight From Feeling: Sociopsychology of Sexual Conflict," *Marxist Perspectives* 1 (1978): 74–95. This essay was brought to my attention by Eugene Rivers.

12. I am indebted to Linda Patrik (Union College) for much of the way that I have put this paragraph.

13. See Genovese.

14. In my "Rawlsian Self-Respect and the Black Consciousness Movement" *(Philosophical Forum* 9 [1978]; 303–14], I have distinguished between having full, partial, and no moral status. A thing has no moral status (e.g., stones) if there are no rights which it can have and there are no duties which it can have or which can be owed to it. A thing has only partial moral status (e.g., animals) if there are duties which can be owed to it, but there are no duties which it can have. A thing has full moral status (e.g., persons) if there are rights and duties which it can have. As for whether or not animals can have rights, suffice it to say that they cannot, unlike persons, have rights against one another. A dog does not violate any rights of the squirrel which it catches and kills or hurts.

15. The doctrine reads thus: "By marriage the husband and the wife are one person in law; that is, the very being or legal existence of the woman is suspended during the marriage, or at least incorporated and consolidated into that of the husband; under whose wing, protection, and cover, she performs everything" (see William Blackstone, *Commentaries on the Laws of England*, reprint ed. [London: Dawsons of Pall Mall, 1966], p. 430).

16. See, among others, Stanley Coopersmith, *The Antecedents of Self-Esteem* (San Francisco: W. H. Freeman & Co, 1967); L. Edward Well and Gerald Marwell, *Self-Esteem: Its Conceptualization and Measurement* (Beverly Hills, Calif.: Sage Publications, 1976); and Robert W. White, "Ego and Reality in Psychoanalytic Theory," *Psychological Issues*, vol. 3, monograph 11 (1963). I have tried to show the importance of distinguishing between self-esteem and self-respect, which I have defined in terms of having the conviction that one has and is deserving of full moral status (see my "Morality and Our Self-Concept," *Journal of Value Inquiry* 12 [1978]: 258–68).

17. In a nonsexist society, perhaps the difference between gender identity and sexual identity would collapse (see Richard Wasserstrom, "Racism, Sexism, and Preferential Treatment: An Approach to the Topics," *UCLA Law Review* 24 [1977]: 581–622). For some illuminating discussions concerning the roles of women, see the collection of articles in Jo Freeman, ed., *Woman:*

A Feminist Perspective (Palo Alto, Calif.: Mayfield Publishing Co., 1975); and Michele Garskof, ed., *Roles Women Play* (Belmont, Calif.: Brooks/Cole Publishing Co., 1971).

18. See, e.g., Patricia Hollis, ed., *Class and Conflict in Nineteenth-Century England, 1815–1850* (London: Routledge & Kegan Paul, 1973).

19. In the use of the word "institutional," I follow John Rawls, "Two Concepts of Rules," *Philosophical Review* 64 (1955): 3-32.

20. Indeed, it would seem that this is true even of the role of slavemaster. Aristotle thought it natural that there should be slaves. I do not see, though, that he thought it natural that the slaves should be black (see *Politics*, bk. 1).

21. Sayers (n. 7 above), pp. 143–45. A later paragraph reads as follows. "If, after a few centuries of this kind of treatment, the male was a little self-conscious, a little on the defensive, I should not blame him. If he traded a little upon his sex, I could forgive him. If he presented the world with a major social problem, I would scarcely be surprised. It would be more surprising if he retained any rag of sanity and self-respect."

22. The fact that a person's self-esteem may be enhanced by the successful pursuit of morally unacceptable ends is often proferred as an explanation as to why those for whom street crime is a way of life do not accept the more traditional moral values (see, e.g., Charles Silberman, *Criminal Violence, Criminal Justice* [New York: Random House, 1978], chaps. 2 and 3).

The Red
and the Black

Vine Deloria, Jr

Vine Deloria, Jr. (Standing Rock Sioux) is a professor of American Indian studies, political science, and law at the University of Colorado at Boulder. Deloria has authored numerous books, including Custer Died for Your Sins *(1969),* God Is Red *(1973),* Behind the Trail of Broken Treaties *(1974), and* American Indian Policy in the Twentieth Century *(1985).*

Deloria criticizes the tradition of viewing civil rights issues as applying solely to African Americans, and broadens our discussion to include American Indians. Deloria distinguishes between the types of conflicts that American Indians and African Americans have had with the federal government. He states that American Indians need to adjust the legal relationship between the various tribes and the government, while African Americans need to work on socioeconomic relations with the government. Deloria suggests that the ultimate understanding of and solution to the racial question lies with the white majority. Whites must examine the past and come to see that they have created the racism dilemma and must take responsibility to cease projecting their fears and their way of life onto other races.

Civil Rights has been the most important and least understood movement of our generation. To some it has seemed to be a simple matter of fulfilling rights outlined by the Constitutional amendments after the Civil War. To others, particularly church people, Civil Rights has appeared to be a fulfillment of the brotherhood of man and the determination of humanity's relationship to God. To those opposing the movement, Civil Rights has been a foreign conspiracy which has threatened the fabric of our society.

For many years the movement to give the black people rights equal to those of their white neighbors was called Race Relations.

The preoccupation with race obscured the real issues that were developing and meant that programs devised to explore the area of race always had a black orientation.

To the Indian people it has seemed quite unfair that churches and government agencies concentrated their efforts primarily on the blacks. By defining the problem as one of race and making race refer solely to black, Indians were systematically excluded from consideration. National church groups have particularly used race as a means of exploring minority-group relations. Whatever programs or policies outlined from national churches to their affiliates and parishes were generally black-oriented programs which had been adapted to include Indians.

There was probably a historical basis for this type of thinking. In many states in the last century, Indians were classified as white by laws passed to exclude blacks. So there was a connotation that Indians might in some way be like whites. But in other areas, particularly marriage laws, Indians were classified as blacks and this connotation really determined the role into which the white man forced the red man. Consequently, as far as most Race Relations were concerned, Indians were classified as non-whites.

There has been no way to positively determine in which category Indians belong when it comes to federal agencies. The Bureau of Indian Affairs consistently defined Indians as good guys who have too much dignity to demonstrate, hoping to keep the Indian people separate from the ongoing Civil Rights movement. Other agencies generally adopted a semi-black orientation. Sometimes Indians were treated as if they were blacks and other times not.

The Civil Rights Commission and the Community Relations Service always gave only lip service to Indians until it was necessary for them to write an annual report. At that time they always sought out some means of including Indians as a group with which they had worked the previous fiscal year. That was the extent of Indian relationship with the agency: a paragraph in the annual report and a promise to do something next year.

Older Indians, as a rule, have been content to play the passive role outlined for them by the bureau. They have wanted to avoid the rejection and bad publicity given activists.

The Indian people have generally avoided confrontations between the different minority groups and confrontations with the American public at large. They have felt that any publicity would inevitably have bad results and since the press seemed dedicated to the perpetuation of sensationalism rather than straight reporting of the facts, great care has been taken to avoid the spotlight. Because of this attitude, Indian people have not become well known in the field of intergroup and race relations. Consequently they have suffered from the attitudes of people who have only a superficial knowledge of minority groups and have attached a certain stigma to them.

The most common attitude Indians have faced has been the unthoughtful Johnny-come-lately liberal who equates certain goals with a dark skin. This type of individual generally defines the goals of all groups by the way he understands what he wants for the blacks. Foremost in this category have been younger social workers and clergymen entering the field directly out of college or seminary. For the most part they have been book-fed and lack experience in life. They depend primarily upon labels and categories of academic import rather than on any direct experience. Too often they have achieved positions of prominence as programs have been expanded to meet needs of people. In exercising their discretionary powers administratively, they have run roughshod over Indian people. They have not wanted to show their ignorance about Indians. Instead, they prefer to place all people with darker skin in the same category of basic goals, then develop their programs to fit these preconceived ideas.

Since the most numerous group has been the blacks, programs designed for blacks were thought adequate for all needs of all groups. When one asks a liberal about minority groups, he unconsciously seems to categorize them all together for purposes of problem solving. Hence, dark-skinned and minority group as categorical concepts have brought about the same basic results—the Indian is defined as a subcategory of black.

Cultural differences have only seemed to emphasize the white liberal's point of view in lumping the different communities together. When Indians have pointed out real differences that do exist, liberals have tended to dismiss the differences as only minor aberrations which distinguish different racial groups.

At one conference on education of minority groups, I once mentioned the existence of some three hundred Indian languages which made bicultural and bilingual education a necessity. I was immediately challenged by several white educators who attempted to prove that blacks also have a language problem. I was never able to make the difference real to them. For the conference people the point had again been established that minority groups all had the same basic problems.

Recently, blacks and some Indians have defined racial problems as having one focal point—the White Man. This concept is a vast oversimplification of the real problem, as it centers on a racial theme rather than on specific facts. And it is simply the reversal of the old prejudicial attitude of the white who continues to define minority groups as problems of his—that is, Indian problem, Negro problem, and so on.

Rather than race or minority grouping, non-whites have often been defined according to their function within the American society. Negroes, as we have said, were considered draft animals, Indians wild animals. So too, Orientals were considered domestic animals and Mexicans humorous lazy animals. The white world has responded to the non-white groups in a number of ways, but primarily according to the man-

ner in which it believed the non-whites could be rescued from their situation.

Thus Orientals were left alone once whites were convinced that they preferred to remain together and presented no basic threat to white social mores. Mexicans were similarly discarded and neglected when whites felt that they preferred to remain by themselves. In both cases there was no direct confrontation between whites and the two groups because there was no way that a significant number of them could be exploited. They owned little; they provided little which the white world coveted.

With the black and the Indian, however, tensions increased over the years. Both groups had been defined as animals with which the white had to have some relation and around whom some attitude must be formed. Blacks were ex-draft animals who somehow were required to become non-black. Indeed, respectability was possible for a black only by emphasizing characteristics and features that were non-black. Indians were the ex-wild animals who had provided the constant danger for the civilizing tendencies of the invading white. They always presented a foreign aspect to whites unfamiliar with the western hemisphere.

The white man adopted two basic approaches in handling blacks and Indians. He systematically excluded blacks from all programs, policies, social events, and economic schemes. He could not allow blacks to rise from their position because it would mean that the evolutionary scheme had superseded the Christian scheme and that man had perhaps truly descended from the ape.

With the Indian the process was simply reversed. The white man had been forced to deal with the Indian in treaties and agreements. It was difficult, therefore, to completely overlook the historical antecedents such as Thanksgiving, the plight of the early Pilgrims, and the desperate straits from which various Indian tribes had often rescued the whites. Indians were therefore subjected to the most intense pressure to become white. Laws passed by Congress had but one goal—the Anglo-Saxonization of the Indian. The antelope had to become a white man.

Between these two basic attitudes, the apelike draft animal and the wild free-running antelope, the white man was impaled on the horns of a dilemma he had created within himself.

It is well to keep these distinctions clearly in mind when talking about Indians and blacks. When the liberals equate the two they are overlooking obvious historical facts. Never did the white man systematically exclude Indians from his schools and meeting places. Nor did the white man ever kidnap black children from their homes and take them off to a government boarding school to be educated as whites. The white man signed no treaties with the black. Nor did he pass any amendments to the Constitution to guarantee the treaties of the Indian.

The basic problem which has existed between the various racial groups has not been one of race but of culture and legal status. The white man systematically destroyed Indian culture where it existed, but separated blacks from his midst so that they were forced to attempt the creation of their own culture.

The white man forbade the black to enter his own social and economic system and at the same time force-fed the Indian what he was denying the black. Yet the white man demanded that the black conform to white standards and insisted that the Indian don feathers and beads periodically to perform for him.

The white man presented the *problem* of each group in contradictory ways so that neither black nor Indian could understand exactly where the problem existed or how to solve it. The Indian was always told that his problem was one of conflicting cultures. Yet, when solutions were offered by the white man, they turned out to be a reordering of the legal relationship between red and white. There was never a time when the white man said he was trying to help the Indian get into the mainstream of American life that he did not also demand that the Indian give up land, water, minerals, timber, and other resources which would enrich the white men.

The black also suffered from the same basic lie. Time after time legislation was introduced which purported to give the black equal rights with the white but which ultimately restricted his life and opportunities, even his acceptance by white people. The initial Civil Rights Act following the thirteenth, fourteenth, and fifteenth amendments was assumed to give the blacks equal rights with "white citizens." In fact, it was so twisted that it took nearly a century to bring about additional legislation to confirm black rights.

In June of 1968 the Supreme Court finally interpreted an ancient statute in favor of blacks in the matter of purchasing a house. Had the right existed for nearly a century without anyone knowing it? Of course not, the white had simply been unwilling to give in to the black. Can one blame the black athletes at the recent Olympic Games for their rebellion against the role cast for them by white society? Should they be considered as specially trained athletic animals suitable only for hauling away tons of gold medals for the United States every four years while equality remains as distant as it ever was?

It is time for both black and red to understand the ways of the white man. The white is after Indian lands and resources. He always has been and always will be. For Indians to continue to think of their basic conflict with the white man as cultural is the height of folly. The problem is and always has been the adjustment of the legal relationship between the Indian tribes and the federal government, between the true owners of the land and the usurpers.

The black must understand that whites are determined to keep him out of their society. No matter how many Civil Rights laws are passed or how many are on the drawing board, the basic thrust is to keep the black out of society and harmless. The problem, therefore, is not one of legal status, it is one of culture and social and economic mobility. It is foolish for a black to depend upon a law to make acceptance of him by the white possible. Nor should he react to the rejection. His problem is social, and economic, and cultural, not one of adjusting the legal relationship between the two groups.

When the black seeks to change his role by adjusting the laws of the nation, he merely raises the hope that progress is being made. But for the majority of blacks progress is not being made. Simply because a middle-class black can eat at the Holiday Inn is not a gain. People who can afford the best generally get it. A socioeconomic, rather than legal adjustment must consequently be the goal.

But the understanding of the racial question does not ultimately involve understanding by either blacks or Indians.

It involves the white man himself. He must examine his past. He must face the problems he has created within himself and within others. The white man must no longer project his fears and insecurities onto other groups, races, and countries. Before the white man can relate to others he must forego the pleasure of defining them. The white man must learn to stop viewing history as a plot against himself.

It was more than religious intolerance that drove the early colonists across the ocean. More than a thousand years before Columbus, the barbaric tribes destroyed the Roman Empire. With utter lack of grace, they ignorantly obliterated classical civilization. Christianity swept across the conquerors like the white man later swept across North America, destroying native religions and leaving paralyzed groups of disoriented individuals in its wake. Then the combination of Christian theology, superstition, and forms of the old Roman civil government began to control the tamed barbaric tribes. Gone were the religious rites of the white tribesmen. Only the Gothic arches in the great cathedrals, symbolizing the oaks under which their ancestors worshiped, remained to remind them of the glories that had been.

Not only did the European tribes lose their religion, they were subjected to a new form of economics which totally destroyed them: feudalism. The freedom that had formerly been theirs became only the freedom to toil on the massive estates. Even their efforts to maintain their ancient ways fell to the requirements of the feudal state as power centered in a few royal houses.

Feudalism saw man as a function of land and not as something in himself. The European tribes, unable to withstand the chaos of medieval social and political forces, were eliminated as power consolidated in a few hands. Far easier than the Indian tribes of this continent, the Europeans gave up the ghost and accepted their fate without questioning it. And they remained in subjection for nearly a millennium.

The religious monolith which Christianity had deviously constructed over the Indo-European peasants eventually showed cracks in its foundations. The revolution in religious thought triggered by Martin Luther's challenge to Papal authority was merely an afterthought. It did no more than acknowledge that the gates had been opened a long time and that it was perfectly natural to walk through them into the new era.

In the sixteenth century Europe opened up the can of worms which had been carefully laid to rest a millennium earlier. The Reformation again brought up the question of the place of Western man in God's scheme of events. Because there was no way the individual could relate to the past, he was told to relate to the other world, leaving this world free for nationalistic exploitation—the real forger of identity.

Because tribes and groups had been unable to survive, the common denominator, the individual, became the focal point of the revolt. Instead of socially oriented individuals, the Reformation produced self-centered individuals. Social and economic Darwinism, the survival of the fittest at any cost, replaced the insipid brotherhood of Christianity not because Christianity's basic thrust was invalid, but because it had been corrupted for so long that it was no longer recognizable.

The centuries following the Reformation were marked with incredible turmoil. But the turmoil was not so much over religious issues as it was over interpretation of religious doctrines. Correctness of belief was preferred over truth itself. Man charged back into the historical mists to devise systems of thought which would connect him with the greats of the past. Fear of the unfamiliar became standard operating procedure.

Today Europe is still feeling the effects of the submersion of its original tribes following the demise of the Roman Empire. Western man smashes that which he does not understand because he never had the opportunity to evolve his own culture. Instead ancient cultures were thrust upon him while he was yet unprepared for them.

There lingers still the unsolved question of the primacy of the Roman Empire as contrasted with the simpler more relaxed life of the Goths, Celts, Franks, and Vikings.

Where feudalism conceived man as a function of land, the early colonists reversed the situation in their efforts to create "new" versions of their motherlands. Early settlers made land a function of man, and with a plentitude of land, democracy appeared to be the inevitable desire of God. It was relatively simple, once they had made this juxtaposition, to define Indians, blacks, and other groups in relation to land.

The first organizing efforts of the new immigrants were directed toward the process of transplanting European social and political systems in the new areas they settled. Thus New England, New France, New Spain, New Sweden, New Haven, New London, New York, New Jersey, Troy, Ithaca, and other names expressed their desire to relive the life they had known on the other side of the Atlantic—but to relive it on their own terms. No one seriously wanted to return to the status of peasant, but people certainly entertained the idea of indigenous royalty. If your ancestor got off the boat, you were one step up the ladder of respectability. Many Indians, of course, believe it would have been better if Plymouth Rock had landed on the Pilgrims than the Pilgrims on Plymouth Rock.

The early colonists did not flee religious persecution so much as they wished to perpetuate religious persecution under circumstances more favorable to them. They wanted to be the persecutors. The rigorous theocracies which quickly originated in New England certainly belie the myth that the first settlers wanted only religious freedom. Nothing was more destructive of man than the early settlements on this continent.

It would have been far better for the development of this continent had the first settlers had no illusions as to their motives. We have seen nearly five centuries of white settlement on this continent, yet the problems brought over from Europe remain unsolved and grow in basic intensity daily. And violence as an answer to the problem of identity has only covered discussion of the problem. . . .

Shared Responsibility
for Racism

Larry May

Larry May is a professor of philosophy at Washington University in St. Louis. He is the author of The Morality of Groups *(1987),* Sharing Responsibility *(1992),* The Socially Responsive Self *(1996), and* Masculinity and Morality *(1997). May is also the co-editor of* Collective Responsibility *(1991),* Rethinking Masculinity *(1992),* Mind and Morals *(1996), and* Hannah Arendt: Twenty Years Later *(1996).*

May investigates the conceptual legitimacy of asserting that one shares moral responsibility for harms that one did not directly cause, particularly harms related to attitudes held in common with those who cause harm. Attitudes, May states, are not merely cognitive states, but affect how a person will behave. Our attitudes often contribute to an atmosphere in which harms are more likely to occur. May argues that moral responsibility for racial harms is to be shared by all members of the community who hold racist attitudes, even those who did not directly perpetrate the harm. Those who hold racist attitudes are like those who risk harm by holding a loaded gun.

At large state universities like the one where I used to teach, there has been an increase in racism. Not only have racial epithets been scrawled on bathroom stalls, but cross burnings and other more violent acts of racism are again occurring. Over the last ten years there has been a steady rise in racist attitudes among white students, faculty, and administrators. Yet the response of members of these academic communities to racially motivated violence is often to say that they do not share in responsibility for those events since they have played no causal role in the incidents. On February 4, 1988, Steven

Beering, president of Purdue University, issued a public statement which read, in part: "The recent cross-burning incident at the Black Cultural Center was outrageous and deplorable. It brings shame to the responsible person, but we must not allow it to bring shame to our community."[1] This is a common response to incidents of racism in America. The individuals who directly perpetrated a harmful act are held to be responsible, to be worthy of shame, but the members of the community, many of whom share the attitudes of the perpetrators, are not held to share in the responsibility. I want to investigate the conceptual legitimacy of claiming that a person shares responsibility for harms that he or she has not directly caused, especially harms that are correlated with certain kinds of attitudes . . . .

OMISSIONS AND RISKS

Negligent omissions concern things left undone that a person had a duty to do. Those who have such duties are responsible for their omissions in ways not true of other people who omitted the same actions but had no duty to do them. The salesperson who sold you your car and omitted to warn you about the danger of operating it in a certain way may well be responsible for the harm resulting from your operating it in that way, even though such harm was not intended by the salesperson and the salesperson's behavior did not directly produce the harm. On the other hand, if I as your neighbor omitted to warn you about the danger of operating your car in that particular way, my omission is not connected to your harm in the way that the car salesperson's is, since I do not stand in a special relationship with you.

Omissions can facilitate and even enhance the ability of others to do certain kinds of things. If I have been designated to supervise your conduct, it will take an omission on my part to allow you to act in ways that my supervisory veto could have negated. By omitting to block your proposed action, I facilitate your behavior, and my action is similar to my contribution to a type of joint venture. Consider a case in which I am supposed to supervise your operation of a forklift truck on a loading dock. If after giving the keys to you, I leave the premises, then any harm caused by your use of the forklift truck is a harm that I facilitated as supervisor. When it is true that I have supervisory duty to block certain of your actions, then my omitting to block your action is similar to my contribution to a joint venture. Hence, it is commonly recognized in law and morality that those who fail in their supervisory duties share in responsibility for harms resulting from such omissions.

When a person's negligent omission contributes to the production of a harmful effect, then it is reasonable to consider that person to be partly responsible for that harm. The reason is that negligent omissions create a situation in which there is much greater likelihood that harmful effects will be produced. Negligence generally creates risks because due care is not being exercised in the prevention of harm. Negligent omissions are a kind of risky behavior even when no harm is actually produced. In all such cases, it does not make much sense to assign full responsibility to each participant since the roles of the participants vary so greatly. Also, negligent omissions do not clearly contribute to a discrete part of the harmful result.

Let us turn now to three cases of risky behavior, in an attempt to assess the plausibility of the claim that risk takers should share in responsibility for certain harms even though their behaviors and attitudes do not directly cause these harms. First of all, consider the case of someone who does not remove the snow from his sidewalk, knowing that his omission risks harm to delivery people; in fact one such person slips and hurts himself. Even if there is no intent to bring about the harm, it is generally thought that the taking of a risk itself renders a person responsible for any harms reasonably expected to follow from the risky omission or commission. This is a key assumption for my analysis and one quite commonly recognized. Such a premise is recognized in tort and criminal law. Certain risk takers are considered liable for various harms because of their recklessness, even though the harm is an unintended consequence of their behavior.

Consider next the case of two people, each of whom does not remove the snow from his or her portion of a common sidewalk, although each knows that harm to delivery people and others is risked. The first person's omission actually results in an accident on his portion of the sidewalk; the second person's omission does not result in harm. If both displayed the same knowledgeability and lack of due care, then the first person is unlucky and the second is lucky. And in law only one, the first person, will have his omission viewed as legally actionable, since only on his portion of the sidewalk was there any harm to be remedied. But it seems that both are at fault for having knowingly engaged in a risky enterprise. From a moral perspective, as I will argue below, both people have engaged in risky omissions and the fact that one of them was unlucky does not seem relevant.[2] One party may be more guilty than the other, but neither should be fully relieved of responsibility for the harm.

As is well known, one of the problems with allowing luck to be considered morally relevant is that a person's moral responsibility then turns on a factor which is completely beyond the control of the person in question. I will later argue for expanding the range of things for which it is relevant to hold people morally responsible, in particular to our attitudes and beliefs. But in arguing for the view that the attitudes and beliefs we choose, not just our overt behaviors, are relevant to judgments of responsibility, I remain committed to the view that people should only be judged morally responsible for those things that are under their control; but control does not necessarily mean that one could have made the world a different

place. Here it remains true that whether one shoveled one's part of the sidewalk or not, the harm on the other part would still have occurred.

The importance of stressing control in moral responsibility is that it correctly puts the emphasis on what people have chosen (to do or to be). But if it should be true, in the cases we are here considering, that a person is relieved of responsibility merely due to good luck, even though her choices are faulty, then the notion of being a moral agent, which includes our choices of who we are and not just of what we do, ceases to have the high moral importance it is normally afforded. . . .

Consider finally the case of someone who owns a portion of a common sidewalk and who observes another person fail to remove the snow from his portion of the sidewalk. The first person then sees that a delivery person is harmed by this omission. Having made this observation, during the next snowstorm the observer nonetheless then decides not to remove the snow from her portion of the sidewalk. Again, due to good luck, the observer's action does not result in harm, even though the similar behavior of another neighbor does result in harm. Yet it seems that the observer is perhaps even more at fault than the person whose behavior resulted in harm. The observer has engaged in omissions in a way that she has already observed to produce harm. Such behavior is best described as morally reckless and probably also blameworthy.

Yet the reckless observer's behavior did not seem to contribute to the perpetration of a harmful result at all. Indeed, it might be claimed that since no harm was produced there is no causal responsibility for harm either. It thus seems odd to say that the reckless observer is morally at fault, since there is no harm of which this person is even partially causally responsible. However, the reckless observer did initiate a causal process that she recognized as likely to result in harm, even though the causal process did not actually result in harm. Following the model of criminal law we might think of this act as involving an attempted harm. In order to be at fault (or guilty) of an attempted harm a person must knowingly initiate a causal process which is likely to produce harm.

It is my contention that those who knowingly risk harm to others, even when their behavior does not directly cause any harm, share responsibility for the harm caused by those whose similar actions directly produce that harm. The reason for this is quite straightforward: the person who merely risks harm and the person who risks *and* actually causes harm have both acted in morally similar ways. When two people both have increased the likelihood of harm and both are equally knowledgeable that their actions increased the likelihood of harm, then their risky behavior creates a greater likelihood than previously existed that harm will occur, and they should share in the responsibility for the harms that result. In the remainder of this chapter I will expand on one particular sort of risk taking, namely, contributing to a climate of racist attitudes in a community.

RACIST ATTITUDES AND RISKS

Various attempts can lead to an increased likelihood of harm. For example, a parent's careless attitude regarding the safety of his children can easily lead to behavior likely to produce harm. Such a careless attitude could lead the parent to operate a car in an area where his children are play-

ing, thereby increasing the likelihood that the automobile will strike and harm one of the children. But the attitude of carelessness can also increase the risk of harm by others. The careless parent is likely to omit taking various precautions, such as removing rusty objects and matches from proximity to children's toys; he thereby increases the likelihood that children would harm themselves.

In discussing potentially harmful attitudes, I am not interested in what may be described as *mere* thoughts. Attitudes are not mere cognitive states, but they are also affective states in which a person is, under normal circumstances, moved to behave in various ways as a result of having a particular attitude. The test for whether someone actually has a particular attitude or not is a behavioral test, or at least a counterfactual behavioral analysis, based on the assumption that if a person really does have a certain attitude, then certain behavior normally results. In this section, I will discuss cases in which a person has an attitude likely to result in harm, in situations in which others with similar attitudes are causing harm.

Certain cultural attitudes, such as racism, can have an effect similar to that produced by the careless parent. Those who have racist attitudes, as opposed to those who do not, create a climate of attitudes in which harm is more likely to occur. We come now to the central applied concern of this chapter, namely, to show that the members of a community who share racist attitudes also share in responsibility for racially motivated harms produced by some of the members because of this climate of racist attitudes. Here is a more extreme case of sharing responsibility for effects one has not directly caused than those previously discussed. Indeed, in the case of cultural racism, it may happen that only a small number of the members of such a community directly perpetrate harm, yet most or all of the members share in responsibility for these harms.

The members of a group who hold racist attitudes, both those who have directly caused harm and those who could directly cause harm but haven't done so yet, share in responsibility for racially motivated harms in their communities by sharing in the attitude that risks harm to others. Consider again the case of racial violence on college campuses. When administrators and faculty condone racist attitudes, sometimes adopting those attitudes themselves, a risk of racial violence is created. The individual racist attitudes considered as an aggregate constitute a climate of attitude and disposition that increases the likelihood of racially motivated harm. The climate of racist attitudes creates an atmosphere in which the members of a community become risk takers concerning racial violence.[3]

My thesis is that insofar as people share in the production of an attitudinal climate, they participate in something like a joint venture that increases the likelihood of harm. Those who hold racist attitudes, but who do not themselves cause harm directly, participate in the racial harms of their societies in two distinct ways: first, by causally contributing to the production of racial violence by others; and second, by becoming, like the reckless observer discussed above, people who choose to risk harm and yet do nothing to offset this risk. I will take up each of these points in turn.

First, those who hold racist attitudes may participate in racial violence by causally contributing to a climate that influences others to cause harm. There are several distinct ways in which having contributed to a climate of opinion may make a person

responsible for the harms perpetrated by others who are influenced by that climate. In some cases there may be a straightforward causal connection between those who contribute to a climate of opinion and those who perpetrate a harm. Think of Thomas Becket, archbishop of Canterbury, who was murdered by Henry II's knights after the king created a climate of opinion simply by asking aloud why he had no followers loyal enough to rid him of the false priest. Here one person's expressed attitudes created in others a hatred that causally contributed to a harm, just as if that person had contributed to a common undertaking. Henry II's attitudes, once publicly known, had a strong impact on the attitudes and behaviors of the members of his court. Even though Henry did not direct his knights to murder Thomas (and may not have intended that his behavior be interpreted as his knights did), few would dispute that Henry shared in the responsibility for the murder of Thomas. Such judgments rely on the causal connection between Henry's attitudes and behavior and the attitudes and behavior of those who murdered Thomas.

In other cases a person's contribution to a climate of opinion has a much less straightforward causal connection with the perpetration of a harm. Consider someone who is a member of a group of people who voice public disapproval of another group of people, knowing that their acts are likely to incite still others to violence against the disapproved group. Such a person may be responsible for the harms that occur even though, due to good luck, his own public disapproval was not the act of disapproval that *directly* provoked the violence. Rather, his contribution was a bit more remote; perhaps he provided the first straw, but not the proverbial last straw that broke the camel's back. Both of these cases concern attitudes that are publicly expressed and that at least indirectly contribute to the production of harm. I turn next to situations in which the resultant harm does not depend on the public expression of racist attitudes.

The second main group of cases concerns members of a group who continue to hold racist attitudes even after similar attitudes in others are known to have produced racially motivated violence. These members share in responsibility for the racially motivated harm even if their attitudes have not been publicly expressed and have not straightforwardly contributed to the harm. If having a certain attitude leads some people to cause harm, then each person who holds that attitude risks being a producer of harm. To do that which risks harm to another, especially if it is known that the harm is highly likely and not merely possible, implicates the risk taker in these harms. And while the share in the responsibility may be greater for one who holds the risky attitude and directly causes harm than it is for one who does not directly cause harm, nonetheless there is a sharing in the responsibility for harm by all those who share the potentially harm-producing attitudes.

In some of these cases, those who hold racist attitudes should share in responsibility for racially motivated violence because their racist attitudes may reinforce, or even contribute, to the legitimation of the racist attitudes of those who do produce racially motivated violence. On college campuses, the racist attitudes of faculty members or administrators often have a clear impact on students who actually engage in racially motivated violence. Here the racist attitudes of the faculty members and administrators might stand in a causal chain, but that chain is tenuous and not normally the

kind of causal contribution that makes someone responsible for a harm. What is important is *not* any direct causal connection but the fact that these attitudes indirectly contribute to a climate of opinion that makes racially motivated violence more likely. Because of this, I believe these faculty members and administrators share in responsibility for the racially motivated harms in their communities.

In other cases, those who hold racist attitudes do not do anything that could be said to stand in the causal chain leading to racially motivated violence. But insofar as these people do not try to decrease the chances of such violence by changing their own attitudes, given that similar attitudes in others have produced harm, they demonstrate a kind of moral recklessness, similar to that of the reckless observer, which implicates them in the racially motivated violence. In these cases, the person with racist attitudes is like someone who aims a gun at another person and pulls the trigger but, unbeknownst to him, there is no bullet in the chamber. The fact that the gun does not go off in his hands, but it does go off in the hands of the next person to pull the trigger, does not eliminate his share in the responsibility for the harm. Both people who act recklessly share responsibility not just for the risk but for the actual harm. While it is true that the one who actually caused the harm is the one who is generally taken to court, the matter is different if we are not primarily interested in choosing who is the most guilty person.

In American law there is a famous case involving a drug, DES which was taken by pregnant women to prevent miscarriages.[4] It turned out that DES caused cancer in a number of the daughters of the women who had taken it. Because of the length of time it took for the harm to manifest itself, it was not clear in a particular woman's case which of several manufacturers had produced the dose of the drug that had caused the cancer. The court decided to apportion damages among all the manufacturers based on the likelihood that each company had produced the dose of DES in question (as determined by each company's share of the market at the time the dose was sold). The manufacturers of DES had each contributed to what had turned out to be a hazardous environment for pregnant women and their daughters. When it is unclear who actually perpetrated a harm, it seems acceptable to apportion responsibility according to likelihood of having been a harm producer. This is especially true when all the members of a group act in identical or relevantly similar ways. I want to suggest that this strategy is equally valid in some cases even when we do have knowledge of which member actually produced the harm in question. To return to the example of pulling the trigger of a partially loaded gun, someone who takes such risks with the health and safety of others should not be relieved of responsibility due to good luck, nor should all of the responsibility fall on the person who has the bad luck to pull the trigger when a bullet has come into the chamber.

It might be objected that having racist attitudes is not like pulling the trigger of a gun that may or may not be loaded.[5] Such an objection might be based on the claim that there is a significant difference between those who act on their attitudes and those who do not, which is not captured in the analogy of two people who both clearly act on the basis of their motivations. I would respond by again emphasizing that there is a difference between those who have mere thoughts or beliefs and those who have attitudes. Attitudes involve dispositions to behave in various ways. And while it is possible to override these dispositions, the cases I am considering involve those who do nothing to prevent their attitudes from leading to behavior that could cause harm. The failure to do anything to prevent one's racist attitudes from leading to racially motivated violence is similar to the failure of the person who aims a loaded gun to do anything to make sure that the gun will not go off. I take it that most people who have racist attitudes have not done anything to make sure that their attitudes do not lead them to racially motivated violence. I would agree that a person who is aware of having racist attitudes and who chooses to suppress them or to allow them to be overridden by other motivations is not like the person who pulls the trigger of a gun that may or may not be loaded. The first person's precautions against violent behavior will normally mitigate his or her responsibility.

The racist who does not directly cause harm, but who chooses to maintain unsuppressed attitudes not significantly different from those of other racists whose attitudes he or she knows, or should know, directly cause harm, should share in responsibility for the racial harms perpetrated by those in society who share the racist attitudes. The racist who directly causes harm, and those racists I have described who do not, are both responsible for racially motivated harm. The racist who does not cause harm is responsible because he or she shares in the attitudes and dispositions that, but for good luck, would cause harm.

In *On Guilt and Innocence,* Herbert Morris tries to make sense of Karl Jasper's claim that all Germans shared guilt for the Holocaust. Morris describes a type of shared guilt concerning

the deeds and characteristics of others. We connect ourselves in some way with these others and when they act we see it not just reflected on them but on us . . . . We are not at fault, but we still see their conduct as reflecting on us, reflecting perhaps on deficiencies we share with them.[6]

Morris correctly identifies one of the sources of shared guilt: a feeling that another's deficiency has produced a harm and that I share this deficiency. Each person with the deficiency shares the risk of harm because each is negligent for risking the harm that the deficiency is known to have produced. The shared risk of being a harm producer is the element which links the members to the harm caused by other members.

All those who hold racist attitudes and have done nothing significant to make it less likely that they will directly cause racial violence, even though they could have, share in responsibility for that violence. This is similar to my claim about those who engage in negligent omissions. But this is not to say that all those who hold racist attitudes share to the same degree in the responsibility as all others who hold these attitudes and have also directly caused racially motivated harm as a result. Those who have not actually caused harm may often find that shame rather than blame or punishment is the proper category to describe what should follow from their sharing responsibility for various harms. Indeed it is often true that *feeling* guilty or responsible is what should properly be the response of those who have these attitudes, rather than being held guilty or responsible. It will also often make sense to employ categories of responsibility here that do not involve the kind of accusatory stance toward the person in question that is involved in talk of guilt or blame. This is why, I take it, Morris talks of a "deficiency" rather than a fault . . . . As

I have argued all those people who hold racist attitudes in communities where racially motivated violence occurs share in the responsibility for these harms. . . .

NOTES

1. President Beering's statement was issued as a memorandum to the entire Purdue faculty.
2. Bernard Williams has argued that luck does matter in the moral assessment of people's behavior and character. See his *Moral Luck,* especially pp. 20–39. Williams is mainly concerned about the kind of case in which luck leads to good consequences that the agent could not have known would occur. In such cases, Williams argues that our moral assessment will be affected by whether these good consequences result or not. But in the cases I am examining, people are not taking risks out of a hope that greatly beneficial consequences for self or others will occur. Rather, they are taking risks hoping, if hoping at all, merely that greatly harmful consequences to others will not occur. Whether or not Williams's position is plausible (I do not find it so), the difference in our cases should lead to different intuitive judgments. In my cases people are taking risks with the lives of others, and without the consent of these others. On this point, Judith Jarvis Thomson provides a basis for seeing the intuitive difference. See her essay "Imposing Risks," in her book *Rights, Restitution and Risk,* ed. William Parent (Cambridge: Harvard University Press, 1986).
3. Judith Jarvis Thomson provides an interesting analysis of the relationship between this case and other examples of risks in "Imposing Risks," especially pp. 181–83, ibid.
4. See Sindell v. Abbott Laboratories, 26 Cal. 3d 588, 163 Cal. Rptr. 132, 607 P. 2d 924 (1980). The *Chicago Tribune* reported that in DES cases the theory of "market-share liability had been adopted in one form or another by the supreme courts of four states–California, Washington, Wisconsin, and New York. But the Illinois Supreme Court rejected the idea in a 5–2 decision." See *Chicago Tribune,* July 4, 1990, sec. 1, p. 7.
5. This was one of many excellent objections raised by Patricia Greenspan, my commentator at the APA Eastern Division meetings, December 1988, where I read a shortened version of this chapter. The point has also been pushed with great vigor by Roger Gardner, to whom I am indebted for lengthy discussions of possible rejoinders.
6. Herbert Morris, *On Guilt and Innocence* (Berkeley and Los Angeles: University of California Press, 1976), p. 135.

QUESTIONS: RACIAL AND ETHNIC DISCRIMINATION

1. Boxill argues that color, like talent, can be the basis of justified discrimination. Reconstruct his argument, explaining how he justifies this type of discrimination. As part of his justification is that color is a form of merit, in that a Black doctor could better serve Black patients *who would otherwise not have that service*, does his argument imply that recipients of color-conscious policies owe their services to the needy of their race? If so, do white doctors have the same duties in Appalachia?

2. Provide Steele's argument against affirmative action being used to address the harms of racism (in the present) and the harms from racism's legacy. (Be sure to make clear the various definitions of affirmative action that he is relying on, and the harm that he argues will result from these forms of affirmative action.) What is Steele's solution? Do you think that racial development is likely without affirmative action?

3. Appiah argues that there are no morally relevant differences between the races. What implications, if any, does his view have for multicultural studies? What does his view imply for ethical principles that hold that people have a stronger ethical duty to those in their own race?

4. What are the primary distinctions Thomas draws between sexism and racism? Why does he argue that sexism will be more difficult to end than racism? Although males' self-concepts might be tied more to being sexists than racists, white males generally cannot avoid living and interacting with women while they can avoid this with Blacks. In light of this, could one make an argument that sexism could be more likely to end than racism? Why or why not?

5. Deloria illuminates many U.S. violations of American Indians' human rights. What are some of these violations? Deloria argues that American Indian issues are fundamentally issues involving sovereignty, while African-American issues are fundamentally socioeconomic. What is white America's responsibility regarding these issues?

6. May addresses the responsibility that those who hold racist attitudes have in racial harms, even if they did not participate directly in those harms. Provide May's argument concerning how racist attitudes risk harm. How does Lawrence Blum's (see essay in the beginning of this book) value of antiracism relate to May's argument about the responsibility of those who hold racist attitudes?

SUPPLEMENTARY READINGS: RACIAL AND ETHNIC DISCRIMINATION

BANTON, MICHAEL. "The International Defense of Racial Equality." *Ethnic and Racial Studies*, vol. 13(4). October 1990.

BOXILL, BERNARD. "Self-Respect and Protest." In *Philosophy Born of Struggle*, Harris, editor. Dubuque, IA: Kendall/Hunt, 1983.

CROW, STEPHEN M., and DINAH PAYNE. "Affirmative Action for a Face Only a Mother Could Love." *Journal of Business Ethics*, vol. 11 (11), 1992.

CORNELL, STEPHEN. "Land, Labour and Group Formation: Blacks and Indians in the United States." *Ethnic and Racial Studies*, vol. 13(3), July 1990.

HARRIS, LEONARD. "The Concept of Racism." In *Exploitation and Exclusion*, Zegeye, Harris, and Maxted, editors. London: Hans Zell, 1991.

KARENGA, MAULANA. "Society, Culture and the Problem of Self-Consciousness: A Kawaida Analysis." In *Philosophy Born of Struggle*, Harris, editor, Dubuque, IA: Kendall/Hunt, 1983.

LAWSON, BILL. "Nobody Knows Our Plight: Moral Discourse, Slavery and Social Progress." *Social Theory and Practice*, vol. 18(1), Spring 1992.

MAPHAI, VINCENT. "Prisoners' Dilemmas: Black Resistance—Government Response." *The Philosophical Forum* (Special Issue on Apartheid), Winter–Spring 1987.

MCGARY, HOWARD. "Race and Class Exploitation." In *Exploitation and Exclusion*, Zegeye, Harris, and Maxted, editors. London: Hans Zell, 1991.

MOSLEY, ALBERT G. *African Philosophy*. Upper Saddle River, NJ: Prentice Hall, 1995.

NAILS, DEBRA. "A Human Being Like Any Other: Like No Other." *The Philosophical Forum*, Winter–Spring 1987.

OUTLAW, LUCIUS. "Toward a Critical Theory of Race." In *Anatomy of Racism*, Goldberg, editor. Minneapolis: University of Minnesota Press, 1990.

SAID, EDWARD W. "Zionism from the Standpoint of Its Victims." In *Anatomy of Racism*, Goldberg, editor. Minneapolis: University of Minnesota Press, 1990.

WEST, CORNEL. *Race Matters*. Boston, MA: Beacon Press, 1993.

VII

THE AIDS EPIDEMIC

AIDS is the plague of the latter half of the twentieth century. AIDS is the acronym for "acquired immune deficiency syndrome." We think we know what causes AIDS, which is more than could be said of the great plagues of earlier centuries. It is believed to be caused by the human immunodeficiency virus (HIV). But as of now, we do not have an effective medicine to counteract HIV. And as with many such viruses, more people have the virus than have the AIDS disease. So testing for the virus does not necessarily tell us who has the disease AIDS. Yet, tragically, those who have AIDS do not survive the disease, for they will die of other ailments caused when their immune systems break down.

The AIDS virus is transmitted through blood or semen (or other bodily fluids). Most people contract AIDS from anal or vaginal intercourse, from intravenous injections or blood transfusions, or from their infected mothers at birth. In the recent past, the most discussed cases in the West were those that were caused by male homosexual contact. Many conservative commentators have sought to portray AIDS as just revenge on those who choose the "unacceptable" lifestyle of homosexuality. Presently, heterosexuals have the fastest growing infection rate. Many health-care workers worry that the disease will reach epidemic proportions if policies are not adopted to curtail its spread.

Curtailing AIDS would seemingly require the identification of those who carry the virus and the isolation of those people from the rest of the population. To identify all of those who have the virus would require massive testing. Furthermore, isolating those individuals would require quarantining in numbers unheard of in the history of modern medicine. Both of these practices are the subject of the bulk of the essays in this section. Ethical questions of confidentiality, coercion, and fairness are raised and considered. In addition, several essays attempt to discuss the controversy surrounding AIDS in Europe and Africa.

The question of unjustified coercion of those suspected of having, or known to have, AIDS raises the important philosophical question of paternalism. Paternalism is the practice of restricting the liberty of a person for that person's own good, yet doing so against the person's will. One of the most commonly cited cases of paternalism concerns legal requirements that motorcycle operators wear helmets. One way to justify this requirement is by reference to the good that will be done to the motorcyclist. Of course, there are many other ways of justifying the requirement, since it turns out that motorcyclists who do not wear helmets are involved in a larger number of, and more serious, accidents, than those who wear helmets. There is greater loss of other's lives and more damage to property in cases where people do not wear helmets than in cases where they do.

Another important philosophical issue concerns privacy and confidentiality. Any plan to curtail AIDS must either be voluntary or it must forcibly identify those who have the AIDS virus. Yet any forcible attempt to obtain information about those who carry the virus would involve either a breach of patient–physician confidentiality or a violation of the privacy rights of the AIDS virus carrier. Both of these strategies are difficult to justify, although the enormity and seriousness of the AIDS crisis surely cannot be easily dismissed.

Our first selection is from John Harris and Søren Holm. They urge us to place the AIDS epidemic in the context of other epidemics and plagues over the ages. The serious health risks of these epidemics in the past was made more difficult by the fact that people could not easily prevent getting the disease from others who were infected since the disease was airborne. Those who were infected could more justifiably be quarantined because if not quarantined they would spread the disease to others against the will of those others. But AIDS is morally different in that the disease is not airborne, and it can be avoided by choosing to restrict one's sexual practices. Contracting AIDS is a matter of choice in ways that were not true for previous epidemics and plagues.

Karen Clifford and Russel Iuculano provide a relatively simple economic argument. Since insurance companies will often be the ones who pay the huge medical bills run up by AIDS victims, surely they should be allowed to test for the virus before deciding whether and at what level to insure, just as is true for all other health conditions. To deny insurance companies the right to test for AIDS would be a violation of their property rights. Of course, such testing must conform to the same standards of fair testing that apply to all other medical screening. They conclude that there is no reason in principle to prohibit testing for the AIDS virus.

Many popular defenders of AIDS testing and quarantining begin with the assumption that homosexuality is unnatural and can be legitimately curtailed, especially if it is connected to the spread of AIDS. Christine Pierce characterizes such an argument as a natural law argument. In her essay she tries to show that such arguments run against the grain of pluralistic viewpoints on ethics that are employed in law and legislation. Pierce points out that in some forms the restrictions on homosexuals' lives countenanced by AIDS legislation amount to paternalism, since they try, supposedly out of a concern for their own good, to force people to change their sexual practices against their wills.

David Conway takes up the same issue by attempting to construct nonpaternalistic arguments in favor of quarantining or closing gay bathhouses. He first considers a justification that would simply urge that we punish those who engage in what are sometimes classified as immoral practices. But here he points out that quarantining AIDS victims would sweep much more broadly than just punishing homosexuals. Secondly, he attacks a rationale such as that proposed by Clifford and Iuculano by pointing out that society may wish to bear the increased costs that result from not violating the privacy rights of AIDS victims. Consent is also a part of his argument against seeing AIDS as a harm to individual members of society. After all, he argues, if individuals do not want to risk the harm of AIDS they need only refrain from having sexual contact. Conway admits that the issue is more complicated than this argument would indicate, but he nonetheless feels that it is not clear that society and its individual members are straightforwardly harmed by the AIDS epidemic.

Carol Tauer enters this debate to point out that in France there is such a high regard for patient confidentiality that France has not even engaged in much data collection, let alone restrictions, on AIDS victims. In Great Britain, paternalism still runs very deep, but there are signs that this is changing. And in the United States, Tauer argues, the individualistic emphasis that favored nearly absolute individual rights is also changing. In all three societies, the AIDS crisis has called into question long-standing traditions of medical ethics. There is a tension between the needs, or felt needs, of the community and the rights of AIDS patients, a tension that has resulted in inconsistent public policies in several countries.

Nicholas Christakis considers a culture with quite a different set of moral traditions from those of Western Europe and the United States. There has never been a strong tradition of individual rights in Africa, and hence questions of informed consent and patient confidentiality have not been given the priority they have received in Western countries. But this is quite troubling, says Christakis, because it opens the African continent up for possible exploitation by Western scientific interests that want drugs and vaccines tested. Christakis worries about what he calls "medical imperialism" in Africa, and argues that precautions need to be taken so that the rights of Africans are not violated in the rush to find and test an AIDS vaccine.

—Larry May

If Only AIDS
Were Different!

John Harris and Søren Holm

John Harris is senior lecturer in philosophy at the University of Manchester in England. Søren Holm is a professor of philosophy at Umea University in Sweden.

These authors set the current AIDS dispute in the context of other epidemics and plagues over the centuries. They explain that most of the other great tragedies of a similar sort were different from the AIDS epidemic because they involved an airborne disease that people could not easily prevent getting. Yet, with AIDS things are different since it is contracted largely by voluntary sexual practices that people could easily choose not to have.

When the plague claimed its first victim in the Derbyshire village of Eyam on 7 September 1665 the villagers were faced with a terrible dilemma, one that presents itself to all those with a communicable disease. The dilemma, simply stated but often agonizingly difficult to resolve, is how those who have the disease or are at acute risk are to understand and discharge their responsibility to limit its spread.

Eyam presents one celebrated and terrible solution. As the infection spread, the rector, William Mompesson, and his nonconformist colleague, Thomas Stanley, persuaded the villagers to impose on themselves a voluntary quarantine, remaining in the village and so reducing the chances of the plague's spreading throughout Derbyshire. In accepting this responsibility the villagers must have known that they would probably contract the plague

John Harris and Søren Holm, "If Only AIDS Were Different!" *Hastings Center Report* 23, no. 6 (1993): 6–12.

and so die. As the plague took hold, Mompesson arranged for supplies of food and other necessities to be left at the boundary stone of the village; the payment was disinfected by placing the coins in running water or vinegar. All in all, about 260 villagers were claimed by the plague, a heroic shouldering of civic and moral responsibility felt and acted upon in the absence of any social welfare provision or reciprocal care for the diseased. Nor was there compensation for those who took on the burdens and dangers of voluntary quarantine.

AIDS has not so far required (or even raised questions about) a comparably dramatic response. In most Western European countries and in North America the response to the AIDS epidemic has been characterized by a relatively liberal approach, thereby distinguishing it from the draconian measures often instituted in the past when an epidemic arose. We do not expel those infected with HIV from society, require them to wear special clothes, or demand that they ring a bell and shout "unclean" when they enter human habitations.[1] Nor for that matter have those infected with HIV imposed such restrictions on themselves. There have of course been departures from the liberal approach, but all in all, the Western European and North American countries have put a value on the individual liberty of citizens higher than that put on the interests of society in controlling the spread of the disease.

The liberal nature of the present response could be taken to indicate that our societies have progressed morally, leaving an old ethics of control, punishment, or self-denial behind and embracing a new morality of individual autonomy and freedom. There is undoubtedly some truth in this interpretation. We would, however, like to suggest that the difference in the response to the AIDS epidemic compared to previous epidemics is not only the result of a change in society's ethics.

Specifically we want to suggest that two crucial features in the natural history of HIV infection have allowed a more liberal response toward this epidemic than would be possible or even desirable toward other actual and possible epidemics with a deadly disease. These features are:

1. the low infection rate of the human immunodeficiency virus, which is a result of
2. the inability of the virus to be transmitted by normal social contact or even through ordinary contact with, for example, excreta from infected persons (see below).

If it is true that the liberal response to the AIDS epidemic is not primarily caused by a change in social ethics, but is predicated on features specific to the natural history of HIV infection, then this fact has major implications, not only for our understanding of how social ethics have evolved but perhaps more crucially for our use of the AIDS epidemic as a model for future policy.

If we consider possible alternative scenarios for the mode of transmission of lethal diseases we will be in a position to see a number of things more clearly. The first of these is what our response to future lethal epidemics of a different character might have to be. Equally important is how our response to AIDS will have to change if the virus mutates so that transmission of the disease takes a different form.

We would therefore like to consider the implications of three different scenarios in which the course of the HIV infection is held constant but the mode of infection is modeled after other existing infectious diseases. We have chosen to use existing infectious diseases as models because these existing diseases exemplify modes of transmission that are not only theoretically possible but actually occur in nature. Many strange modes of transmission are logically and probably physically possible, but by looking at models of real diseases we avoid basing our arguments on pure science fiction.

We know it is very likely that humans will encounter other "new" infectious diseases in the future, either because truly new diseases appear through genetic change in the causative organisms, or because changing modes of agriculture bring human populations into contact with animal populations in which pathogens that have never before been encountered by humans are endemic.[2] It is therefore of considerable practical interest to consider what policies should be chosen if a new epidemic is capable of spreading more quickly than the AIDS epidemic.

THE EPIDEMIOLOGY OF HIV

AIDS has an interesting epidemiology.[3] The human immunodeficiency virus, of which there are two distinct types (HIV I and HIV II), has a very low infection rate, and transmission normally requires contact between excreta or blood from an HIV-infected person and the bloodstream of an uninfected person. There are no insect or other animal vectors carrying this virus. This means that HIV transmission between persons only occurs through certain sexual practices, through direct blood-to-blood contact (transfusions, needle-stick injuries, or needle sharing), and through vertical transmission between mother and fetus. It is known that certain sexual practices such as receptive anal intercourse carry a higher risk of transmission than others, presumably because the lining of the lower intestinal tract is more easily injured during intercourse that the vaginal lining.

The course of HIV infection is considerably protracted. Apart from a transient acute illness with skin rashes and enlarged lymph nodes that occurs in 40 to 60 percent of infected persons, the infection is characterized by a period often lasting several years in which few symptoms appear (the asymptomatic carrier state), followed by the actual symptomatic autoimmune deficiency syndrome, whose duration is also measured in years. It is still believed that all HIV-infected persons will eventually develop AIDS and die, although recent reports of people who have remained in an asymptomatic carrier state for more than ten years cast some doubts on this. There is no cure, and the HIV-infected person is infectious throughout all phases of the infection.

THE PLAGUE MODEL

Plague is a disease that has followed human beings since ancient times. It is mentioned in the Bible and by the early Greek writers. Plague was the cause of the Black Death that exterminated many communities in Europe in the 1300s, and even today plague epidemics occur regularly in developing countries. It is caused by the bacterium *Yersinia pestis*, which affects a range of rodents, including the common brown and black rats. Normally it occurs as an epizootic disease in the rats and is transmitted from the rat population to the human population by fleas that leave their dead hosts and attack humans. In humans the disease can take two forms. Bubonic plague, which is the most common form, is mainly a disease of the lymphatic system and gives rise to high fever and grossly swollen and painful lymph nodes. The other form, pulmonary plague, is our main interest here.

Pulmonary plague occurs when the plague bacterium affects the lymphatic system and the blood vessels in the lungs of the infected person. Here the bacterium gains access to the airways and becomes airborne, with an extremely high transmission rate. Although pulmonary plague is bacterial, its mode of infection is paralleled by several viral infections, including such common ones as measles and flu. Anybody present in the same house or apartment as a victim of one of these diseases will, at least in principle, be infected. Experimental work shows that the inhalation of one single plague bacterium belonging to one of the virulent strains is sufficient to cause a potentially lethal infection. Today, thanks to antibiotics, the mortality rate for pulmonary plague has dropped from virtually 100 percent to approximately 10 percent.

Plague is a relatively short-lasting disease in both its pulmonary and its bubonic form. Within a two-week period the patient will either have recovered or be dead, thus in either case becoming noninfectious. An isolation and quarantine regime is therefore possible, and has been a main feature of the control of plague epidemics since ancient times.

THE HEMORRHAGIC FEVER MODEL

Lassa, Ebola, Junin, Machupo, and Marburg fevers are caused by different vira belonging to the family *filoviridae*. These diseases occur in Africa and South America. They all seem to be enzootic in indigenous rodent populations and are acquired when humans come into contact with these populations, but once the disease has crossed the species boundary, human-to-human transmission does occur, with a high transmission rate through contact with excreta or blood from infected patients. The vira can cross intact mucous membranes, and direct blood-to-blood contact is not necessary. The infection rate of the African hemorrhagic fevers is therefore much higher than for HIV infection.

These diseases have all caused deaths among personnel caring for infected persons,[4] and transmission in the hospital environment can only be prevented through strict barrier procedures. The diseases have a mortality rate of 20 to 50 percent if untreated, but supportive treatment (and antiviral treatment in the case of Lassa fever) brings the mortality rate down to almost zero. In Marburg fever, clinical disease can be followed by a short asymptomatic carrier state.

THE LEPRA MODEL

Lepra has, like plague, been with us for many years and has traditionally been fought by expelling its victims from society. The disease is caused by a mycobacterium distantly related to the bacterium causing tuberculosis and has a very low transmission rate. The bacterium, which cannot be grown in culture, can only infect humans (and, under experimental conditions, nine-banded armadillos). Until the end of the nineteenth century, lepra was still common in Europe; indeed, the lepra bacterium was initially isolated from patients in Bergen, Norway.

Lepra has a wide range of clinical manifestations depending on the cellular immune response of the infected person. Some such persons are virtually noninfectious. Transmission occurs primarily through prolonged exposure to the bacteria, which are shed in large quantities from the nasal lining of victims with the lepromatous form of the disease. The disease is also transmitted through direct inoculation from lepromatous skin lesions. Children are much more susceptible than adults, and the main mode of transmission in populations where lepra is endemic seems to be vertical transmission from infected adults to children living in the same household. Not all persons exposed to the bacterium will become infected. The treatment for the disease, though effective, may last more than ten years. It is impossible to find an exact viral analogue to lepra, but children infected with cytomegalovirus (CMV) or measles in the womb often acquire a permanent infection and continue to shed large quantities of vira for many years.

LIBERTY, SAFETY, AND RECIPROCITY

What would have happened if the mode of transmission for AIDS had conformed to one of the three models mentioned above? It seems safe to assume that both the public policy adopted to cope with the disease and the conception of the individual diseased person's responsibility would have been radically different.

In the debate about AIDS, attention has been focused on questions about testing—including the issue of mandatory testing—on whether there are obligations to inform others about one's HIV status or obligations not knowingly or recklessly to infect others, and on whether enforced quarantine is an appropriate response toward infected persons who persistently engage in behavior that carries risk for others.

Further analysis of the three models of transmission presented above will show that the answers given to these questions in public debate are mainly based on the peculiar mode of transmission of the human immunodeficiency virus, and only to a very limited extent take account of the lethal nature of the disease. Because the risk of transmission, even during anal intercourse, can be minimized (but not abolished) through the use of a condom, it has been possible to choose or permit to develop a public policy where the full autonomy of the individual carrier is at least in principle protected and the protection of others is left, by and large, to their personal sense of responsibility and indeed to their self-regarding prudence.

A liberal public policy of this sort is of course constantly under strain. On the one hand there is pressure, sometimes immense, to encroach on the autonomy, rights, and civil liberties of the individual carrier for the real or imagined protection of society, or indeed of other, less grandiose interests. These will include the real or imagined interests of employers and fellow workers, insurance corporations, and others. On the other hand, the civil rights of the individual carrier are vigilantly protected.

One way of understanding and of trying to reconcile these conflicting pressures within a generally liberal framework has recently been suggested and forms the background to a European initiative in understanding the ethics of AIDS.[5] This approach is basically contractarian in character, but it may also be characterized more beneficently in terms of the recognition of a reciprocity of obligations.

The approach involves the idea that the mutual obligations holding between the person infected by HIV and society should be understood within a framework of reciprocity, and it is argued that:

> Those citizens for whom protection against infection with HIV has failed should be shown the same concern and respect as other citizens; they are entitled to the same consideration in access to employment, health care, and other areas of social provision, as any other citizen.[6]

The *quid pro quo* (in contractarian terms) or the reciprocal obligation on the part of those infected by HIV would involve the obligation to disclose their status to sexual partners and health care professionals where nondisclosure poses any risk to the life or health of these others.

If this were to become the generally accepted basis of relations between those with deadly communicable diseases and others within society, then, in the case of AIDS at least, it might reasonably be expected that the general acceptance of reciprocal obligations would lead to a diffusion of the tension between those who are infected and those who believe they are not. This latter group would be assured that any risks of infection to which they might become exposed would be fully voluntary, and those capable of infecting them would know that responsible disclosure would not result in stigma or discrimination or in the compromise of their civil rights. Of course, the process of achieving such a state of affairs would almost certainly be slow and painful, but as mutual confidence and respect grew and fear receded, one could reasonably expect to arrive at a humane and responsible solution to the problem of containing a deadly disease like AIDS.

But if it seems fruitful to explore this as a model for approaching the ethic of AIDS, to what extent does this intuition depend not on the state of our moral and political theory, or indeed on the moral sensibility of individuals and society, but on the rather more contingent or "brute" facts of the epidemiology of AIDS? One way to answer this question is to see what the implications of the reciprocity thesis would be if it were applied to our three present scenarios.

First, however, we should consider one alternative model for assessing our obligations to people who are infectious in the ways we have been considering. As we have indicated, the response to AIDS, whether by accident or design, has been surprisingly liberal, although this, as we have suggested, may be more a function of the mode of transmission of HIV than of any other single factor. However, the assessment of liberal responses to more contagious diseases must be made in the light of other possible alternatives. While there are many such, the most obvious counterpoise to choose is one that is essentially conservative—a model most likely to appeal in the panic that inevitably follows the identification of a lethal disease with a more threatening mode of transmission.

The conservative model we want to offer for consideration has attracted much philosophical attention, although little in the context of infectious or contagious diseases, or indeed of health care more generally. It is neither contractarian nor beneficent but sees the problem of coping with deadly, communicable disease in terms of threat and self-defense. In addition to the considerations we have just rehearsed, there may be merit in considering such a stark model of social relations against the background of a threatening epidemic because of the many salutary and instructive reminders it offers. Some of these concern the fragility of the cooperative presuppositions of society when faced with a deadly threat; others raise questions about the scope and range of the right to self-defense against the threat of disease or disability both for ourselves and for others.[7] Equally important perhaps are questions about the extent to which the proximity of the threat statistically, psychologically, physically, and geographically engages the right to personal initiatives in self-defense.

ANARCHY, STATE, AND UTOPIA

The title of this section is of course also the title of an influential book by Robert Nozick, in which the model we are about to consider appears. Nozick's book is notorious for containing large measures of anarchy, virtually no state, and a vision of society that few would call utopian. In an early part of the book he considers our obligations to people he characterizes as "innocent threats."

> I shall not pursue here the details of a principle that prohibits physical aggression, except to note that it does not prohibit the use of force in defense against another party who is a threat, even though he is innocent and deserves no retribution. An *innocent threat* is someone who innocently is a causal agent in a process such that he

would be an aggressor had he chosen to become such an agent.[8]

It is clear from the gloss Nozick offers on this passage that he means we are entitled to kill innocent threats where there is no other way of protecting ourselves from the danger they pose. Of course it is crucial in the case of AIDS to understand the scope of the proviso, implicit rather than explicit in Nozick, that there is no other way of protecting ourselves. A crucial moral issue will be the extent of the costs we should be prepared to pay before concluding that they are so high that we cannot afford them. For to conclude that we cannot or need not afford them is to conclude that we are entitled not only to protect ourselves against such costs but also against those who would (albeit innocently and perhaps unwillingly) impose them on us. Thus the idea that force is presumptively a legitimate response to innocent threats is an important background assumption in thinking about the threats posed by communicable disease.

It is also important to understand that the Nozickian model implies the potential for a Hobbesian war of everyman against everyman, because those who would defend themselves against innocent lethal threats also constitute innocent lethal threats to those they see as aggressors. That is, if one may defend oneself against innocent lethal threats by killing, if necessary, those who pose such threats, then both sides to this "defensive war" are aggressors, albeit innocent ones. We use the term "aggressors" because each person in this scenario is a threat to the other, and the threat that each poses is the other's only reason for retaliation and hence for posing a threat in turn. The person with a highly infectious disease poses a threat to others just by walking into transmission distance. The noninfected individual, seeing an infected person approaching and finding no other obvious method of defense, may, to borrow the outmoded language of nuclear deterrence, consider a preemptive strike.

The difference between the Nozickian position and that encapsulated in the reciprocal obligations thesis is perhaps one of emphasis on outlook. Nozick expresses the problem in terms of threats and aggression. The reciprocal obligations approach sees the resolution of the problem of conflicting interests in the recognition of mutual obligations within a shared and consensual morality. But when, if ever, is it appropriate to shift the emphasis? How great must the costs of these other ways of defending ourselves be before they become so unrealistic as to warrant the drastic measures of self-protection defended by Nozick? This is a question to which we must return in the context of the three models of transmission we have outlined.

THE PLAGUE MODEL

If HIV infection followed the plague model of infection we would have large numbers of infected persons walking around for years spreading the infection to everybody in their vicinity. Each infected person could infect thousands before he or she eventually developed symptoms and died, and all those infected would themselves be doomed. Such a state would therefore not only endanger individual persons, but would endanger the entire fabric of society. History tells us about the immense impact of the Black Death on European societies in the 1300s, but the impact of plague-model HIV disease would be much larger.

Stephen King, the well-known writer of horror stories, has captured some of this in his book *The Stand*, describing the aftermath of an epidemic of genetically engineered lethal flu, but even he has probably not been able to capture the full extent of the effects of such an epidemic.

Given the extremely high transmission rate of a plague-model epidemic there is no way infectious persons could participate in social life (unless they were equipped with self-contained space-suits). They would have to be quarantined, but in contrast to real plague, where the necessary duration of isolation is measured in days or weeks, the carriers of this new disease would have to be isolated for years, for the rest of their natural lives.

The only way persons infected with plague-type HIV could discharge their side of the obligations that flow from the reciprocity thesis would be to accept quarantine. It follows from the reciprocity thesis that such a large sacrifice of liberty on the part of the individual must lead to a wide-ranging obligation on society to reciprocate. How could such an obligation be discharged by society? The short answer is, of course, only with great difficulty. A society, an isolation colony if you like, would have to be set up with all the amenities of a small modern state. If infected persons could not sustain all the main services and necessities of such a society from within, then these would have to be provided from without. Medical assistance could of course also be provided from without by suitably space-suited personnel. To say that all this would be less than ideal and more than expensive is an understatement.

One solution on a global scale might be to establish a number of international isolation colonies. If this were to happen, some nation-state or indeed a number of nation-states would have to set aside the space, while the resources would have to be found by the international community. Alternatively, and perhaps more likely in the short term, each individual state would have to find a site, either by evacuating an existing city and its environs or by building a microsociety on a "greenfield" site. This sounds fanciful perhaps, but if the alternative is the Nozickian "war of defense" it may be a cost that every society ought, or ought to try, to pay.[9]

THE HEMORRHAGIC FEVER MODEL

If the hemorrhagic fever model came into reality, the carrier of the disease would not pose any threat in normal social contact, but his or her excreta would be highly infectious. Infectious persons could therefore in principle live a normal life among other people in society, if it could be ensured that nobody came into contact with their excreta. It follows from the reciprocity thesis that these persons would have an obligation to protect other people from infection, and that society would have an obligation to make it possible for the carrier to participate in normal social life.

The discharge of these reciprocal obligations would not be as hard as it would be in the plague model, but it would be very difficult because it would put stringent limits on the behavior of the person with the disease. Not only would the person have to practice safe sex, he or she would have to have a private bathroom that was disinfected regularly. The person could never use a public toilet, could never spit on the street, could never kiss any noninfected person, and could never participate in any activity where he or she could be injured and acquire a bleeding wound.

If carriers of the disease agreed to restrict their social activities in this way, society would have an obligation to provide the necessary facilities—private lavatories in the workplace, and so on—and would also have an obligation to compensate carriers for the restrictions imposed on their lives. Such compensation could take many forms, but it would have to include protection against unfair hiring, insurance, and housing policies.

Given the relatively high infectiousness of the hemorrhagic fevers, it is predictable that the fears of the noninfected part of the population would be even greater than has been the case in the present AIDS epidemic. Those with the disease could therefore only be expected to fulfill their side of the bargain if they were to be protected against the manifestations of this fear.

THE LEPRA MODEL

Finally, the lepra model raises unique problems of its own. It is natural to assume that we ourselves have special obligations toward our own children, obligations that go beyond reciprocity. In the same way, a society's obligation to protect the safety of its citizens must be interpreted to be more significant in those cases where the citizens are not able to protect themselves, and this is notably the case when we think of the problems posed by children and families. This means that both society and the individual parent would have a special obligation to ensure that children were not exposed to risk of infection. In the case of real lepra this is a minor problem because sufferers under treatment are not highly infectious, but in the case of an untreatable lethal viral disease with the same

mode of transmission the problem assumes a different magnitude. Not only would any children living in the same household as a carrier be at high risk, the risk would also be present for a long time (several years), and one can foresee very difficult psychological problems among older children who would be aware of the risk posed for their health by the parent they depended on and loved. On the other hand, a policy whereby children were removed from carrier parents also causes great psychological trauma to both parents and children.

LESSONS FOR THE FUTURE

It should be clear by now that the epidemiology and mode of infection of a given epidemic disease will be crucial in determining the ways in which societies attempt to cope with it. A society may be liberal or conservative, but the response to a plague-model epidemic with a lethal and untreatable disease will necessarily have to be different from the response to an epidemic with an epidemiology like AIDS or like lepra. Although liberal and conservative societies could still differ widely in their coping strategies, it would be within a totally different range of responses.

Further, it is important to realize that the peculiar features of the epidemiology not only determine the range and intensity of the available responses, they also determine part of the specific content of the responses. This is perhaps best illustrated by the lepra model outlined above. The plague and the hemorrhagic fever models differ mainly in the degree of infectiousness of the causal agent, but the lepra model shows some qualitative differences as well. The low rate of infection and the possibility of decreasing this rate even further by simple means (face masks, etc.), on the one hand, and the special sensitivity of children, on the other, mean that sufferers of this kind of disease would probably be able to participate in the daily life of society with very few restrictions, but not within their own homes. Society would have to intervene to protect the interests of the children. Thus, the epidemiology of the disease prompts a very specific social response, neither wholly liberal nor wholly conservative, which threatens the idea that persons have a special right to be protected from the interference of public officials and regulations in their own homes. In short, this particular epidemiology requires the reverse of normal liberal conventions about the role of state and individual. Society would have to intervene in the privacy of the home, but could leave wider social interaction unregulated.

In a similar way, reflection shows that the present reaction to the AIDS epidemic is strongly influenced by the specific features of AIDS epidemiology. The HIV carrier represents no risk to others in normal social and commercial life. However, within the health care sector, where bodily interventions and the attendant risk of blood-to-blood contact are parts of normal daily activity, things are somewhat different. The only real risk of transmission outside the health care setting occurs during sexual intercourse or among needle-sharing drug users, and even there the risk is very small if safe sex practices are used and needle-exchange programs are implemented. In this context reciprocity would demand disclosure of HIV infection to sexual partners, but it is evident that there is limited scope for regulation in general and no foothold for a policy along Nozickian lines. The HIV carrier poses no general threat, and, with effective public educa-

tion, individual citizens can be left to protect themselves.

What follows from these examples when we talk about the general ethics of communicable diseases? If we are right in our assumption that it is not so much any sort of moral progress but rather features peculiar to the natural history of HIV infection that have been responsible for the relatively humane social and political response to AIDS, then we need to think now about what our response should be to future and different epidemics. Or what our response to AIDS might have to be if the virus mutated to mirror one of the disease models we have been considering.

Where the communicable disease is lethal, there seem to be two possibilities. We could move immediately to a Nozickian approach and see things in terms of threats and aggressors and draw our battle lines accordingly. This is perhaps what many people would feel disposed to do. The alternative is of course that we could attempt to discharge our mutual obligations to one another, albeit at some considerable cost.

What we need and so far lack is a conception of the level of cost we ought to be prepared to meet before concluding that we are entitled to see those with communicable diseases as threats against which we must aggressively protect ourselves. This is not only a philosophical question concerning the level of hardship we should be prepared to undergo before resorting to measures that threaten the liberty and the very lives of the innocent, it is also a complex economic question. We will not be able to think adequately and realistically about the level of hardship we should be prepared to bear until we have a sense of the economic costs that will in part create that hardship. There are, however, immense difficulties in the way of our achieving an adequate picture of those costs. Because of the lack of the necessary economic data for the calculation, the analysis would require the incorporation of a great number of ad hoc assumptions and would therefore probably be more misleading than illuminating. And even if valid data could be found, the analysis would have to be specific for one society at one specific point in time.

From our perspective the philosophical problems inherent in the analysis of such a cost threshold are more interesting but just as complex as the economic problems briefly outlined above. What is really at issue here are a number of subproblems, such as, When can a moral society legitimately abandon, imprison, or exterminate innocent citizens? What would the effect be of a public policy of abandonment, confinement, or extermination? Which is the relevant sum to consider—total societal costs for all sufferers or individual lifetime costs for each individual infected person? If the survival of the society as a society were at stake, and if abandonment or extermination were the only possible ways to save it, then the threshold would (probably) have been passed, but even here some would argue that a society that could only survive at such cost would not deserve to survive at all. The question of whether this threshold has been passed at less global levels of hardship is much more complicated.

It is obvious that quite different answers would be given to this question depending on whether, for example, total societal costs or individual lifetime costs were seen as the relevant sum to consider. If total societal costs are what matters, society would be obliged to care for a few people with very expensive needs (a few people with plague-model disease), but not for a lot of people with less expensive needs (many people with hemorrhagic fever-model disease). If individual lifetime costs are what matter, the result would be exactly opposite. Although it is obvious that the two ways of looking at costs give opposite policy solutions, it is unfortunately not equally obvious which of the two points of view is more plausible or even more appealing.

At the lower levels of hardship we will also have to engage with the very old problem about when the life of some persons may be sacrificed for the well-being of other persons. We cannot here present a full solution to this problem, but given the current projections of the number of HIV-infected people in the future, it may be an issue that will soon have to be seriously addressed.

ACKNOWLEDGMENTS

This paper was written in pursuance of the commission of the European Communities Biomedical and Health Research Programme: "AIDS: Ethics, Justice and European Policy." The authors gratefully acknowledge the stimulus and support provided by the commission, the helpful suggestions of the editors of the *Hastings Center Report*, and also the invaluable advice of Dr. John Pickstone.

NOTES

1. Although some people with HIV disease might see this claim more skeptically, we believe that in essence the response has been liberal, particularly when compared with possible alternative scenarios to which we will come in a moment.
2. Stephen S. Morse, "AIDS and Beyond: Defining the Rules for Viral Traffic," in *AIDS: The Making of a Chronic Disease*, ed. Elizabeth Fee and Daniel Fox (Berkeley and Los Angeles: University of California Press, 1992), pp. 23–48.

3. Most medical information in this paper is taken from Ernest Jawetz, Joseph L. Melnick, and Edward A. Adelberg, *Review of Medical Microbiology*, 16th ed. (Los Altos, Calif.: Lange Medical Publishers, 1984); and Dion R. Bell, *Lecture Notes on Tropical Medicine*, 3rd ed. (Oxford: Blackwell Scientific Publications, 1990).

4. For an interesting literary treatment of the first occurrence of Marburg fever see "The Green Monkeys: Revenge in the Rhineland," in *Great Medical Disasters*, ed. Robert Gordon (London: Hutchinson, 1983).

5. Charles A. Erin and John Harris, "AIDS: Ethics, Justice and Social Policy," *The Journal of Applied Philosophy*, in press. It is this idea that forms the background to the Commission of the European Communities Biomedical and Health Research Programme project entitled "AIDS: Ethics, Justice and European Policy."

6. Erin and Harris, "AIDS."

7. This may also have implications for our entitlement to prevent or treat disability by various means, including genetic engineering and prenatal diagnosis. Such concerns are beyond our present remit, but see John Harris, *Wonderwoman and Superman: The Ethics of Human Biotechnology* (New York: Oxford University Press, 1992), chs. 4, 7, and 9; and his "Should We Attempt to Eradicate Disability?" in *Applied Ethics and Its Foundation*, ed. Edgar Morscher, Otto Neumaier, and Peter Simons (Dordrecht: Kluwer, 1993).

8. Robert Nozick, *Anarchy, State, and Utopia* (New York: Basic, 1974), p. 34. For a discussion of Nozick's views in the context of health care see John Harris, *The Value of Life* (London: Routledge, 1985), ch. 4.

9. It is interesting to note that Cuba is already employing quarantine for all citizens with HIV. Other countries such as Sweden have also employed enforced quarantine in the case of those infected with HIV (drug-addicted prostitutes, for example) who are deemed especially liable to engage in unsafe sexual practices.

AIDS and Insurance:
The Rationale
for AIDS-Related Testing

Karen A. Clifford and Russel P. Iuculano

Karen Clifford is assistant counsel, Health Insurance Association of America.
Russel Iuculano is senior counsel, American Council of Life Insurance.

These authors argue that AIDS testing is a quite legitimate and necessary strategy for the insurance industry to pursue in order to protect its economic interests. They begin by pointing out that America's economic health, not merely its medical well-being, is threatened by the AIDS epidemic. The health care system and the medical insurance industry may be put in jeopardy by the tremendously escalating costs involved in treating AIDS patients. AIDS testing will allow insurers to regain their predictive abilities and plan in a rational way. They argue that such testing is not unfair as long as it is conducted according to objective standards. Indeed, if insurers are prohibited from testing for the AIDS virus, this would itself constitute an unfair infringement of their economic rights.

Acquired Immune Deficiency Syndrome (AIDS) is potentially the most serious health threat the United States has ever faced. The disease, although unknown in this nation until 1981, may afflict as many as 270,000 Americans by 1991, causing an estimated 179,000 deaths.[1] Most of these deaths will occur among the 1 to 1.5 millions Americans already infected with the virus, many of whom do not yet show signs of illness.[2]

Although the immediate danger posed by AIDS to Americans has understandably attracted a great deal of attention, the epidemic also threatens the country's economic well-being and the solvency of its health care system. In the rush to ensure that persons with AIDS are treated fairly, some legislatures have enacted and others are considering laws which, by mandating the abandonment of time-honored and sensible underwriting principles, endanger the financial stability of many insurers.

The United States Public Health Service estimates that the annual direct cost of health care for the estimated 171,000 AIDS patients expected to be alive in 1991 will be between eight billion and sixteen billion dollars.[3] This figure assumes a per case cost of $46,000 to $92,000.[4] Some studies predict considerably higher costs.[5] A large portion of these health care costs will be borne by insurance companies. Yet, high as

Reprinted by permission of *The Harvard Law Review*, Karen Clifford, and Russel P. Iuculano, from *The Harvard Law Review*, 1987. [Edited]

they are, these figures underestimate the total impact of AIDS on the insurance industry because they do not include the cost of outpatient health care, including counseling and home health care costs. Moreover, these studies do not reflect claims incurred for loss of income due to disability, and they do not in any way measure the impact on the life insurance business. Insurers expect to pay billions of dollars for AIDS-related claims over the next several years as they fulfill contractual responsibilities to policyholders who are or become AIDS patients.[6] Estimates indicate that the insurance community has already paid a significant portion of the health care costs associated with AIDS, from thirteen to sixty-five percent in some hospitals.[7]

Insurance is founded on the principle that policy holders with the same expected risk of loss should be treated equally. Infection with the AIDS virus is now known to be a highly significant factor, one that cannot be ignored by any actuarially sound insurance system. Yet some lawmakers, understandably motivated by sympathy for persons with AIDS, are giving serious consideration to a prohibition on any use of AIDS-related testing for insurance purposes, a ban that would seriously distort the fair and equitable functioning of the insurance pricing system.

This commentary argues that insurers must be allowed to continue using AIDS-related testing to determine insurability. Part I begins with an explanation of some fundamental principles of insurance and examines how these principles might apply to individuals at risk for developing AIDS. Parts II and III then review both the legal and medical rationales behind testing by insurers and set forth recent actions by several jurisdictions that have prohibited AIDS-related testing for insur-

ance purposes. [We] conclude that such actions present potential dangers to both insurers and the insurance-buying public. Finally, [we] suggest an alternative means of financing the AIDS-related costs of individuals who are denied insurance.

I. BASICS OF INSURANCE UNDERWRITING

Even a cursory review of the fundamentals of insurance underwriting underscores the unprecedented challenges and implications the AIDS crisis holds for the life and health insurance industry. Underwriting is generally defined as the "process by which an insurer determines whether or not and on what basis it will accept an application for insurance."[8] The primary goal of underwriting is the accurate prediction of future mortality and morbidity cost.[9] An insurance company has the responsibility to treat all its policyholders fairly by establishing premiums at a level consistent with the risk represented by each individual policy holder. As one observer has noted, "[b]asic to the concept of providing insurance to persons of different ages, sexes, . . . occupations and health histories . . . [is] the right of the insurer to create classifications to recognize the many differences which exist among individuals."[10] Individual characteristics that have an impact on risk assessment, such as age, health history and general physical condition, gender,[11] occupation, and use of alcohol and tobacco, are analyzed separately and in combination to determine their effects on mortality.[12] "It is the understanding of the way these various [characteristics] influence mortality that enables companies to classify applicants into groups or classes with comparable mortality risks to be charged appropriate premium rates."[13]

At last count, some 158 million Americans under the age of sixty-five were covered by some form of group health insurance, and nine million more were covered solely by individual health insurance.[14] About ninety percent of the insured population is covered by group health insurance and forty-seven percent is covered by group life insurance.[15] Group insurance underwriting involves an evaluation of the risk of a *group*—for example, employees, members of a labor union, or members of an association—to determine the terms on which the insurance contract will be acceptable to the insurer.[16]

In contrast to underwriting for individual insurance, insurers underwriting group life insurance and health insurance consider only the relevant characteristics of the *group*, not of the individuals who comprise the group. Such an approach operates "on the premise that in any large group of individuals there will only be a few individuals who have medical conditions of [significant] severity and frequency which would, using individual underwriting standards, make them either a substandard or noninsurable risk."[17] Thus, the issue of testing for the presence of the AIDS virus, its antibodies, AIDS-related complex (ARC), or the active presence of AIDS relates only to new coverage for which evidence of insurability is required.[18]

II. FAIRNESS AND EQUITY REQUIRED BY INSURANCE LAW

The insurance industry has long been subject to statutory rules requiring the fair and equitable treatment of insured parties in the underwriting process. The Unfair Trade Practices Act (UTPA), developed by the National Association of Insurance Commissioners (NAIC), was, by 1960, enacted in some form in all states and the District of Columbia.[19] The central tenet of the UTPA is its distinction between fair and unfair discrimination. State insurance laws modeled on the NAIC Act both compel discrimination in certain situations and prohibit unfair discrimination in others.[20] For example, the Act deems it inequitable to charge identical premiums for life insurance to a sixty-year-old man in poor health and a twenty-year-old woman in good health.[21] In such a case, an insurer must differentiate between the two to determine an equitable premium: "[r]ates should be adequate but not excessive and should discriminate fairly between insureds . . . so that each insured will pay in accordance with the quality of his risk."[22]

Likewise, section 4(7)(a) of the UTPA prohibits any insurer from "making or permitting any *unfair* discrimination between individuals of the same class and equal expectation of life in the rates charged for any contract of life insurance." Section 4(7)(b) contains a similar provision for health insurance that proscribes "unfair discrimination between individuals of the same class and having essentially the same hazard."[23] We contend that persons who have been infected by the AIDS virus are not of the same class and risk as those who have not been infected.

The proper definition of "fairness" in the underwriting context has been the subject of litigation. In *Physicians Mutual Insurance Co. v. Denenberg*,[24] for example, the Pennsylvania Insurance Commissioner had revoked his approval of several of Physicians Mutual's health insurance policy forms.[25] Each of the policy forms in question provided for an initial premium of one dollar, regardless of the type of risk insured.[26] The Commissioner's action was based on his determination that the policy forms "effected unfair discrimination and . . . were not in accord with sound actuarial principles."[27] Agreeing with the Commissioner's ruling, a Pennsylvania state court found that "[t]he $1.00 premium in the first month in no way relate[d] actuarially to the risk involved and [was] discriminatory."[28] To underwrite within the spirit of state antidiscrimination laws, an insurer is bound to accord similar treatment in the underwriting process to those representing similar health risks.[29]

Last year, Washington became the first state to address the practical application of its Unfair Trade Practices Act to the underwriting of AIDS. The state's insurance department had promulgated a rule establishing minimum standards to be met by insurers in underwriting the AIDS risk. The regulation construed the state's UTPA "to *require* grouping of insureds into classes of like risk and exposure" and the "charg[ing of] a premium commensurate with the risk and exposure."[30] The department's rule stresses the Act's mandate that underwriting considerations for AIDS be consistent with underwriting considerations for other diseases. It notes, by way of example, that "policies issued on a standard basis should not be surcharged to support those issued to insureds suffering from an ailment."[31]

The Washington regulation illustrates that although, on its face, the UTPA seems to impose only a negative duty on insurers, closer examination reveals that under the Act insurers have a positive duty to separate insureds with identifiable, serious health risks from the pool of insureds without those risks. Failure to do so represents a forced subsidy from the healthy to the less healthy. To meet the fundamental fairness requirements of the UTPA and to address the concern for unfair discrimination, insurers must continue to use objective, accurate, and fair standards for appraising the risk of

AIDS. As will be shown below, the tests for infection by the AIDS virus indisputably identify an actuarially significant risk of developing AIDS. If the insuring process is to remain fair to other applicants and policyholders, insurers must be permitted to treat tests for infection by the AIDS virus in the same manner as they treat medical tests for other diseases.[32] To ignore risk levels associated with infection and treat a seropositive individual on the same terms as one not similarly infected would constitute unfair discrimination against noninfected insureds and, therefore, violate the state's Unfair Trade Practices Acts.[33]

III. AIDS ANTIBODY TESTS ARE VALID UNDERWRITING TOOLS

AIDS is caused by a virus that has been given various scientific designations but is chiefly known as HTLV-III. When the HTLV-III virus enters the bloodstream, it begins to attack certain white blood cells (T-lymphocytes) which are vital to the body's immune defenses. In response to infection with the virus, the white blood cells produce antibodies. A person generally develops antibodies two weeks to three months after infection.[34]

A protocol of tests, known as the ELISA-ELISA-Western blot (WB) series, is considered highly accurate for determining the presence of infection with the HTLV-III virus. A person with two positive ELISA tests and a positive WB is a true confirmed positive with 99.9% reliability.[35] The insurance industry and the medical profession commonly administer the ELISA-ELISA-WB series of tests.[36]

Several developments have established the reliability of the series of AIDS antibody tests used by insurers. The blood test series is consistent with the Centers for Disease

Control's (CDC) definition of HTLV-III infection, which provides that "[f]or public health purposes, patients with repeatedly reactive screening tests for HTLV-III/LAV antibody (e.g. [ELISA]) in whom antibody is also identified by the use of supplemental tests [including the Western blot test] should be considered both infected and infective."[37]

Further evidence of the reliability of these tests comes from the findings of the Wisconsin State Epidemiologist, who was recently directed by state law to determine whether any test or series of tests was "medically significant and sufficiently reliable" for detecting the presence of antibodies to HTLV-III.[38] The epidemiologist concluded, after a comprehensive review of the relevant medical literature, that two positive ELISA tests followed by a positive WB are "medically significant and sufficiently reliable" for detecting the presence of HTLV-III antibody.[39]

Nonetheless, when analyzing a test's validity for underwriting purposes, reliability, in and of itself, is not sufficient. A test must also be established as an effective and accurate predictor of future mortality and morbidity costs. In June 1986, the CDC estimated that 20% to 30% of those infected will develop the invariably fatal disease over the next five years.[40] In July of the same year, the National Institutes of Health predicted that, over the next six to eight years, as many as 35% of HTLV-III antibody positive persons may develop AIDS.[41] On October 23, 1986, the Institute of Medicine of the National Academy of Sciences issued a 374-page report, *Confronting AIDS*, which estimated that up to 50% of all those infected with the virus might develop full-scale AIDS within ten years.[42]

Quite apart from signaling the risk of developing AIDS itself, HTLV-III infection may herald the onset of other illnesses such as ARC or neurological disease. Studies

cited by the CDC found that 25% of those who were confirmed positive with the HTLV-III antibody developed ARC within two to five years.[43] An individual suffering from ARC may have a weakened immune system and manifest such symptoms as night sweats, weight loss, fatigue, fever, gastrointestinal symptoms, and enlargement of the lymph nodes, and may become disabled as a result.[44] Due to the chronic nature of these ailments, ARC may, in and of itself, give rise to substantial medical expenses.

Despite the wealth of medical data that lends support to AIDS-related testing for insurance purposes, utilization of such tests is sometimes questioned because there are a significant number of individuals who have tested positive but have not yet developed AIDS. This viewpoint, however, demonstrates a fundamental lack of familiarity with basic insurance principles. Underwriting is, by its very nature, concerned with probabilities, not certainties; no one knows how many infected people will eventually develop AIDS. Even assuming that "only" twenty percent will contract AIDS during the first five years, there is a demonstrable risk that a large percentage of infected individuals will develop AIDS in year six and beyond.

A twenty percent assumption implies that 200 of each 1000 applicants testing positive on the ELISA-ELISA-WB series will develop AIDS within five years and, therefore, die within approximately seven years.[45] In comparison, life insurance mortality tables estimate that, of a standard group of 1000 persons aged thirty-four, only about seven and one-half (as opposed to 200 in 1000) will die within the first seven years from any cause.[46]

The substantially greater risk represented by persons who test positive for HTLV-III infection is obvious. The comparison of 200 deaths to seven and one-half deaths indicates that a person infected with the AIDS virus is, over a seven-year period, twenty-six times more likely to die than is someone in "standard health."[47] The actuarial significance of these percentages is overwhelming and cannot be ignored. Because such tests are reliable, accurate, and effective predictors of risk, they must be considered appropriate as underwriting tools. . . .

CONCLUSION

To operate in a voluntary market, insurance underwriting must appraise the risk of an unknown and unanticipated occurrence and spread that risk over a large number of individuals. The risk must be assessed as accurately as possible because the whole price structure of insurance depends on the principle that individuals who present the same expected risk of loss pay the same premium. When an insurer is able to estimate accurately the risk to which it is exposed, it can, in turn, be more precise in pricing the cost of the insurance.

Contrary to this principle, several jurisdictions have imposed legal constraints which place AIDS outside the normal medical and regulatory rules pertaining to underwriting for other diseases. Although it is legally permissible for an insurer to obtain medical information about an applicant who may contract any other disease, such as heart disease or cancer, some states grant AIDS carriers special treatment by completely exempting them from relevant tests.

The tests for infection by the AIDS virus are extremely accurate in the same sense that any tests used in the insurance business can be accurate: they provide a basis for an objective determination of significantly higher risks and, hence, risk-based pricing. Legislation intended to force life and health insurers to ignore reliable, scientific evidence of a person's increased risk of contracting a fatal disease will result in significant inequities to policyholders. Given the potential magnitude of the AIDS epidemic and the substantial likelihood that gay rights advocates will seek additional legal constraints on AIDS-related testing by insurers, the financial consequences of AIDS to all involved—insurers, policyholders, and the public—will become even more severe.

Because the life and health insurance industry's livelihood is dependent on insuring persons against premature death and the costs of disability, it is as concerned as the public health community with curbing this tragic disease. Although the industry is fully cognizant of the concerns of those who have been infected with the AIDS virus, it must also consider its responsibility to those who have not been infected. If projections of AIDS cases materialize, public policy makers will be faced with an increasingly pressing need to achieve a balance between competing concerns. This balance need not, and indeed should not, be achieved at the expense of an industry that will inevitably bear a substantial amount of the costs associated with the AIDS crisis.

ACKNOWLEDGMENT

The authors would like to acknowledge, with gratitude, the able assistance of J. Bruce Ferguson, Editor, Law Publications, ACLI.

NOTES

1. See *U.S. Public Health Service, Public Health Service Plan for the Prevention and Control of*

AIDS and the Aids Virus 5 (Report of the Coolfont Planning Conference, June 4–6, 1986) [hereinafter *Public Health Service Plan*].

2. See *id.*
3. See Institute of Medicine, National Academy of Sciences, *Confronting AIDS, Directions for Public Health, Health Care, and Research* 21 (1986) [hereinafter *Confronting AIDS*]. This figure substantially underestimates actual expenses associated with AIDS because it does not include aggregate medical expenses associated with AIDS-related complex (ARC) patients or infected individuals. These expenses may outstrip all other costs associated with AIDS because of the large number of ARC or seropositive individuals and because of the length of treatment they undergo. One study estimated that the average hospital stay for AIDS patients to be between 13 and 25 days, at an average charge of from $740 to $950 per hospital day. See Scitovsky and Rice, "Estimates of the Direct and Indirect Costs of Acquired Immunodeficiency Syndrome in the United States, 1985, 1986, & 1991," 102 *Pub. Health Rep.* 10 (1987),
4. See *Public Health Service Plan, supra* note 1, at 15.
5. See, eg. Hardy, Rauch, Echenberg, Morgan & Curran, "The Economic Impact of the First 10,000 Cases of Acquired Immunodeficiency Syndrome in the United States," 255 *J. Am. Med. Ass'n,* 209, 210 (1986) (estimating hospitalization costs of approximately $147,000 per case for the first 10,000 AIDS cases).
6. If, in the year 1991, 54,000 people die of AIDS, as has been projected by the United States Public Health Service, see *Public Health Service Plan, supra* note 1, at 5, and if one-half of those people owned $50,000 of individual life insurance—a conservative estimate—the resulting claim liability of the insurance industry would be $2.7 billion.
7. See *Confronting AIDS, supra* note 3, at 165.
8. Health Insurance Association of America, *A Course In Group Life and Health Insurance* pt. A, at 379 (1985) [hereinafter, HIAA] 1985 ed.
9. "Mortality" is defined as "the death rate at each age as determined from prior experience." "Morbidity" is the "incidence and severity of sickness and accidents in a well-defined class or classes of persons." *Id.* at 366.
10. Bailey, Hutchison & Narber, "The Regulatory Challenge to Life Insurance Classification," 25 *Drake L. Rev.* 779, 780 (1976) (footnote omitted).
11. In *Manufacturers Hanover Trust Co. v, United States,* 775 F.2d 459 (2nd Cir. 1985), *cert. denied,* 106 S. Ct. 1490 (1986), the Second Circuit upheld the Internal Revenue Service's use of gender-based mortality tables to compute the value of reversionary trust interests. The court concluded that categorizing individuals by gender and calculating different costs and benefits on the basis of this group characteristic did not discriminate against individuals and did not involve any intent to discriminate against men and women. See *id.* at 465, 469.

12. See R. Mehr, E. Cammack & T. Rose, *Principles of Insurance* 657–59 (8th ed. 1985), C. Will, *Life Company Underwriting* 6, 8-19 (1974); Bailey, Hutchison & Narber, *supra* note 10, at 785.
13. C. Will, *supra* note 12, at 6.
14. See Letter from Thomas D. Musco, HAA Director of Statistics, to the *Harvard Law Review* (Mar. 31, 1987) (citing unpublished 1986 Health Insurance Association of America Survey) (on file at Harvard Law School Library).
15. See Public Relations Division, Health Insurance Association of America, *Source Book of Health Insurance Data,* 1986 Update 6; Letter from Suzanne K. Sternnock, ACLI Program Director, to the *Harvard Law Review* (Apr. 16, 1987) (citing a forthcoming 1984 Life Insurance Marketing and Research Association Survey) (on file at Harvard Law School Library).
16. Groups must have characteristics that permit the insurance company to predict, within reasonable limits, the probable claim costs under the contracts issued. The underwriting of a new group involves a general assimilation and evaluation of all the relevant factors to be considered. Common factors include, but are not limited to, the size of the group, type of industry, number of eligible lives, cost sharing involved, type of insurance plan, and previous coverage and experience. See *HIAA* 1985 ed., *supra* note 8, at 153.
17. *Id.* Although no screening takes place in most group situations, there are at least three instances in which a group plan may require evidence of insurability. These exceptions include (1) small groups, (2) late entrants to a group plan, and (3) large amounts of life insurance that are used to supplement basic coverage. It is common to use individual underwriting standards in these situations due to the increased danger of adverse selection—the tendency of persons with poorer than average health expectations to apply for insurance to a greater extent than persons with average or better health expectations. Underwriting standards are stricter for small groups, for example, because the size of the group is insufficient to spread the risk broadly enough to absorb the effect of adverse selection. The same rationale supports the use of evidence of insurability in the group area for "late entrants." These are employees who decline coverage when first eligible but later seek to be covered. Finally, every group life insurer has a "guaranteed issue" amount, the maximum face amount it will approve without requiring evidence of insurability. Individuals

seeking coverage above the guaranteed issue amount may be required to furnish a statement of health or to undergo a medical examination. See *id.*, at 204–7.

18. In the United States, individual health insurance accounts for 10% of the health insurance in force, see Health Insurance Association of America, *HIAA Annual Survey of Health Insurance Coverage* (1984) [hereinafter *HIAA Annual Survey*], and individual life insurance approximately 58% of the life insurance in force, *see* American Council of Life Insurance, *1986 Life Insurance Fact Book* 30.

19. See Bailey, Hutchison & Narber, *supra* note 10, at 782.

20. See *id. at* 782.

21. See *id.*

22. *Id.* quoting A. Mowbray, R. Blanchard & C. Williams, *Insurance* 411 (6th ed. 1969) (emphasis omitted); accord *Thompson* v. *IDS Life Ins. Co.,* 274 Or. 649, 654, 549 P.2d 510, 512, (1976) (en banc) ("[I]nsurance, to some extent, always involves discrimination, to a large degree based on statistical differences and actuarial tables. The legislature specifically intended . . . to only prohibit *unfair* discrimination in the sale of insurance policies." (emphasis in original) [footnote omitted]).

23. National Association of Insurance Commissioners, *An Act Relating to Unfair Methods of Competition and Unfair and Deceptive Acts and Practices in the Business of Insurance,* 1972 Proc. NAIC I 493, 495 (as amended).

24. 15 Pa. Commw. 509, 327 A.2d 415 (1974).

25. See *id.* at 511, 327 A.2d at 416.

26. See *id.*

27. *Id.* at 515, 327 A.2d at 418.

28. *Id.* at 516, 327 A.2d at 419.

29. *Cf.* S. Huebner & K. Black, *Life Insurance* 4 (10th ed. 1982) (stating that equitable principles require those with more serious health risks to be charged higher premiums).

30. *Wash. Admin. Code ?* 284-90-010(2) (effective Nov 14. 1986) (emphasis added).

31. *Id.*

32. In opposing AIDS-related testing by insurers, gay rights advocates have placed particular emphasis on laws prohibiting consideration of the sickle cell trait. Sickle cell *trait*, however—as opposed to the disease of sickle cell *anemia*—presents only a minimal increased risk of mortality or morbidity. As a study prepared by the National Academy of Sciences noted, "[s]ickle-cell trait (AS) has been considered—except in situations that involve exposure to significant hypoxia, dehydration, or acidosis—as a benign and relatively innocuous condition." National Research Council, National Academy of Sciences, *The S-Hemoglobinopathies: Their Status in the Armed Forces* 1–2 (1993) (footnote omitted).

33. A different interpretation of the Unfair Trade Practices Act was made in Massachusetts when the Commissioner of Insurance, on December 12, 1986, issued a "Policy Statement," which announced that the use of AIDS antibody tests by life and health insurers constituted an unfair trade practice under that state's version of the Act, see *Mass. Gen. L.* ch. 176D, §3(7) (1984), and that violators would be subject to an enforcement action. See Letter from Peter Hiam, Commissioner of Insurance to All Life/Health Insurance Companies (Dec. 12, 1986) (Policy Statement Re: Application Form Questions Inquiring About AIDS and ARC). The validity of the Policy Statement may be subject to legal challenge because the Massachusetts Legislature expressly declined to enact legislation in 1986 that would have prohibited life and health insurers from requiring AIDS antibody tests as a condition of insurability. See S. 489, Reg. Sess., §2(1986). Moreover, the Policy Statement was issued without any prior notice, opportunity for comment, or public hearing as required by the Massachusetts Administrative Procedures Act. See Mass. Gen. L. ch. 31 §4 (1984).

34. See U.S. Dept of Health and Human Services, *Surgeon General's Report on Acquired Immune Deficiency Syndrome* 10 (1986).

35. See J. Slaff & J. Brubaker, *The AIDS Epidemic* 201 (1985) (citing Dr. Robert Gallo, National Institutes of Health researcher and a co-discoverer of the HTLV-III virus).

36. See American Council of Life Insurance & The Health Insurance Association of America, *AIDS Survey of Member Companies* 2 (Aug. 19, 1986) (unpublished survey) [hereinafter AIDS Survey of Member Companies].

37. "CDC Classification System for HIV Infections," 35 *Morbidity & Mortality Weekly Rep.* 334, 335 (1986).

38. *Wis. Stat. Ann.* §631.90(3)(a) (West Supp. 1986).

39. J. Davis, *Serologic Tests for the Presence of Antibody to Human T-Lymphotropic Virus Type III: Information Pursuant to the Purposes of Wisconsin Statute §631.90 Regarding Their Use in Underwriting Individual Life, Accident and Health Insurance Policies* 22(Wis, Dep't of Health and Social Servs., 1986) [hereinafter Report of Wisconsin Epidemiologist].

40. See *Public Health Insurance Plan, supra* note 1, at 5. In 1985, the CDC cited studies in which 5% to 19% of those infected with the AIDS virus were found to develop AIDS over a period of two to five years, See "Provisional Public Health Service Inter-Agency Recommendations for Screening Donated Blood and Plasma for Antibody to the Virus Causing Acquired Immunodeficiency Syndrome," 34 *Morbidity & Morality Weekly Rep.* 5 (1985) [hereinafter *Recommendations for Screening*].

41. See National Institutes of Health, "The Impact of Routine HTLV-III Antibody Testing on Public Health," 6 *Consensus Development Conference Statement* 10 (1986).

42. See *Confronting AIDS, supra* note 3, at 7.

43. See *Recommendations for Screening, supra* note 40, at 5.

44. See *Report of Wisconsin Epidemiologist, supra* note 39, at 3.

45. See *Confronting AIDS, supra* note 3, at 7. ("Most patients die within *two* years of the appearance of clinical disease; few survive longer than 3 years.")

46. See Society of Actuaries, Transactions: 1982 *Reports of Mortality and Morbidity Experience* 55 (1985). That is the approximate mortality upon which the premium cost of an individual standard class life insurance policy for such a person is based.

47. See Affidavit of Warren L, Kleinsasser, M.D, at 6, American Council of Life Ins. v. District of Columbia, 645 F. Supp. 84 (D.D.C. 1986).

AIDS and
Bowers v. Hardwick

Christine Pierce

Christine Pierce is an associate professor of philosophy at North Carolina State University. She has co-edited People, Penguins and Plastic Trees *(1986) and* AIDS: Ethics and Public Policy *(1988).*

Pierce examines natural law arguments in the debate about AIDS. She argues that there is little basis for thinking that AIDS is naturally transmitted more readily in homosexual relations than in heterosexual relations. Pierce also carefully examines a recent Supreme Court opinion to show the widespread use of natural law arguments to suppress gay rights. She argues that such arguments are incompatible with deontological positions such as those supporting human rights, as well as with consequentialist positions that are espoused by many policy makers. She concludes that laws regulating homosexuality that are supported by natural law arguments are examples of unjustified paternalism.

During the AIDS crisis, natural law arguments have turned up again not only in relation to anti-sodomy arguments, but even as parts of important claims about AIDS prevention made by the medical and scientific community. Such arguments were invoked by the state of Georgia in the 1986 Supreme Court case, *Bowers v. Hardwick*,[1] which the Court held that the Constitution does not confer a fundamental right upon homosexuals to engage in sodomy. As we shall see, the Court accepted a version of legal moralism ignoring both the relevance of a right to privacy and two friend-of-the-Court briefs urging them to consider public health implications of prohibiting homosexual sodomy. I want to argue against legal moralism both in its

Reprinted by permission of *Journal of Social Philosophy*, Vol. 20, No. 3, Winter 1989.

standard form and in a more sophisticated version that permits natural law arguments a place in legal reasoning. Natural law arguments have aggravated the AIDS crisis by contributing not only to bad law but to bad science.

Natural law arguments which attempt to fix blame for AIDS on gay sex are variants of arguments from design. For example, Representative William Dannemeyer (R-California), a leading proponent of AIDS legislation, stated on the House floor that "God's plan for man was Adam and Eve, not Adam and Steve."[2] Ken Kesey, author of *One Flew Over the Cuckoo's Nest*, recently remarked: "It seems to me it's one's job to put sperm in a place that's designed for it. You don't put crankcase oil in your power steering system. And when God says, 'Do not put crankcase oil in your power steering system,' he's not saying, 'if you do, you'll go to hell,' he's saying, 'if you do, you'll blow the seals out of your power steering.'"[3] If blowing the seals out of one's power steering system is analogous to getting AIDS or any sexually transmitted disease, then the only well-designed sex between or among human beings is lesbian sex. As physician Barbara Herbert put it, "Only nuns have less incidence of sexually transmitted diseases (STD's) than lesbians . . . where you see an STD there's been a penis in the picture."[4]

I want now to examine some serious attempts on the part of the contemporary medical and scientific community to use natural law arguments in their effort to show that AIDS will not spread in any significant way into the heterosexual population. The first is the popular so-called efficiency thesis.

The efficiency thesis is important. Understandably, it has been incorporated into safe sex guidelines, for such guidelines need to be explicit as to who is at risk. Some scientists maintain that HIV is more *efficiently* transmitted through anal sex than vaginal sex with the implication that heterosexuals who practice only vaginal intercourse are at very low risk. However, the fact of heterosexual transmission is not in question. *The New England Journal of Medicine* reports an example of sexual transmission of HIV from a man to a woman to a man.[5] A 37-year-old married man engaged in homosexual activity while on business trips to New York. He and his 33-year-old wife had vaginal intercourse accompanied by heavy mouth kissing about twice a month. After her husband died from pneumocystis carinii pneumonia (PCP), she had a sexual relationship with a 26-year-old male neighbor. She too died from PCP. The neighbor, who developed AIDS related complex (ARC), reported no drug use and no sexual contact except the above mentioned relationship which included only vaginal intercourse and deep kissing. Comparatively few cases of vaginal transmission (particularly woman to man) exist today. The efficiency thesis attempts to explain this fact. It is thought that the lining of the anus is easily torn, thus facilitating the entry of infected semen into the bloodstream. "The rugged vagina," in the words of John Langone, unlike "the vulnerable rectum," is *designed* to withstand the trauma of intercourse. . . ."[6] Although it may be true that rectums and vaginas are respectively tender and tough, it has not been demonstrated that a traumatic event is necessary for the transmission of HIV. For example, artificial insemination[7] is not a traumatic procedure and yet women can get AIDS from undergoing this process if the sperm is contaminated. Moreover, if it turns out that HIV can cross mucous membranes, no trauma will be required to transmit AIDS.

Although scientific research already points to the possibility of direct infection of cells without trauma or tears, conventional assumptions about the proper sexuality continue to influence both the design of experiments and the interpretation of results. For instance, in late 1986, a team of federal scientists headed by Dr. Malcolm Martin found that HIV can directly infect cells from the colon and rectum in the test tube, suggesting that AIDS could spread in anal intercourse without any breakage in tissue. Dr. Martin's team tested 13 other types of cells representing a wide range of human tissues such as breast, lung, pancreas and ovary, none of which proved to be susceptible to the AIDS virus. Though he neglected even to test vaginal cells for any susceptibility to HIV, the new finding, according to *The New York Times* interpretation, "may help to explain the high incidence of AIDS among male homosexuals practicing anal intercourse."[8]

Scientist or science reporter, heterosexuals have a vested interest in believing that AIDS will be largely confined to the gay male population—that AIDS really is the "gay plague." Moreover, the efficiency thesis relies, as does the next argument under consideration, on beliefs about the proper place for depositing sperm that historically have been used to support the view that heterosexuality is good and homosexuality is bad.

Steve Witkin and a team of researchers from Cornell conducted experiments intended to show that the mere introduction of semen into the bloodstream during anal intercourse—not the trauma—adversely affects the immune systems of males. Witkin theorized that in order for the species to continue, "females have evolved immunological mechanisms to deal with exposure to sperm."[9] A woman, he thought, was not at risk for AIDS even if her partner ejaculated inside her rectum. Men, however, have not evolved such mechanisms, hence, the implication that gay anal sex from an evolutionary point of view is biologically unnatural. Witkin's thesis explains why rabbits described in the following experiments were male. The researchers engaged in what David Black, author of *The Plague Years*, calls "bunny bondage." In an effort to test the thesis that depositing semen from one male into the rectum of another might cause the receiver to produce antibodies to foreign semen and in turn suppress the immune system, researchers . . . "took rabbits and gave them rabbit semen rectally once a week. . . . Healthy males were restrained and 1 ml of fresh semen . . . was deposited . . . to a depth of 5 cm with a No. 7 French rubber catheter."[10]

Like so many religious explanations for disease, says Richard Goldstein, a reviewer of David Black's book, Witkin's theory "not only wrongly fixes blame but falsely reassures."[11] Views like Witkin's including the efficiency thesis suggest that "prevention may ultimately be a matter of harmonizing with natural order."[12]

In *Bowers*, the court was presented by the petitioner with natural law arguments which were admissible because the Court embraced legal moralism, rejecting, to the surprise of many, the rights approach it had been developing in sex-related cases over the past twenty years. A brief review of the facts surrounding the Bowers case follows:

Michael Hardwick was arrested for sodomy in his own bedroom.[13] Police arrived at Hardwick's door to see him about an unrelated charge—a ticket for public drunkenness which Hardwick claims he had long since paid. Hardwick, a gay bartender, received the ticket as he was leaving his place of work. According to Hardwick, he left at 6:00 a.m. because he had been working on a sound system. Although he did not pay the fine on the appointed date, he did settle the matter in person at a later time. Thus, Hardwick was not expecting to be visited by the police. A house guest answered the door and let the officer in. Not knowing that Hardwick had company, the guest said Hardwick was in his room. The officer went to Hardwick's bedroom, caught him in the act of consensual fellatio, and arrested him. Although the charges were later dropped, Hardwick sued Michael J. Bowers, the attorney general of Georgia, in hopes of achieving Supreme Court review of a law that had, he thought, "inadequate rationale." According to the Georgia statute:

> A person commits the offense of sodomy when he performs or submits to any sexual act involving the sex organs of one person and the mouth or anus of another.

It is important to note at the outset that the issue before the Court in *Bowers v. Hardwick* was whether to affirm a lower court ruling that Georgia, in order to keep its sodomy statute, would have to demonstrate that it promoted a compelling state interest. Michael Hardwick's winning the case would not have made Georgia's sodomy law unconstitutional; it simply would have required Georgia to show that its sodomy statute serves some legitimate state objective and is the most narrowly drawn means of achieving that end.

Bowers is an example of legal moralism par excellence. Legal moralism, as characterized by Joel Feinberg, is the view that "it can be morally legitimate to prohibit conduct on the ground that it is inherently immoral, even though it causes neither harm nor offense to the actor or to others."[14] A view often associated with Patrick Devlin, legal moralism is also put forward in a more sophisticated form by Ronald Dworkin in an article critical of Devlin. I want to argue against Dworkin's proposal that legal moralism might be acceptable as long as certain minimal rational requirements are met. Dworkin distinguishes between moral views that ought not to be legally enforced because they are based on prejudice, emotional reaction, false claims or arguments from authority (what Dworkin calls parroting) and genuine moral convictions that might be legally enforced. As Dworkin puts it, "Not every reason I might give will do."[15] Among the reasons that will do, however, as a legitimate basis for prohibiting X, is "X is unnatural." As we shall see, the reasoning in *Bowers* arguably meets neither the minimal standards outlined by Dworkin, nor even the lower requirements advocated by Devlin.

Patrick Devlin takes the view that, ultimately, morality is a matter of feeling,

in particular, feelings of disgust, indignation, and intolerance on the part of ordinary people. Moreover, he claims that moral views should be legally enforced if these feelings are sufficiently intense (reach "concert pitch," as H.L.A. Hart puts it). These feelings need not be based on any rational considerations. In essence, the majority of the Court said that there is no fundamental right to homosexual sodomy because people have strongly disapproved of it and have done so for a very long time.

For example, the majority says, "Sodomy was a criminal offense at common law and was forbidden by the laws of the original thirteen States. . . . In fact, until 1961, all 50 States outlawed sodomy, and today, 24 States and the District of Columbia continue to provide criminal penalties for sodomy performed in private and between consenting adults."[16] Chief Justice Burger says, "Decisions of individuals relating to homosexual conduct have been subject to state intervention throughout the history of Western civilization."[17]

The Court, in *Bowers*, does not take a critical view of history. It does not consider the possibility that popular prejudices can undermine individual rights in societies that are deeply rooted in sexism, heterosexism and racism. However, the Court has not always thought of history as buttressing moral claims. Twenty years ago, section 20-59 of the Virginia law stated:

> If any white person intermarry with a colored person, or any colored person intermarry with a white person, he shall be guilty of a felony and shall be punished by confinement in the penitentiary for not less than one nor more than five years.[18]

In *Loving v. Virginia*[19] a unanimous Court found Virginia's ban on interracial marriages a product of "invidious racism." In that case, the Court was unpersuaded either by tradition or by the trial court's argument from design that "Almighty God created the races white, black, yellow, malay, and red, and he placed them on separate continents. And but for their interference with his arrangement there would be no cause for such marriages. The fact that he separated the races shows that he did not intend for the races to mix."[20] The Court was also unpersuaded by the fact that anti-miscegenation statutes had been common in Virginia since colonial times and that Virginia was one of 16 states that prohibited interracial marriage. Nonetheless, when Michael Hardwick claimed that "the presumed belief of a majority of the electorate in Georgia that homosexual sodomy is immoral and unacceptable" is an "inadequate rationale to support the law," the Court said simply, "we do not agree."[21]

There is an important feature of Devlin's legal moralism that is relevant to the outcome of *Bowers*. Devlin notes that "the limits of tolerance shift." Although, on his view, we are justified in passing laws on no other basis than deeply held feelings of disapproval, when the limits of tolerance shift, we should change the laws. Polls in 1986 conducted by *Time* and *Newsweek* magazines show an absence of majority approval for the outlawing of any of a variety of specific sexual practices, including oral and anal sex, between consenting adults.[22] Thus, one might argue that the Supreme Court does not even realistically apply legal moralism of the sort articulated by Devlin.

It is also important to note, for example, that the trend of States to repeal laws against sodomy or interracial marriage has been interpreted as cutting both ways. Virginia, as we have seen, was one of the 16 States to prohibit interracial marriage in 1967. Fifteen years earlier 30 States prohibited interracial marriage. This data

was taken by the Court as showing that the limits of tolerance shift. A similar trend vis-a-vis sodomy laws was used by the Court to show that many people still oppose sodomy.[23]

Natural law arguments figure into the case since the petitioner, Bowers, appeals to the beliefs of Western philosophers who thought that homosexuality was unnatural. As Bowers argues, "No universal principle of morality teaches that homosexual sodomy is acceptable conduct. To the contrary, traditional Judeo-Christian values proscribe such conduct. Indeed, there is no validation for sodomy found in the teaching of the ancient Greek philosophers Plato or Aristotle. More recent thinkers, such as Immanuel Kant, have found homosexual sodomy no less unnatural."[24]

In the *Laws* (the work of Plato's cited by Bowers), Plato, himself a homosexual, characterizes homosexual sex as unnatural, whereas in earlier dialogues he portrayed the intensity and delights of homosexuality,[25] even suggesting that homoerotic experience is an important prerequisite for knowing the essence of Beauty.[26] In the *Laws*, Plato's last work, he maintained that heterosexuality—with its procreative end—was inherently orderly; he approved of the use of the law to enforce what he saw as natural, i.e., orderly sexuality. Some commentators on Plato have charged him with inconsistency. Others have said Plato got increasingly conservative in his old age. However, there is another possible interpretation here. Plato, in the *Laws*, was legislating for a public which, by and large, did not consist of philosophers. Not above considerable elitism and (some say) a bit of totalitarianism, Plato thought—as does Petitioner Bowers—that marriage, family and procreation were institutions designed to promote social control. Bowers says that

. . . homosexual sodomy is the anathema of the basic units of our society—marriage and the family. To decriminalize or artificially withdraw the public's expression of its disdain for this conduct does not uplift sodomy, but rather demotes these sacred institutions to merely other alternative lifestyles. One author has described that result as the promotion of indifference toward these foundations of social order, where historically there has been endorsement.[27]

Unlike the Attorney General of Georgia, Plato made an honorable pederastic exception for philosophers—an exception not needed (in the *Laws*) for members of the general public who lived their lives in the realm of opinion, not the realm of knowledge.

Although Bowers cites Kant as a philosopher who disapproved of sodomy,[28] other legal scholars such as David Richards have found support in Kant for the opposite point of view. Richards cites Kant as an author of the idea of human rights, as one "who best articulated its radical implications for the significance of respect for moral personality."[29] Extending the Kantian notion of autonomy to sexuality, Richards says: "Sexuality . . . is not a spiritually empty experience that the state may compulsorily legitimize only in the form of rigid, marital procreational sex, but one of the fundamental experiences through which, as an end in itself, people define the meaning of their lives."[30] Rights, typically, protect certain basic interests or desires of persons even if so doing makes the majority unhappy. Being able to love, according to Richards, is central to human lives. Moreover, "[f]reedom to love means that a mature individual must have the autonomy to decide how and whether to love another."[31]

Despite Kant's talk about rights as guarantees of proper respect for moral personality or rational autonomy, Kant did not see the implications of his theory for sexual autonomy. Of course, whenever one is developing a new theory, one may fail to see the whole range of its possible applications. Kant, for example, never asked whether non-human animals were capable of rational autonomy. In the *Lectures*, he referred to them as "man's instruments."[32] Kant also thought women quite lacking in rational ability and therefore did not see that they had any need for the rights of "man." Thus, in citing Kant, both Bowers and Richards are right. Kant was a very conventional man. He was also one of the originators of a theory of rights with radical implications for moral and social thought.

On a view like Devlin's, there is no theoretical limit to the legal enforcement of morality. Principles—such as Mill's principle of liberty or a right to privacy—are designed to function as just such limits. Blackmun, in his dissent, laments the "overall refusal" of the Court to "consider the broad principles that have informed our treatment of privacy in specific cases."[33]

The word "privacy" does not appear in the Constitution. Nonetheless, a series of Supreme Court decisions has established a right of privacy. It is said to exist in the penumbra of certain Amendments and, more philosophically, in the concept of liberty itself. (The word "liberty" is in the Constitution.)

A number of cases have established the constitutional status of a right of privacy.[34] *Griswold v. Connecticut*[35] held that a right of privacy protects the use of contraceptives by married persons. In this case, much was made of the fact that if contraceptives were illegal, police could enter the bedroom and search for them. *Eisenstadt v. Baird*[36] held that unmarried persons, under the equal protection clause, also have the right to use contraceptives. *Roe v. Wade*[37] held that the right of privacy encompasses a woman's decision to have an abortion. *Stanley v. Georgia*[38] upheld the right to private possession of obscene material. Although a First Amendment case, the Court stressed the importance of the privacy of one's own home. In the words of Justice Marshall, "[Stanley] is asserting the right to read or observe what he pleases—the right to satisfy his intellectual and emotional needs in the privacy of his own home."[39]

One way to explain a connection between the concepts of privacy and liberty is to borrow some thoughts from J.S. Mill. Mill advances roughly the following principle of liberty: People (competent adults, not children) should be allowed to voice their opinion and direct their lives as they see fit as long as no one else is wrongfully harmed. It follows from this principle that what one does to oneself, as long as no harm comes to another, is one's own business. A private action then is one that concerns oneself and does not wrongly harm others. Mill adds that if more than one party is involved, all parties must give their consent. Thus, what consenting adults do, as long as others are not wrongly harmed, is private, i.e., their own business and not the business of the law. On such a view, it would be natural to suppose that a right of privacy would include sexual intimacies between consenting adults in their bedroom. The recognition of a right to sexual autonomy—something very much like Mill's view—was believed by many, including David Richards and dissenting Justice Blackmun, to be the Court's view in its development of privacy law. Thus, many were surprised that the Court did not extend the right of privacy to the facts in *Bowers*.

With respect to prior cases in privacy, the Court said, "None of the rights announced in these cases bears any resemblance to the claimed constitutional right of homosexuals to engage in acts of sodomy. . . . No connection between family, marriage, or procreation on the one hand and homosexual activity on the other has been demonstrated."[40] The majority produced no principle for this distinction. Nan D. Hunter, an ACLU attorney, calls the Court's statement one of "unmasked contempt . . . as if gay people don't create families, belong in families, raise children, or have the staying power for those 9.4-year-long average marriages that are the bedrock of civilized society."[41] It is not insignificant that the majority here aligned itself with Bowers who in turn sided with Plato in thinking it a legitimate function of the law to bolster the conventional institutions of marriage, family, and procreation.

The complaint here is not simply that the Court did not extend the right of privacy to consensual sexual conduct between adults in their bedroom, but that the Court did not even recognize the right of privacy as the fundamental right at issue. Blackmun, in the opening sentence of his dissent, says: "This case is no more about 'a fundamental right to engage in homosexual sodomy,' as the Court purports to declare, than *Stanley v. Georgia*, . . . was about a fundamental right to watch obscene movies . . ."[42] To push the point, in Kansas, in 1986, the legislature passed a law banning sex toys in general and vibrators in particular.[43] If a challenge to this law should ever reach the Supreme Court, no one would expect the Court to find in the Constitution a fundamental right to own a vibrator.[44] Since the legislation was part of a pornography package, we might anticipate that the right of freedom of expression and/or the right of privacy would count as a fundamental right at issue.

Recognition of a fundamental right by the courts triggers heightened judicial scrutiny. Very good reasons (a "compelling interest," in the language of law) must be given by a State if a law is to survive this heightened scrutiny. In a case where no fundamental right is recognized, almost any reason, however weak, will do. As we have seen in *Bowers*, moral beliefs were used as reasons without meeting any rational requirements such as those suggested by Ronald Dworkin. For example, Dworkin would not count as genuine moral convictions those claims based only on arguments from authority such as appeals to the beliefs of Plato, Kant and the Judeo-Christian tradition. Interestingly, in citing Kant as an authority, Bowers also stated Kant's reason for opposing homosexuality by noting that Kant thought homosexuality unnatural. It is unclear, I think, whether one has committed the fallacy of argument from authority if in appealing to an authority one cites as well the authority's reason for opposing whatever is at issue.

Assuming the man on the bus does produce a reason that is not disqualified on Dworkin's grounds, that reason, Dworkin says, "will presuppose some general moral principle or theory even though [the man on the bus] may not be able to state that principle or theory . . ."[45] Presumably, it is unreasonable to make everyone who rides the bus take a course in moral philosophy, hence, Dworkin's standards of rationality are minimal, requiring only that one be able to produce a reason for one's view and use it consistently. "*X* has harmful consequences," "*X* violates my rights," "*X* is unnatural," even "The Bible forbids *X*" count as genuine reasons, and if used con-

sistently, constitute a genuine moral conviction. Joel Feinberg objects to Dworkin's version of legal moralism when he says, "Even if there is a *genuine* moral consensus in a community that certain sorts of 'harmless' activities are wrong, I see no reason why that consensus should be enforced by the criminal law . . . even a genuine 'discriminatory' popular morality might, for all that, be *mistaken. . . .*"[46] Undoubtedly, mistaken moralities and bad reasons will find their way into the criminal law on Dworkin's view. To illustrate the point, reasons of the sort "*X* is unnatural" are bad reasons and yet such reasons surely would pass Dworkin's test for they have a principled form and presuppose a general moral theory. In not requiring the ordinary person to recognize moral reasons in their principle form or to know anything about the moral theories to which the reasons are attached, Dworkin does not and cannot require a citizen to have a *good* reason for his moral point of view, for without a knowledge of ethical theory or metatheory, there is no basis for judging between competing kinds of reason.

It is easy to think that in adopting legal moralism one simply adds a principle of legal moralism to the harm principle, the offense principle, etc., in an effort to sanction increasingly invasive restrictions on personal liberty. In some instances, however, endorsing legal moralism is costly to society, i.e., personal liberty is not the only cost. E.g., a friend-of-the-court brief accompanying *Bowers* filed jointly by the American Psychological Association and the American Public Health Association argued, correctly, I believe, that "from a public health standpoint, the [Georgia] statute is simply counterproductive . . . the statute does not deter conduct that spreads AIDS, but it may deter conduct essential to combating it."[47] Briefly, the Associations of Psychology and Public Health argued that sodomy statutes adversely affect scientific investigation directed toward containing AIDS and finding a cure and interfere with health education efforts designed to encourage safer sexual practices. Specifically, the Associations supported their claims in the following way:

> A statutory scheme that creates a realistic fear of punishment if certain behavior is disclosed runs the risk of obscuring important data, as individuals simply refuse to volunteer for studies or provide needed information, and of creating false data, as individuals try to conform what they reveal to what they believe is legal. . . . With respect to at least two important issues— the existence of potentially high risk to recent immigrants from Haiti and the transmissibility of the AIDS virus from women to men—there is reason to believe that falsification of information, caused by fear of punishment, have distorted the epidemiological picture. Finding these and other crucial pieces of the AIDS puzzle should not have to depend on the ability of the epidemiologist to guess whether patients are not telling the truth because they fear being punished . . . community effort and support [for major educational efforts] are made more difficult in an environment in which a concomitant of participating in educational efforts is self-incrimination. Attending an educational presentation on "safe sex", for example, could be seen as an admission of engaging in sexual practices prohibited by the statute. Criminalization is likely to compromise the efficacy of informal educational networks by making people more cautious about what they reveal about themselves to acquaintances. It also presents state public health officials with the awkward choice of appearing to suppress information about safe sex techniques or appearing to condone felonious conduct.[48]

The Associations also point out that the Georgia statute does not further any mental health objectives and causes substantial psychological harm by fostering homophobia among heterosexuals and internalized homophobia among gay people. Roy Cohn, a queer-baiter in the McCarthy era who recently died of AIDS, is a classic case of the destructive behavior that results from internalized homophobia. It is worthy of note that Cohn's medical records showed him "reluctant to be celibate"[49] and his public statements showed him reluctant to tell the truth.

Rather than relinquish the idea that homosexual sex is wicked, some would even deny condoms to those who need them, preferring to see people die of AIDS. E.g., the Corrections Department in New York State made condoms available to married prisoners enrolled in a family visitation program, whereas condoms were not made available to prisoners not enrolled in the program even though officials realized some prisoners engaged in homosexual sex and could use the condoms to protect themselves against AIDS.[50] Of course, if natural sex is procreative sex, then the use of condoms by heterosexuals is equally unnatural. However, somewhere between Aquinas and Bowers, a new use of "natural" has emerged for convenience-oriented consumers. In defense of a company decision not to portray gay users of condoms in television commercials, Susan Smirnoff, spokesperson for Trojan, recently said "[Condoms] are effective against infection when used properly. A condom's proper use is for vaginal intercourse."[51]

The point I want to make here is that natural law arguments and consequentialist arguments are incompatible. Aquinas said that rape is not as bad as consensual sodomy or interrupting heterosexual intercourse, because (heterosexual) rape allows for the possibility of fulfilling the purpose of sexuality, namely, procreation. At the very least, it seems somewhat peculiar to prefer sexual acts which are by definition unloving, violent abuses of persons to acts which need not be, and may be quite the contrary. Consequences, however destructive of individuals or society, do not matter a whit in the face of what is claimed to be the natural order. To those who care nothing about real consequences, Richard Goldstein says, "Better you should wear a condom. But if a layer of latex is all it takes to still the winds of doom, what kind of moral mystery does AIDS pose?"[52]

Regardless of one's assessment of the foregoing arguments regarding the social costs of prohibiting homosexual sodomy, the fact remains that to advocate the prohibition of homosexual sodomy because it is believed to be wicked or unnatural is to dispense with any discussion of harmful consequences that may result from the prohibition. Had the Court ruled in Hardwick's favor, Georgia could have made its case—on the basis of public health or whatever—for its sodomy statute. But, Georgia did not have to give any good reasons for its law nor did the Court concern itself with arguments to the effect that the public health is ill-served by the prohibition of sodomy. The Court, as we have seen, dismissed these arguments in favor of traditional views that were poorly supported or wholly unsupported: Bowers said that Kant said that homosexuality is unnatural.

NOTES

1. *Bowers v. Hardwick*, 106 S.Ct. 2841 (1986).
2. Note: "The Constitutional Rights of AIDS Carriers," *Harvard Law Review* 99 (1986), p. 1274.
3. Richard Goldstein, "A Plague on All Our Houses," *The Village Voice*, Literary Supplement, September 1986, p. 17.
4. Barbara Herbert, M.D., quoted in "Lesbian/Gay Health Conference," *Off Our Backs*, May 1986, p. 3.
5. *The New England Journal of Medicine*, vol. 314, no. 15, 1986, p. 987.
6. John Langone, "AIDS," *Discover*, December 1985, pp. 40–41.
7. Some prefer the term "alternative insemination" for the obvious and good reason that "artificial" is in opposition to "natural."
8. *The New York Times*, December 14, 1986.
9. David Black, *The Plague Years: A Chronicle of AIDS, The Epidemic of Our Times* (New York: Simon and Schuster, 1986), p. 99.
10. Ibid., p. 97.
11. Goldstein, p. 17.
12. Ibid.
13. The facts surrounding Hardwick's arrest are found in an interview with him in *The Advocate*, September 2, 1986, pp. 38–41, 110. See also Donahue Transcript #07116 (Cincinnati: Multimedia Entertainment, Inc., 1986).
14. Joel Feinberg, *Offense to Others* (Oxford University Press, 1985), p. xiii.
15. Ronald Dworkin, "Lord Devlin and the Enforcement of Morals," *Morality and the Law*, edited by Richard Wasserstrom (Belmont, CA: Wadsworth Publishing Company, 1971), p. 63.
16. 106 S.Ct. 2841, 2844, 2845 (1986).
17. 106 S.Ct, 2841, 2847 (1986).
18. *Loving v. Virginia*, 388 U.S. 1 (1967).
19. 388 U.S. 1, 3 (1967).
20. Ibid.
21. 106 S.Ct 2841, 2846 (1986).
22 "Sex Busters," *Time*, July 21, 1986, p. 22. See also "Poll Shows Americans Disapprove of Ruling," *The Advocate*, August 5, 1986, p. 11.
23. In a footnote, Justice Stevens comments, "Interestingly, miscegenation was once treated as a crime similar to sodomy." 106 S.Ct. 2841, 2857 (1986).
24. Petitioner's Brief, p. 20.
25. See, for example, the *Symposium* and the *Phaedrus*.
26. Gregory Vlastos, foremost authority on Plato, gives this interpretation. See "The Individual as an Object of Love in Plato," *Platonic Studies* (Princeton: Princeton University Press, 1973). See, in particular, Appendix II *(Sex in Platonic Love)*, pp. 38–42.
27. Petitioner's Brief, pp, 37–38.
28. Immanuel Kant, *Lectures on Ethics*, trans. Louis Infield (Cambridge: Hackett Publishing Company, n.d., reprint of the 1979 ed. published by Methuen, London), p. 170.
29. David A.J. Richards, *Sex, Drugs, Death and the Law: An Essay on Human Rights and Overcrimiminalization* (Totowa, N.J.: Rowman and Littlefield, 1982), p. 31.
30. Ibid., p. 52.
31. Ibid., p. 55.
32. Kant, p. 240.
33. 106 S.Ct. 2841, 2852 (1986).

34. The following sketch of the constitutional status of privacy serves only the limited functions of explaining why Blackmun and others thought the Court in earlier cases was developing a right to sexual autonomy and providing some background for the ensuing critical discussion of Dworkin.
35. 381 U.S. 479 (1965).
36. 405 U.S. 438 (1972).
37. 410 U.S. 113 (1973).
38. 394 U.S. 557 (1969).
39. 394 U.S. 557, 565 (1969).
40. 106 S.Ct. 2841, 2844 (1986).
41. Nan D. Hunter, "Banned in the U.S.A.: What the Sodomy Ruling Will Mean," *The Village Voice,* July 22, 1986, pp. 15–16.
42. 106 S.Ct. 2841, 2848 (1986).
43. "Sex Busters," *Time,* p. 21.
44. Thanks to Beth Timson for this point.
45. Ronald Dworkin, p. 64.
46. Joel Feinberg, 'Harmless Immoralities' and Offensive Nuisances," *Rights, Justice, and the Bounds of Liberty* (Princeton: Princeton University Press, 1980), p. 83.
47. Brief of Amici Curiae, American Psychological Association and American Public Health Association in Support of Respondents, pp. 27, 22. A friend-of-the-court brief supporting the petitioners was filed by Professor David Robinson, Jr., George Washington Law School.
48. Ibid., pp. 24–27. The following footnote in the brief explains the Associations' claim that the transmissibility of the AIDS virus from women to men is an area where falsification of information may have occurred: "A study of military personnel done at Walter Reed Army Medical Center shows a much higher incidence of female-to-male transmission of HTLV-III/LAV virus than most other United States reports. The question of the incidence of female-to-male transmission is an important area of current inquiry. It is possible that the other reports show an artificially low incidence of such transmission. But another explanation for the disparity is that the military personnel in the Walter Reed study were reluctant to admit to homosexual activity or intravenous drug use, either of which could lead to discharge."
49. Dale Van Atta, "Faint Light, Dark Point; Roy Cohn, AIDS, and the question of privacy," *Harper's* (November 1986), pp. 56–57.
50. *The Citizen,* Auburn, NY, December 23, 1986.
51. *Gay Community News,* Feb. 1–7, 1987.
52. Goldstein, p. 17.

AIDS and
Legal Paternalism

David A. Conway

David A. Conway is an associate professor of philosophy at the University of Missouri in St.Louis. He is the author of A Farewell to Marx *(1987).*

Conway examines a number of arguments that would provide a nonpaternalistic basis to testing or quarantining AIDS carriers. Most of his essay is concerned with the question: Is it true that not quarantining AIDS carriers poses a serious threat to the society at large? Conway concludes that there are serious risks that are run by members of the population at large due to the nonquarantining of AIDS carriers. But while this provides a possible basis for nonpaternalistic arguments to quarantine AIDS carriers, there are many other factors that would make it unlikely that his argument would work given the specific facts of the current AIDS crisis.

The great majority of the known cases of Acquired Immune Deficiency Syndrome (AIDS) in the United States are believed to have been contracted through homosexual activities.[1] As a result there have been calls for, and in some instances passage of, laws whose purpose is to decrease the number of homosexual contacts and thus at least to slow the spread of this lethal ailment. These actual or suggested laws include those that would close bars and baths where meetings and sexual activities are likely to take place, and those that would provide for the quarantine of carriers of the AIDS virus.[2]

It is frequently maintained, however, that laws such as these provide for unwarranted paternalistic intrusion on the chosen actions of consenting adults. For instance, faced with the threat of being closed down by local government, proprietors of baths and bars have maintained that the men who choose to frequent their establishments and to engage in sexual activities there are well aware of the dangers of doing so. If these people are willing to risk their own health and even lives by frequenting the bars and baths, that is "their own business." It is not the business of the law to interfere with those free choices.

Philosopher Jonathan Lieberson argues in the same vein:

> The New York Post has called the civil rights of bathhouse patrons "irrelevant banter." But AIDS in bathhouses is contracted through consensual acts. . . . While the state government has in principle the right to intervene in private sex activity in order to protect people from an epidemic of highly contagious disease, it . . . has not been shown that AIDS is very contagious. . . .[3]

And widely syndicated columnist Charles Krauthammer says this about the notion that AIDS carriers should be quarantined:

David A. Conway, "AIDS and Legal Paternalism" in *Social Theory and Practice*, Vol. 13, No. 3, Fall 1987.

The fact is plain: AIDS is hard to transmit. It stubbornly sticks to certain high-risk groups engaged in sexual promiscuity and intravenous drug abuse. . . . [B]oth are voluntary. . . . Quarantine is justified when it is the only way to protect citizens from involuntary infection. If Jones can give you his tuberculosis by sneezing on you in a subway car, then society must protect you by locking him up. But if Jones needs your full cooperation in a rather complicated act to give you his AIDS, what possible reason can society have for locking up Jones in the name of protecting you?[4]

The principle that lies behind these positions would seem to be Mill's: "There is no room for [even considering a prohibition] when a person's conduct affects the interests of no persons besides himself, *or needs not affect them unless they like* . . . In all such cases, there should be perfect freedom, legal and social, to do the action and stand the consequences."[5] Mill's principle clearly entails that it is illegitimate to close baths and bars and to quarantine AIDS carriers to protect their potential patrons and lovers from contracting AIDS, since the patrons and lovers consent to take the risks of getting the disease. The opposing doctrine—the one that would have it that it is a proper function of the law to protect the individual from making unwise choices that may bring him harm—has come to be called "legal paternalism." In these terms, Mill's position is that of principled anti-paternalism, and arguments such as those given by Lieberson and Krauthammer against the legitimacy of closing the baths or quarantining carriers appear to rest on anti-paternalistic presuppositions.[6]

It has often been claimed that the sort of anti-paternalism defended by Mill is much too radical to be plausible, since, for instance, it would (so say Mill and others) make it illegitimate to interfere even with

the sale of dangerous drugs.[7] Nonetheless, Mill's position has considerable plausibility. If the only reason that can be given for preventing me from riding a motorcycle without wearing a helmet or from playing the commodities market or from handling poisonous snakes is that the action may bring me harm, then it is hardly far-fetched to think that you do not have adequate reason for interfering with my informed deliberate decision to perform that action. This indicates that paternalistic justifications for interference with individual liberty are, at best, inherently weak, and so nonpaternalistic justifications are almost always to be preferred.

The question that I now want to consider is whether the threat posed by AIDS actually does somehow provide the basis for a coherent non-paternalistic rationale for actions such as closing baths and bars and quarantining carriers of the virus. Here are some possible rationales.

1. The homosexual acts that spread AIDS are immoral in themselves. The aim of laws which would close meeting places or quarantine homosexual carriers is to prevent people from behaving immorally or to punish them for having done so.

This sort of rationale is not paternalistic in our sense, for the purpose here is not the prevention of harm to self but rather the enforcement of morality as such.[8] Many quite understandably find this function of law considerably less palatable than paternalism.[9] While it would justify the closings and quarantines, it also could justify a general repressive anti-gay campaign that would appeal to only the most diligent of moralists. More basic to present purposes, even though AIDS and homosexuality are understandably closely connected in the public mind (it would be naive to think that the recent AIDS panic would have been so severe were it not for fear and loathing of homosexuality), AIDS is one thing and homosexuality is another. Our question is whether the threat of AIDS, not homosexuality itself, can be the basis of a non-paternalistic justification for the closings and quarantines. And so this proposed justification is not really to the point.

2. Many AIDS victims will require protracted hospital or hospice care for which they cannot pay from their own resources. This means that they will be dependent on public funds for support. The aim of closing the baths and quarantining carriers is to protect society from the monetary burden of providing such support.

Reasoning of this sort is common enough in legal cases (for example, as justification for requiring motorcyclists to wear helmets), but it is not at all clear that it can actually provide a non-paternalistic rationale for actions that might slow the spread of AIDS (or, for that matter, for requiring the helmets). If someone is seriously in need of health care which he cannot afford, it may be that society should see to it that the care is provided. But the fact that society should do this does not mean that it does not have a genuine choice as to whether to do it. (Even if I really should give the change in my pocket to the blind street musician, I still have the choice of whether or not to do so. It would, in general, be ethically peculiar to hold that having an obligation to do A interferes with my freedom of choice whether to do A.) If society provides care for AIDS patients and incurs the attendant expenses of doing so, that is something that society consents to do. Thus, a person becoming sick with AIDS (or falling off a motorcycle while not wearing a helmet)

and then needing medical care beyond his ability to pay does not force a harmful financial burden on any unwilling party.

It may yet be possible to develop a non-paternalistic, "burden on society" rationale for closing baths and quarantining carriers.[10] In particular, even given that having an obligation to help someone leaves a person free to help or not to help, it still seems that there should be something more to be said for the view that if I have an obligation to take care of you when you get into trouble (fall off a motorcycle, contract AIDS), than I have some right to prevent you from getting into that trouble (to make you wear a helmet, to prevent you from visiting bathhouses). One form of that "something more" will be suggested below. For now let us just note that any financial "burden on society" rationale would not get to the heart of the matter. For the intuition that there are non-paternalistic grounds for closing the baths and quarantining carriers surely turns on the harm of suffering and dying of AIDS, whereas the relevant harm in the "burden on society" rationale is the quite different harm of monetary loss to those who do not have the disease. Thus, the most that might be said for the "burden on society" rationale is that it would make it possible to get the "right" result albeit for the "wrong" reason. There would be, perhaps, a certain value in this (better to send the gangland dope importer and murderer to jail for nonpayment of income taxes than not to send him at all), but it remains unsatisfying.[11] What we really want to know is whether there is anything behind the intuitive conviction that there are legitimate grounds for closings and quarantines *and* that those grounds are those given in (3).

3. The point of closing the baths or quarantining AIDS carriers is not to protect

society from the financial burden of caring for AIDS sufferers. Nor is it to protect those individuals who would deliberately take the risk of visiting a bath or of having sex with an acknowledged carrier. The point is to protect society at large from involuntarily being subjected to the threat of AIDS.

Despite the intuitive appeal that this has, we have to wonder just how society at large is threatened by AIDS.

(a) The greater the number of people there are who have a highly contagious disease the greater is the threat to those who might become its unwilling victims. Everyone knows, for instance, that the more people there are around with a cold the more likely I am to catch it by being sneezed on. Thus there is clearly a non-paternalistic rationale for laws that would prevent Smith from consenting to engage in an act that could well result in his contracting a highly contagious disease from Jones. The rationale is not paternalistic since the aim is not to protect Smith's welfare but rather to protect society at large from Smith becoming a carrier of a disease that will make him a danger to others.

As cogent as this reasoning is, it is predicated on the disease in question being highly contagious, and AIDS is certainly not that. It is not transmitted by shaking hands, sharing a drinking glass, or even by being sneezed on. AIDS is virtually always passed from one person to another by actions that require the active participation of the potential victim (in the case of homosexual transmission, by participation in what Krauthammer interestingly refers to as "a rather complicated act"). This means that just as the man who would visit the baths chooses to take the risks involved in doing so, anyone "further down the line" who contracts AIDS (such as someone who decides to enter into a homosexual rela-

tionship with the person who frequents the baths) also has consented to engage in the risky conduct that has this unfortunate result. Thus at each stage those who are harmed are harmed as a result of choosing actively to cooperate in the acts that result in this happening. And since no one is harmed without consenting to take the risks, any interference in the process, for instance by closing the baths, must be intended to protect individuals from their own deliberate choices. There is nothing in the process analogous to being sneezed on by a cold carrier. And so any justification that there may be here for closing the baths or for quarantining an AIDS carrier still appears to be a paternalistic one.[12]

(b) It would be far too soon to give up on (3). For while it is both correct and important to realize that AIDS is not spread by casual everyday contact, it is still a mistake to think that only those who consent to take a risk are in fact put at risk by the presence of the AIDS virus in some other individuals. Consider, for instance, a woman "Alice," who does not know that her lover is bisexual and that he visits the baths a dozen or more times each year. In choosing to engage in sexual activities with him she is not deliberately choosing to take the risk of contracting AIDS, for she is unaware that this is a real possibility. In this respect—she is in a very different position from the man who must know the AIDS risk of engaging in multiple sex acts in a gay bath. Perhaps the rationale for closing the baths is to protect members of "the public at large" like Alice from the unknown threat of contracting AIDS.

There are certainly non-paternalistic grounds for doing something on Alice's behalf. Even Mill's reputedly extreme antipaternalism explicitly allows for intervention when the agent is not aware of the risks involved in a choice. "If either a public officer or anyone else saw a person attempting to cross a bridge which had been ascertained to be unsafe, and there was no time to warn him of his danger, they might seize him and turn him back, without any real infringement on his liberty; for liberty consists in doing what one desires, and he does not desire to fall into the river."[13] Since the point of opposition to paternalism is that one should not be prevented from bringing harm or the risk of harm to oneself if one freely chooses to do so; since one is not freely choosing to bring on or to risk a harm one does not know about; and finally, since the interference with the action continues only until the agent is made aware of the risks involved, there is clearly nothing in Mill's position that any anti-paternalist should object to.[14]

Nor, however, is there anything in Mill's position that would justify closing the baths or quarantining AIDS carriers. At most it would be justified to restrict certain activities until requisite information could be disseminated. For instance, the baths could be closed until signs could be printed and posted regarding the danger of AIDS and the precautions necessary for "safe sex." (Such signs have in fact been posted in many establishments.) If Alice's friends knew specifically of her new lover's sexual habits, they could be sure that she had this information, and they might even do what they could to interrupt the relationship until they could bring this about. The role of society in regard to Alice would be that it should come to her aid by promulgating information about whatever dangers there might be in certain sorts of sexual activities.[15]

One may well think that if this is all that an anti-paternalist could allow to be done on Alice's behalf then there is something quite wrong with anti-paternalism.

For we should all feel a considerable sympathy for anyone in Alice's position, and yet the information that society would normally be able to supply is not in fact going to be a great deal of help to Alice. Essentially what she is going to learn is that there is such a disease as AIDS but that only a small percentage of men who have regular relationships with women carry the AIDS virus and that the virus appears to be difficult to transmit through conventional heterosexual activities.[16] Unfortunately, such information would lead Alice to underestimate the actual danger of contracting AIDS from this particular lover who, unknown to her, is a bisexual and a frequenter of the baths. Of course society could see to it that Alice received much more complete information. Detailed records about just who visits baths and who their friends are could be compiled and published on a regular basis. Laws could be enacted requiring that everyone provide any potential partner with the particulars of one's sexual history. But while these are things that could be done, it is unlikely that any of us would want to live in that sort of Draconian society.

So the case of Alice seems to lead the opponent of paternalism to some unhappy alternatives. In the name of anti-paternalism the baths will not be closed, and either Alice will face a much greater possibility of contracting a lethal disease than she realizes or society must intrude upon the private lives of its citizens in order to get the information needed to enlighten Alice about the real risks in her specific case.

The anti-paternalist may simply deny that the first of these alternatives is intolerable. We all have to make many decisions with less than ideal information. The fact that Alice must do so does not justify infringing on liberty by closing baths and bars or quarantining carriers. (Of the many

"Alice's" facing the decision of whether to have sex with a friend, the vast majority in fact will not be in danger of contracting AIDS.) But perhaps the anti-paternalist need not take this possibly "heroic" position, for there is still another way in which we might be able to make a non-paternalistic case for closings or quarantines.

(c) To contract AIDS is to suffer harm. If this is the only harm that persons might suffer as the result of the presence of the AIDS virus in the community, then it is difficult to imagine that any non-paternalistic justification for closing the baths or for quarantining carriers of the virus might be successful, given that the disease is contracted by consensual acts. But actually contracting AIDS is not the only way in which one can be harmed by the presence of the virus in the community. A "desert island" scenario should help to explain why this is so.

> Suppose there exists a certain Harvey, benevolent dictator of a small and entirely isolated society made up of a few thousand highly sensual persons. Some of these prefer their own sex, some the other, but they are all capable of intense enjoyment with anyone else. On the whole their sex lives are extremely satisfying, and they regard this as necessary not only for happiness but for their most basic psychological well-being. One day (as you might have guessed) trouble intrudes into this world in the form of a new and lethal disease. Christening it "The Lethal Ailment," the official doctor quickly determines that just a small handful of inhabitants actually have the disease, that it is transmitted only by sexual activity, and that it is rather hard to transmit at all but it is far more readily transmitted through certain activities preferred by a minority of the population.
>
> Harvey is not only benevolent; he is also wise enough to rely on a staff of skilled advisors when expertise is needed. This time he turns to Jeremy, his resident source of wisdom on matters legal and philosophical. As it happens, Jeremy is a devoted follower of Mill, and so he advises Harvey in this way: "Everybody on the island knows the disease is here and how one can get it. You could lock up the people who have it or close down the places where they are likely to do the things that transmit it, but the only reason for your doing things like this would be to protect the folks from their own choices. If old Smith there chooses to take the risk of contracting this disease it is his own business. You stay out of it."
>
> Harvey follows Jeremy's advice and stays out of it. Shortly thereafter he takes the opportunity for a balloon trip to the outside world. Returning twenty years later he finds a society considerably reduced in number and happiness. Many people have died of the disease, and a very large number of those who are still alive suffer from it. Jeremy, as sick as he is, is sanguine. "It is true that the results have not been too good, but we avoided paternalism. Mill would have been proud of us. No one contracted the disease who did not deliberately choose to take the risk of contracting it. No one who did not consent to do so was ever threatened with the harm of the disease. What we have here is the triumph of a principle of liberty."
>
> "What we have here is an idiot of an advisor."
>
> "But all I did was follow Mill's precepts. I just told you. No one was harmed who did not consent to be harmed."
>
> "What about me?"
>
> "You?"
>
> "I came back from the outside world to my homeland of loving sensuality only to find myself faced with nothing better than a choice between a killer disease and celibacy. No one is harmed who did not consent to be harmed, you say? What greater harm could there be than being faced with those two miserable alternatives? I am getting in my balloon and going back to the outside world."
>
> But Harvey's balloon had burst. He couldn't go anywhere. There are no records of what happened after that on Harvey's Island.

The inhabitants of Harvey's unfortunate island are threatened with a harm: contracting The Lethal Ailment. But they also come to face a related but different harm, having a choice between alternatives each of which is so undesirable that to have to choose between them is itself to be harmed. When the point is reached that everybody else carries the disease or any other person is quite likely to be a carrier, each individual faces the alternatives of celibacy or the likelihood of contracting a disease from which he will not recover. Having to choose between these alternatives is a very real harm, and it is not one to which the individual in any way consents to be subjected. In short, *anyone who gets The Lethal Ailment does so as a result of consenting to take the risk of getting it rather than choosing to be celibate. But no one consents to the harm of being faced with only these miserable alternatives*. Thus, insofar as the aim was to prevent this harm, Harvey did have, despite Jeremy's misguided advice, a non-paternalistic rationale for locking up carriers and closing places where people were likely to engage in the sexual activities by which the disease was most easily transmitted. Both the "burden on society" and "Alice" discussions above were left with the suggestion that there might be more to be said. The Harvey story enables us to see what this would be. Obviously that story suggests a way of reconceptualizing the "Alice" situation so that it really might provide a nonpaternalistic rationale for closing the baths. Given that Alice has all the information that could reasonably be made available to her, when she chooses to have sexual relations with her lover she is consenting in as enlightened a way as practically possible to take whatever AIDS risks there may be. She did not, however, consent to having to face just the alternatives of rejecting her lover or taking those risks, and the existence of the baths contributes to her having

to face these alternatives. If having to face them does indeed constitute a harm, then in the Alice case we really do have a non-paternalistic rationale for the closings.

Perhaps the "burden on society" rationale can be reformulated in a similar though not so obvious way. Understood on the model of the story of Harvey, there may well be a legitimate basis for the intuitive conviction that if I have an obligation to take care of you when you get into trouble, then I have some right to prevent you from getting into that trouble. It is not that your getting into trouble and my resulting obligation forces on me the harm of taking care of you. Obligation or no, I am quite free, after all, just to leave you to fend for yourself. What your getting into trouble does force on me is this set of alternatives: either I neglect my obligation to take care of you or I shoulder the financial burden of your care. If being faced with just these alternatives is counted a harm, then the "burden on society" argument would provide a genuinely non-paternalistic reason for closing the baths or quarantining carriers of the AIDS virus.[17]

What all this tells us is that there *can be* non-paternalistic reasons for closing gay bathhouses and quarantining AIDS virus carriers even though everyone who might get the disease consents to take the risk of doing so. It does not, however, tell us that there really *are* such reasons. That latter point depends on whether the activities of the bath patrons and carriers will actually make it likely that persons (or society) will have to face alternatives so thoroughly unacceptable that having to face them is to be harmed.

Whether in fact this happens depends, first, on what the actual consequences of not closing the baths or quarantining the carriers are likely to be. For instance, is it likely that we would all come to find ourselves, like Harvey, facing a choice between celibacy or a near certainty of contracting a killing disease? Or, perhaps, is the virus so difficult to transmit by heterosexual activity that there is no genuine risk in heterosexual relationships? In this event AIDS would not force a choice between celibacy and the risk of death on anyone but it would force the choice between celibacy, exclusive heterosexuality, and the risk of death on everyone, including homosexuals.

Here questions of a second, a more conceptual/evaluative, nature become crucial. What consequences would constitute a genuine *harm?* While it is clear (at least it seems to me that it would be incredible to deny) that a person is harmed by being faced with a choice between celibacy and contracting a lethal disease, would a homosexual be harmed by being restricted to choosing between celibacy, heterosexual activity, and contracting the disease? If one sees sexual orientation as a matter of (as current terminology often has it) sexual *preference*, being so restricted may not appear to be a harm. (If my *preference* is for blond pudgy sexual partners, am I *harmed* if I am somehow limited to a choice between celibacy and a generous selection of slender dark-haired partners?) On the other hand, most heterosexuals would think it a very great harm indeed to be limited to a choice between celibacy, homosexuality, and contracting a fatal disease. Does not parity dictate that the homosexual is equally harmed by being restricted to a choice between celibacy, heterosexuality and the disease?

Further, it is clearly artificial to think that any activities would absolutely ensure contracting AIDS. Thus, the alternatives posed by the presence of the AIDS virus are not likely to be as simple as celibacy or contracting the disease (or celibacy, heterosexuality, or contracting the disease). They will instead be something more like celibacy or *X* amount of risk of contracting the disease (or celibacy, heterosexuality, or *X* amount of risk of contracting the disease). And so, in considering whether or not having to face some particular set of alternatives constitutes a harm, we must consider not only what the "safe choices" are (celibacy, exclusive heterosexuality, and so on.) but also how great a risk there is in deviating from the safe choices. Harvey is clearly harmed because his choices are celibacy and the *practical certainty* of getting The Lethal Ailment. But if one's choices were between celibacy and a chance of getting AIDS approximately equal to the chance of being devoured by a runaway zoo lion, then only the most paranoid would think herself harmed by having to face those alternatives. Sorting out such conceptual/evaluative considerations is entirely necessary if we are to determine whether the presence of the AIDS virus does indeed threaten members of the community with a harm to which they do not consent.

Suppose that it finally does turn out (as it quite likely will) that not closing the baths and not quarantining carriers brings some degree of harm to unconsenting parties, that not doing these things contributes to people being limited to alternatives so undesirable that having to face them is a harm. In this event, Mill's anti-paternalistic principle that "there is no room for [even considering a prohibition] when a person's conduct affects the interests of no person besides himself, or needs not affect" simply does not come into play. Anti-paternalism does not dictate that it would be in principle illegitimate to close the baths or to quarantine carriers of the AIDS virus. But the fact that closings and quarantines are not in principle illegitimate does not mean that they are warranted overall. For whatever non-paternalistic reasons there may be for closing baths and quarantining carriers, there may be stronger reasons against such actions. For instance, it might be wise to leave the baths open because they serve as locations for educating gays on sexual safety. And quarantining all carriers of the AIDS virus—which some say, could be as many as two million people— would most likely be completely unworkable even if it were somehow desirable.

There are difficult issues of substance here. My aim has not been to argue that they should be resolved in any particular way. It has been to show that even if AIDS is spread exclusively through consensual acts there can be nonpaternalistic grounds for closing the baths or quarantining the carriers. Without question there is a great deal of plausibility in the claim that it is no one's business but Smith's if he freely chooses to frequent the baths or even to have a homosexual relationship with a known carrier. But in spite of the plausibility of this position, it is altogether too simple. The hard social issues posed by AIDS cannot be so easily disposed of by appeal to an anti-paternalistic principle.

NOTES

1. It is often said that approximately 73% of AIDS cases have been contracted through homosexual activities. This figure may be somewhat high, however, since the disease can be and often is spread through the sharing of drug needles, and AIDS victims who are both homosexual and drug users have been classified as homosexual rather than intravenous drug users. This is pointed out by Jonathan Lieberson in "The Reality of AIDS," *The New York Review of Books* (January 16, 1986), p. 44. Insofar as engaging in particular sexual activities and sharing drug needles are equally consensual acts, the relative percentage

of cases contracted in these two ways has no bearing on any issues discussed in this paper.
2. Similar reasoning would support closing "shooting galleries," places where there is widespread sharing of drug needles. The issues regarding paternalism and AIDS discussed here could be equally well discussed in terms of this possibility.
3. Lieberson, "The Reality of AIDS," p. 48.
4. *St. Louis Post Dispatch* (November 5, 1985), p. 3b.
5. John Stuart Mill, *On Liberty* (Indianapolis: Hackett, 1978), pp. 73–74, italics added.
6. Richard D. Mohr also seems to take the position that any rationale for closing gay baths must be an illegitimate paternalistic one ("AIDS: What to Do—And What Not to Do," *Report from the Center for Philosophy and Public Policy* (Fall 1985); 6–7.) *Newsweek* quotes Dr. Dean F. Echenberg, director of San Francisco's Bureau of Communicable Diseases, to a similar effect regarding quarantines (September 23, 1985, p. 23).
7. Mill, *On Liberty,* pp. 94–96; H.L.A. Hart, *Law Liberty, and Mortality* (New York: Random House, 1966), pp. 32–33.
8. Hart *(Law, Liberty, Morality,* pp. 30–34), Joel Feinberg *(Social Pohilosophy)* [Englewood Cliffs: Prentice Hall, 1973] Ch. 2–3), and others take it (rightly I should think) that there is a clear enough distinction between moralism and paternalism. (Lord Devlin, however, rejects the distinction, and John Kleinig questions both its clarity and moral importance. See Kleinig's *Paternalism* [Totowa: Rowan & Allanheld, 1983], pp. 14–16).
9. For instance, Hart, *Law, Liberty, and Morality.*
10. On this question, see Kleinig, *Paternalism,* pp. 92–95.
11. I am not suggesting here that a financial burden is not a harm. Nor am I suggesting that it would not be a harm of the relevant kind to justify non-paternalistic interference. Rather, I am suggesting that any rationale for closings and quarantines in terms of this harm does not explicate our sense that the harm of AIDS itself ought to supply a non-paternalistic rationale for such actions. (Imagine a society in which, somehow, medical care were entirely cost-free on every level. This stipulation does not rid us of our intuition that AIDS poses a threat of harm to society.)
12. The line of reasoning in this paragraph makes explicit what is at least implicit in Lieberson and Krauthammer. In other words they seem to mean not just that the person who visits the bath or has sex with a carrier consents to his action but also anyone further down the line also consents to anything that could result in his getting the disease.
13. Mill, *On Liberty,* p. 95.
14. The view that even such temporary interference with action is justified has been called "weak

paternalism." I take it, however, that this is far too weak a doctrine of interference to be called "paternalism" at all, and so my "anti-paternalist" is not opposed to this sort of interference. (Cf. Feinberg, *Social Philosophy* pp. 49–50; Tom L. Beauchamp, "Paternalism and Biobehavioral Control," *The Monist* 60 (1977): 67–68.

15. Cf. Mohr, "AIDS: What to Do . . . And What Not to Do," p. 6. Rejecting paternalism, he maintains that education is the only appropriate response when a person is unable to assess the AIDS-risks involved in a course of action.

16. Despite the frequently heard alarms that AIDS can be and is rapidly being spread into and through the heterosexual community, "there is no clear evidence that AIDS in the United States has yet spread beyond the known risk groups, notably homosexuals and drug addicts." *(New York Times* editorial, "AIDS Alarms, False Alarms," February 4, 1987, p. 26.) The editorial backs up this claim and gives an extraordinarily sensible analysis of the reasons behind the well-intended alarms to the contrary. (But the actual extent of the risk to heterosexuals is not crucial here. "Alice," in other words, heterosexuals, should be informed of the degree of risk, whatever that might be.)

17. This is not to say that having to face just these alternatives (or those that Alice faces) really should be counted as harm. Whether it should be is a further question. Some of the considerations this further question involves are discussed in the paragraphs that follow above.

AIDS and Human Rights:
An Intercontinental
Perspective

Carol A. Tauer

Carol Tauer is a professor of philosophy at the College of St. Catherine in Minnesota.

Tauer discusses the different responses to the AIDS crisis in France and Great Britain, as compared with the United States. Among the issues she examines in her comparative study are: confidentiality, paternalistic intervention, education about AIDS, testing for AIDS antibodies, quarantining, and protection of the civil rights of the AIDS carriers. She argues that France is much more resistant to collecting data on those who are AIDS carriers, and Great Britain is much more resistant to engaging in testing for AIDS, than is the United States. Tauer links these differences with the different ways in which these countries understand medical ethics issues.

BACKGROUND: INTERCONTINENTAL DIMENSIONS

Persons who suffer from AIDS or AIDS-related conditions fear not only the disease but also violations or deprivations of basic rights. They are concerned about invasions of their personal privacy and possible restrictions on their freedom of movement and activity. They worry that they may be denied employment, health or life insurance, housing, and even health care.

The United States and the various nations of western Europe differ in their responses to the social and ethical problems posed by AIDS. While all of these nations basically subscribe to the same international declarations of human rights (for example, the *Universal Declaration of Human Rights*, the *European Convention on Human Rights*), there are both conceptual and practical differences in their understanding of these statements.

In the international documents on human rights, we find support for three categories of rights which measures to control AIDS may threaten:[1] (1) the right of personal privacy and confidentiality regarding medical and sexual information; (2) the right to free movement within one's country and to associate where and how one chooses; (3) the right to pursue one's economic good, without limitation based on irrelevant grounds ([for example], sex, sexual preference). Providing some contrast to this perspective, the World Health Organization takes a more utilitarian stance in relation to its goal of promoting health as the right of all people. For WHO, health is fundamental to the attainment of international peace and security, and so cooperation in the control of disease, especially communicable disease, is essential.[2] In its 1976 document, *Health Aspects of Human Rights*, WHO explicitly adopts "the Benthamite principle of 'the greatest happiness of the greatest number' " and advocates curtailing personal liberty not only for the sake of the common good, but also to promote the health of the individual in question.[3]

Here we see exemplified in statements from one international forum, the United Nations, the underlying tension found in discussions of public policy on AIDS. What is the appropriate balance between the common good, in this case the public health, and the rights and liberties of individual persons? Each member nation is attempting to answer this question in the light of its own laws and traditions, and, as a result, a variety of different practices and policies are emerging.

But it is not only this question, complex as it is, which contributes to differing approaches to the AIDS crisis. A second crucial issue concerns the practice of medicine itself. Since AIDS is a disease, it is handled within a medical model, not only one of civil liberties. Thus, one's conception of the role and duties of the physician, the nature of the physician-patient relationship, and the physician's responsibility for the health of the individual and the public, will affect one's approach to AIDS. Again, each nation has different traditions and codes on these matters, which will influence its policy regarding AIDS.

In considering human rights and AIDS, this paper will focus on France and Great Britain, relating significant aspects of their responses to that of the United States. As of November 13, 1986, the largest number of AIDS cases reported in European countries were in France (997, not including the overseas departments), the Federal Republic of Germany (715), and the United Kingdom (512).[4] At this time, there had been over 26,500 cases in the U.S.; and the rate of infection in any European country (less than 20 per million population) was still low compared to the U.S. rate (greater than 110 per million).

In both France and Great Britain—in contrast to Italy, for example—very few of the AIDS patients are IV drug abusers. The overwhelming majority are homosexual or bisexual men, as in the United States; hence this paper will focus on the potential for violations of rights within that population.

While the approaches of these three countries illustrate cultural and political divergences rooted in history, two new trends also emerge: As an international bioethical community develops, engaging in discussion and sharing documents, there is movement toward a greater uniformity of response to bioethical problems. And secondly, in the United States there are signs of a movement away from the almost single-minded focus on individual rights and liberties of the recent past. Both of these factors will undoubtedly affect the AIDS debate in the coming years.

CONFIDENTIALITY

Among the human rights which have a traditional link to medical ethics is the right of privacy. While privacy has many dimensions, the aspect of personal control of private information is perhaps the greatest concern of those at risk for AIDS and AIDS-related conditions. Violations of the confidentiality of private information not only trespass on an intimate domain, involving both medical data and information about sexual behavior but, because of the nature of AIDS, they may also lead to denial of employment, insurance, and housing.

Medical professionals of all western societies have traditionally regarded confidentiality of information as a serious obligation. However, within the modern hospital in the United States, it is not unusual for as many as 100 people to have access to the medical records of the patient,[5] in addition to third-party payers of whatever sort. This situation is not unique to the U.S.; a dean of the Newcastle Faculty of Medicine observed that as many as 150 different people could have access to patient notes in hospital![6] Moreover, when a disease is reportable by law to either local or national health authorities, the cases (however they are identified) become part of a data bank, most likely computerized, over which no individual health professional has control.

The Centers for Disease Control, which mandate national reporting of AIDS cases in the United States, have developed a system for coding the identifications of the individuals involved. While authorities say there is no way to reconstruct a person's name from the coded identification, some members of the homosexual or gay community are dubious.[7] Furthermore, local departments of health at the state level have their own reporting regulations. Colorado and several other states even require the results of positive antibody tests to be identified by name, whereas California law explicitly prohibits such reporting unless there is written consent of the person tested.[8] The state of Minnesota, which predicts a major increase in cases, is experimenting with a curious policy: According to state law, positive antibody tests are to be reported by name; however, individuals may circumvent this requirement by being tested at an "alternative testing site" where they may remain anonymous.[9]

As of March 22, 1985, Great Britain included AIDS under some of the provisions of the law governing "notifiable diseases," but decided not to require the reporting of AIDS cases themselves.[10] Health officials said that a policy of voluntary reporting (without names) was operating effectively and was all that was needed.[11] British law gives particular legal protection to all records of sexually transmitted diseases which are held by National Health Service authorities. These records "shall not be disclosed" except to a medical practitioner for purposes of treatment or prevention.[12] In hospitals, records relating to venereal diseases are "locked away separate from the main hospital records,"[13] a unique provision which shows a high degree of sensitivity to the implications of disclosure.

French physicians invest medical confidences with a sacredness linked to a religious tradition, somewhat like the secrecy of the Catholic confessional. This view is expressed in French law, which protects "the professional secret" from disclosure in a court of law and does not even permit the patient to waive confidentiality in his own interest.[14] The duty of confidentiality with respect to all third parties is strongly asserted as part of "Code de déontologie médicale," the statement of medical ethics which is imposed by law on French physicians.[15]

While French law and practice seem to provide essentially absolute protection for medical confidentiality, British and American codes allow exceptions, either to protect a third party or for the sake of the common good. American case law contains precedents of a "duty to warn" a third party who is in danger of harm,[16] and currently there is much discussion as to how this duty would apply to the physician of a person who is infectious for the AIDS virus. The codes of both the British Medical Association and the General

Medical Council permit disclosure for the sake of the public interest and, somewhat surprisingly, for purposes of approved medical research.[17] There appears to be quite a bit of leeway for the British physician to determine what may ethically be revealed, apart from special provisions such as the statutes on sexually transmitted diseases.

Physicians, like other professionals, customarily devise their own ethical codes and enforce them through self-regulation. Even when a professional code is included within statutory law, as in France, the duties are those already recognized by members of the profession in that country. Confidentiality, traditionally one of the most cherished values of the profession of medicine, is challenged today by public policy decisions which mandate its abrogation for a cause which is viewed as a greater good. Thus, required reporting of medical information implies that the good consequences which will follow as a result of gathering this information justify both overriding the patient's privacy right and endangering his related interests (for example, his interest in nondiscriminatory treatment when he seeks insurance).

There are two distinct purposes for which public health agencies may use the data they gather about cases of a communicable disease. Both purposes are preventive, but in different ways. The first purpose is epidemiological research, the tracing of patterns of a disease in order to identify causal agents, modes of transmission, ebbs and flows in the history of the disease. As a result of such research, recommendations on disease control are provided to the public, to physicians, and to local government agencies. The U.S. Centers for Disease Control and the British Communicable Disease Surveillance Centre gather their case data for this purpose. Much epidemiological study can be done without specific information of the individuals involved, but some research requires that at least one investigator have this information. The protection of confidentiality in epidemiological research has been a topic of ethical concern for many years.[18]

But while continuing questions are raised, both Britain and the U.S. show a substantial history of epidemiological research. (See Gordis et al. for an impressive listing of results achieved by this work.) Because of strong insistence on confidentiality, France has been slow to gather the data needed for studies of this type. French investigation of AIDS has therefore focused on virological and immunological research, while epidemiological work has been centered in the U.S. Recently, however, there have been signs of a convergence in bioethical standards. For example, a 1985 recommendation of the French national committee on bioethics, "Recommendations on Medical Registers for Epidemiologic Study and Prevention,"[19] stimulated a detailed response from the National Medical Council, . . . incorporating many of the confidentiality precautions suggested nine years ago by Gordis et al.[20] While France is clearly learning from the Anglo-American experience, its cautiousness and discretion can also be instructive to that tradition.

The second purpose for gathering case data is the exercise of direct intervention into the person-to-person transmission of a communicable disease. This intervention may involve the tracing and warning of contacts of an infectious person and/or surveillance of the activities of this person so as to prevent further possible transmission. While the epidemiological use of data presents a speculative danger of violation of confidentiality, its use for direct intervention (which requires a noncoded record of a person's identity) seems to present an immediate ethical dilemma. Whether this abrogation of confidentiality is justified by the lethal and catastrophic nature of AIDS is hotly contested in the U.S., while such measures seem generally to have been rejected in Great Britain and hardly even considered in France. In the U.S., state and local jurisdictions are in the process of developing a tangle of reporting regulations based on their perceptions of this second function for public health data.

INFORMED CONSENT
AND THE RIGHT TO KNOW

The practice of medicine has traditionally been a paternalistic enterprise. In the past few decades it has become much less so in the United States, and there is now a clearer public recognition of patients' rights, both morally and legally. While the statutory assertions of these rights differ somewhat from state to state, as does case law, the American Hospital Association has promulgated a general statement which is universally accepted by hospitals. Among accepted rights are the right to informed consent to treatment, the right to know one's diagnosis and prognosis, and the right to refuse treatment, even life-sustaining treatment. In competent patients, these rights may not be overridden even for what a professional perceives to be the best interests of the patient.

In contrast, Great Britain and France have retained a more paternalistic view of the role of the physician, so that the physician's duty to promote the best interests of the patient generally takes precedence over the patient's rights related to autonomy. Correlatively, the standard for whether a physician has done his or her duty is established almost exclusively by the medical profession in France and Britain, and lawyers and judges defer to medical judgment and testimony in these matters. In the U.S., the courts often exercise an independent function on behalf of patients' rights, and standards such as that of "the reasonable patient" may be applied.

While the French code of medical ethics is part of statutory law, its formulation is entirely the work of the Conseil National de l'Ordre des Médecins.[21] This "Code de déontologie médicale" is expressed in terms of physician duties, and the only right the patient is specifically granted is that of choosing his or her own physician. While the physician is instructed to respect the wishes of the sick person as far as possible, an extraordinary control over information is retained: "For legitimate reasons, which the physician recognizes in conscience, a sick person may be left in ignorance of a grave diagnosis or prognosis."[22]

Although there is now a multidisciplinary national committee on bioethics in France, the charge of this committee restricts it to matters related to biomedical research; clinical issues remain under the jurisdiction of the medical council.[23] Since the committee interprets its charge rather broadly, its documents show substantive interchange with the medical council ([for example], see above on confidentiality and epidemiological research). Another currently debated issue involves phase I drug trials, in which drugs are given their initial testing for toxicity, dosage, and mode of administration. In the United States, these trials are customarily conducted with healthy volunteers (usually paid). Such a practice has been repugnant to the

French medical profession: "There is no justifiable scientific or medical reason for exposing to risk a subject who has no medical reason to participate in a trial and who can expect no benefit from it. Hence, we condemn . . . all phase I trials conducted on subjects."[24] Most French jurists have also supported the view that a healthy normal subject does not have the right to consent to such involvement, even with full information, understanding, and voluntariness.[25] But the national ethics committee is providing a forum for consideration of a change in this stance; and there is evidence that such trials, with careful safeguards, may become ethically acceptable, as they are in the U.S.[26]

In his perceptive study *The Unmasking of Medicine*, Ian Kennedy has detailed the paternalistic bias of the British medical profession, ranging from control of the "sick note," by which the physician certifies that an absent worker truly was ill, to permission for an abortion, where physicians are unavoidably involved in psychosocial judgments.[27] A recent legal case in Britain has thoroughly examined American case law on informed consent and rejected some of its conclusions. The case, that of Mrs. Amy Sidaway, involved her complaint that her physician had not told her the risks of her surgery. The Court of Appeal decided against her, stating that "the doctrine of informed consent [forms] no part of English law," and that "most [people] prefer to put themselves unreservedly in the hands of their doctors. . . . [This] is simply an acceptance of the doctor-patient relationship as it has developed in this country." Final appeal to the House of Lords supported this view; the Lords determined that what to volunteer to disclose was a matter for the physician's clinical judgment. However, they did allow for a court finding contrary to medical testimony in extreme or blatant cases of nondisclosure, and they also stressed the physician's obligation to answer fully and truthfully any questions which the patient actually asked.[28]

Paternalistic practice in France and Britain represents not only the way the doctor-patient relationship has developed in each country, but, in general, the way the class structure has developed. In Britain, social classes 1 to 5 are defined on the basis of occupational and educational level, with class 1 the professional class. A camaraderie among doctors, lawyers, and professors results from their having enjoyed basically the same background and education; hence they are supposedly able to understand each other's language. On the other hand, those who belong to classes 4 or 5 could not be expected to understand technical information, so are assumed to put their trust in the professional's judgment.[29] In France the class structure is also much more clearly defined than in the U.S., and the rural and working classes have a standard of living and level of culture well below those of the bourgeoisie, which includes the professional class.

European notions of the status and role of the professional have had the practical consequence of determining who controls certain types of information. In *Un Virus Étrange Venu d'Ailleurs*, Jacques Leibowitch describes the current openness of information and discussion about AIDS as the Americanization of the disease. It is not merely that the U.S. Centers for Disease Control have decided what is to count worldwide as AIDS, a matter complained of by a variety of European scientists and clinicians.[30] But also socioculturally, "the disease carries the cultural insignia of its origin," presumably the United States.[31] Continuing in Leibowitch's words:

> To tell, to make known, to announce the disease and death—to inform the patient of the medical procedures that will follow, to obtain his informed consent, to expose and to discuss while exposing—North America has its cultural features. In France, we had another tradition. To say nothing, to know nothing; a father protects us with his mysteries. . . . [Now] everyone will know: Goodbye, mystery; hello, terror.[32]

TESTING OR SCREENING FOR AIDS ANTIBODIES

The American patient's "right to know" is an enunciated extension of a general right claimed by the U.S. citizen. With regard to health matters, this claim is supported by U.S. public health officials, who take the position that full knowledge contributes to prudent personal health decisions. The Centers for Disease Control have based their recommendations regarding such general testing for AIDS antibodies on that assumption.

Emphasizing that such tests should be voluntary and accompanied by thorough counseling, the CDC recommends that serologic testing "be routinely offered to all persons at increased risk when they present [themselves] to health-care settings." These recommendations enumerate first the behaviors counseled for those who test negative, and, second, the behaviors counseled for those who test positive.[33] While these behaviors are similar in many respects, the CDC seems to imply that knowledge of one's antibody status will be determininative if one needs to make changes in lifestyle and behavior.

Local health authorities have made similar recommendations. For example, the Minnesota State Department of Health has published notices with the heading, "Don't Guess about It," encouraging persons who may be infected to take advantage of free testing and counseling. In many localities of the U.S., general testing sites were first made available in order to dissuade persons seeking serologic testing from using blood donation centers for this purpose. But presently, the use of these testing sites is being encouraged on the typically American presupposition that more information is better than less in making the individual medical or lifestyle decisions.

In contrast to the United States, British public health authorities are not urging general serum antibody tests, even for members of high-risk groups. The value of routine testing is questioned by the Chief Medical Officer, Department of Health and Social Security, as well as by staff of the National AIDS Counseling Training Unit.[34] After considering the purposes for which such test results might legitimately be used, these authorities conclude that the possible benefits are highly speculative. There is no concrete evidence that knowledge of test results actually leads to greater behavior change than mass education and focused counseling programs, nor that it would in any other way contribute to halting the spread of the disease. Thus these officials believe that there is no justification for risking the harms ([for example], stigmatization, loss of employment or insurance) to which the test might lead.

Here British health authorities take a position similar to that of many gay organizations in the United States. For example, the Gay Men's Health Crisis (New York City) nationally distributed an advertisement with the headline, "The Test Can Be Almost as Devastating as the Disease."[35]

But there is disagreement within the gay community, and some gay groups, especially in urban centers of continental Europe, are urging use of the test.[36]

Lack of British enthusiasm for routine testing does not mean that there is indifference in the situations in which a confirmed positive test result would call for a clear response. Miller et al.... list settings within which screening ought to be done: with donors of blood and blood products, organs for transplant, semen, and growth hormone[s]; before and during the pregnancy of a woman at risk; and probably with hemodialysis patients. The slowness with which Britain instituted screening of blood donations (not widely introduced until October 1985) should not be attributed to lack of concern. Rather, the delay was due to great care and extensive investigation in order to locate, among available testing methods, the best one, ([that is, the method] with the fewest false positives and with nearly zero false negatives).[37]

Discussion of serological testing in official sources in France is largely limited to its use with blood donors. The national committee on bioethics has proposed a policy on screening blood donors, noting the absolute necessity of such screening to ferret out infection of blood with SIDA (AIDS).[38] The proposal carefully delineates the counseling which must accompany a positive finding: The physician of the blood center must impress upon the seropositive person that he has a heavy responsibility to his family and/or other sexual contacts in order to stop the spread of the disease. The document shows the expected French discretion regarding intimate information; the physician must adjust his discourse to each individual situation, and no reporting requirement is mentioned or recommended.

GOVERNMENT-SPONSORED EDUCATION PROGRAMS

Given their decision not to promote identification of cases of AIDS infections, British health authorities have been consistent in putting resources into mass education and focused counselling programs instead. Chief Medical Officer Acheson specifically includes adolescents, undeclared homosexual and bisexual men, and, in fact, all sexually active men and women among those whom government-sponsored educational programs must reach. He also notes that the national press, radio, and television will provide sexually explicit information if necessary, and that public response (to effectiveness and offensiveness) will be periodically evaluated.[39]

The first stage in the government's educational campaign included full-page advertisements in the national newspapers on March 16 and 17, 1986, advertisements in the gay press, and posters and leaflets provided to groups like the Terrence Higgins Trust (a gay organization formed to deal with AIDS), at a total cost of £2.5 million.[40] The national press advertisements were highly explicit, stating that "rectal sex . . . should be avoided," that "using a sheath [condom] reduces the risk of AIDS and other diseases," and that "any act that damages the penis, vagina, anus, or mouth is dangerous."[41]

While U.S. public health authorities have consistently advocated mass educational programs, their efforts have generally had to be more restrained. They have been able to provide some funding to those who work with the gay community and with IV drug users for the development of clear and direct educational programs. But material provided for mass consumption is directed either at those who will read fairly technical explanations of the disease and its transmission, or at those who are sophisticated enough to read between the lines of a vague, generalized warning. Adolescent, disadvantaged, and semiliterate persons are not apt to be informed by scientific or euphemistic discussions.

Several reasons for this restraint may be cited: (1) The Reagan administration has objections to government funding for sexually explicit materials, particularly regarding homosexual activity, and, as a result a number of CDC programs have not been implemented.[42] (2) There is a strong antipornography movement, and some citizens are highly vocal about educational materials which they view as too explicit sexually.[43] (3) There is a widespread but unconfirmed belief that informing young people about sexual practices will only lead them to experiment with them. (4) Activities which are described in educational materials are often illegal; for example, sodomy is criminal by the laws of about half the states.

One may expect that the tide will turn as a result of Surgeon General C. Everett Koop's report on AIDS, issued October 22, 1986. In this report, Koop calls for AIDS sex education, beginning in the elementary grades, as the central focus of public health efforts against AIDS.[44] This focus is strongly supported by the study of the Institute of Medicine, National Academy of Sciences, which was made public one week later.[45] It is too early, however, to assess the effects of these recommendations.

In France, the reluctance to expose the disease is almost universal. While the gay community in the United States has been a leader in the educational effort there, in France there has been a tendency among gay people to deny the seriousness of the disease. An American reporter describes

Parisian gays as "charmed by what they perceive to be the *vraiment New Yorkaise* overreaction to the situation.... Eyebrows arched wryly at the discussion of safe sex."[46] Association AIDES has found great resistance in its efforts to institute programs to educate patrons of gay bars and bathhouses in Paris.[47]

Gay people of other countries, however, have been particularly critical of French authorities for their meager financial commitment to AIDS education (while France is the European country hardest hit). It was not until late 1985 that the government allocated its first $30,000 for AIDS education, an amount less than one San Francisco foundation spends locally in a month.[48] When Dr. Luc Montagnier of the Pasteur Institute recently wrote an informational pamphlet, the decision was made to produce it as a glossy 94-page pamphlet which would be sold for $4, thus excluding many people who needed the information but would not or could not pay that sum.[49]

A country which has been most highly praised for its government's commitment to education on AIDS, as well as for its national office to coordinate all AIDS policy decisions, is the Netherlands. The director of this office, Jan van Wijngaarden, attributes its success to the integration of homosexuality into Dutch society and the lack of bigotry among the Dutch public.[50]

Reports have also been received about imaginative educational efforts in Norway. For example, an Oslo billboard shows a cartoon face drawn on the top of a male organ to illustrate a text about using condoms to prevent the transmission of AIDS. Publicity of this type shows a realization that masses of people will only be attracted, hence informed and affected, by media presentations which are clever, contemporary, and graphic.[51]

QUARANTINE AND OTHER RESTRICTIVE POLICIES

The ethical conflict between the common good and the rights or freedoms of individuals is perhaps illustrated most clearly in the situation where a restriction on movement or association is imposed or contemplated by public authorities. The quarantine, with its long and controversial history, provides an example of a public health measure which can be highly restrictive, and which in some forms is being proposed for the control of AIDS.

In Britain, the Public Health Act of 1984 has been interpreted specifically for its application to AIDS. The section on detention was amended thus:

> A justice of the peace may on the application of any local authority make an order for the detention in hospital of an inmate of that hospital suffering from acquired immune deficiency syndrome if the justice is satisfied that on his leaving . . . proper precautions to prevent the spread of the disease would not be taken by him.[52]

Two applications of the statute have been reported in British journals, both involving rather unusual circumstances. In one case, a hospitalized AIDS patient was put under detention orders for three weeks by Manchester magistrates. The Manchester medical officer described this man as "bleeding copiously and trying to discharge himself [from hospital]." The legal correspondent reporting to the *British Medical Journal* raised the obvious question: What if it were risky sexual behavior rather than bleeding, which endangered others? Detention for such cause would seem to be within the intent of the law. Yet, as the correspondent notes, "To apply the law in this way would clearly raise grave political difficulties for the central government as well as for any local authority concerned."[53]

Interestingly, the other reported case of detention in England also involved bleeding. In this case, the patient was on a psychiatric ward, and at one point he cut his hands and deliberately smeared blood around his room and into the corridor. The police were called, and the person is now being detained in a prison setting.[54]

Thus far in the United States, actual quarantine or isolation has been seriously considered only in relation to prostitutes who are AIDS carriers. A restrictive measure which has had more impact on the gay community in general involves the closing or regulation of gay bathhouses or other meeting places where casual or anonymous sex is a common activity. San Francisco experienced a series of orders and injunctions; in the end, the California Superior Court prohibited legal closing of such establishments, but ordered safeguards like removal of cubicle doors, inspection by monitors every ten minutes, and expulsion of patrons observed in acts of high-risk sex.[55] New York has adopted an emergency regulation which provides for closing establishments which allow anal or oral sex acts on their premises.[56] While gay rights groups are most incensed at this ruling, it has also been applied to heterosexual gathering places.

French public policy has not yet confronted the issue of quarantine or even of regulation of bathhouse activity. In Paris, the police are reportedly engaging in increased harassment of the gay community, using the threat of AIDS as their justification, but apparently on legitimate grounds (for example, to identify minors practicing prostitution or frequenting bathhouses).[57]

Perhaps the most comprehensive policy among European nations has been established by Sweden. By including AIDS under the provisions of its venereal disease laws, as it did in late 1985, Sweden could be interpreted to require compulsory testing of persons in high-risk groups, and for those with seropositive tests, reporting to health authorities, naming of all sexual partners, prohibition of risky conduct (sexual or drug-related), and, in certain cases, confinement to hospitals. At least one person with a seropositive test has been so confined because he continued to share needles with other drug users and to have sex without taking necessary protective precautions.[58]

Clearly a common thread in laws about AIDS, among states in the U.S., Great Britain, and Sweden, is *some* explicit provision for the mandatory restriction of persons who are judged to be an imminent threat to the health of others. However, major problems exist concerning not only the implementation but also the efficacy of such laws. As with [that of] some American states, British law focuses on persons who actually have AIDS, while scientists believe that those who have been infected with the virus, but have not (yet) developed the disease, may actually be more infectious than those who are ill. One must ask whether a policy calling for legal restriction has any meaning without required testing of large population groups; and since that sort of program is not seriously contemplated by public health officials (except perhaps in Sweden), the legal enactments may be more token than efficacious. At most, they seem to provide legal protection for government officials who may wish to restrain an individual whose behavior is particularly blatant, harmful, and perhaps malicious.

PROTECTIONS FOR CIVIL RIGHTS

Each nation has its own tradition with respect to the protection of civil rights. Both the role of the law, whether constitutional, statutory, or case law, and the atti-

tudes of the citizens, differ from country to country; and these differences engender subtle variations in the national concern for the civil rights of AIDS victims.

As members of the European Community, both France and Great Britain have subscribed to its *Convention on Human Rights* and have accepted the provision whereby an individual citizen may appeal to the Commission of Human Rights in Strasbourg if the citizen believes his or her rights under the Convention have been violated by his or her State. It has been suggested that grievances against the National Health Service with regard to confidentiality could be brought before this body, and cases on detention for psychiatric illness have already been decided.[59]

In Article 8, the *European Convention* gives explicit protection to the individual's private and family life, home and correspondence, and states that public authorities may not interfere with the exercise of this right unless it is necessary for some greater social good.[60] This privacy right has been applied by the European Court against national laws prohibiting homosexual acts between consensual adults in private. Although the rest of the United Kingdom had decriminalized such activity in 1967 (Sexual Offenses Act), Northern Ireland had not. An individual's appeal to the European Commission in the early 1980s resulted in the Court's judgment that the law in Northern Ireland did, in fact, violate Article 8 of the Convention and had to be changed.[61]

It has been noted that persons at risk for AIDS in European countries display a relative lack of concern about the possible loss of their civil rights. This phenomenon could perhaps be linked to the fact that homosexual activity is not illegal in these countries, and also perhaps to the national health care systems by which full medical coverage is provided to citizens of most European nations.[62]

While a privacy right is not specifically enunciated in the United States Constitution, it has been found to be implicit in other protections asserted there. Thus, it has been applied to issues in child-rearing and education, marriage, contraception, abortion (*Roe* v. *Wade*), and termination of medical treatment (*In re Karen Ann Quinlan*). However, recently the U.S. Supreme Court rendered a decision specifying a point beyond which the privacy right did not apply. On June 30, 1986, the Court asserted that individual states were entitled to make laws which prohibit sodomy. While most such state laws apply to both homosexual and heterosexual acts (anal and possibly oral sex acts), the Court's opinion clearly focuses on a possible state interest in prohibiting homosexual sodomy.[63] Although the ruling makes no mention of AIDS, it is possible that the majority justices had this disease in mind, for they seem concerned about decisions states may wish to make to safeguard public welfare. And it is known that at least one amicus brief urged the Court to consider AIDS as a good reason for states to have laws against sodomy.[64]

Though the rights of gay persons are protected in some jurisdictions of the U.S., particularly in liberal urban centers, there is no general protection for the homosexual person as such, as there is for the person of a minority race as such. Until recently, however, there was a belief that the rights of those with AIDS or AIDS-related conditions would be safeguarded under the federal Rehabilitation Act of 1973. Under this law, it is illegal for agencies and programs which receive any federal funds to discriminate against those who are handicapped or perceived to be handicapped, provided these persons are otherwise qualified (for example, to do a particular job). As of June 7, 1986, civil rights lawyers in the Justice Department supported a broad application of the Act to AIDS victims.[65] But shortly thereafter, a different position was taken by the Justice Department itself.

In a ruling of June 22, 1986, the Justice Department asserted that a person may not be excluded from a job or a program on grounds that he or she suffers from the disabling effects of the disease AIDS, but may be excluded if there is a concern that he or she might spread the disease.[66] While adverting to the U.S. Public Health Service's assurances that AIDS is not spread by casual contact, the ruling calls the weight of this opinion into question by putting the burden of proof on the person who claims to have been dismissed unfairly. This decision is currently binding on the executive branch, which is the executor of regulations for federally funded agencies and programs.

However, the ruling will have little effect in cities and states which have already ruled that persons with AIDS or positive antibody tests are protected by local antidiscrimination laws. For example, Minnesota and its two major cities have indicated that the Justice Department ruling is irrelevant there.[67] Nonetheless, the Justice Department's conservative interpretation of the application of the Rehabilitation Act presages a national scenario of inconsistent policies, with discrimination excusable in some jurisdictions if an employer is irrationally fearful regarding the transmission of AIDS.

NOTES

1. See I. Brownlie, Ed., *Basic Documents on Human Rights,* 2nd ed. (Oxford: Clarendon Press, 1981).

2. World Health Organization, "Preamble to the Constitution of the World Health Organization" (1946), in *The First Ten Years of the World Health Organization* (Geneva: WHO, 1958).

3. World Health Organization, *Health Aspects of Human Rights* (Geneva: WHO, 1976), p. 42.

4. Information provided by the WHO Control Progam on AIDS, Geneva.

5. Mark Siegler, "Confidentiality in Medicine: A Decrepit Concept," *New England Journal of Medicine* 307 (1982), pp. 1518–21.

6. Alexander W. Macara, "Confidentiality—A Decrepit Concept? Discussion Paper," *Journal of the Royal Society of Medicine* 77 (1984), p. 579.

7. Charles Marwick, " 'Confidentiality' Issues May Cloud Epidemiologic Studies of AIDS," *Journal of the American Medical Association* 250 (1983), pp. 1945–46.

8. Michael Mills, Constance Wofsy, and John Mills, "The Acquired Immunodeficiency Syndrome: Infection Control and Public Health Law," *New England Journal of Medicine* 314 (April 3, 1986), pp. 931–36.

9. Department of Health (Minnesota), "Rules Governing Communicable Diseases," *Disease Control Newsletter,* Insert 12, No. 5 (June, 1985); Walter Parker, "AIDS Screening Tests Offered Anonymously," *St. Paul Pioneer Press and Dispatch* (November 13, 1985), pp. 1A and 4A.

10. The Public Health (Infectious Diseases) Regulations 1985 (Statutory Instrument 1985, No. 434), England and Wales.

11. Rodney Deitch, "Government's Response to Fears about Acquired Immunodeficiency Syndrome," *Lancet* (March 2, 1985), pp. 530–31.

12. The National Health Service (Venereal Diseases) Regulations 1974 (Statutory Instrument 1974, No. 29), England and Wales.

13. E.D. Acheson, "AIDS: A Challenge for the Public Health," *Lancet* (March 22, 1986), p. 665.

14. John Harvard, "Medical Confidence," *Journal of Medical Ethics* 11 (1985), pp. 8–11; Daniel W. Shuman, "The Privilege Study: The Psychotherapist-Patient Privilege in Civil and Common Law Countries," *Proceedings, Sixth World Congress on Medical Law* (Ghent, Belgium, 1984), pp. 73–77.

15. "Code de déontologie médicale," Décret No. 79–506 du Juin 1979, *Journal Officiel de la Republique Française* (June 30, 1979).

16. California Supreme Court, *Tarasoff v. Regents of the University of California,* 131 Cal. Rptr. 14 (decided July 1, 1976).

17. Raanan Gillon, "Confidentiality," *British Medical Journal* 291 (185), pp. 1634–36; Huw. W.S. Francis, "Of Gossips, Eavesdroppers, and Peeping Toms," *Journal of Medical Ethics* 8 (1982), pp. 134–43.

18. Leon Gordis, Ellen Gold, and Raymond Seltser, "Privacy Protection in Epidemiologic and Medical Research: A Challenge and a Responsibility," *American Journal of Epidemiology* 105 (1977), pp. 163–68; Charles Marwick, "Epidemiologists Strive to Maintain Confidentiality of Some Health Data," *Journal of the American Medical Association* 252 (1984), pp. 2377–83; W.E. Waters, "Ethics and Epidemiological Research," *International Journal of Epidemiology* 14 (1985), pp. 48–51.

19. Comité Consultatif National d'Éthique pour les Sciences de la Vie et de la Sante, "Avis sur les registres médicaux poor études épidémiologiques et de prévention," *Journées Annuelles d'Éthique 1985* (Paris: INSERM, 1985), pp. 13–14.

20. Louis René, "Secret médical et collecte de renseignements médicaux à usage épidémiologique," *Lettre d'Information du Comité Consultatif* No. 4 (April 1986), p. 3.

21. Conversation with Catherine Labrusse-Riou, member of the Comité Consultatif National d'Ethique (June 25, 1986).

22. "Code de déontologie médicale," Titre I, Articles 6 and 7: Titre II, Article 42: "Pous des raisons légitimes que le médicin apprécie en conscience, un malade peut étre laissé dans l'ignorance d'un diagnostic ou un pronostic grave."

23. Conversation with Catherine LaBrusse-Riou.

24. Pierre Arpaillange, Sophie Dion, and Georges Mathe, "Proposal for Ethical Standards in Therapuetic Trials," *British Medical Journal* 291 (1985), pp. 887–89.

25. *Ibid.,* p. 887.

26. Assistance Publique Hôpitaux de Paris, "Recommendations concemant les essais therapuetiques sur des voluntaires sains, *Lettre d'Information du Comité Consultatif* No. 3 (January 1986), p. 2.

27. Ian Kennedy, *The Unmasking of Medicine* (London: Granada, 1983).

28. Robert Schwartz and Andrew Grabb, "Why Britain Can't Afford Informed Consent," *Hastings Center Report* 15, No. 4 (August 1985), pp. 19–25; Diana Brahams, "Doctor's Duty to Inform Patient of Substantial or Special Risks When Offering Treatment," *Lancet* (March 2, 1985), pp. 528–30.

29. Schwartz and Grabb, *op. cit.,* p. 22.

30. J. Seale, "AIDS Virus Infection: Prognosis and Transmission," *Journal of the Royal Society of Medicine* 79 (February 1986), p. 122; Jean-Baptiste Branet *et al.* "Epidemiological Aspects of Acquired Immune Deficiency Syndrome in France," *Annals of the New York Academy of Sciences (A.I.D.S.),* Vol. 437, p. 334.

31. Jacques Leibowitch, *A Strange Virus of Unknown Origin,* trans. by Richard Howard, introduction by Robert C. Gallo (New York: Ballantine Books, 1985), p. 93.

32. *Ibid.*, pp. 92–94.
33. Centers for Disease Control, "Additional Recommendations to Reduce Sexual and Drug Abuse-Related Transmission of Human T-Lymphotropic Virus Type III/Lymphadenopathy-Associated Virus," *Morbidity and Mortality Weekly Report* 35 (March 14, 1986), pp. 152–55.
34. Acheson, *op, cit.* pp. 662–66; David Miller *et al.* "HTLV-III: Should Testing Ever Be Routine? *British Medical Journal* 292 (April 5, 1986), pp. 941–43.
35. Advertisement in *GLC Voice* (Minneapolis, November 4, 1985), p. 10.
36. Michael Helquist, "The State of the Science: Taking the Test in Europe," *Coming Up!* 7, No. 4 (January 1986).
37. See, for example, "Notes and News: HTLV-III Antibody Screening," *Lancet* (August 31, 1985), p. 513.
38. Comité Consultatif National d'Ethique pour les Sciences de la Vie et de la Santé, "Avis concernant les problémes éthiques posés par l'appréciation des risques du SIDA par la recherche d'anticorps specifiques chez les donneurs de sang," *Lettre d'Information du Comité Consultatif* No. 1 (July 1985), p 1.
39. Acheson, *op. cit.*, p. 664.
40. "Notes and News; Public Information Campaign on AIDS," *Lancet* (March 22, 1986), p. 694.
41. "Are You At Risk from AIDS?" full page notice in the *Observer* (March 16–17, 1986),
42. Marlene Cimons, "AIDS Education Plans Halted to Avoid Uproar over Explicit Advice," *Minneapolis Star and Tribune* (December 4, 1985), p. 11A.
43 See, for example, Joe Kimball, "Officials Balk at Paying for AIDS Ad with Unclothed Man," *Minneapolis Star and Tribune* (June 17, 1986), pp. 1B and 5B; Lewis Cope, "Ad Blitz about AIDS Begins," *Minneapolis Star and Tribune* (August 9, 1986), pp. 1C and 6C.
44. "Surgeon General Calls for Early AIDS Education, Opposes Compulsory Tests," *Minneapolis Star and Tribune* (October 22, 1986).
45. "Huge AIDS Effort Urged," *St. Paul Pioneer and Dispatch* (October 30, 1986), pp. 1A and 4A.
46. Otis Stuart, "Ghosts," *New York Native* No. 139 (December 16–22, 1985), pp. 33 and 37.
47. Gerald Koskovich, "Letter from Paris," *The Advocate* No. 441 (March 4, 1986), pp. 31–32.
48. Randy Shilts, "Dutch Speedy, Others Lag on AIDS Warnings," *San Francisco Chronicle* (January 3, 1986).
49. "Lack of Funds Hampers European Efforts to Halt Spread of AIDS," *New York Times* (November 11, 1985).
50. Shilts, *op, cit.*
51. Jim Klobuchar, "Sermonette Would Play Well in Oslo," *Minneapolis Star and Tribune* (July 31, 1986), p. 1B. For an illustration of the use of advertising techniques to educate physicians about control of staph infection when standard educational efforts failed, see "When Wonder Drugs Don't Work," NOVA Broadcast (London: BBC-TV, 1986).
52. The Public Health (Infectious Diseases) Regulations 1985 (Statutory Instrument 1985) No. 434, Section 3.
53. "Detaining Patients with AIDS," *British Medical Journal* 291 (October 19, 1985), p. 1,102.
54. C. Thompson *et al.*, "AIDS: Dilemmas for the Psychiatrist," *Lancet* (February 1, 1986), pp. 269–70; responses in *Lancet* (March 1, 1986), pp. 496–97.
55. Mills, Wofsy, and Mills, *op. cit.*, p. 935.
56. "N.Y. Rule Curbing Gay Sex Practices Becomes Law," *Minneapolis Star and Tribune* (December 21, 1985).
57. "In Search of 'Moral Danger' " *The Body Politic* (July 1985), p. 25.
58 "Swedish Govemment Considering Drastic Action to Stop AIDS," *Equal Time* (November 13, 1985) (reprinted from *New York Native);* Shilts, *op. cit.,* "HTLV-III Carrier Detained in Swedish Hospital," *American Medical News* (February 7, 1986), p. 8.
59. A.H. Robertson, *Human Rights in Europe* (Manchester: Manchester University Press, 1977); Paul Sieghart, *The International Law of Human Rights* (Oxford: Clarendon Press, 1983).
60. Brownlie, *op. cit.*, p. 343.
61. "Just Satisfaction under the Convention: Dudgeon Case," *European Law Review* 8 (1983), p. 205.
62. Helquist, *op. cit.*
63. "Excerpts from the Court Opinions on Homosexual Relations," *New York Times* (July 1, 1986), p. A18.
64. William F. Woo, "AIDS Epidemic and the Georgia Ruling," *St. Louis Post-Dispatch* (July 6, 1986). For a full discussion of this issue, see Chris D. Nichols, "AIDS—A New Reason to Regulate Homosexuality?" *Journal of Contemporary Law* 11 (1984), pp. 315–43.
65. Robert Pear, "AIDS Victims Gain in Fight on Rights," *New York Times* (June 8, 1986), pp. 1 and 19.
66. Robert Pear, "Rights Laws Offer Only Limited Help on AIDS, U.S. Rules," *New York Times* (June 23, 1986), pp. A1 and A13.
67. "AIDS Decision Scorned" *Minneapolis Star and Tribune* (June 22, 1986), p. 10B.

The Ethical Design
of an AIDS Vaccine Trial
in Africa

Nicholas A. Christakis

Nicholas A. Christakis is a Robert Wood Johnson Clinical Scholar at the University of Pennsylvania's Medical School. He has published many essays on cross-cultural medical ethics, clinical decision making, and medical sociology.

    Christakis is interested in the ethical justifiability of testing an AIDS vaccine in Africa. He considers various safeguards that must be employed to guarantee that Africans are not treated as guinea pigs to help medical authorities in the West come to an understanding of the AIDS virus. Among other things, he argues that subjects need to be fully informed of the risks. Given the way some African societies are structured and the traditions involved in those societies, obtaining consent may involve significant interaction with community leaders and a substitution of the leader's consent for that of the individual. But the difficulties in obtaining consent should not make Western scientists lax in their pursuit of a test that is respectful of the trial participants.

On March 19, 1987, a group of French and Zairian scientists published a report in *Nature* stating that one of the investigators, Dr. Daniel Zagury of the Pierre and Marie Curie University in Paris, had immunized himself with an investigational AIDS vaccine.[1] With "the full support of the Zairian Ethics Committee," the investigators also immunized "a small group of Zairians, all of whom were HIV-seronegative volunteers and immunologically normal."

The fact that this first trial of an AIDS vaccine took place in Africa leads to a variety of concerns. Most troubling is the possibility that Africans might serve as "guinea pigs" for clinical trials that would not be allowed in the U.S. or Europe, particularly in view of past cases of disregard for the rights of human subjects of research in Third World countries. Africans, feeling that "Western science often comes to Africa with dirty hands," have been concerned that Western investigators, unchecked by foreign or local supervision, might conduct "savage experiments."[2] Indeed, an unidentified source close to the Zagury group informed a *New York Times* reporter that a major reason they conducted the trial in Zaire was that "It was easier to get official permission [in Zaire] than in France."[3]

Differences in permissibility of trials in developed versus developing countries, however, are not supposed to occur. According to the guidelines for human subjects research established jointly by the World

Reprinted with permission of *The Hastings Center Report*, June/July 1988.

Health Organization (WHO) and the Council for International Organizations of Medical Sciences (CIOMS), when research is conducted by investigators of one country on subjects of another, "the research protocol should be submitted to ethical review by the initiating agency. The ethical standards applied should be no less exacting than they would be for research carried out within the initiating country."[4] Yet the great complexity, varied presentation, and wide distribution of HIV infection challenge this stance. When the epidemiologic and scientific aspects of HIV infection and vaccination are coupled with the cultural differences throughout areas of the world where AIDS is prevalent and AIDS research is conducted, the uniform application of ethical principles in the conduct of an AIDS vaccine trial becomes considerably more complicated.

To some extent, the CIOMS guidelines anticipate this. Their stated purpose is to amend the principles of the Declaration of Helsinki "to suggest how [these principles] may be applied in the special circumstances of many technologically developing countries."[5] There is a tension in the guidelines, however, between the desire for culturally relevant application of ethical principles on the one hand and the belief that "the ethical implications of research involving human subjects are identical in principle wherever the work is undertaken" on the other. If trials of HIV vaccines are to take place worldwide, this tension must be resolved. Are there justifiable differences in research ethics in different sociocultural settings? How are ethical concerns to be met in the face of a pandemic? Is it possible to distinguish "medical imperialism" from legitimate reasons for conducting an AIDS vaccine trial in Africa?

DESIGN OF AN AIDS VACCINE TRIAL

Though several types of AIDS vaccines are being considered, investigation has been largely directed towards using recombinant DNA technology to produce HIV proteins or insert portions of the HIV genome into other viruses (such as the vaccinia virus used by the Zagury group).[6] A protocol for evaluating candidate vaccines would involve: (1) preparing the vaccine in sufficient quantity and purity; (2) testing in animals to see if it results in antibodies able to neutralize HIV *in vitro*; (3) testing in nonhuman primates to establish the ability of the vaccine to protect against subsequent challenge with HIV; (4) testing in a small group of humans (members of AIDS risk groups or others) to evaluate short-term safety and immunogenicity (a phase I trial); (5) determining ideal dose and spacing of the vaccine through larger safety and immunogenicity trials (phase II); and (6) determining protection against HIV infection through large scale efficacy trials involving as many as 1,000 to 2,000 subjects (phase III).[7] A phase III trial would be of the randomized, double-blind, controlled type.

The epidemiology of HIV in Africa will raise special considerations in the scientific design of a trial that will, in turn, affect its ethical design. The ethical design of an AIDS vaccine trial in Africa, that is, must be informed by the scientific parameters of the research and of the study population in the familiar interaction between science and ethics.

As we shall see, however, attention must be focused on specific ethical and cultural constraints prevailing in settings where AIDS research is conducted. Even if the epidemiological and scientific parameters of HIV infection were the same in research settings throughout the world, the proper ethical design of AIDS vaccine trials would still vary with the ethical and cultural parameters of the research populations.

ASSEMBLING A SUITABLE STUDY GROUP

Participants in a phase III trial would have to be followed and assessed for HIV infection through serial testing and examination. Such follow-up is time-consuming and expensive because of the variable expression and long latency period of HIV infection. Proper evaluation of a vaccine will require a large number of subjects drawn from a suitable population. The ease of assembling the requisite number of appropriate subjects and the relatively low cost of conducting a trial in Africa (because of typically low wages) have been explicitly identified by some investigators as benefits of conducting AIDS research in Africa.[8]

Africa has also been offered as a vaccine test site on the basis of certain scientific considerations. Specifically, subjects in a phase III trial would have to meet two important technical requirements: they would have to be free of HIV infection at the beginning of the trial, and they would nevertheless have to be *at risk* for HIV infection.

Subjects must initially be free of HIV infection to assess the vaccine's ability to prevent subsequent infection; a person already infected with HIV who received the vaccine would falsely be identified as a vaccine "failure," that is, as someone in whom the vaccine was ineffective. In addition, absence of HIV infection is necessary to avoid the possibility of serious complications that might arise if an HIV-infected

individual were given a recombinant viral vaccine. An individual infected with HIV and suffering from subtle immunocompromise could develop a serious infection with the non-HIV virus used in the vaccine (such as generalized vaccinia).

At present, determining freedom from HIV infection would be accomplished through testing for HIV antibodies. But freedom from infection is not guaranteed by a single test showing absence of HIV antibodies: the test result may simply be inaccurate—scientific tests are not infallible and there will be false negative results—or the research subject may, in fact, be infected with HIV, but have not yet developed antibodies.[9] Most people infected with HIV develop antibodies within six to twelve months if they are to develop them at all. Research subjects would thus have to be retested at a six to twelve-month interval to assure lack of prior exposure. Of course, during this interval, the study population would ideally need to avoid further exposure to HIV, which could lead to infection that might escape detection at the second testing.

The second requirement, being at risk for HIV infection, is necessary to assess the vaccine's ability to prevent HIV infection: a study population at no risk of infection whatsoever would not permit evaluation of vaccine efficacy since no one at all, in either the vaccine or control groups, would become infected.

Two aspects of the epidemiology of HIV infection in Africa facilitate meeting this requirement. First, the predominant mode of transmission of HIV in Africa is thought to be via heterosexual sex; the identified risk factors include having a large number of sexual partners, having sex with prostitutes, being a prostitute, or being a sexual partner of an infected person.[10] Second, estimates of HIV antibody seroprevalence for various sub-Saharan countries range from 0.5 percent to 8.8 percent for healthy controls and 14.6 percent to 55.6 percent for risk groups such as prostitutes.[11] This high prevalence implies high risk of infection for uninfected members of the society that would allow a trial to detect a difference between the vaccinated and unvaccinated (control) study groups with greater ease in less time. Moreover, the substantial prevalence of HIV infection in the general heterosexual population further facilitates assembling an appropriately large study group.

Thus, the benefit of conducting a phase III AIDS vaccine trial in Africa (because of the high risk) would be at least partially offset by the likely increase in adverse effects attributable to vaccination (because of the high prevalence and consequent increase in the number of falsely negative individuals included in the trial).

Of course, the benefit here is to the conduct of the investigation in the form of a speedier, more accurate trial, and hence to the investigators and society-at-large. The cost, however, is borne by the research subjects. This problem could be minimized— but not eliminated—by a scrupulous testing policy aimed at excluding HIV-seropositive individuals from the study. However, achieving this objective would require a certain degree of intrusion upon the privacy of study subjects to ensure that they abstain from risky behaviors in the six-month interval between the two required HIV tests. Moreover, a degree of accuracy in testing beyond that traditionally seen in laboratories in the developing world would have to be assured.

A final scientific concern in assembling a suitable study group regards the applicability of the findings. The pattern of infection in Africa may reflect as yet unknown biological factors in the population at risk or in the virus that may require testing a vaccine in Africa simply to evaluate vaccine efficacy in circumstances that may be unique. Since an effective vaccine would be of great utility in this continent, some trials in Africa would presumably be essential.

RISKS AND CONSENTS

Eligible research subjects would have to consent to participation in the trial, which would require researchers to provide information regarding both benefits and risks. The salient personal benefit to participation in an AIDS vaccine trial is the possibility of gaining immunity to a deadly infection. An effective vaccine would be very beneficial for society-at-large, but this is not ordinarily seen as a direct benefit to the individual.

The risks involved in trial participation are significant, however. For HIV subunit or recombinant viral vaccines, possible direct adverse consequences of participation in a vaccine trial include: (1) serious infection (generalized vaccinia, for example) in the case of undetected HIV infection in recipients of a viral vaccine; (2) mild or severe systemic reactions to the vaccine (headache, severe febrile reactions, convulsions); and (3) hypersensitivity reactions. A further hazard of such research is the possible increase in risky behaviors because participants feel relatively protected. Finally, it is theoretically possible that receiving one type of an AIDS vaccine might preclude immunization with a more effective vaccine developed subsequently.

The need to test for HIV infection both at the onset and during the conduct of the trial creates a further problem peculiar to participating in an AIDS vaccine trial: that of learning one's antibody status. Some have argued that being HIV positive is burdensome knowledge that should not be imposed.[12] Thus, people *excluded* from vaccine trial participation because of HIV antibody positivity might suffer through acquiring knowledge of their status. For persons *enrolled* in the trial, the necessary surveillance of HIV antibody status might also ultimately result in knowledge of HIV infection that the subject would otherwise have avoided.

Research subjects would also have to be advised that as a consequence of participation they will become HIV seropositive by conventional screening methods. Seroconversion may, in turn, lead to discrimination against the subject. This eventuality has led to some innovative measures. In a trial approved but not yet under way in the U.S., subjects will be issued both a certificate testifying to their participation in the trial and a copy of their Western blot results showing a characteristic pattern identified as being a result of participation and not infection.[13]

BENEFICENT TREATMENT OF SUBJECTS

The risks involved in the trial of an AIDS vaccine mandate beneficent treatment of participants. In the context of human subjects research, beneficence has found two complementary expressions: "(1) do not harm, and (2) maximize possible benefits and minimize possible harms."[14] For the benefits to outweigh the risks in the trial of an AIDS vaccine, an individual would have to be at some risk of HIV infection. The necessity of being at risk thus has both scientific and ethical import.

But beneficent treatment of AIDS vaccine trial subjects has several aspects

beyond a suitable risk/benefit ratio. Volunteers must be informed that vaccination does not provide license to engage in risky behavior, and must be counseled regarding "safe sex" practices. In Africa, counseling should at a minimum consist of strong advice to decrease the number of sexual partners, to avoid prostitutes, and to abstain from sex with individuals known to be infected. Counseling, along with informing participants of their negative antibody status, would likely result in a decrease in risky behavior.[15]

In advanced trials to test vaccine efficacy, however, these interventions could diminish the ability of the study to detect a difference between true vaccine recipients and controls by decreasing the incidence of HIV infection in *all* participants for reasons *unrelated* to vaccine status. To circumvent this problem, a larger study group would be required to detect the relatively smaller measured influence of the vaccine. But increasing the size of the study group has attendant adverse consequences, including the increased risk of exposing more individuals to the experimental vaccine and increased cost. Thus, there will be unavoidable conflict between research design and ethics. This conflict should be resolved in favor of beneficent treatment of subjects: to minimize risk to individual research subjects, study size should be increased and all participants should be counseled to avoid risky behaviors.

Deliberately counseling all participants to avoid risky behaviors will likely also increase the time required to complete the study since researchers would have to wait longer to detect sufficient cases of HIV infection for the results to be significant. This necessity must be seen in light of the considerable pressure to develop an effective HIV vaccine rapidly.

The interpersonal nature of HIV transmission may create an additional ethical problem pertaining to the beneficent treatment of research subjects. The unit of analysis in AIDS vaccine trials, some have suggested, should *not* be the individual.[16] Given that simply participating in AIDS research may offer some benefits, especially if participation serves to lower risky behavior, researchers may be obliged to recruit, insofar as possible, the sexual—and where applicable, needle-sharing—partners of research subjects.

Indeed, there is presently a study under way in Africa that involves deliberate tracking of HIV-discordant couples to determine the natural history and transmissibility of the disease where condom use is the sole preventive measure.[17] The ethics of such a study are questionable, *unless* the seronegative member of the couple is properly informed of the risk continued sex with his or her partner poses despite condom use. The argument that researchers studying progression of HIV infection in groups of individuals are merely observing events that would have taken place regardless of the researchers' presence—a so-called study in nature—is untenable. The mere presence of the researchers disturbs the "natural setting" (certainly it does so in this case since condoms and recommendations regarding their use are distributed). Moreover, physician researchers have incumbent upon them the duty to protect the health of their subjects, even if in so doing they compromise their research.[18]

ETHICAL STANDARDS IN CROSS-CULTURAL PERSPECTIVE

Consideration of Africa as a test site should transcend the standard scientific and ethical concerns outlined above and should incorporate broader concern arising from the conduct of research in disparate socio-cultural settings. The conduct of a vaccine trial in Africa will highlight not only practical and scientific differences, but also ethical and cultural differences between Africa and the West.

Soliciting informed consent to participate in research is one of the major areas where variation in ethical standards will be encountered. The Western principle of informed consent is predicated upon the notions of respect for persons as individuals and as autonomous agents.[19] This is at variance with more relational definitions of the person found in other societies, especially in Africa, which stress the embeddedness of the individual within society and define a person by his or her relations to others.[20]

From this variation in the definition of a person arise important practical implications. Where the notion of persons as individuals is not dominant, the consent process may shift from the individual to the family or to the community.[21] It may be necessary to secure the consent of a subject's family or social group instead of or in addition to the consent of the subject himself.

Culturally-defined views of personhood may also find expression in determinations of who is deemed able to give informed consent for others. This is acknowledged in the CIOMS guidelines:

> Where individual members of a community do not have the necessary awareness of the implications of participation in an experiment to give adequately informed consent directly to the investigators, it is desirable that the decision whether or not to participate should be elicited through the intermediary of a trusted community leader.[22]

There will be considerable variation by culture as to who is acknowledged to be a "community leader" and whether such an individual will meet the investigator's expectation regarding who can appropriately give proxy consent.

The principle of community leader consent may be the only alternative—however unsatisfactory by Western standards—to individual consent in many cases where beneficial research is essential. This alternative may not necessarily be ethically incorrect for the society of which the research subject is a member. Indeed, the desire of research subjects to cooperate with respected local authorities can be instrumental in the success of research in many settings.[23] His or her obedience to a local authority should not be abused, however, by a Western researcher to the detriment of a Third World subject of research. A researcher must respect an individual's manifest refusal to participate, even if consent has been elicited from some other person or group.

Western investigators should also appreciate that what appears to them to be coercion may, from the perspective of local inhabitants, represent cooperation and identification with the group to which the individual belongs. This does not relieve Western investigators of the responsibility to avoid coercion arising from their *own* actions. They must be aware that it is difficult to avoid coercing subjects in most settings where clinical investigation in the developing world is conducted. African subjects with relatively little understanding of medical aspects of research participation, indisposed toward resisting the suggestions of Western doctors, perhaps operating under the mistaken notion that they are being treated, and possibly receiving some ancillary benefits from participation in the research, are very susceptible to coercion. Their vulnerability warrants greater care in procuring consent and necessitates

greater sensitivity to protect this class of research subjects.

It is clear that the type of consent practiced in the West, with the signing of an informed consent document containing medical terms, is inappropriate for illiterate or semi-literate peoples. Indeed, signing or even thumb-printing a consent form may be deemed highly suspect in certain societies, as may a physician's "excessive" explanation of the purpose of the research (which may be taken as indicative of some hidden, detrimental purpose). In some cultural settings it may be extremely difficult to convey an accurate understanding of the idea of randomization or other essential scientific concepts.[24] Moreover, there may be cultural variations in the understanding of disease, at odds with Western scientific notions, that make truly *informed* consent impossible.[25] In the context of an AIDS vaccine trial in Africa, the foregoing concerns will allow for significant variability in the information conveyed in obtaining the subject's consent. Nevertheless, investigators must seek to explain the purpose of the research in culturally relevant terms.

The principle of respect for persons is also ordinarily taken to imply a respect for individual privacy and confidentiality. In some societies, as we have seen, it may be necessary that this individual claim yield to a somewhat larger group, as with, for example, informing a husband of his wife's participation in a research endeavor. Yet, insofar as feasible, confidentiality should be respected. One example of unnecessary violation of this principle that has led to irritation on the part of some African officials is the practice of publishing photographs of African AIDS patients in the Western press.[26]

A relational concept of personhood may also result in ethical decisions that, by

Western standards, unduly favor the interests of society at large over those of the individual. Western ethical standards generally accord considerable import to the welfare of the individual in the conduct of research. The Declaration of Helsinki, for example, states that "concern for the interests of the subject must always prevail over the interests of science and society. . . ."[27] The Belmont Report, an ethical standard developed within the U.S., more explicitly acknowledges the difficulties in balancing the rights of the individual versus those of society and states that ethical codes "have required that risks to subjects be outweighed by the sum of both the anticipated benefit to the subject, if any, and the anticipated benefit to society. . . ." It notes, however, that "in balancing these different elements, the risks and benefits affecting the immediate research subject will normally carry special weight."[28]

The calculus of such balancing will be different in different sociocultural settings. In some situations, cultural expectations may be that the anticipated benefit to society will justifiably outweigh the anticipated risk to the individual. Societal values may be such that the interests of the subject do not take precedence over the interests of society. Thus, furthering the interest of society at large may not necessarily compromise the rights and interests of the individual research participant within the particular value system the individual espouses. Even more fundamentally, an African may perceive that it is "difficult to see how the interests of the subject conflict with the interests of the society except, of course, if the society is not his own."[29] That is, the interest of the subject and of society are necessarily congruent. Problems arise only if the values and expectations of a society of which the individual is not a member

are imposed upon him. In this light, imposing Western ethical values upon African research subjects is inappropriate.

Considerations of beneficent treatment of research subjects are also modified by cultural and social concerns. In developing countries, resources are often so scarce as to force particularly difficult decisions regarding allocation.[30] Moreover, assessment of the acceptability of a particular medical intervention will differ in developed as compared with developing countries as a result of different patterns of illness and different medical and practical constraints acting upon the population. Risk/benefit assessments may yield different outcomes, and hence different acceptabilities, depending on the society.[31] AIDS may be so widespread and deadly a disease in Africa that a higher degree of research risk must perforce be tolerated to deal with the problem, and this may well be socially sanctioned.

But while greater risk may be tolerated in Africa, this does not mean that Westerners should indiscriminately benefit from research conducted in Africa if Africans are systematically subjected to excess research risks with the prospect of deriving but little benefit. This would violate the principle of justice. This principle involves a sense of "fairness in distribution" or "what is deserved," and as applied to human subjects research is usually taken to address the question of who should receive the benefits of the research and who should bear the burdens.

Under the principle of justice, research subjects should be chosen "for reasons directly related to the problem being studied," and not "because of their easy availability, their compromised position, or their manipulability."[32] Thus, the practical concerns that make an AIDS vaccine trial easier to conduct in Africa do not alone constitute sufficient justification to use Africans as subjects. Only the scientific concerns related directly to the problem of establishing the ability of a vaccine to prevent HIV infection are relevant.

The principle of justice also requires that those who stand to benefit from the research should, in fact, be those to bear the burden. Much of the world stands to gain from the development of an effective AIDS vaccine and the burden of research risks should therefore be fairly distributed, as should the benefits. In Central and Western Africa much of the population at large stands to gain by introduction of an effective vaccine. Yet economic constraints may well prevent even moderately extensive distribution of a beneficial vaccine in Africa, should one become available. The benefits to Africans are thus only hypothetical unless there is a financial commitment by the developed world to provide the vaccine. In this light, it would be frankly unethical to subject Africans to a disproportionate share of the research risks. A contingency of any trial of an AIDS vaccine in Africa by Western scientists should thus be to provide access to the technology once it is developed—possibly in the form of free or subsidized vaccine.

RESEARCH ETHICS IN THE FACE OF A PANDEMIC

Conduct of research throughout the world on a pandemic disease—which perforce occurs in disparate sociocultural settings—forces reevaluation of a uniform, international view of research ethics. The straightforward application of the ethical standards across cultural barriers is problematic.[33] Confronting AIDS will require a rethinking of a narrow, parochial formulation of ethics.

This is not to assert that standards for research ethics should be culturally relative, but rather that they should be culturally *relevant*. Some ethical standards can and should be met worldwide. An important challenge to Western scientists conducting AIDS vaccine trials is to conform to certain minimum ethical standards regardless of the setting: (1) The trial should be of suitable design and scientific merit; (2) it should involve the free, and where possible, informed consent of the participants; (3) all participants should benefit from proper counseling regarding avoidance of risky behaviors; (4) due consideration should be given to the risks of research participation, using the highest standard of risk/benefit analysis possible; and (5) the countries participating in the study should be allowed fair access to any vaccine arising from the research.

An equally important—and possibly more difficult—challenge to investigators conducting AIDS vaccine trials throughout the world is to be culturally sensitive. Proper conduct of an AIDS vaccine trial must be informed not only by the epidemiology and biology of HIV infection in different settings, but also by the ethical norms and cultural constraints prevailing in such settings. Beyond certain minimum standards, there should be tolerance of variability. Variability, as we have seen, is especially apt to arise in the informational content of consent, in the acceptability of proxy consent, and in the tolerance of an increased risk/benefit ratio.

What is essential is not that the research meet the same ethical standard worldwide. What is essential is that the research manifest a culturally sensitive and ethically sophisticated concern for the well-being of subjects throughout the world.

ACKNOWLEDGMENTS

I am grateful to Robert J. Levine, M.D., Larry Gostin, J.D., Richard Cash, M.D., Erika Zuckerman, and especially to Allan M. Brandt, Ph.D., for their helpful criticism of earlier drafts of this manuscript. This work was partially supported by a grant from the Harvard School of Public Health Alumni Association.

NOTES

1. Daniel Zagury et al., "Immunization Against AIDS in Humans," Nature 326 (1987), 249–50. See also, "First Human AIDS Vaccine Trial Goes Ahead Without Official OK," Nature 325 (1987), 290.
2. Alfred J. Fortin, "The Politics of AIDS in Kenya," Third World Quarterly 9:3 (1987), 906–19; "Special SIDA: Des Millions D'Africains Condamnés á Mort?" Jeune Afrique Magazine (February 1987), 81–93 (at 87). See also, "Who Will Volunteer for an AIDS Vaccine?" The New York Times, April 15, 1986, C1: "AIDS: Racist Myths, Hard Facts," Afric-Asia (May 1987), 50–55.
3. "Zaire, Ending Secrecy, Attacks AIDS Openly," The New York Times, February 8, 1987, A1.
4. Council for International World Organizations of Medical Sciences and the World Health Organization, Proposed International Guidelines for Biomedical Research Involving Human Subjects (Geneva: CIOMS, 1982), 32.
5. CIOMS, Proposed International Guidelines, 23.
6. Wendy K. Mariner and Robert C. Gallo, "Getting to Market; The Scientific and Legal Climate for Developing an AIDS Vaccine," Law, Medicine & Health Care 15:1–2 (1987), 17–25.
7. Donald P. Francis and John C. Petricciani, "The Prospects for and Pathways Toward a Vaccine for AIDS," New England Journal of Medicine 313:25 (1985), 1586–90.
8. "Zaire, Ending Secrecy, Attacks AIDS Openly."
9. For the accuracy of HIV tests, see: Michael J. Bany, Paul D. Cleary, and Harvey V. Fineberg, "Screening for HIV Infection: Risks, Benefits, and the Burden of Proof," Law, Medicine & Health Care 14:5–6 (1986) 259–67.
10. Thomas C. Quinn et al., "AIDS in Africa: An Epidemiologic Paradigm," Science 234 (1986),

955–63; Gerald H. Friedland and Robert S. Klein, "Tansmission of the Human Immunodeficiency Virus," New England Journal of Medicine 317:18 (1987), 1125–35. Regarding heterosexual transmission in Africa, see Peter Piot, et al., "Acquired Immunodeficiency Syndrome in Heterosexual Population in Zaire," The Lancet ii (1984), 65–69; N. Clumeck et al., "Heterosexual Promiscuity Among African Patients with AIDS," New England Journal of Medicine 313:3 (1985), 182; Jonathan M. Mann et al., "Prevalence of HTLV-III/LAV in Household Contacts of Patients with Confirmed AIDS and Controls in Kinshasa, Zaire," Journal of the American Medical Association 256:6 (1986), 721–24.
11. Phyllis J. Kanki et al., "Human T-Lymphotropic Virus Type 4 and the Human Immunodeficiency Virus in West Africa," Science 236 (1987) 827–31; Joan K. Kreiss et al., "AIDS Virus Infection in Nairobi Prostitutes," New England Journal of Medicine 314:7 (1986), 414–18; Jonathan Mann et al., "Condom Use and HIV Infection Among Prostitutes in Zaire," New England Journal of Medicine 316:6 (1987), 345; and Phylllis J. Kanki et al., "Absence of Antibodies to HIV2/HTLV4 in Six Central African Nations," AIDS Research and Human Retroviruses, Phyllis J. Kanki, ed., in press.
12. Alvin Novick, Nancy Neveloff Dubler, and Sheldon H. Landesman, "Do Research Subjects Have the Right Not to Know Their HIV Antibody Test Results?" IRB: A Review of Human Subjects Research 8:5 (September/October 1986), 6–9.
13. Beverly Merz, "HIV Vaccine Approved for Clinical Trials," Journal of the American Medical Association 258:11 (1987), 1433–34.
14. National Commission for the Protection of Human Subjects of Biomedical and Behavioral Research, The Belmont Report: Ethical Principles and Guidelines for the Protection of Human Subjects of Research (Washington, DC: Department of Health, Education and Welfare, 1979), 4.
15. Don C. Des Jarlais and Samuel R. Friedman, "AIDS Prevention Among IV Drug Users: Potential Conflicts Between Research Design and Ethics," IRB: A Review of Human Subjects Research 9:1 (January/February 1987), 6–8.
16. Des Jarlais and Friedman, "AIDS Prevention Among IV Drug Users."
17. "Zaire, Ending Secrecy, Attacks AIDS Openly."
18. See, for example, Allan M. Brandt, "Racism and Research: The Case of the Tuskegee Syphilis Study," Hastings Center Report 8:6 (December 1978), 21–29.
19. Belmont Report, 4.
20. Willy De Craemer, "A Cross-Cultural Perspective on Personhood," Millbank Memorial Fund Quarterly 61:1 (1983), 19–34; Renee C. Fox and David P. Willis, "Personhood, Medicine, and American Society," Millbank Memorial Fund

Quarterly 61:1 (1983), 127–47; J.M. Janzen, *The Quest for Therapy in Lower Zaire* (Berkeley. The University of California Press, 1978), 169, 189.

21. See, for example, H. Tristram Engelhardt, "Bioethics in the People's Republic of China," *Hastings Center Report* 10:2 (April 1980), 7–10.
22. CIOMS, *Proposed International Guidelines,* 26–27; see also p. 24.
23. See Robert J. Levine, "Validity of Consent Procedures in Technologically Developing Countries" in *Human Experimentation and Medical Ethics,* Z. Bankowski and N. Howard-Jones, eds. (Geneva: CIOMS, 1982), 16–30. There is potential for abuse of authority if a community leader acts to the detriment of his or her constituency; see, for example, Francis Moore Lappe, Joseph Collins, and David Kinley, *Aid as Obstacle* (San Francisco: Food First, 1981), at questions 7, 11.
24. M. Beiser, "Ethics in Cross Cultural Perspective," in E.F. Foulks *et al., Current Perspectives in Cultural Psychiatry* (New York: Spectrum Publications, 1977), 125–37.
25. Ebun O. Ekunwe and Ross Kessel, "Informed Consent in the Developing World," *Hastings Center Report* 14:3 (June, 1984), 23–24.
26. "Racist Bigotry on AIDS," *African Concord,* June 4, 1987, 25. See also Margaret Mead, "Research with Human Beings: A Model Derived from Anthropological Field Practice," *Daedalus* 98 (1969), 361–86.
27. World Medical Assembly, "Declaration of Helsinki," revised 1975, in CIOMS, *Proposed International Guidelines,* Appendix 5: principle I.5.
28. *Belmont Report,* 7.
29. O.O. Ajayi, "Taboos and Clinical Research in West Africa," *Journal of Medical Ethics* 6:1 (1980) 61–63.
30. John F. Kilner, "Who Shall Be Saved? An African Answer," *Hastings Center Report* 14:3 (June 1984), 19–22.
31. See, for example, Carol Levine, "Depo-Provera and Contraceptive Risk: A Case Study of Values in Conflict," *Hastings Center Report* 9:4 (August 1979), 8–11.
32. *Belmont Report,* 5.
33. Regarding international variation in ethical decision-making, see, for example, Arthur I. Eidelman, K.N. Siva Subramanian, and Rihito Kimura, "Caring for Newborns: Three World Views," *Hastings Center Report* 16:4 (August 1986), 18–23; "Biomedical Ethics: A Multinational View," *Hastings Center Report* 17:3 (June 1987), Special Supplement.

QUESTIONS: THE AIDS EPIDEMIC

1. Harris and Holm contend that if a virus is airborne its moral status changes. Indicate why Harris and Holm think that an airborne, as opposed to a nonairborne, virus may license certain types of action. Do you find this plausible? Why?

2. Karen Clifford and Russell Iuculano make an economic argument for mandatory AIDS testing. Of what relevance is economics to ethics? Of what relevance is economics to applied ethics? What criteria might we use to decide when economic considerations are relevant?

3. Great Britain has national health coverage and, on occasion, denies certain treatment to people who have caused their own health problems. For example, an alcoholic man was denied an organ transplant because his drinking had caused his need for an organ transplant and because he was still drinking. Of what relevance is one's personal activity in deciding whether or not one is deserving of medical treatment? Do we have a responsibility to take care of ourselves and to avoid risky behavior? Do we have a responsibility to take care of those who refuse to take care of themselves?

4. What are Christine Pierce's objections to natural law arguments? Do you think that natural law arguments are prima facie unjustified? What might the rejection of natural law arguments imply for environmental ethics?

5. David A. Conway discusses some of the tensions between protecting citizens and individual liberty that result from paternalistic approaches in ethics. How

might these tensions be avoided by emphasizing one's responsibilities rather than one's liberties?

6. Carol A. Tauer discusses the results of mandatory AIDS testing and the many ends to which this information may be put. Do the medical ethics issues of clashing rights adequately address the AIDS crisis? What other approaches might be more appropriate? For instance, does one have the responsibility to get tested (as opposed to the right to refuse testing) if he or she is in a high-risk group? If one tests positive, does that entail special responsibilities to not exercise certain liberties?

7. Nicholas A. Christakis brings many interesting ethical issues to the fore. Given the cultural differences, should Western researchers refrain from doing research in Africa until sufficient consent (sufficient consent as required in Africa) is given? Does Christakis think that sufficient consent will justify such research? What more is needed?

SUPPLEMENTARY READINGS: THE AIDS EPIDEMIC

ALMOND, BRENDA, and CAROLE ULANOWSKY. "HIV and Pregnancy," *Hastings Center Report,* March–April 1990.

ARRAS, JOHN D. "Noncompliance in AIDS Research." *Hastings Center Report,* September–October 1990.

BATTIN, MARGARET PABST. "Going Early, Going Late: The Rationality of Decisions about Suicide in AIDS." *Journal of Medical Ethics,* vol. 19 (6), December 1994.

BELL, NORA KISER. "Women and AIDS: Too Little, Too Late?" *Hypatia,* vol. 4 (3), Fall 1989.

CHAMBERS, DONALD. "AIDS Testing: An Insurers Viewpoint." In *AIDS: Ethics and Public Policy,* Pierce and VanDeVeer, editors, Belmont, CA: Wadsworth, 1988.

CHILDRESS, JAMES. "Mandatory HIV Screening and Testing." In *AIDS and Ethics,* Reamer, editor. New York: Columbia University Press, 1993.

CRISP, ROGER. "Autonomy, Welfare and the Treatment of AIDS." *Journal of Medical Ethics,* vol. 15, June 1989.

DANIELS, NORMAN. "Duty to Treat or Right to Refuse." *The Hastings Center Report,* vol. 21, March–April 1991.

GRADY, CHRISTINE. "HIV Preventive Vaccine Research: Selected Ethical Issues." *Journal of Medical Ethics,* vol. 19 (6), December 1994.

HOSHIO, KAZUSAMA. "HIV+/AIDS Related Bioethical Issues in Japan." *Bioethics,* vol. 9 (3–4), July 1995.

KOPELMAN, LORETTA M. "Informed Consent and Anonymous Tissue Samples: The Case of HIV Seroprevalence Studies." *Journal of Medical Ethics,* vol. 19 (6), December, 1994.

MAYO, DAVID. "AIDS, Quarantines and Noncompliant Positives." In *AIDS: Ethics and Public Policy,* Pierce and VanDeVeer, editors, Belmont, CA: Wadsworth, 1988.

MURPHY, JULIAN. *The Constructed Body: AIDS, Reproductive Technology, and Ethics.* Albany: SUNY Press, 1995.

MURPHY, TIMOTHY F. *Ethics in an Epidemic: AIDS, Morality, and Culture.* Berkeley: University of California Press, 1994.

RIDSDALE, LEONE. "When Keeping Secrets May Cause Harm." *Journal of Medical Ethics,* vol. 16, June 1990.

SCHOEMAN, FREDERICK D. "AIDS and Privacy." In *AIDS and Ethics*, Reamer, editor: New York: Columbia University Press, 1993.

SPOHN, WILLIAM C. "The Moral Dimensions of AIDS." *Theological Studies,* vol. 49, March 1988.

TAPPIN, D.M., and F. COCKBURN. "Ethics and Ethics Committees: HIV Serosurveillance in Scotland." *Journal of Medicine and Philosophy,* vol. 18, March 1992.

WALTERS, LEROY. "Ethical Issues in the Prevention and Treatment of AIDS." *Science,* vol. 239, February 5, 1988.

WAYMACK, MARK. "AIDS, Ethics and Health Insurance." *Business & Professional Ethics Journal,* vol. 10, Spring 1991.

ZION, DEBORAH. "Can Communities Protect Autonomy: Ethical Dilemmas in HIV Preventative Drug Trials." *Cambridge Quarterly of Healthcare Ethics*, vol. 4 (4), Fall 1995.

VIII

ABORTION

In their remarkable joint decision, Justices Sandra Day O'Connor, Anthony M. Kennedy and David H. Souter directly addressed the American people, clearly seeking their support for a compromise legal position . . . the three conservative justices turned middle-of-the-roaders . . . noted that a few times each generation the "Court's interpretation of the Constitution calls the contending sides of a national controversy to end their national division by accepting a common mandate rooted in the Constitution."

—St. Louis Post Dispatch[1]

Abortion has been one of the most controversial issues in the United States over the last 25 years. While many people have an exclusively emotional reaction to this issue, there are many important philosophical questions that need to be addressed. In this section, our essays survey the three main positions that have been taken in the debate and provide philosophical defense for these positions. In addition, we turn to other cultures and find that there has been substantial consensus rather than hostility on this issue.

The liberal position on abortion was well articulated in the U.S. Supreme Court's 1973 ruling in *Roe* v. *Wade*. An overwhelming majority ruled that abortion constituted a "fundamental right" of women. Until the fetus is viable (able to live outside the womb), the court ruled that the woman's right to decide what to do with her own body was paramount. After the fetus attained viability (during the third trimester of gestation), then restrictions could be placed on abortion rights, because only at that point was there a competing (human) right. Abortion was seen as one of many rights to privacy, along with the right to obtain and use birth control devices. These rights were considered to be akin to the rights against unreasonable search and seizure and to speech and peaceable assembly.

The conservative position generally regards all abortions as morally unjustifiable. The fetus is regarded as a full-fledged human person from the moment of conception. And since the fetus is regarded by conservatives as a paradigmatic innocent human being, its rights are thought to outweigh the woman's right to control her body. Many who hold the conservative position also hold that any attempt to interfere with the natural process of gestation and birth, even many forms of birth control, is morally unjustifiable. The paramount concern is for the fetus's right to life, a right so important that it overrides all other considerations. Conservatives argue that if a child is unwanted, adoption rather than abortion is the only morally acceptable solution.

Various difficulties plague both sides of the abortion dispute in the United States. Many conservatives have long been bothered by cases of pregnancy due to rape or incest, as well as pregnancies that threaten the life of the pregnant woman. Liberals have been bothered by the issue of whether, on their own principles, they are committed to justifying some forms of infanticide, such as the killing of greatly deformed newborn babies. A consideration of such problem cases has caused some people to adopt one of many moderate, compromise positions on abortion, accepting some types of abortion while also prohibiting some others.

The recent U.S. Supreme Court decision in *Casey* v. *Planned Parenthood*, referred to above, recognizes a compromise position. Abortion is not regarded as a fundamental right, one which would override most others; but neither is the fetus considered to have an absolute right to life. Instead, abortion is considered to be a relatively important right, but one which can be restricted, as long as the restrictions do not place an "undue burden" on the woman in question. This compromise position is far from being a consensus position in America today, but perhaps it will become so. Yet even if this compromise is accepted by the vast majority, this does not resolve the question of the *moral* justifiability of abortion.

John T. Noonan defends a conservative position of abortion from the standpoint of Catholic theology. Arguing that none of the criteria popularly invoked—viability, experience, quickening, attitudes of adults, and social visibility—to establish when a fetus is human prove to be satisfactory, Noonan claims that the only nonarbitrary basis for determining when a fetus is in possession of the right to life is located at the moment of its conception. For this is the point at which it acquires the full human genetic code and the potential to develop into a full-fledged human being—as opposed to a mere nonfertilized egg or spermatozoa which have very little chance of developing into full-fledged human beings on their own. Noonan, however, concedes that abortion is permissible on grounds of self-defense.

Mary Anne Warren is quite clear in arguing that only human persons have strong rights, and that the notion of personhood needs to be philosophically examined before a decision is reached about whether the fetus is a human person whose rights can override the pregnant woman's rights. Warren argues that there are five features that are central to the concept of human personhood: consciousness, reasoning, self-motivated activity, capacity to communicate, and self-awareness. These are the features that make a being a member of a human community. Fetuses do not generally have enough of these features to be considered human persons even though they may resemble human persons in other respects. Fetuses are merely potential persons and as such have merely potential rights, not the sort of rights that could override a woman's right to control her own body.

Don Marquis takes the opposing, conservative position that what is important about a life is its future possibilities, and that what is so tragic about killing is that it deprives someone of this future. Marquis contends that if this is understood as the main criterion of a valuable life, then fetuses share this feature in common with adult human beings. And what makes it wrong to kill adult human beings is also what makes it wrong to kill fetuses. Marquis thus concludes that most abortions are morally unjustified, and this is true no matter what the current consensus is about abortion.

Christine Overall also provides a challenge to the extreme conservative position by presenting the case of multiple fetuses growing in the same womb where it is highly unlikely that any can be carried to term unless at least one is aborted. If all fetuses have an absolute right to life, how are we to resolve this puzzling case? Overall argues that in this case an antiabortion stance is actually contrary to the conservative prescription to support pregnancy to term. The women who seek abortions in these multiple fetus cases generally do so with a hope of continuing, not ending, their pregnancy. A consideration of such cases certainly makes it harder to hold an unbending conservative position.

In addition, Ren-Zong Qiu, Chun-Zhi Wang, and Yuan Gu raise the question of population control in certain societies as a possible basis for justifying even some late-term abortions. In many parts of the world, hunger and starvation are intimately linked with birth control measures, and abortion is one of the many forms of birth control. It is positions like these that profoundly worry conservatives on the abortion issue. They are afraid that late-term abortion will become an accepted form of birth control. However, Qiu, Wang, and Gu suggest that in many cultures women are so stigmatized if they become pregnant that they will find it difficult to admit their condition until it is too late to have anything but a late-term abortion. And adoption may not always be an alternative, especially if control of population growth is considered a vital social goal.

William LaFleur points us toward a society that has largely reached a consensus about abortion. In contemporary Japan, a strong emphasis on conservative family values has had an effect opposite to that which has occurred in America. Abortion is regarded as a necessary feature in assuring that families will have only those members who are wanted. Interestingly, the consensus reached in Japan is one that is tempered by the feeling that abortion is a tragic necessity. No matter where a consensus compromise is reached on abortion, there will probably always be this tragic dimension to our choices on the abortion issue.

—Kai Wong

NOTE

1. *St. Louis Post Dispatch*, July 1, 1992, p. 12A, concerning *Casey* v. *Planned Parenthood*.

An Almost Absolute
Value in History

John T. Noonan, Jr.

John T. Noonan is a professor of law at the University of California. Berkeley. Among his books are
Contraception: A History of Its Treatment by the Catholic Theologians and Canonists *(1965) and*
A Private Choice: Abortion in America in the Seventies *(1979).*

   Noonan advances a defense of the conservative position on abortion from the standpoint of Catholicism. He argues that the fetus acquires the right to life at the moment of its conception when it receives its human genetic codes from its parents. Moreover, since there is an 80 percent chance that a zygote—as opposed to a spermatozoon or an oocyte—develop into a full-fledged human being, this difference in probabilities provides the only reasonable basis for determining when life begins, while other criteria such as viability, experience, quickening, sentiments, and visibility turn out to be arbitrary on his analysis.

The most fundamental question involved in the long history of thought on abortion is: How do you determine the humanity of a being? To phase the question that way is to put in comprehensive humanistic terms what the theologians either dealt with as an explicitly theological question under the heading of "ensoulment" or dealt with implicitly in their treatment of abortion. The Christian position as it originated did not depend on a narrow theological or philosophical concept. It had no relation to theories of infant baptism.[1] It appealed to no special theory of instantaneous ensoulment. It took the world's view on ensoulment as that view changed from Aristotle to Zacchia. There was, indeed, theological influence affecting the theory of ensoulment finally adopted, and, of course, ensoulment itself was a theological concept, so that the position was always explained in theological terms. But the theological notion of ensoulment could easily be translated into humanistic language by substituting "human" for "rational soul"; the problem of knowing when a man is a man is common to theology and humanism.

If one steps outside the specific categories used by the theologians, the answer they gave can be analyzed as a refusal to discriminate among human beings on the basis of their varying potentialities. Once conceived, the being was recognized as man because he had man's potential. The criterion for humanity, thus, was simple and all-embracing: if you are conceived by human parents, you are human.

The strength of this position may be tested by a review of some of the other distinctions offered in the contemporary controversy over legalizing abortion. Perhaps the most popular distinction is in terms of viability. Before an age of so many months, the fetus is not viable, that is, it cannot be removed from the mothers womb and live apart from her. To that extent, the life of the fetus is absolutely dependent on the life of the mother. This dependence is made the basis of denying recognition to its humanity.

There are difficulties with this distinction. One is that the perfection of artificial incubation may make the fetus viable at any time: it may be removed and artificially sustained. Experiments with animals already show that such a procedure is possible.[2] This hypothetical extreme case relates to an actual difficulty: there is considerable elasticity to the idea of viability. Mere length of life is not an exact measure. The viability of the fetus depends on the extent of its anatomical and functional development.[3] The weight and length of the fetus are better guides to the state of its development than age, but weight and length vary.[4] Moreover, different racial groups have different ages at which their fetuses are viable. Some evidence, for example, suggests that Negro fetuses mature more quickly than white fetuses.[5] If viability is the norm, the standard would vary with race and with many individual circumstances.

The most important objection to this approach is that dependence is not ended by viability. The fetus is still absolutely dependent on someone's care in order to continue existence; indeed a child of one or three or even five years of age is absolutely dependent on anothers care for existence; uncared for, the older fetus or the younger child will die as surely as the early fetus detached from the mother. The unsubstantial lessening in dependence and viability

does not seem to signify any special acquisition of humanity.

A second distinction has been attempted in terms of experience. A being who has had experience, has lived and suffered, who possesses memories, is more human than one who has not. Humanity depends on formation by experience. The fetus is thus "unformed" in the most basic human sense.[6]

This distinction is not serviceable for the embryo which is already experiencing and reacting. The embryo is responsive to touch after eight weeks[7] and at least at this point is experiencing. At an earlier stage the zygote is certainly alive and responding to its environment.[8] The distinction may also be challenged by the rare case where aphasia has erased adult memory: has it erased humanity? More fundamentally, this distinction leaves even the older fetus or the younger child to be treated as an unformed inhuman thing. Finally, it is not clear why experience as such confers humanity. It could be argued that certain central experiences such as loving or learning are necessary to make a man human. But then human beings who have failed to love or to learn might be excluded from the class called man.

A third distinction is made by appeal to the sentiments of adults. If a fetus dies, the grief of the parents is not the grief they would have for a living child. The fetus is an unnamed "it" till birth, and is not perceived as personality until at least the fourth month of existence when movements in the womb manifest a vigorous presence demanding joyful recognition by the parents.

Yet feeling is notoriously an unsure guide to the humanity of others. Many groups of humans have had difficulty in feeling that persons of another tongue, color, religion, sex, are as human as they. Apart from reactions to alien groups, we mourn the loss of a ten-year-old boy more than the loss of his one-day-old brother or his 90-year-old grandfather. The difference felt and the grief expressed vary with the potentialities extinguished, or the experience wiped out; they do not seem to point to any substantial difference in the humanity of baby, boy, or grandfather.

Distinctions are also made in terms of sensation by the parents. The embryo is felt within the womb only after about the fourth month.[9] The embryo is seen only at birth. What can be neither seen nor felt is different from what is tangible. If the fetus cannot be seen or touched at all, it cannot be perceived as man.

Yet experience shows that sight is even more untrustworthy than feeling in determining humanity. By sight, color became an appropriate index for saying who was a man, and the evil of racial discrimination was given foundation. Nor can touch provide the test; a being confined by sickness, "out of touch" with others, does not thereby seem to lose his humanity. To the extent that touch still has appeal as a criterion, it appears to be a survival of the old English idea of "quickening"—a possible mistranslation of the Latin *animatus* used in the canon law. To that extent touch as a criterion seems to be dependent on the Aristoklian notion of ensoulment, and to fall when this notion is discarded.

Finally, a distinction is sought in social visibility. The fetus is not socially perceived as human. It cannot communicate with others. Thus, both subjectively and objectively, it is not a member of society. As moral rules are rules for the behavior of members of society to each other, they cannot be made for behavior toward what is not yet a member. Excluded from the society of men, the fetus is excluded from the humanity of men.[10]

By force of the argument from the consequences, this distinction is to be rejected. It is more subtle than that founded on an appeal to physical sensation, but it is equally dangerous in its implications. If humanity depends on social recognition, individuals or whole groups may be dehumanized by being denied any status in their society. Such a fate is fictionally portrayed in *1984* and has actually been the lot of many men in many societies. In the Roman empire, for example, condemnation to slavery meant the practical denial of most human rights; in the Chinese Communist world, landlords have been classified as enemies of the people and so treated as nonpersons by the state. Humanity does not depend on social recognition, though often the failure of society to recognize the prisoner, the alien, the heterodox as human has led to the destruction of human beings. Anyone conceived by a man and a woman is human. Recognition of this condition by society follows a real event in the objective order, however imperfect and halting the recognition. Any attempt to limit humanity to exclude some group runs the risk of furnishing authority and precedent for excluding other groups in the name of the consciousness or perception of the controlling group in the society.

A philosopher may reject the appeal to the humanity of the fetus because he views "humanity" as a secular view of the soul and because he doubts the existence of anything real and objective which can be identified as humanity.[11] One answer to such a philosopher is to ask how he reasons about moral questions without supposing that there is a sense in which he and the others of whom he speaks are human. Whatever group is taken as the society which determines who may be killed is thereby taken as human. A second answer is to ask if he does not believe that there is a right and wrong way of deciding moral questions. If there is such a difference, experience may be appealed to: to decide who is human on the basis of the sentiment of a given society has led to consequences which rational men would characterize as monstrous.[12]

The rejection of the attempted distinctions based on viability and visibility, experience and feeling, may be buttressed by the following considerations: Moral judgments often rest on distinctions, but if the distinctions are not to appear arbitrary fiat, they should relate to some real difference in probabilities. There is a kind of continuity in all Life, but the earlier stages of the elements of human life possess tiny probabilities of development. Consider for example, the spermatozoa in any normal ejaculate: there are about 200,000,000 in any single ejaculate, of which one has a chance of developing into a zygote.[13] Consider the oocytes which may become ova: there are 100,000 to 1,000,000 oocytes in a female infant, of which a maximum of 390 are ovulated.[14] But once spermatozoon and ovum meet and the conceptus is formed, such studies as have been made show that roughly in only 20 percent of the cases will spontaneous abortion occur.[15] In other words, the chances are about 4 out of 5 that this new being will develop. At this stage in the life of the being there is a sharp shift in probabilities, an immense jump in potentialities. To make a distinction between the rights of spermatozoa and the rights of the fertilized ovum is to respond to an enormous shift in possibilities. For about twenty days after conception the egg may split to form twins or combine with another egg to form a chimera, but the probability of either event happening is very small.

It may be asked, What does a change in biological probabilities have to do with establishing humanity? The argument from probabilities is not aimed at establishing humanity but at establishing an objective discontinuity which may be taken into account in moral discourse. As life itself is a matter of probabilities, as most moral reasoning is an estimate of probabilities, so it seems in accord with the structure of reality and the nature of moral thought to found a moral judgment on the change in probabilities at conception. The appeal to probabilities is the most commonsensical of arguments; to a greater or smaller degree all of us base our actions on probabilities, and in morals, as in law, prudence and negligence are often measured by the account one has taken of the probabilities. If the chance is 200,000,000 to 1 that the movement in the bushes into which you shoot is a man's. I doubt if many persons would hold you careless in shooting; but if the chances are 4 out of 5 that the movement is a human being's, few would acquit you of blame. Would the argument be different if only one out of ten children conceived came to term? Of course this argument would be different. This argument is an appeal to probabilities that actually exist, not to any and all states of affairs which may be imagined.

The probabilities as they do exist do not show the humanity of the embryo in the sense of a demonstration in logic any more than the probabilities of the movement in the bush being a man demonstrate beyond all doubt that the being is a man. The appeal is a "buttressing" consideration, showing the plausibility of the standard adopted. The argument focuses on the decisional factor in any moral judgment and assumes that part of the business of a moralist is drawing lines. One evidence of the nonarbitrary character of the line drawn is the difference of probabilities on either side of it. If a spermatozoon is destroyed, one destroys a being which had a trace of far less than 1 in 200 million of developing into a reasoning being possessed of the genetic code, a heart and other organs, and capable of pain. If a fetus is destroyed, one destroys a being already possessed of the genetic code, organs, and sensitivity to pain, and one which had an 80 percent chance of developing further into a baby outside the womb who, in time, would reason.

The positive argument for conception as the decisive moment of humanization is that at conception the new being receives the genetic code.[16] It is this genetic information which determines his characteristics, which is the biological carrier of the possibility of human wisdom, which makes him a self-evolving being. A being with a human genetic code is man.

This review of current controversy over the humanity of the fetus emphasizes what a fundamental question the theologians resolved in asserting the inviolability of the fetus. To regard the fetus as possessed of equal rights with other humans was not, however, to decide every case where abortion might be employed. It did decide the case where the argument was that the fetus should be aborted for its own good. To say a being was human was to say it had a destiny to decide for itself which could not be taken from it by another man's decision. But human beings with equal rights often come in conflict with each other, and some decision must be made as [to] whose claims are to prevail. Cases of conflict involving the fetus are different only in two respects: the total inability of the fetus to speak for itself and the fact that the right of the fetus regularly at stake is the right to life itself.

The approach taken by the theologians to these conflicts was articulated in terms of "direct" and "indirect." Again, to look at what they were doing from outside their cat-egories, they may be said to have been drawing lines or "balancing values." "Direct" and "indirect" are spatial metaphors; "line-drawing" is another. "To weigh" or "to balance" values is a metaphor of a more complicated mathematical sort hinting at the process which goes on in moral judgments. All the metaphors suggest that, in the moral judgments made, comparisons were necessary, that no value completely controlled. The principle of double effect was no doctrine fallen from heaven, but a method of analysis appropriate where two relative values were being compared. In Catholic moral theology, as it developed, life even of the innocent was not taken as an absolute. Judgments on acts affecting life issued from a process of weighing. In the weighing, the fetus was always given a value greater than zero, always a value separate and independent from its parents. This valuation was crucial and fundamental in all Christian thought on the subject and marked it off from any approach which considered that only the parents' interests needed to be considered.

Even with the fetus weighed as human, one interest could be weighed as equal or superior: that of the mother in her own life. The casuists between 1450 and 1895 were willing to weigh this interest as superior. Since 1895, that interest was given decisive weight only in the two special cases of the cancerous uterus and the ectopic pregnancy. In both of these cases the fetus itself had little chance of survival even if the abortion were not performed. As the balance was once struck in favor of the mother whenever her life was endangered, it could be so struck again. The balance reached between 1895 and 1930 attempted prudentially and pastorally to forestall a multitude of exceptions for interests less than life.

The perception of the humanity of the fetus and the weighing of fetal rights against other human rights constituted the work of the moral analysts. But what spirit animated their abstract judgments? For the Christian community it was the injunction of Scripture to love your neighbor as yourself. The fetus as human was a neighbor; his life had parity with one's own. The commandment gave life to what otherwise would have been only rational calculation.

The commandment could be put in humanistic as well as theological terms: Do not injure your fellow man without reason. In these terms, once the humanity of the fetus is perceived, abortion is never right except in self-defense. When life must be taken to save life, reason alone cannot say that a mother must prefer a child's life to her own. With this exception, now of great rarity, abortion violates the rational humanist tenet of the equality of human lives.

For Christians the commandment to love had received a special imprint in that the exemplar proposed of love was the love of the Lord for his disciples. In the light given by this example, self-sacrifice carried to the point of death seemed in the extreme situations not without meaning. In the less extreme cases, preference for one's own interests to the life of another seemed to express cruelty or selfishness irreconcilable with the demands of love.

NOTES

1. According to Glanville Williams (*The Sanctity of Human Life and the Criminal Law,* 1957, 193), "The historical reason for the Catholic objection to abortion is the same as for the Christian Church's historical opposition to infanticide: the horror of bringing about the death of an unbaptized child." This statement is made without any citation of evidence. As has been seen, desire to administer baptism could, in the Middle Ages, even be urged as a reason for procuring an abortion. It is highly regrettable that the American Law Institute was apparently misled by Williams' account and repeated after him the same baseless statement. See American Law Institute, *Model Penal Code: Tentative Draft No. 9* (1959), p. 148, n. 12.

2. E.g., R. L. Brinsler and J. L. Thomson, "Development of Eight-Cell Mouse Embryos In Vitro," 42 *Experimental Cell Research* 308 (1966).

3. J. Edgar Morison, *Fetal and Neonatal Pathology* 99-100 (1963).

4. Peter Gruenwald, "Growth of the Human Fetus," 94 *American Journal of Obstetrics and Gynecology* 1112 (1966).

5. Morison, *Fetal and Neonatal Pathology supra* n. 3, at 101.

6. This line of thought was advanced by some participants at the International Conference on Abortion sponsored by the Harvard Divinity School in cooperation with the Joseph P. Kennedy, Jr., Foundation in Washington, D.C., Sept, 8-10, 1967.

7. Frank D. Allan, *Essentials of Human Embryology* 165 (1960).

8. Frederick J. Gottlieb, *Developmental Genetics* 28 (1966)

9. Allan, *Essentials of Human Embryology supra* n. 7, at 165.

10. Another line of thought advanced at the Conference mentioned in n. 6. Thomas Aquinas gave an analogous reason against baptizing a fetus in the womb: "As long as it exists in the womb of the mother, it cannot be subject to the operation of the ministers of the Church as it is not known to men" *(In sententias Petri Lombardi* 4.6 1.1.2).

11. Compare John O'Connor, "Humanity and Abortion," 12 *Natural Law Forum* 128-130 (1968), with John T. Noonan, Jr. "Deciding Who Is Human," 12 *Natural Law Forum* 134-138.

12. A famous passage of Montesquieu reads:

    "Ceux dont il s'agit sont noirs depuis les pieds jusqú à la tête; et ils ont le nez si écrasé qu'il est presque impossible de les plaindre.

    "On ne peut se mettre dans l'esprit que Dieu qui est un être très-sage, ait mis une âme, surtout une âme bonne, dans un corps tout noir.

    "Il est si naturel de penser que c'est la couleur qui constituie l'essence de l'humanité, que les peuples d'Asie, qui font des eunuques, privent toujours les noirs du rapport qu'ils ont avec nous d'une façon plus marquée." *Montesquieu, De l'esprit des lois,* in *Oeuvres Complètes* book 15, chap. 5 (Paris, 1843).

13. J. S. Baxter, Frazer's *Manual of Embryology* 5 (1963).

14. Gregory Pincus, *The Control of Fertility* 197 (19a).

15. *Idem.* Apparently there is some small variation by region.

16. Gottleib, *Developmental Genetics supra* n. 8, at 17.

On the Moral and Legal Status of Abortion

Mary Anne Warren

Mary Anne Warren is a professor of philosophy at San Francisco State University. She is the author of The Nature of Woman *(1980) and* Gendercide: The Implications of Sex Selection *(1985).*

Warren provides the classic "liberal" defense of abortion rights. She maintains that once one concedes that the fetus is a person, then one must accept limitations on the right to abortion. But, she argues, the fetus is not a person. Her argument proceeds by examining the various criteria that have been employed to establish personhood. Eventually, Warren constructs what she regards as the most plausible definition of a human person and then shows that a fetus does not conform to the definition. Neither the resemblance of the fetus to a person, not the act that it may become a human person, are sufficient reasons for regarding the fetus as a human person whose rights could override a pregnant woman's right to decide whether or not to have an abortion.

We will be concerned with both the moral status of abortion, which for our purposes we may define as the act which a woman performs in voluntarily terminating, or allowing another person to terminate, her pregnancy, and the legal status which is appropriate for this act. I will argue that, while it is not possible to produce a satisfactory defense of a woman's right to obtain an abortion without showing that a fetus is not a human being, in the morally relevant sense of that term, we ought not to conclude that the difficulties involved in determining whether or not a fetus is human make it impossible to produce any satisfactory solution to the problem of the moral status of abortion. For it is possible to show that, on the basis of intuitions which we may expect even the opponents of abortion to share, a fetus is not a person, and hence

Reprinted from *The Monist.* 1973. [Edited]

not the sort of entity to which it is proper to ascribe full moral rights.

Of course, while some philosophers would deny the possibility of any such proof,[1] others will deny that there is any need for it, since the moral permissibility of abortion appears to them to be too obvious to require proof. But the inadequacy of this attitude should be evident from the fact that both the friends and the foes of abortion consider their position to be morally self-evident. Because proabortionists have never adequately come to grips with the conceptual issues surrounding abortion, most if not all, of the arguments which they advance in opposition to laws restricting access to abortion fail to refute or even weaken the traditional antiabortion argument, i.e., that a fetus is a human being, and therefore abortion is murder.

These arguments are typically of one of two sorts. Either they point to the terrible side effects of the restrictive laws, e.g., the deaths due to illegal abortions, and the fact that it is poor women who suffer the most as a result of these laws, or else they state that to deny a woman access to abortion is to deprive her of her right to control her own body. Unfortunately, however, the fact that restricting access to abortion has tragic side effects does not, in itself, show that the restrictions are unjustified, since murder is wrong regardless of the consequences of prohibiting it; and the appeal to the right to control one's body, which is generally construed as a property right, is at best a rather feeble argument for the permissibility of abortion. Mere ownership does not give me the right to kill innocent people whom I find on my property, and indeed I am apt to be held responsible if such people injure themselves while on my property. It is equally unclear that I have any moral right to expel an innocent person from my property when I know that doing so will result in his death.

Furthermore, it is probably inappropriate to describe a woman's body as her property, since it seems natural to hold that a person is something distinct from her property, but not from her body. Even those who would object to the identification of a person with his body, or with the conjunction of his body and his mind, must admit that it would be very odd to describe, say, breaking a leg, as damaging one's property, and much more appropriate to describe it as injuring *oneself*. Thus it is probably a mistake to argue that the right to obtain an abortion is in any way derived from the right to own and regulate property.

But however we wish to construe the right to abortion, we cannot hope to convince those who consider abortion a form of murder of the existence of any such right unless we are able to produce a clear and convincing refutation of the traditional antiabortion argument, and this has not, to my knowledge, been done. With respect to the two most vital issues which that argument involves, i.e., the humanity of the fetus and its implication for the moral status of abortion, confusion has prevailed on both sides of the dispute.

Thus, both proabortionists and antiabortionists have tended to abstract the question of whether abortion is wrong to that of whether it is wrong to destroy a fetus, just as though the rights of another person were not necessarily involved. This mistaken abstraction has led to the almost universal assumption that if a fetus is a human being, with a right to life, then it follows immediately that abortion is wrong (except perhaps when necessary to save the woman's life), and that it ought to be prohibited. It has also been generally assumed that unless the question about the status of the fetus is answered, the moral status of abortion cannot possibly be determined. . . .

The question which we must answer in order to produce a satisfactory solution to the problem of the moral status of abortion is this: How are we to define the moral community, the set of beings with full and equal moral rights, such that we can decide whether a human fetus is a member of this community or not? What sort of entity, exactly, has the inalienable rights to life, liberty, and the pursuit of happiness? Jefferson attributed these right to all *men*, and it may or may not be fair to suggest that he intended to attribute them *only* to men. Perhaps he ought to have attributed them to all human beings. If so, then we arrive, first, at the problem of defining what makes a being human, and, second, at the equally vital question . . . namely, What reason is there for identifying the moral community with the set of all human beings, in whatever way we have chosen to define that term?

On the Definition of "Human"

One reason why this vital second question is so frequently overlooked in the debate over the moral status of abortion is that the term "human" has two distinct, but not often distinguished, senses. This fact results in a slide of meaning, which serves to conceal the fallaciousness of the traditional argument that since (1) it is wrong to kill innocent human beings, and (2) fetuses are innocent human beings, then (3) it is wrong to kill fetuses. For if "human" is used in the same sense in both (1) and (2) then, whichever of the two senses is meant, one of these premises is question-begging. And if it is used in two different senses then of course the conclusion doesn't follow.

Thus, (1) is a self-evident moral truth.[2] and avoids begging the question about abortion, only if "human being" is used to mean something like "a full-fledged member of the moral community." (It may or may not also be meant to refer exclusively to members of the species *Homo sapiens*.) We may call this the *moral* sense of "human." It is not to be confused with what we will call the *genetic* sense, i.e., the sense in which *any* member of the species is a human being, and no member of any other species could be. If (1) is acceptable only if the moral sense is intended, (2) is non-question-begging only if what is intended is the genetic sense.

In "Deciding Who is Human," Noonan argues for the classification of fetuses with human beings by pointing to the presence of the full genetic code, and the potential capacity for rational thought.[3] It is clear that what he needs to show, for his version of the traditional argument to be valid, is that fetuses are human in the moral sense, the sense in which it is analytically true

that all human beings have full moral rights. But, in the absence of any argument showing that whatever is genetically human is also morally human, and he gives none, nothing more than genetic humanity can be demonstrated by the presence of the human genetic code. And, as we will see, the *potential* capacity for rational thought can at most show that an entity has the potential for *becoming* human in the moral sense.

Defining the Moral Community

Can it be established that genetic humanity is sufficient for moral humanity? I think that there are very good reasons for not defining the moral community in this way. I would like to suggest an alternative way of defining the moral community, which I will argue for only to the extent of explaining why it is, or should be, self-evident. The suggestion is simply that the moral community consists of all and only *people* rather than all and only human beings;[4] and probably the best way of demonstrating its self-evidence is by considering the concept of personhood, to see what sorts of entity are and are not persons, and what the decision that a being is or is not a person implies about its moral rights.

What characteristics entitle an entity to be considered a person? This is obviously not the place to attempt a complete analysis of the concept of personhood, but we do not need such a fully adequate analysis just to determine whether and why a fetus is or isn't a person. All we need is a rough and approximate list of the most basic criteria of personhood, and some idea of which, or how many, of these an entity must satisfy in order to properly be considered a person.

In searching for such criteria, it is useful to look beyond the set of people with whom we are acquainted, and ask how we would decide whether a totally alien being was a person or not. (For we have no right to assume that genetic humanity is necessary for personhood.) Imagine a space traveler who lands on an unknown planet and encounters a race of beings utterly unlike any he has ever seen or heard of. If he wants to be sure of behaving morally toward these beings, he has to somehow decide whether they are people, and hence have full moral rights, or whether they are the sort of thing which he need not feel guilty about treating as, for example, a source of food.

How should he go about making this decision? If he has some anthropological background, he might look for such things as religion, art, and the manufacturing of tools, weapons, or shelters, since these factors have been used to distinguish our human from our prehuman ancestors, in what seems to be closer to the moral than the genetic sense of "human." And no doubt he would be right to consider the presence of such factors as good evidence that the alien beings were people, and morally human. It would, however, be overly anthropocentric of him to take the absence of these things as adequate evidence that they were not, since we can imagine people who have progressed beyond, or evolved without ever developing, these cultural characteristics.

I suggest that the traits which are most central to the concept of personhood, or humanity in the moral sense, are, very roughly, the following:

(1) consciousness (of objects and events external and/or internal to the being), and in particular the capacity to feel pain;
(2) reasoning (the *developed* capacity to solve new and relatively complex problems);
(3) self-motivated activity (activity which is relatively independent of either genetic or direct external control);
(4) the capacity to communicate, by what ever means, messages of an indefinite variety of types, that is, not just with an indefinite number of possible contents, but on indefinitely many possible topics;
(5) the presence of self-concepts, and self-awareness, either individual or racial, or both.

Admittedly, there are apt to be a great many problems involved in formulating precise definitions of these criteria, let alone in developing universally valid behavioral criteria for deciding when they apply. But I will assume that both we and our explorer know approximately what (1)–(5) mean, and that he is also able to determine whether or not they apply. How, then, should he use his findings to decide whether or not the alien beings are people? We needn't suppose that an entity must have *all* of these attributes to be properly considered a person; (1) and (2) alone may well be sufficient for personhood, and quite probably (1)–(3) are sufficient. Neither do we need to insist that any one of these criteria is *necessary* for personhood, although once again (1) and (2) look like fairly good candidates for necessary conditions, as does (3), if "activity" is construed so as to include the activity of reasoning.

All we need to claim, to demonstrate that a fetus is not a person, is that any being which satisfies *none* of (1)–(5) is certainly not a person. I consider this claim to be so obvious that I think anyone who denied it, and claimed that a being which satisfied none of (1)–(5) was a person all the same, would thereby demonstrate that he had no notion at all of what a person is—perhaps because he had confused the concept of a person with that of genetic humanity. If the opponents of abortion were to deny the appropriateness of these five criteria, I do not know what further arguments would convince them. We would probably have to admit that our conceptual schemes were indeed irreconcilably different, and that our dispute could not be settled objectively.

I do not expect this to happen, however, since I think that the concept of a person is one which is very nearly universal (to people), and that it is common to both proabortionists and antiabortionists, even though neither group has fully realized the relevance of this concept to the resolution of their dispute. Furthermore, I think that on reflection even the antiabortionists ought to agree not only that (1)–(5) are central to the concept of personhood, but also that it is a part of this concept that all and only people have full moral rights. The concept of a person is in part a moral concept; once we have admitted that x is a person we have recognized, even if we have not agreed to respect, x's right to be treated as a member of the moral community. It is true that the claim that x is a *human being* is more commonly voiced as part of an appeal to treat x decently than is the claim that x is a person, but this is either because "human being" is here used in the sense which implies personhood, or because the genetic and moral senses of "human" have been confused.

Now if (1)–(5) are indeed the primary criteria of personhood, then it is clear that genetic humanity is neither necessary nor sufficient for establishing that an entity is a person. Some human beings are not people, and there may well be people who are not human beings. A man or woman whose consciousness has been permanently obliterated but who remains alive is a human being which is no longer a person; defective human beings, with no appreciable mental capacity, are not and presumably never will be people; and a fetus is a human being which is not yet a person, and which therefore cannot coherently be said to have full moral rights. Citizens of the next century should be prepared to recognize highly advanced, self-aware robots or computers, should such be developed, and intelligent inhabitants of other worlds, should such be found, as people in the fullest sense, and to respect their moral rights. But to ascribe full moral rights to an entity which is not a person is as absurd as to ascribe moral obligations and responsibilities to such an entity.

Fetal Development and the Right to Life

Two problems arise in the application of these suggestions for the definition of the moral community to the determination of the precise moral status of a human fetus. Given that the paradigm example of a person is a normal adult human being, then (1) How like this paradigm, in particular how far advanced since conception, does a human being need to be before it begins to have a right to life by virtue, not of being fully a person as of yet, but of being *like* a person? and (2) To what extent, if any, does the fact that a fetus has the *potential* for becoming a person endow it with some of the same rights? Each of these questions requires some comment.

In answering the first question, we need not attempt a detailed consideration of the moral rights of organisms which are not developed enough, aware enough, intelligent enough, etc., to be considered people, but which resemble people in some respects. It does seem reasonable to suggest that the more like a person, in the relevant respects, a being is, the stronger is the case for regarding it as having a right to life, and indeed the stronger its right to life is. Thus we ought to take seriously the suggestion that, insofar as "the human individual develops biologically in a continuous fashion . . . the rights of a human person might develop in the same way."[5] But we must keep in mind that the attributes which are relevant in determining whether or not an entity is enough like a person to be regarded as having some of the same moral rights are no different from those which are relevant to determining whether or not it is fully a person—i.e., are no different from (1)–(5)—and that being genetically human, or having recognizably human facial and other physical features, or detectable brain activity, or the capacity to survive outside the uterus, are simply not among these relevant attributes.

Thus it is clear that even though a seven- or eight-month fetus has features which make it apt to arouse in us almost the same powerful protective instinct as is commonly aroused by a small infant, nevertheless it is not significantly more personlike than is a very small embryo. It is *somewhat* more personlike; it can apparently feel and respond to pain, and it may even have a rudimentary form of consciousness, insofar as its brain is quite active. Nevertheless, it seems safe to say that it is not fully conscious, in the way that an infant of a few months is, and that it cannot reason, or communicate messages of indefinitely many sorts, does not engage in self-motivated activity, and has no self-awareness. Thus, in the *relevant* respects, a fetus, even a fully developed one, is considerably less personlike than is the average mature mammal, indeed the average fish. And I think that a rational person must conclude that if the right to life of a fetus is to be based upon its resemblance to a person, then it cannot be said to have any more right to life than, let us say, a new-born guppy (which also seems to be capable of feeling pain), and that a right of that magnitude could never override a woman's right to obtain an abortion, at any stage of her pregnancy.

There may, of course, be other arguments in favor of placing legal limits upon the stage of pregnancy in which an abortion may be performed. Given the relative safety of the new techniques of artificially inducing labor during the third trimester, the danger to the woman's life or health is no longer such an argument. Neither is the fact that people tend to respond to the thought of abortion in the later stages of pregnancy with emotional repulsion, since mere emotional responses cannot take the place of moral reasoning in determining what ought to be permitted. Nor, finally, is the frequently heard argument that legalizing abortion, especially late in the pregnancy, may erode the level of respect for human life, leading, perhaps, to an increase in unjustified euthanasia and other crimes. For this threat, if it is a threat, can be better met by educating people to the kinds of moral distinctions which we are making here than by limiting access to abortion (which limitation may, in its disregard for the rights of women, be just as damaging to the level of respect for human rights).

Thus, since the fact that even a fully developed fetus is not personlike enough to have any significant right to life on the basis of its person-likeness shows that no legal restrictions upon the stage of pregnancy in which an abortion may be performed can be justified on the grounds that we should protect the rights of the older fetus; and since there is no other apparent justification for such restrictions, we may conclude that they are entirely unjustified. Whether or not it would be *indecent* (whatever that means) for a woman in her seventh month to obtain an abortion just to avoid having to postpone a trip to Europe, it would not, in itself, be *immoral* and therefore it ought to be permitted.

Potential Personhood and the Right to Life

We have seen that a fetus does not resemble a person in any way which can support the claim that it has even some of the same rights. But what about its *potential*, the fact that if nurtured and allowed to develop naturally it will very probably become a person? Doesn't that alone give it at least some right to life? It is hard to deny that the fact that an entity is a potential person is a strong prima facie reason for not destroying it; but we need not conclude from this that a potential person has a right to life, by virtue of that potential. It may be that our feeling that it is better, other things being equal, not to destroy a potential person is better explained by the fact that potential people are still (felt to be) an invaluable resource, not to be lightly squandered. Surely, if every speck of dust were a potential person, we would be much less apt to conclude that every potential person has a right to become actual.

Still, we do not need to insist that a potential person has no right to life whatever. There may be something immoral, and not just imprudent, about wantonly destroying potential people, when doing so isn't necessary to protect anyone's rights. But even if a potential person does have some prima facie right to life, such a right could not possibly outweigh the right of a woman to obtain an abortion, since the rights of any actual person invariably outweigh those of any potential person, whenever the two conflict. Since this may not be immediately obvious in the case of a human fetus, let us look at another case.

Suppose that our space explorer falls into the hands of an alien culture, whose scientists decide to create a few hundred thousand or more human beings, by breaking his body into its component cells, and using these to create fully developed human beings, with, of course, his genetic code. We may imagine that each of these newly created men will have all of the original man's abilities, skills, knowledge, and so on, and also have an individual self-concept, in short that each of them will be a bona fide (though hardly unique) person. Imagine that the whole project will take only seconds, and that its chances of success are extremely high, and that our explorer knows all of this, and also knows that these people will be treated fairly. I maintain that in such a situation he would have every right to escape if he could, and thus to deprive all of these potential people of their potential lives; for his right to life outweighs all of theirs together, in spite of the fact that they are all genetically human, all innocent, and all have a very high probability of becoming people very soon, if only he refrains from acting.

Indeed, I think he would have a right to escape even if it were not his life which the alien scientists planned to take, but only a year of his freedom, or, indeed, only a day. Nor would he be obligated to stay if he had gotten captured (thus bringing all these people-potentials into existence) because of his own carelessness, or even if he had done so deliberately, knowing the consequences. Regardless of how he got captured, he is not morally obligated to remain in captivity for *any* period of time for the sake of permitting any number of potential people to come into actuality, so great is the margin by which one actual person's right to liberty outweighs whatever right to life even a hundred thousand potential people have. And it seems reasonable to conclude that the rights of a woman will outweigh by a similar margin whatever right to life a fetus may have by virtue of its potential personhood.

Thus, neither a fetus's resemblance to a person, nor its potential for becoming a person provides any basis whatever for the claim that it has any significant right to life. Consequently, a woman's right to protect her health, happiness, freedom, and even her life,[6] by terminating an unwanted pregnancy, will always override whatever right to life it may be appropriate to ascribe to a fetus, even a fully developed one. And thus, in the absence of any overwhelming social need for every possible child, the laws which restrict the right to obtain an abortion, or limit the period of pregnancy during which an abortion may be performed, are a wholly unjustified violation of a woman's most basic moral and constitutional rights.

ACKNOWLEDGMENT

My thanks to the following people, who were kind enough to read and criticize an earlier version of this paper: Herbert Gold, Gene Glass, Anne Lauterbach, Judith Thomson, Mary Mothersill, and Timothy Binkley.

NOTES

1. For example, Roger Wertheimer, who in "Understanding the Abortion Argument" (*Philosophy and Public Affairs*, 1, No. 1 [Fall, 1971], 67–95), argues that the problem of the moral status of abortion is insoluble, in that the dispute over the status of the fetus is not a question of fact at all, but only a question of how one responds to the facts.
2. Of course, the principle that it is (always) wrong to kill innocent human beings is in need of many other modifications, e.g, that it may be permissible to do so to save a greater number of other innocent human beings, but we may safely ignore these complications here.
3. John Noonan, "Deciding Who Is Human," *Natural Law Forum,* vol. 13 (1968), p 135.
4. From here on, we will use "human" to mean genetically human, since the moral sense seems closely connected to, and perhaps derived from, the assumption that genetic humanity is sufficient for membership in the moral community
5. Thomas L. Hayes, "A Biological View," *Commonweal,* 85 (March 17, 1967), 677–78; quoted by Daniel Callahan, in *Abortion, Law, Choice, and Morality* (London: Macmillan & Co., 1970).
6. That is, insofar as the death rate, for the woman, is higher for childbirth than for early abortion.

Why Abortion Is Immoral

Don Marquis

Don Marquis is a professor of philosophy at the University of Kansas.

Marquis provides a sustained defense of one variation of the "conservative" position that abortion is morally unjustified. He begins by explaining why both sides of the debate engage in serious conceptual mistakes in the way they regard the fetus. Then he argues that "it is wrong to kill us" because such killing deprives us of all the value of our futures. Contrary to Warren, Marquis argues that fetuses are sufficiently like us to permit the assertion that it is just as wrong to kill them as it is to kill us. In both two cases, it is wrong to kill because of the deprivation of a valuable future. Marquis allows, at the end, that this argument does not make all abortion wrong since there may be overriding considerations in some cases.

The view that abortion is, with rare exceptions, seriously immoral has received little support in the recent philosophical literature. No doubt most philosophers affiliated with secular institutions of higher education believe that the anti-abortion position is either a symptom of irrational religious dogma or a conclusion generated by seriously confused philosophical argument. The purpose of this essay is to undermine this general belief. This essay sets out an argument that purports to show, as well as any argument in ethics can show, that abortion is, except possibly in rare cases, seriously immoral, that it is in the same moral category as killing an innocent adult human being.

The argument is based on a major assumption. Many of the most insightful and careful writers on the ethics of abortion—such as Joel Feinberg, Michael Tooley, Mary Anne Warren, H. Tristram Engelhardt, Jr., L. W. Sumner, John T. Noonan, Jr., and Philip Devine[1]—believe that whether or not abortion is morally permissible stands or falls on whether or not a fetus is the sort of being whose life it is seriously wrong to end. The argument of this essay will assume, but not argue, that they are correct.

Also, this essay will neglect issues of great importance to a complete ethics of abortion. Some anti-abortionists will allow that certain abortions, such as abortion before implantation or abortion when the life of a woman is threatened by a pregnancy or abortion after rape, may be morally permissible. This essay will not explore the casuistry of these hard cases. The purpose of this essay is to develop a general argument for the claim that the overwhelming majority of deliberate abortions are seriously immoral.

A sketch of standard anti-abortion and pro-choice arguments exhibits how those arguments possess certain symmetries that explain why partisans of those positions are so convinced of the correctness of their own positions, why they are not successful in convincing their opponents, and why, to oth-

Reprinted with permission of *The Journal of Philosophy* and Donald Marquis, from *The Journal of Philosophy*, April 1989. [Edited]

ers, this issue seems to be unresolvable. An analysis of the nature of this standoff suggests a strategy for surmounting it.

Consider the way a typical anti-abortionist argues. She will argue or assert that life is present from the moment of conception or that fetuses look like babies or that fetuses possess a characteristic such as a genetic code that is both necessary and sufficient for being human. Anti-abortionists seem to believe that (1) the truth of all of these claims is quite obvious, and (2) establishing any of these claims is sufficient to show that abortion is morally akin to murder.

A standard pro-choice strategy exhibits similarities. The pro-choicer will argue or assert that fetuses are not persons or that fetuses are not rational agents or that fetuses are not social beings. Pro-choicers seem to believe that (1) the truth of any of these claims is quite obvious, and (2) establishing any of these claims is sufficient to show that an abortion is not a wrongful killing.

In fact, both the pro-choice and the antiabortion claims do seem to be true, although the "it looks like a baby" claim is more difficult to establish the earlier the pregnancy. We seem to have a standoff. How can it be resolved?

As everyone who has taken a bit of logic knows, if any of these arguments concerning abortion is a good argument, it requires not only some claim characterizing fetuses, but also some general moral principle that ties a characteristic of fetuses to having or not having the right to life or to some other moral characteristic that will generate the obligation or the lack of obligation not to end the life of a fetus. Accordingly, the arguments of the anti-abortionist and the pro-choicer need a bit of filling in to be regarded as adequate.

Note what each partisan will say. The anti-abortionist will claim that her position is supported by such generally accepted moral principles as "It is always prima facie seriously wrong to take a human life" or "It is always prima facie seriously wrong to end the life of a baby." Since these are generally accepted moral principles, her position is certainly not obviously wrong. The pro-choicer will claim that her position is supported by such plausible moral principles as "Being a person is what gives an individual intrinsic moral worth" or "It is only seriously prima facie wrong to take the life of a member of the human community." Since these are generally accepted moral principles, the pro-choice position is certainly not obviously wrong. Unfortunately, we have again arrived at a standoff.

Now, how might one deal with this standoff? The standard approach is to try to show how the moral principles of one's opponent lose their plausibility under analysis. It is easy to see how this is possible. On the one hand, the anti-abortionist will defend a moral principle concerning the wrongness of killing which tends to be broad in scope in order that even fetuses at an early stage of pregnancy will fall under it. The problem with broad principles is that they often embrace too much. In this particular instance, the principle "It is always prima facie wrong to take a human life" seems to entail that it is wrong to end the existence of a living human cancer-cell culture, on the grounds that the culture is both living and human. Therefore, it seems that the antiabortionist's favored principle is too broad.

On the other hand, the pro-choicer wants to find a moral principle concerning the wrongness of killing which tends to be narrow in scope in order that fetuses will *not* fall under it. The problem with narrow principles is that they often do not embrace enough. Hence, the needed principles such as "It is prima facie seriously wrong to kill only persons" or "It is prima facie wrong to kill only rational agents" do not explain why it is wrong to kill infants or young children or the severely retarded or even perhaps the severely mentally ill. Therefore, we seem again to have a standoff. The anti-abortionist charges, not unreasonably, that pro-choice principles concerning killing are too narrow to be acceptable; the pro-choicer charges, not unreasonably, that anti-abortionist principles concerning killing are too broad to be acceptable.

Attempts by both sides to patch up the difficulties in their positions run into further difficulties. The anti-abortionist will try to remove the problem in her position by reformulating her principle concerning killing in terms of human beings. Now we end up with: "It is always prima facie seriously wrong to end the life of a human being." This principle has the advantage of avoiding the problem of the human cancer-cell culture counterexample. But this advantage is purchased at a high price. For although it is clear that a fetus is both human and alive, it is not at all clear that a fetus is a human *being*. There is at least something to be said for the view that something becomes a human being only after a process of development, and that therefore first trimester fetuses and perhaps all fetuses are not yet human beings. Hence, the anti-abortionist, by this move, has merely exchanged one problem for another.[2]

The pro-choicer fares no better. She may attempt to find reasons why killing infants, young children, and the severely retarded is wrong which are independent of her major principle that is supposed to explain the wrongness of taking human life, but which will not also make abortion immoral. This is no easy task. Appeals to social utility will seem satisfactory only to those who resolve not to think of the enormous difficulties with a utilitarian account

of the wrongness of killing and the significant social costs of preserving the lives of the unproductive.[3] A prochoice strategy that extends the definition of "person" to infants or even to young children seems just as arbitrary as an antiabortion strategy that extends the definition of "human being" to fetuses. Again, we find symmetries in the two positions and we arrive at a standoff.

. . . We can start from the following unproblematic assumption concerning our own case: it is wrong to kill *us*. Why is it wrong? Some answers can be easily eliminated. It might be said that what makes killing us wrong is that a killing brutalizes the one who kills. But the brutalization consists of being inured to the performance of an act that is hideously immoral; hence, the brutalization does not explain the immorality. It might be said that what makes killing us wrong is the great loss others would experience due to our absence. Although such hubris is understandable, such an explanation does not account for the wrongness of killing hermits, or those whose lives are relatively independent and whose friends find it easy to make new friends.

A more obvious answer is better. What primarily makes killing wrong is neither its effect on the murderer nor its effect on the victim's friends and relatives, but its effect on the victim. The loss of one's life is one of the greatest losses one can suffer. The loss of one's life deprives one of all the experiences, activities, projects, and enjoyments that would otherwise have constituted one's future. Therefore, killing someone is wrong, primarily because the killing inflicts (one of) the greatest possible losses on the victim. To describe this as the loss of life can be misleading, however. The change in my biological state does not by itself make killing me wrong. The effect of the loss of my biological life is the loss to me of all those activities, projects, experiences, and enjoyments which would otherwise have constituted my future personal life. These activities, projects, experiences, and enjoyments are either valuable for their own sakes or are means to something else that is valuable for its own sake. Some parts of my future are not valued by me now, but will come to be valued by me as I grow older and as my values and capacities change. When I am killed, I am deprived both of what I now value which would have been part of my future personal life, but also what I would come to value. Therefore, when I die, I am deprived of all of the value of my future. Inflicting this loss on me is ultimately what makes killing me wrong. This being the case, it would seem that what makes killing *any* adult human being prima facie seriously wrong is the loss of his or her future.[4]

How should this rudimentary theory of the wrongness of killing be evaluated? It cannot be faulted for deriving an "ought" from an "is," for it does not. The analysis assumes that killing me (or you, reader) is prima facie seriously wrong. The point of the analysis is to establish which natural property ultimately explains the wrongness of the killing, given that it is wrong. A natural property will ultimately explain the wrongness of killing, only if (1) the explanation fits with our intuitions about the matter and (2) there is no other natural property that provides the basis for a better explanation of the wrongness of killing. This analysis rests on the intuition that what makes killing a particular human or animal wrong is what it does to that particular human or animal. What makes killing wrong is some natural effect or other of the killing. Some would deny this. For instance, a divine-command theorist in ethics would deny it. Surely this denial is, however, one of those features of divine-command theory which renders it so implausible.

The claim that what makes killing wrong is the loss of the victim's future is directly supported by two considerations. In the first place, this theory explains why we regard killing as one of the worst of crimes. Killing is especially wrong, because it deprives the victim of more than perhaps any other crime. In the second place, people with AIDS or cancer who know they are dying believe, of course, that dying is a very bad thing for them. They believe that the loss of a future to them that they would otherwise have experienced is what makes their premature death a very bad thing for them. A better theory of the wrongness of killing would require a different natural property associated with killing which better fits with the attitudes of the dying. What could it be?

The view that what makes killing wrong is the loss to the victim of the value of the victim's future gains additional support when some of its implications are examined. In the first place, it is incompatible with the view that it is wrong to kill only beings who are biologically human. It is possible that there exists a different species from another planet whose members have a future like ours. Since having a future like that is what makes killing someone wrong, this theory entails that it would be wrong to kill members of such a species. Hence, this theory is opposed to the claim that only life that is biologically human has great moral worth, a claim which many anti-abortionists have seemed to adopt. This opposition, which this theory has in common with personhood theories, seems to be a merit of the theory.

In the second place, the claim that the loss of one's future is the wrong-making feature of one's being killed entails the possibility that the futures of some actual nonhuman mammals on our own planet are sufficiently like ours that it is seriously wrong to kill them also. Whether some animals do have the same right to life as human beings depends on adding to the account of the wrongness of killing some additional account of just what it is about my future or the futures of other adult human beings which makes it wrong to kill us. No such additional account will be offered in this essay. Undoubtedly, the provision of such an account would be a very difficult matter. Undoubtedly, any such account would be quite controversial. Hence, it surely should not reflect badly on this sketch of an elementary theory of the wrongness of killing that it is indeterminate with respect to some very difficult issues regarding animal rights.

In the third place, the claim that the loss of one's future is the wrong-making feature of one's being killed does not entail, as sanctity of human life theories do, that active euthanasia is wrong. Persons who are severely and incurably ill, who face a future of pain and despair, and who wish to die will not have suffered a loss if they are killed. It is, strictly speaking, the value of a human's future which makes killing wrong in this theory. This being so, killing does not necessarily wrong some persons.who are sick and dying. Of course, there may be other reasons for a prohibition of active euthanasia, but that is another matter. Sanctity-of-human-life theories seem to hold that active euthanasia is seriously wrong even in an individual case where there seems to be good reason for it independently of public policy considerations. This consequence is most implausible, and it is a plus for the claim that the loss of a future of value is what makes killing wrong that it does not share this consequence.

In the fourth place, the account of the wrongness of killing defended in this essay does straight-forwardly entail that it is prima facie seriously wrong to kill children and infants, for we do presume that they have futures of value Since we do believe that it is.wrong to kill defenseless little babies, it is important that a theory of the wrongness of killing easily account for this. Personhood theories of the wrongness of killing, on the other hand, cannot straight-forwardly account for the wrongness of killing infants and young children.[5] Hence, such theories must add special ad hoc accounts of the wrongness of killing the young. The plausibility of such ad hoc theories seems to be a function of how desperately one wants such theories to work. The claim that the primary wrong-making feature of a killing is the loss to the victim of the value of its future accounts for the wrongness of killing young children and infants directly; it makes the wrongness of such acts as obvious as we actually think it is. This is a further merit of this theory. Accordingly, it seems that this value of a future-like-ours theory of the wrongness of killing shares strengths of both sanctity-of-life and personhood accounts while avoiding weaknesses of both. In addition, it meshes with a central intuition concerning what makes killing wrong.

The claim that the primary wrong-making feature of a killing is the loss to the victim of the value of its future has obvious consequences for the ethics of abortion. The future of a standard fetus includes a set of experiences, projects, activities, and such which are identical with the futures of adult human beings and are identical with the futures of young children. Since the reason that is sufficient to explain why it is wrong to kill human beings after the time of birth is a reason that also applies to fetuses, it follows that abortion is prima facie seriously morally wrong.

This argument does not rely on the invalid inference that, since it is wrong to kill persons, it is wrong to kill potential persons also. The category that is morally central to this analysis is the category of having a valuable future like ours; it is not the category of personhood. The argument to the conclusion that abortion is prima facie seriously morally wrong proceeded independently of the notion of person or potential person or any equivalent. Someone may wish to start with this analysis in terms of the value of a human future, conclude that abortion is, except perhaps in rare circumstances, seriously morally wrong, infer that fetuses have the right to life, and then call fetuses "persons" as a result of their having the right to life. Clearly, in this case, the category of person is being used to state the *conclusion* of the analysis rather than to generate the *argument* of the analysis.

The structure of this anti-abortion argument can be both illuminated and defended by comparing it to what appears to be the best argument for the wrongness of the wanton infliction of pain on animals. This latter argument is based on the assumption that it is prima facie wrong to inflict pain on me (or you, reader). What is the natural property associated with the infliction of pain which makes such infliction wrong? The obvious answer seems to be that the infliction of pain causes suffering and that suffering is a misfortune. The suffering caused by the infliction of pain is what makes the wanton infliction of pain on me wrong. The wanton infliction of pain on other adult humans causes suffering. The wanton infliction of pain on animals causes suffering. Since causing suffering is what makes the wanton infliction of pain wrong and since the wanton infliction of pain on animals causes suffering, it follows that the wanton infliction of pain on animals is wrong.

This argument for the wrongness of the wanton infliction of pain on animals shares a number of structural features with the argument for the serious prima facie wrongness of abortion. Both arguments start with an obvious assumption concerning what it is wrong to do to me (or you, reader). Both then look for the characteristic or the consequence of the wrong action which makes the action wrong. Both recognize that the wrong-making feature of these immoral actions is a property of actions sometimes directed at individuals other than postnatal human beings. If the structure of the argument for the wrongness of the wanton infliction of pain on animals is sound, then the structure of the argument for the prima facie serious wrongness of abortion is also sound, for the structure of the two arguments is the same. The structure common to both is the key to the explanation of how the wrongness of abortion can be demonstrated without recourse to the category of person. In neither argument is that category crucial.

This defense of an argument for the wrongness of abortion in terms of a structurally similar argument for the wrongness of the wanton infliction of pain on animals succeeds only if the account regarding animals is the correct account. Is it? In the first place, it seems plausible. In the second place, its major competition is Kant's account. Kant believed that we do not have direct duties to animals at all, because they are not persons. Hence, Kant had to explain and justify the wrongness of inflicting pain on animals on the grounds that "he who is hard in his dealings with animals becomes hard also in his dealing with men."[6] The problem with Kant's account is that there seems to be no reason for accepting this latter claim unless Kant's account is rejected. If the alternative to Kant's account is accepted, then it is easy to understand why someone who is indifferent to inflicting pain on animals is also indifferent to inflicting pain on humans, for one is indifferent to what makes inflicting pain wrong in both cases. But, if Kant's account is accepted, there is no intelligible reason why one who is hard in his dealings with animals (or crabgrass or stones) should also be hard in his dealings with men. After all, men are persons: animals are no more persons than crabgrass or stones. Persons are Kant's crucial moral category. Why, in short, should a Kantian accept the basic claim in Kant's argument?

Hence, Kant's argument for the wrongness of inflicting pain on animals rests on a claim that, in a world of Kantian moral agents, is demonstrably false. Therefore, the alternative analysis, being more plausible anyway, should be accepted. Since this alternative analysis has the same structure as the anti-abortion argument being defended here, we have further support for the argument for the immorality of abortion being defended in this essay.

Of course, this value of a future-like-ours argument, if sound, shows only that abortion is prima facie wrong, not that it is wrong in any and all circumstances. Since the loss of the future to a standard fetus, if killed, is, however, at least as great a loss as the loss of the future to a standard adult human being who is killed, abortion, like ordinary killing, could be justified only by the most compelling reasons. The loss of one's life is almost the greatest misfortune that can happen to one. Presumably abortion could be justified in some circumstances, only if the loss consequent on failing to abort would be at least as great. Accordingly, morally permissible abortions will be rare indeed unless, perhaps, they occur so early in pregnancy that a fetus is not yet definitely an individual. Hence, this argument should be taken as showing that abortion is presumptively very seriously wrong, where the presumption is very strong—as strong as the presumption that killing another adult human being is wrong. . . .

The purpose of this essay has been to set out an argument for the serious presumptive wrongness of abortion subject to the assumption that the moral permissibility of abortion stands or falls on the moral status of the fetus. Since a fetus possesses a property, the possession of which in adult human beings is sufficient to make killing an adult human being wrong, abortion is wrong. This way of dealing with the problem of abortion seems superior to other approaches to the ethics of abortion, because it rests on an ethics of killing which is close to self-evident, because the crucial morally relevant property clearly applies to fetuses, and because the argument avoids the usual equivocations on "human life," "human being," or "person." The argument rests neither on religious claims nor on Papal dogma. It is not subject to the objection of "speciesism." Its soundness is compatible with the moral permissibility of euthanasia and contraception. It deals with our intuitions concerning young children.

Finally, this analysis can be viewed as resolving a standard problem—indeed, *the* standard problem—concerning the ethics of abortion. Clearly, it is wrong to kill adult human beings. Clearly, it is not wrong to end the life of some arbitrarily chosen single human cell. Fetuses seem to be like arbitrarily chosen human cells in some respects and like adult humans in other respects. The problem of the ethics of abortion is the problem of determining the fetal property that settles this moral controversy. The thesis of this essay is that the problem of the ethics of abortion, so understood, is solvable.

NOTES

1. Feinberg, "Abortion," in *Matters of Life and Death: New Introductory Essays in Moral Philosophy,* Tom Regan, ed. (New York: Random House, 1986), pp. 256–293; Tooley, "Abortion and Infanticide,"

Philosophy and Public Affair, II, 1 (1972):37–65, Tooley, *Abortion and Infanticide* (New York: Oxford, 1984); Warren, "On the Moral and Legal Status of Abortion," *The Monist,* I. VII, 1 (1993): 43–61; Engelhardt, "The Ontology of Abortion," *Ethics,* I.XXXIV, 3 (1974):217–234; Summer, *Abortion and Moral Theory* (Princeton: University Press, 1981); Noonan, "An Almost Absolute Value in History," in *The Morality of Abortion: Legal and Historical Perspectives,* Noonan, ed. (Cambridge: Harvard, 1970); and Devine, *The Ethics of Homicide* (Ithaca: Cornell, 1978).

2. For interesting discussions of this issue, see Warren Quinn, "Abortion: Identity and *Loss,*" *Philosophy and Public Affairs,* XIII, 1 (1984): 24–54; and Lawrence C. Becker, "Human Being: The Boundaries of the Concept," *Philcsophy and Public Affairs,* IV, 4 (1975): 334–359.

3. For example, see my "Ethics and The Elderly: Some Problems," in Stuart Spicker, Kathleen Woodward, and David Van Tassel, eds. *Aging and the Elderly: Humanistic Perspectives in Gerontology* (Atlantic Highlands, NJ: Humanities, 1978), pp. 341–355.

4. I have been most influenced on this matter by Jonathan Glover, *Causing Death and Saving Lives* (New York: Penguin, 1977), ch. 3; and Robert Young, "What Is So Wrong with Killing People?" *Philosophy,* 1. IV, 210 (1979):515–528.

5. Feinberg, Tooley, Warren, and Engelhardt have all dealt with this problem.

6. "Duties to Animals and Spirits," in *Lectures on Ethics,* Louis Infeld, trans. (New York: Harper, 1963), p. 239.

Selective Termination of Pregnancy and Women's Reproductive Autonomy

Christine Overall

Christine Overall is a professor of philosophy at Queen's University in Canada. She is the author of Ethics and Human Reproduction: A Feminist Analysis *(1987), and the editor of* Feminist Perspectives *(1988) and* The Future of Human Reproduction *(1989).*

  Overall tackles the difficult question of abortion where a woman is carrying two or more fetuses. The case is difficult, because unlike standard abortion cases, the decision to abort is not a decision to end pregnancy but rather often a decision to enhance the likelihood of continuing a pregnancy full term. Overall also points out that the decision to abort one of the fetuses occurs as a result of a technological intervention which has made it much more likely than otherwise that multiple fetuses will form in the first place. The so-called "demand" for abortion in these cases is actually seen as a necessary effect of the artificially produced hyperfertility of certain women. Overall concludes that fetuses cannot all have a right to be carried to term by a woman.

The development of techniques for selective termination of pregnancy has added further questions to debates about women's reproductive self-determination. The procedure is performed during the first or second trimester in some instances of multiple pregnancy, either to eliminate a fetus found through prenatal diagnosis to be handicapped or at risk of a disability, or simply to reduce the number of fetuses in the uterus. More than two hundred cases of selective termination are known to have been performed around the world.[1]

Physicians and ethicists have expressed reservations about selective termination, both with respect to its moral justification and to the formation of social policy governing access to and resource allocation for this procedure. Selective termination has been viewed as invoking a right to kill a fetus rather than to control one's body, as with abortion,[2] and some commentators have recommended restricting the procedure to pregnancies of three or more[3] and even stipulated a need for national guidelines for the procedure.[4]

Many discussions appear to assume that selective termination is primarily a matter of acting against some fetus(es) on behalf of others. For example, Diana Brahams describes the issue as follows:

> Is it ethical and legally appropriate to carry out a selective reduction of pregnancy—that is, to destroy one or more fetuses in order to give the remaining fetus or fetuses a better chance?[5]

Reprinted with permission of *The Hastings Center Report*, May/June 1990.

However, this construction of the problem is radically incomplete, since it omits attention to the women—their bodies and their lives—who should be at the center of any discussion of selective termination. When Margaret Somerville, for example, expresses concern about "the right to kill a fetus who is competing with another for space," she neglects to mention that the "space" in question is the pregnant woman's uterus. In fact, selective termination vividly instantiates many of the central ethical and policy concerns that must be raised about the technological manipulation of women's reproductive capacities.

Evans and colleagues state that "the ethical issues [of selective termination] are the same in multiple pregnancies whether the cause is spontaneous conception or infertility treatment" (293). Such a claim is typical of many discussions in contemporary bioethics, which abstract specific moral and social problems from the cultural context that produced them. But the issue of selective termination of pregnancy demonstrates the necessity of examining the social and political environment in which issues in biomedical ethics arise.

Selective termination itself must be understood and evaluated with reference to its own particular context. The apparent need or demand for selective termination in fact is created and elaborated in response to prior technological interventions in women's reproductive processes, themselves the result of prevailing cultural interpretations of infertility.

Hence, it is essential to explore the significance of selective termination for women's reproductive autonomy. The issue acquires added urgency at this point in both Canada and the United States when access to and allocation of funding for abortion are the focus of renewed controversy. Although not precisely the same as abortion, selective termination is similar insofar as in both cases one or more fetuses are destroyed. They differ in that in abortion the pregnancy ends whereas in selective termination, ideally, the pregnancy continues with one or more fetuses still present. I will argue that, provided a permissive abortion policy is justified (that is, a policy that allows abortion until the end of the second trimester), a concern for women's reproductive autonomy precludes any general policy restricting access to selective termination of pregnancy, as well as clinical practices that discriminate on nonmedical grounds as to which women will be permitted to choose the procedure or how many fetuses they must retain.

A TECHNOLOGICAL FIX

In recent discussions of selective termination, women with multiple pregnancies are often represented as demanding the procedure—sometimes by threatening to abort the entire pregnancy if they are not allowed selective termination.[6]

The assumption that individual women "demand" selective termination of pregnancy places all moral responsibility for the procedure on the women themselves. However, neither the multiple pregnancies nor the "demands" for selective termination originated *ex nihilo*. An examination of their sources suggests both that moral responsibility for selective termination cannot rest solely on individual women and that the "demand" for selective termination is not just a straightforward exercise of reproductive freedom.

Deliberate societal and medical responses to the perceived problem of female infertility generate much of the demand for selective termination, which is but one result of a complex system of values and beliefs concerning fertility and infertility, maternity and children. Infertility is not merely a physical condition; it is both interpreted and evaluated within cultural contexts that help to specify the appropriate beliefs about and responses to the condition of being unable to reproduce. According to the prevailing ideology of pronatalism, women must reproduce, men must acquire offspring, and both parents should be biologically related to their offspring. A climate of acquisition and commodification encourages and reinforces the notion of child as possession. Infertility is seen as a problem for which the solution must be acquiring a child of one's own, biologically related to oneself, at almost any emotional, physical, or economic costs.[7]

The recent increase in numbers of multiple pregnancies comes largely from two steps taken in the treatment of infertility. The use of fertility drugs to prod women's bodies into ovulating and producing more than one ovum at a time results in an incidence of multiple gestation ranging from 16 to 33 percent.[8] Gamete intrafallopian transfer (GIFT) using several eggs, and in vitro fertilization (IVF) with subsequent implantation of several embryos in the woman's uterus to increase the likelihood that she will become pregnant may also result in multiple gestation. As Brahams notes, "Pregnancy rate increments are about 8 percent for each pre-embryo replaced in IVF, giving expected pregnancy rates of 8, 16, 24, and 32 percent for 1, 2, 3, and 4 pre-embryos, respectively" (1409). A "try anything" mentality is fostered by the fact that prospective IVF patients are often not adequately informed about the very low clinical success rates ("failure rates" would be a more appropriate term) of the procedure.[9] A case reported by Evans and colleagues dramatically illustrates the potential effects of these treatments: One woman's reproductive history included three cesarean sections, a tubal ligation, a tuboplasty (after

which she remained infertile), in vitro fertilization with subsequent implantation of four embryos, selective termination of two of the fetuses, revelation via ultrasound that one of the remaining twins had "severe oligohydramnios and no evidence of a bladder or kidneys," spontaneous miscarriage of the abnormal twin, and intrauterine death of the remaining fetus (291).

In a commentary critical of selective termination, Angela Holder quotes Oscar Wilde's dictum: "In this world, there are only two tragedies. One is not getting what one wants, and the other is getting it" (22). But this begs the question of what is meant by saying that women "want" multiple pregnancy, or "want" selective termination of pregnancy.[10] What factors led these women to take infertility drugs and/or participate in an IVF program? How do they evaluate fertility, pregnancy, motherhood, children? How do they perceive themselves as women, as potential mothers, as infertile, and where do children fit into these visions? To what degree were they adequately informed of the likelihood that they would gestate more than one fetus? Were they provided with adequate support to enable them to clarify their own reasons and goals for seeking reproductive interventions, and to provide assistance throughout the emotionally and physically demanding aspects of the treatment? Barbara Katz Rothman's appraisal of women who abort fetuses with genetic defects has more general applicability:

> They are the victims of a social system that fails to take collective responsibility for the needs of its members, and leaves individual women to make impossible choices. We are spared collective responsibility, because we individualize the problem. We make it the woman's own. She "chooses," and so we owe her nothing.[11]

Uncritical use of the claim that certain women "demand" selective termination implies that they are just selfish, unable to extend their caring to more than one or two infants, particularly if one has a disability. But this interpretation appears unjustified. In general, participants in IVF programs are extremely eager for a child. They are encouraged to be self-sacrificing, to be acquiescent in the manipulations the medical system requires their bodies to undergo. As John C. Hobbins notes, these women "have often already volunteered for innovative treatments and may be desperate to try another." The little evidence so far available suggests that if anything these women are, by comparison to their male partners, somewhat passive in regard to the making of reproductive decisions.[12] There is no evidence to suggest that most are not willing to assume the challenges of multiple pregnancy.

An additional cause of multiple pregnancy is the conflicting attitudes toward the embryo and fetus manifested in infertility research and clinical practice. One report suggests that multiple pregnancies resulting from IVF are generated not only because clinicians are driven by the motive to succeed—and implantation of large numbers of embryos appears to offer that prospect—but also because of "intimidation of medical practitioners by critics and authorities who insist that all fertilized eggs or pre-embryos be immediately returned to the patient."[13] Such "intimidation" does not, of course, excuse clinicians who may sacrifice their patients' well-being. Nevertheless, conservative beliefs in the necessity and inevitability of procreation and the sacredness and "personhood" of the embryo may contribute to the production of multiple pregnancies.

Thus, the technological "solutions" to some forms of female infertility create an additional problem of female hyperfertility—to which a further technological "solution" of selective termination is then offered. Women's so-called "demand" for selective termination of pregnancy is not a primordial expression of individual need, but a socially constructed response to prior medical interventions.

The debate over access to selective pregnancy termination exemplifies a classic no-win situation for women, in which medical technology generates a solution to a problem itself generated by medical technology—yet women are regarded as immoral for seeking that solution. While women have been, in part, victimized through the use of reproductive interventions that fail to respect and facilitate their reproductive autonomy, they are nevertheless unjustifiably held responsible for their attempts to cope with the outcomes of these interventions in the forms made available to them. From this perspective, selective termination is not so much an extension of women's reproductive choice as it is the extension of control over women's reproductive capacity—through the use of fertility drugs, GIFT, and IVF as "solutions" to infertility that often result, when successful, in multiple gestations; through the provision of a technology, selective termination, to respond to multiple gestation that may create much of the same ambivalence for women as is generated by abortion; and finally through the imposition of limitations on women's access to the procedure.

In decisions about selective termination, women are not simply feckless, selfish, and irresponsible. Nor are they mere victims of their social conditioning and the machinations of the medical and scientific establishments. But they must make their choices in the face of extensive socialization for maternity, a limited range of options, and sometimes inadequate information about outcomes. When women "demand" selective termination of pregnancy they are attempting to take action in response to a situation not of their own making, in the only way that seems available to them. Hence my argument is not that women are merely helpless victims and therefore must be permitted access to selective termination, but rather that it would be both socially irresponsible and unjust for a health care system that contributes to the generation of problematic multiple pregnancies to withhold access to a potential, if flawed, response to the situation.

SELECTIVE TERMINATION AND ABORTION

There is reason to believe that women's attitudes toward selective termination may be similar to their attitudes toward abortion. Although abortion is a solution to the problem of unwanted pregnancy, and the general availability of abortion accords women significant and essential reproductive freedom, it is often an occasion for ambivalence, and remains, as Caroline Whitbeck has pointed out, a "grim option" for most women.[14] Women who abort are, after all, undergoing a surgical invasion of their bodies, and some may also experience emotional distress. Moreover, for some women the death of the fetus is a source of grief, particularly when the pregnancy is wanted and the abortion is sought because of severe fetal disabilities.[15]

Comparable factors may contribute to women's reservations about selective termination of pregnancy. Those who resort to this procedure surely do not desire the invasion of their uterus, nor do they make it their aim to kill fetuses. In fact, unlike women who request abortions because their pregnancy is unwanted, most of those who seek selective termination are originally pregnant by choice. And as Evans and colleagues note, such pregnancies are "not only wanted but achieved at great psychological and economic cost after a lengthy struggle with infertility" (292).

For such women a procedure that risks the loss of all fetuses as selective termination does, may be especially troubling. The procedure is still experimental, and its short- and long-term outcomes are largely unknown. Richard C. Berkowitz and colleagues suggest that "[a]lthough the risks associated with selective reduction are known, the dearth of experience with the procedure to date makes it impossible to assess their likelihood" (1046). Further, in their report on four cases of selective termination, Evans and coworkers state that:

> [A]ny attempt to reduce the number of fetuses [is] experimental and [can] result in miscarriage, and . . . infection, bleeding, and other unknown risks [are] possible. If successful, the attempt could theoretically damage the remaining fetuses (290).

Note that "success" in the latter case would be seriously limited, assuming that the pregnant woman's goal is to gestate and subsequently deliver one or more healthy infants. In fact, success in this more plausible sense is fairly low.[16] As a consequence, in their study of first trimester selective termination, Berkowitz *et al.* mention the "psychological difficulty of making the decision [to undergo selective termination]," a difficulty partly resulting from "emotional bonding" with the fetuses after repeated ultrasound examinations (1046).

Thus, women undergoing selective termination, like those undergoing abortion, are choosing a grim option; they are ending the existence of one or more fetuses because the alternatives—aborting all the fetuses (and taking the risk that they will never again succeed in becoming pregnant), or attempting to maintain all the fetuses through pregnancy, delivery, and childbearing—are unacceptable, morally, medically, or practically.

THE CHALLENGES OF MULTIPLE GESTATION

Why don't women who seek selective termination simply continue their pregnancies? No matter how much it is taken for granted, the accomplishment of gestating and birthing even one child is an extraordinary event; perhaps even more praise should be given to the woman who births twins or triplets or quadruplets. Rather than setting policy limits on women who are not able or willing to gestate more than one or two fetuses, we should recognize and understand the extraordinary challenges posed by multiple pregnancies.

There are good consequentialist reasons why a woman might choose to reduce the number of fetuses she carries. For the pregnant woman, continuation of a multiple pregnancy means, Evans notes, "almost certain preterm delivery, prefaced by early and lengthy hospitalization, higher risks of pregnancy-induced hypertension, polyhydramnios, severe anemia, preeclampsia, and postpartum blood transfusions" (292).[17]

The so-called "minor discomforts" of pregnancy are increased in a multiple pregnancy, and women may suffer severe nausea and vomiting or become depressed or anxious. There is also an increased likelihood of cesarean delivery, entailing more pain and a longer recovery time after the birth.[18]

Infants born of multiple pregnancy risk "premature delivery, low infant birthweight, birth defects, and problems of infant immaturity, including physical and mental retardation."[19] Moreover, as Evans and colleagues note, there is a high likelihood that these infants "may . . . suffer a lengthy, costly process of dying in neonatal intensive care" (295). Thus a woman carrying more than one fetus also faces the possibility of becoming a mother to infants who will be seriously physically impaired or will die.

It is also important to count the social costs of bearing several children simultaneously, where the responsibilities, burdens, and lost opportunities occasioned by childrearing fall primarily if not exclusively upon the woman rather than upon her male partner (if any) or more equitably upon the society as a whole—particularly when the infants are disabled. A recent article on Canada's first set of "test-tube quintuplets" reported that the babies' mother, Mae Collier, changes diapers fifty times a day, and goes through twelve liters of milk a day and 150 jars of baby food a week. Her husband works full time outside of the home and "spends much of his spare time building the family's new house."[20]

Moreover, while North American culture is strongly pronatalist, it is simultaneously anti-child. One of the most prevalent myths of the West is that North Americans love and spoil their children. A sensitive examination—perhaps from the perspective of a child or a loving parent—of the conditions in which many children grow up puts the lie to this myth.[21] Children are among the most vulnerable victims of poverty and malnutrition. Subjected to physical and sexual abuse, educated in schools that more often aim for custody and confinement than growth and learning, exploited as opportunities for the mass marketing of useless and sometimes dangerous foods and toys, children, the weakest members of our society, are often the least protected. Children are virtually the last social group in North America for whom discrimination and segregation are routinely countenanced. In many residential areas, businesses, restaurants, hotels, and other "public" places, children are not welcome, and except in preschools and nurseries, there is usually little or no accommodation to their physical needs and capacities.

A society that is simultaneously pronatalist but anti-child and only minimally supportive of mothering is unlikely to welcome quintuplets and other multiples—except for their novelty—any more than it welcomes single children. The issue, then, is not just how many fetuses a woman can be required to gestate, but also how many children she can be required to raise, and under what sort of societal conditions.

To this argument it is no adequate rejoinder to say that such women should continue their pregnancies and then surrender some but not all of the infants for adoption by eager childless and infertile couples. It is one thing for a woman to have the choice of making this decision after careful thought and with full support throughout the pregnancy and afterward when the infants have been given up. Such a choice may be hard enough. It would be another matter, however, to advocate a policy that would restrict selective termination in such a way that gestating all the fetuses and surrendering some becomes a woman's only option.

First, the presence of each additional fetus places further demands on the woman's physical and emotional resources; gestating triplets or quadruplets is not just the same as gestating twins. Second, to compel a woman to continue to gestate fetuses she does not want for the sake of others who do is to treat the woman as a mere breeder, a biological machine for the production of new human beings. Finally, it would be callous indeed to ignore the emotional turmoil

and pain of the woman who must gestate and deliver a baby only to surrender it to others. In the case of a multiple gestation an added distress would arise because of the necessity of somehow choosing which infant(s) to keep and which to give up.

REPRODUCTIVE RIGHTS

Within the existing social context, therefore, access to selective termination must be understood as an essential component of women's reproductive rights. But it is important to distinguish between the right to reproduce and the right not to reproduce. Entitlement to access to selective termination, like entitlement to access to abortion, falls within the right not to reproduce.[22]

Entitlement to choose how many fetuses to gestate, and of what sort, is in this context a limited and negative one. If women are entitled to choose to end their pregnancies altogether, then they are also entitled to choose how many fetuses and of what sort they will carry. If it is unjustified to deny a woman access to an abortion of all fetuses in her uterus, then it is also unjustified to deny her access to the termination of some of those fetuses. Furthermore, if abortion is legally permitted in cases where the fetus is seriously handicapped, it is inconsistent to refuse to permit the termination of one handicapped fetus in a multiple pregnancy.

One way of understanding abortion as an exercise of the right not to reproduce is to see it as the premature emptying of the uterus, or the deliberate termination of the fetus's occupancy of the womb. If a woman has an entitlement to an abortion, that is to the emptying of her uterus of all its occupants, then there is no ground to compel her to maintain all the occupants of her uterus if she chooses to retain only some of them.

While the risks of multiple pregnancy for both the fetuses and the pregnant woman increase with the number of fetuses involved, it does not follow that restrictions on selective termination for pregnancies with smaller numbers of fetuses would be justified. Legal or medical policy cannot consistently say, "you may choose whether to be pregnant, that is, whether your uterus shall be occupied, but you may not choose how many shall occupy your uterus."

More generally, if abortion of a healthy singleton pregnancy is permitted for any reason, as a matter of the woman's choice, within the first five months or so of pregnancy, it is inconsistent to refuse to permit the termination of one or more healthy fetuses in a multiple pregnancy. To say otherwise is unjustifiably to accord the fetuses a right to occupancy of the woman's uterus. It is to say that two or more human entities, at an extremely immature stage in their development, have the right to use a human person's body. But no embryo or fetus has a right to the use of a pregnant woman's body—any more than any other human being, at whatever stage of development, has a right to use another's body.[23] The absence of that right is recognized through state-sanctioned access to abortion. Fetuses do not acquire a right, either collectively or individually, to use a woman's uterus simply because there are several of them present simultaneously. Even if a woman is willingly and happily pregnant she does not surrender her entitlement to bodily self-determination, and she does not, specifically, surrender her entitlement to determine how many human entities may occupy her uterus.

Although I defend a social policy that does not set limits on access to selective termination of pregnancy, there can be no denying that the procedure may raise serious moral problems. As some persons with disabilities have pointed out, there is a special moral significance to the termination of a fetus with a disability such as Down syndrome.[24] The use of prenatal diagnosis followed by abortion or selective termination may have eugenic overtones, when the presupposition is that we can ensure only high quality babies will be born, and that "defective" fetuses can be eliminated before birth.[25] The fetus is treated as a product for which "quality control" measures are appropriate. Moreover, as amniocentesis and chorionic villus sampling reveal the sex of offspring, there is also a possibility that selective termination of pregnancy could be used, as abortion already is, to eliminate fetuses of the "wrong" sex—in most cases, that is, those that are female.[26]

These possibilities are distressing and potentially dangerous to disabled persons and to women generally. The way to deal with these and other moral reservations about selective termination is not to prohibit the procedure or to limit access to it on such grounds as fetal disability or fetal sex choice. Instead, part of the answer is to change the conditions that promote large numbers of embryos and fetuses. For example, since as Evans and colleagues astutely note, "[m]any of the currently known instances of grand multiple pregnancies should have never happened" (296), the administration of fertility drugs to induce ovulation can be carefully monitored, and for IVF and GIFT procedures, more use can be made of the natural ovulatory cycle and of cryopreservation of embryos.[27] The number of eggs implanted through GIFT and the number of embryos implanted after IVF can be limited—not by unilateral decision of the physician, but after careful consultation with the woman about the chances of multiple pregnancy and her attitudes toward it.[28] To that end, there is a need for further research on predicting the likelihood of multiple pregnancy.[29] And, given the experimental nature of selective termination, genuinely informed choice should be mandatory for prospective patients, who need to know both the short- and long-term risks and outcomes of the procedure. Acquiring this information will necessitate the "long-term follow-up of parents and children . . . to assess the psychological and physical effects of fetal reduction."[30] By these means the numbers of selective terminations can be reduced, and the women who seek selective termination can be both protected and empowered.

More generally, however, we should carefully reevaluate both the pronatalist ideology and the system of treatments of infertility that constitute the context in which selective termination of pregnancy comes to seem essential. There is also a need to improve social support for parenting, and to transform the conditions that make it difficult or impossible to be the mother of triplets, quadruplets, etc. or of a baby with a severe disability. Only through the provision of committed care for children and support for women's self-determination will genuine reproductive freedom and responsibility be attained.

ACKNOWLEDGMENT

I would like to acknowledge the assistance of Monica Webster, Queen's University Health Sciences Library, in locating resource material for this paper.

NOTES

1. Marie T. Mulcahy, Brian Roberman, and S.E. Reid, "Chorion Biopsy, Cytogenetic Diagnosis, and Selective Termination in a Twin Pregnancy at Risk of Haemophilia" (letter), *The Lancet,* 13 October 1984, 866; "Selective Fetal Reduction" (review article), *The Lancet,* 1 October 1988, 773; Dorothy Lipovenko, "Infertility Technology Forces People to Make Life and Death Choices," *The Globe and Mail,* 21 January 1989, A4.

2. "Multiple Pregnancies Create Moral Dilemma," *Kingston Whig Standard,* 21 January 1989, 3.

3. Mark I. Evans *et al.* "Selective First-Trimester Termination in Octuplet and Quadruplet Pregnancies: Clinical and Ethical Issues," *Obstetrics and Gynecology* 71:3, pt. I (1988), 289–296, at 293; Richard L. Berkowitz, *et al.,* "Selective Reduction of Multifetal Pregnancies in the First Trimester," *New England Journal of Medicine* 118:16 (1988), 1043. Berkowitz and colleagues regard even triplet pregnancies as constituting a "gray area" for physician and patient. However, it is not clear whether this hesitation is based on moral scruples in addition to the medical risks.

4. Lipovenko, "Infertility Technology."

5. Diana Brahams, "Assisted Reproduction and Selective Reduction of Pregnancy," *The Lancet,* 12 December 1987, 1409; cf. John C Hobbins, "Selective Reduction—A Perinatal Necessity?", *New England Journal of Medicine* 318:16 (1988), 1063; Evans *et al.,* "Selective First-Trimester Termination," 295.

6. One television interviewer who talked to me about this issue described women as "forcing" doctors to provide the procedure! See also "Multiple Pregnancies Create Moral Dilemma"; Angela R. Holder and Mary Sue Henifin, "Selective Termination of Pregnancy," *Hastings Center Report* 18:1 (1988), 21–22.

7. Christine Overall, *Ethics and Human Reproduction: A Feminist Analysis* (Boston: Allen & Unwin, 1987), 139–56.

8. Hobbins, "Selective Reduction," 1062.

9. Gena Corea and Susan Ince, "Report of a Survey of IVF Clinics in the U.S.," in *Made to Order: The Myth of Reproductive and Genetic Progress,* Patricia Spallone and Deborah Lynn Steinberg, eds. (Oxford: Pergamon Press, 1987), 133–45.

10. Compare the ambiguity of the claim "women want it" in connection with in vitro fertilization. See Christine Crowe, "Women Want It: In Vitro Fertilization and Women's Motivations for Participation" in Spallone and Steinberg, *Made to Order,* 84–93.

11. Barbara Katz Rothman, *The Tentative Pregnancy: Prenatal Diagnosis and the Future of Motherhood* (New York: Viking, 1986), 189.

12. Judith Lorber, "In Vitro Fertilization and Gender Politics," in *Embryos, Ethics, and Women's Rights,* Elaine Hoffman Barach, Amadeo F. D'Adamo, Jr., and Joni Seager, eds. (New York: Haworth Press, 1988), 123–26.

13. "Selective Fetal Reduction," 774.

14. Caroline Whitbeck, "The Moral Implications of Regarding Women as People: New Perspectives on Pregnancy and Personhood," in *Abortion and*

the Status of the Fetus, William B. Bondeson *et al.,* eds. (Boston: Reidel, 1984), 251–52.

15. Rothman, *The Tentative Pregnancy,* 177–216. She describes abortion in the case of fetal defect as "the chosen tragedy" (180).

16. Evans *et al.* give a success rate of 50% (p. 289), while Berkowitz *et al.* give 66–2/3% (1043). Angela Holder quotes a success rate of 55% (21).

17. Cf. Berkowitz *et al.,* "Selective Reduction," 1045; and Alastair H. MacLennan, "Multiple Gestation: Clinical Characteristics and Management," in *Maternal-Fetal Medicine: Principles and Practice,* Robert K. Creasy and Robert Resnick, eds. (Philadelphia: W.B. Saunders, 2nd ed., 1989), 581–84.

18. Jose C. Scerbo, Powan Rattan, and Joan E. Drukker, "Twins and Other Multiple Gestations," in *High-Risk Pregnancy: A Team Approach,* Robert A. Knuppel and Joan E. Drukker, eds. (Philadelphia: W.B. Saunders, 1986), 347–46, 358; Martin L. Pernoll, Gerda I. Benda, and S. Gorham Babson, *Diagnosis and Management of the Fetus and Neonate at Risk: A Guide for Team Care* (St. Louis: C.V. Mosby, 5th ed., 1986), 192–93.

19. "Selective Fetal Reduction," 773.

20. Victoria Stevens, "Test-Tube Quints Celebrate First Birthday," *The Toronto Star* 6 February 1989, A7.

21. See Letty Cottin Pogrebin, *Family Politics: Love and Power on an Intimate Frontier* (New York: McGraw-Hill, 1983), 42.

22. Overall, *Ethics and Human Reproduction,* 166–68.

23. Overall, *Ethics and Human Reproduction,* 76–79.

24. Adrienne Asch, "Reproductive Technology and Disability," in *Reproductive Laws for the 1990s,* Sherrill Cohen and Nadine Taub, eds. (Clifton, NJ: Humana Press, 1989), 69–117; Marsha Saxton, "Prenatal Screening and Discriminatory Attitudes About Disability," in *Embryos, Ethics, and Women's Rights,* 217–24.

25. Ruth Hubbard, "Eugenics: New Tools, Old Ideas," in *Embryos, Ethics, and Women's Rights,* 225–35.

26. Cf. Robyn Rowland, "Motherhood, Patriarchal Power, Alienation and the Issue of 'Choice' in Sex Preselection," in *Man-Made Women,* 74–87.

27. Hobbins, "Selective Reduction," 1063; "Selective Fetal Reduction," 773, 774.

28. Brahams, "Assisted Reproduction," 1409.

29. Ian Craft *et al.,* "Multiple Pregnancy, Selective Reduction, and Flexible Treatment" (letter), *The Lancet,* 5 November 1988, 1087.

30. "Selective Fetal Reduction," 775.

Can Late Abortion
Be Ethically Justified?

Ren-Zong Qiu, Chun-Zhi Wang, and Yuan Gu

Ren-Zong Qiu is the director of the Medical Ethics program, Institute of Philosophy, Academy of Social Sciences of China, Beijing, People's Republic of China.

Chun-Zhi Wang is the chief of the Unit for Medical Ethics at Capital Medical College, Beijing, People's Republic of China.

Yuan Gu is chief of the Unit for Philosophy of Science at Capital Medical College, Beijing, People's Republic of China.

Qiu, Wang, and Gu defend the current policy in the People's Republic of China favoring late-term abortions for those who are unmarried or who already have a child. Concerning unmarried women, the authors point out that in China there is no possibility of supporting a child on the wages one person can earn. This consideration makes even late-term abortion potentially justifiable. For women who already have one child, control of the world's largest population is in conflict with considerations of fetal survival and the woman's health. In general, these authors argue for a consequentialist approach to abortion that could, in some circumstances, justify late-term abortion.

THORNY CASES

Miss A is a 25-year-old unmarried woman working in a factory. She lived with her boyfriend and became pregnant. She was not aware of her condition in the early stage of her pregnancy, because she lacked education in reproduction. After she realized that she was pregnant, she was afraid to undergo an abortion. She used a cloth to bind her waist to hide her illegitimate pregnancy from others, and she was burdened with anxieties every day. Her pregnancy was revealed when the fetus was eight months old. Responsible men in her factory escorted her to the hospital and asked the physician to perform an abortion. The physician agreed, because the young woman did not want the child, and because she had no birth quota as an unmarried woman.[1] The physician performed the abortion using an intraamniotic injection of Huangyan Flower,[2] and a 2800 g. dead baby was expelled the next day.

Mrs. B is another story. She is a 30-year-old accountant, the wife of an army officer. She has been pregnant two times, but only gave birth once, to a girl, and was given a "One Child" certificate.[3] When she became aware of being pregnant the third time, she felt a physical difference, and she inferred that the fetus might possibly be a boy. Her husband was performing his duty outside Beijing at that time. She made every effort to hide the truth for seven months. During this period she economized on food and clothing, and she worked very

Reprinted by permission of *The Journal of Medicine and Philosophy*, 1989.

hard to save money for the penalty fine;[4] both courses of action jeopardized her health. When her husband came home to visit, he persuaded her to give up the fetus in the interests of their family and country. Mrs. B. agreed, and was escorted by her husband to the hospital to undergo an abortion. After examination, the physician found her malnourished, dropsical, Hgb 4g., heart rate 120/min., fetal heartbeat quite weak. She was given supportive treatment first, and then an intraamniotic injection of Rivanol several days later. A 1800 g. dead baby was born the next day.

The experience of Mrs. C. is somewhat different. She is a 40-year-old worker in a state-owned factory, with two daughters and one son from five pregnancies. She wanted more children. When she conceived the sixth time, she succeeded in covering the truth until seven months later, when the cadres of her factory discovered her condition. The cadres asked her to give up the fetus, but she refused, because she believed the Chinese maxim "More children, more happiness." She said she did not care if she were fined. One month later she was persuaded to undergo an abortion, but the physician refused to perform the operation. The cadres of her factory complained that if she gave birth to a fourth child, the rewards of all of the workers would be diminished, because they had broken the birth quota assigned to the factory.[5] Finally the physician was convinced, and he performed the abortion with an intraamniotic injection of Huangyan Flower. The next day a 3000 g. live baby was born, and later adopted by an infertile couple.

REASONS FOR LATE ABORTIONS

From the cases described above we know that there are two groups of pregnant women who undergo late abortion: the unmarried woman, and those who want more than one child but who are convinced at a late date to forgo the fetus.

The rate of pregnancy in unmarried women has increased in recent decades. With the wide application and free distribution of contraceptives, and the opening of the door to foreign cultures, China is undergoing its own form of the "sexual revolution." But sex education is still unavailable to young men, including knowledge on how to use contraceptives. According to one study in nine villages of Jiangbei County in the Sichuan Province, the average rate of illegitimate pregnancies was 50–82%. In one village it was as high as 90%; and in another village the rates in 1979, 1980, and 1981 were 44%, 53%, and 71% respectively (Hua, 1984). We think that the figures may not be representative, but only indicative. In a region of Shanghai city, among the pregnant women who underwent abortion, the rate of unmarried women was 8.4%; but in recent years it has been as high as 40% in some hospitals in Beijing and other cities.

In the early stages of pregnancy, these unmarried women made every effort to hide the truth from others. However, it is hardly possible for them to raise a child by themselves, for moral and economic reasons. The average income of a young woman is below 100 yuan ($27) per month. And changes in the moral environment lag behind the change in the sexual behavior of youth. In Chinese public opinion, premarital sexual relations are still considered unethical, an illegitimate pregnancy even more so. In some cities, abortion in hospitals was allowed only for married women, in an attempt to decrease or put an end to illegitimate pregnancies. As a result, however, there was an increase in the rate of late and illegal abortions which usually led to the death of both mother and fetus.

In our opinion, appropriate sex and reproductive education should be provided to young people, and there should be a change of attitude toward premarital sexual relations and illegitimate pregnancies. We believe that the attitude should be more lenient, in order to make it easier for pregnant girls to tell the truth and to have an abortion earlier and more safely, if they do not want to carry the pregnancy to term.

The case of pregnancy in a woman who already has a child is much more complicated. It is the Confucian cultural tradition which encourages the Chinese to have more children. Confucius said "Among the three vices that violate the principle of filial piety, the biggest is to be without offspring." The Chinese turned this negative warning into a positive maxim: "More children, more virtues." In the case of Mrs. B, she wanted a male child. Chinese tradition values male children more highly than females, because genealogy is continued through the male. But the desire to have more children, or a male child, often conflicts with the state policy of "one couple, one child." In Mrs. B's case, it also conflicted with the interests of her colleagues in the factory where she worked. However, Mrs. B and Mrs. C were finally persuaded to agree to undergo an abortion in the interest of their country and their colleagues. Can this be ethically justified?

CONFLICTS OF VALUES

There are conflicts of values around the ethical issue of late abortion which cannot be solved exclusively by deontological theory. The Chinese Ministry of Health has promulgated a regulation to prohibit late abortions after 28 weeks, with the purpose of protecting the health and life of the mother as well as of the fetus. But at the same time, since the beginning of the 1980s, the Chinese government has promulgated a regulation of birth control which permits a couple to have only one child. These two regulations are in conflict, but the latter is the more powerful. It is argued that this regulation ("one couple, one child") is in the maximum interest of the maximum number of people. Rewards in a factory are connected not only with one's work performance, but also with one's reproductive behavior.

If you give birth to a second child, you will be fined *and* the rewards of all of your colleagues will be deducted. This practice forces a fertile married woman to consider the consequences of her reproductive behavior for others before making a decision. Some married women, most of whom are professionals and intellectuals, do not want more than one child. A few of them do not even want to get married. Some want more than one child, but they are reluctant to be in a position to be fined, or they think they should put the interest of their country first by carrying out the birth control policy. But there are still a few women who insist on having another child. The outcome is usually that they are finally persuaded to undergo an abortion, or they give birth to the child in spite of the financial or psychological pressures from their colleagues or their employers.

In our opinion, it is difficult to say which conduct is moral or immoral. For a woman not to have any more children, for whatever reason, may be labeled praiseworthy conduct; but if a woman wants more than one child, it is not a vicious desire. "Moral" or "immoral" may be too strong a label to apply in such cases.

But value conflicts exist. In preceding years, when the technology for late abortion was underdeveloped and no third party intruded, the balance would usually incline towards rejecting late abortion in the interest of protecting the mother and the viable fetus. Now the scale is more evenly stacked. On the one side is the presumed interest of the viable fetus; on the other are the interests of a big third party: the country, the factory and colleagues, and the family. If the mother stands on the latter side, she tips the balance against the fetus. If she insists on giving birth, or if the late abortion would jeopardize the mother's life, the scale could be a match, or the interests of the fetus could even prevail.

PHYSICIAN'S DILEMMAS

In two of the three cases described above, the physician did not hesitate to perform a late abortion. In the third case the physician was persuaded to perform the abortion by cadres of the factory where the pregnant woman worked.

There is a schism between physicians, ethicists, and the public over late abortions.

The first to explicitly defend prohibiting abortions after seven months was an obstetrician, Dr. J.K. Liu, at the 2nd National Conference on Medical Ethics (Liu, 1983, pp. 213–218). We have asked our obstetrician friends their opinions on this issue. They always say, "I don't know what I should do." Some of them prefer not to perform late abortions except for women with particularly troubled pregnancies. Others take their responsibility to society into account first, and perform late abortions with less hesitation. The overwhelming majority of Chinese physicians are employed by state-owned hospitals; they are labeled "state cadres" and have the responsibility of carrying out state policy.

But all of them are perplexed; either way they harm one side, either the mother and fetus or society. Especially thorny is the case in which the aborted fetus is alive. Although the fertility rate is increasing now in China, and infertile couples are willing to adopt such a baby, should the physician tell the truth to the mother who had expressed a desire to give up the fetus? In some cases physicians do not do so, because they are afraid that the mother might change her mind and keep the baby.

The author of *An Outline of Medical Moral Theory* claims that in some cases, because a woman was coerced into an abortion in order to keep the birth rate low, the physician was coerced to perform late abortions, thereby violating both policy and medical morality (p. 80). But the author of *Essential Medical Ethics* claims that, "when the perinatal care came into conflict with birth control and eugenics, it must be subordinated to the needs of the latter, because these are in the interest of the whole nation and the whole of mankind, as well as in accord with the greatest morality" (pp. 191–192).

A questionnaire showed that 16% of the respondents assented to performing late abortions on women with second pregnancies, in order to conform with the state policy, 7% supported respect for the woman's free will without any interference, and 77% believed the late abortion should not be performed, but that a fine should be imposed. As for the question of who should make the decision on late abortion, 32% supported the pregnant woman and her family as the primary decision makers, 32% the physician, 9% the responsible men of the unit (factory, school, institute, etc.) where the woman was working; and 27% an ethical committee (unpublished report).

When making the decision to undergo or perform a late abortion, should the responsible parties take into account the interests of the third party, or only the interest of the woman, or only the interest of the fetus?

SOCIAL GOOD

Even as a member of an individualist society, one should be concerned about the social good, although more attention might be paid to individual rights or interests. If you are a carrier of the AIDS virus, do you have the right to have sex freely and spread the disease to others? No. A socialist country operating under the guiding ideology of Marxism favors a holistic social philosophy which asserts that a society is not merely the sum of its members but a non-additive whole which is more than the sum. Every member should put the interest of society as a whole in the first position and subordinate his or her interest to that of society. The problem is, Who is the representative of society and its interests, and how is the interest of a society as a whole known? Usually, someone claims that he is the representative, and it later turns out that this is not the case. However, in China the "one couple, one child" policy has been accepted by the majority of the Chinese people as in the best interest of the society as a whole. Of course, birth control is not the only factor, but it is one of the most important factors in modernizing underdeveloped countries in Asia, Africa, and Latin America. In a sense, the success or failure of development depends on the use of birth control. Everyone, including the married couple and the physician, should take this into account.

But we should practice birth control in a more human way. We should make every effort to avoid late abortions, i.e., to use effectively the contraceptives and to perform the abortions earlier. In the case of a late abortion, voluntary consent of the mother is indispensable. The physician should determine whether the late abortion would cause any harm to the mother's health or endanger her life, and he should refuse to perform it if there is a high risk.

In preceding years the second pregnancy was treated with more leniency and flexibility than at present. If a couple in a rural area had a child who was disabled, or if they live in a rural area that has a birth rate lower than the quota, they were permitted to give birth to a second child. But this flexibility in policy has raised the birth level, and an upsurge of second births amongst China's rural families is jeopardizing the attempt to limit the population to 1.2 billion by the year 2000. The State Statistics Bureau reports that 40% of rural women have given birth to three or more children over the past several years. Compared with 1985, the number of second births last year climbed by 1.37 million people to 6.92 million, and the number of third or more births topped 2.88 million, 240,000 more than the previous year (*China's Daily*, 1987).

CONCLUSION

Our conclusion is that the late abortion can be justified ethically in China: (1) if the "one couple, one child" policy is justifiable; (2) if the couple and the physician take the social good into account; (3) if the mother expresses her voluntary consent, no matter whether the decision is made on the basis of her own original desire or after persuasion by others that is not coercive; and (4) if the late abortion will entail only a low risk to the mother's health or life.

NOTES

1. Every married woman gets a birth quota before pregnancy; also see note 5.
2. The extraction from an herb used as an effective drug to induce abortion.
3. Whoever has such a certificate enjoys favored treatment, such as additional rewards at the factory, enrollment in a kindergarten for their child, etc.
4. If you give birth to a second child, you will be fined about 1000 yuan ($270), which can be about one year's wages.
5. Every factory, school, or institute has a birth quota set by the authorities. Female workers are allowed to give birth to only a certain number per year, and the quotas are assigned to the married women on the basis of consultation with them each year.

REFERENCES

China's Daily: 1987 (July 1).

Hua, Jinma: 1984, "Sex Education Is an Urgent Need," *Popular Medicine* 12.

Liu, J.K.: 1983, in the *Proceedings of the 2nd National Conference on Medical Ethics. An Outline of Medical Moral Theory:* 1983, The Health Press, Beijing.

Essentials of Medical Ethics: 1985, Jiangxi People's Press, Beijing.

Contestation and Consensus:
The Morality of Abortion in Japan

William R. LaFleur

William R. LaFleur is a professor in the Department of Japanese Studies at the University of Pennsylvania. He is the author of The Karma of Words: Buddhism and Literary Arts in Medieval Japan *(1983) and* Liquid Life: Abortion and Buddhism in Japan *(1992). He is the editor of* Dogen Studies *(1985).*

    LaFleur examines the traditional Buddhist doctrine that abortion is morally justifiable. Even though abortion is considered justifiable, it is nonetheless regarded as a necessary evil and also as a necessary sorrow. Abortion is considered to be an important component in the preservation of family values in Japan as well as in keeping the population in check. Because of these two considerations, there is a consensus in Japan that abortion is morally justifiable. He contends that the controversy in Japan concerns the question of whether retribution or guilt is appropriate for those who have abortions.

. . . The scholarly community, especially in the West, has habitually by-passed or denigrated vast amounts of materials that are important to understand the history of ethical thinking in Japan. It has also led to a systematic pattern of ignoring and downplaying those times and ways in which there was real conflict and contestation in Japanese ethical and religious life. In keeping with the fact that some recent works in Japanese have paid increasing attention to the reality and energy of intellectual contestation in Japanese history,[1] I am here suggesting that we, at least for heuristic purposes, reject as flawed the common assumption that there usually was a neat division of intellectual labor in Japan. To assume that Buddhists merely plugged

Reprinted by permission of the University of Hawaii Press, from its journal *Philosophy East and West*, Vol. 40/4. October, 1990. [Edited]

Confucianism into their teachings as a kind of caretaker for "the world," ethics, and the family is an assumption that tends to flatten the real shape of ethical discourse in Japan. It also reads as complementary and "harmonized" certain points that were, in fact, often fraught with conflict over both principles and practice.

ABORTION IN JAPAN: THE CONTESTATION

I believe this to be eminently true in the case of Japanese thinking about abortion. I have elsewhere narrated what I take to be the history of Japanese Buddhist thinking about abortion as a moral and religious problem.[2] Within that history I have located a phase in the early half of the nineteenth century when what I call a distinct difference between Buddhists on the one hand and Confucians and Shinto-based Kokugaku scholars on the other took shape. I detail why it is clear that the Buddhists for the most part took the position that abortion was what we call a "necessary evil"—although their term was a "necessary sorrow." Their opponents rejected all abortion as morally and religiously wrong. A common Buddhist position, in this sense comparatively "soft" on abortion, is expressed in the tradition of memorial rituals (kuyō) provided in cases of abortion; it can also be known from the materials in which Buddhists were attacked on this point by their opponents.

This is not to say that Buddhists had no qualms about abortion or did not recognize a tension between its practice and the precept against taking life. It is merely to note that they were more flexible on this point than were the Confucians and proponents of late Kokugaku. The latter, especially, mixed religion and politics unabashedly; beginning in the nineteenth century a family's reproductivity was read as an index to patriotism. This became intense in the Meiji (1868–1912) period—an eloquent demonstration of Bellah's observation that in Japan "the family does not stand over against the polity but is integrated into it and to an extent penetrated by it."[3]

Therefore, the Buddhist stance at that time was charged with being a threat to national well-being and as a flagrant offense to the gods—gods that protect the nation and are happiest when people's "seeds" germinate into whole persons in great numbers. Of course, the fact that there was a political aspect to the entire discourse also helps explain why the Buddhists dared to express their "soft" stand only indirectly. In fact, the Buddhist "position" on this was articulated not so much through treatises as through ritual, surely a "safer" medium in their situation. I

would, however, point out that this indirect, mixed, or muted discourse on specific moral questions had by this point already become "traditional" for Japanese Buddhists. Here was an instance where a traditional mode of expression also happened to be the only politically viable one; that it came in a muted form, however, does not mean it was not a distinct and *discernible* position. Its opponents knew it was at odds with their view and we, too, can reconstruct why that was so—and, therefore, its structure as an ethical stance on abortion.

During the later half of the nineteenth century much changed within Japan. What the government perceived as a "population stagnation" conflicted with imperial designs. Japan's growing need for human manpower, a need that was to grow with rapid industrialization and a military buildup for foreign wars, fit hand-in-glove with the antiabortion arguments advanced early in the nineteenth century by Kokugaku advocates and Confucians. This meant that a process was in place that led to the criminalization of abortion soon after the Meiji Restoration in 1868. During the latter half of the nineteenth century and the first half of the twentieth, therefore, the case against abortion, identifiable with this Shinto revival and with Confucian points of view, held sway in Japan. What I call "fecundism" became the order of the day and was associated in the public mind with "family" values.

Given the fact that in 1945 with its total defeat in World War II Japan underwent as thorough and total a crisis as can be imagined, the ban on abortion, too, began to be rethought. Whereas during the decades of rapid industrialization, militarization, colonial expansion, and war, abortion had been proscribed, after the Pacific War things were completely different. To some degree what had been the Kokugaku/Confucian opposition to abortion had been totally discredited by the events of history, most especially Japan's own defeat in 1945. Beginning at that time—especially given the tightness of basic resources—there was a deep concern about an explosion of the population. Thus once again a more "Buddhist" view, traditionally amenable to seeing abortion as a "necessary suffering," was the view that for all practical purposes was adopted when, in 1948, the process was begun to legalize abortion once again. Although what we here call "the Buddhist view" was not articulated in terms of explicit arguments, it was implicit in Buddhism's readiness to provide "rituals of memorial" for aborted fetuses (*mizuko*), a view widely perceived as tolerating abortion. It is probably not an exaggeration to say that, at least since 1948, on this ethical question it has been the Buddhist view which, consciously or not, has been what underlies actual practice.

The point that I want to emphasize here is not the one that ethical positions merely traipse along in the wake of political needs but, in fact, a quite different one—namely, that ethical discourse in Japan has in fact been much more diverse and conflict-ridden than most commentators assume. It also interests me that, once we begin to derive our readings of ethical positions from materials that are "mixed" and do not necessarily come in a genre recognizable as *"the ethical treatise,"* we can more readily reconstruct what clearly seems historically to have been a distinctly Buddhist approach to abortion in Japan, a position in actuality quite different from the total opposition—at least from the early nineteenth to the mid-twentieth centuries—to it by persons self-consciously representing Confucianism and the Neo-Shinto phase of Kokugaku. This is not to say that certain schools of Buddhists, especially those in the Pure Land tradition, have not objected both to abortion and to the

mizuko rites. It is merely to note a trajectory of comparative tolerance of the practice.

ABORTION IN JAPAN: CONSENSUS

What are we to make of the fact that, whereas what I call Japan's conflict over abortion was most aggravated in the middle of the nineteenth century, there is relatively little debate today—when in Europe and America the debate has become strong and often acrimonious?

One might expect that, given the high rate of abortion in Japan as well as the diversity of religious positions represented there, Japan would have been the locus of protracted and spirited debates about the ethics of abortion in recent years. Such, however, has not been the case. What is impressive, at least to the Western scholar looking for such, is the fact that comparatively little has been written on this topic during the past few decades—and that what has appeared has for the most part dealt with the politics of abortion, the legalization of the contraceptive pill, and criticisms of certain entrepreneurial temples for capitalizing on the *mizuko* boom. Voices advocating the repeal of legalized abortion have, by contrast, been almost nonexistent. I think it significant that what a century ago had been strongly expressed Confucian and neo-Shintō objections to legalized abortion have today in Japan largely dissipated and disappeared.

There are groups—such as Seichō no Ie (The House of Life), a "new religion"—that vocally oppose abortion. Such groups during the early 1980s evoked strong opposition from the Women's Movement in Japan, but as far as the general public is concerned these rather small groups opposed to abortion are little more than a blip on the screen of public consciousness. Some Buddhist and

Christian groups express alarm at the *number* of abortions performed, yet in Japan today there could hardly be anything that could rightly be called a real or wide public debate on this issue. Books on abortion as a public policy problem can scarcely be found. Many assume that the legalization of the pill will in time cut back the abortion rate. In fact, it is the *absence* of such a debate at the present time which, in my opinion at least, is the salient datum that deserves exploration and interpretation.

I would contend that this absence of public debate also needs to be interpreted as a sign of something *present*—namely, a fairly wide consensus on this matter. There is a consensus that abortion constitutes a painful social necessity and as such must remain legal and available, although religio-psychological mechanisms for relieving bad feelings about abortion—the *mizuko* rites, for instance—in most cases probably play a positive, therapeutic role. And, of course, this is to say that it is now what I have termed a Buddhist position on abortion which has, for all practical purposes, won the day.

A "position" is expressed not only by what is said but also by what goes unsaid. Therefore, in my view, it is significant that within the Japanese Buddhist community the discussion of abortion is now limited largely to criticisms of those temples and temple like organizations which employ the notion of "fetal retribution" to coerce the "parents" of an aborted fetus into performing rituals that memorialize the fetus, remove its "grudges," and facilitate its rebirth or its Buddhahood. Many Buddhists find repugnant such types of manipulation of parental guilt—especially when expressed in the notion that a fetus in limbo will wreak vengeance (*tatari*) on parents who neglect to memorialize it.

But, of course, the focus here is on the morality of using this concept of retribution; the question of the morality of abortion per se is, by comparison, something that goes almost without discussion. In other words, it seems now widely accepted that the Buddhist praxis developed over centuries on this issue is itself basically a moral and viable way of handling this complex and vexing problem.

Although I cannot here recapitulate things discussed in more detail elsewhere, a very rudimentary statement of the matter is that most Japanese Buddhists have accepted abortion as a necessary sorrow but at the same time have contextualized the termination of pregnancy—and also infanticide in an earlier epoch—through Buddhist ritual. One result of my analysis has been to demonstrate that historically the belief in transmigration and rebirth effectively attenuated any sense of "finality" in abortion—thus giving the "parents" of an aborted fetus the expectation that the fetus' entry into the world had been merely postponed.

Thus parental prayers and ritual memorializations were expected to palliate guilt, create what is taken to be a continuing relationship between parents in this world and a fetus in a Buddhist "limbo," and render close to moot many of the West's protracted debates about life's inception, fetal rights, and ownership of the bodies of women. Although those Japanese Buddhists who take this position face various conceptual and ethical problems in its wake, these are rather different—and in terms of upheaval in the larger society certainly less severe—than the problems we have faced in trying to deal with abortion in the West in general and the United States in particular.[4]

This is not to say that women's rights advocates feel no need for vigilance vis-à-vis Buddhist institutions on this matter. It is merely to call attention to the fact that, even though their acknowledged concerns are political and focus on the danger of being, as women, manipulated, those feminists who have written about Buddhism and abortion have tended to focus their criticisms on those who employ the concept of "fetal retribution," and that is something which, as noted above, many Buddhists themselves are quick to condemn.[5] My sense is that many feminists in Japan find, at least in the present context, a kind of odd, unanticipated ally in the Buddhists. Those feminists who are also ideologically Marxists are troubled by this convergence, but most feminists show reluctance to refuse the Buddhist hand that seems to render indirect help to this part of their cause. Obviously the Marxist critique of religion is itself "softened" in this.

My own personal conversations with representatives of various religious constituencies in Japan leads me to conclude that, especially if the legalization of "the pill" and a wider use of contraceptive devices can effectively reduce the *number* of abortions, there will be no deep objection to the continued legalization of abortion and the tendency to keep in place those Buddhist rituals that ritually memorialize fetuses and may serve as a conscience-solace for parents. The status quo, especially if numbers can be reduced, is acceptable to a surprisingly wide spectrum of persons engaged in discussions of religious and ethical questions. To that degree at least—and in contrast to American society—there is in Japan a fairly wide public consensus on this matter.

MORAL HIGH GROUND

Sometimes on moral questions a consensus forms because the participants in a pro-

tracted debate are exhausted or the issue no longer seems so important. On other occasions, however, consensus comes into being because something tagged as a "higher" value is recognized and respected by those who had earlier been partisans of differing positions; in such instances the "higher" can begin to override the former concern to sharpen differences. If a sense of exhaustion happens to coincide with a sense of moving towards a value deemed "higher" by both sides, the potential for consensus becomes eminently realizable.

My view is that in Japan's consensus on abortion today we can observe an instance where these two motives have, in fact, coincided quite remarkably. Interest in opening the old wounds is minimal—especially given the high social cost of the years of abortion-proscription. In addition, there is a widely generalized perception that abortion, however much regarded as a source of suffering, is not only demographically necessary but even a means for protecting what are felt to be "family" values. In most basic terms it is necessary to prevent the hemorrhaging of population in a land where the density is already unusually high. More importantly, however, abortion is perceived as a mechanism whereby families can maximize the opportunities for their children by a "rational" investment of resources in the education and upbringing of a limited number of children, usually two. It would not be too much to say that in Japan the high emphasis placed upon family life is itself a factor in the current consensus in favor of keeping abortion legal and available.

Religious institutions—perhaps Buddhist ones in particular—articulate and reinforce these family values in Japan. This means that in most instances such institutions cannot be expected to move in any significant way to curtail a practice they perceive as a regrettable but necessary component in ensuring the persistence of good family life and national life. The consensus among religious groups to leave abortion legal and available will, I suspect, remain as long as it seems clear to the majority that, however unpleasant and painful abortion may be, family life in the aggregate is far better served by having it available than by criminalizing it once again. In my own conversations with Buddhist clergy in Japan on this problem I detect two concerns, but they are not, it should be noted, of sufficient weight to prompt any strong movement for a change in the rather liberalized law.

The first concern is that people not become inured to abortion and trivialize it. Many Buddhists are worried that, especially if there is no real grief and ritual, a kind of personal degradation becomes the pattern: from repeated abortions to a flippant acceptance of the practice and from there to a deterioration in a person's (read: woman's) capacity for generalized sensitivity. This consists in a "hardening," something serious because in the psychoethical vocabulary of the Japanese this is a matter of the *kokoro* or "heart." If too many people within society become persons who take abortion as simply a matter of course, then the tenor of society itself will change for the worse.

The legal and social admission of abortion as a practice is different from being psychologically and spiritually inured to it. Japanese Buddhists worry more about the latter than the former and focus their energies accordingly. Japanese Buddhists will often go on to argue that the meaningful performance of remembrance rites can, in fact, offset what is to be most feared. That is, the ritual of *mizuko kuyō*, a kind of "requiem mass" for the fetus, can, it is claimed, do much to prevent this "hardening" of the *kokoro* and dehumanization.

The second concern is for a possible nexus between the accessibility of abortion and an appreciable growth in the numbers of persons who adopt what is now called the "single" (*shingaru*) style of the larger urban centers. Within Buddhist periodicals, for instance, there can be found more and more discussions of the single life-style as a threat to family life. A decline is detected and projected: from the extended family to the nuclear family and from there to the single life-style and the one-parent "family." It is important to note that virtually every Buddhist institution is committed to the superior values of the traditional family and is itself dependent upon such a family's readiness to support temples for the performance of ancestral rites. Partially no doubt because of this, the single life-style is pinpointed as a threat to societal values in general. It is also seen as an index to the growth of a dangerous form of (Western-style) individualism, and fundamentally contrary to traditional values that are at the same time understood to be "national" values.

On the basis of things I have heard and read, it probably can be predicted that, if the single life-style were to become really widespread, the ready accessibility of abortion could eventually come under attack. To date, however, this does not seem likely. The anxiety about a nexus between "liberated sex" and a changing structure of the family has for now focused on the danger of making "the pill" readily available. If that anxiety tends to deepen, it will more likely jeopardize the legalization of the contraceptive pill rather than the availability of abortion.

In fact, "conservative" views in Japan can at times take strikingly unexpected turns—at least when judged by what would be expected if they are thought to be the equivalent of "conservative" views in American public life. For instance, one privately will often be told in Japan that the availability of abortion is in fact *protective of family values* to the degree that it makes unnecessary the birthing of unwanted children. Then, because it is assumed, first, that unwanted children are both pitiable and more prone to become problematic for society itself and, second, that family strength and well-being are maximized when it can be assumed that all persons within it are *wanted* and valued, logic seems to compel the conclusion that abortion is needed as a necessary "safety valve" to ensure familial, societal, and national strength. Buddhists go on from this to argue that, especially if the "hearts" of persons who have had abortions can be "softened" via the rituals that keep alive a sensitivity to the departed fetus as still alive in the Buddhist limbo (*sai no kawara*), the cumulative danger to society is reduced.

In Japan, surprisingly then, it seems to be the case that the most politically effective argument for legalized abortion, even though it comes down in muted forms, is based on fairly "conservative" concerns for the quality of family life. To many persons with fairly traditional religious and social views in Japan it is difficult to imagine why "conservative" Americans can be found favoring a public policy—the criminalization of abortion—that will in effect result not only in giving birth to obviously unwanted children but, beyond that, also to the psychic pain, both individual and social, that is bound to follow such a policy. In addition it is assumed in Japan that there must be some close correlations in any society among the degree to which children are wanted, such children's perceptions of being wanted and loved, the quality of the care they receive, and whether or not their subsequent behavior becomes deviant or criminal.

To criminalize abortion, thus, looks irrational and socially foolhardy. To Japanese ready to express candid views on these things, this scarcely seems to be the direction in which American public life should sensibly be moving today. Given the existing problem of large numbers of unwanted children as well as the exorbitant crime rate in America, those who push for abortion's recriminalization appear to be courting what to some Japanese looks like a kind of social suicide. To some Japanese it is even somewhat baffling why certain Americans, viewing themselves to be "conservative" in their views of the family, do not recognize that forcing others to have children they do not really want is itself a morally questionable stance.

Clearly that location called the "moral high ground" can be approached from different directions. What is interesting—and potentially instructive—in the Japanese case is that interpretations of the relationship between religion and abortion have not been forced down the either/or chutes of "rights of the unborn" or "rights of the woman." In part that is undoubtedly because the Japanese traditional concern for social order (*chitsujo*) still seems almost automatically to take immediate precedence over any public scenario of "rights" and "liberation."

ABORTION AND THE POLIS

I believe the chief value in the study of Japanese thinking about abortion may be heuristic. That is, in this way we can see a society permitting abortion while avoiding interminable debate over conflicting rights. In a sense we can see a society that, through trial and error, has learned to opt for access to abortion as a way of enhancing the quality of social life itself. Neither the rights of the individual fetus nor those of the individual woman are highlighted; instead these claims—often taken in the

West as "opposite"—are both seen as driven by the ideology of individualism. There are other reasons to legitimate abortion, reasons which, it is felt, have to do with the quality of common life of the society itself. The health of the larger society is at issue.

Robert Nisbet grasped this point. As an advocate of the contemporary relevance of the position on these things held by ancient Greeks and Romans rather than by medieval Christians, Nisbet found in the Japanese case a ready instance of exactly what he had in mind. In the entry on "abortion" in his *Prejudices: A Philosophical Dictionary*, he wrote:

> In the contemporary world it would be hard to find a family system more honored and more important in its authority than that of Japan. But abortion there has for long been easily available.[6]

My own analysis has suggested that, although Nisbet did not realize how historically complicated things really had been in Japan and how painful had been the process to legalize abortion there,[7] he was entirely accurate in his grasp of the nexus between tolerance of abortion in Japan and the high valorization of family life there *today*. That is, he grasped that there is an argument for abortion based upon familial and societal values, an argument furthermore that is not bound to prioritize individuals and individual rights.

Alasdair MacIntyre, in his *Whose Justice? Which Rationality?* refers to "the unborn" in a way that suggests how he reads the history of Europe very differently from Nisbet. In depicting what he calls the emergence of the "Augustinian alternative" to Aristotelianism, MacIntyre locates the moral payoff of that alterative as making itself evident in the following way:

> The law of the *civitas Dei* requires a kind of justice to the unborn which Aristotle's pro-

posed measures for controlling the size of the population of a *polis* deny to them.[8]

It would be difficult to find a more pithy statement of what many in the West have often held to be how Christianity gained its own moral high ground, a position assumed to be superior even to that of Aristotle.

The problem, of course, is that the trajectory right into individualism seems to have been prepared at the same time. Augustine, says MacIntyre, had found a way to require "a kind of justice to the unborn" but he neglects to point out that in Augustine the importance of the *polis* was at the same time being drastically reduced. In his *De nuptiis et concupiscentia*, the Bishop Hippo, having declared that childbearing is "the end and aim of marriage," goes on to judge that, unless they have the intent of being fecund, a man and woman, however legally married, are really only having sinful sex. Without the aim of propagation a woman is just her "husband's harlot" and the man is his own "wife's adulterer."[9] Ultimately marriage is something for the Church to define, not the state.

Once such views were injected into the consciousness of the West—and later defined in such a way that something uniquely "Western" and morally "higher" was implied in their observance—it became extremely difficult to go back and recapture Aristotle's important and still valid point about eugenics and the quality of life in the polis. That point had been compromised, of course, because Aristotle had viewed it, unnecessarily I think, as something the polis must force upon its citizens. But the Christians went beyond merely objecting to the coercion. With their polemic against paganism, Christians tended toward the obscuring of the view that the *polis* might have eugenic concerns that are legitimate and, in fact, ethically worthy. In this way, what was important in Aristotle was effectively obliterated by the "Augustinian alternative," and with the articulation of that alternative the course of the West was set.

If eugenics became a matter of consensus rather than coercion, however, the picture changes significantly. Then it appears possible to avoid, on one side, the forced compliance that Aristotle mandated and, on the other, the prizing of individual rights—either to "life" in the fetus' case or to "choice" in the pregnant woman's—at the expense of what is good for the larger social entity.[10] While I do not imply that the Japanese have arrived at a perfect solution to these problems, their present practice with respect to abortion and the family avoids, I wish to suggest, some of the most serious pitfalls of our own practices. In addition, an understanding of how their practice has been put together as an instance of moral "reasoning" is—however initially odd by our usual criteria—itself a reason for studying it with care.

NOTES

1. For example, Imai Jun and Ozawa Tomio, eds., *Nihon shisô ronsôshi* (Tokyo: Perikansha, 1979).
2. William R. LaFleur, *Liquid Life: Buddhism, Abortion, and the family in Japan*, Princeton: Princeton University Press, 1992. Published studies on *mizuko* in English to date include: Anne Page Brooks, "*Mizuko kuyō* and Japanese Buddhism," *Japanese Journal of Religious Studies* 8, nos. 3–4 (September–December 1981): 119–147; Emiko Ohnuki-Tierney, *Illness and Culture in Contemporary Japan: An Anthropological View* (Cambridge: Cambridge University Press, 1984), pp 78–81; Hoshino Eiki and Takeda Dōshō, "Indebtedness and Comfort: The Undercurrents of *Mizuko Kuyō* in Contemporary Japan," *Japanese Journal of Religious Studies* 14, no. 4 (December 1987): 305–320, and Bardwell Smith, "Buddhism and Abortion in Contemporary Japan: *Mizuko kuyō* and the Confrontation with Death," *Japanese Journal of Religious Studies* 15, no. 1 (March 1988): 3–24. There is, of course, an extensive bibliography in Japanese.
3. Robert N. Bellah, *Tokugawa Religion: The Values of Pre-Industrial Japan* (Glencoe, Illinois: The Free Press, 1957), p. 19.
4. For the incredulous, somewhat appalled response of a Japanese woman legal expert present at European debates trying to pinpoint the exact time of a soul's entry into the body, see Nakatani Kinko, "Chūzetsu, Dataizai no Toraekata," in Nihon Kazoku Keikaku Renmei, ed., *Onna no jinken to sei* (Tokyo: Komichi Shobō, 1984), p. 29.
5. See, for example, Anzai Atsuko, "Mizuko kuyō" shōbai no ikagawashisa,: in Nihon Kazoku Keigaku Renmei, ed., *Kanashimi o sabakemasu ka* (Tokyo: Ningen no Kagakusha, 1983), pp. 137–148. The critique of *tatari* from within Buddhism, however, is also strong. There is widespread censure of it, for instance, in a special issue devoted to this problem in the interdenominational Buddhist Journal *Daihōrin*, vol. 54 (July 1987). For details see my *Liquid Life*, pp. 160–176.
6. Robert Nisbet, *Prejudices: A Philosophical Dictionary* (Cambridge, Massachusetts: Harvard University Press, 1982), p. 1.
7. See my *Liquid Life*. pp. 69–139.
8. Alasdair MacIntyre, *Whose Justice? Which Rationality?* (Notre Dame: University of Notre Dame Press, 1988), p. 163.
9. Augustine, "Of Marriage and Concupiscence" in Marcus Dods, ed., *The works of Aurelius Augustine, Bishop of Hippo*, trans. Peter Holmes (Edinburgh: T & T Clark, 1985), vol. 12, p. 116.
10. For a discussion of how, in fact, history shows there is nothing absolute about "respect for life" in the West's religions, see John A. Miles, Jr., "Jain and Judaeo-Christian Respect for Life," *Journal of the American Academy of Religion* 44, no. 3 (1976): 453–457.

QUESTIONS: ABORTION

1. John T. Noonan argues that a fetus possesses the right to life at the moment of conception because it is when it receives the full human genetic code and the potentiality for developing into a full-fledged human being. What problems do you see in his argument?

2. Mary Anne Warren argues that there are five features central to the concept of human personhood. What are these features, and what do you think are the most important? Do you think that one must achieve personhood as she defines it to have rights? Do you agree with her distinction between actual and potential rights?

3. Don Marquis attempts to place himself between two opposing positions with regard to abortion. What are these positions? What problems does he think these positions have? Outline his alternative position. What objections can be made against Marquis?

4. The issue of multiple-fetus pregnancies presents a challenge to the conservative position against abortion. What are the problems this issue presents for those who argue that abortion is morally unjustifiable? What does Christine Overall conclude concerning the right to life in multiple-fetus pregnancies?

5. Ren-Zong Qiu, Chun-Zhi Wang, and Yuan Gu argue that in some circumstances late-term abortion is justifiable. What are their reasons for justifying certain late-term abortions? Do you think that the severe economic constraints and over-population in China are important contextual considerations that could be included in a decision concerning abortion? Does Qiu, Wang, and Gu's justification of certain late-term abortions place them on a slippery slope regarding all late-term abortions?

6. What does William LaFleur think the *mizuko kuyo* ritual accomplishes for the Japanese women who undergo abortions? How is the "necessary sorrow" of abortion connected to the Japanese concern for "family values"? How does this attitude affect the way we view the abortion controversy in the West?

SUPPLEMENTARY READINGS: ABORTION

ARMSTRONG, ROBERT L. "The Right to Life." *Journal of Social Philosophy*, vol. 8(1), January 1977.

BADGER, W. DOUGLAS. "Abortion: The Judeo-Christian Imperative." In *Whose Values? The Battle for Morality in Pluralistic America*, Horn, editor. Ann Arbor, MI: Servant Books, 1985.

BAYLES, MICHAEL D. "Genetic Choice." In *Ethical Issues in the New Reproductive Technologies*, Hull, editor. Belmont. CA: Wadsworth, 1990.

BOLTON, MARTHA BRANDT. "Responsible Women and Abortion Decisions." In *Having Children*, O'Neill and Ruddick, editors. New York: Oxford University Press, 1979.

HURSTHOUSE, ROSALIND. "Virtue Theory and Abortion." *Philosophy and Public Affairs*, vol. 20(3), Summer, 1991.

KARKAL, MALINI. "Abortion Laws and the Abortion Situation in India." *Issues in Reproductive and Genetic Engineering*, vol. 4(1), 1991.

KELLY, JAMES R. "Learning and Teaching Consistency: Catholics and the Right-to-Life Movement." In *Catholic Church and the Politics of Abortion: A View from the States*, Byrnes and Segers, editors. Boulder, CO: Westview Press, 1992.

KOERNER, UWE, and HANNELORE KOERNER. "Ethics in Reproductive Medicine in the German Democratic Republic." *The Journal of Medicine and Philosophy*, vol. 14(3), June 1989.

MARKOWITZ, SALLY. "Abortion and Feminism." *Social Theory and Practice*, Spring 1990.

McCORMICK, RICHARD A., S. J. "Blastomene Separation: Some Concerns." Hastings Center Report vol. 24(2), 1994.

MENKITI, IFANYI A. "Person and Community in African Traditional Thought." In *African Philosophy: An Introduction*, third edition, Wright, editor. Lanham, MD: University Press of America, 1984.

MURRAY, THOMAS H. "Moral Obligations to the Not-Yet Born: The Fetus as Patient." In *Ethical Issues in the New Reproductive Technologies*, Hull, editor. Belmont, CA: Wadsworth, 1990.

NOONAN, JOHN. "Responding to Persons: Methods of Moral Argument in the Debate Over Abortion." *Theology Digest*, 1973.

PAPP, ZOLTAN. "Genetic Counseling and Termination of Pregnancy in Hungary." *Journal of Medicine and Philosophy*, vol. 14(3), June 1989.

ROBERTSON, JOHN A. "The Question of Human Cloning." *Hastings Center Report*, vol. 24(2), 1994.

SISTARE, CHRISTINE. "Reproductive Freedom and Women's Freedom: Surrogacy and Autonomy." *Philosophical Forum*, vol. 19(4), 1987.

SUMNER, L. WAYNE. "The Morality of Abortion." *Abortion and Moral Theory*, Princeton, NJ: Princeton University Press, 1981.

SUTHERLAND, GAIL HINICH. "Abortion and Woman's "Nature": The Idiom of Choice." *Soundings*, vol. 76(4), Winter, 1993.

THOMSON, JUDITH JARVIS. "A Defense of Abortion." *Philosophy and Public Affairs*, vol. 1(1), Fall 1971.

TWORKOV, HELEN. "Anti-abotion/Pro-choice." *Tricycle: The Buddhist Review*, vol. 1(3), Spring 1992.

IX

EUTHANASIA
AND SUSTAINING LIFE

Should his demand to die be respected? . . . Another question occurred to me as I watched this blind, maimed, and totally helpless man defy and baffle everyone: could his adamant stand be the only way available for him to regain his independence after such a prolonged period of helplessness and total dependence? Consequently I decided to assist him . . .

—Robert B. White, M.D.[1]

There is a right to life but is there also a right to die? This is the first question we take up in this section. The second question is this: Given that there is a right to life, what do we do when rights to life conflict, as in situations where not everyone's life can be sustained due to a scarcity of medical resources? These questions push our discussion of human rights into the domain of very difficult cases. Those who demand the right to die are often opposed by those who think that the right to life is too precious to be compromised. Discussions about the allocation of scarce medical resources also involve the right to life, since, when not all can be saved, someone's right to life will seemingly be regarded as not being paramount.

The right to life is often thought to be connected to the right to decide how to live one's life. If one can be killed against one's will, this calls into question the right to decide how to live one's life. Similarly, if one can be forced to stay alive against one's will, then autonomy doesn't amount to much. And yet it seems odd to say that there is a right to die that is on the same level as the right to live. Isn't the right to die in some sense unnatural? Should people be allowed to decide to end their lives whenever they wish? Should the rest of us have to assist them in their decision to die with the same vigor as if the person's right to life were at stake? These are many of the questions that make our final topic such a difficult one.

"Euthanasia" literally means "good or happy death." The term is often equated with mercy killing. There are two types of euthanasia: active and passive. Active euthanasia refers to the practice of directly bringing about a person's death, according to or against that person's wishes. A person who wishes to die may request that a lethal injection be administered, and such an injection would constitute active euthanasia. Passive euthanasia is the practice of doing nothing to prevent death from occurring. If someone is suffering greatly and wants to die, a decision may be made not to treat the person's current pneumonia, for example, thereby allowing the person to die naturally. There are difficult cases that will not easily fit into this scheme, such as the decision to remove someone from life support systems. Some argue that this is a way of directly causing a person's death, while others argue that it is a way of merely allowing a person to die naturally.

In many, but not all societies, active euthanasia is condemned. We will examine the practices and their justification in a number of societies in hopes of understanding the complexities of the morality of euthanasia. We will also examine how decisions are made about whom to save when not all can be saved. In both of these topics we will be forced to confront the possible limits of the right to life, as well as the justification of certain medical practices, such as physician-assisted suicide, that are currently some of the most controversial in Western society and in many other societies.

We begin with a very influential essay written by James Rachels. Rachels argues that the distinction between active and passive euthanasia is not a morally relevant one. He points out that one can directly bring about a person's death with the best of intentions, and one can let someone die with the worst of intentions. The intentions make a moral difference, but whether the death is actively or passively brought about is not relevant. Similarly, from a consequentialist perspective, one can produce very good results by actively bringing about someone's death, and one can produce very bad results by letting someone die. The consequences make a moral difference but the type of euthanasia does not. Rachels contends that those who argue for or against an instance of euthanasia, merely because it is either active or passive, have made a conceptual mistake.

In response to Rachels, Bonnie Steinbock contends that there are at least two kinds of circumstances in which the termination of life-sustaining treatment cannot be equated with intentionally letting die. The first has to do with a physician's respecting a patient's rights to decline treatment and to be free from unjustified intervention. And the second has to do with the ending of extraordinary means of care deemed to be of little benefit to the patient. In neither of these situations, as Steinbock further points out, can the doctor's act of ceasing life-prolonging treatment be construed as one involving intentionally bringing about the death of the patient, the reason being that one can do something knowing what its results will be while having no intention of producing those results.

Margaret Battin argues in favor of a form of euthanasia called physician-assisted suicide. She points out that in the Netherlands various forms of euthanasia have been practiced without major difficulties. Physician-assisted suicide has the advantage of keeping things under a physician's scrutiny, but it also gives the patient a greater range of autonomy, especially for those who are suffering greatly. Battin also talks about the successes in Germany, where assisted suicide but not active euthanasia is allowed. Cultural differences as well as cultural similarities are addressed in urging that the United States allow more forms of euthanasia than it currently does.

Carl Becker enters the debate from a Buddhist perspective. Unlike contemporary Westerners, Buddhists do not regard death as an evil or even as something to be avoided. Indeed, the Buddha is said to have praised certain persons who committed suicide. For Buddhists, what is most important is that a person be mentally and physically prepared to die. Once this has occurred, then the only morally relevant question concerns how this person can best die with dignity. To keep someone alive who is prepared to die and wants to die is generally considered inhumane in Japan, where Buddhism is very strong.

Issues about what is humane and about what rights we have are also of central importance to discussions of scarce medical resource allocation. Indeed, one of the questions raised in the literature on this subject is whether a physician acts wrongly by refusing to save the life of one patient when such a refusal will allow another patient's life to be saved. The refusal to save the one life is, in many respects, similar to euthanasia. But in this case it is not consistent with the wishes of the patient whose life is not sustained. Hence, the issues of explicit coercion arise in the scarce medical resource literature in ways that they do not generally arise in the euthanasia literature.

John Harris presents us with a highly controversial example of scarce resource allocation. He asks what would be wrong if one person were killed so that his organs could be used to save two other people who would otherwise die. This essay presents a similar problem to that presented by John Arthur in the section on hunger and poverty, but Harris takes quite a different tack on this issue. He argues that it may be justified to kill this person, and that the system that would be the most morally unobjectionable for selecting those to be killed is some form of lottery. But, as he admits, it would be a nearly insoluble problem to decide who should be in the lottery, that is, who would be in the class of possible donors.

John Kilner provides an interesting challenge to the standard consequentialist way of deciding who should be saved. From an African perspective an older patient's life is valued over that of a younger patient, in situations where both cannot be saved. Usefulness to society, the category often used in the West to decide hard cases in favor of those who are young, is not valued as much in Africa as is how much one needs help. Equality is also very highly valued, and this is true to such an extent that some form of lottery, such as first-come-first-served, is often a preferred strategy for selection in cases where two people cannot both be saved. If one values need or equality ahead of usefulness, then consequentialist analyses that favor the young are not necessarily those that are viewed as preferable.

Susan Sherwin discusses the way in which gender, race, and class differences contribute to the way that scarce medical resources are allocated. She contends that if one is female or nonwhite or poor, one is much less likely to have access to scarce resources than if one is male, white, and wealthy. And if one is both female and poor, or both female and nonwhite, one is at the bottom of the pool of those who obtain scarce medical resources. Indeed, those at the bottom don't even have studies done about them to determine which resources they most need. Sherwin argues that this situation should be changed by empowering all health consumers so that they can effectively fight for their medical rights.

—Kai Wong

NOTE

1. Robert B. White, M.D., "A Demand To Die," *Hastings Center Report,* June 1975.

Active and Passive Euthanasia

James Rachels

James Rachels is professor of philosophy at the University of Alabama at Birmingham. He is the author of The Elements of Moral Philosophy *(1986),* The End of Life: Euthanasia and Morality *(1986), and* Created from Animals: The Moral Implications of Darwinism *(1990). He is the editor of* The Right Thing To Do *(1989).*

In this essay, Rachels treats the distinction between active and passive euthanasia as an example of the distinction between killing and letting die. Rachels argues that there is no morally relevant difference between actively killing someone and passively letting a person die. He argues that if this is true, then policies of the American Medical Association and other institutions that rely on the distinction need to be changed. What is important morally are the motivations or consequences of actively or passively killing, and only after these factors have been evaluated in each case can it be said that euthanasia is morally justifiable.

The distinction between active and passive euthanasia is thought to be crucial for medical ethics. The idea is that it is permissible, at least in some cases, to withhold treatment and allow a patient to die, but it is never permissible to take any direct action designed to kill the patient. This doctrine seems to be accepted by most doctors, and it is endorsed in a statement adopted by the House of Delegates of the American Medical Association on 4 December 1973:

> The intentional termination of the life of one human being by another—mercy killing—is contrary to that for which the medical profession stands and is contrary to the policy of the American Medical Association.

James Rachels, "Active and Passive Euthanasia," in *The New England Journal of Medicine,* vol. 292, © 1975, pp. 78–80. Reprinted by permission of *The New England Journal of Medicine.*

The cessation of the employment of extraordinary means to prolong the life of the body when there is irrefutable evidence that biological death is imminent is the decision of the patient and/or his immediate family. The advice and judgment of the physician should be freely available to the patient and/or his immediate family.

However, a strong case can be made against this doctine. In what follows I will set out some of the relevant arguments, and urge doctors to reconsider their views on this matter.

To begin with a familiar type of situation, a patient who is dying of incurable cancer of the throat is in terrible pain, which can no longer be satisfactorily alleviated. He is certain to die within a few days, even if present treatment is continued, but he does not want to go on living for those days since the pain is unbearable. So he asks the doctor for an end to it, and his family joins in the request.

Suppose the doctor agrees to withhold treatment, as the conventional doctrine says he may. The justification for his doing so is that the patient is in terrible agony, and since he is going to die anyway, it would be wrong to prolong his suffering needlessly. But now notice this. If one simply withholds treatment, it may take the patient longer to die, and so he may suffer more than he would if more direct action were taken and a lethal injection given. This fact provides strong reason for thinking that, once the initial decision not to prolong his agony has been made, active euthanasia is actually preferable to passive euthanasia, rather than the reverse. To say otherwise is to endorse the option that leads to more suffering rather than less, and is contrary to the humanitarian impulse that prompts the decision not to prolong his life in the first place.

Part of my point is that the process of being "allowed to die" can be relatively slow and painful, whereas being given a lethal injection is relatively quick and painless. Let me give a different sort of example. In the United States about one in 600 babies is born with Down's syndrome. Most of these babies are otherwise healthy—that is, with only the usual pediatric care, they will proceed to an otherwise normal infancy. Some, however, are born with congenital defects such as intestinal obstructions that require operations if they are to live. Sometimes, the parents and the doctor will decide not to operate, and let the infant die. Anthony Shaw describes what happens then:

When surgery is denied [the doctor] must try to keep the infant from suffering while natural forces sap the baby's life away. As a surgeon whose natural inclination is to use the scalpel to fight off death, standing by and watching a salvageable baby die is the most emotionally exhausting experience I know. It is easy at a conference, in a theoretical discussion to decide that such infants should be allowed to die. It is altogether different to stand by in the nursery and watch as dehydration and infection wither a tiny being over hours and days. This is a terrible ordeal for me and the hospital staff—much more so than for the parents who never set foot in the nursery.[1]

I can understand why some people are opposed to all euthanasia, and insist that such infants must be allowed to live. I think I can also understand why other people favor destroying these babies quickly and painlessly. But why should anyone favor letting "dehydration and infection wither a tiny being over hours and days"? The doctrine that says a baby may be allowed to dehydrate and wither, but may not be given an injection that would end its life without suffering, seems so patently cruel as to require no further refutation. The strong language is not intended to offend, but only to put the point in the clearest possible way.

My second argument is that the conventional doctrine leads to decisions concerning life and death made on irrelevant grounds.

Consider again the case of the infants with Down's syndrome who need operations for congenital defects unrelated to the syndrome to live. Sometimes, there is no operation, and the baby dies, but when there is no such defect, the baby lives on. Now an operation such as that to remove an intestinal obstruction is not prohibitively difficult. The reason why such operations are not performed in these cases is, clearly, that the child has Down's syndrome and the parents and the doctor judge that because of that fact it is better for the child to die.

But notice that this situation is absurd, no matter what view one takes of the lives and potentials of such babies. If the life of such an infant is worth preserving what does it matter if it needs a simple operation? Or, if one thinks it better that such a baby should not live on, what difference does it make that it happens to have an unobstructed intestinal tract? In either case, the matter of life and death is being decided on irrelevant grounds. It is the Down's syndrome, and not the intestines, that is the issue. The matter should be decided, if at all, on that basis, and not be allowed to depend on the essentially irrelevant question of whether the intestinal tract is blocked.

What makes this situation possible, of course, is the idea that when there is an intestinal blockage, one can "let the baby die," but when there is no such defect there is nothing that can be done, for one must not "kill" it. The fact that this idea leads to such results as deciding life or death on irrelevant grounds is another good reason why the doctrine would be rejected.

One reason why so many people think that there is an important moral difference between active and passive euthanasia is that they think killing someone is morally worse than letting someone die. But is it? Is killing, in itself, worse than letting die? To investigate this issue, two cases may be considered that are exactly alike except that one involves killing whereas the other involves letting someone die. Then, it can be asked whether this difference makes any difference to the moral assessments. It is important that the cases be exactly alike, except for this one difference, since otherwise one cannot be confident that it is this difference and not some other that accounts for any variation in the assessments of the two cases. So, let us consider this pair of cases:

In the first, Smith stands to gain a large inheritance if anything should happen to his six-year-old cousin. One evening while the child is taking his bath, Smith sneaks into the bathroom and drowns the child, and then arranges things so that it will look like an accident.

In the second, Jones also stands to gain if anything should happen to his six-year-old cousin. Like Smith, Jones sneaks in planning to drown the child in his bath. However, just as he enters the bathroom Jones sees the child slip and hit his head, and fall face down in the water. Jones is delighted; he stands by, ready to push the child's head back under if it is necessary, but it is not necessary. With only a little thrashing about, the child drowns all by himself, "accidentally," as Jones watches and does nothing.

Now Smith killed the child, whereas Jones "merely" let the child die. That is the only difference between them. Did either man behave better, from a moral point of view? If the difference between killing and letting die were in itself a morally important matter, one should say that Jones's behavior was less reprehensible than Smith's. But does one really want to say that? I think not. In the first place, both men acted from the same motive, personal gain, and both had exactly the same end in view when they acted. It may be inferred from Smith's conduct that he is a bad man, although that judgment may be withdrawn or modified if certain further facts are learned about him—for example, that he is mentally deranged. But would not the very same thing be inferred about Jones from his conduct? And would not the same further considerations also be relevant to any modification of this judgment? Moreover, suppose Jones pleaded, in his own defense, "After all, I didn't do anything except just stand there and watch the child drown. I didn't kill him; I only let him die." Again, if letting die were in itself less bad than killing, this defense should have at least some weight. But it does not. Such a "defense" can only be regarded as a grotesque perversion of moral reasoning. Morally speaking, it is no defense at all.

Now, it may be pointed out, quite properly, that the cases of euthanasia with which doctors are concerned are not like this at all. They do not involve personal gain or the destruction of normal healthy children. Doctors are concerned only with cases in which the patient's life is of no further use to him, or in which the patient's life has become or will soon become a terrible burden. However, the point is the same in these cases: the bare difference between killing and letting die does not, in itself, make a moral difference. If a doctor lets a patient die, for humane reasons, he is in the same moral position as if he had given the patient a lethal injection for humane reasons. If his decision was wrong—if, for example, the patient's illness was in fact curable—the decision would be equally regrettable no matter which method was used to carry it out. And if the doctor's decision was the right one, the method used is not in itself important.

The AMA policy statement isolates the crucial issue very well; the crucial issue is "the intentional termination of the life of one human being by another." But after identifying this issue, and forbidding "mercy killing," the statement goes on to deny that the cessation of treatment is the intentional termination of a life. This is where the mistake comes in, for what is the cessation of treatment, in these circumstances, if it is not "the intentional termination of the life of one human being by another"? Of course it is exactly that, and if it were not, there would be no point to it.

Many people will find this judgment hard to accept. One reason, I think, is that it is very easy to conflate the question of whether killing is, in itself, worse than letting die, with the very different question of whether most actual cases of killing are more reprehensible than most actual cases of letting die. Most actual cases of killing are clearly terrible (think, for example, of all the murders reported in the newspapers), and one hears of such cases every day. On the other hand, one hardly ever hears of a case of letting die, except for the actions of doctors who are motivated by humanitarian reasons. So one learns to think of killing in a much worse light than of letting die. But this does not mean that there is something about killing that makes it in itself worse than letting die, for it is not the bare difference between killing and letting die that makes the difference in these cases. Rather, the other factors—the murderer's motive of personal gain, for example, contrasted with the doctor's humanitarian motivation—account for different reactions to the different cases.

I have argued that killing is not in itself worse than letting die; if my contention is right, it follows that active euthanasia is not any worse than passive euthanasia. What arguments can be given on the other side? The most common, I believe, is the following:

> The important difference between active and passive euthanasia is that, in passive euthanasia, the doctor does not do anything to bring about the patient's death. The doctor does nothing, and the patient dies of whatever ills already afflict him. In active euthanasia, however, the doctor does something to bring about the patient's death: he kills him. The doctor who gives the patient with cancer a lethal injection has himself caused his patient's death; whereas if he merely ceases treatment, the cancer is the cause of death.

A number of points need to be made here. The first is that it is not exactly correct to say that in passive euthanasia the doctor does nothing, for he does do one thing that is very important: he lets the patient die. "Letting someone die" is certainly different, in some respects, from other types of action—mainly in that it is a kind of action that one may perform by way of not performing certain other actions. For example, one may let a patient die by way of not giving medication, just as one may insult someone by way of not shaking his hand. But for any purpose of moral assessment, it is a type of action none the less. The decision to let a patient die is subject to moral appraisal in the same way that a decision to kill him would be subject to moral appraisal: it may be assessed as wise or unwise, compassionate or sadistic, right or wrong. If a doctor deliberately let a patient die who was suffering from a routinely curable illness, the doctor would certainly be to blame for what he had done, just as he would be to blame if he had needlessly killed the patient. Charges against him would then be appropriate. If so, it would be no defense at all for him to insist that he didn't "do anything." He would have done something very serious indeed, for he let his patient die.

Fixing the cause of death may be very important from a legal point of view, for it may determine whether criminal charges are brought against the doctor. But I do not think that this notion can be used to show a moral difference between active and passive euthanasia. The reason why it is considered bad to be the cause of someone's death is that death is regarded as a great evil—and so it is. However, if it has been decided that euthanasia—even passive euthanasia—is desirable in a given case, it has also been decided that in this instance death is no greater an evil than the patient's continued existence. And if this is true, the usual reason for not wanting to be the cause of someone's death simply does not apply.

Finally, doctors may think that all of this is only of academic interest—the sort of thing that philosophers may worry about but that has no practical bearing on their own work. After all, doctors must be concerned about the legal consequences of what they do, and active euthanasia is clearly forbidden by the law. But even so, doctors should also be concerned with the fact that the law is forcing upon them a moral doctrine that may be indefensible, and has a considerable effect on their practices. Of course, most doctors are not now in the position of being coerced in this matter, for they do not regard themselves as merely going along with what the law requires. Rather, in statements such as the AMA policy statement that I have quoted, they are endorsing this doctrine as a central point of medical ethics. In that statement, active euthanasia is condemned not merely as illegal but as "contrary to that for which the medical profession stands," whereas passive euthanasia is approved. However, the preceding considerations suggest that there is really no difference between the two, considered in themselves (there may be important moral differences in some cases in their *consequences,* but as I pointed out, these differences may make active euthanasia, and not passive euthanasia, the morally preferable option). So, whereas doctors may have to discriminate between active and passive euthanasia to satisfy the law, they should not do any more than that. In particular, they should not give the distinction any added authority and weight by writing it into official statements of medical ethics.

NOTE

1. Shaw, Anthony, "Doctor, Do We Have a Choice?" *The New York Times Magazine*, 30 Jan. 1972, p. 54.

The Intentional
Termination of Life

Bonnie Steinbock

Bonnie Steinbock is a professor of philosophy at the State University of New York at Albany. She has published articles on ethics regarding life and death and a recent work Life Before Birth: The Moral and Legal Status of Embryos and Fetuses (1992).

Steinbock argues that Rachels misconstrues the American Medical Association policy as endorsing a distinction between active and passive euthanasia by falsely identifying the termination of life-sustaining treatment with passive euthanasia. She claims that this identification cannot hold in situations where the patient chooses to refuse treatment and where the treatment is discontinued when it proves to be of no benefit to the patient. In closing, Steinbock points out that one needs to make a distinction between an act done intentionally and the unintended results brought about by the act.

According to James Rachels and Michael Tooley . . . a common mistake in medical ethics is the belief that there is a moral difference between active and passive euthanasia. This is a mistake, they argue, because the rationale underlying the distinction between active and passive euthanasia is the idea that there is a significant moral difference between intentionally killing and intentionally letting die. "The idea," Tooley says, "is admittedly very common. But I believe that it can be shown to reflect either confused thinking or a moral point of view unrelated to the interests of individuals." Whether or not the belief that there is a significant moral difference is mistaken is not my concern here. For it is far from clear that

From "The Intentional Termination of Life" by Bonnie Steinbock, *Ethics in Science and Medicine* 6, no. 1, 1979, pp. 59–64. Reprinted by permission of Elsevier Science, Ltd.

this distinction *is* the basis of the doctrine of the American Medical Association which Rachels attacks. And if the killing/letting die distinction is not the basis of the AMA doctrine, then arguments showing that the distinction has no moral force do not, in themselves, reveal in the doctrine's adherents either "confused thinking" or "a moral point of view unrelated to the interests of individuals." Indeed, as we examine the AMA doctrine, I think it will become clear that it appeals to and makes use of a number of overlapping distinctions, which may have moral significance in particular cases, such as the distinction between intending and foreseeing, or between ordinary and extraordinary care. Let us then turn to the 1973 statement, from the House of Delegates of the American Medical Association, which Rachels cites:

> The intentional termination of the life of one human being by another—mercy

killing—is contrary to that for which the medical profession stands and is contrary to the policy of the American Medical Association.

The cessation of the employment of extraordinary means to prolong the life of the body when there is irrefutable evidence that biological death is imminent is the decision of the patient and/or his immediate family. The advice and judgment of the physician should be freely available to the patient and/or his immediate family.

Rachels attacks this statement because he believes that it contains a moral distinction between active and passive euthanasia. Tooley also believes this to be the position of the AMA, saying:

Many people hold that there is an important moral distinction between passive euthanasia and active euthanasia. Thus, while the AMA maintains that people have a right "to die with dignity," so that it is morally permissible for a doctor to allow someone to die if that person wants to and is suffering from an incurable illness causing pain that cannot be sufficiently alleviated, the AMA is unwilling to countenance active euthanasia for a person who is in similar straits, but who has the misfortune not to be suffering from an illness that will result in a speedy death.

Both men, then, take the AMA position to prohibit active euthanasia, while allowing, under certain conditions, passive euthanasia.

I intend to show that the AMA statement does not imply support of the active/passive euthanasia distinction. In forbidding the intentional termination of life, the statement rejects both active and passive euthanasia. It does allow for "the cessation of the employment of extraordinary means" to prolong life. The mistake Rachels and Tooley make is in identifying the cessation of life-prolonging treatment with passive euthanasia, or intentionally letting die. If it were right to equate the two, then the

AMA statement would be selfcontradictory, for it would begin by condemning, and end by allowing, the intentional termination of life. But if the cessation of life-prolonging treatment is not always or necessarily passive euthanasia, then there is no confusion and no contradiction.

Why does Rachels think that the cessation of life-prolonging treatment is the intentional termination of life? He says:

The AMA policy statement isolates the crucial issue very well: the crucial issue is "the intentional termination of the life of one human being by another." But after identifying this issue, and forbidding "mercy killing," the statement goes on to deny that the cessation of treatment is the intentional termination of a life. This is where the mistake comes in, for what is the cessation of treatment, in these circumstances, if it is not "the intentional termination of the life of one human being by another"? Of course it is exactly that, and if it were not, there would be no point to it.

However, there can be a point (to the cessation of life-prolonging treatment) other than an endeavor to bring about the patient's death, and so the blanket identification of cessation of treatment with the intentional termination of a life is inaccurate. There are at least two situations in which the termination of life-prolonging treatment cannot be identified with the intentional termination of the life of one human being by another.

The first situation concerns the patient's right to refuse treatment. Both Tooley and Rachels give the example of a patient dying of an incurable disease, accompanied by unrelievable pain, who wants to end the treatment which cannot cure him but can only prolong his miserable existence. Why, they ask, may a doctor accede to the patient's request to stop treatment, but not provide a patient in a similar situation with a lethal dose? The answer lies in the patient's right to refuse treatment. In general, a competent adult has the right to refuse treatment, even where such treatment is necessary to prolong life. Indeed, the right to refuse treatment has been upheld even when the patient's reason for refusing treatment is generally agreed to be inadequate.[1] This right can be overridden (if, for example, the patient has dependent children) but, in general, no one may legally compel you to undergo treatment to which you have not consented. "Historically, surgical intrusion has always been considered a technical battery upon the person and one to be excused or justified by consent of the patient or justified by necessity created by the circumstances of the moment . . . ."[2]

At this point, an objection might be raised that if one has the right to refuse life-prolonging treatment, then consistency demands that one have the right to decide to end his or her life, and to obtain help in doing so. The idea is that the right to refuse treatment somehow implies a right to voluntary euthanasia, and we need to see why someone might think this. The right to refuse treatment has been considered by legal writers as an example of the right to privacy or, better, the right to bodily self-determination. You have the right to decide what happens to your own body, and the right to refuse treatment is an instance of that right. But if you have the right to determine what happens to your own body, then should you not have the right to choose to end your life, and even a right to get help in doing so?

However, it is important to see that the right to refuse treatment is not the same as, nor does it entail, a right to voluntary euthanasia, even if both can be derived from the right to bodily self-determination. The right to refuse treatment is not itself a "right to die"; that one may choose to exercise this right even at the risk of death, or even *in order to die*, is irrelevant. The purpose of the right to refuse medical treatment is not to give persons a right to decide whether to live or die, but to protect them from the unwanted interferences of others. Perhaps we ought to interpret the right to bodily self-determination more broadly, so as to include a right to die; but this would be a substantial extension of our present understanding of the right to bodily self-determination, and not a consequence of it. If we were to recognize a right to voluntary euthanasia, we would have to agree that people have the right not merely to be left alone but also the right to be killed. I leave to one side that substantive moral issue. My claim is simply that there can be a reason for terminating life-prolonging treatment other than "to bring about the patient's death."

The second case in which termination of treatment cannot be identified with intentional termination of life is where continued treatment has little chance of improving the patient's condition and brings greater discomfort than relief.

The question here is what treatment is appropriate to the particular case. A cancer specialist describes it in this way:

> My general rule is to administer therapy as long as a patient responds well and has the potential for a reasonably good quality of life. But when all feasible therapies have been administered and a patient shows signs of rapid deterioration, the continuation of therapy can cause more discomfort than the cancer. From that time I recommend surgery, radiotherapy, or chemotherapy only as a means of relieving pain. But if a patient's condition should once again stabilize after the withdrawal of active therapy and if it should appear that he could still gain some good time, I would immediately reinstitute active therapy. The decision to cease anticancer treatment is never irrevocable, and often the desire to live will push a patient to try for

another remission, or even a few more days of life.[3]

The decision here to cease anticancer treatment cannot be construed as a decision that the patient die, or as the intentional termination of life. It is a decision to provide the most appropriate treatment for that patient at that time. Rachels suggests that the point of the cessation of treatment is the intentional termination of life. But here the point of discontinuing treatment is not to bring about the patient's death but to avoid treatment that will cause more discomfort than the cancer and has little hope of benefiting the patient. Treatment that meets this description is often called "extraordinary."[4] The concept is flexible, and what might be considered "extraordinary" in one situation might be ordinary in another. The use of a respirator to sustain a patient through a severe bout with a respiratory disease would be considered ordinary; its use to sustain the life of a severely brain-damaged person in an irreversible coma would be considered extraordinary.

Contrasted with extraordinary treatment is ordinary treatment, the care a doctor would normally be expected to provide. Failure to provide ordinary care constitutes neglect, and can even be construed as the intentional infliction of harm, where there is a legal obligation to provide care. The importance of the ordinary/extraordinary care distinction lies partly in its connection to the doctor's intention. The withholding of extraordinary care should be seen as a decision not to inflict painful treatment on a patient without reasonable hope of success. The withholding of ordinary care, by contrast, must be seen as neglect. Thus, one doctor says, "We have to draw a distinction between ordinary and extraordinary means. We never withdraw what's

needed to make a baby comfortable, we would never withdraw the care a parent would provide. We never kill a baby . . . . But we may decide certain heroic interventions are not worthwhile."[5]

We should keep in mind the ordinary/extraordinary care distinction when considering an example given by both Tooley and Rachels to show the irrationality of the active/passive distinction with regard to infanticide. The example is this: a child is born with Down's syndrome and also has an intestinal obstruction that requires corrective surgery. If the surgery is not performed, the infant will starve to death, since it cannot take food orally. This may take days or even weeks, as dehydration and infection set in. Commenting on this situation in his article in this book Rachels says:

> I can understand why some people are opposed to all euthanasia, and insist that such infants must be allowed to live. I think I can also understand why other people favor destroying these babies quickly and painlessly. But why should anyone favor letting "dehydration and infection wither a tiny being over hours and days"? The doctrine that says that a baby may be allowed to dehydrate and wither, but may not be given an injection that would end its life without suffering, seems so patently cruel as to require no further refutation.

Such a doctrine perhaps does not need further refutation; but this is not the AMA doctrine. The AMA statement criticized by Rachels allows only for the cessation of extraordinary means to prolong life when death is imminent. Neither of these conditions is satisfied in this example. Death is not imminent in this situation, any more than it would be if a normal child had an attack of appendicitis. Neither the corrective surgery to remove the intestinal obstruction nor the intravenous feeding required to keep the infant alive until such surgery is performed can be regarded as extraordinary means, for neither is particularly expensive, nor does either place an overwhelming burden on the patient or others. (The continued existence of the child might be thought to place an overwhelming burden on its parents, but that has nothing to do with the characterization of the means to prolong its life as extraordinary. If it had, then *feeding* a severely defective child who required a great deal of care could be regarded as extraordinary.) The chances of success if the operation is undertaken are quite good, though there is always a risk in operating on infants. Though the Down's syndrome will not be alleviated, the child will proceed to an otherwise normal infancy.

It cannot be argued that the treatment is withheld for the infant's sake, unless one is prepared to argue that all mentally retarded babies are better off dead. This is particularly implausible in the case of Down's syndrome babies, who generally do not suffer and are capable of giving and receiving love, of learning and playing, to varying degrees.

In a film on this subject entitled, "Who Should Survive?", a doctor defended a decision not to operate, saying that since the parents did not consent to the operation, the doctors' hands were tied. As we have seen, surgical intrusion requires consent, and in the case of infants, consent would normally come from the parents. But, as legal guardians, parents are required to provide medical care for their children, and failure to do so can constitute criminal neglect or even homicide. In general, courts have been understandably reluctant to recognize a parental right to terminate life-prolonging treatment.[6] Although prosecution is unlikely, physicians who comply with invalid instructions from the parents and permit the infant's death could be liable for aiding

and abetting, failure to report child neglect, or even homicide. So it is not true that, in this situation, doctors are legally bound to do as the parents wish.

To sum up, I think that Rachels is right to regard the decision not to operate in the Down's syndrome example as the intentional termination of life. But there is no reason to believe that either the law or the AMA would regard it otherwise. Certainly the decision to withhold treatment is not justified by the AMA statement. That such infants have been allowed to die cannot be denied; but this, I think, is the result of doctors misunderstanding the law and the AMA position.

Withholding treatment in this case is the intentional termination of life because the infant is deliberately allowed to die; that is the point of not operating. But there are other cases in which that is not the point. If the point is to avoid inflicting painful treatment on a patient with little or no reasonable hope of success, this is not the intentional termination of life. The permissibility of such withholding of treatment, then, would have no implications for the permissibility of euthanasia, active or passive.

The decision whether or not to operate, or to institute vigorous treatment, is particularly agonizing in the case of children born with spina bifida, an opening in the base of the spine usually accompanied by hydrocephalus and mental retardation. If left unoperated, these children usually die of meningitis or kidney failure within the first few years of life. Even if they survive, all affected children face a lifetime of illness, operations, and varying degrees of disability. The policy used to be to save as many as possible, but the trend now is toward selective treatment, based on the physician's estimate of the chances of success. If operating is not likely to improve significantly the child's condition, parents and doctors may agree not to operate. This is not the intentional termination of life, for again the purpose is not the termination of the child's life but the avoidance of painful and pointless treatment. Thus, the fact that withholding treatment is justified does not imply that killing the child would be equally justified.

Throughout the discussion, I have claimed that intentionally ceasing life-prolonging treatment is not the intentional termination of life unless the doctor has, as his or her purpose in stopping treatment, the patient's death.

It may be objected that I have incorrectly characterized the conditions for the intentional termination of life. Perhaps it is enough that the doctor intentionally ceases treatment, foreseeing that the patient will die.

In many cases, if one acts intentionally, foreseeing that a particular result will occur, one can be said to have brought about that result intentionally. Indeed, this is the general legal rule. Why, then, am I not willing to call the cessation of life-prolonging treatment, in compliance with the patient's right to refuse treatment, the intentional termination of life? It is not because such an *identification* is necessarily opprobrious; for we could go on to *discuss* whether such cessation of treatment is a *justifiable* intentional termination of life. Even in the law, some cases of homicide are justifiable; e.g., homicide in self-defense.

However, the cessation of life-prolonging treatment, in the cases which I have discussed, is not regarded in law as being justifiable homicide, because it is not homicide at all. Why is this? Is it because the doctor "doesn't do anything," and so cannot be guilty of homicide? Surely not, since, as

I have indicated, the law sometimes treats an omission as the cause of death. A better explanation, I think, has to do with the fact that in the context of the patient's right to refuse treatment, a doctor is not at liberty to continue treatment. It seems a necessary ingredient of intentionally letting die that one could have done something to prevent the death. In this situation, of course, the doctor can physically prevent the patient's death, but since we do not regard the doctor as *free* to continue treatment, we say that there is "nothing he can do." Therefore he does not intentionally let the patient die.

To discuss this suggestion fully, I would need to present a full-scale theory of intentional action. However, at least I have shown, through the discussion of the above examples, that such a theory will be very complex, and that one of the complexities concerns the agent's reason for acting. The reason why an agent acted (or failed to act) may affect the characterization of what he did intentionally. The mere fact that he did *something* intentionally, foreseeing a certain result, does not necessarily mean that he brought about that *result* intentionally.

In order to show that the cessation of life-prolonging treatment, in the cases I've discussed, is the intentional termination of life, one would either have to show that treatment was stopped in order to bring about the patient's death, or provide a theory of intentional action according to which the reason for ceasing treatment is irrelevant to its characterization as the intentional termination of life. I find this suggestion implausible, but am willing to consider arguments for it. Rachels has provided no such arguments: indeed, he apparently shares my view about the intentional termination of life. For when he claims that the cessation of life-prolonging treatment *is* the intentional termination of life, his reason for making the claim is that "if it were not, there would be no point to it." Rachels believes that the point of ceasing treatment, "in these cases," is to bring about the patient's death. If that were not the point, he suggests, why would the doctor cease treatment? I have shown, however, that there can be a point to ceasing treatment which is not the death of the patient. In showing this, I have refuted Rachels' reason for identifying the cessation of life-prolonging treatment with the intentional termination of life, and thus his argument against the AMA doctrine.

Here someone might say: Even if the withholding of treatment is not the intentional termination of life, does that make a difference, morally speaking? If life-prolonging treatment may be withheld, for the sake of the child, may not an easy death be provided, for the sake of the child, as well? The unoperated child with spina bifida may take months or even years to die. Distressed by the spectacle of children "lying around, waiting to die," one doctor has written, "It is time that society and medicine stopped perpetuating the fiction that withholding treatment is ethically different from terminating a life. It is time that society began to discuss mechanisms by which we can alleviate the pain and suffering for those individuals whom we cannot help."[7]

I do not deny that there may be cases in which death is in the best interests of the patient. In such cases, a quick and painless death may be the best thing. However, I do not think that, once active or vigorous treatment is stopped, a quick death is always preferable to a lingering one. We must be cautious about attributing to defective children *our* distress at seeing them linger. Waiting for them to die may be tough on parents, doctors, and nurses—it isn't necessarily tough on the child. The

decision not to operate need not mean a decision to neglect, and it may be possible to make the remaining months of the child's life comfortable, pleasant, and filled with love. If this alternative is possible, surely it is more decent and humane than killing the child. In such a situation, withholding treatment, foreseeing the child's death, is not ethically equivalent to killing the child, and we cannot move from the permissibility of the former to that of the latter. I am worried that there will be a tendency to do precisely that if active euthanasia is regarded as morally equivalent to the withholding of life-prolonging treatment.

CONCLUSION

The AMA statement does not make the distinction Rachels and Tooley wish to attack, that between active and passive euthanasia. Instead, the statement draws a distinction between the intentional termination of life, on the one hand, and the cessation of the employment of extraordinary means to prolong life, on the other. Nothing said by Rachels and Tooley shows that this distinction is confused. It may be that doctors have misinterpreted the AMA statement, and that this has led, for example, to decisions to allow defective infants to starve slowly to death. I quite agree with Rachels and Tooley that the decisions to which they allude were cruel and made on irrelevant grounds. Certainly it is worth pointing out that allowing someone to die *can* be the intentional termination of life, and that it can be just as bad as, or worse than, killing someone. However, the withholding of life-prolonging treatment is not necessarily the intentional termination of life, so that if it is permissible to withhold life-prolonging treatment it does not follow that, other things being equal, it is permissible to kill. Furthermore, most of the time, other things are not equal. In many of the cases in which it would be right to cease treatment, I do not think that it would also be right to kill.

ACKNOWLEDGMENTS

I would like to express my thanks to Jonathan Bennett, Josiah Gould, Deborah Johnson, David Pratt, Bruce Russell, and David Zimmerman, all of whom provided helpful criticism and suggestions for this article. Reprinted with permission of the publisher and author.

NOTES

1. For example, *In re Yetter*, 62 Pa. D. & C. 2d 619 (C.P., Northampton County Ct. 1974).

2. David W. Meyers, "Legal Aspects of Voluntary Euthanasia," in *Dilemmas of Euthanasia*, ed. John Behnke and Sissela Bok (New York: Anchor Books, 1975), p. 56.

3. Ernest H. Rosenbaum, M.D., *Living with Cancer* (New York: Praeger, 1975), p. 27.

4. See Tristram Engelhardt, Jr., "Ethical Issues in Aiding the Death of Young Children," in *Beneficent Euthanasia,* ed. Marvin Kohl (Buffalo, N.Y.: Prometheus Books, 1975).

5. B. D. Colen, *Karen Ann Quinlan: Living and Dying in the Age of Eternal Life* (Los Angeles: Nash, 1976), p. 115.

6. See Norman L. Cantor, "Law and the Termination of an Incompetent Patient's Life-Preserving Care," in *Dilemmas of Euthanasia*, pp. 69–105.

7. John Freeman, "Is There a Right to Die— Quickly?", *Journal of Pediatrics,* 80, no. 5 (1972), 904–905.

Euthanasia: The Way We Do It, the Way They Do It

Margaret Battin

Margaret Battin is a professor of philosophy at the University of Utah. She is the author of Ethical Issues in Suicide *(1982),* Ethics in the Sanctuary *(1990), and* The Least Worst Death *(1994). She is co-editor of* Ethical Issues in the Professions *(1989).*

   Battin examines euthanasia practices in three societies: the Netherlands, where active euthanasia is allowed; Germany where active euthanasia is disallowed but assisted suicide is allowed; and the United States, where neither active euthanasia nor assisted suicide is allowed, but where passive euthanasia in the form of withdrawal or withholding of treatment is common. Battin argues that the United States does not supply an adequate range of options to patients who are near death. After considering arguments from many sides of the issue, Battin concludes that the United States should allow "physician-assisted suicide."

INTRODUCTION

Because we tend to be rather myopic in our discussions of death and dying, especially about the issues of active euthanasia and assisted suicide, it is valuable to place the question of how we go about dying in an international context. We do not always see that our own cultural norms may be quite different from those of other nations, and that our background assumptions, and actual practices, differ dramatically. Thus, I would like to examine the perspectives on end-of-life dilemmas in three countries, the Netherlands, Germany, and the USA.

Reprinted by permission of Elsevier Science Publishing Co., Inc., from "Euthanasia: The Way We Do It, the Way They Do It," by Margaret Battin in *Journal of Pain and Symptom Management*, vol. 6, No. 5, pp. 298–305. Copyright 1991 by the U.S. Cancer Pain Relief Committee.

The Netherlands, Germany, and the United States are all advanced industrial democracies. They all have sophisticated medical establishments and life expectancies over 70 years of age; their populations are all characterized by an increasing proportion of older persons. They are all in what has been called the fourth stage of the epidemiologic transition[1]—that stage of societal development in which it is no longer the case that most people die of acute parasitic or infectious diseases. In this stage, most people do not die of diseases with rapid, unpredictable onsets and sharp fatality curves; rather, the majority of the population—as much as perhaps 70%–80%—dies of degenerative diseases, especially delayed degenerative diseases, that are characterized by late, slow onset and extended decline. Most people in highly industrialized countries die from cancer, atherosclerosis, heart disease (by no means always suddenly fatal), chronic obstructive pulmonary disease, liver, kidney or other organ disease, or degenerative neurological disorders. Thus, all three of these countries are alike in facing a common problem: how to deal with the characteristic new ways in which we die.

DEALING WITH DYING IN THE UNITED STATES

In the United States, we have come to recognize that the maximal extension of life-prolonging treatment in these late-life degenerative conditions is often inappropriate. Although we could keep the machines and tubes—the respirators, intravenous lines, feeding tubes—hooked up for extended periods, we recognize that this is inhumane, pointless, and financially impossible. Instead, as a society we have developed a number of mechanisms for dealing with these hopeless situations, all of which involve withholding or withdrawing various forms of treatment.

Some mechanisms for withholding or withdrawing treatment are exercised by the patient who is confronted by such a situation or who anticipates it; these include refusal of treatment, the patient-executed DNR order, the Living Will, and the Durable Power of Attorney. Others are mechanisms for decision by second parties about a patient who is no longer competent or never was competent. The latter are reflected in a long series of court cases, including *Quinlan, Saikewicz, Spring, Eichner, Barber, Bartling, Conroy, Brophy,* the trio *Farrell, Peter* and *Jobes,* and *Cruzan.* These are cases that attempt to delineate the precise circumstances under which it is appropriate to withhold or withdraw various forms of therapy, including respiratory support, chemotherapy, antibi-

otics in intercurrent infections, and artificial nutrition and hydration. Thus, during the past 15 years or so, roughly since *Quinlan* (1976), we have developed an impressive body of case law and state statute that protects, permits, and facilitates our characteristic American strategy of dealing with end-of-life situations. These cases provide a framework for withholding or withdrawing treatment when we believe there is no medical or moral point in going on. This is sometimes termed *passive euthanasia;* more often, it is simply called *allowing to die,* and is ubiquitous in the United States.

For example, a recent study by Miles and Gomez indicates that some 85% of deaths in the United States occur in health-care institutions, including hospitals, nursing homes, and other facilities, and of these, about 70% involve electively withholding some form of life-sustaining treatment.[2] A 1989 study cited in the *Journal of the American Medical Association* claims that 85%–90% of critical care professionals state that they are withholding and withdrawing life-sustaining treatments from patients who are "deemed to have irreversible disease and are terminally ill."[3] Still another study identified some 115 patients in two intensive-care units from whom care was withheld or withdrawn; 110 were already incompetent by the time the decision to limit care was made. The 89 who died while still in the intensive care unit accounted for 45% of all deaths there.[4] It is estimated that 1.3 million American deaths a year follow decisions to withhold life support;[5] this is a majority of the just over 2 million American deaths per year. Withholding and withdrawing treatment is the way we in the USA go about dealing with dying, and indeed "allowing to die" is the only legally protected alternative to maximal treatment recognized in the United States. We do not legally permit ourselves to actively cause death.

DEALING WITH DYING
IN THE NETHERLANDS

In the Netherlands, voluntary active euthanasia is also an available response to end-of-life situations. Although active euthanasia remains prohibited by statutory law, it is protected by a series of lower and supreme court decisions and is widely regarded as legal, or, more precisely, *gedoeken,* legally "tolerated." These court decisions have the effect of protecting the physician who performs euthanasia from prosecution, provided the physician meets a rigorous set of guidelines.

These guidelines, variously stated, contain five central provisions:

1. that the patient's request be voluntary;
2. that the patient be undergoing intolerable suffering;
3. that all alternatives acceptable to the patient for relieving the suffering have been tried;
4. that the patient have full information;
5. that the physician consult with a second physician whose judgment can be expected to be independent.

Of these criteria, it is the first which is central: euthanasia may be performed only at the voluntary request of the patient. This criterion is also understood to require that the patient's request be a stable, enduring, reflective one—not the product of a transitory impulse. Every attempt is to be made to rule out depression, psychopathology, pressures from family members, unrealistic fears, and other factors compromising voluntariness.

Putting an end to years of inflammatory discussion in which speculation about the frequency of euthanasia had ranged from 2,000 (close to correct) to 20,000 cases a year, a comprehensive study requested by the Dutch government was published in late 1991; an English version appeared in *The Lancet.*[6] Popularly known as the Remmelink Commission report, this study provided the first objective data about the incidence of euthanasia as well as a wider range of medical practices at the end of life: the withholding or withdrawal of treatment, the use of life-shortening doses of opioids for the control of pain, and direct termination, including active euthanasia, physician-assisted suicide, and life-ending procedures not termed euthanasia. This study was supplemented by a second empirical examination, focusing particularly carefully on the characteristics of patients and the nature of their euthanasia requests.[7]

About 130,000 people die in the Netherlands every year, and of these deaths, about 30% are acute and unexpected; 70% are predictable and foreseen, usually the result of degenerative illnesses comparatively late in life. Of the total deaths in the Netherlands, the Remmelink Commission's study found, about 17.5% involved decisions to withhold or withdraw treatment although continuing treatment would probably have prolonged life; another 17.5% involved the use of opioids to relieve pain but in dosages probably sufficient to shorten life. A total of 2.9% of all deaths involved euthanasia and related practices.

About 2,300 people, 1.8% of the total deaths in the Netherlands, died by euthanasia, understood as the termination of the life of the patient at the patient's explicit and persistent request. Another 400 people, 0.03% of the total, chose physician-assisted suicide. About 1,000 additional patients died as the result of "life-terminating procedures," not technically called euthanasia, in virtually all of which euthanasia had either been previously discussed with the patient or the patient had expressed in a previous phase of the disease a wish for euthanasia if his or her suffering became unbearable, or the patient was near death and clearly suffering grievously, yet verbal contact had become impossible.

Although euthanasia is thus not frequent—a small fraction of the total annual mortality—it is nevertheless a conspicuous option in terminal illness, well known to both physicians and the general public. There has been *very* widespread public discussion of the issues in euthanasia during the last several years, especially as the pros and cons of full legalization have been debated, and surveys of public opinion show that the public support for a liberal euthanasia policy has been growing: from 40% in 1966 to 81% in 1988.[8] Doctors too support this practice, and although there is a vocal opposition group, the opposition is in the clear minority. Some 54% of Dutch physicians said that they performed euthanasia or provided assistance in suicide, including 62% of *huisarts* or general practitioners, and an additional 34% said that although they had not actually done so, they could conceive of situations in which they would be prepared to do so. Thus, although many who had practiced euthanasia mentioned that they would be most reluctant to do so again and that "only in the face of unbearable suffering and with no alternatives would they be prepared to take such action,"[9] some 88% of Dutch physicians appear to accept the practice in some cases. As the Remmelink Commission commented, " . . . a large majority of physicians in the Netherlands see euthanasia as an accepted element of medical practice under certain circumstances."[10]

In general, pain alone is not the basis for euthanasia, since pain can, in most cases, be effectively treated. Rather, "intolerable suffering," among the criteria for euthanasia, is understood to mean suffering that is intolerable in the patient's (rather than the physician's) view, and can include a fear of or unwillingness to endure *entluisterung,* that gradual effacement and loss of personal identity that characterizes the end stages of many terminal illnesses. In a year, about 25,000 patients seek reassurance from their physicians that they will be granted euthanasia if their suffering becomes severe; there are about 9,000 explicit requests, and more than two-thirds of these are turned down, usually on the grounds that there is some other way of treating the patient's suffering, and in just 14% on the grounds of psychiatric illness.

In Holland, many hospitals now have protocols for the performance of euthanasia; these serve to ensure that the court-established guidelines have been met. However, euthanasia is often practiced in the patient's home, typically by the *huisarts* or general practitioner who is the patient's long-term family physician. Euthanasia is usually performed after aggressive hospital treatment has failed to arrest the patient's terminal illness; the patient has come home to die, and the family physician is prepared to ease this passing. Whether practiced at home or in the hospital, it is believed that euthanasia usually takes place in the presence of the family members, perhaps the visiting nurse, and often the patient's pastor or priest. Many doctors say that performing euthanasia is never easy, but that it is something they believe a doctor ought to do for his or her patient, when nothing else can help.

Thus, in Holland a patient facing the end of life has an option not openly practiced in the United States: to ask the physician to bring his or her life to an end. Although not everyone does so—indeed, about 97% of people who die in a given year do not—it is a choice widely understood as available.

FACING DEATH IN GERMANY

In part because of its very painful history of Nazism, Germany appears to believe that doctors should have no role in causing death. Although societal generalizations are always risky, it is fair, I think, to say that there is vigorous and nearly universal opposition in Germany to the notion of active euthanasia. Euthanasia is viewed as always wrong, and the Germans view the Dutch as stepping out on a dangerously slippery slope.

However, it is an artifact of German law that, whereas killing on request (including voluntary euthanasia) is prohibited, assisting suicide is not a violation of the law, provided the person is *tatherrschaftsfähig,* capable of exercising control over his or her actions, and also acting out of *freiverantwortliche Wille,* freely responsible choice. Responding to this situation, there has developed a private organization, the *Deutsche Gesellschaft für Humanes Sterben* (DGHS), or German Society for Humane Dying, which provides support to its very extensive membership (over 50,000 persons) in choosing suicide as an alternative to terminal illness.

After a person has been a member of the DGHS for at least a year, and provided that he or she has not received medical or psychotherapeutic treatment for depression or other psychiatric illness during the last two years, he or she may request a copy of DGHS's booklet *Menschenwürdiges und selbstverantworliches Sterben,* or "Dignified and Responsible Death." This booklet provides a list of about ten drugs available by

prescription in Germany, together with the specific dosages necessary for producing a certain, painless death. (The DGHS no longer officially recommends cyanide, though its president, Hans Henning Atrott, was recently charged with selling it.) DGHS recommends that the members approach a physician for a prescription for the drug desired, asking, for example, for a barbiturate to help with sleep, or chloroquine for protection against malaria on a trip to India. If necessary, the DGHS may also arrange for someone to obtain drugs from neighboring countries, including France, Italy, Spain, Portugal, and Greece, where they may be available without prescription. In unusual cases, the DGHS will also provide what it calls *Sterbebegleitung* or "accompaniment in dying," providing a companion to remain with the person during the often extended period that is required for the lethal drug to take full effect. However, the *Sterbebegleiter* is typically a layperson, not someone medically trained, and physicians play no role in assisting in these cases of suicide. To preclude suspicion by providing evidence of the person's intentions, the DGHS also provides a form—printed on a single sheet of distinctive pink paper—to be signed once when joining the organization, expressing the intention to determine the time of one's own death, and to be signed again at the time of the suicide and left beside the body.

Because assisting suicide is not illegal in Germany, provided the person is competent and in control of his or her own will, there is no legal risk for family members, *Sterbebegleiter*, or others in reporting information about the methods and effectiveness of suicide attempts, and the DGHS encourages its network of regional bureaus (five, in major cities throughout the country) to facilitate feedback. On this basis, it regularly updates and revises the drug information it provides. It claims some 2,000–3,000 suicides per year among its members.

To be sure, assisted suicide is not the only option open to the terminally ill patient in Germany, nor is there clear evidence concerning its frequency either within the DGHS or in nonreported cases outside it. There is increasing emphasis on help in dying that does not involve direct termination, and organizations like Omega, offering hospice-style care and an extensive program of companionship, are attracting increasing attention. Furthermore, there has been recent scandal directed towards the founder and president of the DGHS, Hans Henning Atrott, accused in late 1991 of selling cyanide to an attorney hospitalized for mental illness; in May 1992 police raided his office, finding capsules of cyanide, barbiturates, and a large amount of cash. What the outcome of this event will be remains at this writing to be seen, though it is clear that the scandal focuses on Atrott's alleged profiteering and assisting a mentally ill person, rather than with the DGHS's regular practice of assisting competent terminally ill individuals in suicide. Furthermore, the DGHS is a conspicuous, widely known organization, and many Germans appear to be aware that assisted suicide is available even if they do not use the services of the DGHS.

OBJECTIONS TO THE THREE MODELS OF DYING

In response to the dilemmas raised by the new circumstances of death, in which the majority of the population in each of the advanced industrial nations dies of degenerative diseases after an extended period of terminal deterioration, different countries develop different practices. The United States legally permits only withholding and withdrawal of treatment, though of course active euthanasia and assisted suicide do occur. Holland also permits voluntary active euthanasia, and although Germany rejects euthanasia, it tolerates assisted suicide. But there are serious moral objections to be made to each of these practices, objections to be considered before resolving the issue of which practice our own culture ought to adopt.

Objections to the German Practice

German law does not prohibit assisting suicide, but postwar German culture discourages physicians from taking any active role in death. This gives rise to distinctive moral problems. For one thing, it appears that there is little professional help or review provided for patients' choices about suicide; because the patient makes this choice essentially outside the medical establishment, medical professionals are not in a position to detect or treat impaired judgment on the part of the patient, especially judgment impaired by depression. Similarly, if the patient must commit suicide assisted only by persons outside the medical profession, there are risks that the patient's diagnosis and prognosis are inadequately confirmed, that the means chosen for suicide will be unreliable or inappropriately used, that the means used for suicide will fall into the hands of other persons, and that the patient will fail to recognize or be able to resist intrafamilial pressures and manipulation. The DGHS policy for providing assistance requires that the patient be terminally ill and have been a member of the DGHS for at least one year in order to make use of its services, the latter requirement is intended to provide evidence of the stability of such a choice. However, these minimal requirements are hardly sufficient to answer the charge that suicide decisions, which are made for medical reasons but must be made without medical help, may be rendered under less than ideally informed and voluntary conditions.

Objections to the Dutch Practice

The Dutch practice of physician-performed active voluntary euthanasia also raises a number of ethical issues, many of which have been discussed vigorously both in the Dutch press and in commentary on the Dutch practices from abroad. For one thing, it is sometimes said that the availability of physician-performed euthanasia creates a disincentive for providing good terminal care. I have seen no evidence that this is the case; on the contrary, Peter Admiraal, the anesthesiologist who is perhaps Holland's most vocal proponent of voluntary active euthanasia, insists that pain should rarely or never be the occasion for euthanasia, as pain (in contrast to suffering) is comparatively easily treated.[11] Instead, it is a refusal to endure the final stages of deterioration, both mental and physical, that motivates requests.

It is also sometimes said that active euthanasia violates the Hippocratic Oath. Indeed, it is true that the original Greek version of the Oath prohibits the physician from giving a deadly drug, even when asked for it; but the original version also prohibits performing surgery and taking fees for teaching medicine, neither of which prohibitions has survived into contemporary medical practice. Dutch physicians often say that they see performing euthanasia— where it is genuinely requested by the patient and nothing else can be done to

relieve the patient's condition—as part of their duty to the patient, not as a violation of it.

The Dutch are also often said to be at risk of starting down the slippery slope, that is, that the practice of voluntary active euthanasia for patients who meet the criteria will erode into practicing less-than-voluntary euthanasia on patients whose problems are not irremediable, and perhaps by gradual degrees develop into terminating the lives of people who are elderly, chronically ill, handicapped, mentally retarded, or otherwise regarded as undesirable. This risk is often expressed in vivid claims of widespread fear and wholesale slaughter, claims that are repeated in the right-to-life press in both the Netherlands, and the USA, though there is no evidence for these claims. However, the Dutch are now beginning to agonize over the problems of the incompetent patient, the mentally ill patient, the newborn with serious deficits, and other patients who cannot make voluntary choices, though these are largely understood as issues about withholding or withdrawing treatment, not about direct termination.[12]

What is not often understood is that this new and acutely painful area of reflection for the Dutch—withholding and withdrawing treatment from incompetent patients—has already led in the United States to the development of a vast, highly developed body of law: namely that series of cases just cited, beginning with *Quinlan* and culminating in *Cruzan*. Americans have been discussing these issues for a long time, and have developed a broad set of practices that are regarded as routine in withholding and withdrawing treatment. The Dutch see Americans as much further out on the slippery slope than they are, because Americans have already become accustomed to second-party choices about other people. Issues involving second-party choices are painful to the Dutch in a way they are not to us precisely because *voluntariness* is so central in the Dutch understanding of choices about dying. Concomitantly, the Dutch see the Americans, squeamishness about first-party choices—voluntary euthanasia, assisted suicide—as evidence that we are not genuinely committed to recognizing *voluntary* choice after all. For this reason, many Dutch commentators believe that the Americans are at a much greater risk of sliding down the slippery slope into involuntary killing than they are. I fear, I must add, that they are right about this.

Objections to the American Practice

There may be moral problems raised by the German and the Dutch practices, but there are also moral problems raised by the American practice of relying on withholding and withdrawal of treatment in end-of-life situations. The German, Dutch, and American practices all occur within similar conditions—in industrialized nations with highly developed medical systems, where a majority of the population dies of illnesses exhibiting characteristically extended downhill courses—but the issues raised by our own response to this situation may be even more disturbing than those of the Dutch or the Germans. We often assume that our approach is "safer" because it involves only letting someone die, not killing him or her; but it too raises very troubling questions.

The first of these issues is a function of the fact that withdrawing and especially withholding treatment are typically less conspicuous, less pronounced, less evident kinds of actions than direct killing, even though they can equally well lead to death.

Decisions about nontreatment have an invisibility that decisions about directly causing death do not have, even though they may have the same result, and hence there is a much wider range of occasions in which such decisions can be made. One can decline to treat a patient in many different ways, at many different times—by not providing oxygen, by not instituting dialysis, by not correcting electrolyte imbalances, and so on—all of which will cause the patient's death; open medical killing also brings about death, but is a much more overt, conspicuous procedure. Consequently, letting die also invites many fewer protections. In contrast to the standard slippery slope argument which sees killing as riskier than letting die, the more realistic slippery slope argument warns that because our culture relies primarily on decisions about nontreatment, grave decisions about living or dying are not as open to scrutiny as they are under more direct life-terminating practices, and hence, are more open to abuse.

Second, and closely related, reliance on withholding and withdrawing treatment invites rationing in an extremely strong way, in part because of the comparative invisibility of these decisions. When a health care provider does not offer a specific sort of care, it is not always possible to discern the motivation; the line between believing that it would not provide benefit to the patient and that it would not provide benefit worth the investment of resources in the patient can be very thin. This is a particular problem where health care financing is highly decentralized, as in the United States, and where rationing decisions without benefit of principle are not always available for easy review.

Third, relying on withholding and withdrawal of treatment can often be cruel. It requires that the patient who is dying from one of the diseases that exhibits a characteristic extended, downhill course (as the majority of patients in the Netherlands, Germany and the U.S. do) must in effect wait to die until the absence of a certain treatment will cause death. For instance, the cancer patient who foregoes chemotherapy or surgery does not simply die from this choice; he or she continues to endure the downhill course of cancer until the tumor finally destroys some crucial bodily function or organ. The patient with amyotrophic lateral sclerosis who decides in advance to decline respiratory support does not die at the time the choice is made, but continues to endure increasing paralysis until breathing is impaired and suffocation occurs. We often try to ameliorate these situations by administering pain medication or symptom control at the same time we are withholding treatment, but these are all ways of disguising the fact that we are letting the disease kill the patient rather than directly bringing about death. But the ways diseases kill people are far more cruel than the ways physicians kill patients when performing euthanasia or assisting in suicide.

THE PROBLEM: A CHOICE OF CULTURES

Thus we see three similar cultures and countries and three similar sets of circumstances, but three different basic practices in approaching death. All three of these practices generate moral problems; none of them, nor any others we might devise, is free of moral difficulty. But the question that faces us is this: which of these practices is best?

It is not possible to answer this question in a less-than-ideal world without some attention to the specific characteristics and deficiencies of the society in question. In asking which of these practices is best, we must ask which is best *for us*. That we currently employ one set of these practices rather than others does not prove that it is best for us; the question is, would practices developed in other cultures or those not yet widespread in any be better for our own culture than that which has developed here? Thus, it is necessary to consider the differences between our society and these European cultures that have real bearing on which model of approach to dying we ought to adopt.

First, notice that different cultures exhibit different degrees of closeness between physicians and patients—different patterns of contact and involvement. The German physician is sometimes said to be more distant and more authoritarian than the American physician; on the other hand, the Dutch physician is sometimes said to be closer to his or her patients than either the American or the German is. In the Netherlands, basic primary care is provided by the *huisarts,* the general practitioner or family physician, who typically lives in the neighborhood, makes house calls frequently, and maintains an office in his or her own home. The *huisarts* is usually the physician for other members of the patient's family, and will remain the family's physician throughout his or her practice. Thus, the patient for whom euthanasia becomes an issue—say, the terminal cancer patient who has been hospitalized in the past but who has returned home to die—will be cared for by the trusted family physician on a regular basis. Indeed, for a patient in severe distress, the physician, supported by the visiting nurse, may make house calls as often as once a day, twice a day, or more (after all, it is right in the neighborhood), and is in continuous contact with the family. In contrast, the traditional American institution of the family doctor who makes house calls is rapidly becoming a thing of the past, and although some patients who die at home have access to hospice services and house calls from their long-term physician, many have no such long-term care and receive most of it from staff at a clinic or housestaff rotating through the services of a hospital. The degree of continuing contact the patient can have with a familiar, trusted physician clearly influences the nature of his or her dying, and also plays a role in whether physician-performed active euthanasia, assisted suicide, and/or withholding and withdrawing treatment is appropriate.

Second, the United States has a much more volatile legal climate than either the Netherlands or Germany; our medical system is increasingly litigious, much more so than that of any other country in the world. Fears of malpractice action or criminal prosecution color much of what physicians do in managing the dying of their patients. We also tend to evolve public policy through court decisions, and to assume that the existence of a policy puts an end to any moral issue. A delicate legal and moral balance over the issue of euthanasia, as is the case in the Netherlands, would not be possible here.

Third, we in the United States have a very different financial climate in which to do our dying. Both the Netherlands and Germany, as well as every other industrialized nation except South Africa, have systems of national health insurance or national health care. Thus the patient is not directly responsible for the costs of treatment, and consequently the patient's choices about terminal care and/or euthanasia need not take personal financial considerations into account. Even for the patient who does have health insurance

in the United States, many kinds of services are not covered, whereas the national health care or health insurance programs of many other countries variously provide many sorts of relevant services, including at-home physician care, home nursing care, home respite care, care in a nursing-home or other long-term facility, dietitian care, rehabilitation care, physical therapy, psychological counseling, and so on. The patient in the United States needs to attend to the financial aspects of dying in a way patients in many other countries do not, and in this country both the patient's choices and the recommendations of the physician are very often shaped by financial considerations.

There are many other differences between the USA on the one hand and the Netherlands and Germany, with their different models of dying, on the other. There are differences in degrees of paternalism in the medical establishment and in racism, sexism, and ageism in the general cultures, as well as awareness of a problematic historical past, especially Nazism. All of these and the previous factors influence the appropriateness or inappropriateness of practices such as active euthanasia and assisted suicide. For instance, the Netherlands' tradition of close physician/patient contact, its absence of malpractice-motivated medicine, and its provision of comprehensive health insurance, together with its comparative lack of racism and ageism and its experience in resistance to Nazism, suggest that this culture is able to permit the practice of voluntary active euthanasia, performed by physicians, without risking abuse. On the other hand, it is sometimes said that Germany still does not trust its physicians, remembering the example of Nazi experimentation, and given a comparatively authoritarian medical climate in which contact between physician and patient is quite distanced, the population could not be comfortable with the practice of active euthanasia. There, only a wholly patient-controlled response to terminal situations, as in non-physician-assisted suicide, is a reasonable and prudent practice.

But what about the United States? This is a country where (1) sustained contact with the personal physician is decreasing, (2) the risk of malpractice action is increasing, (3) much medical care is hot insured, (4) many medical decisions are financial decisions as well, (5) racism is on the rise, and (6) the public is naive about direct contact with Nazism or similar totalitarian movements. Thus, the United States is in many respects an untrustworthy candidate for practicing active euthanasia. Given the pressures on individuals in an often atomized society, encouraging solo suicide, assisted if at all only by nonprofessionals, might well be open to considerable abuse too.

However, there are several additional differences between the United States and both Holland and Germany that seem relevant here.

So far, the differences cited between the U.S. and both the Netherlands and Germany are negative ones, ones in which the U.S. falls far short. But there are positive differences as well, differences in which distinctive aspects of American culture are more favorable than those of Holland or Germany to the practice of euthanasia and assisted suicide. For example:

First, although the U.S. is indeed afflicted by a great deal of racism and sexism, it is also developing an increasingly strong tradition of independence in women. In many other countries, especially the Far East and the Islamic countries, the role of women still involves much greater disempowerment and expectations of subservience; in contrast,

the U.S. is particularly advanced—though, of course, it has a long way to go. The U.S. may even be ahead of the Netherlands and perhaps Germany in this respect. Whatever the case, this issue is of particular importance with respect to euthanasia, especially among elderly persons, because it is women whose life expectancies are longer than those of men and hence are more likely to be confronted with late-life degenerative terminal conditions.

Second, American culture is more confrontational than many others, including Dutch culture. While the Netherlands prides itself rightly on a long tradition of rational discussion of public issues and on toleration of others' views and practices, the U.S. (and to some degree, also Germany) tends to develop highly partisan, moralizing oppositional groups. In general, this is a disadvantage; but in the case of euthanasia it may serve to alert a public to issues and possibilities it might not otherwise consider, and especially to the risks of abuse.

Third, though this may at first seem to be a trivial difference, it is Americans who are particularly given to personal self-analysis. This tendency is evident not only in America's high rate of utilization of counseling services, including religious counseling, psychological counseling, and psychiatry, but is even more clearly evident in its popular culture: its diet of soap operas, situation comedies, and pop psychology books. It is here that the ordinary American absorbs models for analyzing his or her own personal relationships and individual psychological characteristics. While of course things are changing and our cultural tastes are widely exported, the fact remains that the ordinary American's cultural diet contains more in the way of both professional and do-it-yourself amateur psychology and self-analysis than anyone else's. This long tradition of self-analysis may put us in a better position for certain kinds of end-of-life practices than many other cultures—despite whatever other deficiencies we have, just because we live in a culture that encourages us to inspect our own motives, anticipate the impact of our actions on others and scrutinize our own relationships with others, including our physicians. This disposition is of importance in euthanasia contexts because euthanasia is the kind of fundamental choice about which one may have somewhat mixed motives, be subject to various interpersonal and situational pressures, and so on. If the voluntary character of these choices is to be protected, it may be a good thing to inhabit a culture in which self-inspection of one's own mental habits and motives is encouraged.

Finally, the U.S. is also characterized by a kind of "do-it-yourself" ethic, an ethic that does not rely on others to direct you or provide for you, but encourages individual initiative and responsibility. (To be sure this feature has been somewhat eclipsed in recent years, and is little in evidence in the series of court cases cited earlier, but it is still part, I think, of the American character.) This is coupled with a sort of resistance to authority that is sometimes also said to be basic to the American temperament. If these things are the case, it would seem to suggest that Americans would seek a style of end-of-life practices which would emphasize these characteristics rather than others.

These, of course, are all mere conjectures about features of American culture which would have a positive effect on the practice of euthanasia, or assisted suicide. These are the features that one would want to reinforce, should these practices become general, in part to minimize the effects of the negative features. But, of course, these positive features will differ from one country and culture to another, just as negative features do. In each country, a different architecture of antecedent assumptions and cultural features develops around the issues of the end of life, and in each country the practice of euthanasia, if it is to be free from abuse at all, must be adapted to the culture in which it takes place.

What, then, is appropriate for our own cultural situation? Physician-performed euthanasia, though not in itself morally wrong, is morally jeopardized where the legal, time, and especially financial pressures on both patients and physicians are severe; thus, it is morally problematic in our culture in a way that it is not in the Netherlands. Solo suicide outside the institution of medicine (as in Germany) may be problematic in a culture (like the United States) that is increasingly alienated, offers deteriorating and uneven social services, is increasingly racist, and in other ways imposes unusual pressures on individuals despite opportunities for self-analysis. Reliance only on withholding and withdrawing treatment (as in the United States) can be, as we've seen, cruel, and its comparative invisibility invites erosion under cost containment and other pressures. These are the three principal alternatives we've considered; but none of them seems wholly suited to our actual situation for dealing with the new fact that most of us die of extended-decline, deteriorative diseases. However, permitting physicians to supply patients with the means for ending their own lives grants physicians some control over the circumstances in which this can happen—only, for example, when the prognosis is genuinely grim and the alternatives for symptom control are poor—but leaves the fundamental decision about whether to use these means to the patient alone. It is up to the patient then—the independent, confrontational self-analyzing, do-it-yourself, authority-resisting patient—and his or her advisors, including family, clergy, physician, other health-care providers, and a raft of pop-psychology books, to be clear about whether he or she really wants to use these means or not. Thus, the physician is involved, but not directly; and it is the patient's choice, but the patient is not alone in making it. We live in a quite imperfect world, but, of the alternatives for facing death—which we all eventually must—I think the practice of permitting physician-assisted suicide is the one most nearly suited to the current state of our own somewhat flawed society. This is a model not yet central in any of the three countries examined here—the Netherlands, Germany, or the United States—but it is the one I think suits us best.

NOTES

1. Olshansky SJ, Ault AB. The fourth stage of the epidemiological transition: the age of delayed degenerative diseases. *Milbank Memorial Fund Quarterly/Health and Society* 1986; 64:355–391.

2. Miles S. Gomez C. *Protocols for elective use of life-sustaining treatment.* New York: Springer-Verlag. 1988.

3. Sprung CL, Changing attitudes and practices in foregoing life-sustaining treatments. *JAMA* 1990; 263:2213.

4. Smedira NG et al. Withholding and withdrawal of life support from the critically ill. *N Engl J Med* 1990; 322:309–315.

5. *New York Times,* July 23, 1990, p. A13.

6. Paul J. van der Maas, Johannes J.M. vanDelden, Loes Pijnenborg, and Casper W.N, Looman, "Euthanasia and Other Medical Decisions Concerning the End Of Life," *The Lancet* 338 (Sept, 14, 1991): 669–674.

7. G. van der Wal, J. Th. M. van Eijk, H.J.J. Leenen, and C. Spreeuwenberg, "Euthanasie en hulp bij selfdoding door artsen in de thuissituatie. I. Diagnosen, leeftijd en geslacht van de patienten," *Nederlands Tijdschrift voor Geneesekunde* 135 (1991: 1593–1598: and II. "Lijden van de patienten," 1500–1603.

8. Else Borst-Eilers, paper delivered at the conference "Controversies in the Care of Dying Patients," University of Florida, Orlando, Feb. 14–16, 1991.

9. Van der Maas, p. 673.

10. Van der Maas, p. 671.

11. Admiraal P. *Euthanasia in a general hospital.* Address to the Eighth World Congress of the International Federation of Right-To-Die Societies, Maastricht. Holland. June 8, 1990.

12. Ten Have, H. "Coma: controversy and consensus." *Newsletter of the European Society for Philosophy of Medicine and Health Care* (May 1990) 8:19–20.

Buddhist Views
of Suicide and Euthansia

Carl B. Becker

Carl B. Becker is a professor of Asian studies at the University of Hawaii. He has been a visiting professor of philosophy at University of Tsukuba, Japan. He is the author of Japan: My Teacher, My Love.

Becker explores Buddhist views of death and suicide and attempts to apply these ideas to recent debates about euthanasia. Traditionally, Buddhism does not view death as a bad thing or even as an ending. Rather, death is a transition from one stage of life to another. Because of this, suicide was not condemned, as long as the person had placed *himself or herself in the right state of mind. A key to this is that a person accepts responsibility for his or her own life choices. When suicide or euthanasia is prohibited, it means that a person is deprived of the final act of taking responsibility for his or her own life. Hence, Becker argues, disallowing suicide and euthanasia is inhumane.*

BIOETHICS AND BRAIN DEATH: THE RECENT DISCUSSION IN JAPAN

Japanese scholars of ethics and religions have been slow to come to grips with issues of bioethics, suicide, and death with dignity. Although the practical problems are frequently addressed in the popular press, and scattered citizen groups are beginning to draw attention to the issues, few people outside of the medical community have seriously addressed these issues.[1] As one recent representative example of this situation, consider the 39th annual meeting of the Japan Ethics Association (the academic association of ethicists from the entire country) held at Waseda University in October of

Reprinted by permission of the University of Hawaii Press, from its journal *Philosphy East and West*, Vol. 40/4, October 1990.

1988. The title of the annual meeting, in deference to the late Emperor's ailing condition and growing urgency of bioethical issues, was "Life and Ethics." Ostensibly, this was a chance to further the discussion among medical, religious, and philosophical ethicists on topics such as euthanasia and death with dignity. In fact, more than half of the presentations discussed classical views of life, such as those of Hippocrates, Confucius, Vico, Kant, Nietzsche, and so forth. The periods planned for open discussion were entirely usurped by the panelists' overtime reading of such papers. To their credit, however, there were a few Japanese scholars who boldly attempted to establish some more-Japanese views on the topics in bioethics, particularly euthanasia and death with dignity. While not without their problems, these presentations displayed less a Buddhist than a popular Japanese approach to the issue. The majority agreed with Anzai Kazuhiro's early presentation that brain death should not be equated with human death.[2] Anzai's reasoning runs as follows: If brain death implies human death, then, by contraposition, human life must imply conscious (brain) life. Now there are clearly segments of our lives in which we are alive but not always conscious. Therefore it is wrong to conclude that a human is dead because he or she lacks consciousness. Of course, this argument can be faulted for collapsing conscious life and brain life, and for failing to distinguish periods of unconsciousness with the expectation of future revival (like deep sleep) from periods of unconsciousness with no expectation of future revival (like irreversible coma). But it is representative of a widely seen Japanese rejection of brain-death criteria.

This rejection comes partly from the Japanese association of brain-death criteria with organ transplantation. Many Japanese continue to manifest a distaste for organ transplantation, a distaste which dates back to Confucian teachings that the body, a gift from heaven and from one's parents, must be buried whole, and never cut. For this reason, dissections and autopsies were late in coming to Japan, not widely permitted until the nineteenth century. The modern Japanese practices of universal cremation, of surgical operations, and of flying to other countries to have organ transplants all have superseded the old Confucian prejudice against body-cutting. However, there remains a fear that if brain-death criteria were widely accepted, less conservative elements of society might abuse it for the sake of the "distasteful" practice of organ transplantation.

In his keynote address about Buddhist ethics, Tsukuba Professor Shinjō Kawasaki implied that this rejection of brain-death criteria may also be grounded in a Buddhist view of life and death.[3] He cited the *Visuddhimagga,* which indicates that life energy *(ayus)* is supported by body warmth and conscious faculties (broadly interpretable to include reflexes).[4] If either body heat or reflexes remain, then a person cannot be considered dead. Now Buddhism admits situations (such as meditative trances or hypothermia) in which neither body warmth nor reflexes are externally detectable, but the subject is not yet dead. So lack of warmth and reflexes is a necessary but not sufficient indicator of death; if either persists, it can be said that the body is not yet dead. In other words, Buddhism does not equate life with warmth and reflexes, but holds that body heat and reflexes are the "supports" of life, and therefore life cannot be empirically measurable except through such variables. Kawasaki also reaffirms the widespread Japanese Buddhist view that death is not the end of life, but merely a brief transition to another state, commonly thought to last for forty-nine days, intermediate between life in this body and life in the next. The reluctance to dismiss a body as "dead" prior to its loss of warmth and reflexes is not based on a fear of personal extinction or annihilation, but rather on a Buddhist view of the basic components of the life system.[5]

Chiba's Iida Tsunesuke expands this view by arguing that "persons are not merely the meaningless 'subjects of rights,' but personalities, 'faces,' embodying the possibilities of fulfilling the dreams of their parents or loved ones . . . recipients of love, and therefore worthy of honoring."[6] This argument begs the question of "possibilities," since in the case of brain-dead victims, it is precisely such possibilities which are missing. Logically speaking, the "possibilities" argument has long ago been laid to rest by philosophers like Mary Anne Warren, who have demonstrated that we need not treat potential presidents as presidents, potential criminals as criminals, or potential humans as humans.[7] (Japanese society might differ in this respect; until recently, suspicion of crime or likelihood of committing crime were sufficient grounds for arrest, children of nobles [potential lords] were often honored or killed as real lords.)[8]

However, Iida's argument is important less for its logical persuasion than for its revelation of the Japanese attitude: that persons are not subjects with rights and individual free wills, but rather objects of the attention of others. (Japanese treatment of infants and children reinforces this view that Japanese children are not seen as persons but as possessions of their parents; this was the legal as well as philosophical status of women and servants as well as children prior to the twentieth century.)

This position is further developed by Ohara Nobuo, who argues that "although a body may be treated as a 'thing' or a corpse by physicians, it remains a body of value and meaning, and in that sense, a *person,* to members of its family . . . . In this sense, even vegetative humans and brain-dead corpses can give joy to other people."[9] Of course this point of view is pregnant with problems which Ohara himself seems loath to acknowledge. Only in the most metaphorical of senses can a corpse "give" anything to anyone; rather, it is the family who may *derive* some sense of joy by beholding the face of one dear to them, even though that person is incapable of ever being conscious in that body again.

This attitude is akin to the Japanese reverence for pictures, sculptures, and myths; it provides no useful guidelines whatsoever to the medical faculty as to when to continue or desist from what kinds of treatment for the patient. To the question "When does a body stop being a person?" the Oharan answer, "It never stops being a person to those who love it," may be psychologically correct for some people, but is a dead end in medical ethics, for it fails to answer the question, "When should a body be treated not as a living person but as a dead body?"

Moreover, even if it were thought to have some utility in the case where relatives or "significant others" remain alive and concerned with the fate of the deceased, it values the person (or corpse) entirely in terms of his value *to others.* In cases where old people die alone and uncared for, the absence of concerned others leaves the medical practitioner utterly without guidelines. (This is consistent with the frequently noted proposition that Japanese without social contexts seem morally at a loss.)[10]

This position also presumes a wishful naïveté on the part of the parent or family, a failure to distinguish between a living human with a potential for interaction and a dead body with only the resemblance of a loved one. This may not bother many Japanese parents, for whom children are indeed "objects." In fact, there are "rehabilitation hospitals" in Japan in which anencephalic infants are cared for and raised for as many years as their parents' finances and interest dictate; they are propped up and made to "greet" their parents whenever their parents desire to visit.[11]

Such unwillingness to admit the finality of death or the fundamental suffering of the human condition runs counter to the basic tenets of Buddhism. We are reminded of the famous story of the woman who asked the Buddha to revive her baby. In response, the Buddha instructed her to ask for food from any house in which no one had died. In the process of asking around the entire village, the woman came to realize that all humans must die and deal with death. In this way she gained enlightenment, stopped grieving for her dead child, and became a follower of the Buddha. The relatives who refuse to pronounce dead a relative as long as he has a "face," or the parents who insist on artificially prolonging the appearance of life in an anencephalic infant, cannot claim to understand Buddhism.

A much larger misunderstanding lurks behind the whole discussion between "brain-death advocates" and "brain-dead opposers" in Japan. The real issue is not whether or not every body should immediately be scavenged for spare parts as soon as the brain is isoelectric, as some opponents would purport. Rather, the question is whether it is ever acceptable to desist from treatment after brain death (turning the hospital's valuable and limited resources to other waiting patients). In the absence of brain-death criteria, many otherwise hopeless bodies remain on artificial support systems almost indefinitely. Even if the brain-death criteria were accepted, nothing would prevent families from finding hospitals which would preserve the bodies of their beloved on artificial support systems indefinitely, nor would anything require organ donation if the patient and family did not desire it. Thus the issue, like that of suicide and euthanasia, is not, "Should everyone be forced to follow these criteria?" but rather, "May people who desire it be allowed to follow these criteria?" Groundless fears of widespread organ sales or piracy have made this issue into a much greater hobgoblin than it ever needed to become.

This is not merely to criticize the recently voiced opinions of Japanese ethicists. Rather, I introduce this body of evidence to demonstrate the slow growth of Japanese thought in bioethics, and particularly their concerns with *bodies of value to others*

rather than with *subjects of value to themselves*. This concern finds no support either in Japanese Buddhism nor in samurai teaching, but in the level of popular belief, it may have serious ramifications for Japanese bioethics for many generations to come.

The World Federation of the Right To Die Society held an International Conference in Nice (France) in 1984. Although many Japanese attended this conference, apparently none of them contributed to the West's understanding of Buddhist views of euthanasia. When the President of the Society published a book on world attitudes on euthanasia the following year, only 2 percent (2.5 out of 150 pages) was about Buddhist attitudes, and those ideas were gained from California Buddhists, not from the Japanese Buddhists at Nice.[12]

Buddhists have a big contribution to make to the humanization and naturalization of medicine and bioethics. I may not speak for all of Japanese Buddhism, but I shall be happy if this article inspires further dialogue and contributions from the Japanese Buddhist side.

EARLY BUDDHIST VIEWS OF DEATH, SUICIDE, AND EUTHANASIA

Japan has long been more aware of and sensitive to the dying process than modern Western cultures. Moreover, Japan already has its own good philosophical and experiential background to deal effectively with "new" issues of bioethics, such as euthanasia. Japanese Buddhists have long recognized what Westerners are only recently rediscovering: that the manner of dying at the moment of death is very important. This fundamental premise probably predates Buddhism itself, but is made very explicit in the teachings of the Buddha.[13] In his meditations, the Buddha noticed that even people with good karma were sometimes born into bad situations, and even those with bad karma sometimes found inordinately pleasant rebirths. Buddha declared that the crucial variable governing rebirth was the nature of the consciousness at the moment of death. Thereafter, Buddhists placed high importance on holding the proper thoughts at the moment of death. Many examples of this idea can be found in two works of the Theravāda canon. The *Petavatthu* and the *Vimānavatthu* ("Stories of the Departed"). Indeed, in many sutras, monks visit laymen on their deathbeds to ensure that their dying thoughts are wholesome,[14] and the Buddha recommends that lay followers similarly encourage each other on such occasions.[15]

Buddhism sees death as not the end of life, but simply a transition; suicide is therefore no escape from anything. Thus, in the early *sangha* (community of followers of the Buddha), suicide was in principle condemned as an inappropriate action.[16] But the early Buddhist texts include many cases of suicide which the Buddha himself accepted or condoned. For example, the suicides of Vakkali[17] and of Channa[18] were committed in the face of painful and irreversible sickness. It is significant, however, that the Buddha's praise of the suicides is *not* based on the fact that they were in terminal states, but rather that their minds were selfless, desireless, and enlightened at the moments of their passing.

This theme is more dramatically visible in the example of Godhika. This disciple repeatedly achieved an advanced level of *samādhi*, bordering on *parinirvāna*, and then slipped out of the state of enlightenment into normal consciousness again.

After this happened six times, Godhika at last vowed to pass on to the next realm while enlightened, and quietly committed suicide during his next period of enlightenment. While cautioning his other disciples against suicide, the Buddha nonetheless blessed and praised Godhika's steadiness of mind and purpose, and declared that he had passed on to *nirvāna*. In short, the acceptability of suicide, even in the early Buddhist community, depended not on terminal illness alone, but upon the state of selfless equanimity with which one was able to pass away. It is interesting in passing that all these suicides were committed by the subject knifing himself, a technique which came to be standardized in later Japanese ritual suicide.

When asked about the morality of committing suicide to move on to the next world, the Buddha did not criticize it.[19] He emphasized that only the uncraving mind would be able to move on towards *nirvāna,* and that, conversely, minds desiring to get free or flee something by their death might achieve nothing. Similarly, there are stories in the Jatāka tales of the Buddha giving his own body (in former lives) to save other beings, both animals and humans. Thus death out of compassion for others is also lauded in the scriptures.[20] It is also well known that in the Jain tradition, saints were expected to fast until their deaths,[21] and thereafter there have been those both in China and Japan who have followed this tradition.[22]

In China, it is believed that a disciple of Zendō's jumped out of a tree in order to kill himself and reach the Pure Land. Zendō's response was not that the action of suicide was right or wrong in and of itself, but that the disciple who wanted so strongly to see the Pure Land was doubtless ready to reach it.[23] Other more recent examples may be found in the Buddhist suicides of the Vietnamese monks protesting against the Vietnam government.[24] Whether or not these stories are all historical fact is not at issue here. The point is that they demonstrate the consistent Buddhist position toward suicide: there is nothing intrinsically wrong with taking one's own life, if it is not done in hate, anger, or fear. Equanimity or preparedness of mind is the main issue.

In summary, Buddhism realizes that death is not the end of anything, but a transition. Buddhism has long recognized persons' rights to determine when they should move on from this existence to the next. The important consideration here is not whether the body lives or dies, but whether the mind can remain at peace and in harmony with itself.

The Jōdo, (Pure Land) tradition tends to stress the continuity of life, while the Zen tradition tends to stress the importance of the time and manner of dying. Both of these ideas are deeply rooted in the Japanese consciousness.

RELIGIOUS SUICIDE AND DEATH WITH DIGNITY IN JAPAN

Japanese Buddhists demonstrated an unconcern with death even more than their neighbors. Japanese valued peace of mind and honor of life over length of life. While the samurai often committed suicide on the battlefield or in court to preserve their dignity in death, countless commoners chose to commit suicide in order to obtain a better future life in the Pure Land. On some occasions, whole masses of people committed suicide at the same time. In others, as in the situation depicted in Kurosawa's famous film "Red Beard," a poverty-stricken family would commit suicide in order to escape unbearable suffering in this life and find a better life in the world to come. Often parents would kill their children first, and then kill themselves; this kind of *shinjū* can still be seen in Japan today. The issue for us today is: how does Buddhism appraise such suicide in order to gain heavenly rebirth?

On a popular level, the desire to "leave this dirty world and approach the Pure Land" (*Enri edo, gongu jōdo*) was fostered by wandering itinerant monks such as Kūya in the Heian period, and Ippen in the Kamakura period. The tradition of committing suicide by entering a river or west-facing seashore apparently began in the Kumano area, but rapidly spread throughout the nation along with the Pure Land faith upon which it was based. The common tradition was to enter the water with a rope tied around one's waist, held by one's retainers or horse.[25] If one's nerve and single-minded resolution failed, then one would not achieve rebirth in the Pure Land as desired. In such an instance, either the suicide himself, or his retainers (judging from his countenance), might pull him out of the water and save him from dying with inappropriate thoughts. However, if the suicide retained a peaceful and unperturbed mind and countenance throughout the drowning, the retainers were to let him die in peace, and simply retain the body for funeral purposes. Such situations clearly demonstrate that what is at stake here is not the individual's right to die, but rather his ability to die with peace of mind. If a death with a calm mind is possible, then it is not condemned.

A paradigmatic example of this situation can be found in the records of Saint Ippen.[26] Ajisaka Nyūdō, a Pure Land aspirant possibly of noble descent, gave up his home and family to follow the teachings of Saint Ippen. For unclear reasons, Ippen refused admission to his band of itinerant mendicants, but advised him that the only way to enter the Pure land was to die holding the Nembutsu (name and figure of Amida) in mind. Nyūdō then committed suicide by drowning himself in the Fuji River.

The scene is vividly depicted in the scroll paintings.[27] Here, Ajisaka is seen with a rope around his waist. His attendants on the shore hold one end of the rope. As he bobs above the current, he is seen perfectly preserving the *gasshō* position, at peace and in prayer. Music is heard from the purple clouds above him, a common sign of Ōjō, or rebirth in the Pure Land.

When Ippen heard of this suicide, he praised Ajisaka's faith, interpreting the purple clouds and Ajisaka's unruffled demeanor as proof of his attainment of rebirth in the Pure Land. At the same time, he warned his other disciples, repeating Ajisaka's last words (*nagori o oshimuna*), not to grieve over their master's passing.[28]

When Ippen himself died, six of his disciples also committed suicide in sympathy, hoping to accompany their master to the Pure Land. This occasioned some other debate about the propriety of "sympathy suicide." Shinkyō, Ippen's disciple and second patriarch of the Ji School, declared that the disciples had failed to obtain rebirth in the Pure Land, for their action was seen as "selfwilled," and Pure Land faith relies entirely on the power and will of Amida Buddha. Assertion of self-will is seen as running counter to the reliance on other power demanded by the Amida faith.[29]

Several important points can be learned from these examples. First, suicide is never condemned per se. Rather it is the state of mind which determines the rightness or wrongness of the suicide situation. The dividing line between choosing one's own time and place of death with perfectly assured peace of mind, and self-willing one's own death at the time of one's master's death is perhaps a thin grey one, but this should not obscure the criteria involved: death with desire leads not to rebirth in the Pure Land, but death with calm assurance does. Even the method of water suicide, using a rope as a preventative backup, stresses the importance of the state of mind in this action.

Secondly, Ajisaka's famous phrase, "Nagori o oshimuna," means that Buddhists are not to kill themselves in "sympathy" when others die. A literal translation would be that we are not to cling to what remains of the name or person, but to let the deceased go freely on to the next world. In other words, when someone dies with an assured state of mind, it is not for those who remain either to criticize or to wish that he had not died in this situation. Those who are left behind are to respect and not resent, reject, or grieve for a death which might seem to them untimely.

It is not coincidental that the word for euthanasia in Japanese is *anrakushi,* a term with Buddhist meanings. In Buddhist terminology, *anrakukoku* is another name for the Pure Land, the next world of Amida Bodhisattva, to which each Japanese expects to go after death. German-educated doctor and historical novelist Mori Ōgai's famous book *Takasebune* specifically deals with *anrakushi;* it is the story of Yoshisuke killing his sickly young brother who wants to die but lacks the strength to kill himself,[30] Many famous twentieth-century Japanese authors wrote of suicide, and some, such as Akutagawa, Dazai, Kawabata, and Mishima, actually committed suicide. Following the deaths of each emperor (Meiji, Taishō, and, last year, Shōwa), faithful retainers have also committed suicide in sympathy with their departed leaders. While some of these suicides are not Buddhistic (they show anger, pessimism, nihilism, and so forth), they are still reminders that the Japanese Buddhist world view does not condemn suicide.

Japanese law does not criminalize suicide, and European law is slowly beginning to follow the Japanese model in this regard. However, Japanese law does hold it to be a crime to assist or encourage a suicide. In normal situations, this is only wise and prudent, for healthy people should be encouraged to live and make the most of their lives. But in the situations where *songenshi* (death with dignity) is requested, it is precisely because the person is facing imminent death that it is morally acceptable to assist his suicide, particularly if the motive is mercy.

SAMURAI, *SEPPUKU,* AND EUTHANASIA

Among the warrior elite, who usually followed Zen Buddhism, suicide was considered an honorable alternative to being killed by others or continuing a life in shame or misery. Beginning with the famous *seppuku* of Minamoto no Tametomo and Minamoto no Yorimasi in 1170, *seppuku* became known as the way that a vanquished but proud Buddhist warrior would end his life.[31] Soon thereafter, headed by Taira Noritsune and Tomomori, hundreds of Taira warriors and their families committed suicide in the battle of Dannoura of 1185. Famous suicides included that of Kusunoki Masashige in 1336, in the battle between Nitta and Hosokawa, and that of Hideyori Toyotomi, under siege by Tokugawa Ieyasu in 1615. In the Tokugawa period, love suicides were dramatized in a dozen plays by Chikamatsu Monzaemon including *Sonezaki shinjū,*

Shinjū ten no Amijima, and Shinjū mannensō.[32] The forty-seven Akō *rōnin,* who committed suicide after avenging their master's death, was another famous true story, dramatized in the *Chūshingura* plays and films.[33] The samurai's creed, to be willing to die at any moment, was dramatically spelled out by the *Hag-akure.*[34] According to the *Hagakure,* the important concern was not whether one lived or died, but (1) being pure, simple, single-minded, (2) taking full responsibility for doing one's duty, and (3) unconditionally serving one's master, without concern for oneself.

Although *seppuku* may seem like a violent death to the observer, it was designed to enable the samurai to die with the greatest dignity and peace.

It is particularly noteworthy that the samurai's code of suicide included a provision for euthanasia: the *kaishakunin* (attendant). Cutting of the *hara* alone was very painful, and would not lead to a swift death. After cutting their *hara,* few samurai had enough strength to cut their own necks or spines. Yet without cutting their necks, the pain of the opened *hara* would continue for minutes or even hours prior to death. Therefore, the samurai would make arrangements with one or more *kaishakunin* to assist his suicide. While the samurai steadied his mind and prepared to die in peace, the *kaishakunin* would wait by his side. If the samurai spoke to the *kaishakunin* before or during the *seppuku* ceremony, the standard response was *"go anshin"* (set your mind at peace). All of the interactions and conversations surrounding an officially ordered *seppuku* were also fixed by tradition, so that the suicide might die with the least tension and greatest peace of mind. After the samurai had finished cutting to the prearranged point, or gave some other signal, it was the duty of the *kaishakunin* to cut the neck of the samurai to terminate his pain by administering the coup de grâce.[35]

Many samurai suicides were in fact the moral equivalent of euthanasia. The reasons for a samurai's suicide were either (1) to avoid an inevitable death at the hands of others, or (2) to escape a longer period of unbearable pain or psychological misery, without being an active, fruitful member of society. These are exactly the sorts of situations when euthanasia is desired today: (1) to avoid an inevitable death at the hands of others (including disease, cancer, or bacteria), (2) to escape a longer period of pain or misery without being a fruitful, active member of society.

In regard to (1), most Japanese are now cut down in their seventies by the enemies of cancer and other diseases, rather than in their youth on a battlefield. Regardless of whether the person is hopelessly surrounded by enemies on a battlefield, or hopelessly defeated by enemy organisms within his body, the morality of the situation is the same. In regard to (2), it might be argued that there is a difference between the pain or misery of the permanent incapacitation of a samurai, and the pain or misery of the permanent incapacitation of a hospital patient. But if anything, the hospital patient is in even less of a position to contribute to society or feel valued than is the samurai, so he has even more reason to be granted the option of leaving this arena (world) when he chooses. The samurai tradition shows that the important issue is not the level of physical pain, but the prospect for meaningful and productive interaction with other members of society. If there are no prospects for such interactions, the samurai society claimed no right to prevent the person from seeking more meaningful experiences in another world.

Now in both cases, there may be relatives or retainers in the area who do not wish to see their friend die. The issue in these cases is not whether or not the besieged person will die; it is only a question of how soon, and in what manner. From ancient times, Japanese have respected the right of the individual to choose the moment and manner of dying. The Buddhist principle ought to apply equally well to the modern medical battles against the enemies of the body. The argument that if a body still has a face, it is still a person to those around him, is a basically un-Buddhist failure to understand (a) the difference between body and life, (b) the importance of each person's determination of his own mental states, and (c) the importance of placing mercy over desire in Buddhism.

Of course there need to be safeguards in such situations, and those safeguards have already been spelled out by the decision of the Nagoya High Court. In case of euthanasia, the Nagoya High Court (22 December 1962) defined certain conditions under which euthanasia could be considered acceptable:

1. The disease is considered terminal and incurable by present medicine.
2. The pain is unbearable—both for the patient and those around him.
3. The death is for the purpose of his peaceful passing.
4. The person himself has requested the death, while conscious and sane.
5. The killing is done by a doctor.
6. The method of killing is humane.

If these safeguards are followed, it seems there is no moral reason that Buddhists should oppose euthanasia.

CONCLUSIONS

There are Japanese who hold that the Japanese lack the independent decision-making abilities of Western people, and that therefore doctors should make the decisions for their patients. This logic is backwards. The reason patients cannot make good independent judgments is because the doctors refuse them the information and freedom to do so, not because they lack the mental abilities or personal characteristics to make judgments.[36] Buddhism has always recognized the importance of individual choice, despite social pressures; examples range from the Buddha himself, through Kūkai, Hōnen, Shinran, and Nagamatsu Nissen. The ability of Japanese to take personal responsibility for important decisions in times of stress, danger, or anguish has been repeatedly shown in the historical examples of these bold Buddhist reformers.

In order for the patient to make an intelligent decision about when and how he wants to die, he needs to know the facts about the nature of his disease, not only its real name, but the realistic prospects and alternative outcomes of all available forms of treatment. This means renouncing the paternalistic model held by present Japanese medicine, and granting substantial freedom to the patient in deciding his own case. Some Japanese doctors have argued that (1) patients do not really want to know the bad news about themselves, that (2) knowing the truth may harm their conditions, and that (3) the physicians can judge more intelligently than the patient. However, studies in the West show that none of these claims is true. As Bok points out, "The attitude that what [the patient] doesn't know won't hurt him is proving unrealistic—it is rather what patients do not know but vaguely suspect that causes them corrosive (destructive) worry."[37] People recover faster from surgery and tolerate pain with less medication when they understand their own medical problems and what can and cannot be done about them.[38] In any case, doctors' withholding of information from patients is based not on statistical proof or ethical principles, but on the physician's desires to retain control over patients.[39] This is a situation that clear-thinking Buddhists naturally oppose. There is no reason to believe that these findings, long known and supported in Western medicine, should prove any different for the Japanese.

One important question for Buddhists today remains: what, if any, are the differences between suicide and euthanasia? Obviously one important difference is in the case where the person receiving euthanasia is unconscious. In this case, we have no way of knowing whether the patient genuinely desires euthanasia, unless he or she has previously made a declaration of wishes in a living will. On the other hand, once the consciousness has permanently disassociated itself from the body, there is no reason in Buddhism to continue to nourish or stimulate the body, for the body deprived of its *skandhas* is not a person. The Japan Songenshi Kyōkai (Association for Death with Dignity) has done much to improve the ability of the individual Japanese to choose his time and manner of death.

Another issue is the relation of painkilling to prolonging life and hastening death itself. The Japan Songenshi Kyōkai proposes the administering of painkilling drugs even if they hasten the death of the patient. Buddhists would agree that relief of pain is desirable, and whether the death is hastened or not is not the primary issue. However, consider a case where the pain is extreme and only very strong drugs will stop the pain. Here there may be a choice between: (a) no treatment at all, (b) painkilling which only blurs or confuses the mind of the patient, and (c) treatment which hastens the end while keeping the mind clear. In such a situation, the Buddhist would first prefer the most natural way of (a) no treatment at all. But if his mind were unable to focus or be at peace because of the great pain, the Buddhist would choose (c) over (b), because clarity of consciousness at the moment of death is so important in Buddhism.

Doctors who do not like the idea of shortening a person's life would prefer to prolong the material life-processes, regardless of the mental quality of that life. This is where Buddhists disagree with materialistic Western medicine. But there need be no conflict between Buddhism and medicine. There is no reason to assign the doctor the "responsibility" for the death of the patient. Following the guidelines of the Nagoya court, patients potentially eligible for euthanasia are going to die soon anyway, so that is not the fault of the doctor. And the patient has the right to determine his own death. The fact that he is too weak to hold a sword or to cut short his own life is not morally significant. If his mind is clear, calm, and ready for death, then the one who understands and compassionately assists that person is also following Buddhist morality. In summary, the important issue for Buddhists here is whether or not the person will be allowed responsibility for his own life and fate. The entire Buddhist tradition, and particularly that of suicide within Japan, argues that personal choice in time and manner of death is of extreme importance, and anything done by others to dim the mind or deprive the dying person of such choice is a violation of Buddhist principles. Japanese Buddhists may respect this decision more than Western cultures, and lead humanitarian bioethics in a different perspective towards dignified death.

NOTES

1. Morioka Masahiro, "Nōshi to wa nan de atta ka" (What was brain death?), in *Nihon Rinri Gakkai kenkyū happyō yoshi* (Japanese Ethics Association outline of presentations) (Japan Ethics Association 39th Annual Conference, Waseda University, October 14–15, 1988), p. 7.
2. Anzai Kazuhiro, "Nō to sono ishiki" (Brain and its consciousness), in *Nihon Rinri Gakkai*, p. 6.
3. Kawasaki Shinjō, "Tōyō kodai no seimei juyō" (The accepted understanding of life in the ancient Orient), in *Nihon Rinri Gakkai*, p. 26.
4. *Visuddhimagga*, pp. 229ff.
5. Kawasaki, "Tōyō kodai no seimei juyō." p. 27.
6. Iida Tsunesuke, "Bioethics wa nani o nasu no ka" (What does bioethics accomplish?), in *Nihon Rinri Gakkai*, pp, 40ff.
7. Mary Anne Warren, "Do Potential People Have Moral Rights?" *Canadian Journal of Philosophy* 7 no. 2 (1978): 275–289.
8. Carl Becker, "Old and New: Japan's Mechanisms for Crime Control and Social Justice," *Howard Journal of Criminal Justice,* 27 no. 4 (November 1988): 284–285.
9. Ohara Nobuo, "Sei to shi no rinrigaku" (The ethics of life and death), in *Nihon Rinri Gakkai,* pp. 54–55.
10. Carl Becker, "Religion and Politics in Japan," chap. 13 of *Movements and Issues in World Religions,* ed. C. W-H. Fu and G. S, Spiegler (New York; Greenwood Press, 1987), p. 278.
11. Among the author's students are nurses at such hospitals.
12. Gerald A. Larue, *Euthanasia and Religion: A Survey of the Attitudes of World Religions to the Right-To-Die* (Los Angeles: The Hemlock Society, 1985).
13. Cf. *Hastings Encyclopedia of Religion,* Vol. 4, p. 448.
14. *Majhima Nikāya* II, 91; III, 258.
15. *Samyutta Nikāya* V, 408.
16. Tamaki Koshirō, "Shino oboegaki" (Memoranda on death), in *Bukkyo shisō,* vol. 10, ed. Bukkyō Shiso Kenkyukai, Tokyo (September 1988), pp. 465–475.
17. *Sutta Vibhanga, Vinaya* lII, 74; cf. *Samyutta Nikāya* III, 119–124.
18. *Majhima Nikāya* III, 263–266 *(Channovada-sutta); Samyutta Nikāya* IV, 55–60 *(Channavaga).*
19. *Samyutta Nikāya* I, 121.
20. *Jatakā Suvarna Prabhāsa* 206ff.
21. *Acāranga Sutra* I, 7, 6.
22. A mummified body of one such monk is preserved at the Myorenji temple, close to Tsukuba University.
23. Ogasawara Senshū, *Chūgoku Jōdokyō no kenkyū* (Researches in Chinese Pure Land Buddhism) (Kyoto: Heirakuji, 1951), pp. 60ff.
24. Thich Nhat Hanh, *The Lotus in the Sea of Fire* (London, 1967).
25. Kurita Isamu, *Ippen Shōnin, tabi no shisakuska* (Saint Ippen, the meditative wayfarer) (Tokyo: Shinchosha, 1977), pp. 165–169.

26. Ōhashi Shunnō, *Ippen* (Tokyo: Yoshikawa Kobunkan, 1983), pp. 105ff.

27. *Ippen goroku,* scroll 6, stage 2 *(maki 6, dan 2).*

28. Kurita, *Ippen Shōnin.*

29. Ōhashi, *Ippen,* pp. 107ff.

30. Mori Ōgai, *Takasebune* (Tokyo: Iwanami Bunko, 1978).

31. Jack Seward, *Hara-Kiri: Japanese Ritual Suicide* (Tokyo: Charles E. Tuttle, 1968), Seward describes these and many other significant suicides in detail.

32. Donald Keene, trans., *Major Plays of Chikamatsu* (New York: Columbia University Press, 1961).

33. Fujino Yoshiō, ed., *Kanatehon Chushingura: Kaishaku to kenkyū* (Chushingura) (Tokyo: Ofūsha, 1975).

34. Watsuji Tetsurō, ed., *Hagakure* (Tokyo: Iwanami Bunko, 1970).

35. All condensed from Seward, *Hara-Kiri.*

36. *Kimura Rihito,* "In Japan, Parents Participate but Doctors Decide," *Hastings Center* Report 16, no. 4 (1986): 22–23.

37. Sisela Bok, "Lies to the Sick and Dying," in *Lying: Moral Choice in Public and Private Life* (New York: Pantheon Books, 1978).

38. Lawrence Egbert, George Batitt, et al., "Reduction of Post-operative Pain by Encouragement and Instruction of Patients," *New England Journal of Medicine* 270 (1964): 825–827; and Howard Waitzskin and John Stoeckle, "The Communication of Information About Illness," *Advances in Psychosomatic Medicine* 8 (1972): 185–215.

39. Cf. Bernard Gert and Charles Culver, "Paternalistic Behavior," *Philosophy and Public Affairs* 6 (Summer 1976); and Allen Buchanan, "Medical Paternalism," ibid., vol. 7 (Summer 1978).

The Survival Lottery

John Harris

John Harris is a reader in philosophy at the faculty of education of the University of Manchester, England. He is the author of Violence and Responsibility *(1980),* The Value of Life: An Introduction to Medical Ethics *(1985), and* Wonderwoman and Superman: The Ethics of Human Biotechnology *(1992).*

In this provocative essay, Harris argues that a lottery to determine who should live and who should die, given that organs are scarce, can be justified. Such a justification calls into question many of our deepest intuitions, especially concerning the moral importance of not directly killing a person, even if that person's death will save the lives of others who would die naturally otherwise. Among other things, Harris argues that the person who loses the lottery, and must give up his or her life so that others may be saved, is no more innocent than those who would otherwise die without his or her organs. So, Harris contends, the most obvious objection to such a practice is not defensible.

Let us suppose that organ transplant procedures have been perfected; in such circumstances if two dying patients could be saved by organ transplants then, if surgeons have the requisite organs in stock and no other needy patients, but nevertheless allow their patients to die, we would be inclined to say, and be justified in saying, that the patients died because the doctors refused to save them. But if there are no spare organs in stock and none otherwise available, the doctors have no choice, they cannot save their patients and so must let them die. In this case we would be disinclined to say that the doctors are in any sense the cause of their patients' deaths. But let us further suppose that the two dying patients, Y and Z, are not happy about being left to die. They might argue that it is not strictly true that there

Reprinted with permission of John Harris and Cambridge University Press from *Philosophy, The Journal of the Royal Institute of Philosophy,* Vol. 50, 1975.

are no organs which could be used to save them. Y needs a new heart and Z new lungs. They point out that if just one healthy person were to be killed his organs could be removed and both of them be saved. We and the doctors would probably be alike in thinking that such a step, while technically possible, would be out of the question. We would not say that the doctors were killing their patients if they refused to prey upon the healthy to save the sick. And because this sort of surgical Robin Hoodery is out of the question we can tell Y and Z that they cannot be saved, and that when they die they will have died of natural causes and not of the neglect of their doctors. Y and Z do not agree, however, they insist that if the doctors fail to kill a healthy man and use his organs to save them, then the doctors will be responsible for their deaths.

Many philosophers have for various reasons believed that we must not kill even if by doing so we could save life. They believe that there is a moral difference between killing and letting die. On this view, to kill A so that Y and Z might live is ruled out because we have a strict obligation not to kill but a duty of some lesser kind to save life. A. H. Clough's dictum "Thou shalt not kill but need'st not strive officiously to keep alive" expresses bluntly this point of view. The dying Y and Z may be excused for not being much impressed by Clough's dictum. They agree that it is wrong to kill the innocent and are prepared to agree to an absolute prohibition against so doing. They do not agree, however, that A is more innocent than they are. Y and Z might go on to point out that the currently acknowledged right of the innocent not to be killed, even where their deaths might give life to others, is just a decision to prefer the lives of the fortunate to those of the unfortunate. A is innocent in the sense that he has done nothing to deserve death, but Y and Z are also innocent in this sense. Why should they be the ones to die simply because they are so unlucky as to have diseased organs? Why, they might argue, should their living or dying be left to chance when in so many other areas of human life we believe that we have an obligation to ensure the survival of the maximum number of lives possible?

Y and Z argue that if a doctor refuses to treat a patient, with the result that the patient dies, he has killed that patient as sure as shooting, and that, in exactly the same way, if the doctors refuse Y and Z the transplants that they need, then their refusal will kill Y and Z, again as sure as shooting. The doctors, and indeed the society which supports their inaction, cannot defend themselves by arguing that they are neither expected, nor required by law or convention, to kill so that lives may be saved (indeed, quite the reverse) since this is just an appeal to custom or authority. A

man who does his own moral thinking must decide whether, in these circumstances, he ought to save two lives at the cost of one, or one life at the cost of two. The fact that so-called "third parties" have never before been brought into such calculations, have never before been thought of as being involved, is not an argument against their now becoming so. There are, of course, good arguments against allowing doctors simply to haul passers-by off the streets whenever they have a couple of patients in need of new organs. And the harmful side-effects of such a practice in terms of terror and distress to the victims, the witnesses and society generally, would give us further reasons for dismissing the idea. Y and Z realize this and have a proposal, which they will shortly produce, which would largely meet objections to placing such power in the hands of doctors and eliminate at least some of the harmful side-effects.

In the unlikely event of their feeling obliged to reply to the reproaches of Y and Z, the doctors might offer the following argument: they might maintain that a man is only responsible for the death of someone whose life he might have saved, if, in all the circumstances of the case, he ought to have saved the man by the means available. This is why a doctor might be a murderer if he simply refused or neglected to treat a patient who would die without treatment, but not if he could only save the patient by doing something he ought in no circumstances to do—kill the innocent. Y and Z readily agree that a man ought not to do what he ought not to do, but they point out that if the doctors, and for that matter society at large, ought on balance to kill one man if two can thereby be saved, then failure to do so will involve responsibility for the consequent deaths. The fact that Y's and Z's proposal involves killing the innocent cannot be a reason for refusing to consider their proposal, for this would just be a refusal to face the question at issue and so avoid having to make a decision as to what ought to be done in circumstances like these. It is Y's and Z's claim that failure to adopt their plan will also involve killing the innocent, rather more of the innocent than the proposed alternative.

To back up this last point, to remove the arbitrariness of permitting doctors to select their donors from among the chance passers-by outside hospitals, and the tremendous power this would place in doctors' hands, to mitigate worries about side-effects and lastly to appease those who wonder why poor old A should be singled out for sacrifice, Y and Z put forward the following scheme: they propose that everyone be given a sort of lottery number. Whenever doctors have two or more dying patients who could be saved by transplants, and no suitable organs have come to hand through "natural" deaths, they can ask a central computer to supply a suitable donor. The computer will then pick the number of a suitable donor at random and he will be killed so that the lives of two or more others may be saved. No doubt if the scheme were ever to be implemented a suitable euphemism for "killed" would be employed. Perhaps we would begin to talk about citizens being called upon to "give life" to others. With the refinement of transplant procedures such a scheme could offer the chance of saving large numbers of lives that are now lost. Indeed, even taking into account the loss of the lives of donors, the numbers of untimely deaths each year might be dramatically reduced, so much so that everyone's chance of living to a ripe old age might be increased. If this were to be the consequence of the adoption of such a scheme, and it might well be, it could not be

dismissed lightly. It might of course be objected that it is likely that more old people will need transplants to prolong their lives than will the young, and so the scheme would inevitably lead to a society dominated by the old. But if such a society is thought objectionable, there is no reason to suppose that a program could not be designed for the computer that would ensure the maintenance of whatever is considered to be an optimum age distribution throughout the population.

Suppose that inter-planetary travel revealed a world of people like ourselves, but who organized their society according to this scheme. No one was considered to have an absolute right to life or freedom from interference, but everything was always done to ensure that as many people as possible would enjoy long and happy lives. In such a world a man who attempted to escape when his number was up or who resisted on the grounds that no one had a right to take his life, might well be regarded as a murderer. We might or might not prefer to live in such a world, but the morality of its inhabitants would surely be one that we could respect. It would not be obviously more barbaric or cruel or immoral than our own.

Y and Z are willing to concede one exception to the universal application of their scheme. They realize that it would be unfair to allow people who have brought their misfortune on themselves to benefit from the lottery. There would clearly be something unjust about killing the abstemious B so that W (whose heavy smoking has given him lung cancer) and X (whose drinking has destroyed his liver) should be preserved to over-indulge again.

What objections could be made to the lottery scheme? A first straw to clutch at would be the desire for security. Under such a scheme we would never know when we would hear *them* knocking at the door. Every post might bring a sentence of death, every sound in the night might be the sound of boots on the stairs. But, as we have seen, the chances of actually being called upon to make the ultimate sacrifice might be slimmer than is the present risk of being killed on the roads, and most of us do not lie trembling abed, appalled at the prospect of being dispatched on the morrow. The truth is that lives might well be more secure under such a scheme.

If we respect individuality and see every human being as unique in his own way, we might want to reject a society in which it appeared that individuals were seen merely as interchangeable units in a structure, the value of which lies in its having as many healthy units as possible. But of course Y and Z would want to know why A's individuality was more worthy of respect than theirs.

Another plausible objection is the natural reluctance to play God with men's lives, the feeling that it is wrong to make any attempt to re-allot the life opportunities that fate has determined, that the deaths of Y and Z would be "natural," whereas the death of anyone killed to save them would have been perpetrated by men. But if we are able to change things, then to elect not to do so is also to determine what will happen in the world.

Neither does the alleged moral difference between killing and letting die afford a respectable way of rejecting the claims of Y and Z. For if we really want to counter proponents of the lottery, if we really want to answer Y and Z and not just put them off, we cannot do so by saying that the lottery involves killing and object to it for that reason, because to do so would, as we have seen, just beg the question as to whether the failure to save as many people as possible might not also amount to killing.

To opt for the society which Y and Z propose would be then to adopt a society in which saintliness would be mandatory. Each of us would have to recognize a binding obligation to give up his own life for others when called upon to do so. In such a society anyone who reneged upon this duty would be a murderer. The most promising objection to such a society, and indeed to any principle which required us to kill A in order to save Y and Z, is, I suspect, that we are committed to the right of self-defense. If I can kill A to save Y and Z then he can kill me to save P and Q, and it is only if I am prepared to agree to this that I will opt for the lottery or be prepared to agree to a man's being killed if doing so would save the lives of more than one other man. Of course, there is something paradoxical about basing objections to the lottery scheme on the right of self-defense since, *ex hypothesi,* each person would have a better chance of living to a ripe old age if the lottery scheme were to be implemented. None the less, the feeling that no man should be required to lay down his life for others makes many people shy away from such a scheme, even though it might be rational to accept it on prudential grounds, and perhaps even mandatory on utilitarian grounds. Again, Y and Z would reply that the right of self-defense must extend to them as much as to anyone else, and while it is true that they can only live if another man is killed, they would claim that it is also true that if they are left to die, then someone who lives on does so over their dead bodies.

It might be argued that the institution of the survival lottery has not gone far to mitigate the harmful side-effects in terms of terror and distress to victims, witnesses, and society generally, that would be occasioned by doctors simply snatching passers-by off the streets and disorganizing them for the benefit of the unfortunate. Donors would after all still have to be procured, and this process, however it was carried out, would still be likely to prove distressing to all concerned. The lottery scheme would eliminate the arbitrariness of leaving the life and death decisions to the doctors, and remove the possibility of such terrible power falling into the hands of any individuals, but the terror and distress would remain. The effect of having to apprehend presumably unwilling victims would give us pause. Perhaps only a long period of education or propaganda could remove our abhorrence. What this abhorrence reveals about the rights and wrongs of the situation is, however, more difficult to assess. We might be inclined to say that only monsters could ignore the promptings of conscience so far as to operate the lottery scheme. But the promptings of conscience are not necessarily the most reliable guide. In the present case Y and Z would argue that such promptings are mere squeamishness, an over-nice self-indulgence that costs lives. Death, Y and Z would remind us, is a distressing experience whenever and to whomever it occurs, so the less it occurs the better. Fewer victims and witnesses will be distressed as part of the side-effects of the lottery scheme than would suffer as part of the side-effects of not instituting it.

Lastly, a more limited objection might be made, not to the idea of killing to save lives, but to the involvement of "third parties." Why, so the objection goes, should we not give X's heart to Y or Y's lungs to X, the same number of lives being thereby preserved and no one else's life set at risk? Y's and Z's reply to this objection differs from their previous line of argument. To amend their plan so that the involvement of so called "third parties" is ruled out would, Y and Z claim, violate their right to equal concern and respect with the rest of society. They argue that such a proposal would amount to treating the unfortunate who need new organs as a class within society whose lives are considered to be of less value than those of its more fortunate members. What possible justification could there be for singling out one group of people whom we would be justified in using as donors but not another? The idea in the mind of those who would propose such a step must be something like the following: since Y and Z cannot survive, since they are going to die in any event, there is no harm in putting their names into the lottery, for the chances of their dying cannot thereby be increased and will in fact almost certainly be reduced. But this is just to ignore everything that Y and Z have been saying. For if their lottery scheme is adopted they are not going to die anyway—their chances of dying are no greater and no less than those of any other participant in the lottery whose number may come up. This ground for confining selection of donors to the unfortunate therefore disappears. Any other ground must discriminate against Y and Z as members of a class whose lives are less worthy of respect than those of the rest of society,

It might more plausibly be argued that the dying who cannot themselves be saved by transplants, or by any other means at all, should be the priority selection group for the computer program. But how far off must death be for a man to be classified as "dying"? Those so classified might argue that their last few days or weeks of life are as valuable to them (if not more valuable) than the possibly longer span remaining to others. The problem of narrowing down the class of possible donors without discriminating unfairly against some sub-class of society is, I suspect, insoluble.

Such is the case for the survival lottery. Utilitarians ought to be in favor of it, and absolutists cannot object to it on the ground that it involves killing the innocent, for it is Y's and Z's case that any alternative must also involve killing the innocent. If the absolutist wishes to maintain his objection he must point to some morally relevant difference between positive and negative killing. This challenge opens the door to a large topic with a whole library of literature, but Y and Z are dying and do not have time to explore it exhaustively. In their own case the most likely candidate for some feature which might make this moral difference is the malevolent intent of Y and Z themselves. An absolutist might well argue that while no one intends the deaths of Y and Z, no one necessarily wishes them dead, or aims at their demise for any reason, they do mean to kill A (or have him killed). But Y and Z can reply that the death of A is no part of their plan, they merely wish to use a couple of his organs, and if he cannot live without them . . . *tant pis!* None would be more delighted than Y and Z if artificial organs would do as well, and so render the lottery scheme otiose.

One form of absolutist argument perhaps remains. This involves taking an Orwellian stand on some principle of common decency. The argument would then be that even to enter into the sort of "macabre" calculations that Y and Z propose displays a blunted sensibility, a corrupted and vitiated mind. Forms of this argument have recently been advanced by Noam Chomsky (*American Power and the New Mandarins*) and Stuart Hampshire (*Morality and Pessimism*). The indefatigable Y and Z would of course deny that their calculations are in any sense "macabre," and would pre-

sent them as the most humane course available in the circumstances. Moreover they would claim that the Orwellian stand on decency is the product of a closed mind, and not susceptible to rational argument. Any reasoned defense of such a principle must appeal to notions like respect for human life, as Hampshire's argument in fact does, and these Y and Z could make conformable to their own position.

Can Y and Z be answered? Perhaps only by relying on moral intuition, on the insistence that we do feel there is something wrong with the survival lottery and our confidence that this feeling is prompted by some morally relevant difference between our bringing about the death of A and our bringing about the deaths of Y and Z. Whether we could retain this confidence in our intuitions if we were to be confronted by a society in which the survival lottery operated, was accepted by all, and was seen to save many lives that would otherwise have been lost, it would be interesting to know.

There would of course be great practical difficulties in the way of implementing the lottery. In so many cases it would be agonizingly difficult to decide whether or not a person had brought his misfortune on himself. There are numerous ways in which a person may contribute to his predicament, and the task of deciding how far, or how decisively, a person is himself responsible for his fate would be formidable. And in those cases where we can be confident that a person is innocent of responsibility for his predicament, can we acquire this confidence in time to save him? The lottery scheme would be a powerful weapon in the hands of someone willing and able to misuse it. Could we ever feel certain that the lottery was safe from unscrupulous computer programmers? Perhaps we should be thankful that such practical difficulties make the survival lottery an unlikely consequence of the perfection of transplants. Or perhaps we should be appalled.

It may be that we would want to tell Y and Z that the difficulties and dangers of their scheme would be too great a price to pay for its benefits. It is as well to be clear, however, that there is also a high, perhaps an even higher, price to be paid for the rejection of the scheme. That price is the lives of Y and Z and many like them, and we delude ourselves if we suppose that the reason why we reject their plan is that we accept the sixth commandment.

ACKNOWLEDGMENT

Thanks are due to Ronald Dworkin, Jonathan Glover, M. J. Inwood, and Anne Seller for helpful comments.

Who Shall Be Saved?
An African Answer

John F. Kilner

John F. Kilner is currently at the Parkridge Center for the Study of Health, Faith and Ethics in Chicago. He has taught medical ethics and social ethics at the University of Kentucky. He is the author of Who Lives? Who Dies? Ethical Criteria in Patient Selection *(1990).*

Kilner bases his essay on interviews he conducted in Africa among witch doctors and other traditional healers. The focus of his study is the question: If there are two people who need help and you can only help one, how do you choose? Kilner claims that it is quite common for a health practitioner in Africa to prefer an older to a younger patient. In addition, equality of treatment is extremely important for a number of practitioners. This was true to such an extent that a significant number of healers would not choose one patient over another. In such cases they would not treat either patient, thereby letting them both die.

Daniel Ngwala and I drive our dusty, dented four-wheel drive Subaru into a little market area where cars are not often seen. Getting out, Ngwala wanders over to where several older men are talking while younger faces eye me cautiously. Ngwala asks if there are any traditional healers in the area. With a casual gesture, someone tells him: a witchdoctor named Kavili Nduma lives "out that way," but why does he want to know? After due assurances that we are not government agents come to cause trouble, Ngwala returns to the car and we head "that way."

A mile or so down the rutted dirt road we stop to greet a woman with fifty pounds of firewood on her back, and we ask the whereabouts of Nduma. She says we have gone too far and must return to the second path on (she points) "that" side of the road. We do so, taking the car as far down the path as we can before thornbushes and rocks force us to stop.

We leave the car at a mud and grass hut nearby, but only after we have secured a pledge from an adult to keep the fascinated children from pulling the car apart. Now setting out on foot, we travel twenty minutes through meandering maize fields and up a rocky hill, finally reaching Nduma's home—and she is home, thank God! Ngwala explains the reason we have come, and Nduma calls others to bring us chairs. Though the chairs are rickety and lack upright backs, I quickly forget how uncomfortable they are during the two-and-a-half hour interview that follows.

Questioned about how best to cope with the frequent scarcity of medical resources, which may allow her to save only one of two

Reprinted with permission of *The Hastings Center Report*, June 1984.

dying people, Nduma says to save an old man rather than a young, a man without children rather than a father supporting five. She affirms these priorities even when it is revealed that in both cases those preferred arrived second rather than first for treatment. When she adds that it really would be better to try to save none rather than one, little doubt remains that I have encountered a perspective on scarce resource allocation very different from those generally found in the United States.

In fact, this was precisely the reason for the long journey to Africa. The trip was inspired by my conviction that an ethical analysis of alternative approaches to the microallocation of scarce lifesaving medical resources would be greatly enhanced by discussing the problem with people operating out of a different cultural framework. (Microallocation focuses on determining who gets how much of a particular lifesaving medical resource, once budgetary and other limitations have determined the total amount of the resource available.) With support and guidance both in the United States and Kenya, I decided to investigate in particular the views of the Akamba people of Machakos district, Kenya, by means of personal interviews. Special assistance was provided by Ngwala, one of the Akamba himself, life-long resident of Machakos, and part-time farmer with a variety of skills.

The Akamba are traditionally subsistence farmers and herders. But their young men are increasingly seeking jobs in the district's towns or the nation's capital, Nairobi, as the rapidly growing population of 1.2 million fills the district's 14,183 square kilometers (5,475 sq. mi.). The land is largely semiarid—a major exception being some very hilly areas—so life here is not easy. Moreover, droughts are not unusual; roads and infrastructure are not yet well developed, and government services are limited.

Health care in Machakos reflects the general scarcity of resources. While much development is taking place, the efforts of government and religion (mainly Christian) have so far produced only a few modest hospitals, health centers, and health subcenters (four or five each). Most public health care is provided at the more than fifty small dispensaries scattered throughout the district. But even the most basic critical drugs such as penicillin are frequently out of stock, especially in the dispensaries. Accordingly, many, if not a majority, of the people still depend upon traditional healing even though for the most part it has been forbidden by the government, which is promoting a more "modern" (Western) approach to health care.

Having decided to focus upon the Akamba people, I next had to identify those in the Akamba culture who are most knowledgeable about the ethical as well as medical issues involved in allocating scarce medical resources. I learned that those I was seeking are the "healers" of the culture, for Akamba healers have consistently been concerned with both physical and religious/moral health. Akamba healers are of two types: traditional healers (witchdoctors, herbalists, and midwives) and health workers (those who work in government or mission health care facilities). I randomly selected a sample population of 132 persons, with equal representation of both groups.[1]

Since the Akamba think in terms of stories,[2] it seemed appropriate to pose my questions as a series of stories (see "Two Dying Patients, One Dose of Herbs," on p. 642). The stories focused mainly on a healer named Mutua and two patients, Mbiti and Kioko. Resources are so scarce that only one of the two can be saved. In each situation, Mbiti arrives earlier, which, according to the Akamba, is a presumptive reason for treating him before Kioko. But different facts about the two people are also stated in successive questions—for example, Kioko is helping many people in his area whereas Mbiti is not—in order to see if the Akamba ever view such considerations as more important than order of arrival.

People were generally willing to talk at great length about these matters, with a few notable exceptions. One witchdoctor suddenly stopped in the middle of an answer, and said that she could tell me no more. When asked why, she replied that not she but a spirit had been speaking up to that point and the spirit refused to continue today. Plead as we might, she insisted she had nothing more to say but we could return the next day for more. We did, and she finished the interview. Was she merely eccentric? Another witchdoctor told us she could not be a Christian because whenever she started going to church an evil spirit killed a member of her family after telling her the day the murder would happen. She had lost her husband and two children this way, a fact that others confirmed. If I had not accepted the reality of spiritual beings before going to Kenya I might well have left a believer. Such spiritual involvement added a striking dimension to the tremendous friendliness, hospitality, and thoughtfulness of the Akamba people.

THE AKAMBA VIEW OF LIFE

The answers to our questions proved well worth waiting for, especially where they reflected outlooks different from those commonly encountered in the United States. For instance, where only one person can be saved, many Akamba favor saving an old man before a young, even where the young man is first in line. Whereas in the United States we tend to value the young more highly than the old because they are more productive economically, these Akamba espouse a more relational view of life. Life, they insist, is more than atomistic sums of individual economic contributions; it is a social fabric of interpersonal relation. The older a person becomes, the more intricately interwoven that person becomes in the lives of others, and the greater the damage done if that person is removed. At the same time, the older person has wisdom—a perspective on life that comes only with age—which is considered to be a particularly important social resource.

Another Akamba priority documented by the study is: where only one person can be saved, save a man without children rather than one with five. Whereas in the United States many would favor the opposite choice for the children's sake, many Akamba counter that the man without children faces annihilation and must be allowed to live so he can "raise up a name" for himself by having children. The self, for the Akamba, is not solely an individual, mortal life in the present; it is also a vital link in a chain that teaches through time. To drop a link before subsequent links have been fashioned is to destroy all future links (persons) as well as the perpetual life of the link in question.

A third surprising (by U.S. standards) priority acknowledged by numerous Akamba is the insistence that it is better to give a half-treatment to each of two dying patients—even where experience dictates that a half-treatment is insufficient to save either—than to provide one patient with a full treatment which would almost certainly be lifesaving. Under these circumstances many in the United States would abandon substantive equality (or equal treatment, which would here probably mean equal death) in favor of procedural equality (or equal access, which would here probably entail saving one person according to a first-come, first-served principle).

But many Akamba argue that the whole point of equality is what a person receives. They live according to the proverb, "no matter how many Akamba are gathered the mbilivili will be shared." (A mbilivili is the smallest bird known to Akamba and one that provides very little food.) Their outlook is sustained by the conviction that God is prone to heal not only where medical personnel have faithfully applied all available scientific knowledge but also where they have been faithful to the moral law as they are capable of knowing it. As long as healers remain faithful (that is, moral), they maintain, the responsibility for patients' lives remains God's.

These views bring into question some Western assumptions that dictate allocation decisions in the United States and elsewhere. Moreover, they remind us of the error in too quickly concluding, from the fact that people of different cultures support conflicting policies or actions, that morality is relative and that people's basic moral sensibilities may differ significantly. Often, as here, the difference is one of knowledge or beliefs (about what contributions benefit society most, or the nature of eternal life, or God's role in healing) rather than of moral judgment.

Cultural differences affect more than allocation decisions, however. They help shape the way that medical personnel view and treat patients. For instance, because the Akamba traditionally see God as active in healing and people as both spiritual and material beings, they are more likely than their Western counterparts to perceive a need for treatment that addresses health problems on a spiritual as well as physical

level. While Akamba healers do not generally distinguish a psychological component of illness, their emphasis on relationships (regarding their valuing of the elderly) disposes them, together with the entire community, to provide the care and support required to meet this dimension of illness.

The different approaches of Akamba health workers and Akamba traditional healers reflect similar considerations. Health workers, shaped as they are by Western education and medical training, are much more apt to see an illness in purely physical terms and to be skeptical about spiritual diagnoses, not to mention spiritual treatment. To be sure, of the three types of traditional healer, only the witchdoctors make use of spiritual powers (to help those who have been spiritually victimized by "witches" or "wizards"). Yet, even the more physically oriented herbalists and midwives display a level of caring and personal availability to patients that sets them apart from many of the more Western health workers.

Health workers concentrate more on efficient treatment, and are more apt to devote time to research. They are more likely to employ varied (and scientifically better) treatments, even if their quality of caring does not always equal that of traditional healers. Health workers also use Western developed medicines rather than the traditional herbs, though the administering and even effectiveness of the two do at times appear to be similar.

SCORING VALUES

Though I was eager to understand the full range of Akamba perspectives on the allocation of scarce lifesaving medical resources, I was especially interested to learn what significance, if any, they attach to four basic values frequently invoked in the U.S. allocation debate. Informal preliminary research revealed that the Akamba appeal to these values in the following particular form:

- *Equality:* All people are fundamentally equal where life itself is at stake, so the first to arrive should be treated when only one life can be saved.
- *Usefulness:* The most important goal in deciding whom to treat is to achieve the greatest social benefit possible.
- *Need:* Whoever is in the greatest danger of dying right away should be saved.
- *Life:* The most important goal in deciding who to treat is to save as many lives as possible.

To determine the significance that the Akamba attach to these values, we asked our participants twenty-four questions and assigned value-significance points to their answers according to the values they expressed. Participants could earn a point for equality on twenty-three of the questions. Six questions pertained to usefulness; three to need; three to life; and others to a variety of values such as choice. For example, if a healer maintained that Mbiti, who arrives first, is to be treated rather than the patient Kioko, who is involved in projects to benefit the community, then the healer received an equality point. However, to receive this point the healer had to justify her or his choice with some sort of reference to the notion that people equally

warrant treatment where life-threatening health problems are concerned. The implicit idea expressed here is that treatment should do nothing but proceed according to the natural lottery; first-come, first-served. (As noted previously, a significant number of healers were so strongly egalitarian that they never chose one patient over another. These healers automatically received a high number of equality points.)

Where Kioko rather than Mbiti was chosen because of his greater social usefulness, then the healer received a usefulness point rather than an equality point. Other questions presented the possibility of receiving say, a need or life point as against an equality point. In nearly all of the questions it was possible to accumulate either an equality point or a point of some other type—the three categories mentioned here being the major ones. That virtually every question involved a possible equality point does not mean that equality is in some sense more "important" than the other values but merely reflects the manner in which the moral choice typically arises for the Akamba healers. They must choose between their adopted norm of first-come, first-served and some competing moral claim arising from the particulars of the case before them.

Average Value-Significance Scores by Education

Type of Healer	Level of Education	Average Scores			
		Equality	Usefulness	Need	Life
Health	None-Standard 7	15.5	1.6	2.3	2.1
Workers	Standard 8-Form 2	14.1	2.1	2.4	2.7
	Form 3-Form 4	9.8	3.8	2.4	2.9
Traditional	Non-Standard 8	15.2	1.8	2.4	2.2

Once assigned in this manner, points of each type were summed for each person. The resulting equality scores ranged from 3 to 23 (average 14.3), usefulness scores from 0 to 6 (average 2.1), need scores from 0 to 3 (average 2.4), and life scores from 0 to 3 (average 2.3). (In each case the highest score reflects the number of questions pertaining to that category.)

As the averages suggest, most of those interviewed placed a high value on need and life. Perhaps this is to be expected since the Akamba working in health care settings are dedicated to the health of their people. Another finding was somewhat less predictable. While one-third of those questioned viewed usefulness as completely irrelevant in the context under consideration, the remaining two-thirds saw it as a legitimate consideration, at least sometimes, when deciding whose life to save. This latter outlook had a definite impact upon the significance accorded to equality. Nearly two-thirds of the Akamba scored less than 17 on the equality scale—17 being the score of one who would allow the claims of equality to be set aside only where need, life, or choice (not usefulness) is at stake.[3]

What accounts for a healer's particular set of value-significance scores? Whether a person is a health worker or traditional healer appears to matter, for equality, usefulness, and life scores. But what, more precisely, accounts for the difference between the two groups? In order to attempt a partial answer to this question, personal information was gathered at the start of each participant's interview. Specifically, we ascertained each person's sex, age, marital status, length of marriage, number of children, level of education, length of (medical) training, job responsibility, years worked, and religion. Doing so was not always easy. Age was particularly troublesome since many people did not know their age. Sometimes only through the ingenuity of Ngwala—who quizzed them about their knowledge of certain natural disasters and their estimated age at the time of those they could remember—was it possible to obtain this information. We examined potentially significant relationships between the ten personal factors and the value-significance scores.

With regard to nine of the ten items no consistent correlation emerged between the factors and the value-significance scores. (Perhaps surprisingly, religion was one of the nine. Probably this is because the only two religions our respondents acknowledged were the traditional Akamba religion and Christianity. Both, as the Akamba understand them, promote a fairly egalitarian outlook and place similar degrees of emphasis upon the three other basic values examined in this study.) Only education appeared to make a difference. In the table above, the health workers were divided as evenly as possible into three groups according to the highest level of education completed. (Kenyans completed the "standard" grades and then the "forms" before becoming eligible to enter a college or university.) Because none of the traditional healers interviewed had more than a primary education, they were treated here as a separate group and served as a check upon the other results, as will be explained shortly.

Statistical analysis of the scores suggests that the importance health workers attach to equality, usefulness, and life (not need) is significantly influenced by their education. (In fact, all three correlations are statistically significant at well above a 99 percent confidence level.) The more education one has received, the lower her or his equality score. This drop corresponds to a rise in both usefulness and life scores.

However, when the weight ascribed to equality is changing most rapidly—beyond the primary educational level—the rise in usefulness scores is the primary change associated with the drop in equality scores.

Two other findings would appear to substantiate these conclusions. First, since the educational level of the traditional healers as a whole is only a little above that of the least-educated group of health workers, one would expect their mean value-significance scores to fall between the mean scores of the two least-educated health worker groups, though closer to those of the least-educated group. The table confirms that such is the case for all four values.

Second, in order to obtain a fourth educational level and thereby ascertain whether or not the observed trends continue through university education, the only three Akamba "doctors" (in the Western, university-educated sense) of Machakos district were interviewed. None had previously been selected through the sampling procedure employed. All of the observed trends do in fact persist at this fourth level. To the average equality scores (see the table) of 15.5, 14.1, and 9.8 the doctors add a 7.0; to the average usefulness scores of 1.6, 2.1, and 3.8 they add a 5.3; and to the average life scores of 2.1, 2.7, and 2.9 they add a 3.0.

My language regarding correlations between education and value-significance scores has been purposely tentative. Any quantitative measurement of the significance that people attach to particular values can only be approximate. Furthermore, while the data lead me to think that a decreasing equality-oriented and increasingly usefulness-oriented outlook is traceable directly to the Kenyan educational system, I am aware that this contention has not been conclusively proven. For instance, those who go on for more education may—at least theoretically—be those who already have a more usefulness-oriented outlook.

However, two considerations cast doubt on this alternate explanation. First, this explanation gives no account of what does prompt the values to change. Since the nine other items apparently do not account for the differences in values according to this study, the best explanation seems to be education is affecting values rather than vice-versa. Second, it seems highly unlikely that the reason many people stay in school through secondary school and beyond is their preference for one particular moral value over another. However, this question could be studied empirically.

If in fact basic values are being altered by the educational process in Kenya, then the institution of education, even when "purged" of religious instruction, is not as "value-free" as some contend. The real issue may be *which* values education is going to instill—those that it teaches implicitly, or "better" (if different) values, which are explicitly taught and otherwise encouraged.

A SHARED EXPERIENCE

As we brought the interviewing to a close I did not know exactly what the results of the study would be, but I knew it would be long before I forgot the process by which the results were obtained. One of the greatest challenges came near the very end. We completed the interviews a week ahead of schedule, but the heavy rains came ten days early. Those last three days were quite muddy. I never did get the hang of walking down a steep mud-path in the rain—without the dubious pleasure of sitting down in it at least once. But what a privilege to be able to see the task of healing through very different eyes.

In exchange for sharing their perspective, the Akamba health workers and traditional healers were eager to learn my views of medical resource allocation as well as the views of other Akamba. The problem of allocating scarce lifesaving medical resources, particularly the resource of their own time, is tragically real and urgent. One worker described to me a more than weekly occurrence at the district hospital. In a typical scenario, she is providing "intensive care" for a child who will not survive the night without her when another child who also requires her undivided attention in order to live through the night is unexpectedly brought into the hospital. She herself is the scarce resource, and the allocation decision is hers.

In response to the interest expressed by many of those I interviewed, I decided to write up a final report for the participants. The report was translated into Kikamba and hand-delivered even to the most remotely located participants by persons who could read the reports out loud to those who were not able to read for themselves. The participants were grateful, even as they had been gracious in sharing their outlooks. They also remain eager to learn what others think of their views.

The dusty journey across the plains and hills of central Kenya was more than a strenuous physical trek. It was a moral excursion of the most challenging kind. Confronted by strange, new perspectives on an old and familiar problem, I found that my capacity to wrestle with these perspectives depended upon my willingness to question and struggle anew with my own views and my fixed notions of the range of

viable alternatives. While the study is done, the journey continues.

ACKNOWLEDGEMENTS

In addition to those who were interviewed, many others have made important contributions to this study. I am deeply grateful to Daniel Ngwala, my ever-present Akamba research assistant, as well as to others in Kenya who provided governmental, academic, and personal support and counsel. Francis Massakhalia, James Kagia, Dan Kaseje, Dennis Willms, and Joyce Scott stand out among many others. In the United States, the Danforth Foundation and Harvard University (Sheldon Fellowship) provided major funding for the study, while key planning assistance and critical evaluation were provided by Margot Gill, Ralph Potter, Preston Williams, and Sissela Bok. A special word of thanks belongs to Arthur Dyck who helped guide this project from start to finish.

NOTES

1. For a detailed explanation of the methodology, including a description of the sampling technique and questionnaire pre-testing as well as a copy of the basic questionnaire, see John F. Kilner, "Who Shall Be Saved?: An Ethical Analysis of Major Approaches to the Allocation of Scarce Lifesaving Medical Resources" (Cambridge, MA: Ph.D. dissertation, Harvard University, 1983).

2. Cf. John S. Mbiti, *Akamba Stories* (Oxford: Oxford University Press, 1966).

3. The issue of choice arises once in the questionnaire, when the respondents are asked whether or not patients should be allowed to forego treatment voluntarily (e.g., when they discover that all of the waiting patients cannot be treated). For a normative defense of a United States allocation policy which would more or less allow equality (as expressed in random selection) to be

over-ridden only where need, life, or choice is at stake, see John F. Kilner, "A Moral Allocation of Scarce Lifesaving Medical Resources," *Journal of Religious Ethics* 9 (Fall 1981), 245–85.

TWO DYING PATIENTS, ONE DOSE OF HERBS

Mutua was an herbalist in Ukambani, who treated people for many different illnesses. Some patients such as those with kiathi (a severe bacterial infection), received a rare herb called kitawa. But sometimes Mutua's supply of kitawa would run out. Mutua had seen people die because there was no kitawa. One morning a person dying of kiathi was waiting when Mutua finished treating his first patient. The person's name was Mbiti. But before Mutua called Mbiti in to examine and treat him, another person came in and asked to speak to Mutua. He told Mutua that a man named Kioko was dying from kiathi and had just arrived. The person urged Mutua to see Kioko right away. Mutua knew that there was only enough kitawa left to cure one person.

Suppose that Kioko was involved in a number of projects of great benefit to the people in Mutua's area. Moreover, if he died the projects would probably soon fail. Should Mutua save the life of Kioko or that of Mbiti, who had arrived earlier? Why?

Suppose that Kioko was the father of five children, whereas Mbiti had no children. Should Mutua save the life of Kioko or that of Mbiti, who had arrived earlier? Why?

Suppose that Mbiti was over sixty years old, whereas Kioko was twenty-five. Should Mutua save the life of Kioko or that of Mbiti, who had arrived earlier? Why?

—Example of scenario with some follow-up questions.

Gender, Race, and Class in the Delivery of Health Care

Susan Sherwin

Susan Sherwin is a professor of philosophy and women's studies at Dalhousie University in Canada. She is the author of No Longer Patient: Feminist Ethics and Health Care *(1992). She is a coeditor of* Moral Problems in Medicine, second edition *(1983).*

Sherwin begins by noting that women are the primary users of health care, but they often receive care that is inadequate given their needs. She argues that when a woman is also an ethnic minority member, or if she is poor, this can further compound the problem of discrimination in the delivery of health care. She contends that women as a group are more vulnerable to be harmed by poor health care than are men. The health-care needs of women, especially in the Third World, are simply not being adequately addressed. Sherwin ends by considering various feminist proposals for redressing the problems that women find in seeking adequate health care.

OPPRESSION AND ILLNESS

It is widely recognized throughout the field of biomedical ethics that people's health care needs usually vary inversely with their power and privilege within society. Most bioethical discussions explain these differences solely in economic terms, observing that health and access to health resources are largely dependent on income levels. Poverty is an important determining factor in a person's prospects for health: being poor often means living without access to adequate nutrition, housing, heat, clean water, clothing, and sanitation, and each of these factors may have a negative impact on health (Lewis 1990). Further, the poor are more likely than others to work in

industries that pose serious health risks (Stellman 1988) and to do without adequate health insurance (Tallon and Block 1988). And the poor suffer higher rates of mental illness and addiction (Paltiel 1988) than do other segments of the population. Financial barriers also often force the poor to let diseases reach an advanced state before they seek professional help; by the time these individuals do receive care, recovery may be compromised.

It is not sufficient, however, just to notice the effects of poverty on health; it is also necessary to consider who is at risk of becoming the victim of poverty. In a hierarchical society such as the one we live in, members of groups that are oppressed on the basis of gender, race, sexuality, and so forth are the people who are most likely to be poor. Moreover, not only does being oppressed lead to poverty and poverty to poor health but being oppressed is itself also a significant determining factor in the areas

From *No Longer Patient: Feminist Ethics and Health Care* by Susan Sherwin (Philadelphia: Temple University Press, 1992). Reprinted by permission. [Edited]

of health and health care. Those who are most oppressed in society at large are likely to experience the most severe and frequent health problems and have the least access to adequate medical treatment.[1] One reason for this vulnerability is that oppressed individuals are usually exposed to high levels of stress by virtue of their oppressed status, and excessive stress is responsible for many serious illnesses and is a complicating factor in most diseases. Another important factor to consider, as we shall see, is that the same prejudices that undermine the status of the oppressed members of society may affect the treatment they receive at the hands of health care workers.

North American society is characteristically sexist, racist, classist, homophobic, and frightened of physical or mental imperfections; we can anticipate, then, that those who are oppressed by virtue of their gender, race, class, sexual orientation, or disabilities—and especially, those who are oppressed in a number of different ways—will experience a disproportional share of illness and will often suffer reduced access to resources. Moreover, the connection between illness and oppression can run in both directions; because serious or chronic illness is often met with fear and hostility, it may also precipitate an individual's or family's slide into poverty and can therefore lead to oppression based on class.

The damaging connections between oppression and illness are profoundly unfair. Because this situation is ethically objectionable, bioethicists have a responsibility to consider ways in which existing medical institutions can be modified to challenge and undermine these connections, rather than contribute to them. Ethical analyses of the distribution of health and health care must take into consideration the role that oppression plays in a person's prospects for health and well-being.

PATIENTS AS MEMBERS OF OPPRESSED GROUPS

Throughout . . . I have argued that women constitute an oppressed group, which is at a clear disadvantage in the health care system. Women are the primary consumers of health care, but the care they receive does not always serve their overall health interests. In a report presented to the American Medical Association, Richard McMurray (1990) reviewed recent studies on gender disparities in clinical decision-making; he found that although women are likely to undergo more medical procedures than do men when they present the same symptoms and condition, they have significantly less access than men do to some of the major diagnostic and therapeutic interventions that are considered medically appropriate for their conditions. In some cases the discrepancies were quite remarkable: for example, despite comparable physical needs, women were 30 percent less likely than men to receive kidney transplants, 50 percent as likely to be referred for diagnostic testing for lung cancer, and only 10 percent as likely to be referred for cardiac catheterization. The studies were unable to identify any biological difference that would justify these discrepancies. In addition, even though biological differences are sometimes significant in the course of various diseases and therapies, McMurray found that medical researchers have largely ignored the study of diseases and medications in women; for instance, cardiovascular disease is the leading cause of death in women in the United States, but research in this area has been almost exclusively conducted on men.

Therefore, as a group, it appears that women are particularly vulnerable to poor health care. Although they receive a great deal of medical treatment, the relevant research data are frequently missing, and specific treatment decisions seem to be biased against them. When women are medically treated, they are often overtreated, that is, subjected to excessive testing, surgery, and prescription drugs (Weaver and Garrett 1983). Sometimes they are simply not offered the treatment that physicians have judged to be preferable; for example, most professionals who work in the area of fertility control encourage women seeking birth control to go on the pill, despite its known risks. Interestingly, the majority of practitioners choose barrier methods for themselves and their spouses (Todd 1989); they do not seem to trust ordinary women to be conscientious in the use of the safer, less medically intrusive methods.

Physicians are trained in the stereotypical views of women as people who are excessively anxious, devious, and unintelligent; they are taught not to take all women's complaints seriously (Ehrenreich and English 1979; Corea 1985a; Todd 1989). Researchers have found that physicians are often condescending toward their women patients, and many deliberately withhold medical information from them out of concern for their inability to interpret it correctly (Corea 1985a; Todd 1989). Having medicalized the very condition of being female, many doctors have seized opportunities to intervene and modify those bodies in ways they are unwilling to apply to men—for example, psychosurgery, an exceedingly controversial therapy, is performed twice as often on women as on men, and ultrasound was widely practiced on women before being introduced as a therapy for men (Corea 1985a).

Nevertheless, not all women experience the health care system in the same ways. There are many important differences among women that result in different sorts of experiences within the health care system; in particular, differences that are associated with race, economic class, and ethnicity compound the difficulties most women experience in their various encounters with health care workers. Alexandra Todd observed that "the darker a woman's skin and/or the lower her place on the economic scale, the poorer the care and efforts at explanation she received" (Todd 1989, 77). Other factors that contribute to the sort of health care a woman is likely to receive include age, sexuality, body size, intelligence, disabilities, and a history of mental illness. It is a matter of serious moral concern that social factors play a significant role in determining the quality of health care a woman receives.

If we expand our scope to that of a global perspective, then it is obvious that women in other parts of the world face distinct health problems, such as those created by malnutrition, often to the point of starvation, and by the absence of a safe source of drinking water; many women must cope with the ravages of war or the hazards of living under brutally repressive political regimes. Third World women must frequently rely on unsafe drugs, which have failed to meet minimum safety standards and therefore are dumped in developing countries by manufacturers determined to make a profit from them (McDonnell 1986). Some prominent concerns of bioethicists, such as the need to obtain informed consent for treatment and research, are deemed to be the products of Western ideals and are likely to go unrecognized in nations where all personal liberties are severely curtailed; elsewhere, the ethical "niceties" are often ignored in the face of the pressing demands posed by crippling poverty and illiteracy.

The injustice represented by the differing health options and standards of care based on different levels of power and privilege is not restricted to the Third World. Inadequate prenatal care and birth services are common to poor women everywhere, and the lack of safe, effective birth control and abortion services is more a matter of politics than of economics. In North America women of color are at a higher risk than white women for many life-threatening conditions; for example, black American women are four times more likely to die in childbirth and three times more likely to have their newborns die than are white women (Gordon-Bradshaw 1988, 256). Black women in the United States are twice as likely to die of hypertensive cardiovascular disease as are white women; they have three times the rate of high blood pressure and of lupus as do white women; they are more likely than white women to die from breast cancer (despite having lower rates of incidence); they are twelve times more likely than white women to contract the AIDS virus; and they are four times more likely than white women to die of homicide (Davis 1990).

In the United States the poor usually have (at best) access only to inadequate health services. Many people who find themselves employed full time but receiving annual incomes well below established poverty lines fail to qualify for Medicaid support (Tallon and Block 1988). Those who do receive subsidized health care must confront the fact that many physicians and hospitals refuse to accept Medicaid patients. In 1985, for example, four out of ten physicians who provided obstetrical service refused to take Medicaid patients (McBarnette 1988).

Canadians have so far avoided the two-tiered system of private and public health care. In Canada poor women are not turned away from hospitals or doctors' offices,[2] but they may not be able to afford travel to these facilities. Rural women are often restricted from access to needed health care by lack of transportation. Many Canadian communities lack suitably qualified health care specialists, and some provinces simply refuse to provide needed services, especially abortion, thus making it unavailable to women who cannot travel to a private clinic in another jurisdiction. Despite its guaranteed payment for health care, then, the Canadian health care system still reflects the existence of differential patterns of health and illness, associated with both race and income level (York 1987; Paltiel 1988).

In both countries the services available to women through the health care system are predominantly those that meet the needs of the most privileged and articulate women, namely, those who are white, middle-class, educated, and urban. The health needs of other women are likely to be invisible or to slip through the cracks of the structures and funding of the system. In most cities, for example, prenatal programs, exercise counseling, mammography facilities, and hormone replacement therapy for menopausal women are available, but other urgent services, such as programs for alcohol or drug dependent women, are less easily found. Although some private programs exist for affluent women with substance-abuse problems, poor women have virtually no place to which they can turn. Further, if they should manage to find a program that is not too alienating to their experience to be of value, then they may face the problem of finding child care for the duration of the program, and if they are poor, then they are liable to lose custody of their children to the state when they admit to having a problem with addiction.

Although most urban centers offer nutritional guidance to affluent women trying to lose weight (even if their main goal is to fit the cultural ideals and medically mandated norms of slimness), few programs help women on welfare learn how to stretch their inadequate welfare checks to provide nutritious meals or to locate the resources for a healthy diet. Battered women who arrive at emergency rooms are patched up by the specialists on duty and perhaps referred to local, short-term shelters—if space can be found.[3] Preventive health care, which would help the abuser find nonviolent ways of behaving, is usually not available. As a result, many women get trapped in the cycle of returning home to their violent partner, returning to hospital with increasingly severe injuries (where they encounter frustrated staff members, who frequently blame them for repeat episodes), and recuperating in a temporary shelter. In the meantime, their children become intimately acquainted with violence as a means of addressing personal tensions and become primed to continue the pattern in the next generation.

In bioethics literature the issue of justice is often raised, but most discussions focus on whether or not everyone has a right to health care and, if so, what services this right might entail. Accessibility is viewed as the principal moral concern, but even where there is universal health insurance (for example, in Canada), the system is not designed to respond to the particular health needs of many groups of women. Being subject to violence, at risk of developing addictions to alcohol or other mood-altering drugs, and lacking adequate resources to obtain a nutritious food supply are all factors that affect peoples' prospects for health and their ability to promote their own well-being. Such threats to health are a result of the social system, which promotes oppression of some groups by others. Health care alone will not correct all these social effects, but as long as the damage of oppression continues, it is necessary to help its victims recover from some of the harms to their health that occur as a result of their oppressed status.

Bioethicists share with health care professionals and the rest of the community an ethical responsibility to determine how the health needs generated by oppressive structures can best be met. Medical care per se will not always be the most effective means of restoring or preserving the health of oppressed persons. Investigation of how best to respond to these socially generated needs is a topic that must be added to the traditional agenda of health care ethics.

THE ORGANIZATION OF HEALTH CARE

Much of the explanation for the different ways in which health care providers respond to the needs of different social groups can be found in the very structures of the health care delivery system. The dominance structures that are pervasive throughout society are reproduced in the medical context; both within and without the health care delivery system, sex, race, economic class, and able-bodied status are important predictors in determining someone's place in the hierarchy. The organization of the health care system does not, however, merely mirror the power and privilege structures of the larger society; it also perpetuates them.

Within existing health care structures, women do most of the work associated with health care, but they are, for the most part, excluded from making the policy decisions that shape the system. They are the principal providers of home health care, tending the ill members of their own families, but because this work is unpaid, it is unrecorded labor, not even appearing in statistical studies of health care delivery systems; it carries no social authority, and the knowledge women acquire in caring for the ill is often dismissed by those who have power in the system. Furthermore, support is not made available to provide some relief to women carrying out this vital but demanding work.

In the formal institutions of health care delivery, women constitute over 80 percent of paid health care workers, but men hold almost all the positions of authority.[4] Health policy is set by physicians, directors, and legislators, and these positions are filled overwhelmingly by men. Despite recent dramatic increases in female enrollment in medical schools, most physicians are men (78.8 percent in Canada and 84.8 percent in the United States as of 1986);[5] further, female physicians tend to cluster in less influential specialties, such as family practice and pediatrics, and they are seldom in positions of authority within their fields. Most medical textbooks are written by men, most clinical instructors are men, and most hospital directors are men.[6] The professional fields that women do largely occupy in the health care system are ones associated with traditionally female skills, such as nursing, nutrition, occupational and physical therapy, and public health. Women who work in health administration tend to be situated in middle-management positions, where their mediating skills may be desirable but their influence on policy is limited.

Research, too, is largely concentrated in male hands. Few women have their own labs or the budgets to pursue projects of their own choosing. The standards by which research is evaluated are those that have been developed by privileged men to meet their needs. They do not incorporate considerations that some female scientists and most feminist philosophers of science find important, such as including space in the design of a project for a measure of participant control, reducing the separation between subject and object, and resisting restrictive, medicalized analysis.

When we focus directly on issues of race and economic class, the isolation of health care provider from consumer becomes even more pronounced. Although many members of minority races and plenty of poor people are involved in the delivery of health care, very few hold positions of authority. Working-class and minority employees are concentrated in the nonprofessional ranks of cleaners, nurses' aides, orderlies, kitchen staff, and so forth. Women from these groups generally have the lowest income and status in the whole health care system. They have no opportunity to shape health care policy or voice their concerns about their own health needs or those of persons for whom they are responsible. One result of this unbalanced representation is that there has been virtually no research into the distinct needs of minority women (White 1990). Both those empowered to do medical research and those expected to respond to identified health needs come almost entirely from the socially defined groups and classes most removed from the experiences of women of color and poor and disabled women.

The gender and racial imbalances in the health care system are not accidental; they are a result of specific barriers designed to restrict access to women and minorities to the ranks of physicians.

Regina Morantz-Sanchez (1985) documents how the medical profession organized itself over the last century to exclude and harass women who sought to become doctors, and Margaret Campbell (1973) shows that many of these mechanisms are still with us. Blacks, too, have been subject to systematic barriers, which keep them out of the ranks of physicians. For example, it is necessary to serve as an intern to become licensed to practice medicine, but until the 1960s, few American hospitals would grant internship positions to black physicians; those blacks who did manage to become qualified to practice medicine often encountered hospitals that refused to grant them the opportunity to admit patients (Blount 1990). Because black women must overcome both gender and race barriers, they face nearly insurmountable obstacles to pursuing careers as physicians (Weaver and Garrett 1983; Gamble 1990). Therefore, although blacks make up 12 percent of the population of the United States, they account for only 3 percent of the population of practicing doctors, and black women constitute only 1 percent of the nation's physicians; further, blacks represent only 2 percent of the faculty at medical schools (Gamble 1990).

Racism and sexism in health care have been exacerbated by the fact that different oppressed groups have long been encouraged to perceive their interests as in conflict, so that race often divides women who might otherwise be expected to unite. Darlene Clark Hine (1989) has shown that racial struggles have plagued the nursing profession since 1890. For much of that period, white nurses acted on their own racist views and fought to exclude black women from their ranks. Although their racism is not excusable, it is perhaps understandable: Hine explains that white nurses felt compelled to fight for profes-

sional status and autonomy. Acting within a predominantly racist culture, they feared that their claims for recognition would be undermined if they were to welcome black nurses into the profession on an equal footing. In other words, because the combined forces of racism and sexism made it especially difficult for black nurses to obtain respect as professionals, white nurses chose to accept the implicit judgments behind such attitudes and to distance themselves from their black colleagues, rather than joining them in the struggle to counter racial prejudice.

Moreover, the racial struggles of nurses are just one symptom of a larger problem. The hierarchical structures that operate throughout the health care system motivate each social group to pursue the pragmatic strategy of establishing its relative superiority over yet more disadvantaged groups, rather than working collectively to challenge the structures themselves. Although white nurses did seek to dissociate themselves from black nurses and claimed greater commonality with the higher-ranked (white) male physicians, black nurses were themselves driven to seek distance from other black women who were employed in the system as domestic staff or nurses' aides, by claiming an unreciprocated identity with white nurses. Within hierarchical structures, all participants have reason to foster connections with those ranked higher and to seek distance from those ranked lower. This motive breeds an attitude that encourages submission to those above and hostility and a sense of superiority toward those below; in this way, all but the most oppressed groups become complicit in maintaining the hierarchical structure of the health care system. Thus the organization of the health care system itself helps reinforce the oppressive structures and attitudes of society at large. . . .

The power and authority that society has entrusted to doctors give them the opportunity to destroy many of the patriarchal assumptions about women collectively and the racist, classist, homophobic, and other beliefs about various groups of women that are key to their oppression. Few physicians, however, have chosen to exercise their social power in this way. Many doctors have accepted uncritically the biases of an oppressive society, and some have offered evidence in confirmation of such values. As a group, physicians have held onto their own power and privilege by defending the primacy of the authoritarian medical model as a necessary feature of health care. Most have failed to listen honestly to the alternative perspectives of oppressed people who are very differently situated in society.

The medical model organizes our current attempts at defining and responding to health needs. It has been conceived as a structure that requires a hierarchically organized health care system, in which medical expertise is privileged over other sorts of knowledge. It grants license to an elite class of experts to formulate all matters of health and to determine the means of responding to them. As we have seen, however, there are several serious moral problems with this model. First, it responds differently to the health needs of different groups, offering less and lower-quality care to members of oppressed groups. Second, its structures and presuppositions support the patterns of oppression that shape our society. Finally, it rationalizes the principle of hierarchy in human interactions, rather than one of equality, by insisting that its authoritarian structures are essential to the accomplishment of its specific ends, and it tolerates an uneven distribution of positions within its hierarchy.

We need, then, different models to guide our thinking about ways to organize the delivery of health care. In addition to the many limits to the medical model that have been named in the bioethics literature, the traditional model reflects and perpetuates oppression in society. I conclude by summarizing some feminist suggestions that I believe should be incorporated into alternative models, if they are to be ethically acceptable.

A model that reflects the insights of feminist ethics would expand its conceptions of health and health expertise. It would recognize social as well as physiological dimensions of health. In particular, it would reflect an understanding of both the moral and the health costs of oppression. Thus it would make clear that those who are committed to improving the health status of all members of the population should assume responsibility for avoiding and dismantling the dominance structures that contribute to oppression.

Such a model would require a change in traditional understandings of who has the relevant knowledge to make decisions about health and health policy. Once we recognize the need to include oppression as a factor in health, we can no longer maintain the authoritarian medical model, in which physicians are the experts on all matters of health and are authorized to respond to all such threats. We need also to recognize that experiential knowledge is essential to understanding how oppression affects health and how the damage of oppression can be reduced. Both political and moral understandings may be necessary to address these dimensions of health and health care. Physiological knowledge is still important, but it is not always decisive.

Therefore, a feminist model would resist hierarchical structures and proclaim a commitment to egalitarian alternatives.

Not only would these alternatives be more democratic in themselves and hence more morally legitimate, they would also help to produce greater social equality by empowering those who have been traditionally disempowered. They would limit the scope for domination that is available to those now accustomed to power and control. More egalitarian structures would foster better health care and higher standards of health for those who are now oppressed in society; such structures would recognize voices that are now largely unheard and would be in a position to respond to the needs they express.

The current health care system is organized around the central ideal of pursuing a "cure" in the face of illness, wherein "cure" is interpreted with most of the requisite agency belonging to the health care providers. A feminist alternative would recommend that the health care system be principally concerned with empowering consumers in their own health by providing them with the relevant information and the means necessary to bring about the changes that would contribute to their health. The existing health care system, modeled as it is on the dominance structures of an oppressive society, is closed to many innovative health strategies that would increase the power of patients; a feminist model would be user-controlled and responsive to patient concerns.

Such a change in health care organization would require us to direct our attention to providing the necessities of healthy living, rather than trying only to correct the serious consequences that occur when the opportunities for personal care have been denied. Moreover, as an added benefit, a shift to a more democratized notion of health needs may help to evolve a less expensive, more effective health care delivery system; most patients seem to be less committed than are

their professional health care providers to a costly high-tech, crisis-intervention focus in health care (York 1987).

A health care system that reflects feminist ideals would avoid or at least lessen the contribution that the system of health care makes in the maintenance of oppression. It would be significantly more egalitarian in both organization and effect than anything that we are now accustomed to. This system not only would be fairer in its provision of health services but would also help to undermine the ideological assumptions on which many of our oppressive practices rest. Such an alternative is required as a matter of both ethics and health.

To spell out that model in greater detail and with an appropriate understanding, it is necessary to democratize the discipline of bioethics itself—hence, bioethics, as an area of intellectual pursuit, must also recognize the value of incorporating diverse voices in its discussions and analyses. Like medicine or any other discipline, bioethics is largely defined by the perspective of its participants. If we hope to ensure a morally adequate analysis of the ethics of health care, then we should ensure the participation of many different voices in defining the central questions and exploring the promising paths to answers in the field.

NOTES

1. Writers who are concerned about oppression are likely to make the connection prominent; for example, Beverly Smith states: "The reason that Black women don't have good health in this country is because we are so oppressed. It's just that simple" (quoted in Lewis 1990, 174).
2. Nevertheless many provinces would like to reinstitute a "small" user fee. Quebec has recently announced plans to proceed with a five-dollar charge for each visit to a hospital emergency room.
3. Women who gain entry to shelters learn that there are limits to the amount of time any

woman can stay; most also find that low-cost housing is not available for them to move into once their prescribed time is exhausted, especially if they have children in tow and welfare is their only means of support.

4. Canada census data statistics for 1986 list 104,315 men and 418,855 women employed in the areas of medicine and health. Brown (1983) reports that over 85 percent of all health-service and hospital workers in the United States are women.

5. The Canadian figure is from Statistics Canada census figures; the American figure is taken from Todd (1989).

6. To correct the apparently systematic gender bias in the provision of health care McMurray (1990) recommends that efforts be made to increase "the number of female physicians in leadership roles and other positions of authority in teaching, research and the practice of medicine" (10).

REFERENCES

BLOUNT, MELISSA. 1990. "Surpassing Obstacles: Pioneering Black Women Physicians." In *Black Women's Health Book*. See White.

CAMPBELL, MARGARET. 1973. *Why Would a Woman Go Into Medicine? Medical Education in the United States: A Guide for Women*. Old Westbury, NY: Feminist Press.

COREA, GENA. 1985. *The Hidden Malpractice: How American Medicine Mistreats Women*. rev. ed. New York: Harper Colophon Books.

DAVIS, ANGELA Y. 1990. "Sick and Tired of Being Sick and Tired: The Politics of Black Women's Health." In *Black Women's Health Book*. See White.

EHRENREICH, BARBARA, and DEIDRE ENGLISH. 1979. *For Her Own Good: 150 Years of the Experts' Advice to Women*. Garden City, NY: Anchor Books.

GAMBLE, VANESSA NORTHINGTON. 1990. "On Becoming a Physician: A Dream Not Deferred." In *Black Women's Health Book*. See White.

GORDON-BRADSHAW, RUTH H. 1988. "A Social Essay on Special Issues Facing Poor Women of Color." In *Too Little, Too Late*. See Stellman.

HINE, DARLENE CLARK. 1989. *Black Women in White: Racial Conflict and Cooperation in the Nursing Profession, 1890–1950*. Bloomington: Indiana University Press.

LEWIS, ANDREA. 1990. "Looking at the Total Picture: A Conversation with Health Activist Beverly Smith." In *Black Women's Health Book*. See White.

McBARNETTE, LORNA. 1988. "Women and Poverty: The Effects on Reproductive Status." In *Too Little, Too Late*. See Stellman.

McDONNELL, KATHLEEN. 1984. *Not an Easy Choice: A Feminist Re-examines Abortion*, Toronto: Women's Press.

McMURRAY, RICHARD J. 1990. "Gender Disparities in Clinical Decision-Making." Report to the American Medical Association Council on Ethical and Judicial Affairs.

MORANTZ-SANCHEZ, REGINA MARKELL. 1985. *Sympathy and Science: Women Physicians in American Medicine*. New York: Oxford University Press.

PALTIEL, FREDA L. 1988. "Is Being Poor a Mental Health Hazard?" In *Too Little, Too Late*. See Stellman, 1988.

STELLMAN, JEAN MAGER. 1988. "The Working Environment of the Working Poor: An Analysis based on Worker's Compensation Claims, Census Data and Known Risk Factors." In *Too Little, Too Late: Dealing with the Health Needs of Women in Poverty*, ed. Cesar Perales and Lauren Young. New York: Harrington Park Press.

TALLON, JAMES R. JR., and RACHEL BLOCK. 1988. "Changing Patterns of Health Insurance Coverage: Special Concerns for Women." In *Too Little, Too Late*. See Stellman, 1988.

TODD, ALEXANDRA DUNDAS. 1989. *Intimate Adversaries: Cultural Conflict Between Doctors and Women Patients*. Philadelphia: University of Pennsylvania Press.

WEAVER, JERRY L., and SHARON D. GARRETT. 1983. "Sexism and Racism in the American Health Care Industry: A Comparative Analysis." In *Women and Health: The Politics of Sex in Medicine*, ed. Elizabeth Fee. Farmingdale, NY: Baywood.

WHITE, EVELYN C., ed. 1990. *Black Women's Health Book: Speaking for Ourselves*. Seattle: Seal Press.

YORK, GEOFFREY. 1987. *The High Price of Health: A Patient's Guide to the Hazards of Medical Politics*. Toronto: James Lorimer and Company.

QUESTIONS: EUTHANASIA AND SUSTAINING LIFE

1. Is there any morally relevant difference between killing and letting die, according to James Rachels? Why or why not? Either raise objections to his contention or offer supporting arguments.
2. How does Bonnie Steinbock argue against Rachels's identification of the termination of life-sustaining measures with passive euthanasia? Do you think her arguments are effective? Why or why not?
3. Margaret Battin discusses German, Dutch, and American methods of dealing with euthanasia. How do these different medical practices reflect different views of respect for the patient's autonomy?
4. Outline Carl Becker's discussion of how the traditional Buddhist (Samurai) notion of dying with dignity can be translated into modern medical practice of euthanasia. Is this notion of respect for individual responsibility or autonomy different from or similar to (or different in some ways but similar in others) that of the Western practice of euthanasia? Explain. Are there problems with this view?
5. Imagine two worlds: In World A, Harris's lottery scheme has been set up in an impartial way and with strong safeguards against abuse; in World B, there is only "nature's lottery"—you are stuck with the organs you have, and transplantations are forbidden. Explain what moral reasons there are for preferring one world over the other. How does Harris's World A compare morally to World C in which organs are freely, openly, and widely bought and sold as part of a well-developed commercial market?
6. Consider a slight variation of the scenario presented in John Kilner's account of the African perspective of deciding who should be saved.

   > Mutua has only one dose of herbs to give to one of the two dying patients, Kioko and Mbiti. Kioko is 25 years old, has no children, and arrived first, while Mbiti is 62 years old, has many grandchildren, and arrived later.

   Imagine that Mutua decides to give the last kitawa to Mbiti, ensuring that Mbiti will live and Kioko will die. Keeping in mind the discussion concerning multiculturalism and the problem of relativism, do you think that Mutua's decision was the morally right one?
7. In what ways does current medical practice reproduce and perpetuate the oppression discrimination against women and other minorities? What alternative does Sherwin proposes from her feminist perspective? In what ways do you think medical rights are universal human rights or more related to welfare rights that depend on the economic level of the country where one lives? How is the idea of equality at work in Susan Sherwin's proposal?

SUPPLEMENTARY READINGS: EUTHANASIA AND SUSTAINING LIFE

Battin, Margaret P. "Assisted Suicide: Can We Learn from Germany?" *Hastings Center Report*, March–April 1992.

BAYLES, MICHAEL D. "Allocation of Scarce Medical Resources." *Public Affairs Quarterly*, vol. 4(1), January 1990.

BELL, NORA K. "What Setting Limits Might Mean: A Feminist Critique." *Hypatia*, Summer 1989.

BROADY, BARUCH A., and AMIR HALEVY. "Is Futility a Futile Concept?" *Journal of Medicine and Philosophy*, vol. 20(2), April, 1995.

BROCK, DAN W. "Voluntary Active Euthanasia." *Hastings Center Report*, March–April 1992.

BUCHANAN, ALLEN. "The Right to a Decent Minimum of Health Care." *Philosophy and Public Affairs*, Winter 1984.

FENIGSEN, RICHARD. "A Case Against Dutch Euthanasia." *Hastings Center Report*, January–February 1989.

HARAKAS, STANLEY S. "An Eastern Orthodox Approach to Bioethics." *Journal of Medicine and Philosophy*, vol. 18(6), December, 1993.

HEVI, JACOB. "In Ghana, Conflict and Complementarity." *Hastings Center Report*, July–August 1989.

KIMURA, RIHITO. "Anencephalic Organ Donation: A Japanese Case." *The Journal of Medicine and Philosophy*, vol. 14(1), February 1989.

KUHSE, HELGA, and PETER SINGER. "Age and the Allocation of Medical Resources." *The Journal of Medicine and Philosophy*, vol. 13(1), February 1988.

KUNTZ, TOM. "Helping a Man Kill Himself, as Shown on Dutch TV." *New York Times*, Nov. 13, 1994.

MALM, M.H. "Killing, Letting Die, and Simple Conflicts." *Philosophy and Public Affairs*, vol. 18(3), Summer 1989.

NEWMAN, LONIS E. "Talking Ethics with Strangers: A View from Jewish Tradition." *Journal of Medicine and Philosophy*, vol. 18(6), December, 1993.

POTTS, STEPHEN G. "Looking for the Exit Door: Killing and Caring in Modern Medicine." *Houston Law Review*, vol. 25, 1988.

RESCHER, NICHOLAS. "The Allocation of Exotic Lifesaving Therapy." *Ethics*, April 1969.

SIMONS, MARLISE. "Dutch Doctors to Tighten Rules on Mercy Killings." *New York Times*, September 11, 1995.

SIVA SUBRAMANIAN, K.N. "In India, Nepal and Sri Lanka, Quality of Life Weighs Heavily." *Hastings Center Report*, August 1986.